Philosophic Classics
Volume IV

D1532188

CONTEMPORARY PHILOSOPHY

Walter Kaufmann
Late, of Princeton University

Forrest E. Baird, Editor
Whitworth College

Prentice Hall, Englewood Cliffs, New Jersey 07632

Library of Congress Cataloging-in-Publication Data
(Revised for volume 4)

Philosophic classics.

 Includes bibliographical references.
 Contents: v. 1. Ancient philosophy—v. 3. Modern
philosophy—v. 4. Contemporary philosophy.
 1. Philosophy. I. Kaufmann, Walter Arnold. II. Baird,
Forrest E.
B21.P39 1994   100   93-34534
ISBN 0-13-091316-2 (v. 1)
ISBN 0-13-097551-6 (v. 3)
ISBN 0-13-097601-6 (v. 4)

Acquisitions editor: Ted Bolen
Editorial assistant: Nicole Gray
Editorial/production supervision and
    interior design: Linda B. Pawelchak
Art supervision: Anne Bonanno Nieglos
Chapter introduction sketches: Don Martinetti
Cover design: Donna Wickes
Photo editor: Lori Morris-Nantz
Photo research: Joelle Burrows
Production coordinator: Peter Havens

Cover art: Salvador Dali, The Persistence of Memory,
    1931. Oil on canvas, 9½ × 13″. Collection, The
    Museum of Modern Art, New York. Given anonymously.

© 1994 by Prentice-Hall, Inc.
A Paramount Communications Company
Englewood Cliffs, New Jersey 07632

All rights reserved. No part of this book may
be reproduced, in any form or by any means,
without permission in writing from the publisher.

Printed in the United States of America
10 9 8 7 6 5 4 3 2 1

ISBN 0-13-097601-6

Prentice-Hall International (UK) Limited, *London*
Prentice-Hall of Australia Pty. Limited, *Sydney*
Prentice-Hall Canada Inc., *Toronto*
Prentice-Hall Hispanoamericana, S.A., *Mexico*
Prentice-Hall of India Private Limited, *New Delhi*
Prentice-Hall of Japan, Inc., *Tokyo*
Simon & Schuster Asia Pte. Ltd., *Singapore*
Editora Prentice-Hall do Brasil, Ltda., *Rio de Janeiro*

This volume is dedicated to my children:

Whitney, Sydney, and Soren Baird

Contents

Preface   ix

G.W.F. Hegel   1
Phenomenology of Mind (in part)   4
Who Thinks Abstractly?   10
Introduction to the Philosophy of History (in part)   13

Arthur Schopenhauer   41
The World as Will and Idea (in part)   44

John Stuart Mill   69
Utilitarianism   72
On Liberty (in part)   111
The Subjection of Women (in part)   122

Søren Kierkegaard   128

Fear and Trembling (in part)   132
Concluding Unscientific Postscript (in part)   140

Karl Marx   160

Economic and Philosophical Manuscripts (in part)   163
*A Contribution to the Critique of Political Economy
    (in part)*   176

Charles Sanders Peirce   196

How to Make Our Ideas Clear   199

William James   213

The Will to Believe   216
Pragmatism (in part)   229

Friedrich Nietzsche   243

The Birth of Tragedy (in part)   246
The Genealogy of Morals (in part)   257
The Gay Science (in part)   271
The Anti-Christ (in part)   272

Henri Bergson   277

An Introduction to Metaphysics   279

Edmund Husserl   303

*Ideas: General Introduction to Pure Phenomenology
    (in part)*   306
Philosophy and the Crisis of European Man   314

John Dewey   334

The Quest for Certainty (in part)   337

Bertrand Russell   353

The Problems of Philosophy (in part)   356
Mysticism and Logic   370

Martin Heidegger   385

The Way Back into the Ground of Metaphysics   389
The Question Concerning Technology   398

Ludwig Wittgenstein   415

Tractatus Logico-Philosophicus (in part)   419
Philosophical Investigations (in part)   427

A.J. Ayer   440

Language, Truth and Logic (in part)   443

Jean-Paul Sartre   452

Being and Nothingness (in part)   456
Existentialism Is a Humanism   474

Simone de Beauvoir   489

The Second Sex (in part)   492

Willard Van Orman Quine   504

Two Dogmas of Empiricism   506

Preface

Since 1961, *Philosophic Classics* has provided a generation of students with an anthology of quality in the history of Western philosophy. This latest edition extends the late Professor Kaufmann's work by adding a volume on nineteenth- and early twentieth-century philosophy.

Nineteenth- and twentieth-century philosophy has generally been divided into two groups: Continental thinkers and Anglo-American thinkers. In choosing readings for this volume, I have tried to provide a balance between these two approaches to philosophy. About half the contributors fall on each side of the great divide. Accordingly, it is possible to trace the development of Continental thought beginning with Hegel and moving through Schopenhauer, Kierkegaard, Marx, Nietzsche, Bergson, Husserl, Heidegger, Sartre, and de Beauvior. Likewise, one can follow the Anglo-American concerns beginning with Mill and continuing on through Peirce, James, Dewey, Russell, Wittgenstein, Ayer, and Quine.

Determining what is a "classic" becomes more difficult the closer one gets to the present, and I am sure there will be disagreements about particular selections given (or not included) here. But the choices in this anthology represent the current consensus on the major philosophers and philosophic movements on both sides of the English Channel and Atlantic Ocean (up to the middle of the twentieth century—there is little consensus beyond 1951). Accordingly, this book can be used for variety of courses, including phenomenology/existentialism and analytic philosophy. Unfortunately, space constraints do not allow for works on both sides of the

Pacific Ocean or from the Southern Hemisphere: This is an anthology of *Western* philosophy.

To make the works more accessible to students, most footnotes treating textual matters (variant readings, etc.) have been omitted and all Greek words have been transliterated and put in angle brackets. Introductions for each philosopher are divided into three sections: (1) biographical (a glimpse of the life), (2) philosophical (a résumé of the philosopher's thought), and (3) bibliographical (suggestions for further reading).

*   *   *

I would like to thank the many people who assisted me in this volume, including the library staff of Whitworth College, especially Hans Bynagle, Gail Fielding, Jeanette Langston, and Joan Spanne; my colleagues, F. Dale Bruner, who made helpful suggestions on all the introductions, Barbara Filo, who assisted in making selections for artwork, and John Yoder, for advice on the Marx introduction; David Carr, Emory University, Stephen T. Davis, Claremont McKenna College, Gerald V. Kohls, Wayne Pomerleau, and William F. Ryan, Gonzaga University, and Glen Ross, Franklin & Marshall College, who each read some of the introductions and gave helpful advice; Mark Alfino, Tom Jeannot, and Rosemary Volbrecht, all of Gonzaga University, who made suggestions on the selections; my student assistant, Meredith TeGrotenhuis; my secretary, Lorrie Nelson; and my production editor, Linda Pawelchak, and Ted Bolen of Prentice Hall. I would also like to thank the folowing reviewers: James W. Allard, Montana State University; Robert C. Bennett, El Centro College; Herbert L. Carson, Ferris State University; John Lachs, Vanderbilt University; Helen S. Lang, Trinity College; Michael Losonsky, Colorado State University; Scott MacDonald, University of Iowa; Terry Pinkard, Georgetown University; Robert Redmon, Virginia Commonwealth University; Stephen Scott, Eastern Washington University; Howard N. Tuttle, University of New Mexico; Richard J. Van Iten, Iowa State University; and Donald Phillip Verene, Emory University.

I am especially thankful to my wife, Joy Lynn Fulton Baird, who has supported me in this enterprise.

Finally, I would like to dedicate this last volume to our children, Whitney Jaye Baird, Sydney Tev Baird, and Soren David Baird. Perhaps someday they or their children will chart new courses for philosophy.

Forrest E. Baird
Professor of Philosophy
Whitworth College
Spokane, WA 99251

CONTEMPORARY PHILOSOPHY

Philosophers in This Volume

G.W.F. Hegel
Arthur Schopenhauer
John Stuart Mill
Soren Kierkegaard
Karl Marx
Charles Sanders Pierce
William James
Friedrich Nietzsche
Henri Bergson
Edmund Husserl
John Dewey

Other Important Figures

Napoleon Bonaparte
Queen Victoria
Josiah Royce
Alfred North
Whitehead

A Sampling of Major Events

Napoleon crowns himself emperor
Several Latin American countries achieve independence
Britain and U.S. fight War of 1812
Napoleon defeated at Waterloo
Chaka founds Zulu empire
Revolutions sweep
Europe

| 1750 | 1775 | 1800 | 1825 | 1850 | 1875 |

Bertrand Russell
　　　Martin Heidegger
　　　　　Ludwig Wittgenstein
　　　　　　　Jean-Paul Sartre
　　　　　　　　Simone DeBeauvoir
　　　　　　　A.J. Ayer
　　　　　　　　Willard Van Orman Quine

George Santayana
　　Mahatma Gandhi
　　G.E. Moore
　　　　Joseph Stalin
　　　　　Jacques Maritain
　　　　　Adolf Hitler
　　　　　　Rudolf Carnap
　　　　　　Brand Blanshard
　　　　　　Gilbert Ryle
　　　　　　　J.L. Austin
　　　　　　　Albert Camus

Britain takes over India
American Civil War
　　Suez Canal opens
　　　　　　Boxer Rebellion in China
　　　　　　World War I
　　　　　　　Russian Revolution
　　　　　　　　　Hitler becomes Führer
　　　　　　　　World War II
　　　　　　　　　　Soviet Blockade of
　　　　　　　　　West Berlin
　　　　　　　　　　Mao Zedong gains
　　　　　　　　　power in China
　　　　　　　　　Korean War

1875	1900	1925	1950	1975

G.W.F. Hegel
1770–1831

Georg Wilhelm Friedrich Hegel was born in Stuttgart, in southern Germany. Hegel and his father, a minor government official, his mother, a loving "Haus Frau" (housewife), and his sister and brother were all close, affectionate, and loving. It is easy to see why Hegel would later describe the family as "the immediate Ethical Substance." Following grade school in Stuttgart, at age eighteen, Hegel won a scholarship to Tübingen University, where he studied theology. While there he met and befriended the poet Hölderlin and the philosopher Schelling. The work Hegel submitted to his professors at the university gave no indication of the brilliant philosophical career that was to follow. In fact, his diploma from the university recorded that his knowledge of theology was fair, but his knowledge of philosophy was inadequate. Nevertheless Hegel was already beginning to write insightful essays, not for classroom assignments, but to clarify his own thoughts.

After graduating from the university in 1793, Hegel spent seven years as a tutor for wealthy families in Bern and Frankfurt. During this time he continued to write essays—mostly on religious topics—that indicated he had moved far away from orthodox Christianity. For example, one early essay compared Jesus and Socrates, and Socrates' ethical teaching was seen as superior.

Following his father's death in 1799, Hegel inherited a modest sum of money, quit tutoring, and joined his friend Schelling at the University of Jena. There

1

Hegel became a *Privatdozent* (an unsalaried lecturer) and coedited a philosophic journal with Schelling. While at Jena, Hegel wrote his first great work, *The Phenomenology of Mind* (1807), which laid out the major themes of his philosophy. This work included a critique of Schelling's ideas, ending the friendship. Before this important work could be published, Napoleon's war with Prussia closed the University of Jena, and so Hegel, whose inheritance had now been exhausted, was forced to find other employment.

After a stint as a newspaper editor, Hegel served eight years in Nürnberg as the rector of a *Gymnasium* (high school). There he published his second major work, *Science of Logic* (1812–1816). He also met and married a young woman from a distinguished family who was half his age, and together they had two sons. In 1816 Hegel accepted a chair of philosophy at the University of Heidelberg. He continued his practice of producing a major book at each place he worked by publishing the *Encyclopedia of the Philosophical Sciences in Outline* in 1817. In 1818 Hegel moved to his final institution, the University of Berlin. There he published his *Philosophy of Right* (1821)—and became famous throughout Europe. He remained in Berlin until his death from cholera in 1831.

Following his death, a group of his friends published an eighteen-volume collection of his works, including his early essays and his lectures on aesthetics, history of philosophy, philosophy of history (portions of which are reprinted here), and the philosophy of religion.

* * *

Like all philosophers of his age, Hegel was greatly influenced by Kant. Kant had managed to synthesize two previously disparate realities—the rational world of ideas (emphasized by rationalists) with the phenomenal world of perception (emphasized by empiricists). But in so doing, Kant separated the noumenal world of "things-in-themselves" from the phenomenal world of experience and declared the noumenal world unknowable. In a sense he had reconciled two competing epistemologies—Continental Rationalism and British Empiricism—at the expense of abandoning metaphysics. Hegel sought to go one step further than Kant and effect a complete synthesis that would not only draw together competing epistemologies, but would also show the connection between epistemology and metaphysics. The key to this synthesis is the recognition that consciousness is the ultimate reality, or, to use his famous phrase, "What is real is rational—what is rational is real." That is, metaphysical reality (the real) *is* Idea or Mind (that which knows). The resulting philosophy is called "Absolute Idealism" because all things that exist are essentially related to absolute Idea or Mind or Spirit.

According to Hegel, traditional rationalism (what he calls *raisonnement*) tends to classify all experience formally into abstract, lifeless universals. Taken to its logical extreme, rationalists end up with the abstraction "Being": "But this mere Being, as it is mere abstraction, is therefore the absolutely negative: which, in a similarly immediate aspect, is just NOTHING." By abstracting away the concreteness or particularity of actual experience, one is left with Being which is Nothing. The short article "Who Thinks Abstractly?" (1807–1808?), reprinted here in Walter Kaufmann's translation, clearly conveys Hegel's contempt for the process of abstraction.

While Being and Nothing are both identical and yet contradictory, according to Hegel, "the truth of Being and Nothing is . . . the unity of the two: and this unity is BECOMING." The unity of Becoming does not obliterate Being and

Nothing, but holds both in tension in a higher truth. The two parts of the contradiction, together with that which unites or overcomes them, make up a triad. This method of overcoming contradictions by moving to a higher level of truth is known as the "dialectic." Hegel proposed to develop a complete dialectical System of reality based on the three foundational triads of "Being–Nothing–Becoming," "Being–Essence–Notion," and "Idea–Nature–Spirit." Though he developed several proposals for this System, he never completed any of them. But he did use the dialectical method to explain consciousness.

In the chapter entitled "Lordship and Bondage" from *The Phenomenology of Mind* (1807), reprinted here in the J.B. Baillie translation, Hegel explains one stage in the dialectical development of consciousness. He begins by pointing out that only by acknowledging an "other" is self-consciousness possible. But if there is an other, then the original self-consciousness feels threatened and asserts its freedom by trying to dominate that other and force acknowledgment of its dominance. The ensuing struggle results in a lord who dominates and a bondsman who is dominated. The lord then forces the bondsman to produce material goods for the enjoyment of the lord.

But at this point the lord is now dependent upon the bondsman he has dominated. In the first place, his self-consciousness as lord is subject to his recognition as lord by the bondsman. But more importantly, while the lord has been consuming or destroying what the slave makes, the slave has been learning to create—to bend nature to his will—and so has established his own self-consciousness in relation to what he has created. Furthermore, the labor of the slave has a permanent quality while the master's consumption is again dependent on the slave's production. So by dominating the bondsman, the lord is dominated.

The solution to this contradiction is to acknowledge that neither lord nor bondsman is free and that freedom is not possible in relationships of domination. The next stage in the dialectic is for the mind to seek freedom within itself.

This dialectical development of the consciousness of freedom can also be understood in relation to world history. As Hegel says in his "Introduction" to the *Philosophy of History* (1832), presented here in the J. Sibree translation, "the history of the World . . . has constituted the rational necessary course of the World-Spirit—that Spirit whose nature is always one and the same, but which unfolds this its one nature in the phenomena of the World's existence." In other words, the Absolute Spirit as manifested in history through human consciousness is the World-Spirit *(Weltgeist)* and all of human history is a process whereby this World-Spirit comes to self-consciousness of itself as free. To understand this development of Spirit, Hegel examines the three elements that structure historical movement: (1) the nature of Spirit, (2) its means of actualization, and (3) the shape of its perfect embodiment. This final embodiment of Spirit as freedom is found in the State. As Hegel explains each of these three elements, he makes it clear that the individual is unimportant: ". . . in the history of the World, the *Individuals* we have to do with are *Peoples*." In fact, the individual as an individual is outside of history entirely and only finds freedom and meaning within the unified self-consciousness of a people known as the State.

Hegel's ideas have been both lauded and attacked. His insights on the master–slave relationship made a powerful impression on Marx and Nietzsche. Indeed, Hegel's understanding of dialectical development became a central feature of Marx's thought—though Marx rejected the notion of Absolute Spirit. Phenomenology developed Hegel's insights about the different types of consciousness. The sociology of knowledge developed his notions about the connection between consciousness and the culture of a particular epoch. Chief among Hegel's critics was Kierkegaard, who objected strenuously to the devaluing of the individual, questioned the implicit optimism of the dialectic, and mocked the incompleteness of Hegel's "System." Perhaps Hegel's greatest legacy was not any specific idea, but the vision of a complete historical development of thought.

* * *

For a selection of primary source readings for Hegel, see *Hegel, The Essential Writings,* edited by Frederick G. Weiss (New York: Harper & Row, 1974). Many secondary books about Hegel are difficult for beginning students. Two accessible classics are W.T. Stace, *The Philosophy of Hegel* (1924, reprinted New York: Dover, 1955), and G.R.G. Mure, *An Introduction to Hegel* (Oxford: Clarendon Press, 1940). Recent helpful studies include J.N. Findlay, *Hegel: A Re-examination* (New York: Macmillan, 1958); Walter Kaufmann, *Hegel: Reinterpretation, Texts and Commentary* (Garden City, NY: Doubleday, 1965); and, especially, Peter Singer, *Hegel* (Oxford: Oxford University Press, 1983). Charles Taylor's massive *Hegel* (Cambridge: Cambridge University Press, 1975) can be consulted for particular topics. For specialized topics, see H.A. Reyburn, *Ethical Theory of Hegel* (Oxford: Oxford University Press, 1965); Ivan Soll, *An Introduction to Hegel's Metaphysics* (Chicago: University of Chicago Press, 1969); Walter Kaufmann, ed., *Hegel's Political Philosophy* (New York: Atherton Press, 1970); Quentin Lauer, *Hegel's Idea of Philosophy* (New York: Fordham University Press, 1971); Quentin Lauer, *A Reading of Hegel's "Phenomenology of Spirit"* (New York: Fordham University Press, 1976); Robert C. Solomon, *From Hegel to Existentialism* (New York: Oxford University Press, 1987); Michael N. Forster, *Hegel and Skepticism* (Cambridge, MA: Harvard University Press, 1989); and Merold Westphal, *History and Truth in Hegel's "Phenomenology"* (Atlantic Highlands, NJ: Humanities Press, 1990). Karl Marx, *Critique of Hegel's "Philosophy of Right,"* edited by Joseph O'Malley (Cambridge: Cambridge University Press, 1970), is both a critical review of Hegel's work and a major work in its own right. General collections of critical essays include W.E. Steinkraus, ed., *New Studies in Hegel's Philosophy* (New York: Holt, Rinehart and Winston, 1971); Alasdair MacIntyre, ed., *Hegel: A Collection of Critical Essays* (Notre Dame, IN: University of Notre Dame Press, 1972); and Michael Inwood, ed., *Hegel* (Oxford: Oxford University Press, 1985).

PHENOMENOLOGY OF MIND (in part)

(B, IV, A): LORDSHIP AND BONDAGE

Self-consciousness exists in itself and for itself, in that, and by the fact that it exists for another self-consciousness; that is to say, it *is* only by being acknowledged or "recognized." The conception of this its unity in its duplication, of infinite realizing itself in self-consciousness, has many sides to it and encloses within it elements of varied significance. Thus its moments must on the one hand be strictly kept apart in detailed distinctiveness, and, on the other, in this distinction must, at the same time, also be taken as not distinguished, or must always be accepted and understood in their opposite sense. This double meaning of what is distinguished lies in the nature of self-consciousness:— of its being infinite, or directly the opposite of the determinateness in which it is fixed. The detailed exposition of the notion of this spiritual unity in its duplication will bring before us the process of Recognition.

Self-consciousness has before it another self-consciousness; it has come outside itself. This has a double significance. First it has lost its own self, since it finds itself as an *other* being; secondly, it has thereby sublated that other, for it does not regard the other as essentially real, but sees its own self in the other.

It must cancel this its other. To do so is the sublation of that first double meaning, and is therefore a second double meaning. First, it must set itself to sublate the other independent being, in order thereby to become certain of itself as true being, secondly, it thereupon proceeds to sublate its own self, for this other is itself.

This sublation in a double sense of its otherness in a double sense is at the same time a return in a double sense into its self. For, firstly, through sublation, it gets back itself, because it becomes one with itself again through the canceling of *its* otherness; but secondly, it likewise gives otherness back again to the other self-consciousness, for it was aware of being in the other, it cancels this its own being in the other and thus lets the other again go free.

This process of self-consciousness in relation to another self-consciousness has in this manner been represented as the action of one alone. But this action on the part of the one has itself the double significance of being at once its own action and the action of that other as well. For the other is likewise independent, shut up within itself, and there is nothing in it which is not there through itself. The first does not have the object before it only in the passive form characteristic primarily of the object of desire, but as an object existing independently for itself, over which therefore it has no power to do anything for its own behoof, if that object does not *per se* do what the first does too it. The process then is absolutely the double process of both self-consciousnesses. Each sees the other do the same as itself; each itself does what it demands on the part of the other, and for that reason does what it does only so far as the other does the same. Action from one side only would be useless, because what is to happen can only be brought about by means of both.

The action has then a *double entente* not only in the sense that it is an act done to itself as well as to the other, but also in the sense that the act *simpliciter* is the act of the one as well as of the other regardless of their distinction.

In this movement we see the process repeated which came before us as the play of forces; in the present case, however, it is found in consciousness. What in the former had effect only for us [contemplating experience], holds here for the terms themselves. The middle term is self-consciousness which breaks itself up into the extremes; and each extreme is this interchange of its own determinateness, and complete transition into the opposite. While *qua* consciousness, it no doubt comes outside itself, still, in being outside itself, it is at the same time restrained within itself, it exists for itself, and its self-externalization is for consciousness. *Consciousness* finds that it immediately is and is not another consciousness, as also that this other is for itself only when it cancels itself as existing for itself, and has self-existence only in the self-existence of the other. Each is the mediating term to the other, through which each mediates and unites itself with itself; and each is to itself and to the other an immediate self-existing reality, which, at the same time, exists thus for itself only through this mediation. They recognize themselves as mutually recognizing one another.

This pure conception of recognition, of duplication of self-consciousness within its unity, we must now consider in the way its process appears for self-consciousness. It will, in the first place, present the aspect of the disparity of the two, or the break-up of the middle term into the extremes, which, *qua* extremes, are opposed to one another, and of which one is merely recognized, while the other only recognizes.

Self-consciousness is primarily simple existence for self, self-identity by exclusion of every other from itself. It takes its essential nature and absolute object to be Ego; and in this immediacy, in this bare fact of its self-existence, it is individual. That which for it is other stands as unessential object, as object with the impress and character of negation. But the other is also a self-consciousness; an individual makes its appearance in antithesis to an individual. Appearing thus in their immediacy, they are for each other in the manner of ordinary objects. They are independent individual forms, modes of consciousness that have not risen above the bare level of life (for the existent object here has been determined as life). They are, moreover, forms of consciousness which have not yet accomplished for one another the process of absolute abstraction, of uprooting all immediate existence, and of being merely the bare, negative fact of self-identical consciousness; or, in other words, have not yet revealed themselves to each other as existing purely for themselves, i.e., as self-consciousness. Each is indeed certain of its own self, but not of the other, and hence its own certainty of itself is still without truth. For its truth would be merely that its own individual existence for itself would be shown to it to be an independent object or, which is the same thing, that the object would be exhibited as this pure certainty of itself. By the notion of recognition, however, this is not possible, except in the form that as the other is for it, so it is for the other; each in its self through its own action and again through the action of the other achieves this pure abstraction of existence for self.

The presentation of itself, however, as pure abstraction of self-consciousness consists in showing itself as a pure negation of its objective form, or in showing that it is fettered to no determinate existence, that it is not bound at all by the particularity everywhere characteristic of existence as such, and is *not* tied up with life. The process of bringing all this out involves a twofold action—action on the part of the other and action on the part of itself. In so far as it is the other's action, each aims at the destruction and death of the other. But in this there is implicated also the second kind of action, self-activity; for the former implies that it risks its own life. The relation of both self-consciousnesses is in this way so constituted that they prove themselves and each other through a life-and-death struggle. They must enter into this struggle, for they must bring their certainty of themselves, the certainty of being for themselves, to the level of objective truth, and make this a fact both in the case of the other and in their own case as well. And it is solely by risking life that freedom is obtained; only thus is it tried and proved that the essential nature of self-consciousness is not bare existence, is not the merely immediate form in which it at first makes its appearance, is not its mere absorption in the expanse of life. Rather it is thereby guaranteed that there is nothing present but what might be taken as a vanishing moment—that self-consciousness is merely pure self-existence, being-for-self. The individual, who has not staked his life, may, no doubt, be recognized as a Person; but he has not attained the truth of this recognition as an independent self-consciousness. In the same way each must aim at the death of the other, as it risks its own life thereby; for that other is to it of no more worth than itself; the other's reality is presented to the former as an external other, as outside itself; it must cancel that externality. The other is a purely existent consciousness and entangled in manifold ways; it must view its otherness as pure existence for itself or as absolute negation.

This trial by death, however, cancels both the truth which was to result from it, and therewith the certainty of self altogether. For just as life is the natural "position" of consciousness, independence without absolute negativity, so death is the natural "negation" of consciousness, negation without independence, which thus remains without the requisite significance of actual recognition. Through death, doubtless, there has arisen the certainty that both did stake their life, and held it lightly both in their own case and in the case of the other; but that is not for those who underwent this struggle. They cancel their consciousness which had its place in this alien element of natural existence; in other words, they cancel themselves and are sublated as terms or extremes seeking to have existence on their own account. But along with this there vanishes from the play of change the essential moment, viz. that of breaking up into extremes with opposite characteristics; and the middle term collapses into a lifeless unity which is broken up into lifeless extremes, merely existent and not opposed. And the two do not mutually give and receive one another back from each other through consciousness; they let one another go quite indifferently, like things. Their act is abstract negation, not the negation characteristic of consciousness, which cancels in such a way that it preserves and maintains what is sublated, and thereby survives its being sublated.

In this experience self-consciousness becomes aware that *life* is as essential to it as pure self-consciousness. In immediate self-consciousness the simple ego is absolute object, which, however, is for us or in itself absolute mediation, and has as its essential moment substantial and solid independence. The dissolution of that simple unity is the result of the first experience; through this there is posited a pure self-consciousness, and a consciousness which is not purely for itself, but for another, i.e. as an existent consciousness, consciousness in the form and shape of thinghood. Both moments are essential, since, in the first instance, they are unlike and opposed, and their reflexion into unity has not yet come to light, they stand as two opposed forms or modes of consciousness. The one is independent, and its essential nature is to be for itself; the other is dependent, and its essence is life or existence for another. The former is the Master, or Lord, the latter the Bondsman.

The master is the consciousness that exists for *itself;* but no longer merely the general notion of existence for self. Rather, it is a consciousness existing on its own account which is mediated with itself through an other consciousness, i.e. through an other whose very nature implies that it is bound up with an independent being or with thinghood in general. The master brings himself into relation to both these moments, to a thing as such, the object of desire, and to the consciousness whose essential character is thinghood. And since the master, is *(a) qua* notion of self-consciousness, an immediate relation of self-existence, but *(b)* is now moreover at the same time mediation, or a being-for-self which is for itself only through an other—he [the master] stands in relation *(a)* immediately to both *(b)* mediately to each through the other. The master relates himself to the bondsman mediately through independent existence, for that is precisely what keeps the bondsman in thrall; it is his chain, from which he could not in the struggle get away, and for that reason he proved himself to be dependent, to have his independence in the shape of thinghood. The master, however, is the power controlling this state of existence, for he has shown in the struggle that he holds it to be merely something negative. Since he is the power dominating existence, while this existence again is the power controlling the other [the bondsman], the master holds, *par consequence,* the other in subordination. In the same way the master relates himself to the thing mediately through the bondsman. The bondsman being a self-consciousness in the broad sense, also takes up a negative attitude to things and cancels them; but the thing is, at the same time, independent for him, and, in consequence, he cannot, with all his negating, get so far as to annihilate it outright and be done with it; that is to say, he merely works on it. To the master, on the other hand, by means of this mediating process, belongs the immediate relation, in the sense of the pure negation of it, in other words he gets the enjoyment. What mere desire did not attain, he now succeeds in attaining, viz. to have done with the thing, and find satisfaction in enjoyment. Desire alone did not get the length of this, because of the independence of the thing. The master, however, who has interposed the bondsman between it and himself, thereby relates himself merely to the dependence of the thing, and enjoys it without qualification and without reserve. The aspect of its independence he leaves to the bondsman, who labours upon it.

In these two moments, the master gets his recognition through an other consciousness, for in them the latter affirms itself as unessential, both by working upon the thing, and, on the other hand, by the fact of being dependent on a determinate existence; in neither case can this other get the mastery over existence, and succeed in absolutely negating it. We have thus here this moment of recognition, viz. that the other consciousness cancels itself as self-existent, and, *ipso facto,* itself does what the first does to it. In the same way we have the other moment, that this action on the part of the second is the action proper of the first; for what is done by the bondsman is properly an action on the part of the master. The latter exists only for himself, that is his essential nature; he is the negative power without qualification, a power to which the thing is naught. And he is thus the absolutely essential act in this situation, while the bondsman is not so, he is an unessential activity. But for recognition proper there is needed the moment that what the master does to the other he should also do to himself, and what the bondsman does to himself, he should do to the other also. On that account a form of recognition has arisen that is one-sided and unequal.

In all this, the unessential consciousness is, for the master, the object which embodies the truth of his certainty of himself. But it is evident that this object does not correspond to its notion; for, just where the master has effectively achieved lordship, he really finds that something has come about quite different from an independent consciousness. It is not an independent, but rather a dependent consciousness that he has achieved. He is thus not assured of self-existence as his truth; he finds that his truth is rather the unessential consciousness, and the fortuitous unessential action of that consciousness.

The truth of the independent consciousness is accordingly the consciousness of the bondsman. This doubtless appears in the first instance outside itself, and not as the truth of self-consciousness. But just as lordship showed its essential nature to be the reverse of what it wants to be, so, too, bondage will, when completed, pass into the opposite of what it immediately is: being a consciousness repressed within itself, it will enter into itself, and change round into real and true independence.

We have seen what bondage is only in relation to lordship. But it is a self-consciousness, and we have now to consider what it is, in this regard, in and for itself. In the first instance, the master is taken to be the essential reality for the state of bondage; hence, for it, the truth is the independent consciousness existing for itself, although this truth is not taken yet as inherent in bondage itself. Still, it does in fact contain within itself this truth of pure negativity and self-existence, because it has experienced this reality within it. For this consciousness was not in peril and fear for this element or that, nor for this or that moment of time, it was afraid for its entire being; it felt the fear of death, the sovereign master. It has been in that experience melted to its inmost soul, has trembled throughout its every fibre, and all that was fixed and steadfast has quaked within it. This complete perturbation of its entire substance, this absolute

dissolution of all its stability into fluent continuity, is, however, the simple, ultimate nature of self-consciousness, absolute negativity, pure self-referent existence, which consequently is involved in this type of consciousness. This moment of pure self-existence
is moreover a fact for it; for in the master it finds this as its object. Further, this bondsman's consciousness is not only this total dissolution in a general way; in serving and
toiling the bondsman actually carries this out. By serving he cancels in every particular
aspect his dependence on and attachment to natural existence, and by his work removes
this existence away.

The feeling of absolute power, however, realized both in general and in the particular form of service, is only dissolution implicitly; and albeit the fear of the lord is the
beginning of wisdom, consciousness is not therein aware of being self-existent.
Through work and labour, however, this consciousness of the bondsman comes to itself. In the moment which corresponds to desire in the case of the master's consciousness, the aspect of the non-essential relation to the thing seemed to fall to the lot of the
servant, since the thing there retained its independence. Desire has reserved to itself the
pure negating of the object and thereby unalloyed feeling of self. This satisfaction, however, just for that reason is itself only a state of evanescence, for it lacks objectivity or
subsistence. Labour, on the other hand, is desire restrained and checked, evanescence
delayed and postponed; in other words, labour shapes and fashions the thing. The negative relation to the object passes into the *form* of the object, into something that is permanent and remains; because it is just for the labourer that the object has independence.
This negative mediating agency, this activity giving shape and form, is at the same time
the individual existence, the pure self-existence of that consciousness, which now in the
work it does is externalized and passes into the condition of permanence. The consciousness that toils and serves accordingly attains by this means the directs apprehension of that independent being as its self.

But again, shaping or forming the object has not only the positive significance
that the bondsman becomes thereby aware of himself as factually and objectively self-
existent; this type of consciousness has also a negative import, in contrast with its first
moment, the element of fear. For in shaping the thing it only becomes aware of its own
proper negativity, its existence on its own account, as an object, through the fact that it
cancels the actual form confronting it. But this objective negative element is precisely
the alien, external reality, before which it trembled. Now, however, it destroys this extraneous alien negative, affirms and sets itself up as a negative in the element of permanence, and thereby becomes for itself a self-existent being. In the master, the bondsman
feels self-existence to be something external, an objective fact; in fear self-existence is
present within himself; in fashioning the thing, self-existence comes to be felt explicitly
as his own proper being, and he attains the consciousness that he himself exists in its
own right and on its own account *(an und für sich)*. By the fact that the form is objectified, it does not become something other than the consciousness moulding the thing
through work; for just that form is his pure self-existence, which therein becomes truly
realized. Thus precisely in labour where there seemed to be merely some outsider's
mind and ideas involved, the bondsman becomes aware, through this re-discovery of
himself by himself, of having and being a "mind of his own."

For this reflexion of self into self the two moments, fear and service in general, as
also that of formative activity, are necessary: and at the same time both must exist in a
universal manner. Without the discipline of service and obedience, fear remains formal
and does not spread over the whole known reality of existence. Without the formative
activity shaping the thing, fear remains inward and mute, and consciousness does not
become objective for itself. Should consciousness shape and form the thing without the
initial state of absolute fear, then it has a merely vain and futile "mind of its own"; for

its form or negativity is not negativity *per se,* and hence its formative activity cannot furnish the consciousness of itself as essentially real. If it has endured not absolute fear, but merely some slight anxiety, the negative reality has remained external to it, its substance has not been through and through infected thereby. Since the entire content of its natural consciousness has not tottered and shaken, it is still inherently a determinate mode of being; having a "mind of its own" *(der eigene Sinn)* is simply stubbornness *(Eigensinn),* a type of freedom which does not get beyond the attitude of bondage. As little as the pure form can become its essential nature, so little is that form, considered as extending over particulars, a universal formative activity, an absolute notion; it is rather a piece of cleverness which has mastery within a certain range, but not over the universal power nor over the entire objective reality.

WHO THINKS ABSTRACTLY?

Think? Abstractly?—*Sauve qui peut!* Let those who can save themselves! Even now I can hear a traitor, bought by the enemy, exclaim these words, denouncing this essay because it will plainly deal with metaphysics. For *metaphysics* is a word, no less than *abstract,* and almost *thinking* as well, from which everybody more or less runs away as from a man who has caught the plague.

But the intention here really is not so wicked, as if the meaning of thinking and of abstract were to be explained here. There is nothing the beautiful world finds as intolerable as explanations. I, too, find it terrible when somebody begins to explain, for when worst comes to worst I understand everything myself. Here the explanation of thinking and abstract would in any case be entirely superfluous; for it is only because the beautiful world knows what it means to be abstract that it runs away. Just as one does not desire what one does not know, one also cannot hate it. Nor is it my intent to try craftily to reconcile the beautiful world with thinking or with the abstract as if, under the semblance of small talk, thinking and the abstract were to be put over till in the end they had found their way into society incognito, without having aroused any disgust; even as if they were to be adopted imperceptibly by society, or, as the Swabians say, *hereingezäunselt,* before the author of this complication suddenly exposed this strange guest, namely the abstract, whom the whole party had long treated and recognized under a different title as if he were a good old acquaintance. Such scenes of recognition which are meant to instruct the world against its will have the inexcusable fault that they simultaneously humiliate, and the wirepuller tries with his artifice to gain a little fame; but this humiliation and this vanity destroy the effect, for they push away again an instruction gained at such a price.

In any case, such a plan would be ruined from the start, for it would require that the crucial word of the riddle is not spoken at the outset. But this has already happened in the title. If this essay toyed with such craftiness, these words should not have been allowed to enter right in the beginning; but like the cabinet member in a comedy, they should have been required to walk around during the entire play in their overcoat, unbuttoning it only in the last scene, disclosing the flashing star of

Translated by Walter Kaufmann.

wisdom. The unbuttoning of the metaphysical overcoat would be less effective, to be sure, than the unbuttoning of the minister's: it would bring to light no more than a couple of words, and the best part of the joke ought to be that it is shown that society has long been in possession of the matter itself, so what they would gain in the end would be the mere name, while the minister's star signifies something real—a bag of money.

That everybody present should know what thinking is and what is abstract is presupposed in good society, and we certainly are in good society. The question is merely *who* thinks abstractly. The intent, as already mentioned, is not to reconcile society with these things, to expect it to deal with something difficult, to appeal to its conscience not frivolously to neglect such a matter that befits the rank and status of beings gifted with reason. Rather it is my intent to reconcile the beautiful world with itself, although it does not seem to have a bad conscience about this neglect, still, at least deep down, it has a certain respect for abstract thinking as something exalted, and it looks the other way not because it seems too lowly but because it appears too exalted, not because it seems too mean but rather too noble, or conversely because it seems an *Espèce,* something special; it seems something that does not lend one distinction in general society, like new clothes, but rather something that—like wretched clothes, or rich ones if they are decorated with precious stones in ancient mounts or embroidery that, be it ever so rich, has long become quasi–Chinese—excludes one from society or makes one ridiculous in it.

Who thinks abstractly? The uneducated, not the educated. Good society does not think abstractly because it is too easy, because it is too lowly (not referring to the external status)—not from an empty affectation of nobility that would place itself above that of which it is not capable, but on account of the inward inferiority of the matter.

The prejudice and respect for abstract thinking are so great that sensitive nostrils will begin to smell some satire or irony at this point; but since they read the morning paper they know that there is a prize to be had for satires and that I should therefore sooner earn it by competing for it than give up here without further ado.

I have only to adduce examples for my proposition: everybody will grant that they confirm it. A murderer is led to the place of execution. For the common populace he is nothing but a murderer. Ladies perhaps remark that he is a strong, handsome, interesting man. The populace finds this remark terrible: What? A murderer handsome? How can one think so wickedly and call a murderer handsome; no doubt, you yourselves are something not much better! This is the corruption of morals that is prevalent in the upper classes, a priest may add, knowing the bottom of things and human hearts.

One who knows men traces the development of the criminal's mind: he finds in his history, in his education, a bad family relationship between his father and mother, some tremendous harshness after this human being had done some minor wrong, so he became embittered against the social order—a first reaction to this that in effect expelled him and henceforth did not make it possible for him to preserve himself except through crime.—There may be people who will say when they hear such things: he wants to excuse this murderer! After all I remember how in my youth I heard a mayor lament that writers of books were going too far and sought to extirpate Christianity and righteousness altogether; somebody had written a defense of suicide; terrible, really too terrible!—Further questions revealed that *The Sufferings of Werther* [by Goethe, 1774] were meant.

This is abstract thinking: to see nothing in the murderer except the abstract fact that he is a murderer, and to annul all other human essence in him with this simple quality.

It is quite different in refined, sentimental circles—in Leipzig. There they strewed and bound flowers on the wheel and on the criminal who was tied to it.—But this again is the opposite abstraction. The Christians may indeed trifle with Rosicrucianism, or rather cross-rosism, and wreathe roses around the cross. The cross is the gallows and wheel that have long been hallowed. It has lost its one-sided significance of being the instrument of dishonorable punishment and, on the contrary, suggests the notion of the highest pain and the deepest rejection together with the most joyous rapture and divine honor. The wheel in Leipzig, on the other hand, wreathed with violets and poppies, is a reconciliation à la Kotzebue, a kind of slovenly sociability between sentimentality and badness.

In quite a different manner I once heard a common old woman who worked in a hospital kill the abstraction of the murderer and bring him to life for honor. The severed head had been placed on the scaffold, and the sun was shining. How beautifully, she said, the sun of God's grace shines on Binder's head!—You are not worthy of having the sun shine on you, one says to a rascal with whom one is angry. This woman saw that the murderer's head was struck by the sunshine and thus still worthy of it. She raised it from the punishment of the scaffold into the sunny grace of God, and instead of accomplishing the reconciliation with violets and sentimental vanity, saw him accepted in grace in the higher sun.

Old woman, your eggs are rotten! the maid says to the market woman. What? she replies, my eggs rotten? You may be rotten! You say that about my eggs? You? Did not lice eat your father on the highways? Didn't your mother run away with the French, and didn't your grandmother die in a public hospital? Let her get a whole shirt instead of that flimsy scarf; we know well where she got that scarf and her hats: if it were not for those officers, many wouldn't be decked out like that these days, and if their ladyships paid more attention to their households, many would be in jail right now. Let her mend the holes in her stockings!—In brief, she does not leave one whole thread on her. She thinks abstractly and subsumes the other woman—scarf, hat, shirt, etc., as well as her fingers and other parts of her, and her father and whole family, too—solely under the crime that she has found the eggs rotten. Everything about her is colored through and through by these rotten eggs, while those officers of which the market woman spoke— if, as one may seriously doubt, there is anything to that—may have got to see very different things.

To move from the maid to a servant, no servant is worse off than one who works for a man of low class and low income; and he is better off the nobler his master is. The common man again thinks more abstractly, he gives himself noble airs vis-à-vis the servant and relates himself to the other man merely as to a servant; he clings to this one predicate. The servant is best off among the French. The nobleman is familiar with his servant, the Frenchman is his friend. When they are alone, the servant does the talking: see Diderot's *Jacques et son maître;* the master does nothing but take snuff and see what time it is and lets the servant take care of everything else. The nobleman knows that the servant is not merely a servant, but also knows the latest city news, the girls, and harbors good suggestions; he asks him about these matters, and the servant may say what he knows about these questions. With a French master, the servant may not only do this; he may also broach a subject, have his own opinions and insist on them; and when the master wants something, it is not done with an order but he has to argue and convince the servant of his opinion and add a good word to make sure that this opinion retains the upper hand.

In the army we encounter the same difference. Among the Austrians a soldier may be beaten, he is canaille; for whatever has the passive right to be beaten is canaille.

Thus the common soldier is for the officer this *abstractum* of a beatable subject with whom a gentleman who has a uniform and port *d' epée* must trouble himself—and that could drive one to make a pact with the devil.

INTRODUCTION
TO THE PHILOSOPHY
OF HISTORY (in part)

*   *   *

III

The third kind of history—the *Philosophical*.* No explanation was needed of the two previous classes; their nature was self-evident. It is otherwise with this last, which certainly seems to require an exposition or justification. The most general definition that can be given, is, that the Philosophy of History means nothing but the *thoughtful consideration of it*. Thought is, indeed, essential to humanity. It is this that distinguishes us from the brutes. In sensation, cognition, and intellection; in our instincts and volitions, as far as they are truly human, Thought is an invariable element. To insist upon Thought in this connection with history may, however, appear unsatisfactory. In this science it would seem as if Thought must be subordinate to what is given, to the realities of fact; that this is its basis and guide: while Philosophy dwells in the region of self-produced ideas, without reference to actuality. Approaching history thus prepossessed, Speculation might be expected to treat it as a mere passive material; and, so far from leaving it in its native truth, to force it into conformity with a tyrannous idea, and to construe it, as the phrase is, "*à priori*." But as it is the business of history simply to adopt into its records what is and has been, actual occurrences and transactions; and since it remains true to its character in proportion as it strictly adheres to its data, we seem to have in Philosophy, a process diametrically opposed to that of the historiographer. This contradiction, and the charge consequently brought against speculation, shall be explained and confuted. We do not, however, propose to correct the innumerable special misrepresentations, trite or novel, that are current respecting the aims, the interests, and the modes of treating history, and its relation to Philosophy.

The only Thought which Philosophy brings with it to the contemplation of History, is the simple conception of *Reason;* that Reason is the Sovereign of the World; that the history of the world, therefore, presents us with a rational process. This conviction and intuition is a hypothesis in the domain of history as such. In that of Philosophy it is no hypothesis. It is there proved by speculative cognition, that Reason—and this term may here suffice us, without investigating the relation sustained by the Universe to

---

*[The first two kinds are "Original History" (descriptions of events which the historian has witnessed) and "Reflective History" (a general history which includes events and deeds the historian has not observed).]

the Divine Being—is *Substance,* as well as *Infinite Power;* its own *Infinite Material* underlying all the natural and spiritual life which it originates, as also the *Infinite Form*—that which sets this Material in motion. On the one hand, Reason is the *substance* of the Universe; *viz.,* that by which and in which all reality has its being and subsistence. On the other hand, it is the *Infinite Energy* of the Universe; since Reason is not so powerless as to be incapable of producing anything but a mere ideal, a mere intention-having its place outside reality, nobody knows where; something separate and abstract, in the heads of certain human beings. It is the *infinite complex of things,* their entire Essence and Truth. It is its own material which it commits to its own Active Energy to work up; not needing, as finite action does, the conditions of an external material of given means from which it may obtain its support, and the objects of its activity. It supplies its own nourishment, and is the object of its own operations. While it is exclusively its own basis of existence, and absolute final aim, it is also the energizing power realizing this aim; developing it not only in the phenomena of the Natural, but also of the Spiritual Universe—the History of the World. That this "Idea" or "Reason" is the *True,* the *Eternal,* the absolutely *powerful* essence; that it reveals itself in the World, and that in that World nothing else is revealed but this and its honor and glory—is the thesis which, as we have said, has been proved in Philosophy, and is here regarded as demonstrated.

In those of my hearers who are not acquainted with Philosophy, I may fairly presume, at least, the existence of a *belief* in Reason, a desire, a thirst for acquaintance with it, in entering upon this course of lectures. It is, in fact, the wish for rational insight, not the ambition to amass a mere heap of acquirements, that should be presupposed in every case as possessing the mind of the learner in the study of science. If the clear idea of Reason is not already developed in our minds, in beginning the study of Universal History, we should at least have the firm, unconquerable faith that Reason *does* exist there; and that the World of intelligence and conscious volition is not abandoned to chance, but must show itself in the light of the self-cognizant Idea. Yet I am not obliged to make any such preliminary demand upon your faith. What I have said thus provisionally, and what I shall have further to say, is, even in reference to *our* branch of science, not to be regarded as hypothetical, but as a summary view of the whole; the *result of the investigation* we are about to pursue; a result which happens to be known to *me,* because I have traversed the entire field. It is only an inference from the history of the World, that its development has been a rational process; that the history in question has constituted the rational necessary course of the World-Spirit—that Spirit whose nature is always one and the same, but which unfolds this its one nature in the phenomena of the World's existence. This must, as before stated, present itself as the ultimate *result* of History. But we have to take the latter as it is. We must proceed historically—empirically. Among other precautions we must take care not to be misled by professed historians who (especially among the Germans, and enjoying a considerable authority), are chargeable with the very procedure of which they accuse the Philosopher—introducing *à priori* inventions of their own into the records of the Past. It is, for example, a widely current fiction, that there was an original primeval people, taught immediately by God, endowed with perfect insight and wisdom, possessing a thorough knowledge of all natural laws and spiritual truth; that there have been such or such sacerdotal peoples; or, to mention a more specific averment, that there was a Roman Epos, from which the Roman historians derived the early annals of their city, etc. Authorities of this kind we leave to those talented historians by profession, among whom (in Germany at least) their use is not uncommon. We might then announce it as the first condition to be observed, that we should faithfully adopt all that is historical. But in such general expressions themselves, as "faithfully" and "adopt," lies the ambiguity. Even the ordinary, the "impartial" historiographer, who believes and professes that he maintains a simply receptive attitude; surrendering himself only to the data supplied him—is by no means passive as regards the exercise of his thinking powers. He brings his categories with him, and sees the phenomena presented to his mental vision, exclusively through these media. And, especially in all that pretends to the name of science, it is indispensable that Reason should not sleep—that reflection should be in full play. To him who looks upon the world rationally, the world in its turn presents a rational aspect. The relation is mutual. But the various exercises of reflection, the different points of view, the modes of deciding the simple question of the relative importance of events (the first category that occupies the attention of the historian), do not belong to this place.

I will only mention two phases and points of view that concern the generally diffused conviction that Reason has ruled, and is still ruling in the world, and consequently in the world's history; because they give us, at the same time, an opportunity for more closely investigating the question that presents the greatest difficulty, and for indicating a branch of the subject, which will have to be enlarged on in the sequel.

I. One of these points is, that passage in history, which informs us that the Greek Anaxagoras was the first to enunciate the doctrine that ⟨*nous*⟩, Understanding generally, or Reason, governs the world. It is not intelligence as self-conscious Reason—not a Spirit as such that is meant; and we must clearly distinguish these from each other. The movement of the solar system takes place according to unchangeable laws. These laws are Reason, implicit in the phenomena in question. But neither the sun nor the planets, which revolve around it according to these laws, can be said to have any consciousness of them.

A thought of this kind—that Nature is an embodiment of Reason; that it is unchangeably subordinate to universal laws, appears no wise striking or strange to us. We are accustomed to such conceptions, and find nothing extraordinary in them. And I have mentioned this extraordinary occurrence, partly to show how history teaches, that ideas of this kind, which may seem trivial to us, have not always been in the world; that, on the contrary, such a thought makes an epoch in the annals of human intelligence. Aristotle says of Anaxagoras, as the originator of the thought in question, that he appeared as a sober man among the drunken. Socrates adopted the doctrine from Anaxagoras, and it forthwith became the ruling idea in Philosophy—except in the school of Epicurus, who ascribed all events to chance. "I was delighted with the sentiment"—Plato makes Socrates say—"and hoped I had found a teacher who would show me Nature in harmony with Reason, who would demonstrate in each particular phenomenon its specific aim, and in the whole, the grand object of the Universe. I would not have surrendered this hope for a great deal. But how very much was I disappointed, when, having zealously applied myself to the writings of Anaxagoras, I found that he adduces only external causes, such as Atmosphere, Ether, Water, and the like." It is evident that the defect which Socrates complains of respecting Anaxagoras's doctrine, does not concern the principle itself, but the shortcoming of the propounder in applying it to Nature in the concrete. Nature is not deduced from that principle: the latter remains in fact a mere abstraction, inasmuch as the former is not comprehended and exhibited as a development of it—an organization produced by and from Reason. I wish, at the very outset, to call your attention to the important difference between a conception, a principle, a truth limited to an *abstract* form and its determinate application, and concrete development. This distinction affects the whole fabric of philosophy; and among other bearings of it there is one to which we shall have to revert at the close of our view of Universal History, in investigating the aspect of political affairs in the most recent period.

We have next to notice the rise of this idea—that Reason directs the World—in connection with a further application of it, well known to us—in the form, *viz.,* of the *religious truth,* that the world is not abandoned to chance and external contingent causes, but that a *Providence* controls it. I stated above,that I would not make a demand on your faith, in regard to the principle announced. Yet I might appeal to your belief in it, *in this religious aspect,* if, as a general rule, the nature of philosophical science allowed it to attach authority to presuppositions. To put it in another shape—this appeal is forbidden, because the science of which we have to treat, proposes itself to furnish the proof (not indeed of the abstract *Truth* of the doctrine, but) of its correctness as compared with facts. The truth, then, that a Providence (that of God) presides over the events of the World—consorts with the proposition in question; for *Divine* Providence is Wisdom, endowed with an infinite Power, which realizes its aim, *viz.,* the absolute rational design of the World. Reason is Thought conditioning itself with perfect freedom. But a difference—rather a contradiction—will manifest itself, between this belief and our principle, just as was the case in reference to the demand made by Socrates in the case of Anaxagoras's dictum. For that belief is similarly indefinite; it is what is called a belief in a general Providence, and is not followed out into definite application, or displayed in its bearing on the grand total—the entire course of human history. But to *explain* History is to depict the passions of mankind, the genius, the active powers, that play their part on the great stage; and the providentially determined process which these exhibit, constitutes what is generally called the "plan" of Providence. Yet it is this very plan which is supposed to be concealed from our view: which it is deemed presumption, even to wish to recognize. The ignorance of Anaxagoras, as to how intelligence reveals itself in actual existence, was ingenuous. Neither in his consciousness, nor in that of Greece at large, had that thought been farther expanded. He had not attained the power to apply his general principle to the concrete, so as to deduce the latter from the former. It was Socrates who took the first step in comprehending the union of the Concrete with the Universal. Anaxagoras, then, did not take up a *hostile* position toward such an application. The common belief in Providence *does;* at least it opposes the use of the principle on the large scale, and denies the possibility of discerning the plan of Providence. In isolated cases this plan is supposed to be manifest. Pious persons are encouraged to recognize in particular circumstances, something more than mere chance; to acknowledge the guiding hand of God; *e.g.,* when help has unexpectedly come to an individual in great perplexity and need. But these instances of providential design are of a limited kind, and concern the accomplishment of nothing more than the desires of the individual in question. But in the history of the World, the *Individuals* we have to do with are *Peoples;* Totalities that are States. We cannot, therefore, be satisfied with what we may call this "peddling" view of Providence, to which the belief alluded to limits itself. Equally unsatisfactory is the merely abstract, undefined belief in a Providence, when that belief is not brought to bear upon the details of the process which it conducts. On the contrary our earnest endeavor must be directed to the recognition of the ways of Providence, the means it uses, and the historical phenomena in which it manifests itself; and we must show their connection with the general principle above mentioned. But in noticing the recognition of the plan of Divine Providence generally, I have implicitly touched upon a prominent question. of the day; *viz.,* that of the possibility of knowing God: or rather, since public opinion has ceased to allow it to be a matter of *question,* the *doctrine* that it is impossible to know God. In direct contravention of what is commanded in holy Scripture as the highest duty—that we should not merely love, but *know* God—the prevalent dogma involves the denial of what is there said; *viz.,* that it is the Spirit *(der Geist)* that leads into Truth, knows all things, penetrates even into the deep things of the Godhead. While the Divine Being is thus placed beyond our knowledge, and outside the limit of all human things, we have the convenient license of wandering as far as we list, in the direction of our own fancies. We are freed from the obligation to refer our knowledge to the Divine and True. On the other hand, the vanity and egotism which characterize it, find, in this false position, ample justification; and the pious modesty which puts far from it the knowledge of God, can well estimate how much furtherance thereby accrues to its own wayward and vain strivings. I have been unwilling to leave out of sight the connection between our thesis—that Reason governs and has governed the World—and the question of the possibility of a knowledge of God, chiefly that I might not lose the opportunity of mentioning the imputation against Philosophy of being shy of noticing religious truths, or of having occasion to be so; in which is insinuated the suspicion that it has anything but a clear conscience in the presence of these truths. So far from this being the case, the fact is, that in recent times Philosophy has been obliged to defend the domain of religion against the attacks of several theological systems. In the Christian religion God has revealed Himself, that is, he has given us to understand what He is; so that He is no longer a concealed or secret existence. And this possibility of knowing Him, thus afforded us, renders such knowledge a duty. God wishes no narrowhearted souls or empty heads for his children; but those whose spirit is of itself indeed, poor, but rich in the knowledge of Him; and who regard this knowledge of God as the only valuable possession. That development of the thinking spirit, which has resulted from the revelation of the Divine Being as its original basis, must ultimately advance to the *intellectual* comprehension of what was presented in the first instance, to *feeling* and *imagination*. The time must eventually come for understanding that rich product of active Reason, which the History of the World offers to us. It was for awhile the fashion to profess admiration for the wisdom of God, as displayed in animals, plants, and isolated occurrences. But, if it be allowed that Providence manifests itself in such objects and forms of existence, why not also in Universal History? This is deemed too great a matter to be thus regarded. But Divine Wisdom, *i.e.,* Reason, is one and the same in the great as in the little; and we must not imagine God to be too weak to exercise his wisdom on the grand scale. Our intellectual striving aims at realizing the conviction that what was *intended* by eternal wisdom, is actually *accomplished* in the domain of existent, active Spirit, as well as in that of mere Nature. Our mode of treating the subject is, in this aspect, a *Theodicaea*—a justification of the ways of God—which Leibniz attempted metaphysically, in his method, *i.e.,* in indefinite abstract categories—so that the ill that is found in the World may be comprehended, and the thinking Spirit reconciled with the fact of the existence of evil. Indeed, nowhere is such a harmonizing view more pressingly demanded than in Universal History; and it can be attained only by recognizing the *positive* existence, in which that negative element is a subordinate, and vanquished nullity. On the one hand, the ultimate design of the World must be perceived; and, on the other hand, the fact that this design has been actually realized in it, and that evil has not been able permanently to assert a competing position. But this superintending ⟨*nous*⟩, or in "Providence." "Reason," whose sovereignty over the World has been maintained, is as indefinite a term as "Providence," supposing the term to be used by those who are unable to characterize it distinctly—to show wherein it consists, so as to enable us to decide whether a thing is rational or irrational. An adequate definition of Reason is the first desideratum; and whatever boast may be made of strict adherence to it in explaining phenomena. Without such a definition we get no farther than mere words. With these observations we may proceed to the second point of view that has to be considered in this Introduction.

II. The inquiry into the *essential destiny* of Reason, as far as it is considered in reference to the World, is identical with the question, *what is the ultimate design of the World?* And the expression implies that that design is destined to be realized. Two points of consideration suggest themselves; first, the import of this design—its abstract definition; and secondly, its *realization*.

It must be observed at the outset, that the phenomenon we investigate—Universal History—belongs to the realm of *Spirit*. The term *"World,"* includes both physical and psychical Nature. Physical Nature also plays its part in the World's History, and attention will have to be paid to the fundamental natural relations thus involved. But Spirit, and the course of its development, is our substantial object. Our task does not require us to contemplate Nature as a Rational System in itself, though in its own proper domain it proves itself such, but simply in its relation to *Spirit*. On the stage on which we are observing it—Universal History—Spirit displays itself in its most concrete reality. Notwithstanding this (or rather for the very purpose of comprehending the *general* principles which this, its form of *concrete reality,* embodies) we must premise some abstract characteristics of the *nature of Spirit*. Such an explanation, however, cannot be given here under any other form than that of bare assertion. The present is not the occasion for unfolding the idea of Spirit speculatively; for whatever has a place in an Introduction, must, as already observed, be taken as simply historical; something assumed as having been explained and proved elsewhere; or whose demonstration awaits the sequel of the Science of History itself.

We have therefore to mention here:

1. The abstract characteristics of the nature of Spirit.
2. What means Spirit uses in order to realize its Idea.
3. Lastly, we must consider the shape which the perfect embodiment of Spirit assumes—the State.

(1) The nature of Spirit may be understood by a glance at its direct opposite—*Matter*. As the essence of Matter is Gravity, so, on the other hand, we may affirm that the substance, the essence of Spirit is Freedom. All will readily assent to the doctrine that Spirit, among other properties, is also endowed with Freedom; but philosophy teaches that all the qualities of Spirit exist only through Freedom; that all are but means for attaining Freedom; that all seek and produce this and this alone. It is a result of speculative Philosophy, that Freedom is the sole truth of Spirit. Matter possesses gravity in virtue of its tendency toward a central point. It is essentially composite; consisting of parts that exclude each other. It seeks its Unity; and therefore exhibits itself as self-destructive, as verging toward its opposite [an indivisible point]. If it could attain this, it would be Matter no longer, it would have perished. It strives after the realization of its Idea; for in Unity it exists *ideally*. Spirit, on the contrary, may be defined as that which has its centre in itself. It has not a unity outside itself, but has already found it; it exists *in* and *with itself*. Matter has its essence out of itself; Spirit is *self-contained existence*. Now this is Freedom, exactly. For if I am dependent, my being is referred to something else which I am not; I cannot exist independently of something external. I am free, on the contrary, when my existence depends upon myself. This self-contained existence of Spirit is none other than self-consciousness—consciousness of one's own being. Two things must be distinguished in consciousness; first, the fact *that I know;* secondly, *what I know*. In *self* consciousness these are merged in one; for Spirit *knows* itself. It involves an appreciation of its own nature, as also an energy enabling it to realize itself; to make itself *actually* that which it is *potentially*. According to this abstract definition it may be

said of Universal History, that it is the exhibition of Spirit in the process of working out the knowledge of that which it is potentially. And as the germ bears in Itself the whole nature of the tree, and the taste and form of its fruits, so do the first traces of Spirit virtually contain the whole of that History. The Orientals have not attained the knowledge that Spirit—Man *as such*—is free; and because they do not know this, they are not free. They only know that *one is free*. But on this very account, the freedom of that *one* is only caprice; ferocity—brutal recklessness of passion, or a mildness and tameness of the desires, which is itself only an accident of Nature—mere caprice like the former. That *one* is therefore only a Despot; not a *free man*. The consciousness of Freedom first arose among the Greeks, and therefore they were free; but they, and the Romans likewise, knew only that *some* are free, not man as such. Even Plato and Aristotle did not know this. The Greeks, therefore, had slaves; and their whole life and the maintenance of their splendid liberty, was implicated with the institution of slavery: a fact moreover, which made that liberty on the one hand only an accidental, transient and limited growth; on the other hand, constituted it a rigorous thraldom of our common nature, of the Human. The German nations, under the influence of Christianity, were the first to attain the consciousness, that man, as man, is free: that it is the *freedom* of Spirit which constitutes its essence. This consciousness arose first in religion, the inmost region of Spirit; but to introduce the principle into the various relations of the actual world, involves a more extensive problem than its simple implantation; a problem whose solution and application require a severe and lengthened process of culture. In proof of this, we may note that slavery did not cease immediately on the reception of Christianity. Still less did liberty predominate in States; or Governments and Constitutions adopt a rational organization, or recognize freedom as their basis. That application of the principle to political relations; the thorough moulding and interpenetration of the constitution of society by it, is a process identical with history itself. I have already directed attention to the distinction here involved, between a principle as such, and its *application; i.e.,* its introduction and carrying out in the actual phenomena of Spirit and Life. This is a point of fundamental importance in our science, and one which must be constantly respected as essential. And in the same way as this distinction has attracted attention in view of the *Christian* principle of self-consciousness—Freedom; it also shows itself as an essential one, in view of the principle of Freedom *generally.* The History of the world is none other than the progress of the consciousness of Freedom; a progress whose development according to the necessity of its nature, it is our business to investigate.

The general statement given above, of the various grades in the consciousness of Freedom—and which we applied in the first instance to the fact that the Eastern nations knew only that *one* is free; the Greek and Roman world only that some are free; while we know that all men absolutely (man as *man*) are free—supplies us with the natural division of Universal History, and suggests the mode of its discussion. This is remarked, however, only incidentally and anticipatively; some other ideas must be first explained.

The destiny of the spiritual World, and—since this is the *substantial World,* while the physical remains subordinate to it, or, in the language of speculation, has no truth *as against* the spiritual—*the final cause of the World at large,* we allege to be the *consciousness* of its own freedom on the part of Spirit, and *ipso facto,* the *reality* of that freedom. But that this term "Freedom," without further qualification, is an indefinite, and incalculable ambiguous term; and that while that which it represents is the *ne plus ultra* of attainment, it is liable to an infinity of misunderstandings, confusions and errors, and to become the occasion for all imaginable excesses—has never been more clearly known and felt than in modern times. Yet, for the present, we must content ourselves with the term itself without farther definition. Attention was also directed to the importance of the infinite difference between a principle in the abstract, and its realization in the concrete. In the process before us, the essential nature of freedom—which involves in it absolute necessity—is to be displayed as coming to a consciousness of itself (for it is in its very nature, self-consciousness) and thereby realizing its existence. Itself is its own object of attainment, and the sole aim of Spirit. This result it is, at which the process of the World's History has been continually aiming; and to which the sacrifices that have ever and anon been laid on the vast altar of the earth, through the long lapse of ages, have been offered. This is the only aim that sees itself realized and fulfilled; the only pole of repose amid the ceaseless change of events and conditions, and the sole efficient principle that pervades them. This final aim is God's purpose with the world; but God is the absolutely perfect Being, and can, therefore, will nothing other than himself—his own Will. The Nature of His Will—that is, His Nature itself—is what we here call the Idea of Freedom; translating the language of Religion into that of Thought. The question, then, which we may next put, is: What means does this principle of Freedom use for its realization? This is the second point we have to consider.

(2) The question of the *means* by which Freedom develops itself to a World, conducts us to the phenomenon of History itself. Although Freedom is, primarily, an undeveloped idea, the means it uses are external and phenomenal; presenting themselves in History to our sensuous vision. The first glance at History convinces us that the actions of men proceed from their needs, their passions, their characters and talents; and impresses us with the belief that such needs, passions and interests are the sole springs of action—the efficient agents in this scene of activity. Among these may, perhaps, be found aims of a liberal or universal kind—benevolence it may be, or noble patriotism; but such virtues and general views are but insignificant as compared with the World and its doings. We may perhaps see the Ideal of Reason actualized in those who adopt such aims, and within the sphere of their influence; but they bear only a trifling proportion to the mass of the human race; and the extent of that influence is limited accordingly. Passions, private aims, and the satisfaction of selfish desires, are on the other hand, most effective springs of action. Their power lies in the fact that they respect none of the limitations which justice and morality would impose on them; and that these natural impulses have a more direct influence over man than the artificial and tedious discipline that tends to order and self-restraint, law and morality. When we look at this display of passions, and the consequences of their violence; the Unreason which is associated not only with them, but even (rather we might say *especially*) with *good* designs and righteous aims; when we see the evil, the vice, the ruin that has befallen the most flourishing kingdoms which the mind of man ever created; we can scarce avoid being filled with sorrow at this universal taint of corruption: and, since this decay is not the work of mere Nature, but of the Human Will—a moral embitterment—a revolt of the Good Spirit (if it have a place within us) may well be the result of our reflections. Without rhetorical exaggeration, a simply truthful combination of the miseries that have overwhelmed the noblest of nations and polities, and the finest exemplars of private virtue—forms a picture of most fearful aspect, and excites emotions of the profoundest and most hopeless sadness, counterbalanced by no consolatory result. We endure in beholding it a mental torture, allowing no defence or escape but the consideration that what has happened could not be otherwise; that it is a fatality which no intervention could alter. And at last we draw back from the intolerable disgust with which these sorrowful reflections threaten us, into the more agreeable environment of our individual life—the Present formed by our private aims and interests. In short we retreat into the selfishness that stands on the quiet shore, and thence enjoys in safety the distant spectacle of "wrecks

confusedly hurled." But even regarding History as the slaughter-bench at which the happiness of peoples, the wisdom of States, and the virtue of individuals have been victimized—the question involuntarily arises—to what principle, to what final aim these enormous sacrifices have been offered. From this point the investigation usually proceeds to that which we have made the general commencement of our inquiry. Starting from this we pointed out those phenomena which made up a picture so suggestive of gloomy emotions and thoughtful reflections—as *the very field* which we, for our part, regard as exhibiting only the means for realizing what we assert to be the essential destiny—the absolute aim, or, which comes to the same thing, the true result of the World's History. We have all along purposely eschewed "moral reflections "as a method of rising from the scene of historical specialties to the general principles which they embody. Besides, it is not the interest of such sentimentalities, really to rise above those depressing emotions; and to solve the enigmas of Providence which the considerations that occasioned them, present. It is essential to their character to find a gloomy satisfaction in the empty and fruitless sublimities of that negative result. We return them to the point of view which we have adopted; observing that the successive steps *(Momente)* of the analysis to which it will lead us, will also evolve the conditions requisite for answering the inquiries suggested by the panorama of sin and suffering that history unfolds.

The *first* remark we have to make, and which, though already presented more than once, cannot be too often repeated when the occasion seems to call for it—is that what we call *principle, aim, destiny,* or the nature and idea of Spirit, is something merely general and abstract. Principle—Plan of Existence—Law—is a hidden, undeveloped essence, which *as such,* however true in itself—is not completely real. Aims, principles, etc., have a place in our thoughts, in our subjective design only; but not yet in the sphere of reality. That which exists for itself only, is a possibility, a potentiality; but has not yet emerged into Existence. A *second* element must be introduced in order to produce actuality—*viz.,* actuation, realization; and whose motive power is the Will—the activity of man in the widest sense. It is only by this activity that that Idea as well as abstract characteristics generally, are realized, actualized; for of themselves they are powerless. The motive power that puts them in operation, and gives them determinate existence, is the need, instinct, inclination, and passion of man. That some conception of mine should be developed into act and existence, is my earnest desire: I wish to assert my personality in connection with it: I wish to be satisfied by its execution. If I am to exert myself for any object, it must in some way or other be *my* object. In the accomplishment of such or such designs I must at the same time find *my* satisfaction; although the purpose for which I exert myself includes a complication of results, many of which have no interest for me. This is the absolute right of personal existence—to find *itself* satisfied in its activity and labor. If men are to interest themselves for anything, they must (so to speak) have part of their existence involved in it; find their individuality gratified by its attainment. Here a mistake must be avoided. We intend blame, and justly impute it as a fault, when we say of an individual, that he is "interested" (in taking part in such or such transactions), that is, seeks only his private advantage. In reprehending this we find fault with him for furthering his personal aims without any regard to a more comprehensive design; of which he takes advantage to promote his own interest, or which he even sacrifices with this view. But he who is active in *promoting an object,* is not simply "interested," but interested in that object itself. Language faithfully expresses this distinction. Nothing therefore happens, nothing is accomplished, unless the individuals concerned, seek their own satisfaction in the issue. They are particular units of society; *i.e.,* they have special needs, instincts, and interests generally, peculiar to themselves. Among these needs are not only such as we usually call necessities, the stimuli of individual desire and volition, but also those connected with individual views and convictions; or, to use a term expressing less decision, leanings of opinion; supposing the impulses of reflection, understanding, and reason, to have been awakened. In these cases people demand, if they are to exert themselves in any direction, that the object should commend itself to them; that in point of opinion, whether as to its goodness, justice, advantage, profit, they should be able to "enter into it." This is a consideration of especial importance in our age, when people are less than formerly influenced by reliance on others, and by authority; when, on the contrary, they devote their activities to a cause on the ground of their own understanding, their independent conviction and opinion.

We assert then that nothing has been accomplished without interest on the part of the actors: and—if interest be called passion, inasmuch as the whole individuality, to the neglect of all other actual or possible interests and claims, is devoted to an object with every fibre of volition, concentrating all its desires and powers upon it—we may affirm absolutely that *nothing great in the World* has been accomplished without *passion.* Two elements, therefore, enter into the object of our investigation; the first the Idea, the second the complex of human passions; the one the warp, the other the woof of the vast arras-web of Universal History. The concrete mean and union of the two is Liberty, under the conditions of morality in a State. We have spoken of the Idea of Freedom as the nature of Spirit, and the absolute goal of History. Passion is regarded as a thing of sinister aspect, as more or less immoral. Man is required to have no passions. Passion, it is true, is not quite the suitable word for what I wish to express. I mean here nothing more than the human activity as resulting from private interests—special, or if you will, self-seeking designs—with this qualification, that the whole energy of will and character is devoted to their attainment; that other interests (which would in themselves constitute attractive aims) or rather all things else, are sacrificed to them. The object in question is so bound up with the man's will, that it entirely and alone determines the "hue of resolution," and is inseparable from it. It has become the very essence of his volition. For a person is a specific existence; not man in general (a term to which no real existence corresponds) but a particular human being. The term "character" likewise expresses this idiosyncrasy of Will and Intelligence. But *Character* comprehends all peculiarities whatever; the way in which a person conducts himself in private relations, etc., and is not limited to his idiosyncrasy in its practical and active phase. I shall, therefore, use the term "passions"; understanding thereby the particular bent of character, as far as the peculiarities of volition are not limited to private interest, but supply the impelling and actuating force for accomplishing deeds shared in by the community at large. Passion is in the first instance the *subjective,* and therefore the *formal* side of energy, will, and activity—leaving the object or aim still undetermined. And there is a similar relation of formality to reality in merely individual conviction, individual views, individual conscience. It is always a question of essential importance, what is the purport of my conviction, what the object of my passion, in deciding whether the one or the other is of a true and substantial nature. Conversely, if it is so, it will inevitably attain actual existence—be realized.

From this comment on the second essential element in the historical embodiment of an aim, we infer, glancing at the institution of the State in passing, that a State is then well constituted and internally powerful, when the private interest of its citizens is one with the common interest of the State; when the one finds its gratification and realization in the other—a proposition in itself very important. But in a State many institutions must be adopted, much political machinery invented, accompanied by appropriate political arrangements—necessitating long struggles of the understanding before what is really appropriate can be discovered—involving, moreover, contentions with private interest and passions, and a tedious discipline of these latter, in order to bring about the desired harmony. The epoch when a State attains this harmonious condition, marks the period of its bloom, its virtue, its vigor, and its prosperity. But the history of mankind does not begin with a *conscious* aim of any kind, as it is the case with the particular circles into which men form themselves of set purpose. The mere social instinct implies a conscious purpose of security for life and property; and when society has been constituted, this purpose becomes more comprehensive. The History of the World begins with its general aim, the realization of the Idea of Spirit, only in an *implicit* form that is, as Nature; a hidden, most profoundly hidden, unconscious instinct; and the whole process of History (as already observed), is directed to rendering this unconscious impulse a conscious one. Thus appearing in the form of merely natural existence, natural will— that which has been called the subjective side—physical craving, instinct, passion, private interest, as also opinion and subjective conception—spontaneously present themselves at the very commencement. This vast congeries of volitions, interests and activities, constitute the instruments and means of the World-Spirit for attaining its object; bringing it to consciousness, and realizing it. And this aim is none other than finding itself, coming to itself, and contemplating itself in concrete actuality. But that those manifestations of vitality on the part of individuals and peoples, in which they seek and satisfy their own purposes, are, at the same time, the means and instruments of a higher and broader purpose of which they know nothing—which they realize unconsciously— might be made a matter of question; rather has been questioned, and in every variety of form negatived, decried and condemned as mere dreaming and "Philosophy." But on this point I announced my view at the very outset? and asserted our hypothesis—which, however, will appear in the sequel, in the form of a legitimate inference—and our belief, that Reason governs the world, and has consequently governed its history. In relation to this independently universal and substantial existence—all else is subordinate, subservient to it, and the means for its development. The Union of Universal Abstract Existence generally with the Individual—the Subjective—that this alone is Truth, belongs to the department of speculation, and is treated in this general form in Logic. But in the process of the World's History itself, as still incomplete, the abstract final aim of history is not yet made the distinct object of desire and interest. While these limited sentiments are still unconscious of the purpose they are fulfilling, the universal principle is implicit in them, and is realizing itself through them. The question also assumes the form of the union of *Freedom* and *Necessity;* the latent abstract process of Spirit being regarded as *Necessity,* while that which exhibits itself in the conscious will of men, as their interest, belongs to the domain of *Freedom.* As the metaphysical connection (*i.e.,* the connection in the Idea) of these forms of thought, belongs to Logic, it would be out of place to analyze it here. The chief and cardinal points only shall be mentioned.

Philosophy shows that the Idea advances to an infinite antithesis; that, *viz.,* between the Idea in its free, universal form, in which it exists for itself, and the contrasted form of abstract introversion, reflection on itself, which is formal existence-for-self, personality, formal freedom, such as belongs to Spirit only. The universal Idea exists thus as the substantial totality of things on the one side, and as the abstract essence of free volition on the other side. This reflection of the mind on itself is individual self-consciousness—the polar opposite of the Idea in its general form, and therefore existing in absolute Limitation. This polar opposite is consequently limitation, particularization, for the universal absolute being; it is the side of its *definite existence;* the sphere of its formal reality, the sphere of the reverence paid to God. To comprehend the absolute connection of this antithesis, is the profound task of metaphysics. This Limitation originates all forms of particularity of whatever kind. The formal volition [of which we have spoken] wills itself; desires to make its own personality valid in all that it purposes and does: even the pious individual wishes to be saved and happy. This pole of the antithesis, existing for itself, is—in contrast with the Absolute Universal Being—a special separate existence, taking cognizance of specialty only, and willing that alone. In short it plays its part in the region of mere phenomena. This is the sphere of particular purposes, in effecting which individuals exert themselves on behalf of their individuality, give it full play and objective realization. This is also the sphere of happiness and its opposite. He is happy who finds his condition suited to his special character, will, and fancy, and so enjoys himself in that condition. The History of the World is not the theatre of happiness. Periods of happiness are blank pages in it, for they are periods of harmony, periods when the antithesis is in abeyance. Reflection on self—the Freedom above described—is abstractly defined as the formal element of the activity of the absolute Idea. The realizing *activity* of which we have spoken is the middle term of the Syllogism, one of whose extremes is the Universal essence, the *Idea,* which reposes in the penetralia of Spirit; and the other, the complex of external things—objective matter. That activity is the medium by which the universal latent principle is translated into the domain of objectivity.

I will endeavor to make what has been said more vivid and clear by examples.

The building of a house is, in the first instance, a subjective aim and design. On the other hand we have, as means, the several substances required for the work—Iron, Wood, Stones. The elements are made use of in working up this material: fire to melt the iron, wind to blow the fire, water to set wheels in motion, in order to cut the wood, etc. The result is, that the wind, which has helped to build the house, is shut out by the house; so also are the violence of rains and floods, and the destructive powers of fire, so far as the house is made fireproof. The stones and beams obey the law of gravity, press downward, and so high walls are carried up. Thus the elements are made use of in accordance with their nature, and yet to co-operate for a product, by which their operation is limited. Thus the passions of men are gratified; they develop themselves and their aims in accordance with their natural tendencies, and build up the edifice of human society; thus fortifying a position for Right and Order *against themselves.*

The connection of events above indicated, involves also the fact, that in history an additional result is commonly produced by human actions beyond that which they aim at and obtain—that which they immediately recognize and desire. They gratify their own interest; but something further is thereby accomplished, latent in the actions in question, though not present to their consciousness, and not included in their design. An analogous example is offered in the case of a man who, from a feeling of revenge— perhaps not an unjust one, but produced by injury on the other's part—burns that other man's house. A connection is immediately established between the deed itself and a train of circumstances not directly included in it, taken abstractedly. In itself it consisted in merely presenting a small flame to a small portion of a beam. Events not involved in that simple act follow of themselves. The part of the beam which was set fire to is connected with its remote portions; the beam itself is united with the woodwork of the house generally, and this with other houses; so that a wide conflagration ensues, which destroys the goods and chattels of many other persons besides his against whom the act of revenge was first directed; perhaps even costs not a few men their lives. This lay neither in the deed abstractedly, nor in the design of the man who committed it. But the action has a further general bearing. In the design of the doer it was only revenge executed against an individual in the destruction of his property, but it is moreover a crime, and that involves punishment also. This may not have been present to the mind of the perpetrator, still less in his intention; but his deed itself, the general principles it calls into play, its substantial content entails it. By this example I wish only to impress on you the consideration, that in a simple act, something further may be implicated than lies in the intention and consciousness of the agent. The example before us involves, however, this additional consideration, that the substance of the act, consequently we may say the act itself, recoils upon the perpetrator—reacts upon him with destructive tendency. This union of the two extremes—the embodiment of a general idea in the form of direct reality, and the elevation of a speciality into connection with universal truth—is brought to pass, at first sight, under the conditions of an utter diversity of nature between the two, and an indifference of the one extreme towards the other. The aims which the agents set before them are limited and special; but it must be remarked that the agents themselves are intelligent thinking beings. The purport of their desires is interwoven with *general, essential* considerations of justice, good, duty, etc.; for mere desire, volition in its rough and savage forms, falls not within the scene and sphere of Universal History. Those general considerations, which form at the same time a norm for directing aims and actions, have a determinate purport; for such an abstraction as "good for its own sake," has no place in living reality. If men are to act, they must not only intend the Good, but must have decided for themselves whether this or that particular thing is a Good. What special course of action, however, is good or not, is determined, as regards the ordinary contingencies of private life, by the laws and customs of a State; and here no great difficulty is presented. Each individual has his position; he knows on the whole what a just, honorable course of conduct is. As to ordinary, private relations, the assertion that it is difficult to choose the right and good—the regarding it as the mark of an exalted morality to find difficulties and raise scruples on that score—may be set down to an evil or perverse will, which seeks to evade duties not in themselves of a perplexing nature; or, at any rate, to an idly reflective habit of mind—where a feeble will affords no sufficient exercise to the faculties—leaving them therefore to find occupation within themselves, and to expend themselves on moral self-adulation.

It is quite otherwise with the comprehensive relations that History has to do with. In this sphere are presented those momentous collisions between existing, acknowledged duties, laws, and rights, and those contingencies which are adverse to this fixed system; which assail and even destroy its foundations and existence; whose tenor may nevertheless seem good—on the large scale advantageous—yes, even indispensable and necessary. These contingencies realize themselves in History: they involve a general principle of a different order from that on which depends the *permanence* of a people or a State. This principle is an essential phase in the development of the *creating* Idea, of Truth striving and urging towards [consciousness of] itself. Historical men—*World-Historical Individuals*—are those in whose aims such a general principle lies.

Cæsar, in danger of losing a position, not perhaps at that time of superiority, yet at least of equality with the others who were at the head of the State, and of succumbing to those who were just on the point of becoming his enemies, belongs essentially to this category. These enemies, who were at the same time pursuing *their* personal aims, had the form of the constitution, and the power conferred by an appearance of justice, on their side. Cæsar was contending for the maintenance of his position, honor, and safety; and, since the power of his opponents included the sovereignty over the provinces of the Roman Empire, his victory secured for him the conquest of that entire Empire; and he thus became, though leaving the form of the constitution, the Autocrat of the State. That which secured for him the execution of a design, which in the first instance was of negative import, the Autocracy of Rome, was, however, at the same time an independently necessary feature in the history of Rome and of the world. It was not, then, his private gain merely, but an unconscious impulse that occasioned the accomplishment of that for which the time was ripe. Such are all great historical men—whose own particular aims involve those large issues which are the will of the World-Spirit. They may be called Heroes, inasmuch as they have derived their purposes and their vocation, not from the calm, regular course of things, sanctioned by the existing order; but from a concealed fount—one which has not attained to phenomenal, present existence—from that inner Spirit, still hidden beneath the surface, which, impinging on the outer world as on a shell, bursts it in pieces, because it is another kernel than that which belonged to the shell in question. They are men, therefore, who appear to draw the impulse of their life from themselves; and whose deeds have produced a condition of things and a complex of historical relations which appear to be only *their* interest, and *their* work.

Such individuals had no consciousness of the general Idea they were unfolding, while prosecuting those aims of theirs; on the contrary, they were practical, political men. But at the same time they were thinking men, who had an insight into the requirements of the time—*what was ripe for development*. This was the very Truth for their age, for their world; the species next in order, so to speak, and which was already formed in the womb of time. It was theirs to know this nascent principle; the necessary, directly sequent step in progress, which their world was to take; to make this their aim, and to expend their energy in promoting it. World-historical men—the Heroes of an epoch, must, therefore, be recognized as its clear-sighted ones; *their* deeds, *their* words are the best of that time. Great men have formed purposes to satisfy themselves, not others. Whatever prudent designs and counsels they might have learned from others, would be the more limited and inconsistent features in their career; for it was they who best understood affairs; from whom *others* learned, and approved, or at least acquiesced in their policy. For that Spirit which had taken this fresh step in history is the inmost soul of all individuals; but in a state of unconsciousness which the great men in question aroused. Their fellows, therefore, follow these soul-leaders; for they feel the irresistible power of their own inner Spirit thus embodied. If we go on to cast a look at the fate of these World-Historical persons, whose vocation it was to be the agents of the World-Spirit, we shall find it to have been no happy one. They attained no calm enjoyment; their whole life was labor and trouble; their whole nature was nought else but their master-passion. When their object is attained they fall off like empty hulls from the kernel. They die early, like Alexander; they are murdered, like Cæsar; transported to St. Helena, like Napoleon. This fearful consolation—that historical men have not enjoyed what is called happiness, and of which only private life (and this may be passed under very various external circumstances) is capable—this consolation those may draw from history, who stand in need of it; and it is craved by Envy—vexed at what is great and transcendent—striving, therefore, to depreciate it, and to find some flaw in it. Thus in modern times it has been demonstrated *ad nauseum* that princes are generally unhappy on their thrones; in consideration of which the possession of a throne is tolerated, and men acquiesce in the fact that not themselves but the personages in question are its occupants. The Free Man, we may observe, is not envious, but gladly recognizes what is great and exalted, and rejoices that it exists.

It is in the light of those common elements which constitute the interest and therefore the passions of individuals, that these historical men are to be regarded. They are *great* men, because they willed and accomplished something great; not a mere fancy, a mere intention, but that which met the case and fell in with the needs of the age. This mode of considering them also excludes the so-called "psychological" view, which, serving the purpose of envy most effectually, contrives so to refer all actions to the heart—to bring them under such a subjective aspect—as that their authors appear to have done everything under the impulse of some passion, mean or grand—some *morbid craving*—and on account of these passions and cravings to have been not moral men. Alexander of Macedon partly subdued Greece, and then Asia; therefore he was possessed by a *morbid craving* for conquest. He is alleged to have acted from a craving for fame, for conquest; and the proof that these were the impelling motives is that he did that which resulted in fame. What pedagogue has not demonstrated of Alexander the Great, of Julius Cæsar, that they were instigated by such passions, and were consequently immoral men? Whence the conclusion immediately follows that he, the pedagogue, is a better man than they, because he has not such passions; a proof of which lies in the fact that he does not conquer Asia—vanquish Darius and Porus—but while he enjoys life himself, lets others enjoy it too. These psychologists are particularly fond of contemplating those peculiarities of great historical figures which appertain to them as private persons. Man must eat and drink; he sustains relations to friends and acquaintances; he has passing impulses and ebullitions of temper. "No man is a hero to his valet-de-chambre," is a well-known proverb; I have added—and Goethe repeated it ten years later—"but not because the former is no hero, but because the latter is a valet." He takes off the hero's boots, assists him to bed, knows that he prefers champagne, etc. Historical personages waited upon in historical literature by such psychological valets, come poorly off; they are brought down by these their attendants to a level with, or rather a few degrees below the level of, the morality of such exquisite discerners of spirits. The Thersites of Homer who abuses the kings is a standing figure for all times. Blows, that is beating with a solid cudgel, he does not get in every age, as in the Homeric one; but his envy, his egotism, is the thorn which he has to carry in his flesh; and the undying worm that gnaws him is the tormenting consideration that his excellent views

Coalbrookdale by Night, 1801, by Phillip James De Loutherbourg. The coal furnaces in the background light the sky and illuminate the fragments from the past in the foreground, symbolizing the onward march of history. *(Science Museum, London)*

and vituperations remain absolutely without result in the world. But our satisfaction at the fate of Thersitism also, may have its sinister side.

A World-historical individual is not so unwise as to indulge a variety of wishes to divide his regards. He is devoted to the One Aim, regardless of all else. It is even possible that such men may treat other great, even sacred interests, inconsiderately; conduct which is indeed obnoxious to moral reprehension. But so mighty a form must trample down many an innocent flower, crush to pieces many an object in its path.

The special interest of passion is thus inseparable from the active development of a general principle: for it is from the special and determinate and from its negation, that the Universal results. Particularity contends with its like, and some loss is involved in the issue. *It* is not the general idea that is implicated in opposition and combat, and that is exposed to danger. It remains in the background, untouched and uninjured. This may be called the *cunning of reason*—that it sets the passions to work for itself, while that which develops its existence through such impulsion pays the penalty, and suffers loss. For it is *phenomenal* being that is so treated, and of this, part is of no value, part is positive and real. The particular is for the most part of too trifling value as compared with the general: individuals are sacrificed and abandoned. The Idea pays the penalty of determinate existence and of corruptibility, not from itself, but from the passions of individuals.

But though we might tolerate the idea that individuals, their desires and the gratification of them, are thus sacrificed, and their happiness given up to the empire of chance, to which it belongs; and that as a general rule, individuals come under the category of means to an ulterior end—there is one aspect of human individuality which we should hesitate to regard in that subordinate light, even in relation to the highest; since it is absolutely no subordinate element, but exists in those individuals as inherently eternal and divine. I mean *morality, ethics, religion.* Even when speaking of the realization of the great ideal aim by means of individuals, the *subjective* element in them—their interest and that of their cravings and impulses, their views and judgments, though exhibited as the merely formal side of their existence—was spoken of as having an infinite right to be consulted. The first idea that presents itself in speaking of *means* is that of something external to the object, and having no share in the object itself. But merely natural things—even the commonest lifeless objects—used as means, must be of such a kind as adapts them to their purpose; they must possess something in common with it. Human beings least of all, sustain the bare external relation of mere means to the great ideal aim. Not only do they in the very act of realizing it, make it the occasion of satisfying personal desires, whose purport is diverse from that aim—but they share in that ideal aim itself; and are for that very reason objects of their own existence; not *formally* merely, as the world of living beings generally is—whose individual life is essentially subordinate to that of man, and is properly used *up* as an instrument. Men, on the contrary, are objects of existence to themselves, as regards the intrinsic import of the aim in question. To this order belongs that in them which we would exclude from the category of mere means—Morality, Ethics, Religion. That is to say, man is an object of existence in himself only in virtue of the Divine that is in him—that which was designated at the outset as *Reason;* which, in view of its activity and power of self-determination, was called *Freedom.* And we affirm, without entering at present on the proof of the assertion, that Religion, Morality, etc., have their foundation and source in that principle, and so are essentially elevated above all alien necessity and chance. And here we must remark that individuals, to the extent of their freedom, are responsible for the depravation and enfeeblement of morals and religion. This is the seal of the absolute and sublime destiny of man—that he knows what is good and what is evil; that his Destiny *is* his very ability to will either good or evil—in one word, that he is the subject of moral imputation, imputation not only of evil, but of good; and not only concerning this or that particular matter, and all that happens *ab extra,* but *also* the good and evil attaching to his individual freedom. The brute alone is simply innocent. It would, however, demand an extensive explanation, as extensive as the analysis of moral freedom itself, to preclude or obviate all the misunderstandings which the statement that what is called innocence imports the entire unconsciousness of evil—is wont to occasion.

In contemplating the fate which virtue, morality, even piety experience in history, we must not fall into the Litany of Lamentations, that the good and pious often, or for the most part, fare ill in the world, while the evil-disposed and wicked prosper. The term *prosperity* is used in a variety of meanings—riches, outward honor, and the like. But in speaking of something which in and for itself constitutes an aim of existence, that so-called well or ill-faring of these or those isolated individuals cannot be regarded as an essential element in the rational order of the universe. With more justice than happiness—or a fortunate environment for individuals—it is demanded of the grand aim of the world's existence, that it should foster, nay involve the execution and ratification of good, moral, righteous purposes. What makes men morally discontented (a discontent, by the bye, on which they somewhat pride themselves), is that they do not find the present adapted to the realization of aims which they hold to be right and just (more especially in modern times, ideals of political constitutions); they contrast unfavorably things as they *are,* with their idea of things as they *ought* to be. In this case it is not private interest nor passion that desires gratification, but Reason, Justice, Liberty; and equipped with this title, the demand in question assumes a lofty bearing, and readily adopts a position not merely of discontent, but of open revolt against the actual condition of the world. To estimate such a feeling and such views aright, the demands insisted upon, and the very dogmatic opinions asserted, must be examined. At no time so much as in our own, have such general principles and notions been advanced, or with greater assurance. If in days gone by, history seems to present itself as a struggle of passions; in our time, though displays of passion are not wanting, it exhibits partly a predominance of the struggle of notions assuming the authority of principles; partly that of passions and interests essentially subjective, but under the mask of such higher sanctions. The pretensions thus contended for as legitimate in the name of that which has been stated as the ultimate aim of Reason, pass accordingly, for absolute aims—to the same extent as Religion, Morals, Ethics. Nothing, as before remarked, is now more common than the complaint that the *ideals* which imagination sets up are not realized—that these glorious dreams are destroyed by cold actuality. These Ideals, which in the voyage of life founder on the rocks of hard reality, may be in the first instance only subjective, and belong to the idiosyncrasy of the individual, imagining himself the highest and wisest. Such do not properly belong to this category. For the fancies which the individual in his isolation indulges, cannot be the model for universal reality; just as *universal* law is not designed for the units of the mass. These as such may, in fact, find their interests decidedly thrust into the background. But by the term "Ideal," we also understand the ideal of Reason, of the Good, of the True. Poets, as *e.g.* Schiller, have painted such ideals touchingly and with strong emotion, and with the deeply melancholy conviction that they could not be realized. In affirming, on the contrary, that the Universal Reason does realize itself, we have indeed nothing to do with the individual empirically regarded. That admits of degrees of better and worse, since here chance and speciality have received authority from the Idea to exercise their monstrous power. Much, therefore, in particular aspects of the grand phenomenon might be found fault with. This subjective fault-finding—which, however, only keeps in view the individual and its deficiency, without taking notice of Reason pervading the whole—is easy; and inasmuch as it asserts an excellent intention with regard to the good of the whole, and seems to result from a kindly heart, it feels authorized to give itself airs and assume great consequence. It is easier to discover a deficiency in individuals, in states, and in Providence, than to see their real import and value. For in this merely negative fault–finding a proud position is taken, one which overlooks the object, without having entered into it, without having comprehended its positive aspect. Age generally makes men more tolerant; youth is always discontented. The tolerance of age is the result of the ripeness of a judgment which, not merely as the result of indifference, is satisfied even with what is inferior; but, more deeply taught by the grave experience of life, has been led to perceive the substantial, solid worth of the object in question. The insight then to which—in contradistinction from those ideals—philosophy is to lead us, is, that the real world is as it ought to be, that the truly good, the universal divine reason, is not a mere abstraction, but a vital principle capable of realizing itself. This *Good,* this *Reason,* in its most concrete form, is God. God governs the world; the actual working of his government, the carrying out of his plan, is the History of the World. This plan philosophy strives to comprehend; for only that which has been developed as the result of it, possesses *bona fide* reality. That which does not accord with it, is negative, worthless existence. Before the pure light of this divine Idea, which is no mere Ideal, the phantom of a world whose events are an incoherent concourse of fortuitous circumstances, utterly vanishes. Philosophy wishes to discover the substantial purport, the real side of the divine idea, and to justify the so much despised Reality of things; for Reason is the comprehension of the Divine work. But as to what concerns the perversion, corruption, and ruin of religious, ethical, and moral purposes, and states of society generally, it must be affirmed, that in their *essence* these are infinite and eternal; but that the forms they assume may be of a limited order, and consequently belong to the domain of mere nature, and be subject to the sway of chance. They are therefore perishable, and exposed to decay and corruption. Religion and morality, in the same way as inherently universal essences, have the peculiarity of being present in the individual soul, in the full extent of their Idea, and therefore truly and really; although, they may not manifest themselves in it *in extenso,* and are not applied to fully developed relations. The religion, the morality of a limited sphere of life—that of a shepherd or a peasant, *e.g.,*—in its intensive concentration and limitation to a few perfectly simple relations of life—has infinite worth; the same worth as the religion and morality of extensive knowledge, and of an existence rich in the compass of its relations and actions. This inner focus—this simple region of the claims of subjective freedom—the home of volition, resolution, and action, the abstract sphere of conscience—that which comprises the responsibility and moral value of the individual, remains untouched; and is quite shut out from the noisy din of the World's History—including not merely external and temporal changes, but also those entailed by the absolute necessity inseparable from the realization of the Idea of Freedom itself. But as a general truth this must be regarded as settled, that whatever in the world possesses claims as noble and glorious, has nevertheless a higher existence above it. The claim of the World-Spirit rises above all special claims.

These observations may suffice in reference to the means which the World-Spirit uses for realizing its Idea. Stated simply and abstractly, this mediation involves the activity of personal existences in whom Reason is present as their absolute, substantial being; but a basis, in the first instance, still obscure and unknown to them. But the subject becomes more complicated and difficult when we regard individuals not merely in their aspect of activity, but more concretely, in conjunction with a particular manifestation of that activity in their religion and morality—forms of existence which are intimately connected with Reason, and share in its absolute claims. Here the relation of mere means to an end disappears, and the chief bearings of this seeming difficulty in reference to the absolute aim of Spirit, have been briefly considered.

(3) The third point to be analyzed is, therefore—what is the object to be realized by these means; *i.e.* what is the form it assumes in the realm of reality. We have spoken of *means;* but in the carrying out of a subjective, limited aim, we have also to take into consideration the element of a *material,* either already present or which has to be procured. Thus the question would arise: What is the material in which the Ideal of Reason is wrought out? The primary answer would be—Personality itself—human desires—Subjectivity generally. In human knowledge and volition, as its material element, Reason attains positive existence. We have considered subjective volition where it has an object which is the truth and essence of a reality, *viz.,* where it constitutes a great world-historical passion. As a subjective will, occupied with limited passions, it is dependent, and can gratify its desires only within the limits of this dependence. But the subjective will has also a substantial life—a reality—in which it moves in the region of *essential* being, and has the essential itself as the object of its existence. This essential being is the union of the *subjective* with the *rational* Will: it is the moral Whole, the *State,* which is that form of reality in which the individual has and enjoys his freedom; but on the condition of his recognizing, believing in, and willing that which is common to the Whole. And this must not be understood as if the subjective will of the social unit attained its gratification and enjoyment through that common Will; as if this were a means provided for its benefit; as if the individual, in his relations to other individuals, thus limited his freedom, in order that this universal limitation—the mutual constraint of all—might secure a small space of liberty for each. Rather, we affirm, are Law, Morality, Government, and they alone, the positive reality and completion of Freedom. Freedom of a low and limited order, is mere caprice; which finds its exercise in the sphere of particular and limited desires.

Subjective volition—Passion—is that which sets men in activity, that which effects "practical" realization. The Idea is the inner spring of action; the State is the actually existing, realized moral life. For it is the Unity of the universal, essential Will, with that of the individual; and this is "Morality." The Individual living in this unity has a moral life; possesses a value that consists in this substantiality alone. Sophocles in his *Antigone,* says, "The divine commands are not of yesterday, nor of to-day; no, they have an infinite existence, and no one could say whence they came." The laws of morality are not accidental, but are the essentially Rational. It is the very object of the State that what is essential in the practical activity of men, and in their dispositions, should be duly recognized; that it should have a manifest existence, and maintain its position. It is the absolute interest of Reason that this moral Whole should exist; and herein lies the justification and merit of heroes who have founded states—however rude these may have been. In the history of the World, only those peoples can come under our notice which form a state. For it must be understood that this latter is the realization of Freedom, *i.e.* of the absolute final aim, and that it exists for its own sake. It must further be understood that all the worth which the human being possesses, all spiritual reality, he possesses only through the State. For his spiritual reality consists in this, that his own essence—Reason—is objectively present to him, that it possesses objective immediate existence for him. Thus only is he fully conscious; thus only is he a partaker of morality, of a just and moral social and political life. For Truth is the Unity of the universal and subjective Will; and the Universal is to be found in the State, in its laws, its universal and rational arrangements. The State is the Divine Idea as it exists on Earth. We have in it, therefore, the object of History in a more definite shape than before; that in which Freedom obtains objectivity, and lives in the enjoyment of this objectivity. For Law is the objectivity of Spirit; volition in its true form. Only that will which obeys law, is free; for it obeys itself—it is independent and so free. When the State or our country constitutes a community of existence; when the subjective will of man submits to laws—the contradiction between Liberty and Necessity vanishes. The Rational has necessary existence, as being the reality and substance of things, and we are free in recognizing it as law, and following it as the substance of our own being. The objective and the subjective will are then reconciled, and present one identical homogeneous whole. For the morality of the State is not of that ethical reflective kind, in which one's own conviction bears sway; this latter is rather the peculiarity of the modern time, while the true antique morality is based on the principle of abiding by one's duty [to the state at large]. An Athenian citizen did what was required of him, as it were from instinct: but if I reflect on the object of my activity, I must have the consciousness that my will has been called into exercise. But morality is Duty—substantial Right—a "*second* nature" as it has been justly called; for the *first* nature of man is his primary merely animal existence.

The development *in extenso* of the Idea of the State belongs to the Philosophy of Jurisprudence; but it must be observed that in the theories of our time various errors are current respecting it, which pass for established truths, and have become fixed prejudices. We will mention only a few of them, giving prominence to such as have a reference to the object of our history.

The error which first meets us is the direct contradictory of our principle that the state presents the realization of Freedom; the opinion, *viz.*, that man is free by *nature* but that in *society,* in the State, to which nevertheless he is irresistibly impelled, he must limit this natural freedom. That man is free by Nature is quite correct in one sense; *viz.*, that he is so according to the Idea of Humanity; but we imply thereby that he is such only in virtue of his destiny—that he has an undeveloped power to become such; for the "Nature" of an object is exactly synonymous with its "Idea." But the view in question imports more than this. When man is spoken of as "free by Nature," the mode of his existence as well as his destiny is implied. His merely natural and primary condition is intended. In this sense a "state of Nature" is assumed in which mankind at large are in the possession of their natural rights with the unconstrained exercise and enjoyment of their freedom. This assumption is not indeed raised to the dignity of the historical fact; it would indeed be difficult, were the attempt seriously made, to point out any such condition as actually existing, or as having ever occurred. Examples of a savage state of life can be pointed out, but they are marked by brutal passions and deeds of violence; while, however rude and simple their conditions, they involve social arrangements which (to use the common phrase) *restrain* freedom. That assumption is one of those nebulous images which theory produces; an idea which it cannot avoid originating, but which it fathers upon real existence, without sufficient historical justification.

What we find such a state of Nature to be in actual experience, answers exactly to the Idea of a *merely* natural condition. Freedom as the *ideal* of that which is original and natural, does not exist as *original and natural*. Rather must it be first sought out and won; and that by an incalculable medial discipline of the intellectual and moral powers. The state of Nature is, therefore, predominantly that of injustice and violence, of untamed natural impulses, of inhuman deeds and feelings. Limitation is certainly produced by Society and the State, but it is a limitation of the mere brute emotions and rude instincts; as also, in a more advanced stage of culture, of the premeditated self-will of caprice and passion. This kind of constraint is part of the instrumentality by which only, the consciousness of Freedom and the desire for its attainment, in its true—that is Rational and Ideal form—can be obtained. To the Ideal of Freedom, Law and Morality are indispensably requisite; and they are in and for themselves, universal existences, objects and aims; which are discovered only by the activity of thought, separating itself from the merely sensuous, and developing itself, in opposition thereto; and which must on the other hand, be introduced into and incorporated with the originally sensuous will, and that contrarily to its natural inclination. The perpetually recurring misapprehension of Freedom consists in regarding that term only in its *formal,* subjective sense, abstracted from its essential objects and aims; thus a constraint put upon impulse, desire, passion—pertaining to the particular individual as such—a limitation of caprice and self-will is regarded as a fettering of Freedom. We should on the contrary look upon such limitation as the indispensable proviso of emancipation. Society and the State are the very conditions in which Freedom is realized.

We must notice a second view, contravening the principle of the development of moral relations into a legal form. The *patriarchal* condition is regarded—either in reference to the entire race of man, or to some branches of it—as exclusively that condition of things, in which the legal element is combined with a due recognition of the moral and emotional parts of our nature: and in which justice as united with these, truly and really influences the intercourse of the social units. The basis of the patriarchal condition is the family relation; which develops the *primary* form of conscious morality, succeeded by that of the State as its *second* phase. The patriarchal condition is one of transition, in which the family has already advanced to the position of a race or people; where the union, therefore, has already ceased to be simply a bond of love and confidence, and has become one of plighted service. We must first examine the ethical principle of the Family. The Family may be reckoned as virtually a single person; since its members have either mutually surrendered their individual personality (and consequently their legal position towards each other, with the rest of their particular interests and desires) as in the case of the Parents; or have not yet attained such an independent personality—(the Children, who are primarily in that merely natural condition already mentioned). They live, therefore, in a unity of feeling, love, confidence, and faith in each other. And in a relation of natural love, the one individual has the consciousness of himself in the consciousness of the other; he lives out of self; and in this mutual self-renunciation each regains the life that had been virtually transferred to the other; gains, in fact, that other's existence and his own, as involved with that other. The farther interests connected with the necessities and external concerns of life, as well as the development that has to take place within their circle, *i.e.* of the children, constitute a common object for the members of the Family. The Spirit of the Family—the Penates—form one substantial being, as much as the Spirit of a People in the State; and morality in both cases consists in a feeling, a consciousness, and a will, not limited to individual personality and interest, but embracing the common interests of the members generally. But this unity is in the case of the Family essentially one of *feeling;* not advancing beyond the limits of the merely *natural.* The piety of the Family relation should be respected in the highest degree by the State; by its means the State obtains as its members individuals who are already moral (for as mere *persons* they are not) and who in uniting to form a state bring with them that sound basis of a political edifice—the capacity of feeling one with a Whole. But the expansion of the Family to a patriarchal unity carries us beyond the ties of blood-relationship—the simply natural elements of that basis; and outside of these limits the members of the community must enter upon the position of independent personality. A review of the patriarchal condition, *in extenso,* would lead us to give special attention to the Theocratical Constitution. The head of the patriarchal clan is also its priest. If the Family in its general relations, is not yet separated from civic society and the state, the separation of religion from it has also not yet taken place; and so much the less since the piety of the hearth is itself a profoundly subjective state of feeling.

We have considered two aspects of Freedom,—the objective and the subjective; if, therefore, Freedom is asserted to consist in the individuals of a State all agreeing in its arrangements, it is evident that only the subjective aspect is regarded. The natural inference from this principle is, that no law can be valid without the approval of all. This difficulty is attempted to be obviated by the decision that the minority must yield to the majority; the majority therefore bear the sway. But long ago J.J. Rousseau remarked, that in that case there would be no longer freedom, for the will of the *minority* would cease to be respected. At the Polish Diet each single member had to give his consent before any political step could be taken; and this kind of freedom it was that ruined the State. Besides, it is a dangerous and false prejudice, that the People *alone* have reason and insight, and know what justice is; for each popular faction may represent itself as the People, and the question as to what constitutes the State is one of advanced science, and not of popular decision.

If the principle of regard for the individual will is recognized as the only basis of political liberty, *viz.,* that nothing should be done by or for the State to which all the members of the body politic have not given their sanction, we have, properly speaking, no *Constitution.* The only arrangement that would be necessary, would be, first, a centre having no *will* of its own, but which should take into consideration what appeared to be the necessities of the State; and, secondly, a contrivance for calling the members of the State together, for taking the votes, and for performing the arithmetical operations of reckoning and comparing the number of votes for the different propositions, and thereby deciding upon them. The State is an *abstraction,* having even its generic existence in its citizens; but it is an actuality, and its simply generic existence must embody itself in individual will and activity. The want of government and political administration in general is felt; this necessitates the selection and separation from the rest of those who have to take the helm in political affairs, to decide concerning them, and to give orders to other citizens, with a view to the execution of their plans. If *e.g.* even the people in a Democracy resolve on a war, a general must head the army. It is only by a Constitution that the *abstraction*—the State—attains life and reality; but this involves the distinction between those who command and those who obey. Yet obedience seems inconsistent with liberty, and those who command appear to do the very opposite of that which the fundamental idea of the State, *viz.* that of Freedom, requires. It is, however, urged that—though the distinction between commanding and obeying is absolutely necessary, because affairs could not go on without it—and indeed this seems only a compulsory limitation, external to and even contravening freedom in the abstract—the constitution should be at least so framed, that the citizens may obey as little as possible, and the smallest modicum of free volition be left to the commands of the superiors; that the substance of that for which subordination is necessary, even in its most important bearings, should be decided and resolved on by the People—by the will of many or of all the citizens; though it is supposed to be thereby provided that the State should be possessed of vigor and strength as a reality—an individual unity.

The primary consideration is, then, the distinction between the governing and the governed, and the political constitutions in the abstract have been rightly divided into Monarchy, Aristocracy, and Democracy; which gives occasion, however, to the remark that Monarchy itself must be further divided into Despotism and Monarchy proper; that in all the divisions to which the leading Idea gives rise, only the generic character is to be made prominent—it being not intended thereby that the particular category under review should be exhausted as a Form, Order, or Kind in its *concrete* development. But especially it must be observed, that the above-mentioned divisions admit of a multitude of particular modifications—not only such as lie within the limits of those classes themselves, but also such as are mixtures of several of these essentially distinct classes, and which are consequently misshapen, unstable, and inconsistent forms. In such a collision, the concerning question is, what is the *best constitution;* that is, by what arrangement, organization, or mechanism of the power of the State its object can be most surely attained. This object may indeed be variously understood; for instance, as the calm enjoyment of life on the part of the citizens, or as Universal Happiness. Such aims have suggested the so-called Ideals of Constitutions, and, as a particular branch of the subject, Ideals of the Education of Princes (Fenelon), or of the governing body—the aristocracy at large (Plato); for the chief point they treat of is the condition of those subjects who stand at the head of affairs: and in these Ideals the concrete details of political organization are not at all considered. The inquiry into the best constitution is frequently treated as if not only the theory were an affair of subjective independent conviction, but as if the introduction of a constitution recognized as the best—or as superior to others—could be the result of a resolve adopted in this theoretical manner; as if the form of a constitution were a matter of free choice, determined by nothing else but reflection. Of this artless fashion was that deliberation—not indeed of the Persian *people,* but of the Persian *grandees,* who had conspired to overthrow the pseudo-Smerdis and the Magi, after their undertaking had succeeded, and when there was no scion of the royal family living—as to what constitution they should introduce into Persia; and Herodotus gives an equally naïve account of this deliberation.

In the present day, the Constitution of a country and people is not represented as so entirely dependent on free and deliberate choice. The fundamental but abstractly (and therefore imperfectly) entertained conception of Freedom, has resulted in the Republic being very generally regarded—in *theory*—as the only just and true political constitution. Many even, who occupy elevated official positions under monarchical constitutions, so far from being opposed to this idea, are actually its supporters; only they see that such a constitution, though the best, cannot be realized under all circumstances; and that, while men are what they are, we must be satisfied with less freedom; the monarchical constitution—under the given circumstances, and the present moral condition of the people—being even regarded as the most advantageous. In this view also, the necessity of a particular constitution is made to depend on the condition of the people in such a way as if the latter were non-essential and accidental. This representation is founded on the distinction which the reflective understanding makes between an idea and the corresponding reality; holding to an abstract and consequently untrue idea; not grasping it in its completeness, or—which is virtually, though not in point of form, the same—not taking a concrete view of a people and a state. We shall have to show further on, that the constitution adopted by a people makes one substance—one spirit—with its religion, its art and philosophy, or, at least, with its conceptions and thoughts—its culture generally; not to expatiate upon the additional influences, *ab extra,* of climate, of neighbors, of its place in the World. A State is an individual totality, of which you cannot select any particular side, although a supremely important one, such as its political constitution; and deliberate and decide respecting it in that isolated form. Not only is that constitution most intimately connected with and dependent on those other spiritual forces; but the form of the entire moral and intellectual individuality, comprising all the forces it embodies, is only a step in the development of the grand Whole—with its place preappointed in the process; a fact which gives the highest sanction to the constitution in question, and establishes its absolute necessity. The origin of a state involves imperious lordship on the one hand, instinctive submission on the other. But even obedience—lordly power, and the fear inspired by a ruler—in itself implies some degree of voluntary connection. Even in barbarous states this is the case; it is not the isolated will of individuals that prevails; individual pretensions are relinquished, and the general will is the essential bond of political union. This unity of the general and the particular is the *Idea* itself, manifesting itself as a *state,* and which subsequently undergoes further development within itself. The abstract yet necessitated process in the development of truly independent states is as follows: they begin with regal power, whether of patriarchal or military origin. In the next phase, particularity and individuality assert themselves in the form of Aristocracy and Democracy. Lastly, we have the subjection of these separate interests to a single power; but which can be absolutely none other than one outside of which those spheres have an independent position, *viz.,* the Monarchical. Two phases of royalty, therefore, must be distinguished—a primary and a secondary one. This process is necessitated, so that the form of government assigned to a particular stage of development *must* present itself: it is therefore no matter of choice, but is that form which is adapted to the spirit of the people.

In a Constitution the main feature of interest is the self-development of the *rational,* that is, the *political* condition of a people; the setting free of the successive elements of the Idea: so that the several powers in the State manifest themselves as separate, attain their appropriate and special perfection, and yet in this independent condition, work together for one object, and are held together by it—*i.e.,* form an organic whole. The State is thus the embodiment of rational freedom, realizing and recognizing itself in an objective form. For its objectivity consists in this—that its successive stages are not merely ideal, but are present in an appropriate reality; and that in their separate and several working, they are absolutely merged in that agency by which the totality—the soul—the individuate unity—is produced, and of which it is the result.

The State is the Idea of Spirit in the external manifestation of human Will and its Freedom. It is to the State, therefore, that change in the aspect of History indissolubly attaches itself; and the successive phases of the Idea manifest themselves in it as distinct political *principles.* The Constitutions under which World-Historical peoples have reached their culmination, are peculiar to them; and therefore do not present a generally applicable political basis. Were it otherwise, the differences of similar constitutions would consist only in a peculiar method of expanding and developing that generic basis; whereas they really originate in diversity of principle. From the comparison therefore of the political institutions of the ancient World-Historical peoples, it so happens, that for the most recent principle of a Constitution—for the principle of our own times—nothing (so to speak) can be learned. In science and art it is quite otherwise; *e.g.,* the ancient philosophy is so decidedly the basis of the modern, that it is inevitably contained in the latter, and constitutes its basis. In this case the relation is that of a continuous development of the same structure, whose foundation-stone, walls, and roof have remained what they were. In Art, the Greek itself, in its original form, furnishes us the best models. But in regard to political constitution, it is quite otherwise: here the Ancient and the Modern have not their essential principle in common. Abstract definitions and dogmas respecting just government—importing that intelligence and virtue ought to bear sway—are, indeed, common to both. But nothing is so absurd as to look to Greeks, Romans, or Orientals, for models for the political arrangements of our time. From the East may be derived beautiful pictures of a patriarchal condition, of paternal government, and of devotion to it on the part of peoples; from Greeks and Romans, descriptions of popular liberty. Among the latter we find the idea of a Free Constitution admitting all the citizens to a share in deliberations and resolves respecting the affairs and laws of the Commonwealth. In our times, too, this is its general acceptation; only with this modification, that—since our states are so large, and there are so many of "the Many," the latter, direct action being impossible, should by the indirect method of elective substitution express their concurrence with resolves affecting the common weal; that is, that for legislative purposes generally, the people should be represented by deputies. The so-called Representative Constitution is that form of government with which we connect the idea of a free constitution; and this notion has become a rooted prejudice. On this theory People and Government are separated. But there is a perversity in this antithesis; an ill-intentioned ruse designed to insinuate that the People are the totality of the State. Besides, the basis of this view is the principle of isolated individuality—the absolute validity of the subjective will—a dogma which we have already investigated. The great point is, that Freedom in its Ideal conception has not subjective will and caprice for its principle, but the recognition of the universal will; and that the process by which Freedom is realized is the free development of its successive stages. The subjective will is a merely formal determination—a *carte blanche*—not including what it is that is willed. Only the *rational* will is that universal principle which independently determines and unfolds its own being, and develops its successive elemental phases as organic members. Of this Gothic-cathedral architecture the ancients knew nothing.

At an earlier stage of the discussion we established the two elemental considerations: first, the *idea* of freedom as the absolute and final aim; secondly, the *means* for realizing it, *i.e.,* the subjective side of knowledge and will, with its life, movement, and activity. We then recognized the State as the moral Whole and the Reality of Freedom, and consequently as the objective unity of these two elements. For although we make this distinction into two aspects for our consideration, it must be remarked that they are intimately connected; and that their connection is involved in the idea of each when examined separately. We have, on the one hand, recognized the Idea in the definite form of Freedom conscious of and willing itself—having itself alone as its object: involving at the same time, the pure and simple Idea of Reason, and likewise, that which we have called subject—self-consciousness—Spirit actually existing in the World. If, on the other hand, we consider Subjectivity, we find that subjective knowledge and will is Thought. But by the very act of thoughtful cognition and volition, I will the universal object—the substance of absolute Reason. We observe, therefore, an essential union between the objective side—the Idea—and the subjective side—the personality that conceives and wills it. The *objective* existence of this union is the State, which is therefore the basis and centre of the other concrete elements of the life of a people—of Art, of Law, of Morals, of Religion, of Science. All the activity of Spirit has only this object—the becoming conscious of this union, *i.e.,* of its own Freedom. Among the forms of this conscious union *Religion* occupies the highest position. In it, Spirit—rising above the limitations of temporal and secular existence—becomes conscious of the Absolute Spirit, and in this consciousness of the self-existent Being, renounces its individual interest; it lays this aside in Devotion—a state of mind in which it refuses to occupy itself any longer with the limited and particular. By Sacrifice man expresses his renunciation of his property, his will, his individual feelings. The religious concentration of the soul appears in the form of feeling; it nevertheless passes also into reflection; a form of worship *(cultus)* is a result of reflection. The second form of the union of the objective and subjective in the human spirit is *Art*. This advances farther into the realm of the actual and sensuous than Religion. In its noblest walk it is occupied with representing, not indeed, the Spirit of God, but certainly the Form of God; and in its secondary aims, that which is divine and spiritual generally. Its office is to render visible the Divine; presenting it to the imaginative and intuitive faculty. But the True is the object not only of conception and feeling, as in Religion—and of intuition, as in Art—but also of the thinking faculty; and this gives us the third form of the union in question—*Philosophy*. This is consequently the highest, freest, and wisest phase. Of course we are not intending to investigate these three phases here; they have only suggested themselves in virtue of their occupying the same general ground as the object here considered—the *State*.

The general principle which manifests itself and becomes an object of consciousness in the State, the form under which all that the State includes is brought, is the whole of that cycle of phenomena which constitutes the *culture* of a nation. But the definite substance that receives the form of universality, and exists in that concrete reality which is the State—is the Spirit of the People itself. The actual State is animated by this spirit, in all its particular affairs—its Wars, Institutions, etc. But man must also attain a conscious realization of this his Spirit and essential nature, and of his original identity with it. For we said that morality is the identity of the *subjective* or *personal* with the *universal* will. Now the mind must give itself an express consciousness of this; and the focus of this knowledge is *Religion*. Art and Science are only various aspects and forms of the same substantial being. In considering Religion, the chief point of inquiry is, whether it recognizes the True—the Idea—only in its separate, abstract form, or in its true unity; in *separation*—God being represented in an abstract form as the Highest Being, Lord of Heaven and Earth, living in a remote region far from human actualities— or in its *unity*—God, as Unity of the Universal and Individual; the Individual itself assuming the aspect of positive and real existence in the idea of the Incarnation. Religion is the sphere in which a nation gives itself the definition of that which it regards as the True. A definition contains everything that belongs to the essence of an object; reducing its nature to its simple characteristic predicate, as a mirror for every predicate—the generic soul pervading all its details. The conception of God, therefore, constitutes the general basis of a people's character.

In this aspect, religion stands in the closest connection with the political principle. Freedom can exist only where Individuality is recognized as having its positive and real existence in the Divine Being. The connection may be further explained thus:—Secular existence, as merely temporal—occupied with particular interests—is consequently only relative and unauthorized; and receives its validity only in as far as the universal soul that pervades it—its principle—receives absolute validity; which it cannot have unless it is recognized as the definite manifestation, the phenomenal existence of the Divine Essence. On this account it is that the State rests on Religion. We hear this often repeated in our times, though for the most part nothing further is meant than that individual subjects as Godfearing men would be more disposed and ready to perform their duty; since obedience to King and Law so naturally follows in the train of reverence for God. This reverence, indeed, since it exalts the general over the special, may even turn upon the latter, become fanatical, and work with incendiary and destructive violence against the State, its institutions, and arrangements. Religious feeling, therefore, it is thought, should be sober, kept in a certain degree of coolness, that it may not storm against and bear down that which should be defended and preserved by it. The possibility of such a catastrophe is at least latent in it.

While, however, the correct sentiment is adopted, that the State is based on Religion, the position thus assigned to Religion supposes the State already to exist; and that subsequently, in order to maintain it, Religion must be brought into it—in buckets and bushels as it were—and impressed upon people's hearts. It is quite true that men must be trained to religion, but not as to something whose existence has yet to begin. For in affirming that the State is based on Religion—that it has its roots in it—we virtually assert that the former has proceeded from the latter; and that this derivation is going on now and will always continue; *i.e.,* the principles of the State must be regarded as valid in and for themselves, which can only be in so far as they are recognized as determinate manifestations of the Divine Nature. The form of Religion, therefore, decides that of the State and its constitution. The latter actually originated in the particular religion adopted by the nation; so that, in fact, the Athenian or the Roman State was possible only in connection with the specific form of Heathenism existing among the respective peoples; just as a Catholic State has a spirit and constitution different from that of a Protestant one.

If that outcry—that urging and striving for the implantation of Religion in the community—were an utterance of anguish and a call for help, as it often seems to be, expressing the danger of religion having vanished, or being about to vanish entirely from the State—that would be fearful indeed—worse, in fact, than this outcry supposes; for it implies the belief in a resource against the evil, *viz.,* the implantation and inculcation of religion; whereas religion is by no means a thing to be so produced; its *self-production* (and there can be no other) lies much deeper.

Another and opposite folly which we meet with in our time, is that of pretending to invent and carry out political constitutions independently of religion. The Catholic confession, although sharing the Christian name with the Protestant, does not concede to the State an inherent Justice and Morality—a concession which in the Protestant principle is fundamental. This tearing away of the political morality of the Constitution from its natural connection, is necessary to the genius of that religion, inasmuch as it does not recognize Justice and Morality as independent and substantial. But thus excluded from intrinsic worth—torn away from their last refuge, the sanctuary of conscience, the calm retreat where religion has its abode—the principles and institutions of political legislation are destitute of a real centre, to the same degree as they are compelled to remain abstract and indefinite.

Summing up what has been said of the State, we find that we have been led to call its vital principle, as actuating the individuals who compose it, Morality. The State, its laws, its arrangements, constitute the rights of its members; its natural features, its mountains, air, and waters, are *their* country, their fatherland, their outward material property; the history of this State, *their* deeds; what their ancestors have produced, belongs to them and lives in their memory. All is their possession, just as they are possessed by it; for it constitutes their existence, their being.

Their imagination is occupied with the ideas thus presented, while the adoption of these laws, and of a fatherland so conditioned is the expression of their will. It is this matured totality which thus constitutes *one* Being, the spirit of *one* People. To it the Individual members belong; each unit is the Son of his Nation, and at the same time, in as far as the State to which he belongs is undergoing development, the Son of his Age. None remains behind it, still less advances beyond it. This spiritual Being (the Spirit of his Time) is his; he is a representative of it; it is that in which he originated, and in which he lives. Among the Athenians the word *Athens* had a double import; suggesting primarily, a complex of political institutions, but no less, in the second place, that Goddess who represented the Spirit of the People and its unity.

This Spirit of a People is a *determinate* and particular Spirit, and is, as just stated, further modified by the degree of its historical development. This Spirit, then, constitutes the basis and substance of those other forms of a nation's consciousness, which have been noticed. For Spirit in its self-consciousness must become an object of contemplation to itself, and objectivity involves, in the first instance, the rise of differences which make up a total of distinct spheres of objective spirit; in the same way as the Soul

exists only as the complex of its faculties, which in their form of concentration in a simple unity produce that Soul. It is thus *One Individuality* which, presented in its essence
as God, is honored and enjoyed in *Religion;* which is exhibited as an object of sensuous
contemplation in *Art;* and is apprehended as an intellectual conception, in *Philosophy.*
In virtue of the original identity of their essence, purport, and object, these various
forms are inseparably united with the Spirit of the State. Only in connection with this
particular religion, can this particular political constitution exist; just as in such or such
a State, such or such a Philosophy or order of Art.

The remark next in order is that each particular National genius is to be treated as
only One Individual in the process of Universal History. For that history is the exhibition of the divine, absolute development of Spirit in its highest forms—that gradation
by which it attains its truth and consciousness of itself. The forms which these grades of
progress assume are the characteristic "National Spirits" of History; the peculiar tenor
of their moral life, of their Government, their Art, Religion, and Science. To realize
these grades is the boundless impulse of the World-Spirit—the goal of its irresistible
urging; for this division into organic members, and the full development of each, is its
Idea. Universal History is exclusively occupied with showing how Spirit comes to a
recognition and adoption of the Truth: the dawn of knowledge appears; it begins to discover salient principles, and at last it arrives at full consciousness.

Arthur Schopenhauer
1788–1860

Arthur Schopenhauer was described by his contemporaries as egoistic, vain, arrogant, overbearing, and cynical. He was known to be so anxious that as an adult he always slept with a loaded pistol. His derogatory remarks about women are legendary.* His attacks on the noted professors of his time, especially Hegel, were equally vindictive.** In short, his approach to life and the people around him was as pessimistic as his philosophy. Yet he was a man of strong character and uncompromising honesty who took great pleasure in the theater, in music, and in good food and wine. And ironically, he came to hold that only in sympathy for the sufferings of others and in ascetic holiness can one find release from overwhelming desire. As he was later to say, "I have taught what sainthood is, but I myself am no saint."

*For example, "[women] are childish, frivolous and short-sighted; in a word, they are big children all their life long . . . defective in the powers of reasoning and deliberation." From "Of Women," in *Essays of Schopenhauer*, translated by T. Bailey Saunders (New York: Wiley Book Co., n.d.), pp. 73 and 76.

**He referred to Hegel as "a philosphical creature of ministers . . . manufactured from above with a political but miscalculated purpose, a flat, commonplace, repulsive, ignorant charlatan, who, with unparalleled presumption, conceit, and absurdity, pasted together a system which was trumpeted by his venal adherents as immortal wisdom." From "The History of Philosophy" in *The Wisdom of Life and Other Essays*, translated by T. Bailey Saunders and Ernest Belfort Bax (New York: M. Walter Dunne, 1901), p. 196.

Schopenhauer was born in Danzig, the son of a wealthy merchant father and a noted novelist mother. As a boy, Schopenhauer travelled extensively and attended schools in Germany, France, and England. By the age of sixteen he had visited most of the countries of Europe and was fluent in at least four languages. In 1804 Schopenhauer's father insisted that his son give up travel and school and join him in the family business. Schopenhauer grudgingly agreed—though he continued to study "on the sly." His father's sudden death (apparently by suicide) in 1805 freed Schopenhauer from the drudgery of his father's work and he resumed his studies. He studied at the universities in Göttingen and Berlin before receiving his doctorate from the University of Jena.

Following a period of travel, Schopenhauer moved to Dresden where he wrote his most important work, *The World as Will and Idea* (1818). Given that he believed this work contained the meaning of life, he was sorely disappointed when it received no recognition and sold few copies. He moved to Berlin where he could expound his views verbally in lectures. Receiving a position as *Privatdozent* (unsalaried lecturer), he purposely scheduled his lectures at the same time as those of his nemesis, Hegel, who was then at the height of his fame. Not surprisingly, Schopenhauer's lectures were a failure—no one attended. Within a year he bitterly left Berlin and gave up any aspirations to an academic career.

After more travels in Europe, Schopenhauer eventually settled in Frankfurt am Main. There he published *On the Will in Nature* (1836) as well as a revised and expanded edition of his major work (in 1844). In 1848 a series of democratic revolutions swept Europe. Schopenhauer had no sympathy for the revolutionaries— he even allowed Austrian soldiers to use the windows in his Frankfurt home to shoot at demonstrators below—and asked only that the state preserve law and order. In the aftermath of the failed revolutions, the optimistic philosophy of Hegel passed out of vogue and the pessimism of Schopenhauer came into style. In 1851 Schopenhauer produced a collection of diverse essays, *Parerga and Paralipomena,* which proved quite successful. In the last years of his life, Schopenhauer finally received the fame that he believed he deserved. His final years were spent editing his *magnum opus* for one final edition and receiving and entertaining admirers.

*   *   *

The World as Will and Idea begins with the provocative assertion that, "The world is my idea." Taking seriously Kant's claim that the mind structures the world as it is experienced, Schopenhauer held that the existence of the phenomenal world depends upon my consciousness of it. But whereas Kant had maintained that the *Ding-an-sich* (the thing-in-itself apart from my experience) could not be known, Schopenhauer declared that it is intuitively knowable and identified it as Will. The world as it is projected outward by me, the diversity of phenomena, is idea, while the unity that underlies those phenomena is Will.

The Will is a nonrational force, a blind, meaningless striving after existence, and all of life is a struggle to fulfill its desires. Happiness and pleasure can only be temporary as Will is never satisfied and always wants "more"—more of what it does not know, but it wants more anyway. In the chapter entitled "The Primacy of the Will in Self-Consciousness," reprinted here in the R.B. Haldane and John Kemp translation, Schopenhauer argues that intellect is merely another tool of Will: "The *will* is what is real and essential in man, and the *intellect* only subordinate, conditioned, and produced." The Will, not intellect or memory, is the essential identity of the person. Even our bodies are simply the "objectification" of our wills. Given the nature of this Will, it follows that, as Schopenhauer said elsewhere,

> Man is at bottom a wild, horrible creature. We know him merely as broken and tamed by what we call civilization, and hence the occasional outbreaks of his nature shock us. But where and when the padlock and chain of legal order fall off and anarchy enters, then he shows himself what he is.*

This means, contrary to Hegel, that human history has no purpose, that there is no progressive manifestation of Spirit. Borrowing words from Shakespeare's *Macbeth,* history is no more than "a tale told by an idiot, full of sound and fury, signifying nothing."

How then can we escape the suffering and misery that Will invariably brings us? While the Will becomes "objective" through diverse particular objects that are known in the phenomenal world, it is *immediately* objectified in Platonic Ideas that are expressed in art. We can momentarily overcome the Will by losing ourselves in the aesthetic enjoyment of these Ideas. But in formal, dispassionate music we encounter "the universal imageless language of the heart," which goes beyond Platonic Ideas and reveals the Will as the *Ding-an-sich*. At this point we can experience "pure knowing free from will, which . . . is the only pure happiness."

But for a permanent salvation from desire, we must move beyond aesthetics to ethics and finally to religion. Because the Will is objectified in each of us, we tend to see ourselves as a self-sufficient entity. Borrowing from Hindu thought, Schopenhauer pointed out that perceived individual identity is merely phenomenal, that on the noumenal level all is one. This means that if you suffer, I suffer, which, in turn, leads me to a position of compassionate sympathy as I become one in suffering with you. Yet even such a state of sympathy, which Schopenhauer called "love," is only temporary. What is needed is a "transition from virtue to asceticism" where the individual ceases to feel any concern for earthly things: a "state of voluntary renunciation, resignation, true indifference, and perfect will-lessness." Only when we have reached a mystical state of "denial of the will to live," only when we have become "saints," will we find release from insatiable Will.

While he may not have made the impact his enemy Hegel did, it is difficult to read thinkers such as Nietzsche or Freud and not think of Schopenhauer. Schopenhauer's insistence upon irrational Will as the ground of all human activity is clearly mirrored in Nietzsche's "will to power," and the indeterminacy of the Will's object of desire is the archetype for Freud's "id." Freud himself stated years later that "We have unwittingly steered our course into the harbor of Schopenhauer's philosophy."

*   *   *

For selections from Schopenhauer's work, see *The Works of Schopenhauer,* abridged and edited by Will Durant (New York: Simon & Schuster, 1928).

---

*"On Ethics" in *Wisdom of Life,* op. cit., p. 276

Richard Taylor, "Schopenhauer," in D.J. O'Connor, ed., *A Critical History of Western Philosophy* (New York: Free Press, 1964), provides an excellent short introduction to Schopenhauer's thought, while Patrick Gardiner, *Schopenhauer* (Baltimore, MD: Penguin Books, 1963); V.J. McGill, *Schopenhauer* (New York: Haskell, 1971); David W. Hamlyn, *Schopenhauer* (London: Routledge & Kegan Paul, 1980); Bryan Magee, *The Philosophy of Schopenhauer* (Oxford: Oxford University Press, 1983); and Rudiger Safranski, *Schopenhauer and the Wild Years of Philosophy* (Cambridge, MA: Harvard University Press, 1990), provide helpful book-length studies. For an interesting interpretation from a Catholic viewpoint, see Frederick C. Copleston, *Arthur Schopenhauer: Philosopher of Pessimism* (1946, reprinted New York: Barnes & Noble, 1975). For specialized studies, see Georg Simmel, *Schopenhauer and Nietzsche,* translated by Helmut Loiskandl, Deena Weinstein, and Michael Weinstein (Amherst: University of Massachusetts Press, 1986), and Christopher Janaway, *Self and World in Schopenhauer's Philosophy* (Oxford: Oxford University Press, 1989). For a collection of critical essays, see Michael Fox, ed., *Schopenhauer: His Philosophical Achievement* (Totowa, NJ: Barnes & Noble, 1980).

THE WORLD AS WILL AND IDEA (in part)

CHAPTER 19

On the Primacy of the Will in Self-Consciousness

The will, as the thing in itself, constitutes the inner, true, and indestructible nature of man; in itself, however, it is unconscious. For consciousness is conditioned by the intellect, and the intellect is a mere accident of our being; for it is a function of the brain, which, together with the nerves and spinal cord connected with it, is a mere fruit, a product, nay, so far, a parasite of the rest of the organism; for it does not directly enter into its inner constitution, but merely serves the end of self-preservation by regulating the relations of the organism to the external world. The organism itself, on the other hand, is the visibility, the objectivity, of the individual will, the image of it as it presents itself in that very brain (which in the first book we learned to recognize as the condition of the objective world in general), therefore also brought about by its forms of knowledge, space, time, and causality, and consequently presenting itself as extended, successively acting, and material, *i.e.,* as something operative or efficient. The members are both directly felt and also perceived by means of the senses only in the brain. According to this one may say: The intellect is the secondary phenomenon; the organism the primary phenomenon, that is, the immediate manifestation of the will; the will is metaphysical, the intellect physical;—the intellect, like its objects, is merely phenomenal appearance; the will alone is the thing in itself. Then, in a more and more *figurative sense,* thus by way of simile: The will is the substance of man, the intellect the accident; the will is the matter, the intellect is the form; the will is warmth, the intellect is light.

We shall now first of all verify and also elucidate this thesis by the following facts connected with the inner life of man; and on this opportunity perhaps more will be done for the knowledge of the inner man than is to be found in many systematic psychologies.

1. Not only the consciousness of other things, *i.e.,* the apprehension of the external world, but also *self-consciousness,* contains, as was mentioned already above, a knower and a known; otherwise it would not be *consciousness.* For *consciousness* consists in knowing; but knowing requires a knower and a known; therefore there could be no self-consciousness if there were not in it also a known opposed to the knower and different from it. As there can be no object without a subject, so also there can be no subject without an object, *i.e.,* no knower without something different from it which is known. Therefore a consciousness which is through and through pure intelligence is impossible. The intelligence is like the sun, which does not illuminate space if there is no object from which its rays are reflected. The knower himself, as such, cannot be known; otherwise he would be the known of another knower. But now, as the *known* in self-consciousness we find exclusively the *will.* For not merely willing and purposing in the narrowest sense, but also all striving, wishing, shunning, hoping, fearing, loving, hating, in short, all that directly constitutes our own weal and woe, desire and aversion, is clearly only affection of the will, is a moving, a modification of willing and not-willing, is just that which, if it takes outward effect, exhibits itself as an act of will proper. In all knowledge, however, the known is first and essential, not the knower. Therefore in self-consciousness also the known, thus the will, must be what is first and original; the knower, on the other hand, only what is secondary, that which has been added, the mirror. They are related very much as the luminous to the reflecting body; or, again, as the vibrating strings to the resounding-board, in which case the note produced would be consciousness.

2. But in order not merely to describe consciousness figuratively, but to know it thoroughly, we have first of all to find out what appears in the same way in every consciousness, and therefore, as the common and constant element, will also be the essential. Then we shall consider what distinguishes *one* consciousness from an other, which accordingly will be the adventitious and secondary element.

Consciousness is positively only known to us as a property of animal nature; therefore we must not, and indeed cannot, think of it otherwise than as *animal consciousness,* so that this expression is tautological. Now, that which in every animal consciousness, even the most imperfect and the weakest, is always present, nay, lies at its foundation, is an immediate sense of *longing,* and of the alternate satisfaction and non-satisfaction of it, in very different degrees. This we know to a certain extent *a priori.* For marvellously different as the innumerable species of animals are, and strange as some new form, never seen before, appears to us, we yet assume beforehand its inmost nature, with perfect certainty, as well known, and indeed fully confided to us. We know that the animal *wills,* indeed also *what* it wills, existence, well-being, life, and propagation; and since in this we presuppose with perfect certainty identity with us, we do not hesitate to attribute to it unchanged all the affections of will which we know in ourselves, and speak at once of its desire, aversion, fear, anger, hatred, love, joy, sorrow, longing, &c. On the other hand, whenever phenomena of mere knowledge come to be spoken of we fall at once into uncertainty. We do not venture to say that the animal conceives, thinks, judges, knows: we only attribute to it with certainty ideas in general; because without them its *will* could not have those emotions referred to above. But with regard to the definite manner of knowing of the brutes and the precise limits of it in a given species, we have only indefinite conceptions, and make conjectures. Hence our understanding with them is also often difficult, and is only brought about by skill, in consequence of experience and practice. Here then lie distinctions of consciousness. On the other hand, a longing, desiring, wishing, or a detesting, shunning, and not wishing, is proper to every consciousness: man has it in common with the polyp. This is accordingly the essential element in and the basis of every consciousness. The difference of the manifestations of this in the different species of animal beings depends upon the various extension of their sphere of knowledge, in which the motives of those manifestations lie. We understand directly from our own nature all actions and behaviour of the brutes which express movements of the will; therefore, so far, we sympathize with them in various ways. On the other hand, the gulf between us and them results simply and solely from the difference of intellect. The gulf which lies between a very sagacious brute and a man of very limited capacity is perhaps not much greater than that which exists between a blockhead and a man of genius; therefore here also the resemblance between them in another aspect, which springs from the likeness of their inclinations and emotions, and assimilates them again to each other, sometimes appears with surprising prominence, and excites astonishment. This consideration makes it clear that in all animal natures the *will* is what is primary and substantial, the *intellect* again is secondary, adventitious, indeed a mere tool for the service of the former, and is more or less complete and complicated, according to the demands of this service. As a species of animals is furnished with hoofs, claws, hands, wings, horns, or teeth according to the aims of its will, so also is it furnished with a more or less developed brain, whose function is the intelligence necessary for its endurance. The more complicated the organization becomes, in the ascending series of animals, the more numerous also are its wants, and the more varied and specially determined the objects which are capable of satisfying them; hence the more complicated and distant the paths by which these are to be obtained, which must now be all known and found: therefore in the same proportion the ideas of the animal must be more versatile, accurate, definite, and connected, and also its attention must be more highly strung, more sustained, and more easily roused, consequently its intellect must be more developed and perfected. Accordingly we see the organ of intelligence, the cerebral system, together with all the organs of sense, keep pace with the increasing wants and the complication of the organism; and the increase of the part of consciousness that has to do with ideas (as opposed to the willing part) exhibits itself in a bodily form in the ever-increasing proportion of the brain in general to the rest of the nervous system, and of the cerebrum to the cerebellum; for (according to Flourens) the former is the workshop of ideas, while the latter is the disposer and orderer of movements. The last step which nature has taken in this respect is, however, disproportionately great. For in man not only does the faculty of ideas of *perception,* which alone existed hitherto, reach the highest degree of perfection, but the *abstract* idea, thought, *i.e., reason,* and with it reflection, is added. Through this important advance of the intellect, thus of the secondary part of consciousness, it now gains a preponderance over the primary part, in so far as it becomes henceforward the predominantly active part. While in the brute the immediate sense of its satisfied or unsatisfied desire constitutes by far the most important part of its consciousness, and the more so indeed the lower the grade of the animal, so that the lowest animals are distinguished from plants only by the addition of a dull idea, in man the opposite is the case. Vehement as are his desires, even more vehement than those of any brute, rising to the level of passions, yet his consciousness remains continuously and predominantly occupied and filled with ideas and thoughts. Without doubt this has been the principal occasion of that fundamental error of all philosophers on account of which they make thought that which is essential and primary in the so-called soul, *i.e.,* in the inner or spiritual life of man, always placing it first, but will, as a mere product of thought, they regard as only a subordinate addition and consequence of it. But if willing merely proceeded from knowing, how could the brutes, even the lower grades of them, with so very little knowledge, often show such an unconquerable and vehement will? Accordingly, since that fundamental error of the philosophers makes, as it were, the accident the substance, it leads them into mistaken paths, which there is afterwards no way of getting out of. Now this relative predominance of the *knowing* consciousness over the *desiring,* consequently of the secondary part over the primary, which appears in man, may, in particular exceptionally favoured individuals, go so far that at the moments of its highest ascendancy, the secondary or knowing part of consciousness detaches itself altogether from the willing part, and passes into free activity for itself, *i.e.,* untouched by the will, and consequently no longer serving it. Thus it becomes purely objective, and the clear mirror of the world, and from it the conceptions of genius then arise, which are the subject of our third book.

3. If we run through the series of grades of animals downwards, we see the intellect always becoming weaker and less perfect, but we by no means observe a corresponding degradation of the will. Rather it retains everywhere its identical nature and shows itself in the form of great attachment to life, care for the individual and the species, egoism and regardlessness of all others, together with the emotions that spring from these. Even in the smallest insect the will is present, complete and entire; it wills what it wills as decidedly and completely as the man. The difference lies merely in *what* it wills, *i.e.,* in the motives, which, however, are the affair of the intellect. It indeed, as the secondary part of consciousness, and bound to the bodily organism, has innumerable degrees of completeness, and is in general essentially limited and imperfect. The *will,* on the contrary, as original and the thing in itself, can never be imperfect, but every act of will is all that it can be. On account of the simplicity which belongs to the will as the thing in itself, the metaphysical in the phenomenon, its nature admits of no degrees, but is always completely itself. Only its *excitement* has degrees, from the weakest inclination to the passion, and also its susceptibility to excitement, thus its vehemence from the phlegmatic to the choleric temperament. The *intellect,* on the other hand, has not merely degrees of *excitement,* from sleepiness to being in the vein, and inspiration, but also degrees of its nature, of the completeness of this, which accordingly rises gradually from the lowest animals, which can only obscurely apprehend, up to man, and here again from the fool to the genius. The *will* alone is everywhere completely itself. For its function is of the utmost simplicity; it consists in willing and not willing, which goes on with the greatest ease, without effort, and requires no practice. Knowing, on the contrary, has multifarious functions, and never takes place entirely without effort, which is required to fix the attention and to make clear the object, and at a higher stage is certainly needed for thinking and deliberation; therefore it is also capable of great improvement through exercise and education. If the intellect presents a simple, perceptible object to the will, the latter expresses at once its approval or disapproval of it, and this even if the intellect has laboriously inquired and pondered, in order from numerous data, by means of difficult combinations, ultimately to arrive at the conclusion as to which of the two seems to be most in conformity with the interests of the will. The latter has meanwhile been idly resting, and when the conclusion is arrived at it enters, as the Sultan enters the Divan, merely to express again its monotonous approval or disapproval, which certainly may vary in degree, but in its nature remains always the same.

This fundamentally different nature of the will and the intellect, the essential simplicity and originality of the former, in contrast to the complicated and secondary character of the latter, becomes still more clear to us if we observe their remarkable interaction within us, and now consider in the particular case, how the images and thoughts which arise in the intellect move the will, and how entirely separated and different are the parts which the two play. We can indeed perceive this even in actual events which excite the will in a lively manner, while primarily and in themselves they are merely objects of the intellect. But, on the one hand, it is here not so evident that this reality primarily existed only in the intellect; and, on the other hand, the change does not generally take place so rapidly as is necessary if the thing is to be easily surveyed, and thereby becomes thoroughly comprehensible. Both of these conditions, however, are fulfilled if it is merely thoughts and phantasies which we allow to act on the will. If, for example, alone with ourselves, we think over our personal circumstances, and now perhaps vividly present to ourselves the menace of an actually present danger and the possibility of an unfortunate issue, anxiety at once compresses the heart, and the blood ceases to circulate in the veins. But if then the intellect passes to the possibility of an opposite issue, and lets the imagination picture the long-hoped-for happiness thereby attained, all the pulses quicken at once with joy and the heart feels light as a feather, till the intellect awakes from its dream. Thereupon, suppose that an occasion should lead the memory to an insult or injury once suffered long ago, at once anger and bitterness pour into the breast that was but now at peace. But then arises, called up by accident, the image of a long-lost love, with which the whole romance and its magic scenes is connected; then that anger will at once give place to profound longing and sadness. Finally, if there occurs to us some former humiliating incident, we shrink together, would like to sink out of sight, blush with shame, and often try forcibly to distract and divert our thoughts by some loud exclamation, as if to scare some evil spirit. One sees, the intellect plays, and the will must dance to it. Indeed the intellect makes the will play the part of a child which is alternately thrown at pleasure into joyful or sad moods by the chatter and tales of its nurse. This depends upon the fact that the will is itself without knowledge, and the understanding which is given to it is without will. Therefore the former is like a body which is moved, the latter like the causes which set it in motion, for it is the medium of motives. Yet in all this the primacy of the will becomes clear again, if this will, which, as we have shown, becomes the sport of the intellect as soon as it allows the latter to control it, once makes its supremacy in the last instance felt by prohibiting the intellect from entertaining certain ideas, absolutely preventing certain trains of thought from arising, because it knows, *i.e.,* learns from that very intellect, that they would awaken in it some one of the emotions set forth above. It now bridles the intellect, and compels it to turn to other things. Hard as this often may be, it must yet be accomplished as soon as the will is in earnest about it, for the resisting in this case does not proceed from the intellect, which always remains indifferent, but from the will itself, which in one respect has an inclination towards an idea that in another respect it abhors. It is in itself interesting to the will simply because it excites it, but at the same time abstract knowledge tells it that this idea will aimlessly cause it a shock of painful or unworthy emotion: it now decides in conformity with this abstract knowledge, and compels the obedience of the intellect. This is called "being master of oneself." Clearly the master here is the will, the servant the intellect, for in the last instance the will always keeps the upper hand, and therefore constitutes the true core, the inner being of man. In this respect the title ⟨*Agemonikon*⟩ would belong to the *will;* yet it seems, on the other hand, to apply to the *intellect,* because it is the leader and guide, like the *valet de place* who conducts a stranger. In truth, however, the happiest figure of the relation of the two is the strong blind man who carries on his shoulders the lame man who can see.

The relation of the will to the intellect here explained may also be further recognized in the fact that the intellect is originally entirely a stranger to the purposes of the will. It supplies the motives to the will, but it only learns afterwards, completely *a posteriori,* how they have affected it, as one who makes a chemical experiment applies the reagents and awaits the result. Indeed the intellect remains so completely excluded from the real decisions and secret purposes of its own will that sometimes it can only learn them like those of a stranger, by spying upon them and surprising them, and must catch the will in the act of expressing itself in order to get at its real intentions. For example, I have conceived a plan, about which, however, I have still some scruple, but the feasibleness of which, as regards its possibility, is completely uncertain, for it depends upon external and still undecided circumstances. It would therefore certainly be unnecessary to come to a decision about it at present, and so for the time I leave the matter as it is. Now in such a case I often do not know how firmly I am already attached to that plan in secret, and how much, in spite of the scruple, I wish to carry it out: that is, my intellect does not know. But now only let me receive news that it is practicable, at once there rises within me a jubilant, irresistible gladness, that passes through my whole being and takes permanent possession of it, to my own astonishment. For now my intellect learns for the first time how firmly my will had laid hold of that plan, and how thoroughly the plan suited it, while the intellect had regarded it as entirely problematical, and had with difficulty been able to overcome that scruple. Or in another case, I have entered eagerly into a contract which I believed to be very much in accordance with my wishes. But as the matter progresses the disadvantages and burdens of it are felt, and I begin to suspect that I even repent of what I so eagerly pursued; yet I rid myself of this feeling by assuring myself that even if I were not bound I would follow the same course. Now, however, the contract is unexpectedly broken by the other side, and I perceive with astonishment that this happens to my great satisfaction and relief. Often we don't know what we wish or what we fear. We may entertain a wish for years without even confessing it to ourselves, or even allowing it to come to clear consciousness; for the intellect must know nothing about it, because the good opinion which we have of ourselves might thereby suffer. But if it is fulfilled we learn from our joy, not without shame, that we have wished this. For example, the death of a near relation whose heir we are. And sometimes we do not know what we really fear, because we lack the courage to bring it to distinct consciousness. Indeed we are often in error as to the real motive from which we have done something or left it undone, till at last perhaps an accident discovers to us the secret, and we know that what we have held to be the motive was not the true one, but another which we had not wished to confess to ourselves, because it by no means accorded with the good opinion we entertained of ourselves. For example, we refrain from doing something on purely moral grounds, as we believe, but afterwards we discover that we were only restrained by fear, for as soon as all danger is removed we do it. In particular cases this may go so far that a man does not even guess the true motive of his action, nay, does not believe himself capable of being influenced by such a motive; and yet it is the true motive of his action. We may remark in passing that in all this we have a confirmation and explanation of the rule of La Rochefoucauld: "L'amour-propre est plus habile que le plus habile homme du monde" ["Self-love is cleverer than the cleverest man in the world."]; nay, even a commentary on the Delphic ⟨*gnosi oeauton*⟩ ["Know thyself"] and its difficulty. If now, on the contrary, as all philosophers imagine, the intellect constituted our true nature and the purposes of the will were a mere result of knowledge, then only the motive from which we imagined that we acted would be decisive of our moral worth; in analogy with the fact that the intention, not the result, is in this respect decisive. But really then the distinction between imagined and true motive would be impossible. Thus all cases here set forth, to which every one who pays attention may observe analogous cases in himself, show us how the intellect is so strange to the will that it is sometimes even mystified by it: for it indeed supplies it with motives, but does not penetrate into the secret workshop of its purposes. It is indeed a confidant of the will, but a confidant that is not told everything. This is also further confirmed by the fact, which almost every one will some time have the opportunity of observing in himself, that sometimes the intellect does not thoroughly trust the will. If we have formed some great and bold purpose, which as such is yet really only a promise made by the will to the intellect, there often remains within us a slight unconfessed doubt whether we are quite in earnest about it, whether in carrying it out we will not waver or draw back, but will have sufficient firmness and persistency to fulfil it. It therefore requires the deed to convince us ourselves of the sincerity of the purpose.

All these facts prove the absolute difference of the will and the intellect, the primacy of the former and the subordinate position of the latter.

4. The *intellect* becomes tired; the *will* is never tired. After sustained work with the head we feel the tiredness of the brain, just like that of the arm after sustained bodily work. All *knowing* is accompanied with effort; *willing,* on the contrary, is our very nature, whose manifestations take place without any weariness and entirely of their own accord. Therefore, if our will is strongly excited, as in all emotions, thus in anger, fear, desire, grief, &c., and we are now called upon to know, perhaps with the view of correcting the motives of that emotion, the violence which we must do ourselves for this purpose is evidence of the transition from the original natural activity proper to ourselves to the derived, indirect, and formed activity. For the will alone is . . . is active without being called upon, and therefore often too early and too much, and it knows no weariness. Infants who scarcely show the first weak trace of intelligence are already full of self-will: through unlimited, aimless roaring and shrieking they show the pressure of will with which they swell, while their willing has yet no object, *i.e.,* they will without knowing what they will. What Cabanis has observed is also in point here: ["All these passions, which follow one another so quickly, picture themselves naively on the mobile faces of infants. While their feeble muscles, arms and legs hardly know yet how to make the vaguest movements, the muscles of the face already express, by distinct movements, all the principal emotions proper to human nature; and the attentive observer easily recognizes in this picture the characteristic traits of the future man."]* The intellect, on the contrary, develops slowly, following the completion of the brain and the maturity of the whole organism, which are its conditions, just because it is merely a somatic function. It is because the brain attains its full size in the seventh year that from that time forward children become so remarkably intelligent, inquisitive, and reasonable. But then comes puberty; to a certain extent it affords a support to the brain, or a resounding-board, and raises the intellect at once by a large step, as it were by an octave, corresponding to the lowering of the voice by that amount. But at once the animal desires and passions that now appear resist the reasonableness that has hitherto prevailed and to which they have been added. Further evidence is given of the indefatigable nature of the will by the fault which is, more or less, peculiar to all men by nature, and is only overcome by education—*precipitation.* It consists in this, that the will hurries to its work before the time. This work is the purely active and executive part, which ought only to begin when the explorative and deliberative part, thus the work of knowing, has been completely and thoroughly carried out. But this time is seldom waited for. Scarcely are a few data concerning the circumstances before us, or the event that has occurred, or the opinion of others conveyed to us, superficially comprehended and hastily

*[The actual text here is in French—F.B.] *Rapports du Physique et Moral,* vol. i., p. 123

gathered together by knowledge, than from the depths of our being the will, always ready and never weary, comes forth unasked, and shows itself as terror, fear, hope, joy, desire, envy, grief, zeal, anger, or courage, and leads to rash words and deeds, which are generally followed by repentance when time has taught us that the hegemonicon, the intellect, has not been able to finish half its work of comprehending the circumstances, reflecting on their connection, and deciding what is prudent, because the will did not wait for it, but sprang forward long before its time with "Now it is my turn!" and at once began the active work, without the intellect being able to resist, as it is a mere slave and bondman of the will, and not, like it, ⟨automatos⟩, nor active from its own power and its own impulse; therefore it is easily pushed aside and silenced by a nod of the will, while on its part it is scarcely able, with the greatest efforts, to bring the will even to a brief pause, in order to speak. This is why the people are so rare, and are found almost only among Spaniards, Turks, and perhaps Englishmen, who even under circumstances of provocation *keep the head uppermost,* imperturbably proceed to comprehend and investigate the state of affairs, and when others would already be beside themselves, still ask further questions, which is something quite different from the indifference founded upon apathy and stupidity of many Germans and Dutchmen. Iffland used to give an excellent representation of this admirable quality, as Hetmann of the Cossacks, in Benjowski, when the conspirators have enticed him into their tent and hold a rifle to his head, with the warning that they will fire it if he utters a cry, Iffland blew into the mouth of the rifle to try whether it was loaded. Of ten things that annoy us, nine would not be able to do so if we understood them thoroughly in their causes, and therefore knew their necessity and true nature; but we would do this much oftener if we made them the object of reflection before making them the object of wrath and indignation. For what bridle and bit are to an unmanageable horse the intellect is for the will in man; by this bridle it must be controlled by means of instruction, exhortation, culture, &c., for in itself it is as wild and impetuous an impulse as the force that appears in the descending waterfall, nay, as we know, it is at bottom identical with this. In the height of anger, in intoxication, in despair, it has taken the bit between its teeth, has run away, and follows its original nature. In the *Mania sine delirio* it has lost bridle and bit altogether, and shows now most distinctly its original nature, and that the intellect is as different from it as the bridle from the horse. In this condition it may also be compared to a clock which, when a certain screw is taken away, runs down without stopping.

Thus this consideration also shows us the will as that which is original, and therefore metaphysical; the intellect, on the other hand, as something subordinate and physical. For as such the latter is, like everything physical, subject to *vis inertiæ,* consequently only active if it is set agoing by something else, the will, which rules it, manages it, rouses it to effort, in short, imparts to it the activity which does not originally reside in it. Therefore it willingly rests whenever it is permitted to do so, often declares itself lazy and disinclined to activity; through continued effort it becomes weary to the point of complete stupefaction, is exhausted, like the voltaic pile, through repeated shocks. Hence all continuous mental work demands pauses and rest, otherwise stupidity and incapacity ensue, at first of course only temporarily; but if this rest is persistently denied to the intellect it will become excessively and continuously fatigued, and the consequence is a permanent deterioration of it, which in an old man may pass into complete incapacity, into childishness, imbecility, and madness. It is not to be attributed to age in and for itself, but to long-continued tyrannical overexertion of the intellect or brain, if this misfortune appears in the last years of life. This is the explanation of the fact that Swift became mad, Kant became childish, Walter Scott, and also Wordsworth, Southey, and many *minorum gentium* ["lesser gentry"] became dull and incapable.

Goethe remained to the end clear, strong, and active-minded, because he, who was always a man of the world and a courtier, never carried on his mental occupations with self-compulsion. The same holds good of Wieland and of Knebel, who lived to the age of ninety-one, and also of Voltaire. Now all this proves how very subordinate and physical and what a mere tool the intellect is. Just on this account it requires, during almost a third part of its lifetime, the entire suspension of its activity in sleep, *i.e.,* the rest of the brain, of which it is the mere function, and which therefore just as truly precedes it as the stomach precedes digestion, or as a body precedes its impulsion, and with which in old age it flags and decays. The will, on the contrary, as the thing in itself, is never lazy, is absolutely untiring, its activity is its essence, it never ceases willing, and when, during deep sleep, it is forsaken of the intellect, and therefore cannot act outwardly in accordance with motives, it is active as the vital force, cares the more uninterruptedly for the inner economy of the organism, and as *vis naturæ medicatrix* ["natures healing power"] sets in order again the irregularities that have crept into it. For it is not, like the intellect, a function of the body; *but the body is its function;* therefore it is, *ordine rerum* ["in the order of things"], prior to the body, as its metaphysical substratum, as the in-itself of its phenomenal appearance. It shares its unwearying nature, for the time that life lasts, with the heart, that *primum mobile* of the organism, which has therefore become its symbol and synonym. Moreover, it does not disappear in the old man, but still continues to will what it has willed, and indeed becomes firmer, more inflexible, than it was in youth, more implacable, self-willed, and unmanageable, because the intellect has become less susceptible: therefore in old age the man can perhaps only be matched by taking advantage of the weakness of his intellect.

Moreover, the prevailing *weakness* and *imperfection* of the intellect, as it is shown in the want of judgment, narrow-mindedness, perversity, and folly of the great majority of men, would be quite inexplicable if the intellect were not subordinate, adventitious, and merely instrumental, but the immediate and original nature of the so-called soul, or in general of the inner man: as all philosophers have hitherto assumed it to be. For how could the original nature in its immediate and peculiar function so constantly err and fail? The *truly* original in human consciousness, the *willing,* always goes on with perfect success; every being wills unceasingly, capably, and decidedly. To regard the immorality in the will as an imperfection of it would be a fundamentally false point of view. For morality has rather a source which really lies above nature, and therefore its utterances are in contradiction with it. Therefore morality is in direct opposition to the natural will, which in itself is completely egoistic; indeed the pursuit of the path of morality leads to the abolition of the will.

5. That the *will* is what is real and essential in man, and the *intellect* only subordinate, conditioned, and produced, is also to be seen in the fact that the latter can carry on its function with perfect purity and correctness only so long as the will is silent and pauses. On the other hand, the function of the intellect is disturbed by every observable excitement of the will, and its result is falsified by the intermixture of the latter; but the converse does not hold, that the intellect should in the same way be a hindrance to the will. Thus the moon cannot shine when the sun is in the heavens, but when the moon is in the heavens it does not prevent the sun from shining.

A great *fright* often deprives us of our senses to such an extent that we are petrified, or else do the most absurd things; for example, when fire has broken out run right into the flames. *Anger* makes us no longer know what we do, still less what we say. Zeal, therefore called blind, makes us incapable of weighing the arguments of others, or even of seeking out and setting in order our own. *Joy* makes us inconsiderate, reckless, and foolhardy, and *desire* acts almost in the same way. *Fear* prevents us from seeing,

The Sleep of Reason Produces Monsters, 1796–1798, by Francisco de Goya (1746–1828). In his *Los Caprichos* etching series, Goya questions his own Enlightenment faith in the power of reason to solve the problems of the human condition. In this etching from the frontispiece to the collection, he depicts the nightmarish chaos released when reason sleeps. Goya's work anticipates Schopenhauer's questioning of the intellect's primacy. *(National Gallery of Art, Washington, DC)*

and laying hold of the resources that are still present, and often lie close beside us. Therefore for overcoming sudden dangers, and also for fighting with opponents and enemies, the most essential qualifications are *coolness and presence of mind.* The former consists in the silence of the will so that the intellect can act; the latter in the undisturbed activity of the intellect under the pressure of events acting on the will; therefore the former is the condition of the latter, and the two are nearly related; they are seldom to be found, and always only in a limited degree. But they are of inestimable advantage, because they permit the use of the intellect just at those times when we stand most in need of it, and therefore confer decided superiority. He who is without them knows only what he should have done or said when the opportunity has passed. It is very appropriately said of him who is violently moved, *i.e.,* whose will is so strongly excited that it destroys the purity of the function of the intellect, he is *disarmed;* for the correct knowledge of the circumstances and relations is our defense and weapon in the conflict with things and with men. In this sense Balthazar Gracian says: *"Es la passion enemiga declarada de la cordura"* (Passion is the declared enemy of prudence). If now the intellect were not something completely different from the will, but, as has been hitherto supposed, knowing and willing had the same root, and were equally original functions of an absolutely simple nature, then with the rousing and heightening of the will, in which the emotion consists, the intellect would necessarily also be heightened; but, as we have seen, it is rather hindered and depressed by this; whence the ancients called emotion *animi perturbatio.* The intellect is really like the reflecting surface of water, but the water itself is like the will, whose disturbance therefore at once destroys the clearness of that mirror and the distinctness of its images. The *organism* is the will itself, is embodied will, *i.e.,* will objectively perceived in the brain. Therefore many of its functions, such as respiration, circulation, secretion of bile, and muscular power, are heightened and accelerated by the pleasurable, and in general the healthy, emotions. The *intellect,* on the other hand, is the mere function of the brain, which is only nourished and supported by the organism as a parasite. Therefore every perturbation of the *will,* and with it of the *organism,* must disturb and paralyse the function of the brain, which exists for itself and for no other wants than its own, which are simply rest and nourishment.

But this disturbing influence of the activity of the will upon the intellect can be shown, not only in the perturbations brought about by emotions, but also in many other, more gradual, and therefore more lasting falsifications of thought by our inclinations. *Hope* makes us regard what we wish, and fear what we are apprehensive of, as probable and near, and both exaggerate their object. Plato (according to Ælian, V. H., 13, 28) very beautifully called hope the dream of the waking. Its nature lies in this, that the will, when its servant the intellect is not able to produce what it wishes, obliges it at least to picture it before it, in general to undertake the rôle of comforter, to appease its lord with fables, as a nurse a child, and so to dress these out that they gain an appearance of likelihood. Now in this the intellect must do violence to its own nature, which aims at the truth, for it compels it, contrary to its own laws, to regard as true things which are neither true nor probable, and often scarcely possible, only in order to appease, quiet, and send to sleep for a while the restless and unmanageable *will.* Here we see clearly who is master and who is servant. Many may well have observed that if a matter which is of importance to them may turn out in several different ways, and they have brought all of these into one disjunctive judgment which in their opinion is complete, the actual result is yet quite another, and one wholly unexpected by them: but perhaps they will not have considered this, that this result was then almost always the one which was unfavourable to them. The explanation of this is, that while their *intellect* intended to survey the possibilities completely, the worst of all remained quite invisible to it; because the *will,* as it were, covered it with its hand, that is, it so mastered the intellect that it was quite incapable of glancing at the worst case of all, although, since it actually came to pass, this was also the most probable case. Yet in very melancholy dispositions, or in those that have become prudent through experience like this, the process is reversed, for here apprehension plays the part which was formerly played by hope. The first appearance of danger throws them into groundless anxiety. If the intellect begins to investigate the matter it is rejected as incompetent, nay, as a deceitful sophist, because the heart is to be believed, whose fears are now actually allowed to pass for arguments as to the reality and greatness of the danger. So then the intellect dare make no search for good reasons on the other side, which, if left to itself, it would soon recognize, but is obliged at once to picture to them the most unfortunate issue, even if it itself can scarcely think this issue possible:

> "Such as we know is false, yet dread in sooth,
> Because the worst is ever nearest truth."
>
> —Byron (*Lara,* c, I).

Love and *hate* falsify our judgment entirely. In our enemies we see nothing but faults—in our loved ones nothing but excellences, and even their faults appear to us amiable. Our *interest,* of whatever kind it may be, exercises a like secret power over our judgment; what is in conformity with it at once seems to us fair, just, and reasonable; what runs contrary to it presents itself to us, in perfect seriousness, as unjust and outrageous, or injudicious and absurd. Hence so many prejudices of position, profession, nationality, sect, and religion. A conceived hypothesis gives us lynx-eyes for all that confirms it, and makes us blind to all that contradicts it. What is opposed to our party, our plan, our wish, our hope, we often cannot comprehend and grasp at all, while it is clear to every one else; but what is favourable to these, on the other hand, strikes our eye from afar. What the heart opposes the head will not admit. We firmly retain many errors all through life, and take care never to examine their ground, merely from a fear, of which we ourselves are conscious, that we might make the discovery that we had so long believed and so often asserted what is false. Thus then is the intellect daily befooled and corrupted by the impositions of inclination. This has been very beautifully expressed by Bacon of Verulam in the words: *Intellectus LUMINIS SICCI non est; sed recipit infusionem a voluntate et affectibus: id quod generat ad quod vult scientias: quod enim mavult homo, id potius credit.* ["The intellect is not a dry light, but receives an infusion from the will and the emotions, which results in sciences-as-we-wish; for what a man prefers he will rather believe."] (Org. Nov., i., 14). Clearly it is also this that opposes all new fundamental opinions in the sciences and all refutations of sanctioned errors, for one will not easily see the truth of that which convicts one of incredible want of thought. It is explicable, on this ground alone, that the truths of Goethe's doctrine of colours, which are so clear and simple, are still denied by the physicists; and thus Goethe himself has had to learn what a much harder position one has if one promises men instruction than if one promises them amusement. Hence it is much more fortunate to be born a poet than a philosopher. But the more obstinately an error was held by the other side, the more shameful does the conviction afterwards become. In the case of an overthrown system, as in the case of a conquered army, the most prudent is he who first runs away from it.

A trifling and absurd, but striking, example of that mysterious and immediate power which the will exercises over the intellect, is the fact that in doing accounts we make mistakes much oftener in our own favour than to our disadvantage, and this without the slightest dishonest intention, merely from the unconscious tendency to diminish our *Debit* and increase our *Credit.*

Lastly, the fact is also in point here, that when advice is given the slightest aim or purpose of the adviser generally outweighs his insight, however great it may be; therefore we dare not assume that he speaks from the latter when we suspect the existence of the former. How little perfect sincerity is to be expected even from otherwise honest persons whenever their interests are in any way concerned we can gather from the fact that we so often deceive ourselves when hope bribes us, or fear befools us, or suspicion torments us, or vanity flatters us, or any hypothesis blinds us, or a small aim which is close at hand injures a greater but more distant one; for in this we see the direct and unconscious disadvantageous influence of the will upon knowledge. Accordingly it ought not to surprise us if in asking advice the will of the person asked directly dictates the answer even before the question could penetrate to the forum of his judgment.

I wish in a single word to point out here what will be fully explained in the following book, that the most perfect knowledge, thus the purely objective comprehension of the world, *i.e.,* the comprehension of genius, is conditioned by a silence of the will so profound that while it lasts even the individuality vanishes from consciousness and the man remains *as the pure subject of knowing,* which is the correlative of the *Idea.*

The disturbing influence of the will upon the intellect, which is proved by all these phenomena, and, on the other hand, the weakness and frailty of the latter, on account of which it is incapable of working rightly whenever the will is in any way moved, gives us then another proof that the will is the radical part of our nature, and acts with original power, while the intellect, as adventitious and in many ways conditioned, can only act in a subordinate and conditional manner.

There is no direct disturbance of the will by the intellect corresponding to the disturbance and clouding of knowledge by the will that has been shown. Indeed we cannot well conceive such a thing. No one will wish to construe as such the fact that motives wrongly taken up lead the will astray, for this is a fault of the intellect in its own function, which is committed quite within its own province, and the influence of which upon the will is entirely indirect. It would be plausible to attribute *irresolution* to this, for in its case, through the conflict of the motives which the intellect presents to the will, the latter is brought to a standstill, thus is hindered. But when we consider it more closely, it becomes very clear that the cause of this hindrance does not lie in the activity of the *intellect* as such, but entirely in *external objects* which are brought about by it, for in this case they stand in precisely such a relation to the will, which is here interested, that they draw it with nearly equal strength in different directions. This real cause merely acts *through* the intellect as the medium of motives, though certainly under the assumption that it is keen enough to comprehend the objects in their manifold relations. Irresolution, as a trait of character, is just as much conditioned by qualities of the will as of the intellect. It is certainly not peculiar to exceedingly limited minds, for their weak understanding does not allow them to discover such manifold qualities and relations in things, and moreover is so little fitted for the exertion of reflection and pondering these, and then the probable consequences of each step, that they rather decide at once according to the first impression, or according to some simple rule of conduct. The converse of this occurs in the case of persons of considerable understanding. Therefore, whenever such persons also possess a tender care for their own well-being, *i.e.,* a very sensitive egoism, which constantly desires to come off well and always to be safe, this introduces a certain anxiety at every step, and thereby irresolution. This quality therefore indicates throughout not a want of understanding but a want of courage. Yet very eminent minds survey the relations and their probable developments with such rapidity and certainty, that if they are only supported by some courage they thereby acquire that quick decision and resolution that fits them to play an important part in the affairs of the world, if time and circumstances afford them the opportunity.

The only decided, direct restriction and disturbance which the will can suffer from the intellect as such may indeed be the quite exceptional one, which is the consequence of an abnormally preponderating development of the intellect, thus of that high endowment which has been defined as genius. This is decidedly a hindrance to the energy of the character, and consequently to the power of action. Hence it is not the really great minds that make historical characters, because they are capable of bridling and ruling the mass of men and carrying out the affairs of the world; but for this persons of much less capacity of mind are qualified when they have great firmness, decision, and persistency of will, such as is quite inconsistent with very high intelligence. Accordingly, where this very high intelligence exists we actually have a case in which the intellect directly restricts the will.

6. In opposition to the hindrances and restrictions which it has been shown the intellect suffers from the will, I wish now to show, in a few examples, how, conversely, the functions of the intellect are sometimes aided and heightened by the incitement and spur of the will; so that in this also we may recognize the primary nature of the one and the secondary nature of the other, and it may become clear that the intellect stands to the will in the relation of a tool.

A motive which affects us strongly, such as a yearning desire or a pressing need, sometimes raises the intellect to a degree of which we had not previously believed it capable. Difficult circumstances, which impose upon us the necessity of certain achievements, develop entirely new talents in us, the germs of which were hidden from us, and for which we did not credit ourselves with any capacity. The understanding of the stupidest man becomes keen when objects are in question that closely concern his wishes; he now observes, weighs, and distinguishes with the greatest delicacy even the smallest circumstances that have reference to his wishes or fears. This has much to do with the cunning of half-witted persons, which is often remarked with surprise. On this account Isaiah rightly says, *vexatio dat intellectum,* which is therefore also used as a proverb. Akin to it is the German proverb, *"Die Noth ist die Mutter der Künste"* ("Necessity is the mother of the arts"); when, however, the fine arts are to be excepted, because the heart of every one of their works, that is, the conception, must proceed from a perfectly will-less, and only thereby purely objective, perception, if they are to be genuine. Even the understanding of the brutes is increased considerably by necessity, so that in cases of difficulty they accomplish things at which we are astonished. For example, they almost all calculate that it is safer not to run away when they believe they are not seen; therefore the hare lies still in the furrow of the field and lets the sportsman pass close to it; insects, when they cannot escape, pretend to be dead, &c. We may obtain a fuller knowledge of this influence from the special history of the self-education of the wolf, under the spur of the great difficulty of its position in civilized Europe; it is to be found in the second letter of Leroy's excellent book, *"Lettres sur l'intelligence et la perfectibilité des animaux."* Immediately afterwards, in the third letter, there follows the high school of the fox, which in an equally difficult position has far less physical strength. In its case, however, this is made up for by great understanding; yet only through the constant struggle with want on the one hand and danger on the other, thus under the spur of the will, does it attain that high degree of cunning which distinguishes it especially in old age. In all these enhancements of the intellect the will plays the part of a rider who with the spur urges the horse beyond the natural measure of its strength.

In the same way the memory is enhanced through the pressure of the will. Even if it is otherwise weak, it preserves perfectly what has value for the ruling passion. The lover forgets no opportunity favourable to him, the ambitious man forgets no circumstance that can forward his plans, the avaricious man never forgets the loss he has suffered, the proud man never forgets an injury to his honour, the vain man remembers every word of praise and the most trifling distinction that falls to his lot. And this also extends to the brutes: the horse stops at the inn where once long ago it was fed; dogs have an excellent memory for all occasions, times, and places that have afforded them choice morsels; and foxes for the different hiding-places in which they have stored their plunder.

Self-consideration affords opportunity for finer observations in this regard. Sometimes, through an interruption, it has entirely escaped me what I have just been thinking about, or even what news I have just heard. Now if the matter had in any way even the most distant personal interest, the after-feeling of the impression which it made upon the *will* has remained. I am still quite conscious how far it affected me agreeably or disagreeably, and also of the special manner in which this happened, whether, even in the slightest degree, it vexed me, or made me anxious, or irritated me, or depressed me, or produced the opposite of these affections. Thus the mere relation of the thing to my will is retained in the memory after the thing itself has vanished, and this often becomes the clue to lead us back to the thing itself. The sight of a man sometimes affects us in an analogous manner, for we remember merely in general that we have had something to do with him, yet without knowing where, when, or what it was, or who he is. But the sight of him still recalls pretty accurately the feeling which our dealings with him excited in us, whether it was agreeable or disagreeable, and also in what degree and in what way. Thus our memory has preserved only the response of the will, and not that which called it forth. We might call what lies at the foundation of this process the memory of the heart; it is much more intimate than that of the head. Yet at bottom the connection of the two is so far-reaching that if we reflect deeply upon the matter we will arrive at the conclusion that memory in general requires the support of a will as a connecting point, or rather as a thread upon which the memories can range themselves, and which holds them firmly together, or that the will is, as it were, the ground to which the individual memories cleave, and without which they could not last; and that therefore in a pure intelligence, *i.e.,* in a merely knowing and absolutely will-less being, a memory cannot well be conceived. Accordingly the improvement of the memory under the spur of the ruling passion, which has been shown above, is only the higher degree of that which takes place in all retention and recollection; for its basis and condition is always the will. Thus in all this also it becomes clear how very much more essential to us the will is than the intellect. The following facts may also serve to confirm this.

The intellect often obeys the will; for example, if we wish to remember something, and after some effort succeed; so also if we wish now to ponder something carefully and deliberately, and in many such cases. Sometimes, again, the intellect refuses to obey the will; for example, if we try in vain to fix our minds upon something, or if we call in vain upon the memory for something that was intrusted to it. The anger of the will against the intellect on such occasions makes its relation to it and the difference of the two very plain. Indeed the intellect, vexed by this anger, sometimes officiously brings what was asked of it hours afterwards, or even the following morning, quite unexpectedly and unseasonably. On the other hand, the will never really obeys the intellect; but the latter is only the ministerial council of that sovereign; it presents all kinds of things to the will, which then selects what is in conformity with its nature, though in doing so it determines itself with necessity, because this nature is unchangeable and the motives now lie before it. Hence no system of ethics is possible which moulds and improves the will itself. For all teaching only affects *knowledge,* and knowledge never determines the will itself, *i.e.,* the *fundamental character* of willing, not only its application to the circumstances present. Rectified knowledge can only modify conduct so far as it proves more exactly and judges more correctly what objects of the will's choice are within its reach; so that the will now measures its relation to things more correctly, sees more clearly what it desires, and consequently is less subject to error in its choice. But over the will itself, over the main tendency or fundamental maxim of it, the intellect has no power. To believe that knowledge really and fundamentally determines the will is like believing that the lantern which a man carries by night is the *primum mobile* of his steps. Whoever, taught by experience or the admonitions of others, knows and laments a fundamental fault of his character, firmly and honestly forms the intention to reform and give it up; but in spite of this, on the first opportunity, the fault receives free course. New repentance, new intentions, new transgressions. When this has been gone through several times he becomes conscious that he cannot improve himself, that the fault lies in his nature and personality, indeed is one with this. Now he will blame and curse his nature and personality, will have a painful feeling, which may rise to anguish of consciousness, but to change these he is not able. Here we see that which condemns and that which is condemned distinctly separate: we see the former as a merely theoretical faculty, picturing and presenting the praiseworthy, and therefore desirable, course of life, but the other as something real and unchangeably present, going quite a different way in spite of the former: and then again the first remaining behind with impotent lamentations over the nature of the other, with which, through this very distress, it again identifies itself. Will and intellect here separate very distinctly. But here the will shows itself as the stronger, the invincible, unchangeable, primitive, and at the same time as the essential thing in question, for the intellect deplores its errors, and finds no comfort in the correctness of the *knowledge,* as its own function. Thus the intellect shows itself entirely secondary, as the spectator of the deeds of another, which it accompanies with impotent praise and blame, and also as determinable from without, because it learns from experience, weighs and alters its precepts. Accordingly, a comparison of our manner of thinking at different periods of our life will present a strange mixture of permanence and changeableness. On the one hand, the moral tendency of the man in his prime and the old man is still the same as was that of the boy; on the other hand, much has become so strange to him that he no longer knows himself, and wonders how he ever could have done or said this and that. In the first half of life to-day for the most part laughs at yesterday, indeed looks down on it with contempt; in the second half, on the contrary, it more and more looks back at it with envy. But on closer examination it will be found that the changeable element was the *intellect,* with its functions of insight and knowledge, which, daily appropriating new material from without, presents a constantly changing system of thought, while, besides this, it itself rises and sinks with the growth and decay of the organism. The will on the contrary, the basis of this, thus the inclinations, passions, and emotions, the character, shows itself as what is unalterable in consciousness. Yet we have to take account of the modifications that depend upon physical capacities for enjoyment, and hence upon age. Thus, for example, the eagerness for sensuous pleasure will show itself in childhood as a love of dainties, in youth and manhood as the tendency to sensuality, and in old age again as a love of dainties.

7. If, as is generally assumed, the will proceeded from knowledge, as its result or product, then where there is much will there would necessarily also be much knowledge, insight, and understanding. This, however, is absolutely not the case; rather, we find in many men a strong, *i.e.,* decided, resolute, persistent, unbending, wayward, and vehement will, combined with a very weak and incapable understanding, so that every

one who has to do with them is thrown into despair, for their will remains inaccessible to all reasons and ideas, and is not to be got at, so that it is hidden, as it were, in a sack, out of which it wills blindly. Brutes have often violent, often stubborn wills, but yet very little understanding. Finally, plants will only without any knowledge at all.

If willing sprang merely from knowledge, our *anger* would necessarily be in every case exactly proportionate to the occasion, or at least to our relation to it, for it would be nothing more than the result of the present knowledge. This, however, is rarely the case; rather, anger generally goes far beyond the occasion. Our fury and rage, the *furor brevis*, often upon small occasions, and without error regarding them, is like the raging of an evil spirit which, having been shut up, only waits its opportunity to dare to break loose, and now rejoices that it has found it. This could not be the case if the foundation of our nature were a *knower*, and willing were merely a result of *knowledge*; for how came there into the result what did not lie in the elements? The conclusion cannot contain more than the premises. Thus here also the will shows itself as of a nature quite different from knowledge, which only serves it for communication with the external world, but then the will follows the laws of its own nature without taking from the intellect anything but the occasion.

The intellect, as the mere tool of the will, is as different from it as the hammer from the smith. So long as in a conversation the intellect alone is active it remains *cold*. It is almost as if the man himself were not present. Moreover, he cannot then, properly speaking, compromise himself, but at the most can make himself ridiculous. Only when the will comes into play is the man really present: now he becomes *warm*, nay, it often happens, *hot*. It is always the will to which we ascribe the warmth of life; on the other hand, we say the *cold* understanding, or to investigate a thing *coolly, i.e.,* to think without being influenced by the will. If we attempt to reverse the relation, and to regard the will as the tool of the intellect, it is as if we made the smith the tool of the hammer.

Nothing is more provoking, when we are arguing against a man with reasons and explanation, and taking all pains to convince him, under the impression that we have only to do with his *understanding,* than to discover at last that he *will* not understand; that thus we had to do with his *will,* which shuts itself up against the truth and brings into the field wilful misunderstandings, chicaneries, and sophisms in order to intrench itself behind its understanding and its pretended want of insight. Then he is certainly not to be got at, for reasons and proofs applied against the will are like the blows of a phantom produced by mirrors against a solid body. Hence the saying so often repeated, *"Stat pro ratione voluntas"* ["the will takes the place of reason"]. Sufficient evidence of what has been said is afforded by ordinary life. But unfortunately proofs of it are also to be found on the path of the sciences. The recognition of the most important truths, of the rarest achievements, will be looked for in vain from those who have an interest in preventing them from being accepted, an interest which either springs from the fact that such truths contradict what they themselves daily teach, or else from this, that they dare not make use of them and teach them; or if all this be not the case they will not accept them, because the watchword of mediocrity will always be, *Si quelqu'un excelle parmi nous, qu'il aille exceller ailleurs* ["If anyone excels among us, let him go and excel elsewhere"], as Helvetius has admirably rendered the saying of the Ephesian in the fifth book of Cicero's *"Tusculanæ"* (c. 36), or as a saying of the Abyssinian Fit Arari puts it, "Among quartzes adamant is outlawed." Thus whoever expects from this always numerous band a just estimation of what he has done will find himself very much deceived, and perhaps for a while he will not be able to understand their behaviour, till at last he finds out that while he applied himself to *knowledge* he had to do with the *will,* thus is precisely in the position described above, nay, is really like a man who brings his case before a court the judges of which have all been bribed. Yet in particular cases he will receive the fullest proof that their will and not their insight opposed him, when one or other of them makes up his mind to plagiarism. Then he will see with astonishment what good judges they are, what correct perception of the merit of others they have, and how well they know how to find out the best, like the sparrows, who never miss the ripest cherries.

The counterpart of the victorious resistance of the will to knowledge here set forth appears if in expounding our reasons and proofs we have the will of those addressed with us. Then all are at once convinced, all arguments are telling, and the matter is at once clear as the day. This is well known to popular speakers. In the one case, as in the other, the will shows itself as that which has original power, against which the intellect can do nothing.

8. But now we shall take into consideration the individual qualities, thus excellences and faults of the will and character on the one hand, and of the intellect on the other, in order to make clear, in their relation to each other, and their relative worth, the complete difference of the two fundamental faculties. History and experience teach that the two appear quite independent of each other. That the greatest excellence of mind will not easily be found combined with equal excellence of character is sufficiently explained by the extraordinary rarity of both, while their opposites are everywhere the order of the day; hence we also daily find the latter in union. However, we never infer a good will from a superior mind, nor the latter from the former, nor the opposite from the opposite, but every unprejudiced person accepts them as perfectly distinct qualities, the presence of which each for itself has to be learned from experience. Great narrowness of mind may coexist with great goodness of heart, and I do not believe Balthazar Gracian was right in saying (*Discreto,* p. 406), *"No ay simple, que no sea malicioso"* ("There is no simpleton who would not be malicious"), though he has the Spanish proverb in his favour, *"Nunca la necedad anduvo sin malicia"* ("Stupidity is never without malice"). Yet it may be that many stupid persons become malicious for the same reason as many hunchbacks, from bitterness on account of the neglect they have suffered from nature, and because they think they can occasionally make up for what they lack in understanding through malicious cunning, seeking in this a brief triumph. From this, by the way, it is also comprehensible why almost every one easily becomes malicious in the presence of a very superior mind. On the other hand, again, stupid people have very often the reputation of special good-heartedness, which yet so seldom proves to be the case that I could not help wondering how they had gained it, till I was able to flatter myself that I had found the key to it in what follows. Moved by a secret inclination, every one likes best to choose for his more intimate intercourse some one to whom he is a little superior in understanding, for only in this case does he find himself at his ease, because, according to Hobbes, *"Omnis animi voluptas, omnisque alacritas in eo sita est, quod quis habeat quibuscum conferens se, possit magnifice sentire de se ipso"* ["Every pleasure and vivacity of the mind lies in this, that one has something wherein, comparing himself with others, he can think himself magnificent"] (De Cive, i., 5). For the same reason every one avoids him who is superior to himself; wherefore Lichtenberg quite rightly observes: "To certain men a man of mind is a more odious production than the most pronounced rogue." And similarly Helvetius says: *"Les gens médiocres ont un instinct sür et prompt, pour connáître et fuir les gens d'esprit"* ["Mediocre people have a sure and ready instinct to know and fly from men of genius"]. And Dr. Johnson assures us that "there is nothing by which a man exasperates most people more than by displaying a superior ability of brilliancy in conversation. They seem pleased at the time, but their envy makes them curse him in their hearts" (Boswell;

aet. anno 74). In order to bring this truth, so universal and so carefully concealed, more relentlessly to light, I add the expression of it by Merck, the celebrated friend of Goethe's youth, from his story *"Lindor"* : "He possessed talents which were given him by nature and acquired by himself through learning; and thus it happened that in most society he left the worthy members of it far behind." If, in the moment of delight at the sight of an extraordinary man, the public swallows these superiorities also, without actually at once putting a bad construction upon them, yet a certain impression of this phenomenon remains behind, which, if it is often repeated, may on serious occasions have disagreeable future consequences for him who is guilty of it. Without any one consciously noting that on this occasion he was insulted, no one is sorry to place himself tacitly in the way of the advancement of this man. Thus on this account great mental superiority isolates more than anything else, and makes one, at least silently, hated. Now it is the opposite of this that makes stupid people so generally liked; especially since many can only find in them what, according to the law of their nature referred to above, they must seek. Yet this the true reason of such an inclination no one will confess to himself, still less to others; and therefore, as a plausible pretext for it, will impute to those he has selected a special goodness of heart, which, as we have said, is in reality only very rarely and accidentally found in combination with mental incapacity. Want of understanding is accordingly by no means favourable or akin to goodness of character. But, on the other hand, it cannot be asserted that great understanding is so; nay, rather, no scoundrel has in general been without it. Indeed even the highest intellectual eminence can coexist with the worst moral depravity.

If now it is said of one man, "He has a good heart, though a bad head," but of another, "He has a very good head, yet a bad heart," every one feels that in the first case the praise far outweighs the blame—in the other case the reverse. Answering to this, we see that if some one has done a bad deed his friends and he himself try to remove the guilt from the *will* to the *intellect,* and to give out that faults of the heart were faults of the head; roguish tricks they will call errors, will say they were merely want of understanding, want of reflection, light-mindedness, folly; nay, if need be, they will plead a paroxysm, momentary mental aberration, and if a heavy crime is in question, even madness, only in order to free the *will* from the guilt. And in the same way, we ourselves, if we have caused a misfortune or injury, will before others and ourselves willingly impeach our *stultitia,* simply in order to escape the reproach of *malitia.* In the same way, in the case of the equally unjust decision of the judge, the difference, whether he has erred or been bribed, is so infinitely great. All this sufficiently proves that the *will* alone is the real and essential, the kernel of the man, and the *intellect* is merely its tool, which may be constantly faulty without the will being concerned. The accusation of want of understanding is, at the moral judgment-seat, no accusation at all; on the contrary, it even gives privileges. And so also, before the courts of the world, it is everywhere sufficient to deliver a criminal from all punishment that his guilt should be transferred from his will to his intellect, by proving either unavoidable error or mental derangement, for then it is of no more consequence than if hand or foot had slipped against the will.

Everywhere those who are responsible for any piece of work appeal, in the event of its turning out unsatisfactorily, to their good intentions, of which there was no lack. Hereby they believe that they secure the essential, that for which they are properly answerable, and their true self; the inadequacy of their faculties, on the other hand, they regard as the want of a suitable tool.

If a man is *stupid,* we excuse him by saying that he cannot help it; but if we were to excuse a *bad* man on the same grounds we would be laughed at. And yet the one, like the other, is innate. This proves that the will is the man proper, the intellect merely its tool.

Thus it is always only our *willing* that is regarded as depending upon ourselves, *i.e.,* as the expression of our true nature, and for which we are therefore made responsible. Therefore it is absurd and unjust if we are taken to task for our beliefs, thus for our knowledge: for we are obliged to regard this as something which, although it changes in us, is as little in our power as the events of the external world. And here, also, it is clear that the *will* alone is the inner and true nature of man; the *intellect,* on the contrary, with its operations, which go on as regularly as the external world, stands to the will in the relation of something external to it, a mere tool.

9. High mental capacities have always been regarded as the gift of nature or the gods; and on that account they have been called *Gaben, Begabung, ingenii dotes,* gifts (a man highly gifted), regarding them as something different from the man himself, something that has fallen to his lot through favour. No one, on the contrary, has even taken this view of moral excellences, although they also are innate; they have rather always been regarded as something proceeding from the man himself, essentially belonging to him, nay, constituting his very self. But it follows now from this that the will is the true nature of man; the intellect, on the other hand, is secondary, a tool, a gift.

Answering to this, all religious promise a reward beyond life, in eternity, for excellences of the *will* or heart, but none for excellences of the head or understanding. Virtue expects its reward in that world; prudence hopes for it in this; genius, again, neither in this world nor in that; it is its own reward. Accordingly the will is the eternal part, the intellect the temporal.

Connection, communion, intercourse among men is based, as a rule, upon relations which concern the *will,* not upon such as concern the *intellect.* The first kind of communion may be called the *material,* the other the *formal.* Of the former kind are the bonds of family and relationship, and further, all connections that rest upon any common aim or interest, such as that of trade or profession, of the corporation, the party, the faction, &c. In these it merely amounts to a question of views, of aims; along with which there may be the greatest diversity of intellectual capacity and culture. Therefore not only can any one live in peace and unity with any one else, but can act with him and be allied to him for the common good of both. Marriage also is a bond of the heart, not of the head. It is different, however, with merely formal communion, which aims only at an exchange of thought; this demands a certain equality of intellectual capacity and culture. Great differences in this respect place between man and man an impassable gulf: such lies, for example, between a man of great mind and a fool, between a scholar and a peasant, between a courtier and a sailor. Natures as heterogeneous as this have therefore trouble in making themselves intelligible so long as it is a question of exchanging thoughts, ideas, and views. Nevertheless close *material* friendship may exist between them, and they may be faithful allies, conspirators, or men under mutual pledges. For in all that concerns the will alone, which includes friendship, enmity, honesty, fidelity, falseness, and treachery, they are perfectly homogeneous, formed of the same clay, and neither mind nor culture make any difference here; indeed here the ignorant man often shames the scholar, the sailor the courtier. For at the different grades of culture there are the same virtues and vices, emotions and passions; and although somewhat modified in their expression, they very soon mutually recognize each other even in the most heterogeneous individuals, upon which the similarly disposed agree and the opposed are at enmity.

Brilliant qualities of mind win admiration, but never affection; this is reserved for the moral, the qualities of the character. Every one will choose as his friend the honest, the good-natured, and even the agreeable, complaisant man, who easily concurs, rather than the merely able man. Indeed many will be preferred to the latter, on account of insignificant, accidental, outward qualities which just suit the inclination of another. Only the man who has much mind himself will wish able men for his society; his friendship, on the other hand, he will bestow with reference to moral qualities; for upon this depends his really high appreciation of a man in whom a single good trait of character conceals and expiates great want of understanding. The known goodness of a character makes us patient and yielding towards weaknesses of understanding, as also towards the dullness and childishness of age. A distinctly noble character along with the entire absence of intellectual excellence and culture presents itself as lacking nothing; while, on the contrary, even the greatest mind, if affected with important moral faults, will always appear blamable. For as torches and fireworks become pale and insignificant in the presence of the sun, so intellect, nay, genius, and also beauty, are outshone and eclipsed by the goodness of the heart. When this appears in a high degree it can make up for the want of those qualities to such an extent that one is ashamed of having missed them. Even the most limited understanding, and also grotesque ugliness, whenever extraordinary goodness of heart declares itself as accompanying them, become as it were transfigured, outshone by a beauty of a higher kind, for now a wisdom speaks out of them before which all other wisdom must be dumb. For goodness of heart is a transcendent quality; it belongs to an order of things that reaches beyond this life, and is incommensurable with any other perfection. When it is present in a high degree it makes the heart so large that it embraces the world, so that now everything lies within it, no longer without; for it identifies all natures with its own. It then extends to others also that boundless indulgence which otherwise each one only bestows on himself. Such a man is incapable of becoming angry; even if the malicious mockery and sneers of others have drawn attention to his own intellectual or physical faults, he only reproaches himself in his heart for having been the occasion of such expressions, and therefore, without doing violence to his own feelings, proceeds to treat those persons in the kindest manner, confidently hoping that they will turn from their error with regard to him, and recognize themselves in him also. What is wit and genius against this?—what is Bacon of Verulam?

Our estimation of our own selves leads to the same result as we have here obtained by considering our estimation of others. How different is the self-satisfaction which we experience in a moral regard from that which we experience in an intellectual regard! The former arises when, looking back on our conduct, we see that with great sacrifices we have practiced fidelity and honesty, that we have helped many, forgiven many, have behaved better to others than they have behaved to us; so that we can say with King Lear, "I am a man more sinned against than sinning"; and to its fullest extent if perhaps some noble deed shines in our memory. A deep seriousness will accompany the still peace which such a review affords us; and if we see that others are inferior to us here, this will not cause us any joy, but we will rather deplore it, and sincerely wish that they were as we are. How entirely differently does the knowledge of our intellectual superiority affect us! Its ground bass is really the saying of Hobbes quoted above: *Omnis animi voluptas, omnisque alacritas in eo sita est, quod quis habeat, quibuscum conferens se, possit magnifice sentire de se ipso.* Arrogant, triumphant vanity, proud, contemptuous looking down on others, inordinate delight in the consciousness of decided and considerable superiority, akin to pride of physical advantages,—that is the result here. This opposition between the two kinds of self-satisfaction shows that the one concerns our true inner and eternal nature, the other a more external, merely temporal, and indeed scarcely more than a mere physical excellence. The *intellect* is in fact simply the function of the brain; the will, on the contrary, is that whose function is the whole man, according to his being and nature.

10. Upon what depends the *identity of the person?* Not upon the matter of the body; it is different after a few years. Not upon its form, which changes as a whole and in all its parts; all but the expression of the glance, by which, therefore, we still know a man even after many years; which proves that in spite of all changes time produces in him something in him remains quite untouched by it. It is just this by which we recognize him even after the longest intervals of time, and find the former man entire. It is the same with ourselves, for, however old we become, we yet feel within that we are entirely the same as we were when we were young, nay, when we were still children. This, which unaltered always remains quite the same, and does not grow old along with us, is really the kernel of our nature, which does not lie in time. It is assumed that the identity of the person rests upon that of consciousness. But by this is understood merely the connected recollection of the course of life; hence it is not sufficient. We certainly know something more of our life than of a novel we have formerly read, yet only very little. The principal events, the interesting scenes, have impressed themselves upon us; in the remainder a thousand events are forgotten for one has been retained. The older we become the more do things pass by us without leaving any trace. Great age, illness, injury of the brain, madness, may deprive us of memory altogether, but the identity of the person is not thereby lost. It rests upon the identical *will* and the unalterable character of the person. It is it also which makes the expression of the glance unchangeable. In the *heart* is the man, not in the head. It is true that, in consequence of our relation to the external world, we are accustomed to regard as our real self the subject of knowledge, the knowing I, which wearies in the evening, vanishes in sleep, and in the morning shines brighter with renewed strength. This is, however, the mere function of the brain, and not our own self. Our true self, the kernel of our nature, is what is behind that, and really knows nothing but willing and not willing, being content and not content, with all the modifications of this, which are called feelings, emotions, and passions. This is that which produces the other, does not sleep with it when it sleeps, and in the same way when it sinks in death remains uninjured. Everything, on the contrary, that belongs to *knowledge* is exposed to oblivion; even actions of moral significance can sometimes, after years, be only imperfectly recalled, and we no longer know accurately and in detail how we acted on a critical occasion. But the *character itself,* to which the actions only testify, cannot be forgotten by us; it is now still quite the same as then. The will itself, alone and for itself, is permanent, for it alone is unchangeable, indestructible, not growing old, not physical, but metaphysical, not belonging to the phenomenal appearance, but to that itself which so appears. How the identity of consciousness also, so far as it goes, depends upon it I have shown above, so I need not dwell upon it further here.

11. Aristotle says in passing, in his book on the comparison of the desirable, "To live well is better than to live" (⟨*beltion tou zan to en zan*⟩, Top. iii., 2). From this we might infer, by double contraposition, not to live is better than to live badly. This is also evident to the intellect; yet the great majority live very badly rather than not at all. This clinging to life cannot therefore have its ground in the *object* of life, since life, as was shown in the fourth book, is really a constant suffering, or at the least, as will be shown further on, a business which does not cover its expenses; thus that clinging to life can only be founded in the *subject* of it. But it is not founded in the *intellect,* it is no result of reflection, and in general is not a matter of choice; but this willing of life is something that is taken for granted: it is a *prius* of the intellect itself. We ourselves are the will to live, and therefore we must live, well or ill. Only from the fact that this clinging to a life which is so little worth to them is entirely *a priori* and not *a posteriori* can we

explain the excessive fear of death that dwells in every living thing, which Rochefoucauld has expressed in his last reflection, with rare frankness and naïveté, and upon which the effect of all tragedies and heroic actions ultimately rests, for it would be lost if we prized life only according to its objective worth. Upon this inexpressible *horror mortis* ["horror of death"] is also founded the favourite principle of all ordinary minds, that whosoever takes his own life must be mad; yet not less the astonishment, mingled with a certain admiration, which this action always excites even in thinking minds, because it is so opposed to the nature of all living beings that in a certain sense we are forced to admire him who is able to perform it. For suicide proceeds from a purpose of the intellect, but our will to live is a *prius* of the intellect. Thus this consideration also confirms the primacy of the will in self-consciousness.

12. On the other hand, nothing proves more clearly the secondary, dependent, conditioned nature of the *intellect* than its periodical intermittence. In deep sleep all knowing and forming of ideas ceases. But the kernel of our nature, the metaphysical part of it which the organic functions necessarily presuppose as their *primum mobile,* must never pause if life is not to cease, and, moreover, as something metaphysical and therefore incorporeal, it requires no rest. Therefore the philosophers who set up a *soul* as this metaphysical kernel, *i.e.,* an originally and essentially *knowing* being, see themselves forced to the assertion that this soul is quite untiring in its perceiving and knowing, therefore continues these even in deep sleep; only that we have no recollection of this when we awake. The falseness of this assertion, however, was easy to see whenever one had rejected that *soul* in consequence of Kant's teaching. For sleep and waking prove to the unprejudiced mind in the clearest manner that knowing is a secondary function and conditioned by the organism, just like any other. Only the *heart* is untiring, because its beating and the circulation of the blood are not directly conditioned by nerves, but are just the original manifestation of the will. Also all other physiological functions governed merely by ganglionic nerves, which have only a very indirect and distant connection with the brain, are carried on during sleep, although the secretions take place more slowly; the beating of the heart itself, on account of its dependence upon respiration, which is conditioned by the cerebral system *(medulla oblongata),* becomes with it a little slower. The stomach is perhaps most active in sleep, which is to be attributed to its special consensus with the now resting brain, which occasions mutual disturbances. The *brain* alone, and with it knowing, pauses entirely in deep sleep. For it is merely the minister of foreign affairs, as the ganglion system is the minister of the interior. The brain, with its function of knowing, is only a *vedette* established by the will for its external ends, which, up in the watch-tower of the head, looks round through the windows of the senses and marks where mischief threatens and where advantages are to be looked for, and in accordance with whose report the will decides. This *vedette,* like every one engaged on active service, is then in a condition of strain and effort, and therefore it is glad when, after its watch is completed, it is again withdrawn, as every watch gladly retires from its post. This withdrawal is going to sleep, which is therefore so sweet and agreeable, and to which we are so glad to yield—on the other hand, being roused from sleep is unwelcome, because it recalls the *vedette* suddenly to its post. One generally feels also after the beneficent systole the reappearance of the difficult diastole, the reseparation of the intellect from the will. A so-called soul, which was originally and radically a *knowing* being, would, on the contrary, necessarily feel on awaking like a fish put back into water. In sleep, when merely the vegetative life is carried on, the will works only according to its original and essential nature, undisturbed from without, with no diminution of its power through the activity of the brain and the exertion of knowing, which is the heaviest organic function, yet for the organism merely a means,

not an end; therefore, in sleep the whole power of the will is directed to the maintenance and, where it is necessary, the improvement of the organism. Hence all healing, all favourable crises, take place in sleep; for the *vis naturæ medicatrix* has free play only when it is delivered from the burden of the function of knowledge. The embryo which has still to form the body therefore sleeps continuously, and the new-born child the greater part of its time. In this sense Burdach (*Physiologie,* vol. iii., p. 484) quite rightly declares sleep to be the *original* state.

With reference to the brain itself, I account to myself for the necessity of sleep more fully through an hypothesis which appears to have been first set up in Neumann's book, *"Von den Krankheiten des Menschen,"* 1834, vol. 4, § 216. It is this, that the nutrition of the brain, thus the renewal of its substance from the blood, cannot go on while we are awake, because the very eminent organic function of knowing and thinking would be disturbed or put an end to by the low and material function of nutrition. This explains the fact that sleep is not a purely negative condition, a merely pausing of the activity of the brain, but also shows a positive character. This makes itself known through the circumstance that between sleep and waking there is no mere difference of degree, but a fixed boundary, which, as soon as sleep intervenes, declares itself in dreams which are completely different from our immediately preceding thoughts. A further proof of this is that when we have dreams which frighten us we try in vain to cry out, or to ward off attacks, or to shake off sleep; so that it is as if the connecting-link between the brain and the motor nerves, or between the cerebrum and the cerebullum (as the regulator of movements) were abolished; for the brain remains in its isolation and sleep holds us fast as with brazen claws. Finally, the positive character of sleep can be seen in the fact that a certain degree of strength is required for sleeping. Therefore too great fatigue or natural weakness prevents us from seizing it, *capere somnum.* This may be explained from the fact that the process of nutrition must be introduced if sleep is to ensue: the brain must, as it were, begin to feed. Moreover, the increased flow of blood into the brain during sleep is explicable from the nutritive process; and also the position of the arms laid together above the head, which is instinctively assumed because it furthers this process: also why children, so long as their brain is still growing, require a great deal of sleep, while in old age, on the other hand, when a certain atrophy of the brain, as of all the parts, takes place, sleep is short; and finally why excessive sleep produces a certain dullness of consciousness, the consequence of a certain hypertrophy of the brain, which in the case of habitual excess of sleep may become permanent and produce imbecility: ⟨ania kai polus hypnos⟩ (*noxæ est etiam multus somnus*) ["much sleep is injurous"], Od. 15, 394. The need of sleep is therefore directly proportionate to the intensity of the brain-life, thus to the clearness of the consciousness. Those animals whose brain-life is weak and dull sleep little and lightly; for example, reptiles and fishes: and here I must remind the reader that the winter sleep is sleep only in name, for it is not an inaction of the brain alone, but of the whole organism, thus a kind of apparent death. Animals of considerable intelligence sleep deeply and long. Men also require more sleep the more developed, both as regards quantity and quality, and the more active their brain is. Montaigne relates of himself that he had always been a long sleeper, that he had passed a large part of his life sleeping, and at an advanced age still slept from eight to nine hours at a time (Liv. iii., chap. 13). Descartes also is reported to have slept a great deal (Baillet, *Vie de Descartes,* 1693, p. 288). Kant allowed himself seven hours for sleep, but it was so hard for him to do with this that he ordered his servant to force him against his will, and without listening to his remonstrances, to get up at the set time (Jachmann, *Immanuel Kant,* p. 162). For the more completely awake a man is, *i.e.,* the clearer and more lively his consciousness, the greater for him is the necessity of sleep, thus the deeper and longer he sleeps. Accordingly much thinking or hard brain-work increases the need of sleep. That sustained muscular exertion also makes us sleepy is to be explained from the fact that in this the brain continuously, by means of the *medulla oblongata,* the spinal marrow, and the motor nerves, imparts the stimulus to the muscles which affects their irritability, and in this way it exhausts its strength. The fatigue which we observe in the arms and legs has accordingly its real seat in the brain; just as the pain which these parts feel is really experienced in the brain; for it is connected with the motor nerves, as with the nerves of sense. The muscles which are not actuated from the brain—for example, those of the heart—accordingly never tire. The same grounds explain the fact that both during and after great muscular exertion we cannot think acutely. That one has far less energy in mind in summer than in winter is partly explicable from the fact that in summer one sleeps less; for the deeper one has slept, the more completely awake, the more lively, is one afterwards. This, however, must not mislead us into extending sleep unduly, for then it loses in intension, *i.e.,* in deepness and soundness, what it gains in extension; whereby it becomes mere loss of time. This is what Goethe means when he says (in the second part of "Faust") of morning slumber: "Sleep is husk: throw it off." Thus in general the phenomenon of sleep most specially confirms the assertion that consciousness, apprehension, knowing, thinking, is nothing original in us, but a conditioned and secondary state. It is a luxury of nature, and indeed its highest, which it can therefore the less afford to pursue without interruption the higher the pitch to which it has been brought. It is the product, the efflorescence of the cerebral nerve-system, which is itself nourished like a parasite by the rest of the organism. This also agrees with what is shown in our third book, that knowing is so much the purer and more perfect the more it has freed and severed itself from the will, whereby the purely objective, the aesthetic comprehension, appears. Just as an extract is so much the purer the more it has been separated from that out of which it is extracted and been cleared of all sediment. The opposite is shown by the *will,* whose most immediate manifestation is the whole organic life, and primarily the untiring heart.

This last consideration is related to the theme of the following chapter, to which it therefore makes the transition: yet the following observation belongs to it: In magnetic somnambulism the consciousness is doubled: two trains of knowledge, each connected in itself, but quite different from each other, arise; the waking consciousness knows nothing of the somnambulent. But the will retains in both the same character, and remains throughout identical; it expresses in both the same inclinations and aversions. For the function may be doubled, but not the true nature.

John Stuart Mill
1806–1873

John Stuart Mill was born in London, the eldest of James and Harriet Burrow Mill's nine children. His father, a well-known philosopher and follower of Jeremy Bentham, educated young John at home. Beginning with Greek at age three and Latin at age eight, the younger Mill had read six of Plato's dialogues by the age of ten. John spent most of the day in the study with his father, who was writing a history of India. Each morning, they would go on a walk and James would quiz his son on what he had learned the previous day. During these walks James would often discourse on various topics and then expect his son to prepare a summary of his points for the following day. Given the severity of this schooling—and the fact that his father showed no "signs of feeling"—it is not surprising that John later concluded, "I never was a boy."

The publication of the elder Mill's work on India in 1818 resulted in his receiving a government post as an Assistant Examiner at the East India House. Five years later, James managed to arrange a similar position for his seventeen-year-old son. John worked for the East India House for the next thirty-four years, eventually becoming chief of his department. In his early years as a clerk, John was, like his father, a disciple of Bentham's utilitarianism. John established the Utilitarian Society, contributed articles to the *Westminster Review,* and was active in the London Debating Society. He was developing a reputation as a polemicist for the "philosophic radicals"—those who sought social changes along the lines of Bentham's theories.

But in 1826, at age twenty, Mill suffered a breakdown and went through a period of severe depression. He discovered to his horror that even if all the social changes he was advocating were enacted and all the ideas he had been taught about happiness were proven correct, it would not make *him* happy. As he later wrote in his *Autobiography,* "All my happiness was to have been found in the continual pursuit of this end. The end had ceased to charm, and how could there ever again be any interest in the means? I seemed to have nothing left to live for." He eventually came to the conclusion that his rigorous intellectual training had weakened his ability to feel emotion. Reading such writers as Wordsworth and Coleridge, he began to teach himself to feel as his father had taught him to think. During this period he encountered divergent philosophies, such as those of socialist philosopher Claude-Henry Saint-Simon and positivist thinker Auguste Comte, and he began to see some of the inadequacies of the strict quantificational method of Bentham.

In 1831 Mill was introduced to Harriet Taylor, the wife of a successful merchant. They quickly developed a strong friendship and collaborated on a number of works, including *Principles of Political Economy* (1848) and *On Liberty* (1859). Mill attributed to Taylor a number of his most important ideas, including his liberal feminism, and claimed that next to his father, she was the chief intellectual influence on his life. He even claimed she was the inspiration for his major epistemological work, *A System of Logic* (1843). Following her husband's death in 1849, they were finally married in 1851.

John and Harriet Mill moved to Avignon, France, in 1858, with neither of them in good health. Shortly after arriving Harriet Taylor Mill died, and her daughter came to take care of her stepfather. Over the next seven years Mill published *On Liberty* (1859), *Utilitarianism* (1861), *Considerations on Representative Government* (1861), *Auguste Comte and Positivism* (1865), and *The Subjection of Women* (written 1861, published 1869). In 1865 Mill was surprised by an offer to run for Parliament. Without campaigning he was elected and spent two years working on behalf of women's suffrage, Irish land reform, and the rights of blacks in Jamaica. Returning once again to the south of France, he wrote his *Autobiography* just before dying in 1873.

*   *   *

While Mill wrote on a variety of topics and his work in induction is still used today, he is best known for his modification of Bentham's utilitarianism and his defense of individual liberty. Bentham had taught that ethics should be grounded on maximizing pleasure and minimizing pain, rather than on such abstractions as Kant's "duty" or conscience. Accordingly, Bentham developed a "hedonistic calculus," a mathematical method of determining which actions would most likely provide a greater quantity of pleasure over pain and hence yield happiness. While this system might seem egoistic and individualistic, Bentham claimed that it would be to each individual person's advantage to seek the "greatest happiness of the greatest number."

Mill accepted Bentham's quantitative hedonism and argued that happiness, or pleasure, is the one thing that all people seek. But while Bentham's system merely measured quantities of pleasure and pain, Mill came to believe that the *quality* of a given pleasure or pain had to be considered as well. While a pig might gain a great *quantity* of pleasure from wallowing in the mud, it would be a very low *quality* pleasure; and "It is better to be a human being dissatisfied than a pig satisfied; better to be Socrates dissatisfied than a fool satisfied." According to Mill, the person best able to make a qualitative determination between rival pleasures is the one who has experienced both. Presumably anyone who has both wallowed in the mud *and* studied philosophy would prefer the difficult but fulfilling pleasures of the latter.

In *On Liberty,* Mill asserts that society should maximize individual liberty. In fact, he claims that "the only purpose for which power can be rightfully exercised over any member of a civilized community, against his will, is to prevent harm to others." What an individual does in private does not concern society—even if such actions are not to that individual's own best interests. "Over himself, over his own body and mind, the individual is sovereign," and society should make no paternalistic rules. In Chapter 3, reprinted here, Mill argues that the "free development of individuality is one of the leading essentials of well-being." Mill claims that contrary to the Calvinists, self-will is a fundamental good and "He who chooses his plan for himself, employs all his faculties."

On the Subjection of Women (portions of the first chapter are reprinted here) applies this liberal theory to women. This work points out that for centuries women have been subordinated to men and hence excluded from the kinds of individual choices that *On Liberty* extols. Such subjection is "one of the chief hindrances to human improvement" and only "a principle of perfect equality" will rectify the situation. This work was written in collaboration with Harriet Taylor Mill. Scholars are divided as to how much Mill relied on Taylor—some go so far as to suggest that the work was actually "ghostwritten" by her. Whether or not one accepts that assertion, there is no question that her ideas greatly influenced Mill's version of feminism. Yet Mill never did accept her contention that women should be able to work outside the home after marriage.

Mill's critics pointed out that there seem to be discrepancies between the philosophy of *Utilitarianism* and that of *On Liberty* and *On the Subjection of Women.* For example, following the greatest happiness principle of *Utilitarianism,* wouldn't it make sense for society to increase general happiness by intruding on an individual's liberty? Mill countered this objection by arguing that on balance *laissez-faire* individualism will ultimately benefit society; that the diversity of individual choices is more conducive to general happiness than any socially imposed standard.

More recent critics have questioned Mill's distinction between private and public—for example, what you choose to do to yourself in the privacy of your home may cost the public money if you end up in a tax-supported hospital. Feminist critics have pointed out the potential oppression of the private/public distinction, questioned the possibility of "perfect equality" if paternalistic structures continue, and assailed Mill's "equal opportunity until marriage" doctrine. But there is no question that as a reforming impulse, Mill's beliefs—about the rights of the individual, the rights of women and minorities, freedom from societal intrusion into personal affairs, and utility rather than tradition—have had an enormous influence.

* * *

There are several good overviews of Mill's life and thought, including R.P. Anschutz, *The Philosophy of John Stuart Mill* (Oxford: Oxford University Press, 1953); Karl Britton, *John Stuart Mill* (1953; reprinted New York: Dover, 1969); Alan Ryan, *J.S. Mill* (London: Routledge & Kegan Paul, 1974); and William Thomas, *Mill* (Oxford: Oxford University Press, 1985). F.A. Hayek, *John Stuart Mill and Harriet Taylor* (Chicago: University of Chicago Press, 1951), presents a study of Mill's relationship with Harriet Taylor. For a critical evaluation of his work, see H.J. McCloskey, *John Stuart Mill: A Critical Study* (London: Macmillan, 1971). For more specialized studies, see Denise F. Thompson, *John Stuart Mill and Representative Government* (Princeton, NJ: Princeton University Press, 1976), and Gertrude Himmelfarb, *On Liberty and Liberalism: The Case of John Stuart Mill* (New York: Knopf, 1974). For collections of essays, see J.B. Schneewind, ed., *Mill: A Collection of Critical Essays* (Garden City, NY: Anchor Doubleday, 1968), and J.M. Smith and E. Sosa, eds., *Mill's Utilitarianism* (Belmont, CA: Wadsworth, 1969).

UTILITARIANISM

CHAPTER 1:   GENERAL REMARKS

There are few circumstances among those which make up the present condition of human knowledge, more unlike what might have been expected, or more significant of the backward state in which speculation on the most important subjects still lingers, than the little progress which has been made in the decision of the controversy respecting the criterion of right and wrong. From the dawn of philosophy, the question concerning the *summum bonum,* or, what is the same thing, concerning the foundation of morality, has been accounted the main problem in speculative thought, has occupied the most gifted intellects, and divided them into sects and schools, carrying on a vigorous warfare against one another. And after more than two thousand years the same discussions continue, philosophers are still ranged under the same contending banners, and neither thinkers nor mankind at large seem nearer to being unanimous on the subject, than when the youth Socrates listened to the old Protagoras, and asserted (if Plato's dialogue be grounded on a real conversation) the theory of utilitarianism against the popular morality of the so-called sophist.

It is true that similar confusion and uncertainty, and in some cases similar discordance, exist respecting the first principles of all the sciences, not excepting that which is deemed the most certain of them, mathematics; without much impairing, generally indeed without impairing at all, the trustworthiness of the conclusions of those sciences. An apparent anomaly, the explanation of which is, that the detailed doctrines of a science are not usually deduced from, nor depend for their evidence upon, what are called its first principles. Were it not so, there would be no science more precarious, or whose conclusions were more insufficiently made out, than algebra; which derives none of its certainty from what are commonly taught to learners as its elements, since these, as laid down by some of its most eminent teachers, are as full of fictions as English law, and of mysteries as theology. The truths which are ultimately accepted as the first principles of a science, are really the last results of metaphysical analysis, practised on the elementary notions with which the science is conversant; and their relation to the science is not that of foundations to an edifice, but of roots to a tree, which may perform their office equally well though they be never dug down to and exposed to light. But though in science the particular truths precede the general theory, the contrary might be expected to be the case with a practical art, such as morals or legislation. All action is for the sake of some end, and rules of action, it seems natural to suppose, must take their whole character and colour from the end to which they are subservient. When we engage in a pursuit, a clear and precise conception of what we are pursuing would seem to be the first thing we need, instead of the last we are to look forward to. A test of right and wrong must be the means, one would think, of ascertaining what is right or wrong, and not a consequence of having already ascertained it.

The difficulty is not avoided by having recourse to the popular theory of a natural faculty, a sense or instinct, informing us of right and wrong. For—besides that the existence of such a moral instinct is itself one of the matters in dispute—those believers in it who have any pretensions to philosophy, have been obliged to abandon the idea that it discerns what is right or wrong in the particular case in hand, as our other senses discern the sight or sound actually present. Our moral faculty, according to all those of its interpreters who are entitled to the name of thinkers, supplies us only with the general principles of moral judgments; it is a branch of our reason, not of our sensitive faculty; and must be looked to for the abstract doctrines of morality, not for perception of it in the concrete. The intuitive, no less than what may be termed the inductive, school of ethics, insists on the necessity of general laws. They both agree that the morality of an individual action is not a question of direct perception, but of the application of a law to an individual case. They recognise also, to a great extent, the same moral laws; but differ as to their evidence, and the source from which they derive their authority. According to the one opinion, the principles of morals are evident *à priori,* requiring nothing to command assent, except that the meaning of the terms be understood. According to the other doctrine, right and wrong, as well as truth and falsehood, are questions of observation and experience. But both hold equally that morality must be deduced from principles; and the intuitive school affirm as strongly as the inductive, that there is a science of morals. Yet they seldom attempt to make out a list of the *à priori* principles which are to serve as the premises of the science; still more rarely do they make any effort to reduce those various principles to one first principle, or common ground of obligation. They either assume the ordinary precepts of morals as of *à priori* authority, or they lay down as the common groundwork of those maxims, some generality much less obviously authoritative than the maxims themselves, and which has never succeeded in gaining popular acceptance. Yet to support their pretensions there ought either to be some one fundamental principle or law, at the root of all morality, or if there be several, there should be a determinate order of precedence among them; and the one principle, or the rule for deciding between the various principles when they conflict, ought to be self-evident.

To inquire how far the bad effects of this deficiency have been mitigated in practice, or to what extent the moral beliefs of mankind have been vitiated or made uncertain by the absence of any distinct recognition of an ultimate standard, would imply a complete survey and criticism of past and present ethical doctrine. It would, however, be easy to show that whatever steadiness or consistency these moral beliefs have attained, has been mainly due to the tacit influence of a standard not recognised. Although the non-existence of an acknowledged first principle has made ethics not so much a guide as a consecration of men's actual sentiments, still, as men's sentiments, both of favour and of aversion, are greatly influenced by what they suppose to be the effects of things upon their happiness, the principle of utility, or as Bentham latterly called it, the Greatest Happiness Principle, has had a large share in forming the moral doctrines even of those who most scornfully reject its authority. Nor is there any school of thought which refuses to admit that the influence of actions on happiness is a most material and even predominant consideration in many of the details of morals, however unwilling to acknowledge it as the fundamental principle of morality, and the source of moral obligation. I might go much further, and say that to all those *à priori* moralists who deem it necessary to argue at all, utilitarian arguments are indispensable. It is not my present purpose to criticise these thinkers; but I cannot help referring, for illustration, to a systematic treatise by one of the most illustrious of them, the *Metaphysics of Ethics* by Kant. This remarkable man, whose system of thought will long remain one of the landmarks in the history of philosophical speculation, does, in the treatise in question, lay down a universal first principle as the origin and ground of moral obligation; it is this:—"So act, that the rule on which thou actest would admit of being adopted as a law by all rational beings." But when he begins to deduce from this precept any of the actual duties of morality, he fails, almost grotesquely, to show that there would be any contradiction, any logical (not to say physical) impossibility, in the adoption by all rational beings of the most outrageously immoral rules of conduct. All he shows is that the *consequences* of their universal adoption would be such as no one would choose to incur.

On the present occasion, I shall, without further discussion of the other theories, attempt to contribute something towards the understanding and appreciation of the Utilitarian or Happiness theory, and towards such proof as it is susceptible of. It is evident that this cannot be proof in the ordinary and popular meaning of the term. Questions of ultimate ends are not amenable to direct proof. Whatever can be proved to be good, must be so by being shown to be a means to something admitted to be good without proof. The medical art is proved to be good by its conducing to health; but how is it possible to prove that health is good? The art of music is good, for the reason, among others, that it produces pleasure; but what proof is it possible to give that pleasure is good? If, then, it is asserted that there is a comprehensive formula, including all things which are in themselves good, and that whatever else is good, is not so as an end, but as a mean, the formula may be accepted or rejected, but is not a subject of what is commonly understood by proof. We are not, however, to infer that its acceptance or rejection must depend on blind impulse, or arbitrary choice. There is a larger meaning of the word proof, in which this question is as amenable to it as any other of the disputed questions of philosophy. The subject is within the cognisance of the rational faculty; and neither does that faculty deal with it solely in the way of intuition. Considerations may be presented capable of determining the intellect either to give or withhold its assent to the doctrine; and this is equivalent to proof.

We shall examine presently of what nature are these considerations; in what manner they apply to the case, and what rational grounds, therefore, can be given for accepting or rejecting the utilitarian formula. But it is a preliminary condition of rational acceptance or rejection, that the formula should be correctly understood. I believe that the very imperfect notion ordinarily formed of its meaning, is the chief obstacle which impedes its reception; and that could it be cleared, even from only the grosser misconceptions, the question would be greatly simplified, and a large proportion of its difficulties removed. Before, therefore, I attempt to enter into the philosophical grounds which can be given for assenting to the utilitarian standard, I shall offer some illustrations of the doctrine itself; with the view of showing more clearly what it is, distinguishing it from what it is not, and disposing of such of the practical objections to it as either originate in, or are closely connected with, mistaken interpretations of its meaning. Having thus prepared the ground, I shall afterwards endeavour to throw such light as I can upon the question, considered as one of philosophical theory.

CHAPTER 2:   WHAT UTILITARIANISM IS

A passing remark is all that needs be given to the ignorant blunder of supposing that those who stand up for utility as the test of right and wrong, use the term in that restricted and merely colloquial sense in which utility is opposed to pleasure. An apology is due to the philosophical opponents of utilitarianism, for even the momentary appearance of confounding them with any one capable of so absurd a misconception; which is the more extraordinary, inasmuch as the contrary accusation, of referring everything to pleasure, and that too in its grossest form, is another of the common charges against utilitarianism: and, as has been pointedly remarked by an able writer, the same sort of persons, and often the very same persons, denounce the theory "as impracticably dry when the word 'utility' precedes the word 'pleasure,' and as too practically voluptuous when the word 'pleasure' precedes the word 'utility.'" Those who know anything about the matter are aware that every writer, from Epicurus to Bentham, who maintained the theory of utility, meant by it, not something to be contradistinguished from pleasure, but pleasure itself, together with exemption from pain; and instead of opposing the useful to the agreeable or the ornamental, have always declared that the useful means these, among other things. Yet the common herd, including the herd of writers, not only in newspapers and periodicals, but in books of weight and pretension, are perpetually falling into this shallow mistake. Having caught up the word Utilitarian, while knowing nothing whatever about it but its sound, they habitually express by it the rejection, or the neglect, of pleasure in some of its forms; of beauty, of ornament, or of amusement. Nor is the term thus ignorantly misapplied solely in disparagement, but occasionally in compliment; as though it implied superiority to frivolity and the mere pleasures of the moment. And this perverted use is the only one in which the word is popularly known, and the one from which the new generation are acquiring their sole notion of its meaning. Those who introduced the word, but who had for many years discontinued it as a distinctive appellation, may well feel themselves called upon to resume it, if by doing so they can hope to contribute anything towards rescuing it from this utter degradation.*

The creed which accepts as the foundation of morals Utility or the Greatest Happiness Principle holds that actions are right in proportion as they tend to promote happiness, wrong as they tend to produce the reverse of happiness. By happiness is intended pleasure, and the absence of pain; by unhappiness, pain, and the privation of pleasure. To give a clear view of the moral standard set up by the theory, much more re-

---

*The author of this essay has reason for believing himself to be the first person who brought the word "utilitarian" into use. He did not Invent it, but adopted It from a passing expression in Mr. Galt's *Annals of the Parish*. After using it as a designation for several years, he and others abandoned it from a growing dislike to anything resembling a badge or watchword of sectarian distinction. But as a name for one single opinion, not a set of opinions—to denote the recognition of utility as a standard not any particular way of applying it—the term supplies a want in the language, and offers, in many cases, a convenient mode of avoiding tiresome circumlocution.

quires to be said; in particular, what things it includes in the ideas of pain and pleasure; and to what extent this is left an open question. But these supplementary explanations do not affect the theory of life on which this theory of morality is grounded—namely, that pleasure, and freedom from pain, are the only things desirable as ends; and that all desirable things (which are as numerous in the utilitarian as in any other scheme) are desirable either for the pleasure inherent in themselves, or as means to the promotion of pleasure and the prevention of pain.

Now, such a theory of life excites in many minds, and among them in some of the most estimable in feeling and purpose, inveterate dislike. To suppose that life has (as they express it) no higher end than pleasure—no better and nobler object of desire and pursuit—they designate as utterly mean and grovelling; as a doctrine worthy only of swine, to whom the followers of Epicurus were, at a very early period, contemptuously likened; and modern holders of the doctrine are occasionally made the subject of equally polite comparisons by its German, French, and English assailants.

When thus attacked, the Epicureans have always answered, that it is not they, but their accusers, who represent human nature in a degrading light; since the accusation supposes human beings to be capable of no pleasures except those of which swine are capable. If this supposition were true, the charge could not be gainsaid, but would then be no longer an imputation; for if the sources of pleasure were precisely the same to human beings and to swine, the rule of life which is good enough for the one would be good enough for the other. The comparison of the Epicurean life to that of beasts is felt as degrading, precisely because a beast's pleasures do not satisfy a human being's conceptions of happiness. Human beings have faculties more elevated than the animal appetites, and when once made conscious of them, do not regard anything as happiness which does not include their gratification. I do not, indeed, consider the Epicureans to have been by any means faultless in drawing out their scheme of consequences from the utilitarian principle. To do this in any sufficient manner, many Stoic, as well as Christian elements require to be included. But there is no known Epicurean theory of life which does not assign to the pleasures of the intellect, of the feelings and imagination, and of the moral sentiments, a much higher value as pleasures than to those of mere sensation. It must be admitted, however, that utilitarian writers in general have placed the superiority of mental over bodily pleasures chiefly in the greater permanency, safety, uncostliness, etc., of the former—that is, in their circumstantial advantages rather than in their intrinsic nature. And on all these points utilitarians have fully proved their case; but they might have taken the other, and, as it may be called, higher ground, with entire consistency. It is quite compatible with the principle of utility to recognise the fact, that some kinds of pleasure are more desirable and more valuable than others. It would be absurd that while, in estimating all other things, quality is considered as well as quantity, the estimation of pleasures should be supposed to depend on quantity alone.

If I am asked, what I mean by difference of quality in pleasures, or what makes one pleasure more valuable than another, merely as a pleasure, except its being greater in amount, there is but one possible answer. Of two pleasures, if there be one to which all or almost all who have experience of both give a decided preference, irrespective of any feeling of moral obligation to prefer it, that is the more desirable pleasure. If one of the two is, by those who are competently acquainted with both, placed so far above the other that they prefer it, even though knowing it to be attended with a greater amount of discontent, and would not resign it for any quantity of the other pleasure which their nature is capable of, we are justified in ascribing to the preferred enjoyment a superiority in quality, so far outweighing quantity as to render it, in comparison, of small account.

Now it is an unquestionable fact that those who are equally acquainted with, and equally capable of appreciating and enjoying, both, do give almost marked preference to the manner of existence which employs their higher faculties. Few human creatures would consent to be changed into any of the lower animals, for a promise of the fullest allowance of a beast's pleasures; no intelligent human being would consent to be a fool, no instructed person would be an ignoramus, no person of feeling and conscience would be selfish and base, even though they should be persuaded that the fool, the dunce, or the rascal is better satisfied with his lot than they are with theirs. They would not resign what they possess more than he for the most complete satisfaction of all the desires which they have in common with him. If they ever fancy they would, it is only in cases of unhappiness so extreme, that to escape from it they would exchange their lot for almost any other, however undesirable in their own eyes. A being of higher faculties requires more to make him happy, is capable probably of more acute suffering, and certainly accessible to it at more points, than one of an inferior type; but in spite of these liabilities, he can never really wish to sink into what he feels to be a lower grade of existence. We may give what explanation we please of this unwillingness; we may attribute it to pride, a name which is given indiscriminately to some of the most and to some of the least estimable feelings of which mankind are capable: we may refer it to the love of liberty and personal independence, an appeal to which was with the Stoics one of the most effective means for the inculcation of it; to the love of power, or to the love of excitement, both of which do really enter into and contribute to it: but its most appropriate appellation is a sense of dignity, which all human beings possess in one form or other, and in some, though by no means in exact, proportion to their higher faculties, and which is so essential a part of the happiness of those in whom it is strong, that nothing which conflicts with it could be, otherwise than momentarily, an object of desire to them. Whoever supposes that this preference takes place at a sacrifice of happiness—that the superior being, in anything like equal circumstances, is not happier than the inferior—confounds the two very different ideas, of happiness, and content. It is indisputable that the being whose capacities of enjoyment are low, has the greatest chance of having them fully satisfied; and a highly endowed being will always feel that any happiness which he can look for, as the world is constituted, is imperfect. But he can learn to bear its imperfections, if they are at all bearable; and they will not make him envy the being who is indeed unconscious of the imperfections, but only because he feels not at all the good which those imperfections qualify. It is better to be a human being dissatisfied than a pig satisfied; better to be Socrates dissatisfied than a fool satisfied. And if the fool, or the pig, are of a different opinion, it is because they only know their own side of the question. The other party to the comparison knows both sides.

It may be objected, that many who are capable of the higher pleasures, occasionally, under the influence of temptation, postpone them to the lower. But this is quite compatible with a full appreciation of the intrinsic superiority of the higher. Men often, from infirmity of character, make their election for the nearer good, though they know it to be the less valuable; and this no less when the choice is between two bodily pleasures, than when it is between bodily and mental. They pursue sensual indulgences to the injury of health, though perfectly aware that health is the greater good. It may be further objected, that many who begin with youthful enthusiasm for everything noble, as they advance in years sink into indolence and selfishness. But I do not believe that those who undergo this very common change, voluntarily choose the lower description of pleasures in preference to the higher. I believe that before they devote themselves exclusively to the one, they have already become incapable of the other. Capacity for the nobler feelings is in most natures a very tender plant, easily killed, not only by hostile influences, but by mere want of sustenance; and in the majority of young persons it speedily dies away if the occupations to which their position in life has devoted them, and the society into which it has thrown them, are not favourable to keeping that higher capacity in exercise. Men lose their high aspirations as they lose their intellectual tastes, because they have not time or opportunity for indulging them; and they addict themselves to inferior pleasures, not because they deliberately prefer them, but because they are either the only ones to which they have access, or the only ones which they are any longer capable of enjoying. It may be questioned whether any one who has remained equally susceptible to both classes of pleasures, ever knowingly and calmly preferred the lower; though many, in all ages, have broken down in an ineffectual attempt to combine both.

From this verdict of the only competent judges, I apprehend there can be no appeal. On a question which is the best worth having of two pleasures, or which of two modes of existence is the most grateful to the feelings, apart from its moral attributes and from its consequences, the judgment of those who are qualified by knowledge of both, or, if they differ, that of the majority among them, must be admitted as final. And there needs be the less hesitation to accept this judgment respecting the quality of pleasures, since there is no other tribunal to be referred to even on the question of quantity. What means are there of determining which is the acutest of two pains, or the intensest of two pleasurable sensations, except the general suffrage of those who are familiar with both? Neither pains nor pleasures are homogeneous, and pain is always heterogeneous with pleasure. What is there to decide whether a particular pleasure is worth purchasing at the cost of a particular pain, except the feelings and judgment of the experienced? When, therefore, those feelings and judgment declare the pleasures derived from the higher faculties to be preferable *in kind,* apart from the question of intensity, to those of which the animal nature, disjoined from the higher faculties, is susceptible, they are entitled on this subject to the same regard.

I have dwelt on this point, as being a necessary part of a perfectly just conception of Utility or Happiness, considered as the directive rule of human conduct. But it is by no means an indispensable condition to the acceptance of the utilitarian standard; for that standard is not the agent's own greatest happiness, but the greatest amount of happiness altogether; and if it may possibly be doubted whether a noble character is always the happier for its nobleness, there can be no doubt that it makes other people happier, and that the world in general is immensely a gainer by it. Utilitarianism, therefore, could only attain its end by the general cultivation of nobleness of character, even if each individual were only benefited by the nobleness of others, and his own, so far as happiness is concerned, were a sheer deduction from the benefit. But the bare enunciation of such an absurdity as this last, renders refutation superfluous.

According to the Greatest Happiness Principle, as above explained, the ultimate end, with reference to and for the sake of which all other things are desirable (whether we are considering our own good or that of other people), is an existence exempt as far as possible from pain, and as rich as possible in enjoyments, both in point of quantity and quality; the test of quality, and the rule for measuring it against quantity, being the preference felt by those who in their opportunities of experience, to which must be added their habits of self-consciousness and self-observation, are best furnished with the means of comparison. This, being, according to the utilitarian opinion, the end of human action, is necessarily also the standard of morality; which may accordingly be defined "the rules and precepts for human conduct" by the observance of which an existence such as has been described might be, to the greatest extent possible, secured to all mankind; and not to them only, but, so far as the nature of things admits, to the whole sentient creation.

Against this doctrine, however, arises another class of objectors, who say that happiness, in any form, cannot be the rational purpose of human life and action; because, in the first place, it is unattainable: and they contemptuously ask, what right hast thou to be happy? a question which Mr. Carlyle clenches by the addition, What right, a short time ago, hadst thou even *to be?* Next, they say, that men can do *without* happiness; that all noble human beings have felt this, and could not have become noble but by learning the lesson of *Entsagen,* or renunciation; which lesson, thoroughly learnt and submitted to, they affirm to be the beginning and necessary condition of all virtue.

The first of these objections would go to the root of the matter were it well founded; for if no happiness is to be had at all by human beings, the attainment of it cannot be the end of morality, or of any rational conduct. Though, even in that case, something might still be said for the utilitarian theory; since utility includes not solely the pursuit of happiness, but the prevention or mitigation of unhappiness; and if the former aim be chimerical, there will be all the greater scope and more imperative need for the latter, so long at least as mankind think fit to live, and do not take refuge in the simultaneous act of suicide recommended under certain conditions by Novalis.* When, however, it is thus positively asserted to be impossible that human life should be happy, the assertion, if not something like a verbal quibble, is at least an exaggeration. If by happiness be meant a continuity of highly pleasurable excitement, it is evident enough that this is impossible. A state of exalted pleasure lasts only moments, or in some cases, and with some intermissions, hours or days, and is the occasional brilliant flash of enjoyment, not its permanent and steady flame. Of this the philosophers who have taught that happiness is the end of life were as fully aware as those who taunt them. The happiness which they meant was not a life of rapture; but moments of such, in an existence made up of few and transitory pains, many and various pleasures, with a decided predominance of the active over the passive, and having as the foundation of the whole, not to expect more from life than it is capable of bestowing. A life thus composed, to those who have been fortunate enough to obtain it, has always appeared worthy of the name of happiness. And such an existence is even now the lot of many, during some considerable portion of their lives. The present wretched education, and wretched social arrangements, are the only real hindrance to its being attainable by almost all.

The objectors perhaps may doubt whether human beings, if taught to consider happiness as the end of life, would be satisfied with such a moderate share of it. But great numbers of mankind have been satisfied with much less. The main constituents of a satisfied life appear to be two, either of which by itself is often found sufficient for the purpose: tranquillity, and excitement. With much tranquillity, many find that they can be content with very little pleasure: with much excitement, many can reconcile themselves to a considerable quantity of pain. There is assuredly no inherent impossibility in enabling even the mass of mankind to unite both; since the two are so far from being incompatible that they are in natural alliance, the prolongation of either being a preparation for, and exciting a wish for, the other. It is only those in whom indolence amounts to a vice, that do not desire excitement after an interval of repose: it is only those in whom the need of excitement is a disease, that feel the tranquillity which follows excitement dull and insipid, instead of pleasurable in direct proportion to the excitement which preceded it. When people who are tolerably fortunate in their outward lot do not

*[The German poet Friedrich Leopold Freiherr von Hardenberg (1772–1801).]

find in life sufficient enjoyment to make it valuable to them, the cause generally is, caring for nobody but themselves. To those who have neither public nor private affections, the excitements of life are much curtailed, and in any case dwindle in value as the time approaches when all selfish interests must be terminated by death: while those who leave after them objects of personal affection, and especially those who have also cultivated a fellow-feeling with the collective interests of mankind, retain as lively an interest in life on the eve of death as in the vigour of youth and health. Next to selfishness, the principal cause which makes life unsatisfactory is want of mental cultivation. A cultivated mind—I do not mean that of a philosopher, but any mind to which the fountains of knowledge have been opened, and which has been taught, in any tolerable degree, to exercise its faculties—finds sources of inexhaustible interest in all that surrounds it; in the objects of nature, the achievements of art, the imaginations of poetry, the incidents of history, the ways of mankind, past and present, and their prospects in the future. It is possible, indeed, to become indifferent to all this, and that too without having exhausted a thousandth part of it; but only when one has had from the beginning no moral or human interest in these things, and has sought in them only the gratification of curiosity.

Now there is absolutely no reason in the nature of things why an amount of mental culture sufficient to give an intelligent interest in these objects of contemplation, should not be the inheritance of every one born in a civilised country. As little is there an inherent necessity that any human being should be a selfish egotist, devoid of every feeling or care but those which centre in his own miserable individuality. Something far superior to this is sufficiently common even now, to give ample earnest of what the human species may be made. Genuine private affections, and a sincere interest in the public good, are possible, though in unequal degrees, to every rightly brought up human being. In a world in which there is so much to interest, so much to enjoy, and so much also to correct and improve, every one who has this moderate amount of moral and intellectual requisites is capable of an existence which may be called enviable; and unless such a person, through bad laws, or subjection to the will of others, is denied the liberty to use the sources of happiness within his reach, he will not fail to find this enviable existence, if he escape the positive evils of life, the great sources of physical and mental suffering—such as indigence, disease, and the unkindness, worthlessness, or premature loss of objects of affection. The main stress of the problem lies, therefore, in the contest with these calamities, from which it is a rare good fortune entirely to escape; which, as things now are, cannot be obviated, and often cannot be in any material degree mitigated. Yet no one whose opinion deserves a moment's consideration can doubt that most of the great positive evils of the world are in themselves removable, and will, if human affairs continue to improve, be in the end reduced within narrow limits. Poverty, in any sense implying suffering, may be completely extinguished by the wisdom of society, combined with the good sense and providence of individuals. Even that most intractable of enemies, disease, may be indefinitely reduced in dimensions by good physical and moral education, and proper control of noxious influences; while the progress of science holds out a promise for the future of still more direct conquests over this detestable foe. And every advance in that direction relieves us from some, not only of the chances which cut short our own lives, but, what concerns us still more, which deprive us of those in whom our happiness is wrapt up. As for vicissitudes of fortune, and other disappointments connected with worldly circumstances, these are principally the effect either of gross imprudence, of ill-regulated desires, or of bad or imperfect social institutions. All the grand sources, in short, of human suffering are in a great degree, many of them almost entirely, conquerable by human care and effort; and though their removal is grievously slow—though a long succession of generations will perish in the breach

Crystal Palace, London, 1851, designed by Joseph Paxton
(1801–1865). Built for the Works of Industry of All Nations exhibit, the
building covered ninteen acres and enclosed over thirty million cubic
feet. *(The Bettman Archive)*

Interior, Crystal Palace. The palace was a shrine to science,
industrialization, and progress. This architectural marvel represented in
concrete form Mill's optimism when he spoke of the "the wisdom of
society" and the "progress of science [which] holds out a promise for the
future." *(Courtesy of the Trustees of the Victoria and Albert Museum,
London)*

81

before the conquest is completed, and this world becomes all that, if will and knowledge were not wanting, it might easily be made—yet every mind sufficiently intelligent and generous to bear a part, however small and unconspicuous, in the endeavour, will draw a noble enjoyment from the contest itself, which he would not for any bribe in the form of selfish indulgence consent to be without.

And this leads to the true estimation of what is said by the objectors concerning the possibility, and the obligation, of learning to do without happiness. Unquestionably it is possible to do without happiness; it is done involuntarily by nineteen-twentieths of mankind, even in those parts of our present world which are least deep in barbarism; and it often has to be done voluntarily by the hero or the martyr, for the sake of something which he prizes more than his individual happiness. But this something, what is it, unless the happiness of others, or some of the requisites of happiness? It is noble to be capable of resigning entirely one's own portion of happiness, or chances of it: but, after all, this self-sacrifice must be for some end; it is not its own end; and if we are told that its end is not happiness, but virtue, which is better than happiness, I ask, would the sacrifice be made if the hero or martyr did not believe that it would earn for others immunity from similar sacrifices? Would it be made if he thought that his renunciation of happiness for himself would produce no fruit for any of his fellow creatures, but to make their lot like his, and place them also in the condition of persons who have renounced happiness? All honour to those who can abnegate for themselves the personal enjoyment of life, when by such renunciation they contribute worthily to increase the amount of happiness in the world; but he who does it, or professes to do it, for any other purpose, is no more deserving of admiration than the ascetic mounted on his pillar. He may be an inspiriting proof of what men *can* do, but assuredly not an example of what they *should*.

Though it is only in a very imperfect state of the world's arrangements that any one can best serve the happiness of others by the absolute sacrifice of his own, yet so long as the world is in that imperfect state, I fully acknowledge that the readiness to make such a sacrifice is the highest virtue which can be found in man. I will add, that in this condition of the world, paradoxical as the assertion may be, the conscious ability to do without happiness gives the best prospect of realising such happiness as is attainable. For nothing except that consciousness can raise a person above the chances of life, by making him feel that, let fate and fortune do their worst, they have not power to subdue him: which, once felt, frees him from excess of anxiety concerning the evils of life, and enables him, like many a Stoic in the worst times of the Roman Empire, to cultivate in tranquillity the sources of satisfaction accessible to him, without concerning himself about the uncertainty of their duration, any more than about their inevitable end.

Meanwhile, let utilitarians never cease to claim the morality of self devotion as a possession which belongs by as good a right to them, as either to the Stoic or to the Transcendentalist. The utilitarian morality does recognise in human beings the power of sacrificing their own greatest good for the good of others. It only refuses to admit that the sacrifice is itself a good. A sacrifice which does not increase, or tend to increase, the sum total of happiness, it considers as wasted. The only self-renunciation which it applauds, is devotion to the happiness, or to some of the means of happiness, of others; either of mankind collectively, or of individuals within the limits imposed by the collective interests of mankind.

I must again repeat, what the assailants of utilitarianism seldom have the justice to acknowledge, that the happiness which forms the utilitarian standard of what is right in conduct, is not the agent's own happiness, but that of all concerned. As between his own happiness and that of others, utilitarianism requires him to be as strictly impartial as a disinterested and benevolent spectator. In the golden rule of Jesus of Nazareth, we read the complete spirit of the ethics of utility. "To do as you would be done by," and "to love your neighbour as yourself," constitute the ideal perfection of utilitarian morality. As the means of making the nearest approach to this ideal, utility would enjoin, first, that laws and social arrangements should place the happiness, or (as speaking practically it may be called) the interest, of every individual, as nearly as possible in harmony with the interest of the whole; and secondly, that education and opinion, which have so vast a power over human character, should so use that power as to establish in the mind of every individual an indissoluble association between his own happiness and the good of the whole; especially between his own happiness and the practice of such modes of conduct, negative and positive, as regard for the universal happiness prescribes; so that not only he may be unable to conceive the possibility of happiness to himself, consistently with conduct opposed to the general good, but also that a direct impulse to promote the general good may be in every individual one of the habitual motives of action, and the sentiments connected therewith may fill a large and prominent place in every human being's sentient existence. If the impugners of the utilitarian morality represented it to their own minds in this its true character, I know not what recommendation possessed by any other morality they could possibly affirm to be wanting to it; what more beautiful or more exalted developments of human nature any other ethical system can be supposed to foster, or what springs of action, not accessible to the utilitarian, such systems rely on for giving effect to their mandates.

The objectors to utilitarianism cannot always be charged with representing it in a discreditable light. On the contrary, those among them who entertain anything like a just idea of its disinterested character, sometimes find fault with its standard as being too high for humanity. They say it is exacting too much to require that people shall always act from the inducement of promoting the general interests of society. But this is to mistake the very meaning of a standard of morals, and confound the rule of action with the motive of it. It is the business of ethics to tell us what are our duties, or by what test we may know them; but no system of ethics requires that the sole motive of all we do shall be a feeling of duty; on the contrary, ninety-nine hundredths of all our actions are done from other motives, and rightly so done, if the rule of duty does not condemn them. It is the more unjust to utilitarianism that this particular misapprehension should be made a ground of objection to it, inasmuch as utilitarian moralists have gone beyond almost all others in affirming that the motive has nothing to do with the morality of the action, though much with the worth of the agent. He who saves a fellow creature from drowning does what is morally right, whether his motive be duty, or the hope of being paid for his trouble; he who betrays the friend that trusts him, is guilty of a crime, even if his object be to serve another friend to whom he is under greater obligations. But to speak only of actions done from the motive of duty, and in direct obedience to principle: it is a misapprehension of the utilitarian mode of thought, to conceive it as implying that people should fix their minds upon so wide a generality as the world, or society at large. The great majority of good actions are intended not for the benefit of the world, but for that of individuals, of which the good of the world is made up; and the thoughts of the most virtuous man need not on these occasions travel beyond the particular persons concerned, except so far as is necessary to assure himself that in benefiting them he is not violating the rights, that is, the legitimate and authorised expectations, of any one else. The multiplication of happiness is, according to the utilitarian ethics, the object of virtue: the occasions on which any person (except one in a thousand) has it in his power to do this on an extended scale, in other words to be a public benefactor, are but exceptional; and on these occasions alone is he called on to consider public utility; in every other case, private utility, the interest or happiness of some few persons, is all he has to attend to. Those alone the influence of whose actions extends to society in general, need concern themselves habitually about so large an object. In the case of abstinences indeed—of things which people forbear to do from moral considerations, though the consequences in the particular case might be beneficial—it would be unworthy of an intelligent agent not to be consciously aware that the action is of a class which, if practised generally, would be generally injurious, and that this is the ground of the obligation to abstain from it. The amount of regard for the public interest implied in this recognition, is no greater than is demanded by every system of morals, for they all enjoin to abstain from whatever is manifestly pernicious to society.

The same considerations dispose of another reproach against the doctrine of utility, founded on a still grosser misconception of the purpose of a standard of morality, and of the very meaning of the words "right" and "wrong." It is often affirmed that utilitarianism renders men cold and unsympathising; that it chills their moral feelings towards individuals; that it makes them regard only the dry and hard consideration of the consequences of actions, not taking into their moral estimate the qualities from which those actions emanate. If the assertion means that they do not allow their judgment respecting the rightness or wrongness of an action to be influenced by their opinion of the qualities of the person who does it, this is a complaint not against utilitarianism, but against having any standard of morality at all; for certainly no known ethical standard decides an action to be good or bad because it is done by a good or a bad man, still less because done by an amiable, a brave, or a benevolent man, or the contrary. These considerations are relevant, not to the estimation of actions, but of persons; and there is nothing in the utilitarian theory inconsistent with the fact that there are other things which interest us in persons besides the rightness and wrongness of their actions. The Stoics, indeed, with the paradoxical misuse of language which was part of their system, and by which they strove to raise themselves above all concern about anything but virtue, were fond of saying that he who has that has everything; that he, and only he, is rich, is beautiful, is a king. But no claim of this description is made for the virtuous man by the utilitarian doctrine. Utilitarians are quite aware that there are other desirable possessions and qualities besides virtue, and are perfectly willing to allow to all of them their full worth. They are also aware that a right action does not necessarily indicate a virtuous character, and that actions which are blamable, often proceed from qualities entitled to praise. When this is apparent in any particular case, it modifies their estimation, not certainly of the act, but of the agent. I grant that they are, notwithstanding, of opinion, that in the long run the best proof of a good character is good actions; and resolutely refuse to consider any mental disposition as good, of which the predominant tendency is to produce bad conduct. This makes them unpopular with many people; but it is an unpopularity which they must share with every one who regards the distinction between right and wrong in a serious light; and the reproach is not one which a conscientious utilitarian need be anxious to repel.

If no more be meant by the objection than that many utilitarians look on the morality of actions, as measured by the utilitarian standard, with too exclusive a regard, and do not lay sufficient stress upon the other beauties of character which go towards making a human being lovable or admirable, this may be admitted. Utilitarians who have cultivated their moral feelings, but not their sympathies nor their artistic perceptions, do fall into this mistake; and so do all other moralists under the same conditions. What can be said in excuse for other moralists is equally available for them, namely, that, if there is to be any error, it is better that it should be on that side. As a matter of fact, we may affirm that among utilitarians as among adherents of other systems, there is every imaginable degree of rigidity and of laxity in the application of their standard: some are even puritanically rigorous, while others are as indulgent as can possibly be desired by sinner or by sentimentalist. But on the whole, a doctrine which brings prominently forward the interest that mankind have in the repression and prevention of conduct which violates the moral law, is likely to be inferior to no other in turning the sanctions of opinion again such violations. It is true, the question, "What does violate the moral law?" is one on which those who recognise different standards of morality are likely now and then to differ. But difference of opinion on moral questions was not first introduced into the world by utilitarianism, while that doctrine does supply, if not always an easy, at all events a tangible and intelligible mode of deciding such differences.

It may not be superfluous to notice a few more of the common misapprehensions of utilitarian ethics, even those which are so obvious and gross that it might appear impossible for any person of candour and intelligence to fall into them; since persons, even of considerable mental endowments, often give themselves so little trouble to understand the bearings of any opinion against which they entertain a prejudice, and men are in general so little conscious of this voluntary ignorance as a defect, that the vulgarest misunderstandings of ethical doctrines are continually met with in the deliberate writings of persons of the greatest pretensions both to high principle and to philosophy. We not uncommonly hear the doctrine of utility inveighed against as a godless doctrine. If it be necessary to say anything at all against so mere an assumption, we may say that the question depends upon what idea we have formed of the moral character of the Deity. If it be a true belief that God desires, above all things, the happiness of his creatures, and that this was his purpose in their creation, utility is not only not a godless doctrine, but more profoundly religious than any other. If it be meant that utilitarianism does not recognise the revealed will of God as the supreme law of morals, I answer, that a utilitarian who believes in the perfect goodness and wisdom of *God,* necessarily believes that whatever God has thought fit to reveal on the subject of morals, must fulfil the requirements of utility in a supreme degree. But others besides utilitarians have been of opinion that the Christian revelation was intended, and is fitted, to inform the hearts and minds of mankind with a spirit which should enable them to find for themselves what is right, and incline them to do it when found, rather than to tell them, except in a very general way, what it is; and that we need a doctrine of ethics, carefully followed out, to *interpret* to us the will of God. Whether this opinion is correct or not, it is superfluous here to discuss; since whatever aid religion, either natural or revealed, can afford to ethical investigation, is as open to the utilitarian moralist as to any other. He can use it as the testimony of God to the usefulness or hurtfulness of any given course of action, by as good a right as others can use it for the indication of a transcendental law, having no connection with usefulness or with happiness.

Again, Utility is often summarily stigmatised as an immoral doctrine by giving it the name of "expediency," and taking advantage of the popular use of that term to contrast it with Principle. But the Expedient, in the sense in which it is opposed to the Right, generally means that which is expedient for the particular interest of the agent himself; as when a minister sacrifices the interests of his country to keep himself in place. When it means anything better than this, it means that which is expedient for some immediate object, some temporary purpose, but which violates a rule whose observance is expedient in a much higher degree. The Expedient, in this sense, instead of being the same thing with the useful, is a branch of the hurtful. Thus, it would often be expedient, for the purpose of getting over some momentary embarrassment, or attaining some object immediately useful to ourselves or others, to tell a lie. But inasmuch as the cultivation in ourselves of a sensitive feeling on the subject of veracity, is one of the most useful, and the enfeeblement of that feeling one of the most hurtful, things to which our conduct can be instrumental; and inasmuch as any, even unintentional, deviation from truth, does that much towards weakening the trustworthiness of human assertion, which is not only the principal support of all present social well-being, but the insufficiency of which does more than any one thing that can be named to keep back civilisation, virtue, everything on which human happiness on the largest scale depends; we feel that the violation, for a present advantage, of a rule of such transcendant expediency, is not expedient, and that he who, for the sake of a convenience to himself or to some other individual, does what depends on him to deprive mankind of the good, and inflict upon them the evil, involved in the greater or less reliance which they can place in each other's word, acts the part of one of their worst enemies. Yet that even this rule, sacred as it is, admits of possible exceptions, is acknowledged by all moralists; the chief of which is when the withholding of some fact (as of information from a malefactor, or of bad news from a person dangerously ill) would save an individual (especially an individual other than oneself) from great and unmerited evil, and when the withholding can only be effected by denial. But in order that the exception may not extend itself beyond the need, and may have the least possible effect in weakening reliance on veracity, it ought to be recognised, and, if possible, its limits defined; and if the principle of utility is good for anything, it must be good for weighing these conflicting utilities against one another, and marking out the region within which one or the other preponderates.

Again, defenders of utility often find themselves called upon to reply to such objections as this—that there is not time, previous to action, for calculating and weighing the effects of any line of conduct on the general happiness. This is exactly as if any one were to say that it is impossible to guide our conduct by Christianity, because there is not time, on every occasion on which anything has to be done, to read through the Old and New Testaments. The answer to the objection is, that there has been ample time, namely, the whole past duration of the human species. During all that time, mankind have been learning by experience the tendencies of actions; on which experience all the prudence, as well as all the morality of life, are dependent. People talk as if the commencement of this course of experience had hitherto been put off, and as if, at the moment when some man feels tempted to meddle with the property or life of another, he had to begin considering for the first time whether murder and theft are injurious to human happiness. Even then I do not think that he would find the question very puzzling; but, at all events, the matter is now done to his hand. It is truly a whimsical supposition that, if mankind were agreed in considering utility to be the test of morality, they would remain without any agreement as to what is useful, and would take no measures for having their notions on the subject taught to the young, and enforced by law and opinion. There is no difficulty in proving any ethical standard whatever to work ill, if we suppose universal idiocy to be conjoined with it; but on any hypothesis short of that, mankind must by this time have acquired positive beliefs as to the effects of some actions on their happiness; and the beliefs which have thus come down are the rules of morality for the multitude, and for the philosopher until he has succeeded in finding better. That philosophers might easily do this, even now, on many subjects; that the received code of ethics is by no means of divine right; and that mankind have still much to learn as to the effects of actions on the general happiness, I admit, or rather, earnestly maintain. The corollaries from the principle of utility, like the precepts of every practical art, admit of indefinite improvement, and, in a progressive state of the human mind, their improvement is perpetually going on. But to consider the rules of morality as improvable, is one thing; to pass over the intermediate generalisations entirely, and endeavour to test each individual action directly by the first principle, is another. It is a strange notion that the acknowledgment of a first principle is inconsistent with the admission of secondary ones. To inform a traveller respecting the place of his ultimate destination, is not to forbid the use of landmarks and direction-posts on the way. The proposition that happiness is the end and aim of morality, does not mean that no road ought to be laid down to that goal, or that persons going thither should not be advised to take one direction rather than another. Men really ought to leave off talking a kind of nonsense on this subject, which they would neither talk nor listen to on other matters of practical concernment, Nobody argues that the art of navigation is not founded on astronomy, because sailors cannot wait to calculate the Nautical Almanac. Being rational creatures, they go to sea with it ready calculated; and all rational creatures go out upon the sea of life with their minds made up on the common questions of right and wrong, as well as on many of the far more difficult questions of wise and foolish. And this, as long as foresight is a human quality, it is to be presumed they will continue to do. Whatever we adopt as the fundamental principle of morality, we require subordinate principles to apply it by; the impossibility of doing without them, being common to all systems, can afford no argument against any one in particular; but gravely to argue as if no such secondary principles could be had, and as if mankind had remained till now, and always must remain, without drawing any general conclusions from the experience of human life, is as high a pitch, I think, as absurdity has ever reached in philosophical controversy.

The remainder of the stock arguments against utilitarianism mostly consist in laying to its charge the common infirmities of human nature, and the general difficulties which embarrass conscientious persons in shaping their course through life. We are told that a utilitarian will be apt to make his own particular case an exception to moral rules, and, when under temptation, will see a utility in the breach of a rule, greater than he will see in its observance. But is utility the only creed which is able to furnish us with excuses for evil doing, and means of cheating our own conscience? They are afforded in abundance by all doctrines which recognise as a fact in morals the existence of conflicting considerations; which all doctrines do, that have been believed by sane persons. It is not the fault of any creed, but of the complicated nature of human affairs, that rules of conduct cannot be so framed as to require no exceptions, and that hardly any kind of action can safely be laid down as either always obligatory or always condemnable. There is no ethical creed which does not temper the rigidity of its laws, by giving a certain latitude, under the moral responsibility of the agent, for accommodation to peculiarities of circumstances; and under every creed, at the opening thus made, self-deception and dishonest casuistry get in. There exists no moral system under which there do not arise unequivocal cases of conflicting obligation. These are the real difficulties, the knotty points both in the theory of ethics, and in the conscientious guidance of personal conduct. They are overcome practically, with greater or with less success, according to the intellect and virtue of the individual; but it can hardly be pretended that any one will be the less qualified for dealing with them, from possessing an ultimate standard to which conflicting rights and duties can be referred. If utility is the ultimate source of moral obligations, utility may be invoked to decide between them when their demands are incompatible. Though the application of the standard may be difficult, it is better than none at all: while in other systems, the moral laws all claiming independent authority, there is no common umpire entitled to interfere between them; their claims to precedence one over another rest on little better than sophistry, and unless determined, as they generally are, by the unacknowledged influence of considerations of utility, afford a free scope for the action of personal desires and partialities. We must remember that only in these cases of conflict between secondary principles is it requisite that first principles should be appealed to. There is no case of moral obligation in which some secondary principle is not involved; and if only one, there can seldom be any real doubt which one it is, in the mind of any person by whom the principle itself is recognised.

CHAPTER 3:   OF THE ULTIMATE SANCTION OF THE PRINCIPLE OF UTILITY

The question is often asked, and properly so, in regard to any supposed moral standard—What is its sanction? what are the motives to obey it? or more specifically, what is the source of its obligation? whence does it derive its binding force? It is a necessary part of moral philosophy to provide the answer to this question; which, though frequently assuming the shape of an objection to the utilitarian morality, as if it had some special applicability to that above others, really arises in regard to all standards. It arises, in fact, whenever a person is called on to *adopt* a standard, or refer morality to any basis on which he has not been accustomed to rest it. For the customary morality, that which education and opinion have consecrated, is the only one which presents itself to the mind with the feeling of being *in itself* obligatory; and when a person is asked to believe that this morality *derives* its obligation from some general principle round which custom has not thrown the same halo, the assertion is to him a paradox; the supposed corollaries seem to have a more binding force than the original theorem; the superstructure seems to stand better without, than with, what is represented as its foundation. He says to himself, I feel that I am bound not to rob or murder, betray or deceive; but why am I bound to promote the general happiness? If my own happiness lies in something else, why may I not give that the preference?

If the view adopted by the utilitarian philosophy of the nature of the moral sense be correct, this difficulty will always present itself, until the influences which form moral character have taken the same hold of the principle which they have taken of some of the consequences—until, by the improvement of education, the feeling of unity with our fellow-creatures shall be (what it cannot be denied that Christ intended it to be) as deeply rooted in our character, and to our own consciousness as completely a part of our nature, as the horror of crime is in an ordinarily well brought up young person. In the meantime, however, the difficulty has no peculiar application to the doctrine of utility, but is inherent in every attempt to analyse morality and reduce it to principles; which, unless the principle is already in men's minds invested with as much sacredness as any of its applications, always seems to divest them of a part of their sanctity.

The principle of utility either has, or there is no reason why it might not have, all the sanctions which belong to any other system of morals. Those sanctions are either external or internal. Of the external sanctions it is not necessary to speak at any length. They are, the hope of favour and the fear of displeasure, from our fellow-creatures or from the Ruler of the Universe, along with whatever we may have of sympathy or affection for them, or of love and awe of Him, inclining us to do his will independently of selfish consequences. There is evidently no reason why all these motives for observance should not attach themselves to the utilitarian morality, as completely and as powerfully as to any other. Indeed, those of them which refer to our fellow-creatures are sure to do so, in proportion to the amount of general intelligence; for whether there be any other ground of moral obligation than the general happiness or not, men do desire happiness; and however imperfect may be their own practice, they desire and commend all conduct in others towards themselves, by which they think their happiness is promoted. With regard to the religious motive, if men believe, as most profess to do, in the goodness of God, those who think that conduciveness to the general happiness is the essence, or even only the criterion of good, must necessarily believe that it is also that which God approves. The whole force therefore of external reward and punishment, whether physical or moral, and whether proceeding from God or from our fellow men, together with all that the capacities of human nature admit of disinterested devotion to either, become available to enforce the utilitarian morality, in proportion as that morality is recognised; and the more powerfully, the more the appliances of education and general cultivation are bent to the purpose.

So far as to external sanctions. The internal sanction of duty, whatever our standard of duty may be, is one and the same—a feeling in our own mind; a pain, more or less intense, attendant on violation of duty, which in properly cultivated moral natures rises, in the more serious cases, into shrinking from it as an impossibility. This feeling, when disinterested, and connecting itself with the pure idea of duty, and not with some particular form of it, or with any of the merely accessory circumstances, is the essence of Conscience; though in that complex phenomenon as it actually exists, the simple fact is in general all encrusted over with collateral associations, derived from sympathy, from love, and still more from fear; from all the forms of religious feeling; from the recollections of childhood and of all our past life; from self-esteem, desire of the esteem of others, and occasionally even self-abasement. This extreme complication is, I apprehend, the origin of the sort of mystical character which, by a tendency of the human mind of which there are many other examples, is apt to be attributed to the idea of moral obligation, and which leads people to believe that the idea cannot possibly attach itself to any other objects than those which, by a supposed mysterious law, are found in our present experience to excite it. Its binding force, however, consists in the existence of a mass of feeling which must be broken through in order to do what violates our standard of right, and which, if we do nevertheless violate that standard, will probably have to be encountered afterwards in the form of remorse. Whatever theory we have of the nature or origin of conscience, this is what essentially constitutes it.

The ultimate sanction, therefore, of all morality (external motives apart) being a subjective feeling in our own minds, I see nothing embarrassing to those whose standard is utility, in the question, "What is the sanction of that particular standard?" We may answer, the same as of all other moral standards—the conscientious feelings of mankind. Undoubtedly this sanction has no binding efficacy on those who do not possess the feelings it appeals to; but neither will these persons be more obedient to any other moral principle than to the utilitarian one. On them morality of any kind has no hold but through the external sanctions. Meanwhile the feelings exist, a fact in human nature, the reality of which, and the great power with which they are capable of acting on those in whom they have been duly cultivated, are proved by experience. No reason has ever been shown why they may not be cultivated to as great intensity in connection with the utilitarian, as with any other rule of morals.

There is, I am aware, a disposition to believe that a person who sees in moral obligation a transcendental fact, an objective reality belonging to the province of "things in themselves," is likely to be more obedient to it than one who believes it to be entirely subjective, having its seat in human consciousness only. But whatever a person's opinion may be on this point of Ontology, the force he is really urged by is his own subjective feeling, and is exactly measured by its strength. No one's belief that duty is an objective reality is stronger than the belief that God is so; yet the belief in God, apart from the expectation of actual reward and punishment, only operates on conduct through, and in proportion to, the subjective religious feeling. The sanction, so far as it is disinter-

ested, is always in the mind itself; and the notion therefore of the transcendental moralists must be, that this sanction will not exist *in* the mind unless it is believed to have its
root out of the mind; and that if a person is able to say to himself, "This which is re-
straining me, and which is called my conscience, is only a feeling in my own mind," he
may possibly draw the conclusion that when the feeling ceases the obligation ceases,
and that if he find the feeling inconvenient, he may disregard it, and endeavour to get rid
of it. But is this danger confined to the utilitarian morality? Does the belief that moral
obligation has its seat outside the mind make the feeling of it too strong to be got rid
of? The fact is so far otherwise, that all moralists admit and lament the ease with
which, in the generality of minds, conscience can be silenced or stifled. The question,
"Need I obey my conscience?" is quite as often put to themselves by persons who
never heard of the principle of utility, as by its adherents. Those whose conscientious
feelings are so weak as to allow of their asking this question, if they answer it affir-
matively, will not do so because they believe in the transcendental theory, but because
of the external sanctions.

It is not necessary, for the present purpose, to decide whether the feeling of duty
is innate or implanted. Assuming it to be innate, it is an open question to what objects it
naturally attaches itself; for the philosophic supporters of that theory are now agreed
that the intuitive perception is of principles of morality and not of the details. If there be
anything innate in the matter, I see no reason why the feeling which is innate should not
be that of regard to the pleasures and pains of others. If there is any principle of morals
which is intuitively obligatory, I should say it must be that. If so, the intuitive ethics
would coincide with the utilitarian, and there would be no further quarrel between them.
Even as it is, the intuitive moralists, though they believe that there are other intuitive
moral obligations, do already believe this to be one; for they unanimously hold that a
large *portion* of morality turns upon the consideration due to the interests of our fellow-
creatures. Therefore, if the belief in the transcendental origin of moral obligation gives
any additional efficacy to the internal sanction, it appears to me that the utilitarian principle has already the benefit of it.

On the other hand, if, as is my own belief, the moral feelings are not innate, but
acquired, they are not for that reason the less natural. It is natural to man to speak, to
reason, to build cities, to cultivate the ground, though these are acquired faculties. The
moral feelings are not indeed a part of our nature, in the sense of being in any perceptible degree present in all of us; but this, unhappily, is a fact admitted by those who
believe the most strenuously in their transcendental origin. Like the other acquired capacities above referred to, the moral faculty, if not a part of our nature, is a natural
outgrowth from it; capable, like them, in a certain small degree, of springing up spontaneously; and susceptible of being brought by cultivation to a high degree of development. Unhappily it is also susceptible, by a sufficient use of the external sanctions
and of the force of early impressions, of being cultivated in almost any direction: so
that there is hardly anything so absurd or so mischievous that it may not, by means of
these influences, be made to act on the human mind with all the authority of conscience.
To doubt that the same potency might be given by the same means to the principle of
utility, even if it had no foundation in human nature, would be flying in the face of all
experience.

But moral associations which are wholly of artificial creation, when intellectual
culture goes on, yield by degrees to the dissolving force of analysis: and if the feeling of
duty, when associated with utility, would appear equally arbitrary; if there were no
leading department of our nature, no powerful class of sentiments, with which that as-

sociation would harmonise, which would make us feel it congenial, and incline us not only to foster it in others (for which we have abundant interested motives), but also to cherish it in ourselves; if there were not, in short, a natural basis of sentiment for utilitarian morality, it might well happen that this association also, even after it had been implanted by education, might be analysed away.

But there *is* this basis of powerful natural sentiment; and this it is which, when once the general happiness is recognised as the ethical standard, will constitute the strength of the utilitarian morality. This firm foundation is that of the social feelings of mankind; the desire to be in unity with our fellow creatures, which is already a powerful principle in human nature, and happily one of those which tend to become stronger, even without express inculcation, from the influences of advancing civilisation. The social state is at once so natural, so necessary, and so habitual to man, that, except in some unusual circumstances or by an effort of voluntary abstraction, he never conceives himself otherwise than as a member of a body; and this association is riveted more and more, as mankind are further removed from the state of savage independence. Any condition, therefore, which is essential to a state of society, becomes more and more an inseparable part of every person's conception of the state of things which he is born into, and which is the destiny of a human being. Now, society between human beings, except in the relation of master and slave, is manifestly impossible on any other footing than that the interests of all are to be consulted. Society between equals can only exist on the understanding that the interests of all are to be regarded equally. And since in all states of civilisation, every person, except an absolute monarch, has equals, every one is obliged to live on these terms with somebody; and in every age some advance is made towards a state in which it will be impossible to live permanently on other terms with anybody. In this way people grow up unable to conceive as possible to them a state of total disregard of other people's interests. They are under a necessity of conceiving themselves as at least abstaining from all the grosser injuries, and (if only for their own protection) living in a state of constant protest against them. They are also familiar with the fact of co-operating with others and proposing to themselves a collective, not an individual interest as the aim (at least for the time being) of their actions. So long as they are co-operating, their ends are identified with those of others; there is at least a temporary feeling that the interests of others are their own interests. Not only does all strengthening of social ties, and all healthy growth of society, give to each individual a stronger personal interest in practically consulting the welfare of others; it also leads him to identify his *feelings* more and more with their good, or at least with an even greater degree of practical consideration for it. He comes, as though instinctively, to be conscious of himself as a being who *of course* pays regard to others. The good of others becomes to him a thing naturally and necessarily to be attended to, like any of the physical conditions of our existence. Now, whatever amount of this feeling a person has, he is urged by the strongest motives both of interest and of sympathy to demonstrate it, and to the utmost of his power encourage it in others; and even if he has none of it himself, he is as greatly interested as any one else that others should have it. Consequently the smallest germs of the feeling are laid hold of and nourished by the contagion of sympathy and the influences of education; and a complete web of corroborative association is woven round it, by the powerful agency of the external sanctions. This mode of conceiving ourselves and human life, as civilisation goes on, is felt to be more and more natural. Every step in political improvement renders it more so, by removing the sources of opposition of interest, and levelling those inequalities of legal privilege between individuals or classes, owing to which there are large portions of mankind whose happiness it is still practicable to disregard. In an improving state of the human mind, the influences are constantly on the increase, which tend to generate in each individual a feeling of unity with all the rest; which, if perfect, would make him never think of, or desire, any beneficial condition for himself, in the benefits of which they are not included. If we now suppose this feeling of unity to be taught as a religion, and the whole force of education, of institutions, and of opinion, directed, as it once was in the case of religion, to make every person grow up from infancy surrounded on all sides both by the profession and the practice of it, I think that no one, who can realise this conception, will feel any misgiving about the sufficiency of the ultimate sanction for the Happiness morality. To any ethical student who finds the realisation difficult, I recommend, as a means of facilitating it, the second of M. Comte's two principal works, the *Traité de Politique Positive.* I entertain the strongest objections to the system of politics and morals set forth in that treatise; but I think it has superabundantly shown the possibility of giving to the service of humanity, even without the aid of belief in a Providence, both the psychological power and the social efficacy of a religion; making it take hold of human life, and colour all thought, feeling, and action, in a manner of which the greatest ascendancy ever exercised by any religion may be but a type and foretaste; and of which the danger is, not that it should be insufficient, but that it should be so excessive as to interfere unduly with human freedom and individuality.

Neither is it necessary to the feeling which constitutes the binding force of the utilitarian morality on those who recognise it, to wait for those social influences which would make its obligation felt by mankind at large. In the comparatively early state of human advancement in which we now live, a person cannot indeed feel that entireness of sympathy with all others, which would make any real discordance in the general direction of their conduct in life impossible; but already a person in whom the social feeling is at all developed, cannot bring himself to think of the rest of his fellow-creatures as struggling rivals with him for the means of happiness, whom he must desire to see defeated in their object in order that he may succeed in his. The deeply rooted conception which every individual even now has of himself as a social being, tends to make him feel it one of his natural wants that there should be harmony between his feelings and aims and those of his fellow-creatures. If differences of opinion and of mental culture make it impossible for him to share many of their actual feelings—perhaps make him denounce and defy those feelings—he still needs to be conscious that his real aim and theirs do not conflict; that he is not opposing himself to what they really wish for, namely their own good, but is, on the contrary, promoting it. This feeling in most individuals is much inferior in strength to their selfish feelings, and is often wanting altogether. But to those who have it, it possesses all the characters of a natural feeling. It does not present itself to their minds as a superstition of education, or a law despotically imposed by the power of society, but as an attribute which it would not be well for them to be without. This conviction is the ultimate sanction of the greatest happiness morality. This it is which makes any mind, of well-developed feelings, work with, and not against, the outward motives to care for others, afforded by what I have called the external sanctions; and when those sanctions are wanting, or act in an opposite direction, constitutes in itself a powerful internal binding force, in proportion to the sensitiveness and thoughtfulness of the character; since few but those whose mind is a moral blank, could bear to lay out their course of life on the plan of paying no regard to others except so far as their own private interest compels.

CHAPTER 4:   OF WHAT SORT OF PROOF
THE PRINCIPLE OF UTILITY IS SUSCEPTABLE

It has already been remarked, that questions of ultimate ends do not admit of proof, in the ordinary acceptation of the term. To be incapable of proof by reasoning is common to all first principles; to the first premises of our knowledge, as well as to those of our conduct. But the former, being matters of fact, may be the subject of a direct appeal to the faculties which judge of fact—namely, our senses, and our internal consciousness. Can an appeal be made to the same faculties on questions of practical ends? Or by what other faculty is cognisance taken of them?

Questions about ends are, in other words, questions what things are desirable. The utilitarian doctrine is, that happiness is desirable, and the only thing desirable, as an end; all other things being only desirable as means to that end. What ought to be required of this doctrine—what conditions is it requisite that the doctrine should fulfil—to make good its claim to be believed?

The only proof capable of being given that an object is visible, is that people actually see it. The only proof that a sound is audible, is that people hear it: and so of the other sources of our experience. In like manner, I apprehend, the sole evidence it is possible to produce that anything is desirable, is that people do actually desire it. If the end which the utilitarian doctrine proposes to itself were not, in theory and in practice, acknowledged to be an end, nothing could ever convince any person that it was so. No reason can be given why the general happiness is desirable, except that each person, so far as he believes it to be attainable, desires his own happiness. This, however, being a fact, we have not only all the proof which the case admits of, but all which it is possible to require, that happiness is a good: that each person's happiness is a good to that person, and the general happiness, therefore, a good to the aggregate of all persons. Happiness has made out its title as *one* of the ends of conduct, and consequently one of the criteria of morality.

But it has not, by this alone, proved itself to be the sole criterion. To do that, it would seem, by the same rule, necessary to show, not only that people desire happiness, but that they never desire anything else. Now it is palpable that they do desire things which, in common language, are decidedly distinguished from happiness. They desire, for example, virtue, and the absence of vice, no less really than pleasure and the absence of pain. The desire of virtue is not as universal, but it is as authentic a fact, as the desire of happiness. And hence the opponents of the utilitarian standard deem that they have a right to infer that there are other ends of human action besides happiness, and that happiness is not the standard of approbation and disapprobation.

But does the utilitarian doctrine deny that people desire virtue, or maintain that virtue is not a thing to be desired? The very reverse. It maintains not only that virtue is to be desired, but that it is to be desired disinterestedly, for itself. Whatever may be the opinion of utilitarian moralists as to the original conditions by which virtue is made virtue; however they may believe (as they do) that actions and dispositions are only virtuous because they promote another end than virtue; yet this being granted, and it having been decided, from considerations of this description, what is virtuous, they not only place virtue at the very head of the things which are good as means to the ultimate end, but they also recognise as a psychological fact the possibility of its being, to the individual, a good in itself, without looking to any end beyond it; and hold, that the mind is not in a right state, not in a state conformable to Utility, not in the state most conducive to the general happiness, unless it does love virtue in this manner—as a thing desirable in itself, even although, in the individual instance, it should not produce those other desirable consequences which it tends to produce, and on account of which it is held to be virtue. This opinion is not, in the smallest degree, a departure from the Happiness principle. The ingredients of happiness are very various, and each of them is desirable in itself, and not merely when considered as swelling an aggregate. The principle of utility does not mean that any given pleasure, as music, for instance, or any given exemption from pain, as for example health, is to be looked upon as means to a collective something termed happiness, and to be desired on that account. They are desired and desirable in and for themselves; besides being means, they are a part of the end. Virtue, according to the utilitarian doctrine, is not naturally and originally part of the end, but it is capable of becoming so; and in those who love it disinterestedly it has become so, and is desired and cherished, not as a means to happiness, but as a part of their happiness.

To illustrate this farther, we may remember that virtue is not the only thing, originally a means, and which if it were not a means to anything else, would be and remain indifferent, but which by association with what it is a means to, comes to be desired for itself, and that too with the utmost intensity. What, for example, shall we say of the love of money? There is nothing originally more desirable about money than about any heap of glittering pebbles. Its worth is solely that of the things which it will buy; the desires for other things than itself, which it is a means of gratifying. Yet the love of money is not only one of the strongest moving forces of human life, but money is, in many cases, desired in and for itself; the desire to possess it is often stronger than the desire to use it, and goes on increasing when all the desires which point to ends beyond it, to be compassed by it, are falling off. It may, then, be said truly, that money is desired not for the sake of an end, but as part of the end. From being a means to happiness, it has come to be itself a principal ingredient of the individual's conception of happiness. The same may be said of the majority of the great objects of human life—power, for example, or fame; except that to each of these there is a certain amount of immediate pleasure annexed, which has at least the semblance of being naturally inherent in them; a thing which cannot be said of money. Still, however, the strongest natural attraction, both of power and of fame, is the immense aid they give to the attainment of our other wishes; and it is the strong association thus generated between them and all our objects of desire, which gives to the direct desire of them the intensity it often assumes, so as in some characters to surpass in strength all other desires. In these cases the means have become a part of the end, and a more important part of it than any of the things which they are means to. What was once desired as an instrument for the attainment of happiness, has come to be desired for its own sake. In being desired for its own sake it is, however, desired as *part* of happiness. The person is made, or thinks he would be made, happy by its mere possession; and is made unhappy by failure to obtain it. The desire of it is not a different thing from the desire of happiness, any more than the love of music, or the desire of health. They are included in happiness. They are some of the elements of which the desire of happiness is made up. Happiness is not an abstract idea, but a concrete whole; and these are some of its parts. And the utilitarian standard sanctions and approves their being so. Life would be a poor thing, very ill provided with sources of happiness, if there were not this provision of nature, by which things originally indifferent, but conducive to, or otherwise associated with, the satisfaction of our primitives desires, become in themselves sources of pleasure more valuable than the primitive pleasures, both in permanency, in the space of human existence that they are capable of covering, and even in intensity.

Virtue, according to the utilitarian conception, is a good of this description. There was no original desire of it, or motive to it, save its conduciveness to pleasure, and especially to protection from pain. But through the association thus formed, it may be felt a good in itself, and desired as such with as great intensity as any other good; and with this difference between it and the love of money, of power, or of fame, that all of these may, and often do, render the individual noxious to the other members of the society to which he belongs, whereas there is nothing which makes him so much a blessing to them as the cultivation of the disinterested love of virtue. And consequently, the utilitarian standard, while it tolerates and approves those other acquired desires, up to the point beyond which they would be more injurious to the general happiness than promotive of it, enjoins and requires the cultivation of the love of virtue up to the greatest strength possible, as being above all things important to the general happiness.

It results from the preceding considerations, that there is in reality nothing desired except happiness. Whatever is desired otherwise than as a means to some end beyond itself, and ultimately to happiness, is desired as itself a part of happiness, and is not desired for itself until it has become so. Those who desire virtue for its own sake, desire it either because the consciousness of it is a pleasure, or because the consciousness of being without it is a pain, or for both reasons united; as in truth the pleasure and pain seldom exist separately, but almost always together, the same person feeling pleasure in the degree of virtue attained, and pain in not having attained more. If one of these gave him no pleasure, and the other no pain, he would not love or desire virtue, or would desire it only for the other benefits which it might produce to himself or to persons whom he cared for.

We have now, then, an answer to the question, of what sort of proof the principle of utility is susceptible. If the opinion which I have now stated is psychologically true— if human nature is so constituted as to desire nothing which is not either a part of happiness or a means of happiness—we can have no other proof, and we require no other, that these are the only things desirable. If so, happiness is the sole end of human action, and the promotion of it the test by which to judge of all human conduct; from whence it necessarily follows that it must be the criterion of morality, since a part is included in the whole.

And now to decide whether this is really so; whether mankind do desire nothing for itself but that which is a pleasure to them, or of which the absence is a pain; we have evidently arrived at a question of fact and experience, dependent, like all similar questions, upon evidence. It can only be determined by practised self-consciousness and self-observation, assisted by observation of others. I believe that these sources of evidence, impartially consulted, will declare that desiring a thing and finding it pleasant, aversion to it and thinking of it as painful, are phenomena entirely inseparable, or rather two parts of the same phenomenon—in strictness of language, two different modes of naming the same psychological fact: that to think of an object as desirable (unless for the sake of its consequences), and to think of it as pleasant, are one and the same thing; and that to desire anything, except in proportion as the idea of it is pleasant, is a physical and metaphysical impossibility.

So obvious does this appear to me, that I expect it will hardly be disputed: and the objection made will be, not that desire can possibly be directed to anything ultimately except pleasure and exemption from pain, but that the will is a different thing from desire; that a person of confirmed virtue, or any other person whose purposes are fixed, carries out his purposes without any thought of the pleasure he has in contemplating them, or expects to derive from their fulfilment; and persists in acting on them, even though these pleasures are much diminished, by changes in his character or decay of his passive sensibilities, or are out weighed by the pains which the pursuit of the purposes may bring upon him. All this I fully admit, and have stated it elsewhere, as positively and emphatically as any one. Will, the active phenomenon, is a different thing from desire, the state of passive sensibility, and though originally an offshoot from it, may in time take root and detach itself from the parent stock; so much so, that in the case of an habitual purpose, instead of willing the thing because we desire it, we often desire it only because we will it. This, however, is but an instance of that familiar fact, the power of habit, and is no wise confined to the case of virtuous actions. Many indifferent things, which men originally did from a motive of some sort, they continue to do from habit. Sometimes this is done unconsciously, the consciousness coming only after the action: at other times with conscious volition, but volition which has become habitual, and is put in operation by the force of habit, in opposition perhaps to the deliberate preference, as often happens with those who have contracted habits of vicious or hurtful indulgence. Third and last comes the case in which the habitual act of will in the individual instance is not in contradiction to the general intention prevailing at other times, but in fulfilment of it; as in the case of the person of confirmed virtue, and of all who pursue deliberately and consistently any determinate end. The distinction between will and desire thus understood is an authentic and highly important psychological fact; but the fact consists solely in this—that will, like all other parts of our constitution, is amenable to habit, and that we may will from habit what we no longer desire for itself, or desire only because we will it. It is not the less true that will, in the beginning, is entirely produced by desire; including in that term the repelling influence of pain as well as the attractive one of pleasure. Let us take into consideration, no longer the person who has a confirmed will to do right, but him in whom that virtuous will is still feeble, conquerable by temptation, and not to be fully relied on; by what means can it be strengthened? How can the will to be virtuous, where it does not exist in sufficient force, be implanted or awakened? Only by making the person *desire* virtue—by making him think of it in a pleasurable light, or of its absence in a painful one. It is by associating the doing right with pleasure, or the doing wrong with pain, or by eliciting and impressing and bringing home to the person's experience the pleasure naturally involved in the one or the pain in the other, that it is possible to call forth that will to be virtuous, which, when confirmed, acts without any thought of either pleasure or pain. Will is the child of desire, and passes out of the dominion of its parent only to come under that of habit. That which is the result of habit affords no presumption of being intrinsically good; and there would be no reason for wishing that the purpose of virtue should become independent of pleasure and pain, were it not that the influence of the pleasurable and painful associations which prompt to virtue is not sufficiently to be depended on for unerring constancy of action until it has acquired the support of habit. Both in feeling and in conduct, habit is the only thing which imparts certainty; and it is because of the importance to others of being able to rely absolutely on one's feelings and conduct, and to oneself of being able to rely on one's own, that the will to do right ought to be cultivated into this habitual independence. In other words, this state of the will is a means to good, not intrinsically a good; and does not contradict the doctrine that nothing is a good to human beings but in so far as it is either itself pleasurable, or a means of attaining pleasure or averting pain.

But if this doctrine be true, the principle of utility is proved. Whether it is so or not, must now be left to the consideration of the thoughtful reader.

CHAPTER 5:   ON THE CONNECTION
BETWEEN JUSTICE AND UTILITY

In all ages of speculation, one of the strongest obstacles to the reception of the doctrine that Utility or Happiness is the criterion of right and wrong, has been drawn from the idea of Justice. The powerful sentiment, and apparently clear perception, which that word recalls with a rapidity and certainty resembling an instinct, have seemed to the majority of thinkers to point to an inherent quality in things; to show that the Just must have an existence in Nature as something absolute, generically distinct from every variety of the Expedient, and, in idea, opposed to it, though (as is commonly acknowledged) never, in the long run, disjoined from it in fact.

In the case of this, as of our other moral sentiments, there is no necessary connection between the question of its origin, and that of its binding force. That a feeling is bestowed on us by Nature, does not necessarily legitimate all its promptings. The feeling of justice might be a peculiar instinct, and might yet require, like our other instincts, to be controlled and enlightened by a higher reason. If we have intellectual instincts, leading us to judge in a particular way, as well as animal instincts that prompt us to act in a particular way, there is no necessity that the former should be more infallible in their sphere than the latter in theirs: it may as well happen that wrong judgments are occasionally suggested by those, as wrong actions by these. But though it is one thing to believe that we have natural feelings of justice, and another to acknowledge them as an ultimate criterion of conduct, these two opinions are very closely connected in point of fact. Mankind are always predisposed to believe that any subjective feeling, not otherwise accounted for, is a revelation of some objective reality. Our present object is to determine whether the reality, to which the feeling of justice corresponds, is one which needs any such special revelation; whether the justice or injustice of an action is a thing intrinsically peculiar, and distinct from all its other qualities, or only a combination of certain of those qualities, presented under a peculiar aspect. For the purpose of this inquiry it is practically important to consider whether the feeling itself, of justice and injustice, is *sui generis* like our sensations of colour and taste, or a derivative feeling, formed by a combination of others. And this it is the more essential to examine, as people are in general willing enough to allow, that objectively the dictates of Justice coincide with a part of the field of General Expediency; but inasmuch as the subjective mental feeling of Justice is different from that which commonly attaches to simple expediency, and, except in the extreme cases of the latter, is far more imperative in its demands, people find it difficult to see, in Justice, only a particular kind or branch of general utility, and think that its superior binding force requires a totally different origin.

To throw light upon this question, it is necessary to attempt to ascertain what is the distinguishing character of justice, or of injustice: what is the quality, or whether there is any quality, attributed in common to all modes of conduct designated as unjust (for justice, like many other moral attributes, is best defined by its opposite), and distinguishing them from such modes of conduct as are disapproved, but without having that particular epithet of disapprobation applied to them. If in everything which men are accustomed to characterise as just or unjust, some one common attribute or collection of attributes is always present, we may judge whether this particular attribute or combination of attributes would be capable of gathering round it a sentiment of that peculiar character and intensity by virtue of the general laws of our emotional constitution, or whether the sentiment is inexplicable, and requires to be regarded as a special provision of Nature. If we find the former to be the case, we shall, in resolving this question, have resolved also the main problem: if the latter, we shall have to seek for some other mode of investigating it.

To find the common attributes of a variety of objects, it is necessary to begin by surveying the objects themselves in the concrete. Let us therefore advert successively to the various modes of action, and arrangements of human affairs, which are classed, by universal or widely spread opinion, as Just or as Unjust. The things well known to excite the sentiments associated with those names are of a very multifarious character. I shall pass them rapidly in review, without studying any particular arrangement.

In the first place, it is mostly considered unjust to deprive any one of his personal liberty, his property, or any other thing which belongs to him by law. Here, therefore, is one instance of the application of the terms "just" and "unjust" in a perfectly definite sense, namely, that it is just to respect, unjust to violate, the *legal rights* of any one. But this judgment admits of several exceptions, arising from the other forms in which the notions of justice and injustice present themselves. For example, the person who suffers the deprivation may (as the phrase is) have *forfeited* the rights which he is so deprived of: a case to which we shall return presently. But also,

Secondly; the legal rights of which he is deprived, may be rights which *ought* not to have belonged to him; in other words, the law which confers on him these rights, may be a bad law. When it is so, or when (which is the same thing for our purpose) it is supposed to be so, opinions will differ as to the justice or injustice of infringing it. Some maintain that no law, however bad, ought to be disobeyed by an individual citizen; that his opposition to it, if shown at all, should only be shown in endeavouring to get it altered by competent authority. This opinion (which condemns many of the most illustrious benefactors of mankind, and would often protect pernicious institutions against the only weapons which, in the state of things existing at the time, have any chance of succeeding against them) is defended, by those who hold it, on grounds of expediency; principally on that of the importance, to the common interest of mankind, of maintaining inviolate the sentiment of submission to law. Other persons, again, hold the directly contrary opinion, that any law, judged to be bad, may blamelessly be disobeyed, even though it be not judged to be unjust, but only inexpedient; while others would confine the licence of disobedience to the case of unjust laws: but again, some say, that all laws which are inexpedient are unjust; since every law imposes some restriction on the natural liberty of mankind, which restriction is an injustice, unless legitimated by tending to their good. Among these diversities of opinion, it seems to be universally admitted that there may be unjust laws, and that law, consequently, is not the ultimate criterion of justice, but may give to one person a benefit, or impose on another an evil, which justice condemns. When, however, a law is thought to be unjust, it seems always to be regarded as being so in the same way in which a breach of law is unjust, namely, by infringing somebody's right; which, as it cannot in this case be a legal right, receives a different appellation, and is called a moral right. We may say, therefore, that a second case of injustice consists in taking or withholding from any person that to which he has a *moral right*.

Thirdly, it is universally considered just that each person should obtain that (whether good or evil) which he *deserves* and unjust that he should obtain a good, or be made to undergo an evil, which he does not deserve. This is, perhaps, the clearest and most emphatic form in which the idea of justice is conceived by the general mind. As it involves the notion of desert, the question arises, what constitutes desert? Speaking in a general way, a person is understood to deserve good if he does right, evil if he does wrong; and in a more particular sense, to deserve good from those to whom he does or has done good, and evil from those to whom he does or has done evil. The precept of returning good for evil has never been regarded as a case of the fulfilment of justice, but as one in which the claims of justice are waived, in obedience to other considerations.

Fourthly, it is confessedly unjust to *break faith* with any one: to violate an engagement, either express or implied, or disappoint expectations raised by our own conduct, at least if we have raised those expectations knowingly and voluntarily. Like the other obligations of justice already spoken of, this one is not regarded as absolute, but as capable of being overruled by a stronger obligation of justice on the other side; or by such conduct on the part of the person concerned as is deemed to absolve us from our obligation to him, and to constitute a *forfeiture* of the benefit which he has been led to expect.

Fifthly, it is, by universal admission, inconsistent with justice to be *partial*—to show favour or preference to one person over another, in matters to which favour and preference do not properly apply. Impartiality, however, does not seem to be regarded as a duty in itself, but rather as instrumental to some other duty; for it is admitted that favour and preference are not always censurable, and indeed the cases in which they are condemned are rather the exception than the rule. A person would be more likely to be blamed than applauded for giving his family or friends no superiority in good offices over strangers, when he could do so without violating any other duty; and no one thinks it unjust to seek one person in preference to another as a friend, connection, or companion. Impartiality where rights are concerned is of course obligatory, but this is involved in the more general obligation of giving to every one his right. A tribunal, for example, must be impartial, because it is bound to award, without regard to any other consideration, a disputed object to the one of two parties who has the right to it. There are other cases in which impartiality means, being solely influenced by desert; as with those who, in the capacity of judges, preceptors, or parents, administer reward and punishment as such. There are cases, again, in which it means, being solely influenced by consideration for the public interest; as in making a selection among candidates for a government employment. Impartiality, in short, as an obligation of justice, may be said to mean, being exclusively influenced by the considerations which it is supposed ought to influence the particular case in hand; and resisting the solicitation of any motives which prompt to conduct different from what those considerations would dictate.

Nearly allied to the idea of impartiality is that of *equality,* which often enters as a component part both into the conception of justice and into the practice of it, and, in the eyes of many persons, constitutes its essence. But in this, still more than in any other case, the notion of justice varies in different persons, and always conforms in its variations to their notion of utility. Each person maintains that equality is the dictate of justice, except where he thinks that expediency requires inequality. The justice of giving equal protection to the rights of all, is maintained by those who support the most outrageous inequality in the rights themselves. Even in slave countries it is theoretically admitted that the rights of the slave, such as they are, ought to be as sacred as those of the master; and that a tribunal which fails to enforce them with equal strictness is wanting in justice; while, at the same time, institutions which leave to the slave scarcely any rights to enforce, are not deemed unjust, because they are not deemed inexpedient. Those who think that utility requires distinctions of rank, do not consider it unjust that riches and social privileges should be unequally dispensed; but those who think this inequality inexpedient, think it unjust also. Whoever thinks that government is necessary, sees no injustice in as much inequality as is constituted by giving to the magistrate powers not granted to other people. Even among those who hold levelling doctrines, there are as many questions of justice as there are differences of opinion about expediency.

Some Communists consider it unjust that the produce of the labour of the community should be shared on any other principle than that of exact equality; others think it just that those should receive most whose wants are greatest; while others hold that those who work harder, or who produce more, or whose services are more valuable to the community, may justly claim a larger quota in the division of the produce. And the sense of natural justice may be plausibly appealed to in behalf of every one of these opinions.

Among so many diverse applications of the term "justice," which yet is not regarded as ambiguous, it is a matter of some difficulty to seize the mental link which holds them together, and on which the moral sentiment adhering to the term essentially depends. Perhaps, in this embarrassment, some help may be derived from the history of the word, as indicated by its etymology.

In most, if not in all, languages, the etymology of the word which corresponds to "just" points distinctly to an origin connected with the ordinances of law. *Justum* is a form of *jussum,* that which has been ordered. ⟨*Dikaion*⟩ comes directly from ⟨*dike*⟩, a suit at law. *Recht,* from which came *right* and *righteous,* is synonymous with law. The courts of justice, the administration of justice, are the courts and the administration of law. *La justice,* in French, is the established term for judicature. I am not committing the fallacy imputed with some show of truth to Horne Tooke,* of assuming that a word must still continue to mean what it originally meant. Etymology is slight evidence of what the idea now signified is, but the very best evidence of how it sprang up. There can, I think, be no doubt that the *idée mère,* the primitive element, in the formation of the notion of justice, was conformity to law. It constituted the entire idea among the Hebrews, up to the birth of Christianity; as might be expected in the case of a people whose laws attempted to embrace all subjects on which precepts were required, and who believed those laws to be a direct emanation from the Supreme Being. But other nations, and in particular the Greeks and Romans, who knew that their laws had been made originally, and still continued to be made, by men, were not afraid to admit that those men might make bad laws; might do, by law, the same things, and from the same motives, which if done by individuals without the sanction of law, would be called unjust. And hence the sentiment of injustice came to be attached, not to all violations of law, but only to violations of such laws as *ought* to exist, including such as ought to exist, but do not; and to laws themselves, if supposed to be contrary to what ought to be law. In this manner the idea of law and of its injunctions was still predominant in the notion of justice, even when the laws actually in force ceased to be accepted as the standard of it.

It is true that mankind consider the idea of justice and its obligations as applicable to many things which neither are, nor is it desired that they should be, regulated by law. Nobody desires that laws should interfere with the whole detail of private life; yet every one allows that in all daily conduct a person may and does show himself to be either just or unjust. But even here, the idea of the breach of what ought to be law, still lingers in a modified shape. It would always give us pleasure, and chime in with our feelings of fitness, that acts which we deem unjust should be punished, though we do not always think it expedient that this should be done by the tribunals. We forego that gratification on account of incidental inconveniences. We should be glad to see just conduct enforced and injustice repressed, even in the minutest details, if we were not, with reason, afraid of trusting the magistrate with so unlimited an amount of power over individuals.

---

*[John Tooke (1736–1812), a radical writer and close friend of Bentham.]

When we think that a person is bound in justice to do a thing, it is an ordinary form of language to say, that he ought to be compelled to do it. We should be gratified to see the obligation enforced by anybody who had the power. If we see that its enforcement by law would be inexpedient, we lament the impossibility, we consider the impunity given to injustice as an evil, and strive to make amends for it by bringing a strong expression of our own and the public disapprobation to bear upon the offender. Thus the idea of legal constraint is still the generating idea of the notion of justice, though undergoing several transformations before that notion, as it exists in an advanced state of society, becomes complete.

The above is, I think, a true account, as far as it goes, of the origin and progressive growth of the idea of justice. But we must observe, that it contains, as yet, nothing to distinguish that obligation from moral obligation in general. For the truth is, that the idea of penal sanction, which is the essence of law, enters not only into the conception of injustice, but into that of any kind of wrong. We do not call anything wrong, unless we mean to imply that a person ought to be punished in some way or other for doing it; if not by law, by the opinion of his fellow-creatures; if not by opinion, by the reproaches of his own conscience. This seems the real turning point of the distinction between morality and simple expediency. It is a part of the notion of Duty in every one of its forms, that a person may rightfully be compelled to fulfil it. Duty is a thing which may be *exacted* from a person, as one exacts a debt. Unless we think that it may be exacted from him, we do not call it his duty. Reasons of prudence, or the interest of other people, may militate against actually exacting it; but the person himself, it is clearly understood, would not be entitled to complain. There are other things, on the contrary, which we wish that people should do, which we like or admire them for doing, perhaps dislike or despise them for not doing, but yet admit that they are not bound to do; it is not a case of moral obligation; we do not blame them, that is, we do not think that they are proper objects of punishment. How we come by these ideas of deserving and not deserving punishment, will appear, perhaps, in the sequel; but I think there is no doubt that this distinction lies at the bottom of the notions of right and wrong; that we call any conduct wrong, or employ, instead, some other term of dislike or disparagement, according as we think that the person ought, or ought not, to be punished for it; and we say, it would be right to do so and so, or merely that it would be desirable or laudable, according as we would wish to see the person whom it concerns, compelled, or only persuaded and exhorted, to act in that manner.*

This, therefore, being the characteristic difference which marks off, not justice, but morality in general, from the remaining provinces of Expediency and Worthiness; the character is still to be sought which distinguishes justice from other branches of morality. Now it is known that ethical writers divide moral duties into two classes, denoted by the ill-chosen expressions, duties of perfect and of imperfect obligation; the latter being those in which, though the act is obligatory, the particular occasions of performing it are left to our choice; as in the case of charity or beneficence, which we are indeed bound to practise, but not towards any definite person, nor at any prescribed time. In the more precise language of philosophic jurists, duties of perfect obligation are those duties in virtue of which a correlative *right* resides in some person or persons; duties of imperfect obligation are those moral obligations which do not give birth to any

---

*I see this point enforced and illustrated by Professor Bain, in an admirable chapter (entitled "The Ethical Emotions, or the Moral Sense"), of the second of the two treatises composing his elaborate and profound work on the Mind.

right. I think it will be found that this distinction exactly coincides with that which exists between justice and the other obligations of morality. In our survey of the various popular acceptations of justice, the term appeared generally to involve the idea of a personal right—a claim on the part of one or more individuals, like that which the law gives when it confers a proprietary or other legal right. Whether the injustice consists in depriving a person of a possession, or in breaking faith with him, or in treating him worse than he deserves, or worse than other people who have no greater claims, in each case the supposition implies two things—a wrong done, and some assignable person who is wronged. Injustice may also be done by treating a person better than others; but the wrong in this case is to his competitors, who are also assignable persons. It seems to me that this feature in the case—a right in some person, correlative to the moral obligation—constitutes the specific difference between justice, and generosity or beneficence. Justice implies something which it is not only right to do, and wrong not to do, but which some individual person can claim from us as his moral right. No one has a moral right to our generosity or beneficence, because we are not morally bound to practise those virtues towards any given individual. And it will be found with respect to this as to every correct definition, that the instances which seem to conflict with it are those which most confirm it. For if a moralist attempts, as some have done, to make out that mankind generally, though not any given individual, have a right to all the good we can do them, he at once, by that thesis, includes generosity and beneficence within the category of justice. He is obliged to say, that our utmost exertions are due to our fellow-creatures, thus assimilating them to a debt; or that nothing less can be a sufficient *return* for what society does for us, thus classing the case as one of gratitude; both of which are acknowledged cases of justice. Wherever there is a right, the case is one of justice, and not of the virtue of beneficence: and whoever does not place the distinction between justice and morality in general, where we have now placed it, will be found to make no distinction between them at all, but to merge all morality in justice.

Having thus endeavoured to determine the distinctive elements which enter into the composition of the idea of justice, we are ready to enter on the inquiry, whether the feeling, which accompanies the idea, is attached to it by a special dispensation of nature, or whether it could have grown up, by any known laws, out of the idea itself; and in particular, whether it can have originated in considerations of general expediency.

I conceive that the sentiment itself does not arise from anything which would commonly, or correctly, be termed an idea of expediency; but that though the sentiment does not, whatever is moral in it does.

We have seen that the two essential ingredients in the sentiment of justice are, the desire to punish a person who has done harm and the knowledge or belief that there is some definite individual or individuals to whom harm has been done.

Now it appears to me, that the desire to punish a person who has done harm to some individual is a spontaneous outgrowth from two sentiments, both in the highest degree natural, and which either are or resemble instincts; the impulse of self-defence, and the feeling of sympathy.

It is natural to resent, and to repel or retaliate, any harm done or attempted against ourselves, or against those with whom we sympathise. The origin of this sentiment it is not necessary here to discuss. Whether it be an instinct or a result of intelligence, it is, we know, common to all animal nature; for every animal tries to hurt those who have hurt, or who it thinks are about to hurt, itself or its young. Human beings, on this point, only differ from other animals in two particulars. First, in being capable of sympathising, not solely with their offspring, or, like some of the more noble animals, with some superior animal who is kind to them, but with all human, and even with all sentient, beings. Secondly, in having a more developed intelligence, which gives a wider range to the whole of their sentiments, whether self-regarding or sympathetic. By virtue of his superior intelligence, even apart from his superior range of sympathy, a human being is capable of apprehending a community of interest between himself and the human society of which he forms a part, such that any conduct which threatens the security of the society generally, is threatening to his own, and calls forth his instinct (if instinct it be) of self-defence. The same superiority of intelligence, joined to the power of sympathising with human beings generally, enables him to attach himself to the collective idea of his tribe, his country, or mankind, in such a manner that any act hurtful to them, raises his instinct of sympathy, and urges him to resistance.

The sentiment of justice, in that one of its elements which consists of the desire to punish, is thus, I conceive, the natural feeling of retaliation or vengeance, rendered by intellect and sympathy applicable to those injuries, that is, to those hurts, which wound us through, or in common with, society at large. This sentiment, in itself, has nothing moral in it; what is moral is, the exclusive subordination of it to the social sympathies, so as to wait on and obey their call. For the natural feeling would make us resent indiscriminately whatever any one does that is disagreeable to us; but when moralised by the social feeling, it only acts in the directions conformable to the general good: just persons resenting a hurt to society, though not otherwise a hurt to themselves, and not resenting a hurt to themselves, however painful, unless it be of the kind which society has a common interest with them in the repression of.

It is no objection against this doctrine to say, that when we feel our sentiment of justice outraged, we are not thinking of society at large, or of any collective interest, but only of the individual case. It is common enough certainly, though the reverse of commendable, to feel resentment merely because we have suffered pain; but a person whose resentment is really a moral feeling, that is, who considers whether an act is blamable before he allows himself to resent it—such a person, though he may not say expressly to himself that he is standing up for the interest of society, certainly does feel that he is asserting a rule which is for the benefit of others as well as for his own. If he is not feeling this—if he is regarding the act solely as it affects him individually—he is not consciously just; he is not concerning himself about the justice of his actions. This is admitted even by anti-utilitarian moralists. When Kant (as before remarked) propounds as the fundamental principle of morals, "So act, that thy rule of conduct might be adopted as a law by all rational beings," he virtually acknowledges that the interest of mankind collectively, or at least of mankind indiscriminately, must be in the mind of the agent when conscientiously deciding on the morality of the act. Otherwise he uses words without a meaning: for, that a rule even of utter selfishness could not *possibly* be adopted by all rational beings—that there is any insuperable obstacle in the nature of things to its adoption—cannot be even plausibly maintained. To give any meaning to Kant's principle, the sense put upon it must be, that we ought to shape our conduct by a rule which all rational beings might adopt *with benefit to their collective interest*.

To recapitulate: the idea of justice supposes two things—a rule of conduct, and a sentiment which sanctions the rule. The first must be supposed common to all mankind, and intended for their good. The other (the sentiment) is a desire that punishment may be suffered by those who infringe the rule. There is involved, in addition, the conception of some definite person who suffers by the infringement; whose rights (to use the expression appropriated to the case) are violated by it. And the sentiment of justice appears to me to be, the animal desire to repel or retaliate a hurt or damage to oneself, or to those with whom one sympathises, widened so as to include all persons, by the human capacity of enlarged sympathy, and the human conception of intelligent self-interest. From the latter elements, the feeling derives its morality; from the former, its peculiar impressiveness, and energy of self-assertion.

I have, throughout, treated the idea of a *right* residing in the injured person, and violated by the injury, not as a separate element in the composition of the idea and sentiment, but as one of the forms in which the other two elements clothe themselves. These elements are, a hurt to some assignable person or persons on the one hand, and a demand for punishment on the other. An examination of our own minds, I think, will show, that these two things include all that we mean when we speak of violation of a right. When we call anything a person's right, we mean that he has a valid claim on society to protect him in the possession of it, either by the force of law, or by that of education and opinion. If he has what we consider a sufficient claim, on whatever account, to have something guaranteed to him by society, we say that he has a right to it. If we desire to prove that anything does not belong to him by right, we think this done as soon as it is admitted that society ought not to take measures for securing it to him, but should leave him to chance, or to his own exertions. Thus, a person is said to have a right to what he can earn in fair professional competition; because society ought not to allow any other person to hinder him from endeavouring to earn in that manner as much as he can. But he has not a right to three hundred a year, though he may happen to be earning it; because society is not called on to provide that he shall earn that sum. On the contrary, if he owns ten thousand pounds three-per-cent stock, he *has* a right to three hundred a-year because society has come under an obligation to provide him with an income of that amount.

To have a right, then, is, I conceive, to have something which society ought to defend me in the possession of. If the objector goes on to ask, why it ought? I can give him no other reason than general utility. If that expression does not seem to convey a sufficient feeling of the strength of the obligation, nor to account for the peculiar energy of the feeling, it is because there goes to the composition of the sentiment, not a rational only, but also an animal element, the thirst for retaliation; and this thirst derives its intensity, as well as its moral justification, from the extraordinarily important and impressive kind of utility which is concerned. The interest involved is that of security, to every one's feelings the most vital of all interests. All other earthly benefits are needed by one person, not needed by another; and many of them can, if necessary, be cheerfully foregone, or replaced by something else; but security no human being can possibly do without; on it we depend for all our immunity from evil, and for the whole value of all and every good, beyond the passing moment; since nothing but the gratification of the instant could be of any worth to us, if we could be deprived of anything the next instant by whoever was momentarily stronger than ourselves. Now this most indispensable of all necessaries, after physical nutriment, cannot be had, unless the machinery for providing it is kept unintermittedly in active play. Our notion, therefore, of the claim we have on our fellow-creatures to join in making safe for us the very groundwork of our existence, gathers feelings around it so much more intense than those concerned in any of the more common cases of utility, that the difference in degree (as is often the case in psychology) becomes a real difference in kind. The claim assumes that character of absoluteness, that apparent infinity, and incommensurability with all other considerations, which constitute the distinction between the feeling of right and wrong and that of ordinary expediency and inexpediency. The feelings concerned are so powerful, and we count so positively on finding a responsive feeling in others (all being alike interested), that *ought* and *should* grow into *must*, and recognised indispensability becomes a moral necessity, analogous to physical, and often not inferior to it in binding force.

If the preceding analysis, or something resembling it, be not the correct account of the notion of justice; if justice be totally independent of utility, and be a standard *per se,* which the mind can recognise by simple introspection of itself; it is hard to understand why that internal oracle is so ambiguous, and why so many things appear either just or unjust, according to the light in which they are regarded.

We are continually informed that Utility is an uncertain standard, which every different person interprets differently, and that there is no safety but in the immutable, ineffaceable, and unmistakable dictates of Justice, which carry their evidence in themselves, and are independent of the fluctuations of opinion. One would suppose from this that on questions of justice there could be no controversy; that if we take that for our rule, its application to any given case could leave us in as little doubt as a mathematical demonstration. So far is this from being the fact, that there is as much difference of opinion, and as much discussion, about what is just, as about what is useful to society. Not only have different nations and individuals different notions of justice, but in the mind of one and the same individual, justice is not some one rule, principle, or maxim, but many, which do not always coincide in their dictates, and in choosing between which, he is guided either by some extraneous standard, or by his own personal predilections.

For instance, there are some who say, that it is unjust to punish any one for the sake of example to others; that punishment is just, only when intended for the good of the sufferer himself. Others maintain the extreme reverse, contending that to punish persons who have attained years of discretion, for their own benefit, is despotism and injustice, since if the matter at issue is solely their own good, no one has a right to control their own judgment of it; but that they may justly be punished to prevent evil to others, this being the exercise of the legitimate right of self-defence. Mr. Owen,* again, affirms that it is unjust to punish at all; for the criminal did not make his own character; his education, and the circumstances which surrounded him, have made him a criminal, and for these he is not responsible. All these opinions are extremely plausible; and so long as the question is argued as one of justice simply, without going down to the principles which lie under justice and are the source of its authority, I am unable to see how any of these reasoners can be refuted. For in truth every one of the three builds upon rules of justice confessedly true. The first appeals to the acknowledged injustice of singling out an individual, and making him a sacrifice, without his consent, for other people's benefit. The second relies on the acknowledged justice of self-defence, and the admitted injustice of forcing one person to conform to another's notions of what constitutes his good. The Owenite invokes the admitted principle, that it is unjust to punish any one for what he cannot help. Each is triumphant so long as he is not compelled to take into consideration any other maxims of justice than the one he has selected; but as soon as their several maxims are brought face to face, each disputant seems to have exactly as much to say for himself as the others. No one of them can carry out his own notion of justice without trampling upon another equally binding. These are difficulties; they have always been felt to be such; and many devices have been invented to turn rather than to overcome them. As a refuge from the last of the three, men imagined what they called the freedom of the will; fancying that they could not justify punishing a man whose will is in a thoroughly hateful state, unless it be supposed to have come into that state through no influence of anterior circumstances. To escape from the other difficulties, a favourite contrivance has been the fiction of a contract, whereby at some un-

---

*[Robert Owen (1771–1858), a British reformer who argued for environmental determinism.]

known period all the members of society engaged to obey the laws, and consented to be punished for any disobedience to them; thereby giving to their legislators the right, which it is assumed they would not otherwise have had, of punishing them, either for their own good or for that of society. This happy thought was considered to get rid of the whole difficulty, and to legitimate the infliction of punishment, in virtue of another received maxim of justice, *volenti non fit injuria;* that is not unjust which is done with the consent of the person who is supposed to be hurt by it. I need hardly remark, that even if the consent were not a mere fiction, this maxim is not superior in authority to the others which it is brought in to supersede. It is, on the contrary, an instructive specimen of the loose and irregular manner in which supposed principles of justice grow up. This particular one evidently came into use as a help to the coarse exigencies of courts of law, which are sometimes obliged to be content with very uncertain presumptions, on account of the greater evils which would often arise from any attempt on their part to cut finer. But even courts of law are not able to adhere consistently to the maxim, for they allow voluntary engagements to be set aside on the ground of fraud, and sometimes on that of mere mistake or misinformation.

Again, when the legitimacy of inflicting punishment is admitted, how many conflicting conceptions of justice come to light in discussing the proper apportionment of punishments to offences. No rule on the subject recommends itself so strongly to the primitive and spontaneous sentiment of justice, as the *lex talionis,* an eye for an eye and a tooth for a tooth. Though this principle of the Jewish and of the Mahommedan law has been generally abandoned in Europe as a practical maxim, there is, I suspect, in most minds, a secret hankering after it; and when retribution accidentally falls on an offender in that precise shape, the general feeling of satisfaction evinced bears witness how natural is the sentiment to which this repayment in kind is acceptable. With many, the test of justice in penal infliction is that the punishment should be proportioned to the offence; meaning that it should be exactly measured by the moral guilt of the culprit (whatever be their standard for measuring moral guilt): the consideration, what amount of punishment is necessary to deter from the offence, having nothing to do with the question of justice, in their estimation: while there are others to whom that consideration is all in all; who maintain that it is not just, at least for man, to inflict on a fellow-creature, whatever may be his offences, any amount of suffering beyond the least that will suffice to prevent him from repeating, and others from imitating, his misconduct.

To take another example from a subject already once referred to. In a co-operative industrial association, is it just or not that talent or skill should give a title to superior remuneration? On the negative side of the question it is argued, that whoever does the best he can, deserves equally well, and ought not in justice to be put in a position of inferiority for no fault of his own; that superior abilities have already advantages more than enough, in the admiration they excite, the personal influence they command, and the internal sources of satisfaction attending them, without adding to these a superior share of the world's goods; and that society is bound in justice rather to make compensation to the less favoured, for this unmerited inequality of advantages, than to aggravate it. On the contrary side it is contended, that society receives more from the more efficient labourer; that his services being more useful, society owes him a larger return for them; that a greater share of the joint result is actually his work, and not to allow his claim to it is a kind of robbery; that if he is only to receive as much as others, he can only be justly required to produce as much, and to give a smaller amount of time and exertion, proportioned to his superior efficiency. Who shall decide between these appeals to conflicting principles of justice? Justice has in this case two sides to it, which it is impossible to bring into harmony, and the two disputants have chosen opposite sides;

the one looks to what it is just that the individual should receive, the other to what it is just that the community should give. Each, from his own point of view, is unanswerable; and any choice between them, on grounds of justice, must be perfectly arbitrary. Social utility alone can decide the preference.

How many, again, and how irreconcilable, are the standards of justice to which reference is made in discussing the repartition of taxation. One opinion is, that payment to the State should be in numerical proportion to pecuniary means. Others think that justice dictates what they term graduated taxation; taking a higher percentage from those who have more to spare. In point of natural justice a strong case might be made for disregarding means altogether, and taking the same absolute sum (whenever it could be got) from every one: as the subscribers to a mess, or to a club, all pay the same sum for the same privileges, whether they can all equally afford it or not. Since the protection (it might be said) of law and government is afforded to, and is equally required by all, there is no injustice in making all buy it at the same price. It is reckoned justice, not injustice, that a dealer should charge to all customers the same price for the same article, not a price varying according to their means of payment. This doctrine, as applied to taxation, finds no advocates, because it conflicts so strongly with man's feelings of humanity and of social expediency; but the principle of justice which it invokes is as true and as binding as those which can be appealed to against it. Accordingly it exerts a tacit influence on the line of defence employed for other modes of assessing taxation. People feel obliged to argue that the State does more for the rich than for the poor, as a justification for its taking more from them: though this is in reality not true, for the rich would be far better able to protect themselves, in the absence of law or government, than the poor, and indeed would probably be successful in converting the poor into their slaves. Others, again, so far defer to the same conception of justice, as to maintain that all should pay an equal capitation tax for the protection of their persons (these being of equal value to all), and an unequal tax for the protection of their property, which is unequal. To this others reply, that the all of one man is as valuable to him as the all of another. From these confusions there is no other mode of extrication than the utilitarian.

Is, then, the difference between the Just and the Expedient a merely imaginary distinction? Have mankind been under a delusion in thinking that justice is a more sacred thing than policy, and that the latter ought only to be listened to after the former has been satisfied? By no means. The exposition we have given of the nature and origin of the sentiment, recognises a real distinction; and no one of those who profess the most sublime contempt for the consequences of actions as an element in their morality, attaches more importance to the distinction than I do. While I dispute the pretensions of any theory which sets up an imaginary standard of justice not grounded on utility, I account the justice which is grounded on utility to be the chief part, and incomparably the most sacred and binding part, of all morality. Justice is a name for certain classes of moral rules, which concern the essentials of human well-being more nearly, and are therefore of more absolute obligation, than any other rules for the guidance of life; and the notion which we have found to be of the essence of the idea of justice, that of a right residing in an individual, implies and testifies to this more binding obligation.

The moral rules which forbid mankind to hurt one another (in which we must never forget to include wrongful interference with each other's freedom) are more vital to human well-being than any maxims, however important, which only point out the best mode of managing some department of human affairs. They have also the peculiarity, that they are the main element in determining the whole of the social feelings of mankind. It is their observance which alone preserves peace among human beings: if obedience to them were not the rule, and disobedience the exception, every one would see in every one else an enemy, against whom he must be perpetually guarding himself. What is hardly less important, these are the precepts which mankind have the strongest and the most direct inducements for impressing upon one another. By merely giving to each other prudential instruction or exhortation, they may gain, or think they gain, nothing: in inculcating on each other the duty of positive beneficence they have an unmistakable interest, but far less in degree: a person may possibly not need the benefits of others; but he always needs that they should not do him hurt. Thus the moralities which protect every individual from being harmed by others, either directly or by being hindered in his freedom of pursuing his own good, are at once those which he himself has most at heart, and those which he has the strongest interest in publishing and enforcing by word and deed. It is by a person's observance of these that his fitness to exist as one of the fellowship of human beings is tested and decided; for on that depends his being a nuisance or not to those with whom he is in contact. Now it is these moralities primarily which compose the obligations of justice. The most marked cases of injustice, and those which give the tone to the feeling of repugnance which characterises the sentiment, are acts of wrongful aggression, or wrongful exercise of power over some one; the next are those which consist in wrongfully withholding from him something which is his due; in both cases, inflicting on him a positive hurt, either in the form of direct suffering, or of the privation of some good which he had reasonable ground, either of a physical or of a social kind, for counting upon.

The same powerful motives which command the observance of these primary moralities, enjoin the punishment of those who violate them; and as the impulses of self-defence, of defence of others, and of vengeance, are all called forth against such persons, retribution, or evil for evil, becomes closely connected with the sentiment of justice, and is universally included in the idea. Good for good is also one of the dictates of justice; and this, though its social utility is evident, and though it carries with it a natural human feeling, has not at first sight that obvious connection with hurt or injury, which, existing in the most elementary cases of just and unjust, is the source of the characteristic intensity of the sentiment. But the connection, though less obvious, is not less real. He who accepts benefits, and denies a return of them when needed, inflicts a real hurt, by disappointing one of the most natural and reasonable of expectations, and one which he must at least tacitly have encouraged, otherwise the benefits would seldom have been conferred. The important rank, among human evils and wrongs, of the disappointment of expectation, is shown in the fact that it constitutes the principal criminality of two such highly immoral acts as a breach of friendship and a breach of promise. Few hurts which human beings can sustain are greater, and none wound more, than when that on which they habitually and with full assurance relied, fails them in the hour of need; and few wrongs are greater than this mere withholding of good; none excite more resentment, either in the person suffering, or in a sympathising spectator. The principle, therefore, of giving to each what they deserve, that is, good for good as well as evil for evil, is not only included within the idea of Justice as we have defined it, but is a proper object of that intensity of sentiment, which places the Just, in human estimation, above the simply Expedient.

Most of the maxims of justice current in the world, and commonly appealed to in its transactions, are simply instrumental to carrying into effect the principles of justice which we have now spoken of. That a person is only responsible for what he has done voluntarily, or could voluntarily have avoided; that it is unjust to condemn any person unheard; that the punishment ought to be proportioned to the offence, and the like, are maxims intended to prevent the just principle of evil for evil from being perverted to the infliction of evil without that justification. The greater part of these common maxims have come into use from the practice of courts of justice, which have been naturally led to a more complete recognition and elaboration than was likely to suggest itself to others, of the rules necessary to enable them to fulfil their double function, of inflicting punishment when due, and of awarding to each person his right.

That first of judicial virtues, impartiality, is an obligation of justice, partly for the reason last mentioned; as being a necessary condition of the fulfilment of the other obligations of justice. But this is not the only source of the exalted rank, among human obligations, of those maxims of equality and impartiality, which, both in popular estimation and in that of the most enlightened, are included among the precepts of justice. In one point of view, they may be considered as corollaries from the principles already laid down. If it is a duty to do to each according to his deserts, returning good for good as well as repressing evil by evil, it necessarily follows that we should treat all equally well (when no higher duty forbids) who have deserved equally well of *us,* and that society should treat all equally well who have deserved equally well of *it,* that is, who have deserved equally well absolutely. This is the highest abstract standard of social and distributive justice; towards which all institutions, and the efforts of all virtuous citizens, should be made in the utmost possible degree to converge. But this great moral duty rests upon a still deeper foundation, being a direct emanation from the first principle of morals, and not a mere logical corollary from secondary or derivative doctrines. It is involved in the very meaning of Utility, or the Greatest Happiness Principle. That principle is a mere form of words without rational signification, unless one person's happiness, supposed equal in degree (with the proper allowance made for kind), is counted for exactly as much as another's. Those conditions being supplied, Bentham's dictum, "everybody to count for one, nobody for more than one," might be written under the principle of utility as an explanatory commentary.* The

*This implication, in the first principle of the utilitarian scheme, of perfect impartiality between persons, is regarded by Mr. Herbert Spencer (in his *Social Statics*) as a disproof of the pretensions of utility to be a sufficient guide to right, since (he says) the principle of utility presupposes the anterior principle that everybody has an equal right to happiness. It may be more correctly described as supposing that equal amounts of happiness are equally desirable whether felt by the same or by different persons. This, however, is not a *pre-*supposition; not a premise needful to support the principle of utility, but the very principle itself; for what is the principle of utility, if it be not that "happiness" and "desirable" are synonymous terms? If there Is any anterior principle Implied, it can be no other than this, that the truths of arithmetic are applicable to the valuation of happiness, as of all other measurable quantities.

(Mr. Herbert Spencer in a private communication on the subject of the preceding note, objects to being considered an opponent of utilitarianism, and states that he regards happiness as the ultimate end of morality; but deems that end only partially attainable by empirical generalisations from the observed results of conduct, and completely attainable only by deducing, from the laws of life and the conditions of existence, what kinds of action necessarily tend to produce happiness, and what kinds to produce unhappiness. With the exception of the word "necessarily," I have no dissent to express from this doctrine; and (omitting that word) I am not aware that any modern advocate of utilitarianism is of a different opinion. Bentham, certainly, to whom in the *Social Statics* Mr. Spencer particularly referred, is, least of all writers, chargeable with unwillingness to deduce the effect of actions on happiness from the laws of human nature and the universal conditions of human life. The common charge against him is of relying too exclusively upon such deductions, and declining altogether to be bound by the generalisations from specific experience which Mr. Spencer thinks that utilitarians generally confine themselves to. My own opinion (and, as I collect, Mr. Spencer's) is, that in ethics, as in all other branches of scientific study, the consilience of the results of both these processes, each corroborating and verifying the other, is requisite to give to any general proposition the kind and degree of evidence which constitutes scientific proof.)

equal claim of everybody to happiness in the estimation of the moralist and of the legislator, involves an equal claim to all the means of happiness, except in so far as the inevitable conditions of human life, and the general interest, in which that of every individual is included, set limits to the maxim; and those limits ought to be strictly construed. As every other maxim of justice, so this is by no means applied or held applicable universally; on the contrary, as I have already remarked, it bends to every person's ideas of social expediency. But in whatever case it is deemed applicable at all, it is held to be the dictate of justice. All persons are deemed to have a *right* to equality of treatment, except when some recognised social expediency requires the reverse. And hence all social inequalities which have ceased to be considered expedient, assume the character not of simple inexpediency, but of injustice, and appear so tyrannical, that people are apt to wonder how they ever could have been tolerated; forgetful that they themselves perhaps tolerate other inequalities under an equally mistaken notion of expediency, the correction of which would make that which they approve seem quite as monstrous as what they have at last learnt to condemn. The entire history of social improvement has been a series of transitions, by which one custom or institution after another, from being a supposed primary necessity of social existence, has passed into the rank of a universally stigmatised injustice and tyranny. So it has been with the distinctions of slaves and freemen, nobles and serfs, patricians and plebeians; and so it will be, and in part already is, with the aristocracies of colour, race, and sex.

It appears from what has been said, that justice is a name for certain moral requirements, which, regarded collectively, stand higher in the scale of social utility, and are therefore of more paramount obligation, than any others; though particular cases may occur in which some other social duty is so important, as to overrule any one of the general maxims of justice. Thus, to save a life, it may not only be allowable, but a duty, to steal, or take by force, the necessary food or medicine, or to kidnap, and compel to officiate, the only qualified medical practitioner. In such cases, as we do not call anything justice which is not a virtue, we usually say, not that justice must give way to some other moral principle, but that what is just in ordinary cases is, by reason of that other principle, not just in the particular case. By this useful accommodation of language, the character of indefeasibility attributed to justice is kept up, and we are saved from the necessity of maintaining that there can be laudable injustice.

The considerations which have now been adduced resolve, I conceive, the only real difficulty in the utilitarian theory of morals. It has always been evident that all cases of justice are also cases of expediency: the difference is in the peculiar sentiment which attaches to the former, as contradistinguished from the latter. If this characteristic sentiment has been sufficiently accounted for; if there is no necessity to assume for it any peculiarity of origin; if it is simply the natural feeling of resentment, moralised by being made coextensive with the demands of social good; and if this feeling not only does but ought to exist in all the classes of cases to which the idea of justice corresponds; that idea no longer presents itself as a stumbling-block to the utilitarian ethics. Justice remains the appropriate name for certain social utilities which are vastly more important, and therefore more absolute and imperative, than any others are as a class (though not more so than others may be in particular cases); and which, therefore, ought to be, as well as naturally are, guarded by a sentiment not only different in degree, but also in kind; distinguished from the milder feeling which attaches to the mere idea of promoting human pleasure or convenience, at once by the more definite nature of its commands, and by the sterner character of its sanctions.

ON LIBERTY (in part)

CHAPTER 3: OF INDIVIDUALITY, AS ONE
OF THE ELEMENTS OF WELL-BEING

Such being the reasons which make it imperative that human beings should be free to form opinions and to express their opinions without reserve; and such the baneful consequences to the intellectual, and through that to the moral nature of man, unless this liberty is either conceded, or asserted in spite of prohibition; let us next examine whether the same reasons do not require that men should be free to act upon their opinions—to carry these out in their lives, without hindrance, either physical or moral, from their fellow men, so long as it is at their own risk and peril. This last proviso is of course indispensable. No one pretends that actions should be as free as opinions. On the contrary, even opinions lose their immunity, when the circumstances in which they are expressed are such as to constitute their expression a positive instigation to some mischievous act. An opinion that corn dealers are starvers of the poor, or that private property is robbery, ought to be unmolested when simply circulated through the press, but may justly incur punishment when delivered orally to an excited mob assembled before the house of a corn dealer, or when handed about among the same mob in the form of a placard. Acts, of whatever kind, which, without justifiable cause, do harm to others, may be, and in the more important cases absolutely require to be, controlled by the unfavourable sentiments, and, when needful, by the active interference of mankind. The liberty of the individual must be thus far limited; he must not make himself a nuisance to other people. But if he refrains from molesting others in what concerns them, and merely acts according to his own inclination and judgement in things which concern himself, the same reasons which show that opinion should be free, prove also that he should be allowed without molestation, to carry his opinions into practice at his own cost. That mankind are not infallible that their truths, for the most part, are only half-truths; that unity of opinion, unless resulting from the fullest and freest comparison of opposite opinions is not desirable, and diversity not an evil, but a good, until mankind are much more capable than at present of recognizing all sides of the truth, are principles applicable to men's modes of action, not less than to their opinions. As it is useful that while mankind are imperfect there should be different opinions, so is it that there should be different experiments of living; that free scope should be given to varieties of character short of injury to others; and that the worth of different modes of life should be proved practically, when any one thinks fit to try them. It is desirable, in short, that in things which do not primarily concern others, individuality should assert itself. Where, not the person's own character, but the traditions or customs of other people are the rule of conduct, there is wanting one of the principal ingredients of human happiness, and quite the chief ingredient of individual and social progress.

In maintaining this principle, the greatest difficulty to be encountered does not lie in the appreciation of means towards an acknowledged end, but in the indifference of persons in general to the end itself. If it were felt that the free development of individuality is one of the leading essentials of well-being; that it is not only a co-ordinate element with all that is designated by the terms civilization, instruction, education culture, but is itself a necessary part and condition of all those things; there would be no danger that liberty should be undervalued, and the adjustment of the boundaries between it and social control would present no extraordinary difficulty. But the evil is, that individual spontaneity is hardly recognized by the common modes of thinking, as having any intrinsic worth, or deserving any regard on its own account. The majority being satisfied with the ways of mankind as they now are (for it is they who make them what they are), cannot comprehend why those ways should not be good enough for everybody; and what is more, spontaneity forms no part of the ideal of the majority of moral and social reformers, but is rather looked on with jealousy as a troublesome and perhaps rebellious obstruction to the general acceptance of what these reformers, in their own judgement, think would be best for mankind. Few persons, out of Germany, even comprehend the meaning of the doctrine which Wilhelm von Humboldt, so eminent both as a *savant* and as a politician, made the text of a treatise—that "the end of man, or that which is prescribed by the eternal or immutable dictates of reason, and not suggested by vague and transient desires, is the highest and most harmonious development of his powers to a complete and consistent whole"; that, therefore, the object "towards which every human being must ceaselessly direct his efforts, and on which especially those who design to influence their fellow men must ever keep their eyes, is the individuality of power and development"; that for this there are two requisites, "freedom, and variety of situations," and that from the union of these arise "individual vigour and manifold diversity," which combine themselves in "originality."*

Little, however, as people are accustomed to a doctrine like that of Von Humboldt, and surprising as it may be to them to find so high a value attached to individuality, the question, one must nevertheless think, can only be one of degree. No one's idea of excellence in conduct is that people should do absolutely nothing but copy one another. No one would assert that people ought not to put into their mode of life, and into the conduct of their concerns, any impress whatever of their own judgement, or of their own individual character. On the other hand it would be absurd to pretend that people ought to live as if nothing whatever had been known in the world before they came into it; as if experience had as yet done nothing towards showing that one mode of existence, or of conduct, is preferable to another. Nobody denies that people should be so taught and trained in youth, as to know and benefit by the ascertained results of human experience. But it is the privilege and proper condition of a human being, arrived at the maturity of his faculties, to use and interpret experience in his own way. It is for him to find out what part of recorded experience is properly applicable to his own circumstances and character. The traditions and customs of other people are, to a certain extent, evidence of what their experience has taught *them;* presumptive evidence, and as such, have a claim to his deference: but, in the first place, their experience may be too narrow; or they may not have interpreted it rightly. Secondly, their interpretation of experience may be correct, but unsuitable to him. Customs are made for customary circumstances, and customary characters; and his circumstances or his character may be uncustomary. Thirdly, though the customs be both good as customs, and suitable to him, yet to conform to custom, merely *as* custom, does not educate or develop in him any of the qualities which are the distinctive endowment of a human being. The human faculties of perception, judgement, discriminative feeling, mental activity, and even moral preference, are exercised only in making a choice. He who does anything because it is the custom, makes no choice. He gains no practice either in discerning or in desiring what is best. The mental and moral, like the muscular powers, are improved only by being used.

*The Sphere and Duties of Government, from the German of Baron Wilhelm von Humboldt, pp. 11–13.

The faculties are called into no exercise by doing a thing merely because others do it, no more than by believing a thing only because others believe it. If the grounds of an opinion are not conclusive to the person's own reason, his reason cannot be strengthened, but is likely to be weakened, by his adopting it: and if the inducements to an act are not such as are consentaneous to his own feelings and character (where affection, or the rights of others, are not concerned) it is so much done towards rendering his feelings and character inert and torpid, instead of active and energetic.

He who lets the world, or his own portion of it, choose his plan of life for him, has no need of any other faculty than the ape-like one of imitation. He who chooses his plan for himself, employs all his faculties. He must use observation to see, reasoning and judgement to foresee, activity to gather materials for decision, discrimination to decide, and when he has decided, firmness and self-control to hold to his deliberate decision. And these qualities he requires and exercises exactly in proportion as the part of his conduct which he determines according to his own judgement and feelings is a large one. It is possible that he might be guided in some good path, and kept out of harm's way, without any of these things. But what will be his comparative worth as a human being? It really is of importance, not only what men do, but also what manner of men they are that do it. Among the works of man, which human life is rightly employed in perfecting and beautifying, the first in importance surely is man himself. Supposing it were possible to get houses built, corn grown, battles fought, causes tried, and even churches erected and prayers said, by machinery—by automatons in human form—it would be a considerable loss to exchange for these automatons even the men and women who at present inhabit the more civilized parts of the world, and who assuredly are but starved specimens of what nature can and will produce. Human nature is not a machine to be built after a model, and set to do exactly the work prescribed for it, but a tree, which requires to grow and develop itself on all sides, according to the tendency of the inward forces which make it a living thing.

It will probably be conceded that it is desirable people should exercise their understandings, and that an intelligent following of custom, or even occasionally an intelligent deviation from custom, is better than a blind and simply mechanical adhesion to it. To a certain extent it is admitted, that our understanding should be our own: but there is not the same willingness to admit that our desires and impulses should be our own likewise; or that to possess impulses of our own, and of any strength, is anything but a peril and a snare. Yet desires and impulses are as much a part of a perfect human being, as beliefs and restraints: and strong impulses are only perilous when not properly balanced; when one set of aims and inclinations is developed into strength, while others, which ought to coexist with them, remain weak and inactive. It is not because men's desires are strong that they act ill; it is because their consciences are weak. There is no natural connexion between strong impulses and a weak conscience. The natural connexion is the other way. To say that one person's desires and feelings are stronger and more various than those of another, is merely to say that he has more of the raw material of human nature, and is therefore capable, perhaps of more evil, but certainly of more good. Strong impulses are but another name for energy. Energy may be turned to bad uses; but more good may always be made of an energetic nature, than of an indolent and impassive one. Those who have most natural feeling, are always those whose cultivated feelings may be made the strongest. The same strong susceptibilities which make the personal impulses vivid and powerful, are also the source from whence are generated the most passionate love of virtue, and the sternest self-control. It is through the cultivation of these, that society both does its duty and protects its interests: not by rejecting the stuff of which heroes are made, because it knows not how to make them. A person whose desires and impulses are his own—are the expression of his own nature, as it has been developed and modified by his own culture—is said to have a character. One whose desires and impulses are not his own, has no character, no more than a steam engine has a character. If, in addition to being his own, his impulses are strong, and are under the government of a strong will, he has an energetic character. Whoever thinks that individuality of desires and impulses should not be encouraged to unfold itself, must maintain that society has no need of strong natures—is not the better for containing many persons who have much character—and that a high general average of energy is not desirable.

In some early states of society, these forces might be, and were, too much ahead of the power which society then possessed of disciplining and controlling them. There has been a time when the element of spontaneity and individuality was in excess, and the social principle had a hard struggle with it. The difficulty then was to induce men of strong bodies or minds to pay obedience to any rules which required them to control their impulses. To overcome this difficulty, law and discipline, like the Popes struggling against the Emperors, asserted a power over the whole man, claiming to control all his life in order to control his character—which society had not found any other sufficient means of binding. But society has now fairly got the better of individuality; and the danger which threatens human nature is not the excess, but the deficiency, of personal impulses and preferences. Things are vastly changed, since the passions of those who were strong by station or by personal endowment were in a state of habitual rebellion against laws and ordinances, and required to be rigorously chained up to enable the persons within their reach to enjoy any particle of security. In our times, from the highest class of society down to the lowest, every one lives as under the eye of a hostile and dreaded censorship. Not only in what concerns others, but in what concerns only themselves, the individual or the family do not ask themselves—what do I prefer? or, what would suit my character and disposition? or, what would allow the best and highest in me to have fair play, and enable it to grow and thrive? They ask themselves, what is suitable to my position? what is usually done by persons of my station and pecuniary circumstances? or (worse still) what is usually done by persons of a station and circumstances superior to mine? I do not mean that they choose what is customary, in preference to what suits their own inclination. It does not occur to them to have any inclination, except for what is customary. Thus the mind itself is bowed to the yoke: even in what people do for pleasure, conformity is the first thing thought of; they like in crowds, they exercise choice only among things commonly done: peculiarity of taste, eccentricity of conduct, are shunned equally with crimes: until by dint of not following their own nature, they have no nature to follow: their human capacities are withered and starved: they become incapable of any strong wishes or native pleasures, and are generally without either opinions or feelings of home growth, or properly their own. Now is this, or is it not, the desirable condition of human nature?

It is so, on the Calvinistic theory. According to that, the one great offence of man is self-will. All the good of which humanity is capable, is comprised in obedience. You have no choice; thus you must do, and no otherwise: "Whatever is not a duty, is a sin." Human nature being radically corrupt, there is no redemption for any one until human nature is killed within him. To one holding this theory of life, crushing out any of the human faculties, capacities, and susceptibilities, is no evil: man needs no capacity, but that of surrendering himself to the will of God: and if he uses any of his faculties for any other purpose but to do that supposed will more effectually, he is better without them. This is the theory of Calvinism; and it is held, in a mitigated form, by many who do not consider themselves Calvinists; the mitigation consisting in giving a less ascetic interpretation to the alleged will of God, asserting it to be his will that mankind should gratify some of their inclinations; of course not in the manner they themselves prefer, but in the way of obedience, that is, in a way prescribed to them by authority, and, therefore by the necessary conditions of the case, the same for all.

In some such insidious form there is at present a strong tendency to this narrow theory of life, and to the pinched and hidebound type of human character which it patronizes. Many persons, no doubt, sincerely think that human beings thus cramped and dwarfed, are as their Maker designed them to be, just as many have thought that trees are a much finer thing when clipped into pollards, or cut out into figures of animals, than as nature made them. But if it be any part of religion to believe that man was made by a good Being, it is more consistent with that faith to believe that this Being gave all human faculties that they might be cultivated and unfolded, not rooted out and consumed, and that he takes delight in every nearer approach made by his creatures to the ideal conception embodied in them, every increase in any of their capabilities of comprehension, of action, or of enjoyment. There is a different type of human excellence from the Calvinistic, a conception of humanity as having its nature bestowed on it for other purposes than merely to be abnegated. "Pagan self-assertion" is one of the elements of human worth, as well as "Christian self-denial."* There is a Greek ideal of self-development, which the Platonic and Christian ideal of self-government blends with, but does not supersede. It may be better to be a John Knox than an Alcibiades, but it is better to be a Pericles** than either, nor would a Pericles, if we had one in these days, be without anything good which belonged to John Knox.

It is not by wearing down into uniformity all that is individual in themselves but by cultivating it and calling it forth, within the limits imposed by the rights and interests of others, that human beings become a noble and beautiful object of contemplation; and as the works partake the character of those who do them, by the same process human life also becomes rich, diversified, and animating, furnishing more abundant aliment [sustenance] to high thoughts and elevating feelings, and strengthening the tie which binds every individual to the race, by making the race infinitely better worth belonging to. In proportion to the development of his individuality, each person becomes more valuable to himself, and is therefore capable of being more valuable to others. There is a greater fullness of life about his own existence, and when there is more life in the units there is more in the mass which is composed of them. As much compression as is necessary to prevent the stronger specimens of human nature from encroaching on the rights of others, cannot be dispensed with; but for this there is ample compensation even in the point of view of human development. The means of development which the individual loses by being prevented from gratifying his inclinations to the injury of others are chiefly obtained at the expense of the development of other people. And even to himself there is a full equivalent in the better development of the social part of his nature, rendered possible by the restraint put upon the selfish part. To be held to rigid rules of justice for the sake of others develops the feelings and capacities which have the good of others for their object. But to be restrained in things not affecting their good, by their mere displeasure, develops nothing valuable, except such force of character as may unfold itself in resisting the restraint. If acquiesced in, it dulls and blunts the whole nature. To give any fair play to the nature of each, it is essential that different persons

*Sterling's *Essays*. [John Sterling (1806–1844) was a British writer.]
**[John Knox (1505–1572) was a leader of the Reformation and the founder of the Scottish Presbyterian Church; Alcibiades (ca. 450–404 B.C.) was a disreputable Athenian general who symbolized for many the decline of Athens; Pericles (ca. 495–429 B.C.) was a famous and beloved Athenian statesman.]

should be allowed to lead different lives. In proportion as this latitude has been exercised in any age, has that age been noteworthy to posterity. Even despotism does not produce its worst effects, so long as individuality exists under it; and whatever crushes individuality is despotism, by whatever name it may be called, and whether it professes to be enforcing the will of God or the injunctions of men.

Having said that individuality is the same thing with development, and that it is only the cultivation of individuality which produces, or can produce, well-developed human beings, I might here close the argument: for what more or better can be said of any condition of human affairs, than that it brings human beings themselves nearer to the best thing they can be? Or what worse can be said of any obstruction to good, than that it prevents this? Doubtless, however, these considerations will not suffice to convince those who most need convincing; and it is necessary further to show that these developed human beings are of some use to the undeveloped—to point out to those who do not desire liberty, and would not avail themselves of it, that they may be in some intelligible manner rewarded for allowing other people to make use of it without hindrance.

In the first place, then, I would suggest that they might possibly learn something from them. It will not be denied by anybody, that originality is a valuable element in human affairs. There is always need of persons not only to discover new truths, and point out when what were once truths are true no longer, but also to commence new practices, and set the example of more enlightened conduct, and better taste and sense in human life. This cannot well be gainsaid by anybody who does not believe that the world has already attained perfection in all its ways and practices. It is true that this benefit is not capable of being rendered by everybody alike: there are but few persons, in comparison with the whole of mankind, whose experiments, if adopted by others, would be likely to be any improvement on established practice. But these few are the salt of the earth, without them human life would become a stagnant pool. Not only is it they who introduce good things which did not before exist; it is they who keep the life in those which already existed. If there were nothing new to be done would human intellect cease to be necessary? Would it be a reason why those who do the old things should forget why they are done, and do them like cattle, not like human beings? There is only too great a tendency in the best beliefs and practices to degenerate into the mechanical; and unless there were a succession of persons whose ever-recurring originality prevents the grounds of those beliefs and practices from becoming merely traditional, such dead matter would not resist the smallest shock from anything really alive, and there would be no reason why civilization should not die out, as in the Byzantine Empire. Persons of genius, it is true, are, and are always likely to be, a small minority; but in order to have them, it is necessary to preserve the soil in which they grow. Genius can only breathe freely in an *atmosphere* of freedom. Persons of genius are, *ex vi termini* [by definition], more individual than any other people—less capable, consequently, of fitting themselves, without hurtful compression, into any of the small number of moulds which society provides in order to save its members the trouble of forming their own character. If from timidity they consent to be forced into one of these moulds, and to let all that part of themselves which cannot expand under the pressure remain unexpanded, society will be little the better for their genius. If they are of a strong character, and break their fetters, they become a mark for the society which has not succeeded in reducing them to commonplace, to point at with solemn warning as "wild," "erratic," and the like, much as if one should complain of the Niagara river for not flowing smoothly between its banks like a Dutch canal.

I insist thus emphatically on the importance of genius, and the necessity of allowing it to unfold itself freely both in thought and in practice, being well aware that no one will deny the position in theory, but knowing also that almost every one, in reality, is totally indifferent to it. People think genius a fine thing if it enables a man to write an exciting poem, or paint a picture. But in its true sense, that of originality in thought and action, though no one says that it is not a thing to be admired, nearly all, at heart, think that they can do very well without it. Unhappily this is too natural to be wondered at. Originality is the one thing which unoriginal minds cannot feel the use of. They cannot see what it is to do for them: how should they? If they could see what it would do for them, it would not be originality. The first service which originality has to render them, is that of opening their eyes: which being once fully done, they would have a chance of being themselves original. Meanwhile, recollecting that nothing was ever yet done which some one was not the first to do, and that all good things which exist are the fruits of originality let them be modest enough to believe that there is something still left for it to accomplish, and assure themselves that they are more in need of originality the less they are conscious of the want.

In sober truth, whatever homage may be professed, or even paid, to real or supposed mental superiority, the general tendency of things throughout the world is to render mediocrity the ascendant power among mankind. In ancient history, in the middle ages, and in a diminishing degree through the long transition from feudality to the present time, the individual was a power in himself; and if he had either great talents or a high social position, he was a considerable power. At present individuals are lost in the crowd. In politics it is almost a triviality to say that public opinion now rules the world. The only power deserving the name is that of masses, and of governments while they make themselves the organ of the tendencies and instincts of masses. This is as true in the moral and social relations of private life as in public transactions. Those whose opinions go by the name of public opinion, are not always the same sort of public: in America they are the whole white population; in England, chiefly the middle class. But they are always a mass, that is to say, collective mediocrity. And what is a still greater novelty, the mass do not now take their opinions from dignitaries in Church or State, from ostensible leaders, or from books. Their thinking is done for them by men much like themselves, addressing them or speaking in their name, on the spur of the moment, through the newspapers. I am not complaining of all this. I do not assert that anything better is compatible, as a general rule, with the present low state of the human mind. But that does not hinder the government of mediocrity from being mediocre government. No government by a democracy or a numerous aristocracy, either in its political acts or in the opinions, qualities, and tone of mind which it fosters, ever did or could rise above mediocrity, except in so far as the sovereign Many have let themselves be guided (which in their best times they always have done) by the counsels and influence of a more highly gifted and instructed *One* or *Few*. The initiation of all wise or noble things, comes and must come from individuals; generally at first from some one individual. The honour and glory of the average man is that he is capable of following that initiative; that he can respond internally to wise and noble things, and be led to them with his eyes open. I am not countenancing the sort of "hero-worship" which applauds the strong man of genius for forcibly seizing on the government of the world and making it do his bidding in spite of itself. All he can claim is freedom to point out the way. The power of compelling others into it is not only inconsistent with the freedom and development of all the rest, but corrupting to the strong man himself. It does seem, however, that when the opinions of masses of merely average men are everywhere become or becoming the dominant power, the counterpoise and corrective to that tendency would be the more and more pronounced individuality of those who stand on the higher eminences of thought. It is in these circumstances most especially, that exceptional individuals, instead of being deterred, should be encouraged in acting differently from the mass. In other times there was no advantage in their doing so unless they acted not only differently, but better. In this age, the mere example of nonconformity, the mere refusal to bend the knee to custom, is itself a service. Precisely because the tyranny of opinion is such as to make eccentricity a reproach, it is desirable, in order to break through that tyranny, that people should be eccentric. Eccentricity has always abounded when and where strength of character has abounded; and the amount of eccentricity in a society has generally been proportional to the amount of genius, mental vigour; and moral courage which it contained. That so few now dare to be eccentric marks the chief danger of the time.

I have said that it is important to give the freest scope possible to uncustomary things, in order that it may in time appear which of these are fit to be converted into customs. But independence of action, and disregard of custom, are not solely deserving of encouragement for the chance they afford that better modes of action, and customs more worthy of general adoption, may be struck out; nor is it only persons of decided mental superiority who have a just claim to carry on their lives in their own way. There is no reason that all human existence should be constructed on some one or some small number of patterns. If a person possesses any tolerable amount of common sense and experience, his own mode of laying out his existence is the best, not because it is the best in itself, but because it is his own mode. Human beings are not like sheep; and even sheep are not undistinguishably alike. A man cannot get a coat or a pair of boots to fit him, unless they are either made to his measure or he has a whole warehouseful to choose from: and is it easier to fit him with a life than with a coat, or are human beings more like one another in their whole physical and spiritual conformation than in the shape of their feet? If it were only that people have diversities of taste, that is reason enough for not attempting to shape them all after one model. But different persons also require different conditions for their spiritual development; and can no more exist healthily in the same moral, than all the variety of plants can in the same physical, atmosphere and climate. The same things which are helps to one person towards the cultivation of his higher nature are hindrances to another. The same mode of life is a healthy excitement to one, keeping all his faculties of action and enjoyment in their best order, while to another it is a distracting burden, which suspends or crushes all internal life. Such are the differences among human beings in their sources of pleasure, their susceptibilities of pain, and the operation on them of different physical and moral agencies, that unless there is a corresponding diversity in their modes of life, they neither obtain their fair share of happiness, nor grow up to the mental, moral, and aesthetic stature of which their nature is capable. Why then should tolerance, as far as the public sentiment is concerned, extend only to tastes and modes of life which extort acquiescence by the multitude of their adherents? Nowhere (except in some monastic institutions) is diversity of taste entirely unrecognized; a person may, without blame, either like or dislike rowing, or smoking, or music, or athletic exercises, or chess, or cards, or study, because both those who like each of these things, and those who dislike them, are too numerous to be put down. But the man, and still more the woman, who can be accused either of doing "what nobody does," or of not doing "what everybody does," is the subject of as much depreciatory remark as if he or she had committed some grave moral delinquency. Persons require to possess a title, or some other badge of rank, or of the consideration of people of rank, to be able to indulge somewhat in the luxury of doing as they like without detriment to their estimation. To indulge somewhat, I repeat: for whoever allow themselves much of that indulgence, incur the risk of something worse than disparaging speeches—they are in peril of a commission *de lunatico,* and of having their property taken from them and given to their relations.*

There is one characteristic of the present direction of public opinion, peculiarly calculated to make it intolerant of any marked demonstration of individuality. The general average of mankind are not only moderate in intellect, but also moderate in inclinations: they have no tastes or wishes strong enough to incline them to do anything unusual, and they consequently do not understand those who have, and class all such with the wild and intemperate whom they are accustomed to look down upon. Now in addition to this fact which is general, we have only to suppose that a strong movement has set in towards the improvement of morals, and it is evident what we have to expect. In these days such a movement has set in; much has actually been effected in the way of increased regularity of conduct, and discouragement of excesses; and there is a philanthropic spirit abroad, for the exercise of which there is no more inviting field than the moral and prudential improvement of our fellow creatures. These tendencies of the times cause the public to be more disposed than at most former periods to prescribe general rules of conduct, and endeavour to make every one conform to the approved standard. And that standard, express or tacit, is to desire nothing strongly. Its ideal of character is to be without any marked character; to maim by compression, like a Chinese lady's foot, every part of human nature which stands out prominently, and tends to make the person markedly dissimilar in outline to commonplace humanity.

As is usually the case with ideals which exclude one-half of what is desirable, the present standard of approbation produces only an inferior imitation of the other half. Instead of great energies guided by vigorous reason, and strong feelings strongly controlled by a conscientious will, its result is weak feelings and weak energies, which therefore can be kept in outward conformity to rule without any strength either of will or of reason. Already energetic characters on any large scale are becoming merely traditional. There is now scarcely any outlet for energy in this country except business. The energy expended in this may still be regarded as considerable. What little is left from that employment is expended on some hobby; which may be a useful, even a philanthropic hobby, but is always some one thing, and generally a thing of small dimensions. The greatness of England is now all collective: individually small, we only appear capable of anything great by our habit of combining; and with this our moral and

---

*There is something both contemptible and frightful in the sort of evidence on which, of late years, any person can be judicially declared unfit for the management of his affairs, and after his death, his disposal of his property can be set aside, if there is enough of it to pay the expenses of litigation—which are charged on the property itself. All the minute details of his daily life are pried into, and whatever is found which, seen through the medium of the perceiving and describing faculties of the lowest of the low, bears an appearance unlike absolute commonplace, is laid before the jury as evidence of insanity, and often with success; the jurors being little, if at all, less vulgar and ignorant that the witnesses; while the judges, with that extraordinary want of knowledge of human nature and life which continually astonishes us in English lawyers, often help to mislead them. These trials speak volumes as to the state of feeling and opinion among the vulgar with regard to human liberty. So far from setting any value on individuality—so far from respecting the right of each individual to act, in things indifferent, as seems good to his own judgement and inclinations, judges and juries cannot even conceive that a person in a state of sanity can desire such freedom. In former days when it was proposed to burn atheists, charitable people used to suggest putting them in a madhouse instead: it would be nothing surprising nowadays were we to see this done and the doers applauding themselves, because, instead of persecuting for religion, they had adopted so humane and Christian a mode of treating these unfortunates, not without a silent satisfaction at their having thereby obtained their deserts.

religious philanthropists are perfectly contented. But it was men of another stamp than this that made England what it has been; and men of another stamp will be needed to prevent its decline.

The despotism of custom is everywhere the standing hindrance to human advancement, being in unceasing antagonism to that disposition to aim at something better than customary, which is called, according to circumstances, the spirit of liberty, or that of progress or improvement. The spirit of improvement is not always a spirit of liberty, for it may aim at forcing improvements on an unwilling people, and the spirit of liberty, in so far as it resists such attempts, may ally itself locally and temporarily with the opponents of improvement, but the only unfailing and permanent source of improvement is liberty, since by it there are as many possible independent centres of improvement as there are individuals. The progressive principle, however, in either shape, whether as the love of liberty or of improvement, is antagonistic to the sway of Custom, involving at least emancipation from that yoke; and the contest between the two constitutes the chief interest of the history of mankind. The greater part of the world has, properly speaking, no history, because the despotism of Custom is complete. This is the case over the whole East. Custom is there, in all things, the final appeal; justice and right mean conformity to custom; the argument of custom no one, unless some tyrant intoxicated with power, thinks of resisting. And we see the result. Those nations must once have had originality; they did not start out of the ground populous, lettered, and versed in many of the arts of life, they made themselves all this, and were then the greatest and most powerful nations of the world. What are they now? The subjects or dependants of tribes whose forefathers wandered in the forests when theirs had magnificent palaces and gorgeous temples, but over whom custom exercised only a divided rule with liberty and progress. A people, it appears, may be progressive for a certain length of time, and then stop: when does it stop? When it ceases to possess individuality. If a similar change should befall the nations of Europe, it will not be in exactly the same shape: the despotism of custom with which these nations are threatened is not precisely stationariness. It proscribes singularity, but it does not preclude change, provided all change together. We have discarded the fixed costumes of our forefathers, every one must still dress like other people, but the fashion may change once or twice a year. We thus take care that when there is change it shall be for change's sake, and not from any idea of beauty or convenience; for the same idea of beauty or convenience would not strike all the world at the same moment, and be simultaneously thrown aside by all at another moment. But we are progressive as well as changeable: we continually make new inventions in mechanical things, and keep them until they are again superseded by better; we are eager for improvement in politics, in education, even in morals, though in this last our idea of improvement chiefly consists in persuading or forcing other people to be as good as ourselves. It is not progress that we object to; on the contrary, we flatter ourselves that we are the most progressive people who ever lived. It is individuality that we war against: we should think we had done wonders if we had made ourselves all alike; forgetting that the unlikeness of one person to another is generally the first thing which draws the attention of either to the imperfection of his own type, and the superiority of another, or the possibility, by combining the advantages of both, of producing something better than either. We have a warning example in China—a nation of much talent, and, in some respects, even wisdom, owing to the rare good fortune of having been provided at an early period with a particularly good set of customs, the work, in some measure, of men to whom even the most enlightened European must accord, under certain limitations, the title of sages and philosophers. They are remarkable, too, in the excellence of their apparatus for impressing, as far as possible, the best wisdom they possess upon every mind in the community, and securing that those who have appropriated most of it shall occupy the posts of honour and power. Surely the people who did this have discovered the secret of human progressiveness, and must have kept themselves steadily at the head of the movement of the world. On the contrary, they have become stationary—have remained so for thousands of years; and if they are ever to be farther improved, it must be by foreigners. They have succeeded beyond all hope in what English philanthropists are so industriously working at—in making a people all alike, all governing their thoughts and conduct by the same maxims and rules; and these are the fruits. The modern regime of public opinion is, in an unorganized form, what the Chinese educational and political systems are in an organized, and unless individuality shall be able successfully to assert itself against this yoke, Europe, notwithstanding its noble antecedents and its professed Christianity, will tend to become another China.

What is it that has hitherto preserved Europe from this lot? What has made the European family of nations an improving, instead of a stationary portion of mankind? Not any superior excellence in them which, when it exists, exists as the effect, not as the cause; but their remarkable diversity of character and culture. Individuals, classes, nations, have been extremely unlike one another: they have struck out a great variety of paths, each leading to something valuable; and although at every period those who travelled in different paths have been intolerant of one another, and each would have thought it an excellent thing if all the rest could have been compelled to travel his road, their attempts to thwart each other's development have rarely had any permanent success, and each has in time endured to receive the good which the others have offered. Europe is, in my judgement, wholly indebted to this plurality of paths for its progressive and many-sided development. But it already begins to possess this benefit in a considerably less degree. It is decidedly advancing towards the Chinese ideal of making all people alike. M. de Tocqueville, in his last important work,* remarks how much more the Frenchmen of the present day resemble one another, than did those even of the last generation. The same remark might be made of Englishmen in a far greater degree. In a passage already quoted from Wilhelm von Humboldt, he points out two things as necessary conditions of human development, because necessary to render people unlike one another; namely, freedom, and variety of situations. The second of these two conditions is in this country every day diminishing. The circumstances which surround different classes and individuals, and shape their characters, are daily becoming more assimilated. Formerly, different ranks, different neighbourhoods, different trades and professions, lived in what might be called different worlds; at present, to a great degree in the same. Comparatively speaking, they now read the same things, listen to the same things, see the same things, go to the same places, have their hopes and fears directed to the same objects, have the same rights and liberties, and the same means of asserting them. Great as are the differences of position which remain, they are nothing to those which have ceased. And the assimilation is still proceeding. All the political changes of the age promote it, since they all tend to raise the low and to lower the high. Every extension of education promotes it, because education brings people under common influences, and gives them access to the general stock of facts and sentiments. Improvements in the means of communication promote it, by bringing the inhabitants of distant places into personal contact, and keeping up a rapid flow of changes of residence between one place and another. The increase of commerce and manufactures promotes it,

*[Alexis de Tocqueville (1805–1859), *The Old Régime and the French Revolution.* De Tocqueville was a Frenchman who wrote *Democracy in America,* an insightful analysis of American culture.]

by diffusing more widely the advantages of easy circumstances, and opening all objects of ambition, even the highest, to general competition, whereby the desire of rising becomes no longer the character of a particular class but of all classes. A more powerful agency than even all these, in bringing about a general similarity among mankind, is the complete establishment, in this and other free countries, of the ascendancy of public opinion in the State. As the various social eminences which enabled persons entrenched on them to disregard the opinion of the multitude, gradually become levelled; as the very idea of resisting the will of the public, when it is positively known that they have a will, disappears more and more from the minds of practical politicians; there ceases to be any social support for nonconformity—any substantive power in society, which, itself opposed to the ascendancy of numbers, is interested in taking under its protection opinions and tendencies at variance with those of the public.

The combination of all these causes forms so great a mass of influences hostile to individuality, that it is not easy to see how it can stand its ground. It will do so with increasing difficulty, unless the intelligent part of the public can be made to feel its value—to see that it is good there should be differences, even though not for the better, even though, as it may appear to them, some should be for the worse. If the claims of individuality are ever to be asserted, the time is now, while much is still wanting to complete the enforced assimilation. It is only in the earlier stages that any stand can be successfully made against the encroachment. The demand that all other people shall resemble ourselves, grows by what it feeds on. If resistance waits till life is reduced *nearly* to one uniform type, all deviations from that type will come to be considered impious, immoral, even monstrous and contrary to nature. Mankind speedily become unable to conceive diversity, when they have been for some time unaccustomed to see it.

THE SUBJECTION OF WOMEN (in part)

CHAPTER 1

The object of this Essay is to explain as clearly as I am able the grounds of an opinion which I have held from the very earliest period when I had formed any opinions at all on social or political matters, and which, instead of being weakened or modified, has been constantly growing stronger by the progress of reflection and the experience of life: That the principle which regulates the existing social relations between the two sexes—the legal subordination of one sex to the other—is wrong in itself, and now one of the chief hindrances to human improvement; and that it ought to be replaced by a principle of perfect equality, admitting no power or privilege on the one side, nor disability on the other.

*   *   *

The truth is that people of the present and the last two or three generations have lost all practical sense of the primitive condition of humanity; and only the few who have studied history accurately, or have much frequented the parts of the world occupied by the living representatives of ages long past, are able to form any mental picture of what so-

"The Ladies' Advocate." This cartoon from *Punch* magazine ridicules John Stuart Mill for his advocacy of women's rights. The woman informs Mill that "Prior to your speech I was unaware that women were such miserable creatures." *(Library of Congress/Instructional Resources)*

ciety then was. People are not aware how entirely, in former ages, the law of superior strength was the rule of life; how publicly and openly it was avowed, I do not say cynically or shamelessly—for these words imply a feeling that there was something in it to be ashamed of, and no such notion could find a place in the faculties of any person in those ages, except a philosopher or a saint. History gives a cruel experience of human nature, in showing how exactly the regard due to the life, possessions, and entire earthly happiness of any class of persons, was measured by what they had the power of enforcing; how all who made any resistance to authorities that had arms in their hands, however dreadful might be the provocation, had not only the law of force but all other laws, and all the notions of social obligation against them; and in the eyes of those whom they resisted, were not only guilty of crime, but of the worst of all crimes, deserving the most cruel chastisement which human beings could inflict. The first small vestige of a feeling of obligation in a superior to acknowledge any right in inferiors began when he had been induced, for convenience, to make some promise to them. Though these promises, even when sanctioned by the most solemn oaths, were for many ages revoked or violated on the most trifling provocation or temptation, it is probable that this, except by persons of still worse than the average morality, was seldom done without some twinges of conscience.*

*   *   *

How different are these cases from that of the power of men over women! I am not now prejudging the question of its justification. I am showing how vastly more permanent it could not but be, even if not justifiable, than these other dominations which have nevertheless lasted down to our own time. Whatever gratification of pride there is in the possession of power, and whatever personal interest in its exercise, is in this case not confined to a limited class, but common to the whole male sex. Instead of being, to most of its supporters, a thing desirable chiefly in the abstract, or, like the political ends usually contended for by factious, of little private importance to any but the leaders; it comes home to the person and hearth of every male head of a family, and of every one who looks forward to being so. The clodhopper exercises, or is to exercise, his share of the power equally with the highest nobleman. And the case is that in which the desire of power is the strongest: for every one who desires power, desires it most over those who are nearest to him, with whom his life is passed, with whom he has most concerns in common, and in whom any independence of his authority is most often likely to interfere with his individual preferences. If, in the other cases specified, powers manifestly grounded only on force, and having so much less to support them, are so slowly and with so much difficulty got rid of, much more must it be so with this, even if it rests on no better foundation than those. We must consider, too, that the possessors of the power have facilities in this case, greater than in any other, to prevent any uprising against it. Every one of the subjects lives under the very eye, and almost, it may be said, in the hands, of one of the masters—in closer intimacy with him than with any of her fellow-subjects; with no means of combining against him, no power of even locally overmastering him, and, on the other hand, with the strongest motives for seeking his favour and avoiding to give him offence. In struggles for political emancipation, everybody knows how often its champions are bought off by bribes, or daunted by terrors. In the case of women, each individual of the subject-class is in a chronic state of bribery and intimidation combined. In setting up the standard of resistance, a large number of the leaders, and still more of the followers, must make an almost complete sacrifice of the pleasures or the alleviations of their own individual lot. If ever any system of privilege and enforced subjection had its yoke tightly riveted on the necks of those who are kept down by it, this has.

*   *   *

*[The brief history of the use of force to establish power that follows this paragraph has been deleted.]

But, it will be said, the rule of men over women differs from all these others in not being a rule of force: it is accepted voluntarily; women make no complaint, and are consenting parties to it. In the first place, a great number of women do not accept it. Ever since there have been women able to make their sentiments known by their writings (the only mode of publicity which society permits to them), an increasing number of them have recorded protests against their present social condition: and recently many thousands of them, headed by the most eminent women known to the public, have petitioned Parliament for their admission to the Parliamentary Suffrage. The claim of women to be educated as solidly, and in the same branches of knowledge, as men, is urged with growing intensity, and with a great prospect of success; while the demand for their admission into professions and occupations hitherto closed against them, becomes every year more urgent. Though there are not in this country, as there are in the United States, periodical Conventions and an organized party to agitate for the Rights of Women, there is a numerous and active Society organized and managed by women, for the more limited object of obtaining the political franchise. Nor is it only in our own country and in America that women are beginning to protest, more or less collectively, against the disabilities under which they labour. France, and Italy, and Switzerland, and Russia now afford examples of the same thing. How many more women there are who silently cherish similar aspirations, no one can possibly know; but there are abundant tokens how many *would* cherish them, were they not so strenuously taught to repress them as contrary to the proprieties of their sex. It must be remembered, also, that no enslaved class ever asked for complete liberty at once. When Simon de Montfort called the deputies of the commons to sit for the first time in Parliament, did any of them dream of demanding that an assembly, elected by their constituents, should make and destroy ministries, and dictate to the king in affairs of state? No such thought entered into the imagination of the most ambitious of them. The nobility had already these pretensions; the commons pretended to nothing but to be exempt from arbitrary taxation, and from the gross individual oppression of the king's officers. It is a political law of nature that those who are under any power of ancient origin never begin by complaining of the power itself, but only of its oppressive exercise. There is never any want of women who complain of ill usage by their husbands. There would be infinitely more, if complaint were not the greatest of all provocatives to a repetition and increase of the ill usage. It is this which frustrates all attempts to maintain the power but protect the woman against its abuses. In no other case (except that of a child) is the person who has been proved judicially to have suffered an injury replaced under the physical power of the culprit who inflicted it. Accordingly wives, even in the most extreme and protracted cases of bodily ill usage hardly ever dare avail themselves of the laws made for their protection: and if, in a moment of irrepressible indignation, or by the interference of neighbours, they are induced to do so, their whole effort afterwards is to disclose as little as they can, and to beg off their tyrant from his merited chastisement.

All causes, social and natural, combine to make it unlikely that women should be collectively rebellious to the power of men. They are so far in a position different from all other subject classes, that their masters require something more from them than actual service. Men do not want solely the obedience of women, they want their sentiments. All men, except the most brutish, desire to have, in the woman most nearly connected with them, not a forced slave but a willing one, not a slave merely, but a favourite. They have therefore put everything in practice to enslave their minds. The masters of all other slaves rely, for maintaining obedience, on fear; either fear of themselves, or religious fears. The masters of women wanted more than simple obedience, and they turned the whole force of education to effect their purpose. All women are brought up from the very earliest years in the belief that their ideal of character is the very opposite to that of men; not self-will, and government by self-control, but submission, and yielding to the control of others. All the moralities tell them that it is the duty of women, and all the current sentimentalities that it is their nature, to live for others; to make complete abnegation of themselves, and to have no life but in their affections. And by their affections are meant the only ones they are allowed to have—those to the men with whom they are connected, or to the children who constitute an additional and indefeasible tie between them and a man. When we put together three things—first, the natural attraction between opposite sexes; secondly, the wife's entire dependence on the husband, every privilege or pleasure she has being either his gift, or depending entirely on his will; and lastly, that the principal object of human pursuit, consideration, and all objects of social ambition, can in general be sought or obtained by her only through him, it would be a miracle if the object of being attractive to men had not become the polar star of feminine education and formation of character. And, this great means of influence over the minds of women having been acquired, an instinct of selfishness made men avail themselves of it to the utmost as a means of holding women in subjection, by representing to them meekness, submissiveness, and resignation of all individual will into the hands of a man, as an essential part of sexual attractiveness. Can it be doubted that any of the other yokes which mankind have succeeded in breaking would have subsisted till now if the same means had existed, and had been as sedulously used, to bow down their minds to it? If it had been made the object of the life of every young plebeian to find personal favour in the eyes of some patrician, of every young serf with some seigneur; if domestication with him, and a share of his personal affections, had been held out as the prize which they all should look out for, the most gifted and aspiring being able to reckon on the most desirable prizes; and if, when this prize had been obtained, they had been shut out by a wall of brass from all interests not centering in him, all feelings and desires but those which he shared or inculcated; would not serfs and seigneurs, plebeians and patricians, have been as broadly distinguished at this day as men and women are? and would not all but a thinker here and there, have believed the distinction to be a fundamental and unalterable fact in human nature?

*   *   *

At present, in the more improved countries, the disabilities of women are the only case, save one, in which laws and institutions take persons at their birth, and ordain that they shall never in all their lives be allowed to compete for certain things. The one exception is that of royalty. Persons still are born to the throne; no one, not of the reigning family, can ever occupy it, and no one even of that family can, by any means but the course of hereditary succession, attain it. All other dignities and social advantages are open to the whole male sex: many indeed are only attainable by wealth, but wealth may be striven for by any one, and is actually obtained by many men of the very humblest origin. The difficulties, to the majority, are indeed insuperable without the aid of fortunate accidents; but no male human being is under any legal ban: neither law nor opinion superadd artificial obstacles to the natural ones. Royalty, as I have said, is excepted: but in this case every one feels it to be an exception—an anomaly in the modern world, in marked opposition to its customs and principles, and to be justified only by extraordinary special expediencies, which, though individuals and nations differ in estimating their weight, unquestionably do in fact exist. But in this exceptional case, in which a high social function is, for important reasons, bestowed on birth instead of being put up to competition, all free nations contrive to adhere in substance to the principle from which they nominally derogate; for they circumscribe this high function by conditions avowedly intended to prevent the person to whom it ostensibly belongs from really performing it; while the person by whom it is performed, the responsible minister, does obtain the post by a competition from which no full-grown citizen of the male sex is legally excluded. The disabilities, therefore, to which women are subject from the mere fact of their birth are the solitary examples of the kind in modern legislation. In no instance except this, which comprehends half the human race, are the higher social functions closed against any one by a fatality of birth which no exertions, and no change of circumstances, can overcome; for even religious disabilities (besides that in England and in Europe they have practically almost ceased to exist) do not close any career to the disqualified person in case of conversion.

The social subordination of women thus stands out an isolated fact in modern social institutions; a solitary breach of what has become their fundamental law; a single relic of an old world of thought and practice exploded in everything else, but retained in the one thing of most universal interest; as if a gigantic dolmen [monument], or a vast temple of Jupiter Olympius, occupied the site of St. Paul's and received daily worship, while the surrounding Christian churches were only resorted to on fasts and festivals. This entire discrepancy between one social fact and all those which accompany it, and the radical opposition between its nature and the progressive movement which is the boast of the modern world, and which has successively swept away everything else of an analogous character, surely affords, to a conscientious observer of human tendencies, serious matter for reflection.

The preceding considerations are amply sufficient to show that custom, however universal it may be, affords in this case no presumption, and ought not to create any prejudice, in favour of the arrangements which place women in social and political subjection to men.

Søren Kierkegaard
1813–1855

Søren Aabye Kierkegaard was born in Copenhagen, Denmark, the youngest child of middle-aged parents. His father, Michael, had been an impoverished serf in a bleak area of northern Denmark. While still a boy, Michael had cursed God for the dreariness of his life and from that point on considered himself and his descendants to be under God's condemnation. The external events of Michael's life gave little indication of such a curse, however, as he worked his way to great wealth as a merchant in Copenhagen. Following the death of his first wife, and before the period of mourning was over, Michael was forced to marry his first wife's maid, Anne Lund, and five months later she bore the first of their five children.

Michael was already fifty-six and retired from business when Søren was born in 1813. Like James Mill, Michael educated young Søren at home, and also like Mill, he put his son through rigorous intellectual endeavors. But unlike his predecessor, Michael also communicated to his son a strong religious sentiment and deep, though perhaps warped, emotional feelings. Michael would often take Søren on "trips of fantasy" while conversing in the family library.

In 1830, at his father's urging, Kierkegaard entered the University of Copenhagen to study theology. While there he encountered the work of Hegel and reacted strongly against it. Kierkegaard objected to the implicit optimism and the "swallowing up" of contradictions in Hegel's dialectic. But more importantly, Kierkegaard claimed that while Hegel's "System" was an impressive philosophical *tour de force,* it did not relate to the lived existence of the individual—it did not give any guidance as to what a person should *do.* A famous entry from Kierkegaard's journal at this time is worth quoting at length:

> What I really lack is to be clear in my mind *what I am to do,* not what I am to know, except in so far as a certain understanding must precede every action. The thing is to understand myself, to see what God really wishes *me* to do; the thing is to find a truth which is true *for me,* to find *the idea for which I can live and die.* What would be the use of discovering so-called objective truth, of working through all the systems of philosophy and of being able, if required, to review them all and show up the inconsistencies within each system;—what good would it do me to be able to develop a theory of the state and combine all the details into a single whole, and so construct a world in which I did not live, but only held up to the view of others;— what good would it do me to be able to explain the meaning of Christianity if it had *no* deeper significance *for me and for my life;*—what good would it do me if truth stood before me, cold and naked, not caring whether I recognised her or not, and producing in me a shudder of fear rather than a trusting devotion? I certainly do not deny that I still recognise an *imperative of understanding* and that through it one can work upon men, *but it must be taken up into my life,* and *that is* what I now recognise as *the most important thing.**

Kierkegaard did not find the answer for "what to do" in his studies in theology and soon began living what he would later call an "aesthetic" life as a rich merchant's son. He spent large sums of money on food, drink, and clothing. He frequented parties and appeared to be having a great time. But hedonistic indulgence did not really give an answer for "what to do" either, and he plunged into despair. Another entry from his journals makes this clear:

> I have just returned from a party of which I was the life and soul; wit poured from my lips, everyone laughed and admired me—but I went away—and the dash should be as long as the earth's orbit ————————————————————
> ——————————— and wanted to shoot myself.**

On his son's twenty-fifth birthday, May 15, 1838, Michael revealed to Søren his sexual sins as well as his understanding of God's condemnation of their family. Four days later, Søren Kierkegaard underwent a religious conversion and was reconciled to his father, who died shortly afterward. Kierkegaard now had an answer for "what to do"—he would live as a penitent seeking to "become a Christian." Kierkegaard finished his theological studies, prepared to become a Lutheran pastor, and became engaged to marry seventeen-year-old Regine Olsen.

But by 1841 Kierkegaard realized that he could never live the life of a Lutheran pastor and devoted husband. He came to believe that the Danish Lutheran church had made religion a matter of intellectual assent to certain objective truths and no longer deserved to be called "Christian." For the rest of his life, he would be an opponent of institutional Christianity. The decision to break his engagement to Regine Olsen was a torturous one, but one he felt he had to

---

*Søren Kierkegaard, *The Journals of Søren Kierkegaard,* edited and translated by Alexander Dru (London: Oxford University Press, 1938), p. 15 [entry from August 1, 1835].
**Ibid., p. 27 [entry from early spring, 1836].

make. He decided that a "divine veto" had been cast against this marriage, that his role as penitent was incompatible with that of husband.

Kierkegaard spent the rest of his short life as a writer, publishing a number of books including *Either/Or* (1843), *Fear and Trembling* (1843), *Philosophical Fragments* (1844), *Stages on Life's Way* (1845), *Concluding Unscientific Postscript* (1846), *The Sickness unto Death* (1849), *Training in Christianity* (1850), and *The Attack upon "Christendom"* (1854–1855). All but the last of these works were written under various pseudonyms, and virtually all of them included attacks on the prevailing Hegelian philosophy of his time. In 1855, while returning from the bank with the last of his considerable inheritance, Kierkegaard collapsed on the street and died soon thereafter.

*   *   *

Kierkegaard's biography is reflected in his philosophical quest to establish what it means to be an individual. In such works as *Either/Or, Stages on Life's Way,* and *Fear and Trembling,* he describes a process of self-actualization through three stages in life: the aesthetic, the ethical, and the religious. At the aesthetic stage, an individual's life centers around either hedonistic pleasure or abstract philosophical speculation. The hedonist lives for the immediate pleasures of the moment without concern for the future. The abstract intellectual (Hegel being the prime example) lives in a theoretical world removed from concrete existence. The hedonist reduces existence to immediate pleasure while the abstract speculator reduces existence to thought; but in both cases the aesthete has avoided the either/or decisions of real life, and authentic selfhood has not been achieved. The result, says Kierkegaard, is a life of boredom—and the pointless pursuit of diversions to alleviate such boredom. This was the life Kierkegaard himself lived in his early years at the university.

Those who move beyond the aesthetic to the ethical level choose to accept moral standards and attempt to do their duty. By choosing decisively and accepting responsibility for that choice, an individual's life becomes centralized and unified. For example, the seducing man operates on the aesthetic level where every woman he meets is merely a general source of momentary pleasure. He has no past, no future, only the present desire for fulfillment. He is not really a complete person since he is living life as a series of disconnected "nows." On the other hand, the man who has chosen to fulfill the duties of a faithful husband operates on the ethical level. He has a memory of the past and a hope for the future based on his commitments, which gives an integrated wholeness to his present.

But even though universal moral standards can become personal when chosen by an individual, the ethical stage is not sufficient to bring a person to complete self-actualization. The ethical stage leads to a point at which one realizes that one cannot entirely fulfill the moral law, that one is sinful in the presence of God. Only in the religious stage, where one "leaps" to passionate commitment to God, is one totally free from meaninglessness and dread. In the religious stage a person must be willing to give up everything—even abstract ethical universals—to God. In the selection reprinted here from *Fear and Trembling,* in the Howard and Edna Hong translation, Kierkegaard illustrates this movement from the ethical to the religious stage by contrasting the stories of Agamemnon and Abraham. While both were called upon by a divinity to sacrifice a child, Agamemnon's sacrifice would serve a higher ethical purpose while Abraham's would not. In fact, Abraham was in the odd position of being *tempted* to do the ethical: to not murder/sacrifice Isaac. Yet Abraham had faith in God, rather than Agamemnon's resignation to the gods, and continued to believe that God would return his son to him. Abraham performed a "teleological [i.e., considering the end or goal] suspension of the ethical," giving up what was most dear to him, and by virtue of the absurd, God gave it all back. It is interesting to note that Kierkegaard wrote this work right after he had given up to God what was most dear to him: Regine Olsen. Apparently believing that God would give her back to him, Kierkegaard was shocked when she became engaged to another man.

In the selection from *Concluding Unscientific Postscript* reprinted here in the Howard and Edna Hong translation, Kierkegaard argues that while a logical system is possible, an existential system is not. Hegel's entire systematic enterprise is misguided because it assumes a finality that lived existence never has. When it comes to the important issues of life, such as knowledge of God, no system, no set of objective truths will give any real guidance. According to Kierkegaard, only subjective truth, "An objective uncertainty, held fast through appropriation with the most passionate inwardness," can be the truth for an existing person. So while one can never have objective certainty that God exists, one can make it true in one's own life by committing oneself completely and living as if it were true.

Written in Danish and presenting a pessimistic view of objective reason that was out of touch with the spirit of his time, it is not surprising that Kierkegaard's works were ignored for decades. The horror of World War I, together with the work done by Martin Heidegger in philosophy and Karl Barth in theology, brought Kierkegaard's pessimistic assessment of objectivism to prominence. Today Kierkegaard is acknowledged as the "father of existentialism" and is studied widely.

*   *   *

For representative collections of Kierkegaard's writings, see *A Kierkegaard Anthology,* edited by Robert Bretall (New York: Modern Library, 1936) and Walter A. Kaufmann, ed., *Existentialism from Dostoevsky to Sartre* (New York: Meridian Books, 1956). For biographies of Kierkegaard see Walter Lowrie, *Kierkegaard* (Oxford: Oxford University Press, 1938), for comprehensive coverage or Walter Lowrie, *A Short Life of Kierkegaard* (Princeton, NJ: Princeton University Press, 1942), for a more succinct study. There are a number of general overviews of Kierkegaard's thought, including H. Diem, *Kierkegaard: An Introduction,* translated by David Green (Richmond, VA: John Knox Press, 1966); Josiah Thompson, *Kierkegaard* (New York: Knopf, 1973); Alastair Hannay, *Kierkegaard* (London: Routledge & Kegan Paul, 1982); Diogenes Allen, *Three Outsiders: Pascal, Kierkegaard, Simone Weil* (Cambridge, MA: Cowley Publications, 1983); and Patrick Gardiner, *Kierkegaard* (Oxford: Oxford University Press, 1988). For studies of specific aspects of Kierkegaard's thought, see Louis K. Dupre, *Kierkegaard as Theologian* (New York: Sheed and Ward, 1964); Niels Thulstrup, *Kierkegaard's Relation to Hegel,* translated by George L. Stengren (Princeton, NJ: Princeton University Press, 1980); John W. Elrod, *Kierkegaard and Christendom* (Princeton, NJ: Princeton University Press, 1981); C. Stephen Evans, *Kierkegaard's "Fragments" and "Postscript": The Religious Philosophy of Johannes Climacus* (Atlantic Highlands, NJ: Humanities Press, 1983); and Merold Westphal, *Kierkegaard's Critique of Reason and Society* (Macon, GA:

Mercer University Press, 1987). For collections of essays, see H.A. Johnson and N. Thulstrup, eds., *A Kierkegaard Critique* (Chicago: Henry Regnery, 1967); Jerry H. Gill, ed., *Essays on Kierkegaard* (Minneapolis, MN: Burgess, 1969); Josiah Thompson, ed., *Kierkegaard: A Collection of Critical Essays* (Garden City, NY: Anchor Books, 1972); and Harold Bloom, ed., *Søren Kierkegaard* (New York: Chelsea House Publishers, 1989).

FEAR AND TREMBLING (in part)

IS THERE A TELEOLOGICAL SUSPENSION OF THE ETHICAL?

The ethical as such is the universal, and as the universal it applies to everyone, which from another angle means that it applies at all times. It rests immanent in itself, has nothing outside itself that is its ⟨*telos*⟩ [end, purpose] but is itself the ⟨*telos*⟩ for everything outside itself, and when the ethical has absorbed this into itself, it goes not further. The single individual, sensately and psychically qualified in immediacy, is the individual who has his ⟨*telos*⟩ in the universal, and it is his ethical task continually to express himself in this, to annul his singularity in order to become the universal. As soon as the single individual asserts himself in his singularity before the universal, he sins, and only by acknowledging this can he be reconciled again with the universal. Every time the single individual, after having entered the universal, feels an impulse to assert himself as the single individual, he is in a spiritual trial [*Anfægtelse*], from which he can work himself only by repentantly surrendering as the single individual in the universal. If this is the highest that can be said of man and his existence, then the ethical is of the same nature as a person's eternal salvation, which is his ⟨*telos*⟩ forevermore and at all times, since it would be a contradiction for this to be capable of being surrendered (that is, teleologically suspended), because as soon as this is suspended it is relinquished, whereas that which is suspended is not relinquished but is preserved in the higher, which is its ⟨*telos*⟩.

If this is the case, then Hegel is right in "The Good and Conscience," where he qualifies man only as the individual and considers this qualification as a "moral form of evil" (see especially *The Philosophy of Right*), which must be annulled [*ophævet*] in the teleology of the moral in such a way that the single individual who remains in that stage either sins or is immersed in spiritual trial. But Hegel is wrong in speaking about faith; he is wrong in not protesting loudly and clearly against Abraham's enjoying honor and glory as a father of faith when he ought to be sent back to a lower court and shown up as a murderer.

Faith is namely this paradox that the single individual is higher than the universal—yet, please note, in such a way that the movement repeats itself, so that after having been in the universal he as the single individual isolates himself as higher than the

Søren Kierkegaard, *Fear and Trembling* ("Teleological Suspension of the Ethical"), edited and translated by Howard V. Hong and Edna H. Hong (Princeton, NJ: Princeton University Press). Copyright © 1983 by PUP. Reprinted by permission of Princeton University Press.

universal. If this is not faith, then Abraham is lost, then faith has never existed in the world precisely because it has always existed. For if the ethical—that is, social morality—is the highest and if there is in a person no residual incommensurability in some way such that this incommensurability is not evil (i.e., the single individual, who is to be expressed in the universal), then no categories are needed other than what Greek philosophy had or what can be deduced from them by consistent thought. Hegel should not have concealed this, for, after all, he had studied Greek philosophy.

People who are profoundly lacking in learning and are given to clichés are frequently heard to say that a light shines over the Christian world, whereas a darkness enshrouds paganism. This kind of talk has always struck me as strange, inasmuch as every more thorough thinker, every more earnest artist still regenerates himself in the eternal youth of the Greeks. The explanation for such a statement is that one does not know what one should say but only that one must say something. It is quite right to say that paganism did not have faith, but if something is supposed to have been said thereby, then one must have a clearer understanding of what faith is, for otherwise one falls into such clichés. It is easy to explain all existence, faith along with it, without having a conception of what faith is, and the one who counts on being admired for such an explanation is not such a bad calculator, for it is as Boileau says: *Un sot trouve toujours un plus sot, qui l'admire* [One fool always finds a bigger fool, who admires him].

Faith is precisely the paradox that the single individual as the single individual is higher than the universal, is justified before it, not as inferior to it but as superior—yet in such a way, please note, that it is the single individual who, after being subordinate as the single individual to the universal, now by means of the universal becomes the single individual who as the single individual is superior, that the single individual as the single individual stands in an absolute relation to the absolute. This position cannot be mediated, for all mediation takes place only by virtue of the universal; it is and remains for all eternity a paradox, impervious to thought. And yet faith is this paradox, or else (and I ask the reader to bear these consequences *in mente* [in mind] even though it would be too prolix for me to write them all down) or else faith has never existed simply because it has always existed, or else Abraham is lost.

It is certainly true that the single individual can easily confuse this paradox with spiritual trial [*Anfægtelse*], but it ought not to be concealed for that reason. It is certainly true that many persons may be so constituted that they are repulsed by it, but faith ought not therefore to be made into something else to enable one to have it, but one ought rather to admit to not having it, while those who have faith ought to be prepared to set forth some characteristics whereby the paradox can be distinguished from a spiritual trial.

The story of Abraham contains just such a teleological suspension of the ethical. There is no dearth of keen minds and careful scholars who have found analogies to it. What their wisdom amounts to is the beautiful proposition that basically everything is the same. If one looks more closely, I doubt very much that anyone in the whole wide world will find one single analogy, except for a later one, which proves nothing if it is certain that Abraham represents faith and that it is manifested normatively in him, whose life not only is the most paradoxical that can be thought but is also so paradoxical that it simply cannot be thought. He acts by virtue of the absurd, for it is precisely the absurd that he as the single individual is higher than the universal. This paradox cannot be mediated, for as soon as Abraham begins to do so, he has to confess that he was in a spiritual trial, and if that is the case, he will never sacrifice Isaac, or if he did sacrifice Isaac, then in repentance he must come back to the universal. He gets Isaac back

Wanderer Above the Mist,
1817–1918, by Caspar David
Friedrich (1774–1840). "Faith
is precisely the paradox that
the single individual as the
single individual is higher
than the universal. . . . This
position cannot be mediated
. . . it is and remains for all
eternity a paradox,
impervious to thought."
Kierkegaard, *Fear and
Trembling. (Marburg/Art
Resource)*

again by virtue of the absurd. Therefore, Abraham is at no time a tragic hero but is something entirely different, either a murderer or a man of faith. Abraham does not have the middle term that saves the tragic hero. This is why I can understand a tragic hero but cannot understand Abraham, even though in a certain demented sense I admire him more than all others.

In ethical terms, Abraham's relation to Isaac is quite simply this: the father shall love the son more than himself. But within its own confines the ethical has various gradations. We shall see whether this story contains any higher expression for the ethical that can ethically explain his behavior, can ethically justify his suspending the ethical obligation to the son, but without moving beyond the teleology of the ethical.

When an enterprise of concern to a whole nation is impeded, when such a project is halted by divine displeasure, when the angry deity sends a dead calm that mocks every effort, when the soothsayer carries out his sad task and announces that the deity demands a young girl as sacrifice—then the father must heroically bring this sacrifice. He must nobly conceal his agony, even though he could wish he were "the lowly man who dares to weep" and not the king who must behave in a kingly manner. Although the lonely agony penetrates his breast and there are only three persons in the whole nation who know his agony, soon the whole nation will be initiated into his agony and also into his deed, that for the welfare of all he will sacrifice her, his daughter, this lovely young girl. O bosom! O fair cheeks, flaxen hair (v. 687). And the daughter's tears will agitate him, and the father will turn away his face, but the hero must raise the knife. And when the news of it reaches the father's house, the beautiful Greek maidens will blush with enthusiasm, and if the daughter was engaged, her betrothed will not be angry but will be proud to share in the father's deed, for the girl belonged more tenderly to him than to the father.

When the valiant judge who in the hour of need saved Israel binds God and himself in one breath by the same promise, he will heroically transform the young maiden's jubilation, the beloved daughter's joy to sorrow, and all Israel will sorrow with her over her virginal youth. But every freeborn man will understand, every resolute woman will admire Jephthah, and every virgin in Israel will wish to behave as his daughter did, because what good would it be for Jephthah to win the victory by means of a promise if he did not keep it—would not the victory be taken away from the people again?

When a son forgets his duty, when the state entrusts the sword of judgment to the father, when the laws demand punishment from the father's hand, then the father must heroically forget that the guilty one is his son, he must nobly hide his agony, but no one in the nation, not even the son, will fail to admire the father, and every time the Roman laws are interpreted, it will be remembered that many interpreted them more learnedly but no one more magnificently than Brutus.

But if Agamemnon, while a favorable wind was taking the fleet under full sail to its destination, had dispatched that messenger who fetched Iphigenia to be sacrificed; if Jephthah, without being bound by any promise that decided the fate of the nation, had said to his daughter: Grieve now for two months over your brief youth, and then I will sacrifice you; if Brutus had had a righteous son and yet had summoned the lictors to put him to death—who would have understood them? If, on being asked why they did this, these three men had answered: It is an ordeal in which we are being tried [forsøges]—would they have been better understood?

When in the crucial moment Agamemnon, Jephthah, and Brutus heroically have overcome the agony, heroically have lost the beloved, and have only to complete the task externally, there will never be a noble soul in the world without tears of compassion for their agony, of admiration for their deed. But if in the crucial moment these three men were to append to the heroic courage with which they bore the agony the little phrase: But it will not happen anyway—who then would understand them? If they went on to explain: This we believe by virtue of the absurd—who would understand them any better, for who would not readily understand that it was absurd, but who would understand that one could then believe it?

The difference between the tragic hero and Abraham is very obvious. The tragic hero is still within the ethical. He allows an expression of the ethical to have its ⟨telos⟩ in a higher expression of the ethical; he scales down the ethical relation between father and son or daughter and father to a feeling that has its dialectic in its relation to the idea of moral conduct. Here there can be no question of a teleological suspension of the ethical itself.

Abraham's situation is different. By his act he transgressed the ethical altogether and had a higher <telos> outside it, in relation to which he suspended it. For I certainly would like to know how Abraham's act can be related to the universal, whether any point of contact between what Abraham did and the universal can be found other than that Abraham transgressed it. It is not to save a nation, not to uphold the idea of the state that Abraham does it; it is not to appease the angry gods. If it were a matter of the deity's being angry, then he was, after all, angry only with Abraham, and Abraham's act is totally unrelated to the universal, is a purely private endeavor. Therefore, while the tragic hero is great because of his moral virtue, Abraham is great because of a purely personal virtue. There is no higher expression for the ethical in Abraham's life than that the father shall love the son. The ethical in the sense of the moral is entirely beside the point. Insofar as the universal was present, it was cryptically in Isaac, hidden, so to speak, in Isaac's loins, and must cry out with Isaac's mouth: Do not do this, you are destroying everything.

Why, then, does Abraham do it? For God's sake and—the two are wholly identical—for his own sake. He does it for God's sake because God demands this proof of his faith; he does it for his own sake so that he can prove it. The unity of the two is altogether correctly expressed in the word already used to describe this relationship. It is an ordeal, a temptation. A temptation—but what does that mean? As a rule, what tempts a person is something that will hold him back from doing his duty, but here the temptation is the ethical itself, which would hold him back from doing God's will. But what is duty? Duty is simply the expression for God's will.

Here the necessity of a new category for the understanding of Abraham becomes apparent. Paganism does not know such a relationship to the divine. The tragic hero does not enter into any private relationship to the divine, but the ethical is the divine, and thus the paradox therein can be mediated in the universal.

Abraham cannot be mediated; in other words, he cannot speak. As soon as I speak, I express the universal, and if I do not do so, no one can understand me. As soon as Abraham wants to express himself in the universal, he must declare that his situation is a spiritual trial [*Anfægtelse*], for he has no higher expression of the universal that ranks above the universal he violates.

Therefore, although Abraham arouses my admiration, he also appalls me. The person who denies himself and sacrifices himself because of duty gives up the finite in order to grasp the infinite and is adequately assured; the tragic hero gives up the certain for the even more certain, and the observer's eye views him with confidence. But the person who gives up the universal in order to grasp something even higher that is not the universal—what does he do? Is it possible that this can be anything other than a spiritual trial? And if it is possible, but the individual makes a mistake, what salvation is there for him? He suffers all the agony of the tragic hero, he shatters his joy in the world, he renounces everything, and perhaps at the same time he barricades himself from the sublime joy that was so precious to him that he would buy it at any price. The observer cannot understand him at all; neither can his eye rest upon him with confidence. Perhaps the believer's intention cannot be carried out at all, because it is inconceivable. Or if it could be done but the individual has misunderstood the deity—what salvation would there be for him? The tragic hero needs and demands tears, and where is the envious eye so arid that it could not weep with Agamemnon, but where is the soul so gone astray that it has the audacity to weep for Abraham? The tragic hero finishes his task at a specific moment in time, but as time passes he does what is no less significant: he visits the person encompassed by sorrow, who cannot breathe because of his anguished sighs, whose thoughts oppress him, heavy with tears. He appears to him, breaks the witchcraft of sorrow, loosens the bonds, evokes the tears, and the suffering one forgets his own sufferings in those of the tragic hero. One cannot weep over Abraham. One approaches him with a *horror religiosus*, as Israel approached Mount Sinai. What if he himself is distraught, what if he had made a mistake, this lonely man who climbs Mount Moriah, whose peak towers sky-high over the flatlands of Aulis, what if he is not a sleepwalker safely crossing the abyss while the one standing at the foot of the mountain looks up, shakes with anxiety, and then in his deference and horror does not even dare to call to him?—Thanks, once again thanks, to a man who, to a person overwhelmed by life's sorrows and left behind naked, reaches out the words, the leafage of language by which he can conceal his misery. Thanks to you, great Shakespeare, you who can say everything, everything, everything just as it is—and yet, why did you never articulate this torment? Did you perhaps reserve it for yourself, like the beloved's name that one cannot bear to have the world utter, for with his little secret that he cannot divulge the poet buys this power of the word to tell everybody else's dark secrets. A poet is not an apostle; he drives out devils only by the power of the devil.

But if the ethical is teleologically suspended in this manner, how does the single individual in whom it is suspended exist? He exists as the single individual in contrast to the universal. Does he sin, then, for from the point of view of the idea, this is the form of sin. Thus, even though the child does not sin, because it is not conscious of its existence as such, its existence, from the point of view of the idea, is nevertheless sin, and the ethical makes its claim upon it at all times. If it is denied that this form can be repeated in such a way that it is not sin, then judgment has fallen upon Abraham. How did Abraham exist? He had faith. This is the paradox by which he remains at the apex, the paradox that he cannot explain to anyone else, for the paradox is that he as the single individual places himself in an absolute relation to the absolute. Is he justified? Again, his justification is the paradoxical, for if he is, then he is justified not by virtue of being something universal but by virtue of being the single individual.

How does the single individual reassure himself that he is legitimate? It is a simple matter to level all existence to the idea of the state or the idea of a society. If this is done, it is also simple to mediate, for one never comes to the paradox that the single individual as the single individual is higher than the universal, something I can also express symbolically in a statement by Pythagoras to the effect that the odd number is more perfect than the even number. If occasionally there is any response at all these days with regard to the paradox, it is likely to be: One judges it by the result. Aware that he is a paradox who cannot be understood, a hero who has become a ⟨skandalon⟩ [offense] to his age will shout confidently to his contemporaries: The result will indeed prove that I was justified. This cry is rarely heard in our age, inasmuch as it does not produce heroes—this is its defect—and it likewise has the advantage that it produces few caricatures. When in our age we hear these words: It will be judged by the result—then we know at once with whom we have the honor of speaking. Those who talk this way are a numerous type whom I shall designate under the common name of assistant professors. With security in life, they live in their thoughts: they have a *permanent* position and a *secure* future in a well-organized state. They have hundreds, yes, even thousands of years between them and the earthquakes of existence; they are not afraid that such things can be repeated, for then what would the police and the newspapers say? Their life task is to judge the great men, judge them according to the result. Such behavior toward greatness betrays a strange mixture of arrogance and wretchedness—arrogance because they feel called to pass judgment, wretchedness because they feel that their lives are in no way allied with the lives of the great. Anyone with even a smattering *erectioris ingenii* [of nobility of nature] never becomes an utterly cold and clammy worm, and when he approaches greatness, he is never devoid of the thought that since the creation of the world it has been customary for the result to come last and that if one is truly going to learn something from greatness one must be particularly aware of the beginning. If the one who is to act wants to judge himself by the result, he will never begin. Although the result may give joy to the entire world, it cannot help the hero, for he would not know the result until the whole thing was over, and he would not become a hero by that but by making a beginning.

Moreover, in its dialectic the result (insofar as it is finitude's response to the infinite question) is altogether incongruous with the hero's existence. Or should Abraham's receiving Isaac by a *marvel* be able to prove that Abraham was justified in relating himself as the single individual to the universal? If Abraham actually had sacrificed Isaac, would he therefore have been less justified?

But we are curious about the result, just as we are curious about the way a book turns out. We do not want to know anything about the anxiety, the distress, the paradox. We carry on an esthetic flirtation with the result. It arrives just as unexpectedly but also just as effortlessly as a prize in a lottery, and when we have heard the result, we have built ourselves up. And yet no manacled robber of churches is so despicable a criminal as the one who plunders holiness in this way, and not even Judas, who sold his Lord for thirty pieces of silver, is more contemptible than someone who peddles greatness in this way.

It is against my very being to speak inhumanly about greatness, to make it a dim and nebulous far-distant shape or to let it be great but devoid of the emergence of the humanness without which it ceases to be great, for it is not what happens to me that makes me great but what I do, and certainly there is no one who believes that someone became great by winning the big lottery prize. A person might have been born in lowly circumstances, but I would still require him not to be so inhuman toward himself that he could imagine the king's castle only at a distance and ambiguously dream of its greatness, and destroy it at the same time he elevates it because he elevated it so basely. I require him to be man enough to tread confidently and with dignity there as well. He must not be so inhuman that he insolently violates everything by barging right off the street into the king's hall—he loses more thereby than the king. On the contrary, he should find a joy in observing every bidding of propriety with a happy and confident enthusiasm, which is precisely what makes him a free spirit. This is merely a metaphor, for that distinction is only a very imperfect expression of the distance of spirit. I require every person not to think so inhumanly of himself that he does not dare to enter those palaces where the memory of the chosen ones lives or even those where they themselves live. He is not to enter rudely and foist his affinity upon them. He is to be happy for every time he bows before them, but he is to be confident, free of spirit, and always more than a charwoman, for if he wants to be no more than that, he will never get in. And the very thing that is going to help him is the anxiety and distress in which the great were tried, for otherwise, if he has any backbone, they will only arouse his righteous envy. And anything that can be great only at a distance, that someone wants to make great with empty and hollow phrases—is destroyed by that very person.

Who was as great in the world as that favored woman, the mother of God, the Virgin Mary? And yet how do we speak of her? That she was the favored one among women does not make her great, and if it would not be so very odd for those who listen to be able to think just as inhumanly as those who speak, then every young girl might ask: Why am I not so favored? And if I had nothing else to say, I certainly would not dismiss such a question as stupid, because, viewed abstractly, vis-à-vis a favor, every person is just as entitled to it as the other. We leave out the distress, the anxiety, the paradox. My thoughts are as pure as anybody's, and he who can think this way surely has pure thoughts, and, if not, he can expect something horrible, for anyone who has once experienced these images cannot get rid of them again, and if he sins against them, they take a terrible revenge in a silent rage, which is more terrifying than the stridency of ten ravenous critics. To be sure, Mary bore the child wondrously, but she nevertheless did it "after the manner of women," and such a time is one of anxiety, distress, and paradox. The angel was indeed a ministering spirit, but he was not a meddlesome spirit who went to the other young maidens in Israel and said: Do not scorn Mary, the extraordinary is happening to her. The angel went only to Mary, and no one could understand her. Has any woman been as infringed upon as was Mary, and is it not true here also that the one whom God blesses he curses in the same breath? This is the spirit's view of Mary, and she is by no means—it is revolting to me to say it but even more so that people have inanely and unctuously made her out to be thus—she is by no means a lady idling in her finery and playing with a divine child. When, despite this, she said: Behold, I am the handmaid of the Lord—then she is great, and I believe it should not be difficult to explain why she became the mother of God. She needs worldly admiration as little as Abraham needs tears, for she was no heroine and he was no hero, but both of them became greater than these, not by being exempted in any way from the distress and the agony and the paradox, but became greater by means of these.

It is great when the poet in presenting his tragic hero for public admiration dares to say: Weep for him, for he deserves it. It is great to deserve the tears of those who deserve to shed tears. It is great that the poet dares to keep the crowd under restraint, dares to discipline men to examine themselves individually to see if they are worthy to weep for the hero, for the slop water of the snivellers is a debasement of the sacred.—But even greater than all this is the knight of faith's daring to say to the noble one who wants to weep for him: Do not weep for me, but weep for yourself.

We are touched, we look back to those beautiful times. Sweet sentimental longing leads us to the goal of our desire, to see Christ walking about in the promised land. We forget the anxiety, the distress, the paradox. Was it such a simple matter not to make a mistake? Was it not terrifying that this man walking around among the others was God? Was it not terrifying to sit down to eat with him? Was it such an easy matter to become an apostle? But the result, the eighteen centuries—that helps, that contributes to this mean deception whereby we deceive ourselves and others. I do not feel brave enough to wish to be contemporary with events like that, but I do not for that reason severely condemn those who made a mistake, nor do I depreciate those who saw what was right.

But I come back to Abraham. During the time before the result, either Abraham was a murderer every minute or we stand before a paradox that is higher than all mediations.

The story of Abraham contains, then, a teleological suspension of the ethical. As the single individual he became higher than the universal. This is the paradox, which cannot be mediated. How he entered into it is just as inexplicable as how he remains in it. If this is not Abraham's situation, then Abraham is not even a tragic hero but a murderer. It is thoughtless to want to go on calling him the father of faith, to speak of it to men who have an interest only in words. A person can become a tragic hero through his own strength—but not the knight of faith. When a person walks what is in one sense the hard road of the tragic hero, there are many who can give him advice, but he who walks the narrow road of faith has no one to advise him—no one understands him. Faith is a marvel, and yet no human being is excluded from it; for that which unites all human life is passion, and faith is a passion.

CONCLUDING UNSCIENTIFIC
POSTSCRIPT (in part)

SECTION I, CHAPTER 2: POSSIBLE AND ACTUAL
THESES BY LESSING

*   *   *

*(A) A logical system can be given; (B) but a system of existence [Tilværelsens System]
cannot be given.*

(A) A logical system can be given.

α.   If, however, a logical system is to be constructed, special care must be taken
not to incorporate anything that is subject to the dialectic of existence, accordingly, anything that is [*er*] solely by existing [*være til*] or by having existed [*have været til*], not
something that is [*er*] simply by being [*være*]. It follows quite simply that Hegel's
matchless and matchlessly admired invention—the importation of movement into logic
(not to mention that in every other passage one misses even his own attempt to make
one believe that it is there)—simply confuses logic.* It is indeed curious to make movement the basis in a sphere in which movement is inconceivable or to have movement
explain logic, whereas logic cannot explain movement.

On this point, however, I am very happy to be able to refer to a man who thinks
soundly and fortunately is educated by the Greeks (rare qualities in our age!); a man
who has known how to extricate himself and his thought from every trailing, groveling
relation to Hegel, from whose fame everyone usually seeks to profit, if in no other way,
then by going further, that is, by having absorbed Hegel; a man who has preferred to be
content with Aristotle and with himself—I mean Trendlenburg (*Logische Untersuchun-
gen*). One of his merits is that he comprehended movement as the inexplicable presupposition, as the common denominator in which being and thinking are united, and as

---

*The light-mindedness with which systematicians admit that Hegel has perhaps not been successful
everywhere in importing movement into logic, much like the grocer who thinks that a few raisins do not matter when the purchase is large—his farcical docility is, of course, contempt for Hegel that not even his most
vehement attacker has allowed himself. There have certainly been logical attempts prior to Hegel, but his
method is everything. For him and for everyone who has intelligence enough to comprehend what it means to
will something great, the absence of it at this or that point cannot be a trivial matter, as when a grocer and a
customer bicker about whether there is a little underweight or overweight. Hegel himself has staked his whole
reputation on the point of the method. But a method possesses the peculiar quality that, viewed abstractly, it
is nothing at all; it is a method precisely in the process of being carried out; in being carried out it is a method,
and where it is not carried out, it is not a method, and if there is no other method, there is no method at all. To
turn Hegel into a rattlebrain must be reserved for his admirers; an attacker will always know how to honor
him for having willed something great and having failed to achieve it.

Søren Kierkegaard, *Concluding Unscientific Postscript*, Section I, Chapter 2, "Possible and Actual Theses by
Lessing"; Section II, Chapter 2, "Subjective Truth, Inwardness; Truth is Subjectivity," edited and translated
by Howard V. Hong and Edna H. Hong (Princeton, NJ: Princeton University Press). Copyright © 1992 by
Howard V. Hong. Reprinted by permission of Princeton University Press.

their continued reciprocity. I cannot attempt here to show the relation of his conception to the Greeks, to Aristotelian thought, or to what, oddly enough, although in a popular sense only, bears a certain resemblance to his presentation: a small section in Plutarch's work on Isis and Osiris. It is by no means my view that Hegelian philosophy has not had a salutary influence on Trendlenburg, but it is fortunate that he has perceived that wanting to improve Hegel's structure, to go further etc., will not do (a mendacious approach by which many a botcher in our age arrogates Hegel's celebrity to himself and mendicantly fraternizes with him); on the other hand, it is fortunate that Trendlenburg, sober like a Greek thinker, without promising everything and without claiming to beatify all humankind, does indeed accomplish much and beatifies whoever would need his guidance in learning about the Greeks.

In a logical system, nothing may be incorporated that has a relation to existence, that is not indifferent to existence. The infinite advantage that the logical, by being the objective, possesses over all other thinking is in turn, subjectively viewed, restricted by its being a hypothesis, simply because it is indifferent to existence understood as actuality. This duplexity distinguishes the logical from the mathematical, which has no relation whatever toward or from existence [*Tilværelse*] but has only objectivity—not objectivity and the hypothetical as unity and contradiction in which it is negatively related to existence [*Existents*].

The logical system must not be a mystification, a ventriloquism, in which the content of existence [*Tilværelse*] emerges cunningly and surreptitiously, where logical thought is startled and finds what the Herr Professor or the licentiate has had up his sleeve. Judging between the two can be done more sharply by answering the question: In what sense is a category an abbreviation of existence, whether logical thinking is abstract after existence or abstract without any relation to existence. I would like to treat this question a little more extensively elsewhere, and even if it is not adequately answered, it is always something to have inquired about it in this way.

β. The dialectic of the beginning must be clarified. The almost amusing thing about it, that the beginning is and then in turn is not, because it is the beginning—this true dialectical remark has long enough been like a game that has been played in Hegelian society.

The system, so it is said, begins with the immediate; some, failing to be dialectical, are even oratorical enough to speak of the most immediate of all, although the comparative reflection contained here might indeed become dangerous for the beginning.* The system begins with the immediate and therefore without presuppositions and therefore absolutely, that is, the beginning of the system is the absolute beginning. This is entirely correct and has indeed also been adequately admired. But why, then, before the system is begun, has that other equally important, definitely equally important, question not been clarified and its clear implications honored: *How does the system begin with the immediate, that is, does it begin with it immediately?* The answer to this must certainly be an unconditional no. If the system is assumed to be after existence (whereby a confusion with a system of existence is created), the system does indeed come afterward and consequently does not begin immediately with

---

*To show how would become too prolix here. Frequently it is not worth the trouble either, because, after a person has laboriously advanced an objection sharply, from a philosopher's rejoinder he discovers that his misunderstanding was not that he could not understand the idolized philosophy but rather that he had allowed himself to be persuaded to believe that the whole thing was supposed to be something—and not flabby thinking concealed by the most overbearing expressions.

the immediate with which existence began, even though in another sense existence did not begin with it, because the immediate never is but is annulled when it is. The beginning of the system that begins with the immediate *is then itself achieved through reflection.*

Here is the difficulty, for if one does not let go of this one thought, deceptively or thoughtlessly or in breathless haste to have the system finished, this thought in all its simplicity is capable of deciding that there can be no system of existence and that a logical system must not boast of an absolute beginning, because such a beginning is just like pure being, a pure chimera.

In other words, if a beginning cannot be made immediately with the immediate (which would then be conceived as a fortuitous event or a miracle, that is, which would mean not to think), but this beginning must be achieved through reflection, then the question arises very simply (alas, if only I am not put in the doghouse on account of my simplicity, because everyone can understand my question—and consequently must feel ashamed of the questioner's popular knowledge): How do I bring to a halt the reflection set in motion in order to reach that beginning? Reflection has the notable quality of being infinite. But being infinite must in any case mean that it cannot stop of its own accord, because in stopping itself it indeed uses itself and can be stopped only in the same way as a sickness is cured if it is itself allowed to prescribe the remedy, that is, the sickness is promoted. Perhaps this infinity of reflection is the bad or spurious infinity. In that case, we are indeed almost finished, since the spurious infinity is reputedly something despicable that one must give up, the sooner the better. In that connection, may I not ask a question: How is it that Hegel and all Hegelians, who are generally supposed to be dialecticians, at this point become angry, yes, as angry as Germans? Or is "spurious" a dialectical qualification? From where does such a predicate enter logic? How do scorn and contempt and ways of frightening find a place as legitimate means of movement within logic, so that the absolute beginning is assumed by the individual because he is afraid of what his neighbors on all sides will think of him if he does not do it? Is not "spurious" an ethical category?*

What do I mean by speaking of the spurious infinity? I am charging the individual in question with not willing to stop the infinity of reflection. Am I requiring something of him, then? But on the other hand, in a genuinely speculative way, I assume that reflection stops of its own accord. Why, then, do I require something of him? And what do I require of him? I require a resolution. And in that I am right, for only in that way can reflection be stopped. But, on the other hand, it is never right for a philosopher to make sport of people and at one moment have reflection stop of its own accord in the absolute beginning and at the next moment taunt someone who has only one flaw, that he is obtuse enough to believe the first, taunt him so as to help him in this fashion to the absolute beginning, which then occurs in two ways. But if a resolution is required, presuppositionlessness is abandoned. The beginning can occur only when reflection is stopped, and reflection can be stopped only by something else, and this something else is something altogether different from the logical, since it is a resolution. Only when the beginning, at which point reflection comes to a halt, is a breakthrough, so that the absolute beginning itself breaks forth through the endlessly perpetuated reflection—only then is the beginning presuppositionless. But if it is a break

---

*And if it is not that, it is in any case an esthetic category, as when Plutarch states that some have assumed one world because thay feared that otherwise the result would be an unlimited and embarrassing infinity of worlds <*euthus aoristou kai ksalepas apeirias hypolambanousas*>. (*De defectu oraculorum,* XXII).

whereby reflection is broken off in order that the beginning can emerge, then this beginning is not absolute, since it has occurred by a <*metabasis eis allo genos*> [shifting from one genus to another].

When a beginning with the immediate is achieved by reflection, the immediate must mean something different from what it usually does. Hegelian logicians have correctly discerned this, and therefore they define the immediate, with which logic begins, as follows: the most abstract remainder after an exhaustive abstraction. There is no objection to this definition, but it is certainly objectionable that they do not respect what they themselves are saying, inasmuch as this definition indirectly states that there is no absolute beginning. "How is that?" I hear someone say. "When one has abstracted from everything, is there not then, etc.?" Indeed, *when* one has abstracted from everything. Let us be human beings. Like the act of reflection, this act of abstraction is infinite; so how do I bring it to a halt—and it is indeed first when. . . . . that. . . . . Let us even venture an imaginary construction in thought. Let that act of infinite abstraction be *in actu* [in actuality]; the beginning is not an act of abstraction but comes afterward. But then with what do I begin, now that there has been an abstraction from everything? Alas, at this point a Hegelian, deeply moved, perhaps would collapse on my chest and blissfully stammer: With nothing. And this is precisely what the system declares—that it begins with nothing. But I must pose my second question: How do I begin with this nothing? If, namely, the act of infinite abstraction is not the kind of trick of which two can very well be done at the same time, if, on the contrary, it is the most strenuous work that can be done—what then? Then all my strength will go into maintaining it. If I do not use all my strength, I do not abstract from everything. If, then, on this presupposition I make a beginning, I do not begin with nothing, simply because at the moment of beginning I did not abstract from everything. This means that if it is possible for a human being, thinking, to abstract from everything, it is impossible for him to do more, since this act, provided that it does not surpass human strength altogether, in any case completely exhausts it. To become tired of the act of abstraction and thus to manage to begin is only an explanation befitting grocers, who are not particular about a little irregularity.

The expression "to begin with nothing," even apart from its relation to the infinite act of abstraction, is itself deceptive. That is, to begin with nothing is neither more nor less than a new paraphrasing of the very dialectic of beginning. The beginning is and in turn is not, simply because it is the beginning, something that can also be expressed in this way: the beginning begins with nothing. It is merely a new expression, not a single step ahead. In the one instance, I only think a beginning *in abstracto*; in the other instance, I think the relation of the equally abstract beginning to a something with which a beginning is made. Now it is quite properly manifest that this something, indeed, the only something that corresponds to such a beginning, is nothing. But this is merely a tautological paraphrasing of the second thesis: the beginning is not. "The beginning is not" and "the beginning begins with nothing" are altogether identical theses, and I do not move from the spot.

What if, rather than speaking or dreaming of an absolute beginning, we speak of a leap? To want to be satisfied with a "mostly," an "as good as," a "one can almost say that," an "if you sleep on it until tomorrow, you may well say that" merely shows that one is related to Trop, who little by little went so far as to assume that having almost taken the bar examination was the same as having taken it. Everyone laughs at this, but when one chatters speculatively in the same manner in the realm of truth, in the shrine of science and scholarship, then it is good philosophy—genuine speculative philosophy. Lessing was no speculative philosopher; therefore he assumed the opposite, that an infinitely little distance makes the ditch infinitely broad, because the leap itself makes the ditch that broad.

It is very odd—the Hegelians, who in logic know that reflection is stopped by itself and that doubting everything flips over into its opposite by itself (a true sailor's yarn, that is, truly a sailor's yarn), know for daily use, however, when they are pleasant people, when they are like the rest of us (only more learned and gifted etc., something I shall always be willing to admit)—they know that reflection can be stopped only by a leap. Let us dwell on this point for a moment. If the individual does not stop reflection, he will be infinitized in reflection, that is, no decision is made.* By thus going astray in reflection, the individual really becomes objective, more and more he loses the decision of subjectivity and the return into himself. Yet it is assumed that reflection can stop itself objectively, whereas it is just the other way around; reflection cannot be stopped objectively, and when it is stopped subjectively, it does not stop of its own accord, but it is the subject who stops it.

For example, as soon as Rötscher (who in his book on Aristophanes does indeed understand the necessity of transition in the world-historical development, and who in the realm of logic must have understood the passage of reflection through itself to the absolute beginning) sets himself the task of interpreting Hamlet, he knows that reflection is stopped only by a resolution. He does not assume (shall I say "oddly enough"?), oddly enough, he does not assume that Hamlet finally arrived at the absolute beginning by continuing to reflect; but in logic he assumes (shall I say "oddly enough"?), oddly enough, there he most likely assumes that the passage of reflection through itself comes to a halt at the absolute beginning. This I do not understand, and it pains me not to understand it, because I have admiration for Rötscher's talent, for his classical education, for his esthetically sensitive and yet primitive conception of psychological phenomena.

What has been said here about a beginning in logic (that the same thing shows that there is no system of existence will be pursued in detail in *b*) is very plain and simple. I am almost embarrassed to say it or embarrassed to have to say it, embarrassed because of my situation—that a poor pamphlet writer, who would rather be worshiping on his knees before the system, should be constrained to say such a thing. What has been said could be stated in yet another way whereby it would perhaps make an impression on someone or other because the presentation would recall more specifically the scholarly disputes in the past. It would then become a question of the importance of the Hegelian phenomenology for the system, whether it is an introduction, whether it remains outside, and if it is an introduction, whether it is in turn incorporated in the system; further, whether Hegel may not even have the amazing merit of having written not only the system but two or even three systems, which always takes a matchless systematic head, and which nevertheless seems to be the case, since the system is completed more than once etc. Actually, all this has been said often enough, but frequently it has also been said in a confusing way. A large book has been written about it. First everything is said that Hegel has said, and thereafter consideration is given to this or that later addition, all of which merely diverts attention and shrouds in distracting prolixity what can be stated very briefly.

γ.   In order to shed light on logic, it might be desirable to become oriented psychologically in the state of mind of someone who thinks the logical—what kind of dy-

---

*Perhaps the reader will recall that when the issue becomes objective, there is no question of an eternal happiness, because this lies precisely in subjectivity and in decision.

ing to oneself is required for that purpose, and to what extent the imagination plays a part in it. The following is again another meager and very simple comment, but it may be quite true and not at all superfluous: a philosopher has gradually come to be such a marvelous creature that not even the most prodigal imagination has invented anything quite so fabulous. How, if at all, is the empirical *I* related to the pure *I-I*? Whoever wants to be a philosopher will certainly also want to be somewhat informed on this point and above all not want to become a ludicrous creature by being transmogrified— *eins, zwei, drei, kokolorum* [one, two, three, hocus pocus]—into speculative thought. If the person occupied with logical thought is also human enough not to forget that he is an existing individual, even if he has finished the system, the fantasticality and the char- latanry will gradually vanish. And even though it takes an eminently logical head to re- cast Hegel's logic, only sound common sense is needed for the person who at one time enthusiastically believed in the great thing Hegel claimed to have done and who demon- strated his enthusiasm by believing [*tro*] it, and his enthusiasm for Hegel by crediting [*tiltro*] him with it—and it takes only sound common sense to perceive that in many places Hegel behaved irresponsibly—not toward grocers, who believe only half of what a person says anyway, but toward enthusiastic youths who believed him. Even if such a young person was not exceptionally and splendidly endowed, yet when he has had the enthusiasm to believe the highest, as attributed to Hegel, when he has had the enthusi- asm to despair over himself in a dubious moment in order not to abandon Hegel—when such a young person comes to himself again, he has a right to demand the nemesis of having laughter consume in Hegel what laughter may legitimately claim as its own. And such a young person has indeed vindicated Hegel in a way much different from that of many an adherent who in deceptive asides would now make Hegel everything, now a trifle.

(B) A system of existence cannot be given.

A system of existence [*Tilværelsens System*] cannot be given. Is there, then, not such a system? That is not at all the case. Neither is this implied in what has been said. Existence itself is a system—for God, but it cannot be a system for any existing [*bexis- terende*] spirit. System and conclusiveness correspond to each other, but existence is the very opposite. Abstractly viewed, system and existence cannot be thought conjointly, because in order to think existence, systematic thought must think it as annulled and consequently not as existing. Existence is the spacing that holds apart; the systematic is the conclusiveness that combines.

Actually there now develops a deception, an illusion, which *Fragments* has at- tempted to point out. I must now refer to this work, namely, to the question of whether the past is more necessary than the future. That is, when an existence is a thing of the past, it is indeed finished, it is indeed concluded, and to that extent it is turned over to the systematic view. Quite so—but for whom? Whoever is himself existing cannot gain this conclusiveness outside existence, a conclusiveness that corresponds to the eternity into which the past has entered. Even if a good-natured thinker is so absent- minded as to forget that he himself is existing, speculative thought and absentminded- ness are still not quite the same thing. On the contrary, that he himself is existing implies the claim of existence upon him and that his existence, yes, if he is a great in- dividual, that his existence at the present time may, as past, in turn have the validity of conclusiveness for a systematic thinker. But who, then, is this systematic thinker? Well, it is he who himself is outside existence and yet in existence, who in his eternity is forever concluded and yet includes existence within himself—it is God. So why the deception! Just because the world has lasted now for six thousand years, does existence therefore not have the very same claim upon the existing individual that it has always had, which is not that he in make-believe should be a contemplating spirit but that he in actuality should be an existing spirit. All understanding comes afterward. Whereas an individual existing now undeniably comes afterward in relation to the six thousand years that preceded, the curiously ironic consequence would emerge—if we assumed that he came to understand them systematically—that he would not come to understand himself as an existing being, because he himself would acquire no existence, because he himself would have nothing that should be understood afterward. It follows that such a thinker must be either the good Lord or a fantastical *quodlibet* [anything]. Certainly everyone will perceive the immorality in this, and certainly everyone will also perceive that what another author has observed regarding the Hegelian system is entirely in order: that through Hegel a system, the absolute system, was brought to completion—without having an ethics. By all means, let us smile at the ethical-religious fantasies of the Middle Ages in asceticism and the like, but above all let us not forget that the speculative, farcical exaggeration of becoming an *I-I*—and then *qua* human being often such a philistine that no enthusiast would have cared to lead such a life—is equally ludicrous.

So let us ask very simply, as a Greek youth would ask his master (and if the lofty wisdom can explain everything else but cannot answer a simple question, one surely sees that the world is out of joint), about the impossibility of a system of existence: Who is supposed to write or finish such a system? Surely a human being, unless we are to resume the peculiar talk about a human being's becoming speculative thought, a subject-object. Consequently, a human being—and surely a living, that is, an existing, human being. Or if the speculative thought that produces the system is the joint effort of these various thinkers, in what final conclusion does this fellowship combine? How does it come to light? Surely through a human being? And how, in turn, do the individual thinkers relate themselves to this effort; what are the middle terms between the particular and the world-historical; and in turn what sort of being is the one who is stringing it all on the systematic thread? Is he a human being or is he speculative thought? But if he is a human being, then he is indeed existing. Now, all in all, there are two ways for an existing individual: either he can do everything to forget that he is existing and thereby manage to become comic (the comic contradiction of wanting to be what one is not, for example, that a human being wants to be a bird is no more comic than the contradiction of not wanting to be what one is, as *in casu* [in this case] an existing individual, just as in the use of language it is comic when someone forgets his name, which signifies not so much forgetting his name as the singularity of his nature), because existence possesses the remarkable quality that an existing person exists whether he wants to or not; or he can direct all his attention to his existing. It is from this side that an objection must first be made to modern speculative thought, that it has not a false presupposition but a comic presupposition, occasioned by its having forgotten in a kind of world-historical absentmindedness what it means to be a human being, not what it means to be human in general, for even speculators might be swayed to consider that sort of thing, but what it means that we, you and I and he, are human beings, each one on his own.

The existing individual who directs all his attention to the actuality that *he* is existing will approvingly look upon those words of Lessing about a continued striving as a beautiful saying, not as something that gained its author immortal fame, because the saying is so very simple, but as something every attentive person must certify. The existing individual who forgets that he is existing will become more and more absent-minded, and just as people occasionally set down the fruits of their *otium* [leisure] in books, so we may expect the expected existential system as the fruit of his absentmind-edness—well, not all of us, but only those who are as absentminded as he is. Whereas the Hegelian system in absentmindedness goes ahead and becomes a system of exis-tence, and what is more, is finished—without having an ethics (the very home of exis-tence), that other simpler philosophy, presented by an existing individual for existing individuals, is especially intent upon advancing the ethical.

As soon as it is remembered that philosophizing is not speaking fantastically to fantastical beings but speaking to existing individuals, consequently that a decision about whether a continued striving is somewhat inferior to systematic conclusiveness is not to be made fantastically *in abstracto*, but that the question is what existing beings have to be satisfied with insofar as they are existing—then the continued striving will be unique in not involving illusion. Even if a person has achieved the highest, the repeti-tion by which he must indeed fill out his existence, if he is not to go backward (or be-come a fantastical being), will again be a continued striving, because here in turn the conclusiveness is moved ahead and postponed. This is just like the Platonic conception of love; it is a want, and not only does that person feel a want who craves something he does not have but also that person who desires the continued possession of what he has. In the system and in the fifth act of the drama, one has a positive conclusiveness specu-latively-fantastically and esthetically-fantastically, but such a conclusiveness is only for fantastical beings.

The continued striving is the expression of the existing subject's ethical life-view. The continued striving must therefore not be understood metaphysically, but neither is there any individual who exists metaphysically. Thus through a misunderstanding a contrast could be drawn between systematic conclusiveness and the continued striving for truth. One might then be able, and perhaps has even tried, to bear in mind the Greek notion of continually wanting to be a learner. But that is only a misunderstanding in this sphere. On the contrary, ethically understood, the continued striving is the conscious-ness of being an existing individual, and the continued learning the expression of the perpetual actualization, which at no moment is finished as long as the subject is exist-ing; the subject is aware of this and is therefore not deluded. But Greek philosophy had a continual relation to ethics. That was why continually wanting to be a learner was not regarded as a great discovery or the inspired undertaking of an exceptional individual, since it was neither more nor less than the understanding that one is existing and that to be conscious of this is no merit but to forget it is thoughtlessness.

So-called pantheistic systems have frequently been cited and attacked by saying that they cancel freedom and the distinction between good and evil. This is perhaps ex-pressed just as definitely by saying that every such system fantastically volatilizes the concept *existence*. But this should be said not only of pantheistic systems, for it would have been better to show that every system must be pantheistic simply because of the conclusiveness. Existence must be annulled in the eternal before the system concludes itself. No existing remainder may be left behind, not even such a tiny little dingle-dangle as the existing Herr Professor who is writing the system. But the issue is not presented this way. No, the pantheistic systems are contested, partly with tumultuous aphorisms that again and again promise a new system, partly with a compilation that is supposed to be a system and has a separate paragraph in which it is declared that em-phasis is placed on the concepts "existence" and "actuality." That such a paragraph mocks the entire system, that instead of being a paragraph in the system it is an absolute protest against the system, is of no consequence to busy systematic triflers. If the concept of existence is actually to be emphasized, this cannot be stated directly in a paragraph in a system, and all direct oaths and "the devil take me" only make the didacticizing upside-downness even more ludicrous. That existence is actually emphasized must be expressed in an essential form, and in relation to the illusiveness of existence this is an indirect form—that there is no system. Yet this must not in turn become a reassuring standardized formula, because the indirect expression will always be regenerated in the form. In committee deliberations, it is quite all right to include a dissenting vote, but a system that has a dissenting vote as a paragraph within it is a queer monstrosity. No wonder, then, that the system survives. It proudly ignores objections; and if it comes across a particular objection that appears to draw a little attention, the systematic entrepreneurs proceed to have a copyist make a copy of the objection, which is thereupon recorded in the system, and with the bookbinding the system is finished.

The systematic idea is subject-object, is the unity of thinking and being; existence, on the other hand, is precisely the separation. From this it by no means follows that existence is thoughtless, but existence has spaced and does space subject from object, thought from being. Objectively understood, thinking is pure thinking, which just as abstractly-objectively corresponds to its object, which in turn is therefore itself, and truth is the correspondence of thinking with itself. This objective thinking has no relation to the existing subjectivity, and while the difficult question always remains— namely, how the existing subject gains entrance into this objectivity in which subjectivity is pure abstract subjectivity (which again is an objective qualification and does not signify any existing human being)—it is certain that the existing subjectivity evaporates more and more. And finally, if it is possible that a human being can become such a thing and that all this is not something of which he at best can become cognizant through imagination, this existing subjectivity becomes a pure abstract co-knowledge [*Medviden*] in and knowledge of this pure relation between thinking and being, this pure identity, indeed this tautology, because here being does not mean that the thinking person is, but basically only that he is a thinker.

The existing subject, however, is existing, and so indeed is every human being. Yet let us not do the wrong of calling the objective tendency impious, pantheistic self-worship but rather view it as a venture in the comic, because the idea that from now on to the end of the world nothing should be said except what would suggest a further improvement in a nearly finished system is simply a systematic consequence for systematizers.

By beginning straightway with ethical categories against the objective tendency, one does wrong and fails to hit the mark, because one has nothing in common with the attacked. But by remaining within the metaphysical, one can employ the comic, which also is in the metaphysical sphere, in order to overtake such a transfigured professor. If a dancer could leap very high, we would admire him, but if he wanted to give the impression that he could fly—even though he could leap higher than any dancer had ever leapt before—let laughter overtake him. Leaping means to belong essentially to the earth and to respect the law of gravity so that the leap is merely the momentary, but flying means to be set free from telluric conditions, something that is reserved exclusively for winged creatures, perhaps also for inhabitants of the moon, perhaps—and perhaps that is also where the system will at long last find its true readers. To be a human being has been abolished, and every speculative thinker confuses himself with humankind, whereby he becomes something infinitely great and nothing at all. In absentmindedness, he confuses himself with humankind, just as the opposition press uses "we" and the skippers say "the devil take me." But having cursed for a long time, one finally returns to the direct statement, because all swearing cancels itself; and when one has learned that every urchin can say "we," one learns that it nevertheless means a little more to be *one*; and when one sees that every cellar dweller can play the game of being humankind, one finally perceives that to be simply and solely a human being means something more than playing party games this way. And one thing more—when a cellar dweller plays this game, everyone thinks it ludicrous; and yet it is just as ludicrous when the greatest human being does it. And in that regard one may laugh at him and, as is fitting, still have respect for his abilities, his learning, etc.

SECTION II, CHAPTER 2: SUBJECTIVE TRUTH, INWARDNESS; TRUTH IS SUBJECTIVITY

*   *   *

When the question about truth is asked objectively, truth is reflected upon objectively as an object to which the knower relates himself. What is reflected upon is not the relation but that what he relates himself to is the truth, the true. If only that to which he relates himself is the truth, the true, then the subject is in the truth. When the question about truth is asked subjectively, the individual's relation is reflected upon subjectively. If only the how of this relation is in truth, the individual is in truth, even if he in this way were to relate himself to untruth.*

Let us take the knowledge of God as an example. Objectively, what is reflected upon is that this is the true God; subjectively, that the individual relates himself to a something in *such a way* that his relation is in truth a God-relation. Now, on which side is the truth? Alas, must we not at this point resort to mediation and say: It is on neither side; it is in the mediation? Superbly stated, if only someone could say how an existing person goes about being in mediation, because to be in mediation is to be finished; to exist is to become. An existing person cannot be in two places at the same time, cannot be subject-object. When he is closest to being in two places at the same time, he is in passion; but passion is only momentary, and passion is the highest pitch of subjectivity.

The existing person who chooses the objective way now enters upon all approximating deliberation intended to bring forth God objectively, which is not achieved in all eternity, because God is a subject and hence only for subjectivity in inwardness. The existing person who chooses the subjective way instantly comprehends the whole dialectical difficulty because he must use some time, perhaps a long time, to find God objectively. He comprehends this dialectical difficulty in all its pain, because he must resort to God at that very moment, because every moment in which he does not have God is wasted.** At that very moment he has God, not by virtue of any objective de-

---

*The reader will note that what is being discussed here is essential truth, or the truth that is related essentially to existence, and that it is specifically in order to clarify it as inwardness or as subjectivity that the contrast is pointed out.

**In this way God is indeed a postulate, but not in the loose sense in which it is ordinarily taken. Instead, it becomes clear that this is the only way an existing person enters into a relationship with God: when the dialectical contradiction brings passion to despair and assists him in grasping God with "the category of despair" (faith), so that the postulate, far from being the arbitrary, is in fact *necessary* defense [Nødværge], self defense; in this way God is not a postulate, but the existing person's postulating of God is—a necessity [Nødvendighed].

liberation but by virtue of the infinite passion of inwardness. The objective person is not bothered by dialectical difficulties such as what it means to put a whole research period into finding God, since it is indeed possible that the researcher would die tomorrow, and if he goes on living, he cannot very well regard God as something to be taken along at his convenience, since God is something one takes along a *tout prix* [at any price], which, in passion's understanding, is the true relationship of inwardness with God.

It is at this point, dialectically so very difficult, that the road swings off for the person who knows what it means to think dialectically and, existing, to think dialectically, which is quite different from sitting as a fantastical being at a desk and writing about something one has never done oneself, quite different from writing *de omnibus dubitandum* and then as an existing person being just as credulous as the most sensate human being. It is here that the road swings off, and the change is this: whereas objective knowledge goes along leisurely on the long road of approximation, itself not actuated by passion, to subjective knowledge every delay is a deadly peril and the decision so infinitely important that it is immediately urgent, as if the opportunity had already passed by unused.

Now, if the problem is to calculate where there is more truth (and, as stated, simultaneously to be on both sides equally is not granted to an existing person but is only a beatifying delusion for a deluded *I-I*), whether on the side of the person who only objectively seeks the true God and the approximating truth of the God-idea or on the side of the person who is infinitely concerned that he in truth relate himself to God with the infinite passion of need—then there can be no doubt about the answer for anyone who is not totally botched by scholarship and science. If someone who lives in the midst of Christianity enters, with knowledge of the true idea of God, the house of God, the house of the true God, and prays, but prays in untruth, and if someone lives in an idolatrous land but prays with all the passion of infinity, although his eyes are resting upon the image of an idol—where, then, is there more truth? The one prays in truth to God although he is worshiping an idol; the other prays in untruth to the true God and is therefore in truth worshiping an idol.

If someone objectively inquires into immortality, and someone else stakes the passion of the infinite on the uncertainty—where, then, is there more truth, and who has more certainty? The one has once and for all entered upon an approximation that never ends, because the certainty of immortality is rooted in subjectivity; the other is immortal and therefore struggles by contending with the uncertainty.

Let us consider Socrates. These days everyone is dabbling in a few proofs or demonstrations—one has many, another fewer. But Socrates! He poses the question objectively, problematically: if there is an immortality. So, compared with one of the modern thinkers with the three demonstrations, was he a doubter? Not at all. He stakes his whole life on this "if"; he dares to die, and with the passion of the infinite he has so ordered his whole life that it might be acceptable—if there is an immortality. Is there any better demonstration for the immortality of the soul? But those who have the three demonstrations do not order their lives accordingly. If there is an immortality, it must be nauseated by their way of living—is there any better counter-demonstration to the three demonstrations? The "fragment" of uncertainty helped Socrates, because he himself helped with the passion of infinity. The three demonstrations are of no benefit whatever to those others, because they are and remain slugs and, failing to demonstrate anything else, have demonstrated it by their three demonstrations.

In the same way a girl has perhaps possessed all the sweetness of being in love through a weak hope of being loved by the beloved, because she herself staked everything on this weak hope; on the other hand, many a wedded matron, who more than once has submitted to the strongest expression of erotic love, has certainly had demonstrations and yet, strangely enough, has not possessed *quod erat demonstrandum* [that which was to be demonstrated]. The Socratic ignorance was thus the expression, firmly maintained with all the passion of inwardness, of the relation of the eternal truth to an existing person, and therefore it must remain for him a paradox as long as he exists. Yet it is possible that in the Socratic ignorance there was more truth in Socrates than in the objective truth of the entire system that flirts with the demands of the times and adapts itself to assistant professors.

Objectively the emphasis is on what is said; subjectively the emphasis is on how it is said. This distinction applies even esthetically and is specifically expressed when we say that in the mouth of this or that person something that is truth can become untruth. Particular attention should be paid to this distinction in our day, for if one were to express in a single sentence the difference between ancient times and our time, one would no doubt have to say: In ancient times there were only a few individuals who knew the truth; now everyone knows it, but inwardness has an inverse relation to it. Viewed esthetically, the contradiction that emerges when truth becomes untruth in this and that person's mouth is best interpreted comically. Ethically-religiously, the emphasis is again on: *how*. But this is not to be understood as manner, modulation of voice, oral delivery, etc., but it is to be understood as the relation of the existing person, in his very existence, to what is said. Objectively, the question is only about categories of thought; subjectively, about inwardness. At its maximum, this "how" is the passion of the infinite, and the passion of the infinite is the very truth. But the passion of the infinite is precisely subjectivity, and thus subjectivity is truth. From the objective point of view, there is no infinite decision, and thus it is objectively correct that the distinction between good and evil is canceled, along with the principle of contradiction, and thereby also the infinite distinction between truth and falsehood. Only in subjectivity is there decision, whereas wanting to become objective is untruth. The passion of the infinite, not its content, is the deciding factor, for its content is precisely itself. In this way the subjective "how" and subjectivity are the truth.

But precisely because the subject is existing, the "how" that is subjectively emphasized is dialectical also with regard to time. In the moment of the decision of passion, where the road swings off from objective knowledge, it looks as if the infinite decision were thereby finished. But at the same moment, the existing person is in the temporal realm, and the subjective "how" is transformed into a striving that is motivated and repeatedly refreshed by the decisive passion of the infinite, but it is nevertheless a striving.

When subjectivity is truth, the definition of truth must also contain in itself an expression of the antithesis to objectivity, a memento of that fork in the road, and this expression will at the same time indicate the resilience of the inwardness. Here is such a definition of truth: *An objective uncertainty, held fast through appropriation with the most passionate inwardness, is the truth*, the highest truth there is for an *existing* person. At the point where the road swings off (and where that is cannot be stated objectively, since it is precisely subjectivity), objective knowledge is suspended. Objectively he then has only uncertainty, but this is precisely what intensifies the infinite passion of inwardness, and truth is precisely the daring venture of choosing the objective uncertainty with the passion of the infinite. I observe nature in order to find God, and I do indeed see omnipotence and wisdom, but I also see much that troubles and disturbs. The *summa summarum* [sum total] of this is an objective uncertainty, but the inwardness is so very great, precisely because it grasps this objective uncertainty with all the passion of the infinite. In a mathematical proposition, for example, the objectivity is given, but therefore its truth is also an indifferent truth.

But the definition of truth stated above is a paraphrasing of faith. Without risk, no faith. Faith is the contradiction between the infinite passion of inwardness and the objective uncertainty. If I am able to apprehend God objectively, I do not have faith; but because I cannot do this, I must have faith. If I want to keep myself in faith, I must continually see to it that I hold fast the objective uncertainty, see to it that in the objective uncertainty I am "out on 70,000 fathoms of water" and still have faith.

The thesis that subjectivity, inwardness, is truth contains the Socratic wisdom, the undying merit of which is to have paid attention to the essential meaning of existing, of the knower's being an existing person. That is why, in his ignorance, Socrates was in the truth in the highest sense within paganism. To comprehend this, that the misfortune of speculative thought is simply that it forgets again and again that the knower is an existing person, can already be rather difficult in our objective age. "But to go beyond Socrates when one has not even comprehended the Socratic—that, at least, is not Socratic." See "The Moral" in *Fragments*.

Just as in *Fragments*, let us from this point try a category of thought that actually does go beyond. Whether it is true or false is of no concern to me, since I am only imaginatively constructing, but this much is required, that it be clear that the Socratic is presupposed in it, so that I at least do not end up behind Socrates again.

When subjectivity, inwardness, is truth, then truth, objectively defined, is a paradox; and that truth is objectively a paradox shows precisely that subjectivity is truth, since the objectivity does indeed thrust away, and the objectivity's repulsion, or the expression for the objectivity's repulsion, is the resilience and dynamometer of inwardness. The paradox is the objective uncertainty that is the expression for the passion of inwardness that is truth. So much for the Socratic. The eternal, essential truth, that is, the truth that is related essentially to the existing person by pertaining essentially to what it means to exist (viewed Socratically, all other knowledge is accidental, its degree and scope indifferent), is a paradox. Nevertheless the eternal, essential truth is itself not at all a paradox, but it is a paradox by being related to an existing person. Socratic ignorance is an expression of the objective uncertainty; the inwardness of the existing person is truth. In anticipation of what will be discussed later, the following comment is made here: Socratic ignorance is an analogue to the category of the absurd, except that there is even less objective certainty in the repulsion exerted by the absurd, since there is only the certainty that it is absurd, and for that very reason there is infinitely greater resilience in the inwardness. The Socratic inwardness in existing is an analogue to faith, except that the inwardness of faith, corresponding not to the repulsion exerted by ignorance but to the repulsion exerted by the absurd, is infinitely deeper.

Viewed Socratically, the eternal essential truth is not at all paradoxical in itself, but only by being related to an existing person. This is expressed in another Socratic thesis: that all knowing is a recollecting. This thesis is an intimation of the beginning of speculative thought, but for that very reason Socrates did not pursue it; essentially it became Platonic. This is where the road swings off, and Socrates essentially emphasizes existing, whereas Plato, forgetting this, loses himself in speculative thought. Socrates' infinite merit is precisely that of being an *existing* thinker, not a speculative thinker who forgets what it means to exist. To Socrates, therefore, the thesis that all knowing is a recollecting has, at the moment of parting and as a continually annulled possibility of speculating, a double significance: (1) that the knower is essentially *integer* [uncorrupted] and that for him there is no other dubiousness with regard to knowledge of the eternal truth than this, that he exists, a dubiousness so essential and decisive to him that it signifies that existing, the inward deepening in and through existing, is truth; (2) that existence in temporality has no decisive significance, because there is continually the possibility of taking oneself back into eternity by recollecting, even though this possibility is continually annulled because the inward deepening in existing fills up time.*

The great merit of the Socratic was precisely to emphasize that the knower is an existing person and that to exist is the essential. To go beyond Socrates by failing to understand this is nothing but a mediocre merit. This we must keep *in mente* [in mind] and then see whether the formula cannot be changed in such a way that one actually does go beyond the Socratic.

So, then, subjectivity, inwardness, is truth. Is there a *more inward* expression for it? Yes, if the discussion about "Subjectivity, inwardness, is truth" begins in this way: "Subjectivity is untruth." But let us not be in a hurry. Speculative thought also says that subjectivity is untruth but says it in the very opposite direction, namely, that objectivity is truth. Speculative thought defines subjectivity negatively in the direction of objectivity. The other definition, however, puts barriers in its own way at the very moment it wants to begin, which makes the inwardness so much more inward. Viewed Socratically, subjectivity is untruth if it refuses to comprehend that subjectivity is truth but wants, for example, to be objective. Here, on the other hand, in wanting to begin to become truth by becoming subjective, subjectivity is in the predicament of being untruth. Thus the work goes backward, that is, backward in inwardness. The way is so far from being in the direction of the objective that the beginning only lies even deeper in subjectivity.

*This may be the proper place to elucidate a dubiousness in the design of Fragments, a dubiousness that was due to my not wanting immediately to make the matter as dialectically difficult as it is, because in our day terminologies and the like are so muddled that it is almost impossible to safeguard oneself against confusion. In order, if possible, to elucidate properly the difference between the Socratic (which was supposed to be the philosophical, the pagan philosophical position) and the category of imaginatively constructed thought, which actually goes beyond the Socraic, I carried the Socratic back to the thesis that all knowing is a recollecting. It is commonly accepted as such, and only for the person who with a very special interest devotes himself to the Socratic, always returning to the sources, only for him will it be important to distinguish between Socrates and Plato on this point. The thesis certainly belongs to both of them, but Socrates continually parts with it because he wants to exist. By holding Socrates to the thesis that all knowing is recollecting, one turns him into a speculative philosopher instead of what he was, an existing thinker who understood existing as the essential. The thesis that all knowing is recollecting belongs to speculative thought, and recollecting is immanence, and from the point of view of speculation and the eternal there is no paradox. The difficulty, however, is that no human being is speculation, but the speculating person is an existing human being, subject to the claims of existence. To forget this is no merit, but to hold this fast is indeed a merit and that is precisely what Socrates did. To emphasize existence, which contains within it the qualification of inwardness, is the Socratic, whereas the Platonic is to purse recollection and immanence. Basically Socrates is thereby beyond all speculation, because he does not have a fantastical beginning where the speculating person changes clothes and then goes on and on and speculates, forgetting the most important thing, to exist. But precisely because Socrates is in this way beyond speculative thought, he acquires, when rightly depicted, a certain analogous likeness to what the imaginary construction set forth as that which truly goes beyond the Socratic: the truth as paradox is an analog to the paradox *sensu eminetiori* [in the more eminent sense]; the passion of inwardness in existing is then an analog to faith *sensu eminentiori*. That the difference is infinite nevertheless, that the designations in *Fragments* of that which truly goes beyond the Socratic are unchanged, I can easily show, but I was afraid to make complications by promptly using what seem to be the same designations, at least the same words, about the different things when the imaginary construction was to be presented as different from these. Now, I think there would be no objection to speaking of the paradox in connection with Socrates and faith, since it is quite correct to do so, provided that it is understood correctly. Besides, the ancient Greeks also use the word <*pistis*> [Faith], although by no means in the sense of the imaginary construction, and use it so as to make possible some very illuminating observations beraring upon its dissimilarity to faith *sensu eminentiori*, especially with reference to one of Aristotle's works where the term is employed.

But the subject cannot be untruth eternally or be presupposed to have been untruth eternally; he must have become that in time or he becomes that in time. The Socratic paradox consisted in this, that the eternal truth was related to an existing person. But now existence has accentuated the existing person a second time; a change so essential has taken place in him that he in no way can take himself back into eternity by Socratically recollecting. To do this is to speculate; to be able to do this but, by grasping the inward deepening in existence, to annul the possibility of doing it is the Socratic. But now the difficulty is that what accompanied Socrates as an annulled possibility has become an impossibility. If speculating was already of dubious merit in connection with the Socratic, it is now only confusion.

The paradox emerges when the eternal truth and existing are placed together, but each time existing is accentuated, the paradox becomes clearer and clearer. Viewed Socratically, the knower was an existing person, but now the existing person is accentuated in such a way that existence has made an essential change in him.

Let us now call the individual's untruth *sin*. Viewed eternally, he cannot be in sin or be presupposed to have been eternally in sin. Therefore, by coming into existence (for the beginning was that subjectivity is untruth), he becomes a sinner. He is not born as a sinner in the sense that he is presupposed to be a sinner before he is born, but he is born in sin and as a sinner. Indeed, we could call this *hereditary sin*. But if existence has in this way obtained power over him, he is prevented from taking himself back into eternity through recollection. If it is already paradoxical that the eternal truth is related to an existing person, now it is absolutely paradoxical that it is related to such an existing person. But the more difficult it is made for him, recollecting, to take himself out of existence, the more inward his existing can become in existence; and when it is made impossible for him, when he is lodged in existence in such a way that the back door of recollection is forever closed, then the inwardness becomes the deepest. But let us never forget that the Socratic merit was precisely to emphasize that the knower is existing, because the more difficult the matter becomes, the more one is tempted to rush along the easy road of speculative thought, away from terrors and decisions, to fame, honor, a life of ease, etc. If even Socrates comprehended the dubiousness of taking himself speculatively out of existence back into eternity, when there was no dubiousness for the existing person except that he existed and, of course, that existing was the essential—now it is impossible. He must go forward; to go backward is impossible.

Subjectivity is truth. The paradox came into existence through the relating of the eternal, essential truth to the existing person. Let us now go further; let us assume that the eternal, essential truth is itself the paradox. How does the paradox emerge? By placing the eternal, essential truth together with existing. Consequently, if we place it together in the truth itself, the truth becomes a paradox. The eternal truth has come into existence in time. That is the paradox. If the subject just mentioned was prevented by sin from taking himself back into eternity, now he is not to concern himself with this, because now the eternal, essential truth is not behind him but has come in front of him by existing itself or by having existed, so that if the individual, existing, does not lay hold of the truth in existence, he will never have it.

Existence can never be accentuated more sharply than it has been here. The fraud of speculative thought in wanting to recollect itself out of existence has been made impossible. This is the only point to be comprehended here, and every speculation that insists on being speculation shows *eo ipso* [precisely thereby] that it has not comprehended this. The individual can thrust all this away and resort to speculation, but to accept it and then want to cancel it through speculation is impossible, because it is specifically designed to prevent speculation.

When the eternal truth relates itself to an existing person, it becomes the paradox. Through the objective uncertainty and ignorance, the paradox thrusts away in the inwardness of the existing person. But since the paradox is not in itself the paradox, it does not thrust away intensely enough, for without risk, no faith; the more risk, the more faith; the more objective reliability, the less inwardness (since inwardness is subjectivity); the less objective reliability, the deeper is the possible inwardness. When the paradox itself is the paradox, it thrusts away by virtue of the absurd, and the corresponding passion of inwardness is faith.

But subjectivity, inwardness, is truth; if not, we have forgotten the Socratic merit. But when the retreat out of existence into eternity by way of recollection has been made impossible, then, with the truth facing one as the paradox, in the anxiety of sin and its pain, with the tremendous risk of objectivity, there is no stronger expression for inwardness than—to have faith. But without risk, no faith, not even the Socratic faith, to say nothing of the kind we are discussing here.

When Socrates believed that God is, he held fast the objective uncertainty with the entire passion of inwardness, and faith is precisely in this contradiction, in this risk. Now it is otherwise. Instead of the objective uncertainty, there is here the certainty that, viewed objectively, it is the absurd, and this absurdity, held fast in the passion of inwardness, is faith. Compared with the earnestness of the absurd, the Socratic ignorance is like a witty jest, and compared with the strenuousness of faith, the Socratic existential inwardness resembles Greek nonchalance.

What, then, is the absurd? The absurd is that the eternal truth has come into existence in time, that God has come into existence, has been born, has grown up, etc., has come into existence exactly as an individual human being, indistinguishable from any other human being, inasmuch as all immediate recognizability is pre-Socratic paganism and from the Jewish point of view is idolatry. Every qualification of that which actually goes beyond the Socratic must essentially have a mark of standing in relation to the god's having come into existence, because faith, *sensu strictissimo* [in the strictest sense], as explicated in *Fragments*, refers to coming into existence. When Socrates believed that God is [*er til*], he no doubt perceived that where the road swings off there is a road of objective approximation, for example, the observation of nature, world history, etc. His merit was precisely to shun this road, where the quantifying siren song spellbinds and tricks the existing person. In relation to the absurd, the objective approximation resembles the comedy *Misforstaaelse paa Misforstaaelse* [Misunderstanding upon Misunderstanding], which ordinarily is played by assistant professors and speculative thinkers.

It is by way of the objective repulsion that the absurd is the dynamometer of faith in inwardness. So, then, there is a man who wants to have faith; well, let the comedy begin. He wants to have faith, but he wants to assure himself with the aid of objective deliberation and approximation. What happens? With the aid of approximation, the absurd becomes something else; it becomes probable, it becomes more probable, it may become to a high degree and exceedingly probable. Now he is all set to believe it, and he dares to say of himself that he does not believe as shoemakers and tailors and simple folk do, but only after long deliberation. Now he is all set to believe it, but, lo and behold, now it has indeed become impossible to believe it. The almost probable, the probable, the to-a-high-degree and exceedingly probable—that he can almost know, or as good as know, to a higher degree and exceedingly almost *know*—

but *believe* it, that cannot be done, for the absurd is precisely the object of faith and only that can be believed.

Or there is a man who says he has faith, but now he wants to make his faith clear to himself; he wants to understand himself in his faith. Now the comedy begins again. The object of faith becomes almost probable, it becomes as good as probable, it becomes probable, it becomes to a high degree and exceedingly probable. He has finished; he dares to say of himself that he does not believe as shoemakers and tailors or other simple folk do but that he has also understood himself in his believing. What wondrous understanding! On the contrary, he has learned to know something different about faith than he believed and has learned to know that he no longer has faith, since he almost knows, as good as knows, to a high degree and exceedingly almost knows.

Inasmuch as the absurd contains the element of coming into existence, the road of approximation will also be that which confuses the absurd fact of coming into existence, which is the object of faith, with a simple historical fact, and then seeks historical certainty for that which is absurd precisely because it contains the contradiction that something that can become historical only in direct opposition to all human understanding has become historical. This contradiction is the absurd, which can only be believed. If a historical certainty is obtained, one obtains merely the certainty that what is certain is not what is the point in question. A witness can testify that he has believed it and then testify that, far from being a historical certainty, it is in direct opposition to his understanding, but such a witness repels in the same sense as the absurd repels, and a witness who does not repel in this way is *eo ipso* a deceiver or a man who is talking about something altogether different; and such a witness can be of no help except in obtaining certainty about something altogether different. One hundred thousand individual witnesses, who by the special nature of their testimony (that they have believed the absurd) remain individual witnesses, do not become something else *en masse* so that the absurd becomes less absurd. Why? Because one hundred thousand people individually have believed that it was absurd? Quite the contrary, those one hundred thousand witnesses repel exactly as the absurd does.

But I do not need to develop this further here. In *Fragments* (especially where the difference between the follower at first hand and the follower at second hand is annulled) and in Part One of this book, I have with sufficient care shown that all approximation is futile, since the point is rather to do away with introductory observations, reliabilities, demonstrations from effects, and the whole mob of pawnbrokers and guarantors, in order to get the absurd clear—so that one can believe if one will—I merely say that this must be extremely strenuous.

If speculative thought wants to become involved in this and, as always, say: From the point of view of the eternal, the divine, the theocentric, there is no paradox—I shall not be able to decide whether the speculative thinker is right, because I am only a poor existing human being who neither eternally nor divinely nor theocentrically is able to observe the eternal but must be content with existing. This much, however, is certain, that with speculative thought everything goes backward, back past the Socratic, which at least comprehended that for an existing person existing is the essential; and much less has speculative thought taken the time to comprehend what it means to be *situated* in existence the way the existing person is in the imaginary construction.

The difference between the Socratic position and the position that goes beyond the Socratic is clear enough and is essentially the same as in *Fragments*, for in the latter nothing has changed, and in the former the matter has only been made somewhat more difficult, but nevertheless not more difficult than it is. It has also become somewhat more difficult because, whereas in *Fragments* I set forth the thought-category of the paradox only in an imaginary construction, here I have also latently made an attempt to make clear the necessity of the paradox, and even though the attempt is somewhat weak, it is still something different from speculatively canceling the paradox.

Christianity has itself proclaimed itself to be the eternal, essential truth that has come into existence in time; it has proclaimed itself as *the paradox* and has required the inwardness of faith with regard to what is an offense to the Jews, foolishness to the Greeks—and an absurdity to the understanding. It cannot be expressed more strongly that subjectivity is truth and that objectivity only thrusts away, precisely by virtue of the absurd, and it seems strange that Christianity should have come into the world in order to be explained, alas, as if it were itself puzzled about itself and therefore came into the world to seek out the wise man, the speculative thinker, who can aid with the explanation. It cannot be expressed more inwardly that subjectivity is truth than when subjectivity is at first untruth, and yet subjectivity is truth.

*   *   *

The direct relationship with God is simply paganism, and only when the break has taken place, only then can there be a true God-relationship. But this break is indeed the first act of inwardness oriented to the definition that truth is inwardness. Nature is certainly the work of God, but only the work is directly present, not God. With regard to the individual human being, is this not acting like an illusive author, who nowhere sets forth his result in block letters or provides it beforehand in a preface? And why is God illusive? Precisely because he is truth and in being illusive seeks to keep a person from untruth. The observer does not glide directly to the result but on his own must concern himself with finding it and thereby break the direct relation. But this break is the actual breakthrough of inwardness, an act of self-activity, the first designation of truth as inwardness.

Or is it not the case that God is so unnoticeable, so hidden yet present in his work, that a person might very well live on, marry, be respected and esteemed as husband, father, and captain of the popinjay shooting club, without discovering God in his work, without ever receiving any impression of the infinitude of the ethical, because he managed with an analogy to the speculative confusion of the ethical and the world-historical by managing with custom and tradition in the city where he lived? Just as a mother admonishes her child who is about to attend a party, "Now, mind your manners and watch the other polite children and behave as they do," so he, too, could live on and behave as he saw others behave. He would never do anything first and would never have any opinion unless he first knew that others had it, because "the others" would be his very first. On special occasions he would act like someone who does not know how to eat a course that is served at a banquet; he would reconnoiter until he saw how the others did it etc. Such a person could perhaps know ever so much, perhaps even know the system by rote; he could perhaps live in a Christian country, know how to bow his head every time God's name was mentioned, perhaps also see God in nature if he was in the company of others who saw God; in short, well, he could be a congenial party goer—and yet he would be deceived by the direct relation to truth, to the ethical, to God.

If one were to portray such a person in an imaginary construction, he would be a satire on what it is to be a human being. It is really the God-relationship that makes a human being a human being, but this is what he would lack. Yet no one would hesitate to consider him an actual human being (for the absence of inwardness is not seen directly), although he would be more like a puppet character that very deceptively imitates all the human externalities—would even have children with his wife. At the end of his life, one would have to say that one thing had escaped him: he had not become aware of God. If God could have permitted a direct relationship, he would certainly have become aware. If God had taken the form, for example, of a rare, enormously large green bird, with a red beak, that perched in a tree on the embankment and perhaps even whistled in an unprecedented manner—then our party going man would surely have had his eyes opened; for the first time in his life he would have been able to be the first.

All paganism consists in this, that God is related directly to a human being, as the remarkably striking to the amazed. But the spiritual relationship with God in truth, that is, inwardness, is first conditioned by the actual breakthrough of inward deepening that corresponds to the divine cunning that God has nothing remarkable, nothing at all remarkable, about him—indeed, he is so far from being remarkable that he is invisible, and thus one does not suspect that he is there [*er til*], although his invisibility is in turn his omnipresence. But an omnipresent being is the very one who is seen everywhere, for example, as a police officer is—how illusive, then, that an omnipresent being is cognizable precisely by his being invisible,* simply and solely by this, because his very visibility would annul his omnipresence. This relation between omnipresence and invisibility is like the relation between mystery and revelation, that the mystery expresses that the revelation is revelation in the stricter sense, that the mystery is the one and only mark by which it can be known, since otherwise a revelation becomes something like a police officer's omnipresence.

If God [*Gud*] wants to reveal himself in human form and provide a direct relation by taking, for example, the form of a man who is twelve feet tall, then that imaginatively constructed party goer and captain of the popinjay shooting club will surely become aware. But since God is unwilling to deceive, the spiritual relation in truth specifically requires that there be nothing at all remarkable about his form; then the party goer must say: There is nothing to see, not the slightest. If the god [*Guden*] has nothing whatever that is remarkable about him, the party goer is perhaps deceived in not becoming aware at all. But the god is without blame in this, and the actuality of this deception is continually also the possibility of the truth. But if the god has something remarkable about him, he deceives, inasmuch as a human being thus becomes aware of the untruth, and this awareness is also the impossibility of the truth.

In paganism, the direct relation is idolatry; in Christianity, everyone indeed knows that God cannot manifest himself in this way. But this knowledge is not inwardness at all, and in Christianity it can certainly happen with a rote knower that he becomes utterly "without God in the world," which was not the case in paganism, where there was still the untrue relation of idolatry. Idolatry is certainly a dismal substitute, but that the rubric "God" disappears completely is even more mistaken.

Accordingly, not even God relates himself directly to a derived spirit (and this is the wondrousness of creation: not to produce something that is nothing in relation to the Creator, but to produce something that is something and that in the true worship of God

---

*In order to indicate how illusive the rhetorical can be, I shall show here how one could perhaps produce an effect upon a listener rhetorically, even though what was said would be a dialectical retrogression. Suppose a pagan religious orator says that here on earth the god's temple is actually empty, but (and here the rhetorical begins) in heaven, where everything is more perfect, where water is air, and air is ether, there are also temples and shrines for the gods, but the difference is that the gods actually dwell in these temples—that the god actually dwells in the temple is dialectical retrogression, because his not dwelling in the temple is an expression for the spiritual relation to the invisible. But rhetorically it produces the effect.—Incidentally, I had in mind a specific passage by a Greek author, but I shall not quote him.

can use this something to become by itself nothing before God); even less can one human being relate himself in this way to another *in truth*. Nature, the totality of creation, is God's work, and yet God is not there, but within the individual human being there is a possibility (he is spirit according to his possibility) that in inwardness is awakened to a God-relationship, and then it is possible to see God everywhere. Compared with the spiritual relationship in inwardness, the sensate distinctions of the great, the amazing, the most crying-to-heaven superlatives of a southern nation are a retrogression to idolatry. Is it not as if an author wrote 166 folio volumes and the reader read and read, just as when someone observes and observes nature but does not discover that the meaning of this enormous work lies in the reader himself, because amazement at the many volumes and the five hundred lines to the page, which is similar to amazement at how immense nature is and how innumerable the animal species are, is not understanding.

With regard to the essential truth, a direct relation between spirit and spirit is unthinkable. If such a relation is assumed, it actually means that one party has ceased to be spirit, something that is not borne in mind by many a genius who both assists people *en masse* into the truth and is good-natured enough to think that applause, willingness to listen, signatures, etc. mean accepting the truth. Just as important as the truth, and of the two the even more important one, is the mode in which the truth is accepted, and it is of slight help if one gets millions to accept the truth if by the very mode of their acceptance they are transposed into untruth. And therefore all good-naturedness, all persuasion, all bargaining, all direct attraction with the aid of one's own person in consideration of one's suffering so much for the cause, of one's weeping over humankind, of one's being so enthusiastic, etc.—all such things are a misunderstanding, in relation to the truth a forgery by which, according to one's ability, one helps any number of people to acquire a semblance of truth.

Karl Marx
1818–1883

It is hard to think of a more influential—or more controversial—nineteenth-century thinker than Karl Marx. Not content simply to develop a theory, Marx sought fundamental change in social, economic, and political structures. As he put it, "The philosophers have only *interpreted* the world in various ways; the point is, to *change* it."

Marx was the third of nine children born to Heinrich and Henrietta Marx in the Rhineland town of Trier. His parents were of Jewish ancestry but had converted to Protestant Christianity to protect Heinrich's job as a government lawyer. In 1835 Karl went to the University of Bonn to study law. Hardly the model student, he spent much of his time drinking or writing love letters to his childhood sweetheart and then fiancée, Jenny von Westphalen. At his father's insistence, Marx transferred to the University of Berlin and began to focus on his studies. While there, he abandoned his legal training and began preparing for an academic career as a philosophy professor. He wrote a dissertation contrasting Democritus and Epicurus that was accepted by the University of Jena and in 1841 Marx received his doctorate in philosophy.

But the leftist politics Marx had adopted while in Berlin made it impossible for him to obtain a university post, so in 1842 he took a position as editor of the *Rheinische Zeitung (Rhenish Gazette),* a liberal middle-class newspaper in Cologne. Marx was very successful as an editor—too successful for the government censors who suppressed the pa-

INTRODUCITON **161**

per after an article by Marx on the poverty of the Mosel wine makers. Marx moved to Paris where he became coeditor of the new journal, the *Deutsch-Französische Jahrbücher (German-French Annals)*. With his future seeming secure, Marx finally felt free to marry his fiancée, Jenny, in 1843. But the *Jahrbücher* closed almost immediately and once again Marx was unemployed. Fortunately, at about the same time Marx received a sizable settlement from the shareholders of the *Rheinishe Zeitung,* and he and his new bride were able to live comfortably. Freed from his editing duties, Marx wrote extensively on economic and political matters. He also met the man who was to be his lifelong friend, collaborator, and financial backer: Friedrich Engels (1820–1895). Engels came from a family of wealthy textile industrialists and was, himself, the manager of his family's Manchester, England, branch. Together Marx and Engels produced *The Holy Family* (1845), Marx's first published book, which criticized a number of their fellow leftists.

While pursuing his writing projects, Marx was politically active among German communists living in Paris—activity that led to his expulsion from France in 1845. Living for a time in Brussels, Marx produced *The German Ideology* (1846) and *The Poverty of Philosophy* (1847) while continuing his political involvement. In 1847 he attended the congress of the newly formed Communist League in London. He and Engels were commissioned to produce an easy-to-read pamphlet outlining the league's doctrines. The result was the immensely influential work *The Communist Manifesto* (1848).

Following another attempt at editing an opposition newspaper in Cologne—and another expulsion by the government—Marx eventually settled in London. The next two decades were a time of poverty and hardship for the Marx family due as much to financial mismanagement as to lack of income. (Marx reflected often on the irony of his extensive work on capital when he had so little talent for managing it personally.) Marx received some income as a correspondent for the *New York Tribune;* but for the rest of his life, his primary source of income was Engels's gifts. In London, Marx became a fixture in the reading room of the British Museum, where he pored over government records, histories, and the writings of other economists, gathering data to document his thought. There he wrote *Critique of Political Economy* (1859) and began his magnum opus, *Capital* (1867). He also continued his political involvement, becoming the leader of the International Working Men's Association. He worked with the International until factional strife, particularly conflict with the anarchist Mikhail Aleksandrovich Bakunin (1814–1876), led Marx to dismantle the organization in 1872.

It wasn't until Marx's final years that he managed to gain some financial stability and lived the life of a bourgeois Victorian gentleman. But these years also brought tragedy and hardship of a different kind. Marx developed boils over his entire body and used creosote, opium, and arsenic among other remedies in a futile attempt to effect a cure. His beloved Jenny died in 1881 and his eldest daughter two years later. Marx himself developed bronchitis and also died in 1883.

* * *

While a student in Berlin, Marx had come under the influence of Hegelian philosophy. Hegel had understood *history* as a progressive actualization of the Absolute, but he was somewhat ambiguous about the future. One group of followers, the "Old Hegelians," argued in a reactionary way that this progressive actualization was now complete and that Christianity was the Absolute Religion,

Hegelianism the Absolute Philosophy, and Prussia the Absolute State. Another group, the "Young Hegelians," led by Bruno Bauer, argued that the dialectical movement of history was continuing. To move to the next stage in this historical dialectic, they sought to expose the contradictions of the existing order.

But while Marx accepted Hegel's dialectical understanding of history, he became convinced that Hegel's philosophy (and that of the Young Hegelians) devalued humanity by its emphasis on the Absolute. Instead Marx drew on the materialism espoused in Ludwig Feuerbach's work, *The Essence of Christianity* (1841). Feuerbach had argued that Hegel's philosophy was nothing more than rationalized religion, asserting that humans were merely the "self-alienation," or loss of identity, of God. Instead Feuerbach advocated an atheistic materialism that claimed that "God" was simply the "self-alienation" of humans. That is, all the divine characteristics were nothing more than idealized human characteristics objectified and projected onto an imagined deity.

In *The Critique of Hegel's Dialectic and General Philosophy* (from the *Economic and Philosophical Manuscripts of 1844*), reprinted here in the Tom Bottomore translation, Marx presents his criticism of Hegel on the basis of Feuerbach's work. Marx expresses appreciation for Hegel's dialectical understanding of the "self-creation of man as a process" and points out that Hegel conceives of "objective man" as the result of "his own labor." But Hegel understood labor as being "abstract mental" labor, not the natural, embodied interaction with real objects that concerned Marx. On the other hand, while he appreciated Feuerbach's materialism, Marx held that his predecessor did not tie his criticism to historical development. As Marx wrote in *The German Ideology,* "As far as Feuerbach is a materialist he does not deal with history, and as far as he considers history he is not a materialist." Synthesizing the historical development of Hegel and the materialism of Feuerbach, Marx's theory has often been called "dialectical materialism" (though Marx himself did not use that term).

Marx also adapted Feuerbach's concept of alienation, applying it to political, social, and economic interactions. According to Marx, a capitalist system results in alienation for the worker. The worker's labor is alien to the worker because it belongs to the capitalist. In return for the worker's labor, the capitalist pays the worker a wage—a wage that Marx claimed competition kept at a subsistence level. Yet the worker must continue to labor in order to survive. This means the worker is now self-alienated since the life activity, the essence of the worker, becomes "only a means for his existence." But alienation is not limited to individuals. Because they have different interests, workers, as an economic class, are alienated from those who own the means of production. This, in turn, gives rise to class struggle as the interests of one class are always in opposition to the interests of other economic classes. Only by having communal ownership of the means of production, that is, by the abolition of private property, will such conflict be overcome. Only then will those who work control both the process and the product of their labor.

Throughout his analysis of the human situation, Marx continually returned to the material forces of production, distribution, exchange, and consumption. While previous thinkers had seen philosophy, art, religion, morality, science, and law as the foundation of society, Marx claimed that these elements of "higher culture" are actually the superstructure. In the Preface and Introduction to *A Contribution to the Critique of Political Economy,* reprinted here in the N.I. Stone translation, Marx explains that the real foundations of society are the productive forces and the relations of production. His brief overview of these forces of production serves as a helpful introduction to his method and program.

* * *

For good selections of primary source writings, see *Karl Marx: Early Writings,* edited and translated by Tom Bottomore (London: C.A. Watts, 1963), and *The Marx-Engels Reader,* edited by Robert C. Tucker (New York: Norton, 1978). For a collection of writings by Marx's followers, see David McLellan, ed., *Marxism: Essential Writings* (Oxford: Oxford University Press, 1988). Isaiah Berlin's *Karl Marx: His Life and Environment* (1963, reprinted Oxford: Oxford University Press, 1978) is still considered by many to be the best general introduction to Marx's life and philosophy, while more recent studies include David McLellan, *Karl Marx: His Life and Thought* (New York: Harper & Row, 1973); David McLellan, *Karl Marx* (New York: Penguin Books, 1975); Peter Singer, *Marx* (Oxford: Oxford University Press, 1980); Allen W. Wood, *Karl Marx* (London: Routledge & Kegan Paul, 1981); and Jon Elster, *An Introduction to Karl Marx* (Cambridge: Cambridge University Press, 1986). The following are samples of the many recent studies in particular areas of Marx's thought: Nicholas Lash, *A Matter of Hope: A Theologian's Reflections on the Thought of Karl Marx* (Notre Dame, IN: University of Notre Dame Press, 1982); Nancy Sue Love, *Marx, Nietzsche, and Modernity* (New York: Columbia University Press, 1986); Harold Mah, *The End of Philosophy, The Origin of "Ideology": Karl Marx and the Crisis of the Young Hegelians* (Berkeley: University of California Press, 1987); and Robert Meister, *Political Identity: Thinking Through Marx* (Cambridge, MA: Basil Blackwell, 1990). For an interesting criticism of Marx by one of his contemporaries, see M.A. Bakunin, *Bakunin on Anarchy: Selected Works by the Activist-Founder of World Anarchism,* edited and translated by Sam Dolgoff (New York: Knopf, 1972). For collections of critical essays, see Tom Bottomore, ed., *Modern Interpretations of Marx* (Oxford: B. Blackwell, 1981); David McLellan, ed., *Marx: The First Hundred Years* (New York: St. Martin's Press, 1983); and Terence Ball and James Farr, eds., *After Marx* (Cambridge: Cambridge University Press, 1984).

ECONOMIC AND PHILOSOPHICAL MANUSCRIPTS (in part)

CRITIQUE OF HEGEL'S DIALECTIC AND GENERAL PHILOSOPHY

This is perhaps an appropriate point at which to explain and substantiate what has been said, and to make some general comments upon Hegel's dialectic, especially as it is expounded in the *Phenomenology* and *Logic,* and upon its relation to the modern critical movement.

Economic and Philosophical Manuscripts (1844), from *Karl Marx: Early Writings,* edited and translated by T.B. Bottomore (New York: McGraw-Hill, 1964). Reprinted by permission of McGraw-Hill.

Modern German criticism was so much concerned with the past, and was so hampered by its involvement with its subject-matter, that it had a wholly uncritical attitude to the methods of criticism and completely ignored the partly formal, but in fact *essential* question—how do we now stand with regard to the Hegelian *dialectic?* This ignorance of the relationship of modern criticism to Hegel's general philosophy and his dialectic in particular was so great that critics such as Strauss and Bruno Bauer (the former in all his writings; the latter in his *Synoptiker,* where, in opposition to Strauss, he substitutes the "self-consciousness" of abstract man for the substance of "abstract nature," and even in *Das entdeckte Christentum)* were, at least implicitly, ensnared in Hegelian logic. Thus, for instance, in *Das entdeckte Christentum* it is argued: "As if self-consciousness in positing the world, that which is different, did not produce itself in producing its object; for it then annuls the difference between itself and what it has produced, since it exists only in this creation and movement, has its purpose only in this movement, etc." Or again: "They (the French materialists) could not see that the movement of the universe has only become real and unified in itself in so far as it is the movement of self-consciousness." These expressions not only do not differ from the Hegelian conception, but reproduce it textually.

[XII] How little these writers, in undertaking their criticism (Bauer in his *Synoptiker*), were aware of their relation to Hegel's dialectic, and how little such an awareness emerged from the criticism, is demonstrated by Bauer in his *Gute Sache der Freiheit* when, instead of replying to the indiscreet question put by Gruppe, "And now what is to be done with logic?," he transmits it to future critics.

Now that Feuerbach, in his "Thesen" in the *Anecdotis* and in greater detail in his *Philosophie der Zukunft,* has demolished the inner principle of the old dialectic and philosophy, the "Critical School," which was unable to do this itself but has seen it accomplished, has proclaimed itself the pure, decisive, absolute, and finally enlightened criticism, and in its spiritual pride has reduced the whole historical movement to the relation existing between itself and the rest of the world, which comes into the category of "the mass." It has reduced all dogmatic antitheses to the single dogmatic antithesis between its own cleverness and the stupidity of the world, between the critical Christ and mankind—"the rabble." At every moment of the day it has demonstrated its own excellence *vis-à-vis* the stupidity of the mass, and it has finally announced the critical *last judgment* by proclaiming that the day is at hand when the whole of fallen mankind will assemble before it and will be divided up into groups each of which will be handed its *testimonium paupertatis* (certificate of poverty). The Critical School has made public its superiority to all human feelings and to the world, above which it sits enthroned in sublime solitude, content to utter occasionally from its sarcastic lips the laughter of the Olympian gods. After all these entertaining antics of idealism (of Young Hegelianism) which is expiring in the form of criticism, the Critical School has not even now intimated that it was necessary to discuss critically its own source, the dialectic of Hegel; nor has it given any indication of its relation with the dialectic of Feuerbach. This is a procedure totally lacking in critical sense.

Feuerbach is the only person who has a *serious* and *critical* relation to Hegel's dialectic, who has made real discoveries in this field, and above all, who has vanquished the old philosophy. The magnitude of Feuerbach's achievement and the unassuming simplicity with which he presents his work to the world are in striking contrast with the behaviour of others.

Feuerbach's great achievement is—

1. to have shown that philosophy is nothing more than religion brought into thought and developed by thought, and that it is equally to be condemned as another form and mode of existence of human alienation;

2. to have founded *genuine materialism* and *positive science* by making the social relationship of "man to man" the basic principle of his theory;

3. to have opposed to the negation of the negation which claims to be the absolute positive, a self-subsistent principle positively founded on itself.

Feuerbach explains Hegel's dialectic, and at the same time justifies taking the positive phenomenon, that which is perceptible and indubitable, as the starting-point, in the following way.

Hegel begins from the alienation of substance (logically, from the infinite, the abstract universal) from the absolute and fixed abstraction; i.e. in ordinary language, from religion and theology. Secondly, he supersedes the infinite, and posits the real, the perceptible, the finite, and the particular. (Philosophy, supersession of religion and theology.) Thirdly, he then supersedes the positive and reestablishes the abstraction, the infinite. (Re-establishment of religion and theology.)

Thus Feuerbach conceives the negation of the negation as being *only* a contradiction within philosophy itself, which affirms theology (transcendence, etc.) after having superseded it, and thus affirms it in opposition to philosophy.

For the positing or self-affirmation and self-confirmation which is implied in the negation of the negation is regarded as a positing which is still uncertain, burdened with its contrary, doubtful of itself and thus incomplete, not demonstrated by its own existence, and implicit. [XIII] The positing which is perceptually indubitable and grounded upon itself is directly opposed to it.

In conceiving the negation of the negation, from the aspect of the positive relation inherent in it, as the only true positive, and from the aspect of the negative relation inherent in it, as the only true act and the self-confirming act of all being, Hegel has merely discovered an *abstract, logical* and *speculative* expression of the historical process, which is not yet the real history of man as a given subject, but only the history of the *act of creation,* of the *genesis of man.*

We shall explain both the abstract form of this process and the difference between the process as conceived by Hegel and by modern criticism, by Feuerbach in *Das Wesen des Christentums;* or rather, the critical form of this process which is still so uncritical in Hegel.

Let us examine Hegel's system. It is necessary to begin with the *Phenomenology,* because it is there that Hegel's philosophy was born and that its secret is to be found. [Marx's version of the table of contents from Hegel's *Phenomenology* which follows here has been deleted—F.B.]

*   *   *

Hegel's *Encyclopaedia* begins with logic, with *pure speculative thought,* and ends with *absolute knowledge,* the self-conscious and self-conceiving philosophical or absolute mind, i.e. the superhuman, abstract mind. The whole of the *Encyclopaedia* is nothing but the extended being of the philosophical mind, its self-objectification; and the philosophical mind is nothing but the alienated world-mind thinking within the bounds of its self-alienation, i.e. conceiving itself in an abstract manner. *Logic* is the *money* of the mind, the speculative *thought-value* of man and of nature, their essence indifferent to any real determinate character and thus unreal; *thought* which is *alienated* and abstract and ignores real nature and man. *The external character of this abstract thought . . . nature* as it exists for this abstract thought. Nature is external to it, loss of itself, and is only conceived as something external, as abstract thought, but alienated abstract thought. Finally, spirit, this thought which returns to its own origin and which, as anthropological, phenomenological, psychological, customary, artistic-religious spirit, is not valid for itself until it discovers itself and relates itself to itself as absolute knowledge in the absolute (i.e. abstract) spirit, and so receives its conscious and fitting existence. For its real mode of existence is *abstraction*.

Hegel commits a double error. The first appears most clearly in the *Phenomenology,* the birthplace of his philosophy. When Hegel conceives wealth, the power of the state, etc. as entities alienated from the human being, he conceives them only in their thought form. They are entities of thought and thus simply an alienation of *pure* (i.e. abstract) philosophical thought. The whole movement, therefore, ends in absolute knowledge. It is precisely abstract thought from which these objects are alienated, and which they confront with their presumptuous reality. The *philosopher,* himself an abstract form of alienated man, sets himself up as the *measure* of the alienated world. The whole *history of alienation,* and of the retraction of alienation, is, therefore, only the *history of the production* of abstract thought, i.e. of absolute, logical, speculative thought. *Estrangement,* which thus forms the real interest of this alienation and of the supersession of this alienation, is the opposition of *in itself* and *for itself,* of *consciousness* and *self-consciousness,* of *object* and *subject,* i.e. the opposition in thought itself between abstract thought and sensible reality or real sensuous existence. All other contradictions and movements are merely the *appearance,* the *cloak,* the *exoteric* form of these two opposites which are alone important and which constitute the *significance* of the other, profane contradictions. It is not the fact that the human being *objectifies* himself *inhumanly,* in opposition to himself, but that he *objectifies* himself by *distinction* from and in *opposition* to abstract thought, which constitutes alienation as it exists and as it has to be transcended.

[XVIII] The appropriation of man's objectified and alienated faculties is thus, in the first place, only an *appropriation* which occurs in *consciousness,* in *pure thought,* i.e. in abstraction. It is the appropriation of these objects as *thoughts* and as *movements of thought.* For this reason, despite its thoroughly negative and critical appearance, and despite the genuine criticism which it contains and which often anticipates later developments, there is already implicit in the *Phenomenology,* as a germ, as a potentiality and a secret, the uncritical positivism and uncritical idealism of Hegel's later works— the philosophical dissolution and restoration of the existing empirical world. *Secondly,* the vindication of the objective world for man (for example, the recognition that sense perception is not *abstract* sense perception but *human* sense perception, that religion, wealth, etc. are only the alienated reality of *human* objectification, of *human* faculties put to work, and are, therefore, a way to genuine *human* reality), this appropriation, or the insight into this process, appears in Hegel as the recognition of *sensuousness, religion,* state power, etc. as *mental* phenomena, for *mind* alone is the true essence of man, and the true form of mind is thinking mind, the logical, speculative mind. The *human character* of nature, of historically produced nature, of man's products, is shown by their being *products* of abstract mind, and thus phases of *mind, entities of thought.* The *Phenomenology is* a concealed, unclear and mystifying criticism, but in so far as it grasps the *alienation* of man (even though man appears only as mind) all the elements of criticism are contained in it, and are often *presented* and *worked out* in a manner which goes far beyond Hegel's own point of view. The sections devoted to the "unhappy consciousness," the "honest consciousness," the struggle between the "noble" and the "base" consciousness, etc., etc. contain the *critical* elements (though still in an alienated form) of whole areas such as religion, the state, civil life, etc. Just as the *entity*, the *object*, appears as an entity of thought, so also the *subject* is always *consciousness* or *self-consciousness;* or rather, the object appears only as abstract consciousness and man as *self-consciousness*. Thus the distinctive forms of alienation which are manifested are only different forms of consciousness and self-consciousness. Since abstract consciousness (the form in which the object is conceived) is in *itself* merely a distinctive moment of self-consciousness, the outcome of the movement is the identity of self-consciousness and consciousness—absolute knowledge—the movement of abstract thought not directed outwards but proceeding within itself; i.e. the dialectic of pure thought is the result.

[XXIII] The outstanding achievement of Hegel's *Phenomenology*—the dialectic of negativity as the moving and creating principle—is, first, that Hegel grasps the self-creation of man as a process, objectification as loss of the object, as alienation and transcendence of this alienation, and that he, therefore, grasps the nature of *labour,* and conceives objective man (true, because real man) as the result of his *own* labour. The *real,* active orientation of man to himself as a species-being, or the affirmation of himself as a real species-being (i.e. as a human being) is only possible so far as he really brings forth all his *species-powers* (which is only possible through the co-operative endeavours of mankind and as an outcome of history) and treats these powers as objects, which can only be done at first in the form of alienation.

We shall next show in detail Hegel's one-sidedness and limitations, as revealed in the final chapter of the *Phenomenology,* on absolute knowledge; a chapter which contains the concentrated spirit of the *Phenomenology,* its relation to the dialectic, and also Hegel's *consciousness* of both and of their interrelations.

For the present, let us make these preliminary observations: Hegel's standpoint is that of modern political economy. He conceives *labour* as the *essence,* the self-confirming essence of man; he observes only the positive side of labour, not its negative side. Labour is *man's coming to be for himself* within *alienation,* or as an alienated man. Labour as Hegel understands and recognizes it is *abstract mental labour.* Thus, that which above all constitutes the *essence* of philosophy, the *alienation of man knowing himself,* or *alienated* science *thinking* itself, Hegel grasps as its essence. Consequently, he is able to bring together the separate elements of earlier philosophy and to present his own as the philosophy. What other philosophers did, that is, to conceive separate elements of nature and of human life as phases of self-consciousness and indeed of abstract self-consciousness, Hegel *knows* by doing philosophy; therefore, his science is absolute.

Let us now turn to our subject.

Absolute knowledge. The final chapter
of the "Phenomenology."

The main point is that the *object of consciousness* is nothing else but *self-consciousness,* that the object is only *objectified* self-consciousness, self-consciousness as an object. (Positing man = self-consciousness.)

It is necessary, therefore, to surmount the *object of consciousness. Objectivity* as such is regarded as an alienated human relationship which does not correspond with the *essence of man,* self-consciousness. The reappropriation of the objective essence of man, which was produced as something alien and determined by alienation, signifies the supersession not only of *alienation* but also of *objectivity;* that is, man is regarded as a *non-objective, spiritual* being.

The process of *overcoming the object of consciousness* is described by Hegel as follows: The *object* does not reveal itself only as *returning* into the Self (according to Hegel that is a *one-sided* conception of the movement, considering only one aspect). Man is equated with self. The Self, however, is only man conceived *abstractly* and produced by abstraction. Man is self-referring. His eye, his ear, etc. are *self-referring;* every one of his faculties has this quality of *self*-reference. But it is entirely false to say on that account, "*Self-consciousness* has eyes, ears, faculties." Self-consciousness is rather a quality of human nature, of the human eye, etc.; human nature is not a quality of [XXIV] *self-consciousness.*

The Self, abstracted and determined for itself, is man as an *abstract egoist,* purely abstract *egoism* raised to the level of thought. (We shall return to this point later.)

For Hegel, *human life, man,* is equivalent to *self-consciousness.* All alienation of human life is, therefore, *nothing* but *alienation of self-consciousness.* The alienation of self-consciousness is not regarded as the *expression,* reflected in knowledge and thought, of the *real* alienation of human life. Instead, *actual* alienation, that which appears real, is in its *innermost* hidden nature (which philosophy first discloses) only the *phenomenal being* of the alienation of real human life, of *self-consciousness.* The science which comprehends this is therefore called *Phenomenology.* All reappropriation of alienated objective life appears, therefore, as an incorporation in self-consciousness. The person who takes possession of his being is only the self-consciousness which takes possession of objective being; the return of the object into the Self is, therefore, the reappropriation of the object.

Expressed in a *more comprehensive* way the *supersession of the object of consciousness* means: (1) that the object as such presents itself to consciousness as something disappearing; (2) that it is the alienation of self-consciousness which establishes "thinghood"; (3) that this alienation has *positive* as well as *negative* significance; (4) that it has this significance not only *for us* or in itself, but also *for self-consciousness itself;* (5) that for *self-consciousness* the negative of the object, its self-supersession, has *positive* significance, or self-consciousness *knows* thereby the nullity of the object in that self-consciousness alienates itself, for in this alienation it establishes *itself* as object or, for the sake of the indivisible unity of *being-for-itself,* establishes the object as itself; (6) that, on the other hand, this other "moment" is equally present, that self-consciousness has superseded and reabsorbed this alienation and objectivity, and is thus *at home* in its other being as such; (7) that this is the movement of consciousness, and consciousness is, therefore, the totality of its "moments"; (8) that similarly, consciousness must have related itself to the object in all its determinations, and have conceived it in terms of each of them. This totality of determinations makes the object *intrinsically* a *spiritual being,* and it becomes truly so for consciousness by the apprehension of every one of these determinations as the Self, or by what was called earlier the *spiritual* attitude towards them.

ad (1) That the object as such presents itself to consciousness as something disappearing is the above-mentioned *return of the object into the Self.*

ad (2) *The alienation of self-consciousness* establishes "thinghood." Because man equals self-consciousness, his alienated objective being or "*thinghood*" is equivalent to *alienated self-consciousness,* and "thinghood" is established by this alienation. ("Thinghood" is that which is *an object for him,* and an object for him is really only that which is an essential object, consequently his *objective* essence. And since it is not the real *man,* nor *nature*—man being *human nature*—who becomes as such a subject, but only an abstraction of man, self-consciousness, "thinghood" can only be *alienated self-consciousness.*) It is quite understandable that a living, natural being endowed with objective (i.e. material) faculties should have *real natural objects* of its being, and equally that its self-alienation should be the establishment of a *real,* objective world, but in the form of *externality,* as a world which does not belong to, and dominates, its being. There is nothing incomprehensible or mysterious about this. The converse, rather, would be mysterious. But it is equally clear that a self-consciousness, i.e. its alienation, can only establish *"thinghood,"* i.e. only an abstract thing, a thing created by abstraction and not a real thing. It is [XXVI] clear, moreover, that "thinghood" is totally lacking in *independence,* in *being, vis-à-vis* self-consciousness; it is a mere *construct* established by self-consciousness. And what is established is not self-confirming; it is the confirmation of the act of establishing, which for an instant, but only for an instant, fixes its energy as a product and *apparently* confers upon it the role of an independent, real being.

When real, corporeal *man,* with his feet firmly planted on the solid ground, inhaling and exhaling all the powers of nature, *posits* his real objective faculties, as a result of his alienation, as alien objects, the *positing* is not the subject of this act but the subjectivity of *objective* faculties whose action must also, therefore, be *objective.* An objective being acts objectively, and it would not act objectively if objectivity were not part of its essential being. It creates and establishes *only objects, because* it is established by objects, and because it is fundamentally *natural.* In the act of establishing it does not descend from its "pure activity" to the *creation of objects;* its *objective* product simply confirms its *objective* activity, its activity as an objective, natural being.

We see here how consistent naturalism or humanism is distinguished from both idealism and materialism, and at the same time constitutes their unifying truth. We see also that only naturalism is able to comprehend the process of world history.

Man is directly a *natural being.* As a natural being, and as a living natural being he is, on the one hand, endowed with *natural powers* and *faculties,* which exist in him as tendencies and abilities, as *drives.* On the other hand, as a natural, embodied, sentient, objective being he is a *suffering,* conditioned and limited being, like animals and plants. The *objects* of his drives exist outside himself as *objects* independent of him, yet they are *objects* of his *needs,* essential *objects* which are indispensable to the exercise and confirmation of his faculties. The fact that man is an *embodied,* living, real, sentient, objective being with natural powers, means that he has *real, sensuous objects* as the objects of his being, or that he can only express his being in real, sensuous objects. *To be* objective, natural, sentient and at the same time to have object, nature and sense outside oneself, or to be oneself object, nature and sense for a third person, is the same thing. *Hunger* is a natural *need;* it requires, therefore, a *nature* outside itself, an *object* outside itself, in order to be satisfied and stilled. Hunger is the objective need of a body for an *object* which exists outside itself and which is essential for its integration and the expression of its nature. The sun is an *object,* a necessary and life-assuring object, for the plant, just as the plant is an object for the sun, an *expression* of the sun's life-giving power and *objective* essential powers.

A being which does not have its nature outside itself is not a *natural* being and does not share in the being of nature. A being which has no object outside itself is not an objective being. A being which is not itself an object for a third being has no being for its *object,* i.e. it is not objectively related and its being is not objective.

[XXVII] A non-objective being is a *non-being.* Suppose a being which neither is an object itself nor has an object. In the first place, such a being would be the *only* being; no other being would exist outside itself and it would be solitary and alone. For as soon as there exist objects outside myself, as soon as I am not *alone,* I am *another, another reality* from the object outside me. For this third object I am thus an *other reality* than itself, i.e. *its object.* To suppose a being which is not the object of another being would be to suppose that *no* objective being exists. As soon as I have an object, this object has me for its object. But a *non-objective* being is an unreal, non-sensuous, merely conceived being; i.e. a merely imagined being, an abstraction. To be *sensuous,* i.e. real, is to be an object of sense or *sensuous* object, and thus to have sensuous objects outside oneself, objects of one's sensations. To be sentient is to *suffer* (to experience).

Man as an objective sentient being is a *suffering* being, and since he feels his suffering, a *passionate* being. Passion is man's faculties striving to attain their object.

But man is not merely a natural being; he is a *human* natural being. He is a being for himself, and, therefore, a *species-being;* and as such he has to express and authenticate himself in being as well as in thought. Consequently, *human* objects are not natural objects as they present themselves directly, nor is *human sense,* as it is immediately and objectively *given, human* sensibility and human objectivity. Neither objective nature nor subjective nature is directly presented in a form adequate to the *human* being. And as everything natural must have its *origin* so *man* has his process of genesis, *history,* which is for him, however, a conscious process and thus one which is consciously self-transcending. (We shall return to this point later.)

Thirdly, since this establishment of "thinghood" is itself only an appearance, an act which contradicts the nature of pure activity, it has to be annulled again and "thinghood" has to be denied.

ad 3, 4, 5, 6. (3) This alienation of consciousness has not only a negative but also a positive significance, and (4) it has this positive significance not only for us or in itself, but for consciousness itself. (5) For *consciousness* the negation of the object, or its annulling of itself by that means, has positive significance; it *knows* the nullity of the object by the fact that it alienates *itself,* for in this alienation it *knows* itself as the object or, for the sake of the indivisible unit of *being-for self,* knows the object as itself. (6) On the other hand, this other "moment" is equally present, but consciousness has superseded and reabsorbed this alienation and objectivity and is thus *at home in its other being as such.*

We have already seen that the appropriation of alienated objective being, or the supersession of objectivity in the form of *alienation* (which has to develop from indifferent otherness to real antagonistic alienation), signifies for Hegel also, or primarily, the supersession of *objectivity,* since it is not the determinate character of the object but its *objective* character which is the scandal of alienation for self-consciousness. The object is therefore negative, self-annulling, a *nullity.* This nullity of the object has a positive significance because it knows this nullity, objective being, as its *self-alienation,* and knows that this nullity exists only through its self-alienation. . . .

The way in which consciousness is, and in which something is for it, is *knowing.* Knowing is its only act. Thus something comes to exist for consciousness so far as it *knows* this *something.* Knowing is its only objective relation. It knows, then, the nullity of the object (i.e. knows the nonexistence of the distinction between itself and the object, the non-existence of the object for it) because it knows the object as its *self-alienation.* That is to say, it knows itself (knows knowing as an object), because the object is only the semblance of an object, a deception, which is intrinsically nothing but knowing itself which has confronted itself with itself, has established in face of itself a *nullity,* a "something" which has no objective existence outside the knowing itself. Knowing knows that in relating itself to an object it is only *outside* itself, alienates itself, and that *it* only *appears* to itself as an object; or in other words, that that which appears to it as an object is only itself.

On the other hand, Hegel says, this other "moment" is present at the same time; namely, that consciousness has equally superseded and reabsorbed this alienation and objectivity, and consequently is at *home in its other being as such.*

In this discussion all the illusions of speculation are assembled.

First, consciousness—self-consciousness—is *at home in its other being as such.* It is, therefore—if we abstract from Hegel's abstraction and substitute the self-consciousness of man for self-consciousness—*at home in its other being as such.* This implies, first, that consciousness (knowing as knowing, thinking as thinking) claims to be directly the *other* of itself, the sensuous world, reality, life; it is thought over-reaching itself in thought (Feuerbach). This aspect is contained in it, in so far as consciousness as mere consciousness is offended not by the alienated objectivity but by *objectivity* as such.

Secondly, it implies that self-conscious man, in so far as he has recognized and superseded the spiritual world (or the universal spiritual mode of existence of his world) then confirms it again in this alienated form and presents it as his true existence; he re-establishes it and claims to *be at home in his other being.* Thus, for example, after superseding religion, when he has recognized religion as a product of self-alienation, he then finds a confirmation of himself in *religion as religion. This is* the root of Hegel's false positivism, or of his merely *apparent* criticism; what Feuerbach calls the positing, negation and re-establishment of religion or theology, but which has to be conceived in a more general way. Thus reason is at home in unreason as such. Man, who has recognized that he leads an alienated life in law, politics, etc. leads his true human life in this alienated life as such. Self-affirmation, in contradiction with itself, with the knowledge and the nature of the object, is thus the true *knowledge* and *life.*

There can no longer be any question about Hegel's compromise with religion, the state, etc., for this falsehood is the falsehood of his whole argument.

[XXIX] If I *know* religion as *alienated* human self-consciousness what I know in it as religion is not my self-consciousness but my alienated self-consciousness confirmed in it. Thus my own self, and the self-consciousness which is its essence, is not confirmed in *religion* but in the *abolition* and *supersession* of religion.

In Hegel, therefore, the negation of the negation is not the confirmation of true being by the negation of illusory being. It is the confirmation of illusory being, or of self-alienating being in its denial; or the denial of this illusory being as an objective being existing outside man and independently of him, and its transformation into a subject.

The act of *supersession* plays a strange part in which denial and preservation, denial and affirmation, are linked together. Thus, for example, in Hegel's *Philosophy of Right, private right* superseded equals *morality,* morality superseded equals the *family,* the family superseded equals *civil society,* civil society superseded equals the *state,* and the state superseded equals *world history.* But in *actuality* private right, morality, the family, civil society, the state, etc. remain; only they have become "moments," modes of existence of man, which have no validity in isolation but which mutually dissolve and engender one another. *They are "moments" of the movement.*

In their actual existence this mobile nature is concealed. It is first revealed in thought, in philosophy; consequently, my true religious existence is my existence in the *philosophy of religion,* my true political existence is my existence in the *philosophy of right,* my true natural existence is my existence in the *philosophy of nature,* my true artistic existence is my existence in the *philosophy of art,* and my true human existence is my existence in *philosophy.* In the same way, the true existence of religion, the state, nature and art, is the *philosophy* of religion, of the state, of nature, and of art. But if the philosophy of religion is the only true existence of religion I am only truly religious as a *philosopher of religion,* and I deny actual religious sentiment and the actual *religious* man. At the same time, however, I *confirm* them, partly in my own existence or in the alien existence with which I confront them (for this *is* only their philosophical expression), and partly in their own original form, since they are for me the merely *apparent* other being, allegories, the lineaments of their own true existence (i.e. of my *philosophical* existence) concealed by sensuous draperies.

In the same way, *quality* superseded equals *quantity,* quantity superseded equals measure, measure superseded equals *being,* being superseded equals *phenomenal being,* phenomenal being superseded equals *actuality,* actuality superseded equals the *concept,* the concept superseded equals *objectivity,* objectivity superseded equals the *absolute* idea, the absolute idea superseded equals *nature,* nature superseded equals *subjective* spirit, subjective spirit superseded equals *ethical* objective spirit, *ethical* spirit superseded equals *art,* art superseded equals *religion,* and religion superseded equals *absolute knowledge.*

On the other hand, this supersession is supersession of an entity of thought; thus, private property as *thought* is superseded in the *thought* of morality. And since thought imagines itself to be, without mediation, the other aspect of itself, namely *sensuous reality,* and takes its own action for *real, sensuous action,* this supersession in thought, which leaves its object in existence in the real world, believes itself to have really overcome it. On the other hand, since the object has now become for it a "moment" of thought, it is regarded in its real existence as a confirmation of thought, of self-consciousness, of abstraction.

[XXX] From the one aspect the existent which Hegel *supersedes* in philosophy is not therefore the *actual* religion, state or nature, but religion itself as an object of knowledge, i.e. *dogmatics;* and similarly with *jurisprudence, political science* and *natural science.* From this aspect, therefore, he stands in opposition both to the actual being and to the direct, non-philosophical science (or the non-philosophical *concepts*) of this being. Thus he contradicts the conventional conceptions.

From the other aspect, the religious man, etc. can find in Hegel his ultimate confirmation.

We have now to consider the *positive* moments of Hegel's dialectic, within the condition of alienation.

(a) Supersession as an objective movement which reabsorbs alienation into itself. This is the insight, expressed within alienation, into the *appropriation* of the objective being through the supersession of its alienation. It is the alienated insight into the *real objectification* of man, into the real appropriation of his objective being by the destruction of the *alienated* character of the objective world, by the annulment of its alienated mode of existence. In the same way, atheism as the annulment of God is the emergence of theoretical humanism, and communism as the annulment of private property is the vindication of real human life as man's property. The latter is also the emergence of practical humanism, for atheism is humanism mediated to itself by the annulment of religion, while communism is humanism mediated to itself by the annulment of private property. It is only by the supersession of this mediation (which is, however, a necessary pre-condition) that the self-originating *positive* humanism can appear.

But atheism and communism are not flight or abstraction from, nor loss of, the objective world which men have created by the objectification of their faculties. They are not an impoverished return to unnatural, primitive simplicity. They are rather the first real emergence, the genuine actualization, of man's nature as something real.

Thus Hegel, in so far as he sees the positive significance of the self-referring negation (though in an alienated mode) conceives man's self-estrangement, alienation of being, loss of objectivity and reality, as self-discovery, change of nature, objectification and realization. In short, Hegel conceives labour as man's *act of self-creation* (though in abstract terms); he grasps man's relation to himself as an alien being and the emergence of *species-consciousness* and *species-life* as the demonstration of his alien being.

(b) But in Hegel, apart from, or rather as a consequence of, the inversion we have already described, this act of genesis appears, in the first place, as one which is merely *formal,* because it is abstract, and because human nature itself is treated as merely *abstract, thinking nature,* as self-consciousness.

Secondly, because the conception is *formal* and *abstract* the annulment of alienation becomes a confirmation of alienation. For Hegel, this movement of *self-creation* and *self-objectification* in the form of *self-estrangement* is the *absolute* and hence final *expression of human life,* which has its end in itself, is at peace with itself and at one with its own nature.

This movement, in its abstract [XXXI] form as dialectic, is regarded therefore as *truly human life,* and since it is nevertheless an abstraction, an alienation of human life, it is regarded as a divine process and thus as the *divine process* of mankind; it is a process which man's abstract, pure, absolute being, as distinguished from himself, traverses.

Thirdly, this process must have a bearer, a subject; but the subject first emerges as a result. This result, the subject knowing itself as absolute self-consciousness, is therefore *God, absolute spirit, the self-knowing and self-manifesting idea.* Real man and real nature become mere predicates, symbols of this concealed unreal man and unreal nature. Subject and predicate have, therefore, an inverted relation to each other; *a mystical subject-object,* or a *subjectivity reaching beyond the object,* the *absolute subject* as a process of self-alienation and of return from alienation into itself, and at the same time of reabsorption of this alienation, the *subject* as this process; pure, *unceasing* revolving within itself.

First, the formal and abstract conception of man's act of self-creation or self-objectification.

Since Hegel equates man with self-consciousness, the alienated object, the alienated real being of man, is simply *consciousness,* merely the thought of alienation, its abstract and hence vacuous and unreal expression, the *negation.* The annulment of alienation is also, therefore, merely an abstract and vacuous annulment of this empty abstraction, the *negation of the negation.* The replete, living, sensuous, concrete activity of self-objectification is, therefore, reduced to a mere abstraction, *absolute negativity,* an abstraction which is then crystallized as such and is conceived as an independent activity, as activity itself. Since this so-called negativity is merely the *abstract, vacuous* form of that real living act, its content can only be a formal content produced by abstraction from all content. They are, therefore, general, abstract *forms of abstraction* which refer to any content and are thus neutral towards, and valid for, any content; forms of thought, logical forms which are detached from *real* spirit and *real* nature. (We shall expound later the *logical* content of absolute negativity.)

Hegel's positive achievement in his speculative logic is to show that the *determinate concepts,* the universal *fixed thought-forms,* in their independence from nature and spirit, are a necessary result of the general alienation of human nature and also of human thought; and to depict them as a whole as moments in the process of abstraction. For example, being superseded is essence, essence superseded is concept, the concept superseded is . . . the absolute idea. But what is the absolute idea? It must supersede itself if it does not want to traverse the whole process of abstraction again from the beginning and to rest content with being a totality of abstractions or a self-comprehending abstraction. But the self-comprehending abstraction knows itself to be nothing; it must abandon itself, the abstraction, and so arrives at an entity which is its exact opposite, *nature*. The whole *Logic* is therefore, a demonstration that abstract thought is nothing for itself, that the absolute idea is nothing for itself, that only *nature* is something.

[XXXII] The absolute idea, the *abstract* idea which *"regarded* from the aspect of its unity with itself, is *intuition"* (Hegel's *Encyclopaedia,* 3rd ed., p. 222), and which "in its own absolute truth *resolves* to let the moment of its particularity or of initial determination and other-being, the *immediate idea,* as its reflection, *emerge freely from itself as nature"* (ibid.); this whole idea which behaves in such a strange and fanciful way and which has given the Hegelians such terrible headaches is throughout nothing but *abstraction,* i.e. the abstract thinker. It is abstraction which, made wise by experience and enlightened about its own truth, resolves under various (false and still abstract) conditions to *abandon* itself, and to establish its other being, the particular, the determinate, in place of its self-absorption, non-being, universality and indeterminateness; and which resolves to let nature, which it concealed within itself only as an abstraction, as an entity of thought, *emerge freely from itself*. That is, it decides to forsake abstraction and to observe nature free from abstraction. The abstract idea, which without mediation becomes *intuition,* is nothing but abstract thought which abandons itself and decides for *intuition*. This whole transition from logic to the philosophy of nature is simply the transition from *abstracting* to *intuiting,* a transition which is extremely difficult for the abstract thinker to accomplish and which he therefore describes in such strange terms. The *mystical feeling* which drives the philosopher from abstract thinking to intuition is *ennui,* the longing for a content.

(Man alienated from himself is also the thinker alienated from his *being,* i.e. from his natural and human life. His thoughts are consequently spirits existing outside nature and man. In his *Logic* Hegel has imprisoned all these spirits together, and has conceived each of them first as negation, i.e. as *alienation of human* thought, and secondly as negation of the negation, i.e. as the supersession of this alienation and as the real expression of human thought. But since this negation of the negation is itself still confined within the alienation, it is in part a restoration of these fixed spiritual forms in their alienation, in part an immobilization in the final act, the act of self-reference, as the true being of these spiritual forms.* Further, in so far as this abstraction conceives itself, and experiences an increasing weariness of itself, there appears in Hegel an abandonment of abstract thought which moves solely in the sphere of thought, devoid of eyes, ears, teeth, everything, and a resolve to recognize *nature* as being and to go over to intuition.)

[XXXIII] But *nature* too, taken abstractly, for itself, and rigidly separated from man, is *nothing* for man. It goes without saying that the abstract thinker who has committed himself to intuition, intuits nature abstractly. As nature lay enclosed in the thinker in a form which was obscure and mysterious even to himself, as absolute idea, as an entity of thought, so in truth, when he let it emerge from himself it was still only

---

*That is, Hegel substitutes the act of abstraction revolving within itself, for these fixed abstractions. In so doing, he has first of all the merit of having indicated the source of all these inappropriate concepts which originally belonged to different philosophies, and of having brought them together and established the comprehensive range of abstractions, instead of some particular abstraction, as the object of criticism. We shall see later why Hegel separates though from the *subject*. It is already clear, however, that if man is not human the expression of his nature cannot be human, and consequently thought itself could not be conceived as an expression of man's nature, as the expression of a human and natural subject, with eyes, ears, etc. living in society, in the world, and in nature.

abstract nature, nature as an *entity of thought,* but now with the significance that it is the other-being of thought, is real, intuited nature, distinguished from abstract thought. Or, to speak in human language, the abstract thinker discovers from intuiting nature that the entities which he thought to create out of nothing, out of pure abstraction, to create in the divine dialectic as the pure products of thought endlessly shuttling back and forth in itself and never regarding external reality, are simply *abstractions* from *natural characteristics.* The whole of nature, therefore, reiterates to him the logical abstractions, but in a sensuous, external form. He *analyses* nature and these abstractions again. His intuition of nature is, therefore, simply the act of confirmation of his abstraction from the intuition of nature; his conscious re-enactment of the process of generating his abstraction. Thus, for example, Time equals Negativity which refers to itself (loc. cit., p. 238). In the natural form, superseded Movement as Matter corresponds to superseded Becoming as Being. In the *natural* form Light is *Reflection-in-itself.* Body as *Moon* and *Comet* is the natural form of the antithesis which, according to the *Logic,* is on the one hand the *positive grounded upon itself,* and on the other hand, the *negative grounded upon itself.* The Earth is the *natural* form of the logical *ground,* as the negative unity of the antithesis, etc.

Nature as nature, i.e. so far as it is sensuously distinguished from that secret sense concealed within it, nature separated and distinguished from these abstractions is *nothing* (a *nullity demonstrating its nullity*), is *devoid of sense,* or has only the sense of an external thing which has been superseded.

"In the finite-*teleological* view is to be found the correct premise that nature does not contain within itself the absolute purpose" (loc. cit., p. 225). Its purpose is the confirmation of abstraction. "Nature has shown itself to be the idea in the *form* of *other-being.* Since the idea is in this form the negative of itself, or *external to itself,* nature is not just relatively external *vis-à-vis* this idea, but *externality* constitutes the form in which it exists as nature" (loc. cit., p. 227).

Externality should not be understood here as the *self-externalizing world of sense,* open to the light and to man's senses. It has to be taken here in the sense of alienation, as error, a defect, that which ought not to be. For that which is true is still the idea. Nature is merely the form of its other-being. And since abstract thought is *being,* that which is external to it is by its nature a merely *external thing.* The abstract thinker recognizes at the same time that *sensuousness, externality* in contrast to thought which shuttles back and forth *within itself,* is the essence of nature. But at the same time he expresses this antithesis is such a way that this *externality* of nature, and its *contrast* with thought, appears as a deficiency, and that nature distinguished from abstraction appears as a deficient being. [XXXIV] A being which is deficient, not simply for me or in my eyes, but in itself, has something outside itself which it lacks. That is to say, its being is something other than itself. For the abstract thinker, nature must therefore supersede itself, because it is already posited by him as a potentially *superseded* being.

"*For us,* spirit has *nature as its premise,* being the truth of nature and thereby its *absolute primus.* In this truth nature has *vanished,* and spirit has surrendered itself as the idea which has attained being-for-itself, whose *object,* as well as the *subject,* is the *concept.* This identity is *absolute negativity,* for whereas in nature the concept has its perfect external objectivity, here its alienation has been superseded and the concept has become identical with itself. It is this identity only so far as it is a return from nature" (loc. cit., p. 392).

"*Revelation,* as the *abstract* idea, is unmediated transition to, the *coming-to-be* of, nature; as the revelation of the spirit, which is free, it is the establishment of nature as *its own* world, an establishment which, as reflection, is simultaneously the *presupposition* of the world as independently existing nature. Revelation in conception is the creation of nature as spirit's own being, in which it acquires the *affirmation* and *truth* of its freedom." "*The absolute is spirit;* this is the highest definition of the absolute."

A CONTRIBUTION TO THE CRITIQUE OF POLITICAL ECONOMY (in part)

AUTHOR'S PREFACE

* * *

In the social production which men carry on they enter into definite relations that are indispensable and independent of their will; these relations of production correspond to a definite stage of development of their material powers of production. The sum total of these relations of production constitutes the economic structure of society—the real foundation, on which rise legal and political superstructures and to which correspond definite forms of social consciousness. The mode of production in material life determines the general character of the social, political and spiritual processes of life. It is not the consciousness of men that determines their existence, but, on the contrary, their social existence determines their consciousness. At a certain stage of their development, the material forces of production in society come in conflict with the existing relations of production, or—what is but a legal expression for the same thing—with the property relations within which they had been at work before. From forms of development of the forces of production these relations turn into their fetters. Then comes the period of social revolution. With the change of the economic foundation the entire immense superstructure is more or less rapidly transformed. In considering such transformations the distinction should always be made between the material transformation of the economic conditions of production which can be determined with the precision of natural science, and the legal, political, religious, aesthetic or philosophic—in short ideological forms in which men become conscious of this conflict and fight it out. Just as our opinion of an individual is not based on what he thinks of himself, so can we not judge of such a period of transformation by its own consciousness; on the contrary, this consciousness must rather be explained from the contradictions of material life, from the existing conflict between the social forces of production and the relations of production. No social order ever disappears before all the productive forces, for which there is room in it, have been developed; and new higher relations of production never appear before the material conditions of their existence have matured in the womb of the old society. Therefore, mankind always takes up only such problems as it can solve; since, looking at the matter more closely, we will always find that the problem itself arises only when the material conditions necessary for its solution already exist or are at least in the process of formation. In broad outlines we can designate the Asiatic, the ancient, the feudal, and the modern bourgeois methods of production as so many epochs in the progress of the economic formation of society. The bourgeois relations of production are the last an-

"Capital and Labour," cartoon from *Punch* magazine, 1843. The cartoon
shows the suffering of the workers and their families that makes
possible the bourgeois capitalists' high life. It was in response to
conditions such as this that Marx and Engels wrote in *The Communist
Manifesto* (1848), "The proletarians have nothing to lose but their
chains. They have a world to win. Workingmen of all countries, unite!"
(Library of Congress)

tagonistic form of the social process of production—antagonistic not in the sense of individual antagonism, but of one arising from conditions surrounding the life of individuals in society; at the same time the productive forces developing in the womb of
bourgeois society create the material conditions for the solution of that antagonism.
This social formation constitutes, therefore, the closing chapter of the prehistoric stage
of human society.

* * *

INTRODUCTION

1. PRODUCTION IN GENERAL

The subject of our discussion is first of all *material* production by individuals as determined by society, naturally constitutes the starting point. The individual and isolated
hunter or fisher who forms the starting point with Smith and Ricardo, belongs to the in-

sipid illusions of the eighteenth century. They are Robinsonades which do not by any means represent, as students of the history of civilization imagine, a reaction against over-refinement and a return to a misunderstood natural life. They are no more based on such a naturalism than is Rosseau's "contrat social," which makes naturally independent individuals come in contact and have mutual intercourse by contract. They are the fiction and only the aesthetic fiction of the small and great Robinsonades. They are, moreover, the anticipation of "bourgeois society," which had been in course of development since the sixteenth century and made gigantic strides towards maturity in the eighteenth. In this society of free competition the individual appears free from the bonds of nature, etc., which in former epochs of history made him a part of a definite, limited human conglomeration. To the prophets of the eighteenth century, on whose shoulders Smith and Ricardo are still standing, this eighteenth century individual, constituting the joint product of the dissolution of the feudal form of society and of the new forces of production which had developed since the sixteenth century, appears as an ideal whose existence belongs to the past; not as a result of history, but as its starting point.

Since that individual appeared to be in conformity with nature and [corresponded] to their conception of human nature, [he was regarded] not as a product of history, but of nature. This illusion has been characteristic of every new epoch in the past. Steuart, who, as an aristocrat, stood more firmly on historical ground, contrary to the spirit of the eighteenth century, escaped this simplicity of view. The further back we go into history, the more the individual and, therefore, the producing individual seems to depend on and constitute a part of a larger whole: at first it is, quite naturally, the family and the clan, which is but an enlarged family; later on, it is the community growing up in its different forms out of the clash and the amalgamation of clans. It is but in the eighteenth century, in "bourgeois society," that the different forms of social union confront the individual as a mere means to his private ends, as an outward necessity. But the period in which this view of the isolated individual becomes prevalent, is the very one in which the interrelations of society (general from this point of view) have reached the highest state of development. Man is in the most literal sense of the word a *zoon politikon,* not only a social animal, but an animal which can develop into an individual only in society. Production by isolated individuals outside of society—something which might happen as an exception to a civilized man who by accident got into the wilderness and already dynamically possessed within himself the forces of society—is as great an absurdity as the idea of the development of language without individuals living together and talking to one another. We need not dwell on this any longer. It would not be necessary to touch upon this point at all, were not the vagary which had its justification and sense with the people of the eighteenth century transplanted in all earnest into the field of political economy by Baatiat, Carey, Proudhon and others. Proudhon and others naturally find it very pleasant, when they do not know the historical origin of a certain economic phenomenon, to give it a quasi historico-philosophical explanation by going into mythology. Adam or Prometheus hit upon the scheme cut and dried, whereupon it was adopted, etc. Nothing is more tediously dry than the dreaming *locus communis.*

Whenever we speak, therefore, of production, we always have in mind production at a certain stage of social development, or production by social individuals. Hence, it might seem that in order to speak of production at all, we must either trace the historical process of development through its various phases, or declare at the outset that we are dealing with a certain historical period, as, e.g., with modern capitalistic production which, as a matter of fact, constitutes the subject proper of this work. But all stages of production have certain landmarks in common, common purposes. *Production in general* is an abstraction, but it is a rational abstraction, in so far as it singles out and fixes the common features, thereby saving us repetition. Yet these general or common features discovered by comparison constitute something very complex, whose constituent elements have different destinations. Some of these elements belong to all epochs, others are common to a few. Some of them are common to the most modern as well as to the most ancient epochs. No production is conceivable without them; but while even the most completely developed languages have laws and conditions in common with the least developed ones, what is characteristic of their development are the points of departure from the general and common. The conditions which generally govern production must be differentiated in order that the essential points of difference be not lost sight of in view of the general uniformity which is due to the fact that the subject, mankind, and the object, nature, remain the same. The failure to remember this one fact is the source of all the wisdom of modern economists who are trying to prove the eternal nature and harmony of existing social conditions. Thus they say, e.g., that no production is possible without some instrument of production, let that instrument be only the hand; that none is possible without past accumulated labor, even if that labor consist of mere skill which has been accumulated and concentrated in the hand of the savage by repeated exercise. Capital is, among other things, also an instrument of production, also past impersonal labor. Hence capital is a universal, eternal natural phenomenon; which is true if we disregard the specific properties which turn an "instrument of production" and "stored up labor" into capital. The entire history of production appears to a man like Carey, e.g., as a malicious perversion on the part of governments.

If there is no production in general, there is also no general production. Production is always some special branch of production or an aggregate, as, e.g., agriculture, stock raising, manufactures, etc. But political economy is not technology. The connection between the general destinations of production at a given stage of social development and the particular forms of production, is to be developed elsewhere (later on).

Finally, production is not only of a special kind. It is always a certain body politic, a social personality that is engaged on a larger or smaller aggregate of branches of production. The connection between the real process and its scientific presentation also falls outside of the scope of this treatise. [We must thus distinguish between] production in general, special branches of production and production as a whole.

It is the fashion with economists to open their works with a general introduction, which is entitled "production" (see, e.g., John Stuart Mill) and deals with the general "requisites of production."

This general introductory part treats or is supposed to treat:

1. Of the conditions without which production is impossible, i.e., of the most essential conditions of production. As a matter of fact, however, it dwindles down, as we shall see, to a few very simple definitions, which flatten out into shallow tautologies;

2. Of conditions which further production more or less, as, e.g., Adam Smith's [discussion of] a progressive and stagnant state of society.

In order to give scientific value to what serves with him as a mere summary, it would be necessary to study the *degree of productivity* by periods in the development of individual nations; such a study falls outside of the scope of the present subject, and in so far as it does belong here is to be brought out in connection with the discussion of competition, accumulation, etc. The commonly accepted view of the matter gives a general answer to the effect that an industrial nation is at the height of its production at the moment when it reaches its historical climax in all respects. Or, that certain races, climates, natural conditions, such as distance from the sea, fertility of the soil, etc., are more favorable to production than others. That again comes down to the tautology that the facility of creating wealth depends on the extent to which its elements are present both subjectively and objectively. As a matter of fact a nation is at its industrial height so long as its main object is not gain, but the process of gaining. In that respect the Yankees stand above the English.

But all that is not what the economists are really after in the general introductory part. Their object is rather to represent production in contradistinction to distribution—see Mill, e.g.—as subject to eternal laws independent of history, and then to substitute bourgeois relations, in an underhand way, as immutable natural laws of society *in abstracto*. This is the more or less conscious aim of the entire proceeding. On the contrary, when it comes to distribution, mankind is supposed to have indulged in all sorts of arbitrary action. Quite apart from the fact that they violently break the ties which bind production and distribution together, so much must be clear from the outset: that, no matter how greatly the systems of distribution may vary at different stages of society, it should be possible here, as in the case of production, to discover the common features and to confound and eliminate all historical differences in formulating *general human* laws. E.g., the slave, the serf, the wage-worker—all receive a quantity of food, which enables them to exist as slave, serf, and wage-worker. The conqueror, the official, the landlord, the monk, or the levite, who respectively live on tribute, taxes, rent, alms, and the tithe,—all receive [a part] of the social product which is determined by laws different from those which determine the part received by the slave, etc. The two main points which all economists place under this head, are: first, property; second, the protection of the latter by the administration of justice, police, etc. The objections to these two points can be stated very briefly.

1. All production is appropriation of nature by the individual within and through a definite form of society. In that sense it is a tautology to say that property (appropriation) is a condition of production. But it becomes ridiculous, when from that one jumps at once to a definite form of property, e.g. private property (which implies, besides, as a prerequisite the existence of an opposite form, viz. absence of property). History points rather to common property (e.g. among the Hindus, Slavs, ancient Celts, etc.) as the primitive form, which still plays an important part at a much later period as communal property. The question as to whether wealth grows more rapidly under this or that form of property, is not even raised here as yet. But that there can be no such a thing as production, nor, consequently, society, where property does not exist in any form, is a tautology. Appropriation which does not appropriate is a *contradictio* in *subjecto*.

2. Protection of property, etc. Reduced to their real meaning, these commonplaces express more than what their preachers know, namely, that every form of production creates its own legal relations, forms of government, etc. The crudity and the shortcomings of the conception lie in the tendency to see but an accidental reflective connection in what constitutes an organic union. The bourgeois economists have a vague notion that it is better to carry on production under the modern police, than it was, e.g. under club-law. They forget that club law is also law, and that the right of the stronger continues to exist in other forms even under their "government of law."

When the social conditions corresponding to a certain stage of production are in a state of formation or disappearance, disturbances of production naturally arise, although differing in extent and effect.

To sum up: all the stages of production have certain destinations in common, which we generalize in thought; but the so-called general conditions of all production are nothing but abstract conceptions which do not go to make up any real stage in the history of production.

2. THE GENERAL RELATION OF PRODUCTION TO DISTRIBUTION, EXCHANGE, AND CONSUMPTION

Before going into a further analysis of production, it is necessary to look at the various divisions which economists put side by side with it. The most shallow conception is as follows: By production, the members of society appropriate (produce and shape) the products of nature to human wants; distribution determines the proportion in which the individual participates in this production; exchange brings him the particular products into which he wishes to turn the quantity secured by him through distribution; finally, through consumption the products become objects of use and enjoyment, of individual appropriation. Production yields goods adopted to our needs; distribution distributes them according to social laws; exchange distributes further what has already been distributed, according to individual wants; finally, in consumption the product drops out of the social movement, becoming the direct object of the individual want which it serves and satisfies in use. Production thus appears as the starting point; consumption as the final end; and distribution and exchange as the middle; the latter has a double aspect, distribution being defined as a process carried on by society, while exchange, as one proceeding from the individual. In production the person is embodied in things, in [consumption] things are embodied in persons; in distribution, society assumes the part of go-between of production and consumption in the form of generally prevailing rules; in exchange this is accomplished by the accidental make-up of the individual.

Distribution determines what proportion (quantity) of the products the individual is to receive; exchange determines the products in which the individual desires to receive his share allotted to him by distribution.

Production, distribution, exchange, and consumption thus form a perfect connection, production standing for the general, distribution and exchange for the special, and consumption for the individual, in which all are joined together. To be sure this is a connection, but it does not go very deep. Production is determined [according to the economists] by universal natural laws, while distribution depends on social chance: distribution can, therefore, have a more or less stimulating effect on production: exchange lies between the two as a formal social movement, and the final act of consumption which is considered not only as a final purpose, but also as a final aim, falls, properly, outside of the scope of economics, except in so far as it reacts on the starting point and causes the entire process to begin all over again.

The opponents of the economists—whether economists themselves or not—who reproach them with tearing apart, like barbarians, what is an organic whole, either stand on common ground with them or are *below* them. Nothing is more common than the charge that the economists have been considering production as an end in itself, too much to the exclusion of everything else. The same has been said with regard to distribution. This accusation is itself based on the economic conception that distribution exists side by side with production as a self-contained, independent sphere. Or [they are accused] that the various factors are not treated by them in their connection as a whole. As though it were the text books that impress this separation upon life and not life upon the text books; and the subject at issue were a dialectic balancing of conceptions and not an analysis of real conditions.

a. Production is at the same time also consumption. Twofold consumption, subjective and objective. The individual who develops his faculties in production, is also expending them, consuming them in the act of production, just as procreation is in its way a consumption of vital powers. In the second place, production is consumption of means of production which are used and used up and partly (as e.g. in burning) reduced to their natural elements. The same is true of the consumption of raw materials which do not remain in their natural form and state, being greatly absorbed in the process. The act of production is, therefore, in all its aspects an act of consumption as well. But this is admitted by economists. Production as directly identical with consumption, consumption as directly coincident with production, they call productive consumption. This identity of production and consumption finds its expression in Spinoza's proposition, *Determinatio est negatio*. But this definition of productive consumption is resorted to just for the purpose of distinguishing between consumption as identical with production and consumption proper, which is defined as its destructive counterpart. Let us then consider consumption proper.

Consumption is directly also production, just as in nature the consumption of the elements and of chemical matter constitutes production of plants. It is clear, that in nutrition, e.g., which is but one form of consumption, man produces his own body; but it is equally true of every kind of consumption, which goes to produce the human being in one way or another. [It is] consumptive production. But, say the economists, this production which is identical with consumption, is a second production resulting from the destruction of the product of the first. In the first, the producer transforms himself into things; in the second, things are transformed into human beings. Consequently, this consumptive production—although constituting a direct unity of production and consumption—differs essentially from production proper. The direct unity in which production coincides with consumption and consumption with production, does not interfere with their direct duality.

Production is thus at the same time consumption, and consumption is at the same time production. Each is directly its own counterpart. But at the same time an intermediary movement goes on between the two. Production furthers consumption by creating material for the latter which otherwise would lack its object. But consumption in its turn furthers production, by providing for the products the individual for whom they are products. The product receives its last finishing touches in consumption. A railroad on which no one rides, which is, consequently not used up, not consumed, is but a potential railroad, and not a real one. Without production, no consumption; but, on the other hand, without consumption, no production; since production would then be without a purpose. Consumption produces production in two ways.

In the first place, in that the product first becomes a real product in consumption; e.g., a garment becomes a real garment only through the act of being worn; a dwelling which is not inhabited, is really no dwelling; consequently, a product as distinguished from a mere natural object, proves to be such, first *becomes* a product in consumption. Consumption gives the product the finishing touch by annihilating it, since a product is the [result] of production not only as the material embodiment of activity, but also as a mere object for the active subject.

In the second place, consumption produces production by creating the necessity for new production, i.e. by providing the ideal, inward, impelling cause which constitutes the prerequisite of production. Consumption furnishes the impulse for production as well as its object, which plays in production the part of its guiding aim. It is clear that while production furnishes the material object of consumption, consumption provides the ideal object of production, as its image, its want, its impulse and its purpose. It furnishes the object of production in its subjective form. No wants, no production. But consumption reproduces the want.

In its turn, production—

First, furnishes consumption with its material, its object. Consumption without an object is no consumption, hence production works in this direction by producing consumption.

Second. But it is not only the object that production provides for consumption. It gives consumption its definite outline, its character, its finish. Just as consumption gives the product its finishing touch as a product, production puts the finishing touch on consumption. For the object is not simply an object in general, but a definite object, which is consumed in a certain definite manner prescribed in its turn by production. Hunger is hunger; but the hunger that is satisfied with cooked meat eaten with fork and knife is a different kind of hunger from the one that devours raw meat with the aid of hands, nails, and teeth. Not only the object of consumption, but also the manner of consumption is produced by production; that is to say, consumption is created by production not only objectively, but also subjectively. Production thus creates the consumers.

Third. Production not only supplies the want with material, but supplies the material with a want. When consumption emerges from its first stage of natural crudeness and directness—and its continuation in that state would in itself be the result of a production still remaining in a state of natural crudeness—it is itself furthered by its object as a moving spring. The want of it which consumption experiences is created by its appreciation of the product. The object of art, as well as any other product, creates an artistic and beauty-enjoying public. Production thus produces not only an object for the individual, but also an individual for the object.

Production thus produces consumption: first, by furnishing the latter with material; second, by determining the manner of consumption; third, by creating in consumers a want for its products as objects of consumption. It thus produces the object, the manner, and the moving spring of consumption. In the same manner, consumption [creates] the *disposition* of the producer by setting him up as an aim and by stimulating wants. The identity of consumption and production thus appears to be a three fold one.

First, direct identity: production is consumption; consumption is production. Consumptive production. Productive consumption. Economists call both productive consumption, but make one distinction by calling the former reproduction, and the latter productive consumption. All inquiries into the former deal with productive and unproductive labor; those into the latter treat of productive and unproductive consumption.

Second. Each appears as the means of the other and as being brought about by the other, which is expressed as their mutual interdependence; a relation, by virtue of which they appear as mutually connected and indispensable, yet remaining outside of each other.

Production creates the material as the outward object of consumption; consumption creates the want as the inward object, the purpose of production. Without production, no consumption; without consumption, no production; this maxim figures in political economy in many forms.

Third. Production is not only directly consumption and consumption directly production; nor is production merely a means of consumption and consumption the purpose of production. In other words, not only does each furnish the other with its object; production, the material object of consumption; consumption, the ideal object of production. On the contrary, either one is not only directly the other, not only a means of furthering the other, but while it is taking place, creates the other as such for itself. Consumption completes the act of production by giving the finishing touch to the product as such, by destroying the latter, by breaking up its independent material form; by bringing to a state of readiness, through the necessity of repetition, the disposition to produce developed in the first act of production; that is to say, it is not only the concluding act through which the product becomes a product, but also [the one] through which the producer becomes a producer. On the other hand, production produces consumption, by determining the manner of consumption, and further, by creating the incentive for consumption, the very ability to consume, in the form of want. This latter identity mentioned under point 3, is much discussed in political economy in connection with the treatment of the relations of demand and supply, of objects and wants, of natural wants and those created by society.

Hence, it is the simplest matter with a Hegelian to treat production and consumption as identical. And this has been done not only by socialist writers of fiction but even by economists, e.g. Say; the latter maintained that if we consider a nation as a whole, or mankind *in abstracto*—her production is at the same time her consumption. Storch pointed out Say's error by calling attention to the fact that a nation does not entirely consume her product, but also creates means of production, fixed capital, etc. To consider society as a single individual is moreover a false mode of speculative reasoning. With an individual, production and consumption appear as different aspects of one act. The important point to be emphasized here is that if production and consumption be considered as activities of one individual or of separate individuals, they appear at any rate as aspects of one process in which production forms the actual starting point and is, therefore, the predominating factor. Consumption, as a natural necessity, as a want, constitutes an internal factor of productive activity, but the latter is the starting point of realization and, therefore, its predominating factor, the act into which the entire process resolves itself in the end. The individual produces a certain article and turns again into himself by consuming it; but he returns as a productive and a self-reproducing individual. Consumption thus appears as a factor of production.

In society, however, the relation of the producer to his product, as soon as it is completed, is an outward one, and the return of the product to the individual depends on his relations to other individuals. He does not take immediate possession of it. Nor does the direct appropriation of the product constitute his purpose, when he produces in society. Between the producer and the product distribution steps in, which determines by social laws his share in the world of products; that is to say, distribution steps in between production and consumption.

Does distribution form an independent sphere standing side by side with and outside of production?

b. Production and Distribution. In perusing the common treatises on economics one can not help being struck with the fact that everything is treated there twice; e.g., under distribution, there figure rent, wages, interest, and profit; while under production we find land, labor, and capital as agents of production. As regards capital, it is at once clear that it is counted twice: first, as an agent of production; second, as a source of income; as determining factors and definite forms of distribution, interest and profit figure as such also in production, since they are forms, in which capital increases and grows, and are consequently factors of its own production. Interest and profit, as forms of distribution, imply the existence of capital as an agent of production. They are forms of distribution which have for their prerequisite capital as an agent of production. They are also forms of reproduction of capital.

In the same manner, wages is wage-labor when considered under another head; the definite character which labor has in one case as an agent of production, appears in the other as a form of distribution. If labor were not fixed as wage-labor, its manner of participation in distribution would not appear as wages, as is the case e.g. under slavery. Finally, rent—to take at once the most developed form of distribution—by means of which landed property receives its share of the products, implies the existence of large landed property (properly speaking, agriculture on a large scale) as an agent of production, and not simply land, no more than wages represents simply labor. The relations and methods of distribution appear, therefore, merely as the reverse sides of the agents of production. An individual who participates in production as a wage laborer, receives his share of the products, i.e. of the results of production, in the form of wages. The subdivisions and organization of distribution are determined by the subdivisions and organization of production. Distribution is itself a product of production, not only in so far as the material goods are concerned, since only the results of production can be distributed; but also as regards its form, since the definite manner of participation in production determines the particular form of distribution, the form under which participation in distribution takes place. It is quite an illusion to place land under production, rent under distribution, etc.

Economists, like Ricardo, who are accused above all of having paid exclusive attention to production, define distribution, therefore, as the exclusive subject of political economy, because they instinctively regard the forms of distribution as the clearest forms in which the agents of production find expression in a given society.

To the single individual distribution naturally appears as a law established by society determining his position in the sphere of production, within which he produces, and thus antedating production. At the outset the individual has no capital, no landed property. From his birth he is assigned to wage-labor by the social process of distribution. But this very condition of being assigned to wage-labor is the result of the existence of capital and landed property as independent agents of production.

From the point of view of society as a whole, distribution seems to antedate and to determine production in another way as well, as a pre-economic fact, so to say. A conquering people divides the land among the conquerors establishing thereby a certain division and form of landed property and determining the character of production; or, it turns the conquered people into slaves and thus makes slave labor the basis of production. Or, a nation, by revolution, breaks up large estates into small parcels of land and by this new distribution imparts to production a new character. Or, legislation perpetuates land ownership in large families or distributes labor as an hereditary privilege and thus fixes it in castes.

In all of these cases, and they are all historic, it is not distribution that seems to be organized and determined by production, but on the contrary, production by distribution.

In the most shallow conception of distribution, the latter appears as a distribution of products and to that extent as further removed from and quasi-independent of production. But before distribution means distribution of products, it is first, a distribution of the means of production, and second, what is practically another wording of the same fact, it is a distribution of the members of society among the various kinds of production (the subjection of individuals to certain conditions of production). The distribution of products is manifestly a result of this distribution, which is bound up with the process of production and determines the very organization of the latter. To treat of production apart from the distribution which is comprised in it, is plainly an idle abstraction. Conversely, we know the character of the distribution of products the moment we are given the nature of that other distribution which forms originally a factor of production. Ricardo, who was concerned with the analysis of production as it is organized in modern society and who was the economist of production *par excellence,* for that very reason declares not production but distribution as the subject proper of modern economics. We have here another evidence of the insipidity of the economists who treat production as an eternal truth, and banish history to the domain of distribution.

What relation to production this distribution, which has a determining influence on production itself, assumes, is plainly a question which falls within the province of production. Should it be maintained that at least to the extent that production depends on a certain distribution of the instruments of production, distribution in that sense precedes production and constitutes its prerequisite; it may be replied that production has in fact its prerequisite conditions, which form factors of it. These may appear at first to have a natural origin. By the very process of production they are changed from natural to historical, and if they appear during one period as a natural prerequisite of production, they formed at other periods its historical result. Within the sphere of production itself they are undergoing a constant change. E.g., the application of machinery produces a change in the distribution of the instruments of production as well as in that of products, and modern land ownership on a large scale is as much the result of modern trade and modern industry, as that of the application of the latter to agriculture.

All of these questions resolve themselves in the last instance to this: How do general historical conditions affect production and what part does it play at all in the course of history? It is evident that this question can be taken up only in connection with the discussion and analysis of production.

Yet in the trivial form in which these questions arc raised above, they can be answered just as briefly. In the case of all conquests three ways lie open. The conquering people may impose its own methods of production upon the conquered (e.g. the English in Ireland in the nineteenth century, partly also in India); or, it may allow everything to remain as it was contenting itself with tribute (e.g. the Turks and the Romans); or, the two systems by mutually modifying each other may result in something new, a synthesis (which partly resulted from the Germanic conquests). In all of these conquests the method of production, be it of the conquerors, the conquered, or the one resulting from a combination of both, determines the nature of the new distribution which comes into play. Although the latter appears now as the prerequisite condition of the new period of production, it is in itself but a product of production, not of production belonging to history in general, but of production relating to a definite historical period. The Mongols with their devastations in Russia e.g. acted in accordance with their system of production, for which sufficient pastures on large uninhabited stretches of country are the main prerequisite. The Germanic barbarians, with whom agriculture carried on with the aid of serfs was the traditional system of production and who were accustomed to lonely life in the country, could introduce the same conditions in the Roman provinces so much easier since the concentration of landed property which had taken place there, did away completely with the older systems of agriculture. There is a prevalent tradition that in certain periods robbery constituted the only source of living. But in order to be able to plunder, there must be something to plunder, i.e. there must be production. And even the method of plunder is determined by the method of production. A stockjobbing nation e.g. can not be robbed in the same manner as a nation of shepherds.

In the case of the slave the instrument of production is robbed directly. But then the production of the country in whose interest he is robbed, must be so organized as to admit of slave labor, or (as in South America, etc.) a system of production must be introduced adapted to slavery.

Laws may perpetuate an instrument of production, e.g. land, in certain families. These laws assume an economic importance if large landed property is in harmony with the system of production prevailing in society, as is the case e.g. in England. In France agriculture had been carried on on a small scale in spite of the large estates, and the latter were, therefore, broken up by the Revolution. But how about the legislative attempt to perpetuate the minute subdivision of the land? In spite of these laws land ownership is concentrating again. The effect of legislation on the maintenance of a system of distribution and its resultant influence on production are to be determined elsewhere.

   c. Exchange and Circulation. Circulation is but a certain aspect of exchange, or it may be defined as exchange considered as a whole. Since *exchange* is an intermediary factor between production and its dependent distribution, on the one hand, and consumption, on the other; and since the latter appears but as a constituent of production, exchange is manifestly also a constituent part of production.

   In the first place, it is clear that the exchange of activities and abilities which takes place in the sphere of production falls directly within the latter and constitutes one of its essential elements. In the second place, the same is true of the exchange of products, in so far as it is a means of completing a certain product, designed for immediate consumption. To that extent exchange constitutes an act included in production. Thirdly, the so-called exchange between dealers and dealers' is by virtue of its organization determined by production, and is itself a species of productive activity. Exchange appears to be independent of and indifferent to production only in the last stage when products are exchanged directly for consumption. But in the first place, there is no exchange without a division of labor, whether natural or as a result of historical development; secondly, private exchange implies the existence of private production; thirdly, the intensity of exchange, as well as its extent and character are determined by the degree of development and organization of production, as e.g. exchange between city and country, exchange in the country, in the city, etc. Exchange thus appears in all its aspects to be directly included in or determined by production.

   The result we arrive at is not that production, distribution, exchange, and consumption are identical, but that they are all members of one entity, different sides of one unit. Production predominates not only over production itself in the opposite sense of that term, but over the other elements as well. With it the process constantly starts over again. That exchange and consumption can not be the predominating elements is self evident. The same is true of distribution in the narrow sense of distribution of products; as for distribution in the sense of distribution of the agents of production, it is itself but a factor of production. A definite [form of] production thus determines the [forms of] consumption, distribution, exchange, and *also the mutual relations between these various elements*. Of course, production *in its one-sided form* is in its turn influenced by other elements; e.g. with the expansion of the market, i.e. of the sphere of exchange, production grows in volume and is subdivided to a greater extent.

   With a change in distribution, production undergoes a change; as e.g. in the case of concentration of capital, of a change in the distribution of population in city and country, etc. Finally, the demands of consumption also influence production. A mutual interaction takes place between the various elements. Such is the case with every organic body.

3. THE METHOD OF POLITICAL ECONOMY

When we consider a given country from a politico-economic standpoint, we begin with its population, then analyze the latter according to its subdivision into classes, location in city, country, or by the sea, occupation in different branches of production; then we study its exports and imports, annual production and consumption, prices of commodities, etc. It seems to be the correct procedure to commence with the real and concrete aspect of conditions as they are; in the case of political economy, to commence with population which is the basis and the author of the entire productive activity of society. Yet, on closer consideration it proves to be wrong. Population is an abstraction, if we leave out e.g. the classes of which it consists. These classes, again, are but an empty word, unless we know what are the elements on which they are based, such as wage-labor, capital. etc. These imply, in their turn, exchange, division of labor, prices, etc. Capital, e.g. does not mean anything without wage-labor, value, money, price, etc. If we start out, therefore, with population, we do so with a chaotic conception of the whole, and by closer analysis we will gradually arrive at simpler ideas; thus we shall proceed from the imaginary concrete to less and less complex abstractions, until we get at the simplest conception. This once attained, we might start on our return journey until we would finally come back to population, but this time not as a chaotic notion of an integral whole, but as a rich aggregate of many conceptions and relations. The former method is the one which political economy had adopted in the past at its inception. The economists of the seventeenth century, e.g., always started out with the living aggregate: population, nation, state, several states, etc., but in the end they invariably arrived, by means of analysis, at certain leading, abstract general principles, such as division of labor, money, value, etc. As soon as these separate elements had been more or less established by abstract reasoning, there arose the systems of political economy which start from simple conceptions, such as labor, division of labor, demand, exchange value, and conclude with state, international exchange and world market. The latter is manifestly the scientifically correct method. The concrete is concrete, because it is a combination of many objects with different destinations, i.e. a unity of diverse elements. In our thought, it therefore appears as a process of synthesis, as a result, and not as a starting point, although it is the real starting point and, therefore, also the starting point of observation and conception. By the former method the complete conception passes into an abstract definition; by the latter, the abstract definitions lead to the reproduction of the concrete subject in the course of reasoning. Hegel fell into the error, therefore, of considering the real as the result of self-coordinating, self-absorbed, and spontaneously operating thought, while the method of advancing from the abstract to the concrete is but a way of thinking by which the concrete is grasped and is reproduced in our mind as a concrete. It is by no means, however, the process which itself generates the concrete. The simplest economic category, say, exchange value, implies the existence of population, population that is engaged in production under certain conditions; it also implies the existence of certain types of family, clan, or state, etc. It can have no other existence except as an abstract one-sided relation of an already given concrete and living aggregate.

As a category, however, exchange value leads an antediluvian existence. And since our philosophic consciousness is so arranged that only the image of the man that it conceives appears to it as the real man and the world as it conceives it, as the real world; it mistakes the movement of categories for the real act of production (which unfortunately receives only its impetus from outside) whose result is the world; that is true—here we have, however, again a tautology—in so far as the concrete aggregate is a thought aggregate, in so far as the concrete subject of our thought is in fact a product of thought, of comprehension; not, however, in the sense of a product of a self-emanating conception which works outside of and stands above observation and imagination, but of a mental consummation of observation and imagination. The whole, as it appears in our heads as a thought-aggregate, is the product of a thinking mind which grasps the world in the only way open to it, a way which differs from the one employed by the artistic, religious, or practical mind. The concrete subject continues to lead an independent existence after it has been grasped, as it did before, outside of the head, so long as the head contemplates it only speculatively, theoretically. So that in the employment of the theoretical method [in political economy], the subject, society, must constantly be kept in mind as the premise from which we start.

But have these simple categories no independent historical or natural existence antedating the more concrete ones? *Ça depend.* For instance, in his *Philosophy of Law* Hegel rightly starts out with possession, as the simplest legal relation of individuals. But there is no such thing as possession before the family or the relations of lord and serf, which are a great deal more concrete relations, have come into existence. On the other hand, one would be right in saying that there are families and clans which only *possess,* but do not *own* things. The simpler category thus appears as a relation of simple family and clan communities with respect to property. In earlier society the category appears as a simple relation of a developed organism, but the concrete substratum from which springs the relation of possession, is always implied. One can imagine an isolated savage in possession of things. But in that case possession is no legal relation. It is not true that the family came as the result of the historical evolution of possession. On the contrary, the latter always implies the existence of this "more concrete category of law." Yet so much may be said, that the simple categories are the expression of relations in which the less developed concrete entity may have been realized without entering into the manifold relations and bearings which are mentally expressed in the concrete category; but when the concrete entity attains fuller development it will retain the same category as a subordinate relation.

Money may exist and actually had existed in history before capital, or banks, or wage-labor came into existence. With that in mind, it may be said that the more simple category can serve as an expression of the predominant relations of an undeveloped whole or of the subordinate relations of a more developed whole, [relations] which had historically existed before the whole developed in the direction expressed in the more concrete category. In so far, the laws of abstract reasoning which ascends from the most simple to the complex, correspond to the actual process of history.

On the other hand, it may be said that there are highly developed but historically unripe forms of society in which the highest economic forms are to be found, such as co-operation, advanced division of labor, etc., and yet there is no money in existence, e.g. Peru.

In Slavic communities also, money, as well as exchange to which it owes its existence, does not appear at all or very little within the separate communities, but it appears on their boundaries in their inter-communal traffic; in general, it is erroneous to consider exchange as a constituent element originating within the community. It appears at first more in the mutual relations between different communities, than in those between the members of the same community. Furthermore, although money begins to play its part everywhere at an early stage, it plays in antiquity the part of a predominant element only in one-sidedly developed nations, viz. trading nations, and even in most cultured antiquity, in Greece and Rome, it attains its full development, which constitutes the prerequisite of modern bourgeois society, only in the period of their decay. Thus, this quite simple category attained its culmination in the past only at the most advanced stages of society. Even then it did not pervade all economic relations; in Rome e.g. at the time of its highest development taxes and payments in kind remained the basis. As a matter of fact, the money system was fully developed there only so far as the army was concerned; it never came to dominate the entire system of labor.

Thus, although the simple category may have existed historically before the more concrete one, it can attain its complete internal and external development only in complex forms of society, while the more concrete category has reached its full development in a less advanced form of society.

Labor is quite a simple category. The idea of labor in that sense, as labor in general, is also very old. Yet, "labor" thus simply defined by political economy is as much a modern category, as the conditions which have given rise to this simple abstraction. The monetary system, e.g. defines wealth quite objectively, as a thing in money. Compared with this point of view, it was a great step forward, when the industrial or commercial system came to see the source of wealth not in the object hut in the activity of persons, viz. in commercial and industrial labor. But even the latter was thus considered only in the limited sense of a money producing activity. The physiocratic system [marks still further progress] in that it considers a certain form of labor, viz. agriculture, as the source of wealth, and wealth itself not in the disguise of money, but as a product in general, as the general result of labor. But corresponding to the limitations of the activity, this product is still only a natural product. Agriculture is productive, land is the source of production *par excellence*. It was a tremendous advance on the part of Adam Smith to throw aside all limitations which mark wealth-producing activity and [to define it] as labor in general, neither industrial, nor commercial, nor agricultural, or one as much as the other. Along with the universal character of wealth-creating activity we have now the universal character of the object defined as wealth, viz. product in general, or labor in general, but as past incorporated labor. How difficult and great was the transition, is evident from the way Adam Smith himself falls back from time to time into the physiocratic system. Now, it might seem as though this amounted simply to finding an abstract expression for the simplest relation into which men have been mutually entering as producers from times of yore, no matter under what form of society. In one sense this is true. In another it is not.

The indifference as to the particular kind of labor implies the existence of a highly developed aggregate of different species of concrete labor, none of which is any longer the predominant one. So do the most general abstractions commonly arise only where there is the highest concrete development, where one feature appears to be jointly possessed by many, and to be common to all. Then it can not be thought of any longer in one particular form. On the other hand, this abstraction of labor is but the result of a concrete aggregate of different kinds of labor. The indifference to the particular kind of labor corresponds to a form of society in which individuals pass with ease from one kind of work to another, which makes it immaterial to them what particular kind of work may fall to their share. Labor has become here, not only categorically but really, a means of creating wealth in general and is no longer grown together with the individual into one particular destination. This state of affairs has found its highest development in the most modern of bourgeois societies, the United States. It is only here that the abstraction of the category "labor," "labor in general," labor *sans phrase,* the starting point of modern political economy, becomes realized in practice. Thus, the simplest abstraction which modern political economy sets up as its starting point, and which expresses a relation dating back to antiquity and prevalent under all forms of society, appears in this abstraction truly realized only as a category of the most modern society. It might be said that what appears in the United States as an historical product,—viz. the indifference as to the particular kind of labor—appears among the Russians e.g. as a natural disposition. But it makes all the difference in the world whether barbarians have a natural predisposition which makes them applicable alike to everything, or whether civilized people apply themselves to everything. And, besides, this indifference of the Russians as to the kind of work they do, corresponds to their traditional practice of remaining in the rut of a quite definite occupation until they are thrown out of it by external influences.

This example of labor strikingly shows how even the most abstract categories, in spite of their applicability to all epochs—just because of their abstract character—are by the very definiteness of the abstraction a product of historical conditions as well, and are fully applicable only to and under those conditions.

The bourgeois society is the most highly developed and most highly differentiated historical organization of production. The categories which serve as the expression of its conditions and the comprehension of its own organization enable it at the same time to gain an insight into the organization and the conditions of production which had prevailed under all the past forms of society, on the ruins and constituent elements of which it has arisen, and of which it still drags along some unsurmounted remnants, while what had formerly been mere intimation has now developed to complete significance. The anatomy of the human being is the key to the anatomy of the ape. But the intimations of a higher animal in lower ones can be understood only if the animal of the higher order is already known. The bourgeois economy furnishes a key to ancient economy, etc. This is, however, by no means true of the method of those economists who blot out all historical differences and see the bourgeois form in all forms of society. One can understand the nature of tribute, tithes, etc., after one has learned the nature of rent. But they must not be considered identical.

Since, furthermore, bourgeois society is but a form resulting from the development of antagonistic elements, some relations belonging to earlier forms of society are frequently to be found in it but in a crippled state or as a travesty of their former self, as e.g. communal property. While it may be said, therefore, that the categories of bourgeois economy contain what is true of all other forms of society, the statement is to be taken *cum grano salis*. They may contain these in a developed, or crippled, or caricatured form, but always essentially different. The so-called historical development amounts in the last analysis to this, that the last form considers its predecessors as stages leading up to itself and perceives them always one-sidedly, since it is very seldom and only under certain conditions that it is capable of self-criticism; of course, we do not speak here of such historical periods which appear to their own contemporaries as periods of decay. The Christian religion became capable to assist us to an objective view of past mythologies as soon as it was ready for self-criticism to a certain extent, *dynamei* so-to-say. In the same way bourgeois political economy first came to understand the feudal, the ancient, and the oriental societies as soon as the self-criticism of the bourgeois society had commenced. So far as bourgeois political economy has not gone into the mythology of purely identifying the bourgeois system with the past, its criticism of the feudal system against which it still had to wage war resembled Christian criticism of the heathen religions or Protestant criticism of Catholicism.

In the study of economic categories, as in the case of every historical and social science, it must be borne in mind that as in reality so in our mind the subject, in this case modern bourgeois society, is given and that the categories are therefore but forms of expression, manifestations of existence, and frequently but one-sided aspects of this subject, this definite society; and that, therefore, the origin of [political economy] as a science does not by any means date from the time to which it is referred *as such*. This is to be firmly held in mind because it has an immediate and important bearing on the matter of the subdivisions of the science.

For instance, nothing seems more natural than to start with rent, with landed property, since it is bound up with land, the source of all production and all existence, and with the first form of production in all more or less settled communities, viz. agriculture. But nothing would be more erroneous. Under all forms of society there is a certain industry which predominates over all the rest and whose condition therefore determines the rank and influence of all the rest.

It is the universal light with which all the other colors are tinged and are modified through its peculiarity. It is a special ether which determines the specific gravity of everything that appears in it.

Let us take for example pastoral nations (mere hunting and fishing tribes are not as yet at the point from which real development commences). They engage in a certain form of agriculture, sporadically. The nature of land-ownership is determined thereby. It is held in common and retains this form more or less according to the extent to which these nations hold on to traditions; such e.g. is land-ownership among the Slavs. Among nations whose agriculture is carried on by a settled population—the settled state constituting a great advance—where agriculture is the predominant industry, such as in ancient and feudal societies, even the manufacturing industry and its organization, as well as the forms of property which pertain to it, have more or less the characteristic features of the prevailing system of land ownership; [society] is then either entirely dependent upon agriculture, as in the case of ancient Rome, or, as in the middle ages, it imitates in its city relations the forms of organization prevailing in the country. Even capital, with the exception of pure money capital, has, in the form of the traditional working tool, the characteristics of land ownership in the Middle Ages.

The reverse is true of bourgeois society. Agriculture comes to be more and more merely a branch of industry and is completely dominated by capital. The same is true of rent. In all the forms of society in which land ownership is the prevalent form, the influence of the natural element is the predominant one. In those where capital predominates the prevailing element is the one historically created by society. Rent can not be understood without capital, nor can capital, without rent. Capital is the all dominating economic power of bourgeois society. It must form the starting point as well as the end and be developed before land-ownership is. After each has been considered separately, their mutual relation must be analyzed.

It would thus be impractical and wrong to arrange the economic categories in the order in which they were the determining factors in the course of history. Their order of sequence is rather determined by the relation which they bear to one another in modern bourgeois society, and which is the exact opposite of what seems to be their natural order or the order of their historical development. What we are interested in is not the place which economic relations occupy in the historical succession of different forms of society. Still less are we interested in the order of their succession "in idea" *(Proudhon),* which is but a hazy conception of the course of history. We are interested in their organic connection within modern bourgeois society.

The sharp line of demarkation (abstract precision) which so clearly distinguished the trading nations of antiquity, such as the Phoenicians and the Carthagenians, was due to that very predominance of agriculture. Capital as trading or money capital appears in that abstraction, where capital does not constitute as yet the predominating element of society. The Lombardians and the Jews occupied the same position among the agricultural nations of the middle ages.

As a further illustration of the fact that the same category plays different parts at different stages of society, we may mention the following: one of the latest forms of bourgeois society, viz. stock companies, appear also at its beginning in the form of the great chartered monopolistic trading companies.

The conception of national wealth which is imperceptibly formed in the minds of the economists of the seventeenth century, and which partly continues to be entertained by those of the eighteenth century, is that wealth is produced solely for the state, but that the power of the latter is proportional to that wealth. It was as yet an unconsciously hypocritical way in which wealth announced itself and its own production as the aim of modern states considering the latter merely as a means to the production of wealth.

The order of treatment must manifestly be as follows: first, the general abstract definitions which are more or less applicable to all forms of society, but in the sense indicated above. Second, the categories which go to make up the inner organization of bourgeois society and constitute the foundations of the principal classes; capital, wage-labor, landed property; their mutual relations; city and country; the three great social classes, the exchange between them; circulation, credit (private). Third, the organization of bourgeois society in the form of a state, considered in relation to itself; the "unproductive" classes; taxes; public debts; public credit; population; colonies; emigration. Fourth, the international organization of production; international division of labor; international exchange; import and export; rate of exchange. Fifth, the world market and crises.

4. PRODUCTION, MEANS OF PRODUCTION, AND CONDITIONS OF PRODUCTION. THE RELATIONS OF PRODUCTION AND DISTRIBUTION. THE CONNECTION BETWEEN FORM OF STATE AND PROPERTY ON THE ONE HAND AND RELATIONS OF PRODUCTION AND DISTRIBUTION ON THE OTHER. LEGAL RELATIONS. FAMILY RELATIONS.

Notes on the points to be mentioned here and not to be omitted:*

1. *War* attains complete development before peace; how certain economic phenomena, such as wage-labor, machinery, etc., are developed at an earlier date through war and in armies than within bourgeois society. The connection between productive force and the means of communication is made especially plain in the case of the army.

2. The relation between the idealistic and realistic methods of writing history; namely, the so-called history of civilization which is all a history of religion and states.

In this connection something may be said of the different methods hitherto employed in writing history. The so-called objective [method]. The subjective. (The moral and others). The philosophic.

3. *Secondary and tertiary*. Conditions of production which have been taken over or transplanted; in general, those that are not original. Here [is to be treated] the effect of international relations.

4. Objections to the materialistic character of this view. Its relation to naturalistic materialism.

---

*[The "notes" Marx includes here are extremely fragmentary giving only a listing of issues he plans to discuss later.]

5. The dialectics of the conceptions productive force (means of production) and relation of production, dialectics whose limits are to be determined and which does not do away with the concrete difference.

6. The unequal relation between the development of material production and art, for instance. In general, the conception of progress is not to be taken in the sense of the usual abstraction. In the case of art, etc., it is not so important and difficult to understand this disproportion as in that of practical social relations, e.g. the relation between education in the United States and Europe. The really difficult point, however, that is to be discussed here is that of the unequal development of relations of production as legal relations. As, e.g., the connection between Roman civil law (this is less true of criminal and public law) and modern production.

7. This conception of development appears to imply necessity. On the other hand, justification of accident. Varia. (Freedom and other points). (The effect of means of communication). World history does not always appear in history as the result of world history.

8. The starting point [is to be found] in certain facts of nature embodied subjectively and objectively in clans, races, etc.

It is well known that certain periods of highest development of art stand in no direct connection with the general development of society, nor with the material basis and the skeleton structure of its organization. Witness the example of the Greeks as compared with the modern nations or even Shakespeare. As regards certain forms of art, as e.g. the epos, it is admitted that they can never be produced in the world-epoch making form as soon as art as such comes into existence; in other words, that in the domain of art certain important forms of it are possible only at a low stage of its development. If that be true of the mutual relations of different forms of art within the domain of art itself, it is far less surprising that the same is true of the relation of art as a whole to the general development of society. The difficulty lies only in the general formulation of these contradictions. No sooner are they specified than they are explained. Let us take for instance the relation of Greek art and of that of Shakespeare's time to our own. It is a well known fact that Greek mythology was not only the arsenal of Greek art, but also the very ground from which it had sprung. Is the view of nature and of social relations which shaped Greek imagination and Greek [art] possible in the age of automatic machinery, and railways, and locomotives, and electric telegraphs? Where does Vulcan come in as against Roberts & Co.; Jupiter, as against the lightning rod; and Hermes, as against the Credit Mobilier? All mythology masters and dominates and shapes the forces of nature in and through the imagination; hence it disappears as soon as man gains mastery over the forces of nature. What becomes of the Goddess Fame side by side with Printing House Square?* Greek art presupposes the existence of Greek mythology, i.e. that nature and even the form of society are wrought up in popular fancy in an unconsciously artistic fashion. That is its material. Not, however, any mythology taken at random, nor any accidental unconsciously artistic elaboration of nature (including under the latter all objects, hence [also] society). Egyptian mythology could never be the soil or womb which would give birth to Greek art. But in any event [there had to be] a mythology. In no event [could Greek art originate] in a society which excludes any mythological explanation of nature, any mythological attitude towards it and which requires from the artist an imagination free from mythology.

*[The *Times* building in London.]

Looking at it from another side: is Achilles possible side by side with powder and lead? Or is the Iliad at all compatible with the printing press and steam press? Does not singing and reciting and the muses necessarily go out of existence with the appearance of the printer's bar, and do not, therefore, disappear the prerequisites of epic poetry?

But the difficulty is not in grasping the idea that Greek art and epos are bound up with certain forms of social development. It rather lies in understanding why they still constitute with us a source of aesthetic enjoyment and in certain respects prevail as the standard and model beyond attainment. A man can not become a child again unless he becomes childish. But does he not enjoy the artless ways of the child and must he not strive to reproduce its truth on a higher plane? Is not the character of every epoch revived perfectly true to nature in child nature? Why should the social childhood of mankind, where it had obtained its most beautiful development, not exert an eternal charm as an age that will never return? There are ill-bred children and precocious children. Many of the ancient nations belong to the latter class. The Greeks were normal children. The charm their art has for us does not conflict with the primitive character of the social order from which it had sprung It is rather the product of the latter, and is rather due to the fact that the unripe social conditions under which the art arose and under which alone it could appear can never return.

Charles Sanders Peirce

1839–1914

Charles Sanders Peirce (pronounced "Purse") was born in Cambridge, Massachusetts, to Benjamin and Sarah Hunt Mills Peirce. His father was a noted mathematician and professor of astronomy and mathematics at Harvard. Like John Stuart Mill and Søren Kierkegaard, Charles Peirce received his most significant schooling from his father. From an early age his father taught him mathematics and science, encouraging Peirce in his youthful laboratory experiments. Though Peirce did graduate from both Cambridge High School and Harvard, he did not distinguish himself academically at either institution and had trouble adapting socially. During his college years he spent much of his time with his father, discussing the elder Peirce's mathematical studies. Following graduation from Harvard in 1859, Peirce studied chemistry at the Lawrence Scientific School. There he met and married his first wife, Harriet Melusina Fay. In addition to this change in his social life, Peirce's academic performance improved, and in 1863 he graduated from Lawrence *summa cum laude*.

While Peirce was still in school, his father arranged a job for him with the United States Coast and Geodetic Survey. Peirce worked for this agency over the next thirty years but nevertheless found time for a number of other pursuits. He worked as an astronomer at Harvard, continued to perform scientific experiments, read and wrote extensively in philosophy, and lectured on logic at Johns Hopkins University. Peirce also helped form the

"Metaphysical Club," an informal gathering of friends to discuss philosophical matters. The club included such well-known thinkers as William James and Oliver Wendell Holmes. Though esteemed by his fellow philosophers, Peirce's difficult personality and reputation for "loose living" kept him from a professorship. Peirce's "inability to exercise the proper moral self-control" (James's description) eventually led to a divorce from Harriet Fay in 1883. The following year Peirce married a French woman named Juliette Froisy.

In 1891 Peirce received a small legacy, retired from his job with the Coast and Geodetic Survey, and moved to Milford, Pennsylvania, where he lived a reclusive life while writing on philosophical themes. His works received virtually no recognition during his lifetime, and on his death his second wife sold all his papers to Harvard for five hundred dollars.

* * *

Peirce has been called a "philosopher's philosopher." His writings are often difficult for beginning students, partly because of the technical way in which he expresses his ideas. In addition he developed four more-or-less complete systems, abandoning each in favor of the next. Despite his esoteric and variegated writing, in 1877 and 1878 Peirce published a series of essays for a general audience in *Popular Science Monthly*. These became his most important works.

In the essay "How to Make Our Ideas Clear," reprinted here (complete), Peirce develops his famous theory of pragmatism. He explains that all inquiry begins with doubt. This doubt must be "real and living," the actual state in which we find ourselves, not the invented doubt of thinkers such as Descartes, if it is to lead to genuine inquiry. He defines doubt as an irritating condition that "most frequently . . . arise[s] from some indecision, however momentary, in our action." This doubt stimulates the mind, leading us to seek relief—to find the "calm and satisfactory" state of belief. "Belief" has three properties: (1) "It is something that we are aware of"; (2) "it appeases the irritation of doubt"; and (3) "it involves the establishment in our nature of a rule of action, or, say for short, a *habit*." Belief, then, not only cuts off doubt, it involves and leads to action, so that "different beliefs are distinguished by the different modes of action to which they give rise."

To understand what a belief *means*, then, we must look at what actions or habits it produces:

> Consider what effects, that might conceivably have practical bearings, we conceive the object of our conception to have. Then, our conception of these effects is the whole of our conception of the object.

While one writer has called this famous quotation from our reading "the least clear recommendation of how to make our ideas clear in the history of philosophy," it nevertheless gives the essence of Peirce's pragmatism. To conceive of an object clearly is to anticipate certain practical effects that can be empirically verified. Any idea that cannot be empirically verified and that is without "practical anticipations" is meaningless; "only practical distinctions have a meaning." Furthermore, if two apparently disparate ideas have the same practical effects, they are in fact only one idea.

Peirce then explained four methods of moving from doubt to belief: (1) tenacity, accepting one alternative to the doubt and rejecting all possible criticism of it;

(2) authority, submitting to the state's or the church's tenaciously held beliefs; (3) the *a priori* method, relying on the inclination to believe; and (4) science. Peirce argued for the scientific method, since it was concerned with examining the practical effects that make up one's conception of an object. Furthermore, unlike the other three methods, scientific inquiry is "animated by a cheerful hope that the processes of investigation, if only pushed far enough, will give one certain solution to each question to which they apply it." Peirce assumed that in any diligently pursued scientific study, "a force outside of themselves" will lead all scientists involved in the investigation to the same conclusion.

Peirce has been called the father of pragmatism, and his work clearly influenced William James and John Dewey. Apart from the pragmatists, echoes of Peirce's writing can be heard in the verification criterion of meaning of the logical positivists and in the mandate of the later Wittgenstein that "the meaning is the use." Since the publication of his collected essays in the middle of the century, there has been renewed interest in Peirce's thought.

*   *   *

For general works on pragmatism (which include sections on Peirce and place his thought in a wider context), see Edward C. Moore, *American Pragmatism: Peirce, James and Dewey* (New York: Columbia University Press, 1961); H.S. Thayer, "Pragmatism," in D.J. O'Connor, ed., *A Critical History of Western Philosophy* (New York: The Free Press, 1964); Amelie O. Rorty, ed., *Pragmatic Philosophy* (New York: Anchor Doubleday, 1966); Frederick Copleston, *A History of Philosophy,* Vol. VIII (Garden City, NY: Anchor Doubleday, 1967); A.J. Ayer, *The Origins of Pragmatism: Studies in the Philosophy of Charles Sanders Peirce and William James* (San Francisco: Freeman, Cooper & Co., 1968); H.S. Thayer, *Meaning and Action: A Critical History of Pragmatism* (Indianapolis, IN: Bobbs-Merrill, 1968); Charles Moore, *The Pragmatic Movement in America* (New York: George Braziller, 1970); Israel Scheffler, *Four Pragmatists: A Critical Introduction to Peirce, James, Mead, and Dewey* (New York: Humanities Press, 1974); John E. Smith, *Purpose and Thought: The Meaning of Pragmatism* (New Haven, CT: Yale University Press, 1978); and Richard Rorty, *The Consequences of Pragmatism* (Minneapolis: University of Minnesota Press, 1982).

All of Peirce's works have been collected in the eight-volume set, *Collected Papers of Charles Sanders Peirce,* edited by Charles Hartshorne and Paul Weiss (Cambridge, MA: Harvard University Press, 1931–1935, 1958)—Volumes I, V, and VI contain the most important philosophical material. For a biography of Peirce, see Joseph Brent, *Charles Sanders Peirce, A Life* (Bloomington: Indiana University Press, 1993). The most comprehensive study of Peirce is James Feibleman, *An Introduction to Peirce's Philosophy* (New York: Harper & Brothers, 1946), while Manley Thompson, *The Pragmatic Philosophy of C.S. Peirce* (Chicago: University of Chicago Press, 1953); W.B. Gallie, *Peirce and Pragmatism* (New York: Dover, 1966); Robert F. Almeder, *The Philosophy of Charles S. Peirce: A Critical Introduction* (Totowa, NJ: Rowman and Littlefield, 1980); and Christopher Hookway, *Peirce* (New York: Routledge, 1985), provide helpful introductions. For collections of essays, see Philip P. Wiener and Frederic H. Young, eds., *Studies in the Philosophy of Charles Sanders Peirce* (Cambridge, MA: Harvard University Press, 1952); Edward C. Moore and Richard S. Robin, eds., *Studies in the Philosophy of Charles*

Sanders Peirce, Second Series (Amherst: University of Massachusetts Press, 1964); and Richard J. Bernstein, ed., *Perspectives on Peirce* (New Haven, CT: Yale University Press, 1965),

HOW TO MAKE OUR IDEAS CLEAR

Whoever has looked into a modern treatise on logic of the common sort, will doubtless remember the two distinctions between *clear* and *obscure* conceptions, and between *distinct* and *confused* conceptions. They have lain in the books now for nigh two centuries, unimproved and unmodified, and are generally reckoned by logicians as among the gems of their doctrine.

A clear idea is defined as one which is so apprehended that it will be recognized wherever it is met with, and so that no other will be mistaken for it. If it fails of this clearness, it is said to be obscure.

This is rather a neat bit of philosophical terminology; yet, since it is clearness that they were defining, I wish the logicians had made their definition a little more plain. Never to fail to recognize an idea, and under no circumstances to mistake another for it, let it come in how recondite a form it may, would indeed imply such prodigious force and clearness of intellect as is seldom met with in this world. On the other hand, merely to have such an acquaintance with the idea as to have become familiar with it, and to have lost all hesitancy in recognizing it in ordinary cases, hardly seems to deserve the name of clearness of apprehension, since after all it only amounts to a subjective feeling of mastery which may be entirely mistaken. I take it, however, that when the logicians speak of "clearness," they mean nothing more than such a familiarity with an idea, since they regard the quality as but a small merit, which needs to be supplemented by another, which they call *distinctness.*

A distinct idea is defined as one which contains nothing which is not clear. This is technical language; by the *contents* of an idea logicians understand whatever is contained in its definition. So that an idea is *distinctly* apprehended, according to them, when we can give a precise definition of it, in abstract terms. Here the professional logicians leave the subject; and I would not have troubled the reader with what they have to say, if it were not such a striking example of how they have been slumbering through ages of intellectual activity, listlessly disregarding the enginery of modern thought, and never dreaming of applying its lessons to the improvement of logic. It is easy to show that the doctrine that familiar use and abstract distinctness make the perfection of apprehension has its only true place in philosophies which have long been extinct; and it is now time to formulate the method of attaining to a more perfect clearness of thought, such as we see and admire in the thinkers of our own time.

When Descartes set about the reconstruction of philosophy, his first step was to (theoretically) permit scepticism and to discard the practice of the schoolmen of looking to authority as the ultimate source of truth. That done, he sought a more natural fountain of true principles, and thought he found it in the human mind; thus passing, in the directest way, from the method of authority to that of apriority, as described in my first paper. Self-consciousness was to furnish us with our fundamental truths, and to decide what was agreeable to reason. But since, evidently, not all ideas are true, he was led to note, as the first condition of infallibility, that they must be clear. The distinction between an idea *seeming* clear and really being so, never occurred to him. Trusting to introspection, as he did, even for a knowledge of external things, why should he question its testimony in respect to the contents of our own minds? But then, I suppose, seeing men, who seemed to be quite clear and positive, holding opposite opinions upon fundamental principles, he was further led to say that clearness of ideas is not sufficient, but that they need also to be distinct, i.e., to have nothing unclear about them. What he probably meant by this (for he did not explain himself with precision) was, that they must sustain the test of dialectical examination; that they must not only seem clear at the outset, but that discussion must never be able to bring to light points of obscurity connected with them.

Such was the distinction of Descartes, and one sees that it was precisely on the level of his philosophy. It was somewhat developed by Leibniz. This great and singular genius was as remarkable for what he failed to see as for what he saw. That a piece of mechanism could not do work perpetually without being fed with power in some form, was a thing perfectly apparent to him; yet he did not understand that the machinery of the mind can only transform knowledge, but never originate it, unless it be fed with facts of observation. He thus missed the most essential point of the Cartesian philosophy, which is, that to accept propositions which seem perfectly evident to us is a thing which, whether it be logical or illogical, we cannot help doing. Instead of regarding the matter in this way, he sought to reduce the first principles of science to two classes, those which cannot be denied without self-contradiction, and those which result from the principle of sufficient reason (of which more anon), and was apparently unaware of the great difference between his position and that of Descartes. So he reverted to the old trivialities of logic; and, above all, abstract definitions played a great part in his philosophy. It was quite natural, therefore, that on observing that the method of Descartes laboured under the difficulty that we may seem to ourselves to have clear apprehensions of ideas which in truth are very hazy, no better remedy occurred to him than to require an abstract definition of every important term. Accordingly, in adopting the distinction of *clear* and *distinct* notions, he described the latter quality as the clear apprehension of everything contained in the definition; and the books have ever since copied his words. There is no danger that his chimerical scheme will ever again be over-valued. Nothing new can ever be learned by analyzing definitions. Nevertheless, our existing beliefs can be set in order by this process, and order is an essential element of intellectual economy, as of every other. It may be acknowledged, therefore, that the books are right in making familiarity with a notion the first step toward clearness of apprehension, and the defining of it the second. But in omitting all mention of any higher perspicuity of thought, they simply mirror a philosophy which was exploded a hundred years ago. That much-admired "ornament of logic"—the doctrine of clearness and distinctness—may be pretty enough, but it is high time to relegate to our cabinet of curiosities the antique *bijou,* and to wear about us something better adapted to modern uses.

The very first lesson that we have a right to demand that logic shall teach us is, how to make our ideas clear; and a most important one it is, depreciated only by minds who stand in need of it. To know what we think, to be masters of our own meaning, will make a solid foundation for great and weighty thought. It is most easily learned by those whose ideas are meagre and restricted; and far happier they than such as wallow helplessly in a rich mud of conceptions. A nation, it is true, may, in the course of generations overcome the disadvantage of an excessive wealth of language and its natural concomitant, a vast, unfathomable deep of ideas. We may see it in history, slowly perfecting its literary forms, sloughing at length its metaphysics, and, by virtue of the untirable patience which is often a compensation, attaining great excellence in every branch of mental acquirement. The page of history is not yet unrolled that is to tell us whether such a people will or will not in the long run prevail over one whose ideas (like the words of their language) are few, but which possesses a wonderful mastery over those which it has. For an individual, however, there can be no question that a few clear ideas are worth more than many confused ones. A young man would hardly be persuaded to sacrifice the greater part of his thoughts to save the rest; and the muddled head is the least apt to see the necessity of such a sacrifice. Him we can usually only commiserate, as a person with a congenital defect. Time will help him, but intellectual maturity with regard to clearness is apt to come rather late. This seems an unfortunate arrangement of Nature, inasmuch as clearness is of less use to a man settled in life, whose errors have in great measure had their effect, than it would be to one whose path lay before him. It is terrible to see how a single unclear idea, a single formula without meaning, lurking in a young man's head, will sometimes act like an obstruction of inert matter in an artery, hindering the nutrition of the brain, and condemning its victim to pine away in the fullness of his intellectual vigour and in the midst of intellectual plenty. Many a man has cherished for years as his hobby some vague shadow of an idea, too meaningless to be positively false; he has, nevertheless, passionately loved it, has made it his companion by day and by night, and has given to it his strength and his life, leaving all other occupations for its sake, and in short has lived with it and for it, until it has become, as it were, flesh of his flesh and bone of his bone; and then he has waked up some bright morning to find it gone, clean vanished away like the beautiful Melusina of the fable, and the essence of his life gone with it. I have myself known such a man; and who can tell how many histories of circle-squarers, metaphysicians, astrologers, and what not, may not be told in the old German [French!] story?

The principles set forth in the first part of this essay lead, at once, to a method of reaching a clearness of thought of higher grade than the "distinctness" of the logicians. It was there noticed that the action of thought is excited by the irritation of doubt, and ceases when belief is attained; so that the production of belief is the sole function of thought. All these words, however, are too strong for my purpose. It is as if I had described the phenomena as they appear under a mental microscope. Doubt and Belief, as the words are commonly employed, relate to religious or other grave discussions. But here I use them to designate the starting of any question, no matter how small or how great, and the resolution of it. If, for instance, in a horse-car, I pull out my purse and find a five-cent nickel and five coppers, I decide, while my hand is going to the purse, in which way I will pay my fare. To call such a question Doubt, and my decision Belief, is certainly to use words very disproportionate to the occasion. To speak of such a doubt as causing an irritation which needs to be appeased, suggests a temper which is uncomfortable to the verge of insanity. Yet, looking at the matter minutely, it must be admitted that, if there is the least hesitation as to whether I shall pay the five coppers or the nickel (as there will be sure to be, unless I act from some previously contracted habit in the matter), though irritation is too strong a word, yet I am excited to such small mental activity as may be necessary to deciding how I shall act. Most frequently doubts arise from some indecision, however momentary, in our action. Sometimes it is not so. I have, for example, to wait in a railway-station, and to pass the time I read the advertisements on the walls. I compare the advantages of different trains and different routes which I never expect to take, merely fancying myself to be in a state of hesitancy, because I am bored with having nothing to trouble me. Feigned hesitancy, whether feigned for mere amusement or with a lofty purpose, plays a great part in the production of scientific inquiry. However the doubt may originate, it stimulates the mind to an activity which may be slight or energetic, calm or turbulent. Images pass rapidly through consciousness, one incessantly melting into another, until at last, when all is over—it may be in a fraction of a second, in an hour, or after long years—we find ourselves decided as to how we should act under such circumstances as those which occasioned our hesitation. In other words, we have attained belief.

In this process we observe two sorts of elements of consciousness, the distinction between which may best be made clear by means of an illustration. In a piece of music there are the separate notes, and there is the air. A single tone may be prolonged for an hour or a day, and it exists as perfectly in each second of that time as in the whole taken together; so that, as long as it is sounding, it might be present to a sense from which everything in the past was as completely absent as the future itself. But it is different with the air, the performance of which occupies a certain time, during the portions of which only portions of it are played. It consists in an orderliness in the succession of sounds which strike the ear at different times; and to perceive it there must be some continuity of consciousness which makes the events of a lapse of time present to us. We certainly only perceive the air by hearing the separate notes; yet we cannot be said to directly hear it, for we hear only what is present at the instant, and an orderliness of succession cannot exist in an instant. These two sorts of objects, what we are *immediately* conscious of and what we are *mediately* conscious of, are found in all consciousness. Some elements (the sensations) are completely present at every instant so long as they last, while others (like thought) are actions having beginning, middle, and end, and consist in a congruence in the succession of sensations which flow through the mind. They cannot be immediately present to us, but must cover some portion of the past or future. Thought is a thread of melody running through the succession of our sensations.

We may add that just as a piece of music may be written in parts, each part having its own air, so various systems of relationship of succession subsist together between the same sensations. These different systems are distinguished by having different motives, ideas, or functions. Thought is only one such system, for its sole motive, idea, and function is to produce belief, and whatever does not concern that purpose belongs to some other system of relations. The action of thinking may incidentally have other results; it may serve to amuse us, for example, and among *dilettanti* it is not rare to find those who have so perverted thought to the purposes of pleasure that it seems to vex them to think that the questions upon which they delight to exercise it may ever get finally settled; and a positive discovery which takes a favourite subject out of the arena of literary debate is met with ill-concealed dislike. This disposition is the very debauchery of thought. But the soul and meaning of thought, abstracted from the other elements which accompany it, though it may be voluntarily thwarted, can never be made to direct itself toward anything but the production of belief. Thought in action has for its only possible motive the attainment of thought at rest; and whatever does not refer to belief is no part of the thought itself.

And what, then, is belief? It is the demi-cadence which closes a musical phrase in the symphony of our intellectual life. We have seen that it has just three properties: First, it is something that we are aware of; second, it appeases the irritation of doubt; and, third, it involves the establishment in our nature of a rule of action, or, say for short, a *habit*. As it appeases the irritation of doubt, which is the motive for thinking, thought relaxes, and comes to rest for a moment when belief is reached. But, since belief is a rule for action, the application of which involves further doubt and further thought, at the same time that it is a stopping-place, it is also a new starting-place for thought. That is why I have permitted myself to call it thought at rest, although thought is essentially an action. The *final* upshot of thinking is the exercise of volition, and of this thought no longer forms a part; but belief is only a stadium of mental action, an effect upon our nature due to thought, which will influence future thinking.

The essence of belief is the establishment of a habit; and different beliefs are distinguished by the different modes of action to which they give rise. If beliefs do not differ in this respect, if they appease the same doubt by producing the same rule of action, then no mere differences in the manner of consciousness of them can make them different beliefs, any more than playing a tune in different keys is playing different tunes. Imaginary distinctions are often drawn between beliefs which differ only in their mode of expression;—the wrangling which ensues is real enough, however. To believe that any objects are arranged among themselves as in Fig. 1, and to believe that they are arranged [as] in Fig. 2, are one and the same belief; yet it is conceivable that a man should assert one proposition and deny the other.

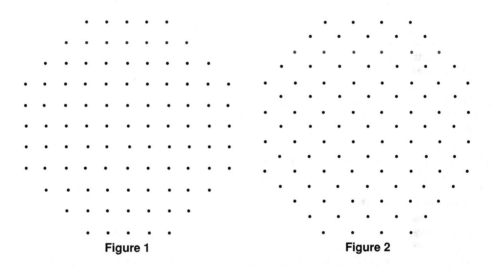

Figure 1   **Figure 2**

Such false distinctions do as much harm as the confusion of beliefs really different, and are among the pitfalls of which we ought constantly to beware, especially when we are upon metaphysical ground. One singular deception of this sort, which often occurs, is to mistake the sensation produced by our own unclearness of thought for a character of the object we are thinking. Instead of perceiving that the obscurity is purely subjective, we fancy that we contemplate a quality of the object which is essentially mysterious; and if our conception be afterward presented to us in a clear form we do not recognize it as the same, owing to the absence of the feeling of unintelligibility. So long as this deception lasts, it obviously puts an impassable barrier in the way of perspicuous thinking; so that it equally interests the opponents of rational thought to perpetuate it, and its adherents to guard against it.

Another such deception is to mistake a mere difference in the grammatical construction of two words for a distinction between the ideas they express. In this pedantic age, when the general mob of writers attend so much more to words than to things, this error is common enough. When I just said that thought is an *action,* and that it consists in a *relation,* although a person performs an action but not a relation, which can only be the result of an action, yet there was no inconsistency in what I said, but only a grammatical vagueness.

From all these sophisms we shall be perfectly safe so long as we reflect that the whole function of thought is to produce habits of action; and that whatever there is connected with a thought, but irrelevant to its purpose, is an accretion to it, but no part of it. If there be a unity among our sensations which has no reference to how we shall act on a given occasion, as when we listen to a piece of music, why we do not call that thinking. To develop its meaning, we have, therefore, simply to determine what habits it produces, for what a thing means is simply what habits it involves. Now, the identity of a habit depends on how it might lead us to act, not merely under such circumstances as are likely to arise, but under such as might possibly occur, no matter how improbable they may be. What the habit is depends on *when* and *how* it causes us to act. As for the *when,* every stimulus to action is derived from perception; as for the *how,* every purpose of action is to produce some sensible result. Thus, we come down to what is tangible and conceivably practical, as the root of every real distinction of thought, no matter how subtle it may be; and there is no distinction of meaning so fine as to consist in anything but a possible difference of practice.

To see what this principle leads to, consider in the light of it such a doctrine as that of transubstantiation. The Protestant churches generally hold that the elements of the sacrament are flesh and blood only in a tropical sense; they nourish our souls as meat and the juice of it would our bodies. But the Catholics maintain that they are literally just meat and blood; although they possess all the sensible qualities of wafer-cakes and diluted wine. But we can have no conception of wine except what may enter into a belief, either—

1. That this, that, or the other, is wine; or,
2. That wine possesses certain properties.

Such beliefs are nothing but self-notifications that we should, upon occasion, act in regard to such things as we believe to be wine according to the qualities which we believe wine to possess. The occasion of such action would be some sensible perception, the motive of it to produce some sensible result. Thus our action has exclusive reference to what affects the senses, our habit has the same bearing as our action, our belief the same as our habit, our conception the same as our belief; and we can consequently mean nothing by wine but what has certain effects, direct or indirect, upon our senses; and to talk of something as having all the sensible characters of wine, yet being in reality blood, is senseless jargon. Now, it is not my object to pursue the theological question; and having used it as a logical example I drop it, without caring to anticipate the theologian's reply. I only desire to point out how impossible it is that we should have an idea in our minds which relates to anything but conceived sensible effects of things. Our idea of anything *is* our idea of its sensible effects; and if we fancy that we have any other we deceive ourselves, and mistake a mere sensation accompanying the thought for a part of the thought itself. It is absurd to say that thought has any meaning unrelated to its only function. It is foolish for Catholics and Protestants to fancy themselves in disagreement about the elements of the sacrament, if they agree in regard to all their sensible effects, here and hereafter.

It appears, then, that the rule for attaining the third grade of clearness of apprehension is as follows: Consider what effects, that might conceivably have practical bearings, we conceive the object of our conception to have. Then, our conception of these effects is the whole of our conception of the object.

Let us illustrate this rule by some examples; and, to begin with the simplest one possible, let us ask what we mean by calling a thing *hard*. Evidently that it will not be scratched by many other substances. The whole conception of this quality, as of every other, lies in its conceived effects. There is absolutely no difference between a hard thing and a soft thing so long as they are not brought to the test. Suppose, then, that a diamond could be crystallized in the midst of a cushion of soft cotton, and should remain there until it was finally burned up. Would it be false to say that that diamond was soft? This seems a foolish question, and would be so, in fact, except in the realm of logic. There such questions are often of the greatest utility as serving to bring logical principles into sharper relief than real discussions ever could. In studying logic we must not put them aside with hasty answers, but must consider them with attentive care, in order to make out the principles involved. We may, in the present case, modify our question, and ask what prevents us from saying that all hard bodies remain perfectly soft until they are touched, when their hardness increases with the pressure until they are scratched. Reflection will show that the reply is this: there would be no *falsity* in such modes of speech. They would involve a modification of our present usage of speech with regard to the words hard and soft, but not of their meanings. For they represent no fact to be different from what it is; only they involve arrangements of facts which would be exceedingly maladroit. This leads us to remark that the question of what would occur under circumstances which do not actually arise is not a question of fact, but only of the most perspicuous arrangement of them. For example, the question of free-will and fate in its simplest form, stripped of verbiage, is something like this: I have done something of which I am ashamed; could I, by an effort of the will, have resisted the temptation, and done otherwise? The philosophical reply is, that this is not a question of fact, but only of the arrangement of facts. Arranging them so as to exhibit what is particularly pertinent to my question—namely, that I ought to blame myself for having done wrong—it is perfectly true to say that, if I had willed to do otherwise than I did, I should have done otherwise. On the other hand, arranging the facts so as to exhibit another important consideration, it is equally true that, when a temptation has once been allowed to work, it will, if it has a certain force, produce its effect, let me struggle how I may. There is no objection to a contradiction in what would result from a false supposition. The *reductio ad absurdum* consists in showing that contradictory results would follow from a hypothesis which is consequently judged to be false. Many questions are involved in the free-will discussion, and I am far from desiring to say that both sides are equally right. On the contrary, I am of opinion that one side denies important facts, and that the other does not. But what I do say is, that the above single question was the origin of the whole doubt; that, had it not been for this question, the controversy would never have arisen; and that this question is perfectly solved in the manner which I have indicated.

Let us next seek a clear idea of Weight. This is another very easy case. To say that a body is heavy means simply that, in the absence of opposing force, it will fall. This (neglecting certain specifications of how it will fall, etc., which exist in the mind of the physicist who uses the word) is evidently the whole conception of weight. It is a fair question whether some particular facts may not account for gravity; but what we mean by the force itself is completely involved in its effects.

This leads us to undertake an account of the idea of Force in general. This is the great conception which, developed in the early part of the seventeenth century from the rude idea of a cause, and constantly improved upon since, has shown us how to explain all the changes of motion which bodies experience, and how to think about all physical phenomena; which has given birth to modern science, and changed the face of the globe; and which, aside from its more special uses, has played a principal part in directing the course of modern thought, and in furthering modern social development. It is, therefore, worth some pains to comprehend it. According to our rule, we must begin by asking what is the immediate use of thinking about force; and the answer is, that we thus account for changes of motion. If bodies were left to themselves, without the intervention of forces, every motion would continue unchanged both in velocity and in direction. Furthermore, change of motion never takes place abruptly; if its direction is changed, it is always through a curve without angles; if its velocity alters, it is by degrees. The gradual changes which are constantly taking place are conceived by geometers to be compounded together according to the rules of the parallelogram of forces. If the reader does not already know what this is, he will find it, I hope, to his advantage to endeavour to follow the following explanation; but if mathematics are insupportable to him, pray let him skip three paragraphs rather than that we should part company here.

A *path* is a line whose beginning and end are distinguished. Two paths are considered to be equivalent, which, beginning at the same point, lead to the same point. Thus the two paths, A B C D E and A F G H E (Fig. 3), are equivalent. Paths which do *not* begin at the same point are considered to be equivalent, provided that, on moving either of them without turning it, but keeping it always parallel to its original position, when its beginning coincides with that of the other path, the ends also coincide. Paths are considered as geometrically added together, when one begins where the other ends; thus the path A E is conceived to be a sum of A B, B C, C D, and D E. In the parallelogram of Fig. 4 the diagonal A C is the sum of A B and B C; or, since A D is geometrically equivalent to B C, A C is the geometrical sum of A B and A D.

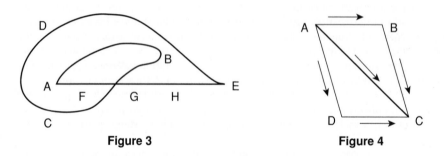

Figure 3   **Figure 4**

All this is purely conventional. It simply amounts to this: that we choose to call paths having the relations I have described equal or added. But, though it is a convention, it is a convention with a good reason. The rule for geometrical addition may be applied not only to paths, but to any other things which can be represented by paths. Now, as a path is determined by the varying direction and distance of the point which moves over it from the starting-point, it follows that anything which from its beginning to its end is determined by a varying direction and a varying magnitude is capable of being represented by a line. Accordingly, *velocities* may be represented by lines, for they have only directions and rates. The same thing is true of *accelerations,* or changes of velocities. This is evident enough in the case of velocities; and it becomes evident for accelerations if we consider that precisely what velocities are to positions—namely, states of change of them—that accelerations are to velocities.

The so-called "parallelogram of forces" is simply a rule for compounding accelerations. The rule is, to represent the accelerations by paths, and then to geometrically add the paths. The geometers, however, not only use the "parallelogram of forces" to compound different accelerations, but also to resolve one acceleration into a sum of several. Let A B (Fig. 5) be the path which represents a certain acceleration—say, such a change in the motion of a body that at the end of one second the body will, under the influence of that change, be in a position different from what it would have had if its motion had continued unchanged such that a path equivalent to A B would lead from the latter position to the former.

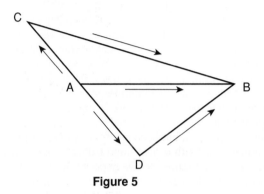

Figure 5

This acceleration may be considered as the sum of the accelerations represented by A C and C B. It may also be considered as the sum of the very different accelerations represented by A D and D B, where A D is almost the opposite of A C. And it is clear that there is an immense variety of ways in which A B might be resolved into the sum of two accelerations.

After this tedious explanation, which I hope, in view of the extraordinary interest of the conception of force, may not have exhausted the reader's patience, we are prepared at last to state the grand fact which this conception embodies. This fact is that if the actual changes of motion which the different particles of bodies experience are each resolved in its appropriate way, each component acceleration is precisely such as is prescribed by a certain law of Nature, according to which bodies, in the relative positions which the bodies in question actually have at the moment, always receive certain accelerations, which, being compounded by geometrical addition, give the acceleration which the body actually experiences.

This is the only fact which the idea of force represents, and whoever will take the trouble clearly to apprehend what this fact is, perfectly comprehends what force is. Whether we ought to say that a force *is* an acceleration, or that it *causes* an acceleration, is a mere question of propriety of language, which has no more to do with our real meaning than the difference between the French idiom *"Il fait froid"* and its English equivalent *"It is cold."* Yet it is surprising to see how this simple affair has muddled men's minds. In how many profound treatises is not force spoken of as a "mysterious entity," which seems to be only a way of confessing that the author despairs of ever getting a clear notion of what the word means! In a recent admired work on *Analytic Mechanics* it is stated that we understand precisely the effect of force, but what force itself is we do not understand! This is simply a self-contradiction. The idea which the word force excites in our minds has no other function than to affect our actions, and these actions can have no reference to force otherwise than through its effects. Consequently, if we know what the effects of force are, we are acquainted with every fact which is implied in saying that a force exists, and there is nothing more to know. The truth is, there is some vague notion afloat that a question may mean something which the mind cannot conceive; and when some hair-splitting philosophers have been confronted with the absurdity of such a view, they have invented an empty distinction between positive and negative conceptions, in the attempt to give their non-idea a form not obviously nonsensical. The nullity of it is sufficiently plain from the considerations given a few pages back; and, apart from those considerations, the quibbling character of the distinction must have struck every mind accustomed to real thinking.

Let us now approach the subject of logic, and consider a conception which particularly concerns it, that of *reality*. Taking clearness in the sense of familiarity, no idea could be clearer than this. Every child uses it with perfect confidence, never dreaming that he does not understand it. As for clearness in its second grade, however, it would probably puzzle most men, even among those of a reflective turn of mind, to give an abstract definition of the real. Yet such a definition may perhaps be reached by considering the points of difference between reality and its opposite, fiction. A figment is a product of somebody's imagination; it has such characters as his thought impresses upon it. That those characters are independent of how you or I think is an external reality. There are, however, phenomena within our own minds, dependent upon our thought, which are at the same time real in the sense that we really think them. But though their characters depend on how we think, they do not depend on what we think those characters to be. Thus, a dream has a real existence as a mental phenomenon, if somebody has really dreamt it; that he dreamt so and so, does not depend on what anybody thinks was dreamt, but is completely independent of all opinion on the subject. On the other hand, considering, not the fact of dreaming, but the thing dreamt, it retains its peculiarities by virtue of no other fact than that it was dreamt to possess them. Thus we may define the real as that whose characters are independent of what anybody may think them to be.

But, however satisfactory such a definition may be found, it would be a great mistake to suppose that it makes the idea of reality perfectly clear. Here, then, let us apply our rules. According to them, reality, like every other quality, consists in the peculiar sensible effects which things partaking of it produce. The only effect which real things have is to cause belief, for all the sensations which they excite emerge into consciousness in the form of beliefs. The question therefore is, how is true belief (or belief in the real) distinguished from false belief (or belief in fiction). Now, as we have seen in the former paper,* the ideas of truth and falsehood, in their full development, appertain exclusively to the experiential method of settling opinion. A person who arbitrarily chooses the propositions which he will adopt can use the word truth only to emphasize the expression of his determination to hold on to his choice. Of course, the method of tenacity never prevailed exclusively; reason is too natural to men for that. But in the literature of the dark ages we find some fine examples of it. When Scotus Erigena is commenting upon a poetical passage in which Helleborus is spoken of as having caused the death of Socrates, he does not hesitate to inform the inquiring reader that Helleborus and Socrates were two eminent Greek philosophers, and that the latter, having been overcome in argument by the former, took the matter to heart and died of it! What sort of an idea of truth could a man have who could adopt and teach, without the qualification of a perhaps, an opinion taken so entirely at random? The real spirit of Socrates, who I hope would have been delighted to have been "overcome in argument," because

---

*["The Fixation of Belief" (1877).]

he would have learned something by it, is in curious contrast with the naive idea of the glossist, for whom (as for "the born missionary" of today) discussion would seem to have been simply a struggle. When philosophy began to awake from its long slumber, and before theology completely dominated it, the practice seems to have been for each professor to seize upon any philosophical position he found unoccupied and which seemed a strong one, to intrench himself in it, and to sally forth from time to time to give battle to the others. Thus, even the scanty records we possess of those disputes enable us to make out a dozen or more opinions held by different teachers at one time concerning the question of nominalism and realism. Read the opening part of the *Historia Calamitatum* of Abelard, who was certainly as philosophical as any of his contemporaries, and see the spirit of combat which it breathes. For him, the truth is simply his particular stronghold. When the method of authority prevailed, the truth meant little more than the Catholic faith. All the efforts of the scholastic doctors are directed toward harmonizing their faith in Aristotle and their faith in the Church, and one may search their ponderous folios through without finding an argument which goes any further. It is noticeable that where different faiths flourish side by side, renegades are looked upon with contempt even by the party whose belief they adopt; so completely has the idea of loyalty replaced that of truth seeking. Since the time of Descartes, the defect in the conception of truth has been less apparent. Still, it will sometimes strike a scientific man that the philosophers have been less intent on finding out what the facts are, than on inquiring what belief is most in harmony with their system. It is hard to convince a follower of the *a priori* method by adducing facts; but show him that an opinion he is defending is inconsistent with what he has laid down elsewhere, and he will be very apt to retract it. These minds do not seem to believe that disputation is ever to cease; they seem to think that the opinion which is natural for one man is not so for another, and that belief will, consequently, never be settled. In contenting themselves with fixing their own opinions by a method which would lead another man to a different result, they betray their feeble hold of the conception of what truth is.

On the other hand, all the followers of science are animated by a cheerful hope that the processes of investigation, if only pushed far enough, will give one certain solution to each question to which they apply it. One man may investigate the velocity of light by studying the transits of Venus and the aberration of the stars; another by the oppositions of Mars and the eclipses of Jupiter's satellites; a third by the method of Fizeau; a fourth by that of Foucault; a fifth by the motions of the curves of Lissajoux; a sixth, a seventh, an eighth, and a ninth, may follow the different methods of comparing the measures of statical and dynamical electricity. They may at first obtain different results, but, as each perfects his method and his processes, the results are found to move steadily together toward a destined centre. So with all scientific research. Different minds may set out with the most antagonistic views, but the progress of investigation carries them by a force outside of themselves to one and the same conclusion. This activity of thought by which we are carried, not where we wish, but to a fore-ordained goal, is like the operation of destiny. No modification of the point of view taken, no selection of other facts for study, no natural bent of mind even, can enable a man to escape the predestinate opinion. This great hope is embodied in the conception of truth and reality. The opinion which is fated to be ultimately agreed to by all who investigate, is what we mean by the truth, and the object represented in this opinion is the real. That is the way I would explain reality.

But it may be said that this view is directly opposed to the abstract definition which we have given of reality, inasmuch as it makes the characters of the real depend on what is ultimately thought about them. But the answer to this is that, on the one hand, reality is independent, not necessarily of thought in general, but only of what you or I or any finite number of men may think about it; and that, on the other hand, though the object of the final opinion depends on what that opinion is, yet what that opinion is does not depend on what you or I or any man thinks. Our perversity and that of others may indefinitely postpone the settlement of opinion; it might even conceivably cause an arbitrary proposition to be universally accepted as long as the human race should last. Yet even that would not change the nature of the belief, which alone could be the result of investigation carried sufficiently far; and if, after the extinction of our race, another should arise with faculties and disposition for investigation, that true opinion must be the one which they would ultimately come to. "Truth crushed to earth shall rise again," and the opinion which would finally result from investigation does not depend on how anybody may actually think. But the reality of that which is real does depend on the real fact that investigation is destined to lead, at last, if continued long enough, to a belief in it.

But I may be asked what I have to say to all the minute facts of history, forgotten never to be recovered, to the lost books of the ancients, to the buried secrets.

> Full many a gem of purest ray serene
>   The dark, unfathomed caves of ocean bear;
> Full many a flower is born to blush unseen,
>   And waste its sweetness on the desert air.

Do these things not really exist because they are hopelessly beyond the reach of our knowledge? And then, after the universe is dead (according to the prediction of some scientists), and all life has ceased forever, will not the shock of atoms continue though there will be no mind to know it? To this I reply that, though in no possible state of knowledge can any number be great enough to express the relation between the amount of what rests unknown to the amount of the known, yet it is unphilosophical to suppose that, with regard to any given question (which has any clear meaning), investigation would not bring forth a solution of it, if it were carried far enough. Who would have said, a few years ago, that we could ever know of what substances stars are made whose light may have been longer in reaching us than the human race has existed? Who can be sure of what we shall not know in a few hundred years? Who can guess what would be the result of continuing the pursuit of science for ten thousand years, with the activity of the last hundred? And if it were to go on for a million, or a billion, or any number of years you please, how is it possible to say that there is any question which might not ultimately be solved?

But it may be objected, "Why make so much of these remote considerations, especially when it is your principle that only practical distinctions have a meaning?" Well, I must confess that it makes very little difference whether we say that a stone on the bottom of the ocean, in complete darkness, is brilliant or not—that is to say, that it *probably* makes no difference, remembering always that that stone *may* be fished up tomorrow. But that there are gems at the bottom of the sea, flowers in the untravelled desert, etc., are propositions which, like that about a diamond being hard when it is not pressed, concern much more the arrangement of our language than they do the meaning of our ideas.

It seems to me, however, that we have, by the application of our rule, reached so clear an apprehension of what we mean by reality, and of the fact which the idea rests on, that we should not, perhaps, be making a pretension so presumptuous as it would be singular, if we were to offer a metaphysical theory of existence for universal acceptance

Guaranty Building, Buffalo, New York, 1895, designed by Louis Sullivan
(1856–1924). Sullivan's building epitomizes the pragmatic approach to
architecture summarized in his famous dictum, "form follows function."
Both the exterior and interior designs complement the purpose for which
this building was constructed. *(The Buffalo and Erie County Historical
Society)*

among those who employ the scientific method of fixing belief. However, as metaphysics is a subject much more curious than useful, the knowledge of which, like that of a sunken reef, serves chiefly to enable us to keep clear of it, I will not trouble the reader with any more Ontology at this moment. I have already been led much further into that path than I should have desired; and I have given the reader such a dose of mathematics, psychology, and all that is most abstruse, that I fear he may already have left me, and that what I am now writing is for the compositor and proofreader exclusively. I trusted to the importance of the subject. There is no royal road to logic, and really valuable ideas can only be had at the price of close attention. But I know that in the matter of ideas the public prefer the cheap and nasty; and in my next paper I am going to return to the easily intelligible, and not wander from it again. The reader who has been at the pains of wading through this paper, shall be rewarded in the next one by seeing how beautifully what has been developed in this tedious way can be applied to the ascertainment of the rules of scientific reasoning.

We have, hitherto, not crossed the threshold of scientific logic. It is certainly important to know how to make our ideas clear, but they may be ever so clear without being true. How to make them so, we have next to study. How to give birth to those vital and procreative ideas which multiply into a thousand forms and diffuse themselves everywhere, advancing civilization and making the dignity of man, is an art not yet reduced to rules, but of the secret of which the history of science affords some hints.

William James
1842–1910

William James was born into one of the leading families of New York City. His grandfather, a strict Calvinist also named William, was an Irish immigrant who had amassed a fortune in real estate. His father, Henry, rejected the grandfather's religion and became an unorthodox mystic. His mother, Mary, was also a child of wealth, and his brother, Henry Jr., became a famous novelist. The life of the James family was one of creative anarchy. Their dinner table was animated with lively debate in which the children were expected to hold their own with such guests as Ralph Waldo Emerson, Washington Irving, and Oliver Wendell Holmes. To encourage intellectual freedom, and to avoid the rigidity of his own joyless upbringing, Henry Sr. put his children into as many different schools as possible. The family moved often, restlessly wandering back and forth across the Atlantic, alighting temporarily in London, Paris, New York, Geneva, Newport, Bonn, and Albany.

William James reflected his family's wanderlust in his academic pursuits. He studied art for a time before joining an expedition to the Amazon basin as an apprentice naturalist. He then travelled to Germany to study physiology, before returning to the United States to complete a degree in medicine at Harvard Medical School in 1869. In 1872 James was appointed to teach physiology and anatomy at Harvard. His intellectual roving and his unwillingness to be bound by the usual academic disciplines continued when he moved in 1875 to psychology and later to philosophy. He subsequently marvelled at his audacity:

> I originally studied medicine in order to be a physiologist, but I drifted into psychology and philosophy from a sort of fatality. I never had any philosophic instruction and the first lecture on psychology I ever heard was the first one I ever gave.

In 1878 James married Alice Howe Gibbens, and together they had five children. While James had experienced ill health as a young man (including smallpox contracted in Brazil), his strength seemed to improve following marriage.

In 1890 William James published his first major work, *The Principles of Psychology*. A two-volume work, *Principles* was one of the first attempts to treat psychology as a legitimate, experimental science, and it quickly became the standard work in the field. Over the next seventeen years James did intense philosophical research and published his results: *The Will to Believe and Other Essays* (1897), *Varieties of Religious Experience* (1902), and *Pragmatism* (1907). During this period he continued to teach at Harvard and to lecture throughout the United States and Europe. Resigning from Harvard in 1907, James gave a series of lectures published as *A Pluralistic Universe* (1909) and *The Meaning of Truth* (1909). James died in 1910, and his last complete work, *Essays in Radical Empiricism,* was published posthumously.

At the time of his death, James was considered the embodiment of American philosophy. All accounts indicate that in addition to his large intellect and breadth of learning, James was a generous, open-minded, and sociable person. One historian of philosophy went so far as to describe him as "one of the sweetest men who ever lived."

* * *

If Peirce is a philosopher's philosopher, then James is the common person's philosopher. What his thought may lack in technical precision, it makes up for both in expressiveness and in concern for common problems. Yet James's engaging style and lack of jargon left him open to charges of imprecision and carelessness.

In the series of lectures published as *Pragmatism,* James began by distinguishing between two human temperaments: the tough-minded and the tender-minded. The tough-minded are those who are empirically oriented—those who "go by facts." By contrast, the tender-minded are rationalists who "go by principles." According to James, the history of philosophy is largely the story of the clash between these two attitudes: "The tough think of the tender as sentimentalists and softheads. The tender feel the tough to be unrefined, callous, or brutal." The tough-minded approach to philosophy has the virtue of being connected to "facts," but it tends to exclude religion. The tender-minded approach allows for religion but is unconnected to the realities of everyday life. The result is that for the common person, "Empiricist writers give him materialism, rationalists give him something religious, but to that religion 'actual things are blank.'"

James believed that pragmatism is a method that reconciles these opposing temperaments. Borrowing from Peirce, James developed pragmatism as "a method of settling metaphysical disputes that otherwise might be interminable." As a theory of meaning, pragmatism asks what practical effects a belief has, whether that belief is tough- or tender-minded. To discover what a belief *means* is to find what difference such a belief makes "in concrete fact and in conduct consequent upon that fact, imposed on somebody, somehow, somewhere, and some-when." The proper goal of philosophy is to discover "what definite difference it will make to you and me, at definite instants of our life, if this world-formula or that world-formula be the true one."

But James went further than Peirce and claimed that pragmatism provides a theory of *truth* as well as of meaning. Peirce had continued to hold a traditional correspondence theory of truth: An assertion was true if it corresponded with a fact. Instead, James said that an idea *becomes* true if it allows the individual to gain "satisfactory relations with other parts of our experience." These relations are not fixed—they are dynamic, just as our experience is dynamic. As James put it,

> *True ideas are those that we can assimilate, validate, corroborate, and verify. False*
> *ideas are those that we cannot.* That is the practical difference it makes to us to have
> true ideas, that therefore is the meaning of truth. . . .

Though it was written earlier, James's famous essay on religion, "The Will to Believe," anticipated elements of his mature pragmatism. Defining a genuine op-tion as one that is living, forced, and momentous, James argued that there is no reason not to make such a choice for religious belief. Those who would argue that one should withhold religious beliefs until there is sensible proof are "telling us . . . that to yield to our fear of it being error is wiser and better than to yield to our hope that it may be true." Instead, said James, we have the "right to believe"— even if the data are inconclusive.

Critics have pointed out that James's "will to believe" could lead to virtually *any* conclusion one considers living, forced, and momentous. Furthermore, his theory of pragmatism could be used to make any belief true—provided it pro-duced beneficial results. As H.S. Thayer pointed out, "Standards of veracity thus go slack on the very occasions in which, ordinarily, they need the tightest reign, where passion and personal interests are most in play."* This fact, along with a number of other objections, led Peirce to change the name of *his* philosophy to "pragmaticism" to distinguish it from James's thought. For his part, James claimed that he was only presenting a way of discovering truth, not redefining it. It was left to others such as John Dewey to reformulate the pragmatic theory of truth more precisely.

* * *

For general works on pragmatism, see the introduction to Peirce (page 198). For biographies of James, see Gay Wilson Allen, *William James: A Biography* (New York: Viking Press, 1967); Jacques Barzun, *A Stroll with William James* (New York: Harper & Row, 1983); and Daniel W. Bjork, *William James: The Center of His Vision* (New York: Columbia University Press, 1988). The standard study of James's thought is Ralph Barton Perry, *The Thought and Character of William James,* 2 vols. (Boston: Little, Brown, 1935). Other general introductions to his thought include Bernard P. Brennan, *William James* (New York: Twayne, 1968); Ellen Kappy Suckiel, *The Pragmatic Philosophy of William James* (Notre Dame, IN: University of Notre Dame Press, 1982); Graham Bird, *William James* (Lon-don: Routledge & Kegan Paul, 1986); and Gerald E. Myers, *William James: His*

---

*H.S. Thayer, "Pragmatism," in D.J. O'Connor, ed., *A Critical History of Western Philosophy* (New York: The Free Press, 1964), p. 451.

Life and Thought (New Haven, CT: Yale University Press, 1986). For studies devoted to James's religious theories, see Stephen T. Davis, *Faith, Skepticism, and Evidence: An Essay in Religious Epistemology* (Lewisburg, PA: Bucknell University Press, 1978); Robert J. Vanden Burgt, *The Religious Philosophy of William James* (Chicago: Nelson-Hall, 1981); Robert J. O'Connell, *William James on the Courage to Believe* (New York: Fordham University Press, 1984); and Eugene Fontinell, *Self, God, and Immortality: A Jamesian Investigation* (Philadelphia: Temple University Press, 1986). For studies of James's psychology, see Bruce Wilshire, *William James and Phenomenology: A Study of "The Principles of Psychology"* (Bloomington: Indiana University Press, 1968); John Wild, *The Radical Empiricism of William James* (Garden City, NY: Doubleday, 1969); and James M. Edie, *William James and Phenomenology* (Bloomington: Indiana University Press, 1987).

THE WILL TO BELIEVE

In the recently published Life by Leslie Stephen of his brother, Fitz-James, there is an account of a school to which the latter went when he was a boy. The teacher, a certain Mr. Guest, used to converse with his pupils in this wise: "Gurney, what is the difference between justification and sanctification?—Stephen, prove the omnipotence of God!" etc. In the midst of our Harvard freethinking and indifference we are prone to imagine that here at your good old orthodox College conversation continues to be somewhat upon this order; and to show you that we at Harvard have not lost all interest in these vital subjects, I have brought with me to-night something like a sermon on justification by faith to read to you,—I mean an essay in justification of faith, a defence of our right to adopt a believing attitude in religious matters, in spite of the fact that our merely logical intellect may not have been coerced. "The Will to Believe," accordingly, is the title of my paper.

I have long defended to my own students the lawfulness of voluntarily adopted faith; but as soon as they have got well imbued with the logical spirit, they have as a rule refused to admit my contention to be lawful philosophically, even though in point of fact they were personally all the time chock-full of some faith or other themselves. I am all the while, however, so profoundly convinced that my own position is correct, that your invitation has seemed to me a good occasion to make my statements more clear. Perhaps your minds will be more open than those with which I have hitherto had to deal. I will be as little technical as I can, though I must begin by setting up some technical distinctions that will help us in the end.

I.

Let us give the name of *hypothesis* to anything that may be proposed to our belief; and just as the electricians speak of live and dead wires, let us speak of any hypothesis as either *live* or *dead*. A live hypothesis is one which appeals as a real possibility to him to whom it is proposed. If I ask you to believe in the Mahdi, the notion makes no electric connection with your nature,—it refuses to scintillate with any credibility at all. As an hypothesis it is completely dead. To an Arab, however (even if he be not one of the Mahdi's followers), the hypothesis is among the mind's possibilities: it is alive. This shows that deadness and liveness in an hypothesis are not intrinsic properties, but relations to the individual thinker. They are measured by his willingness to act. The maximum of liveness in an hypothesis means willingness to act irrevocably. Practically, that means belief; but there is some believing tendency wherever there is willingness to act at all.

Next, let us call the decision between two hypotheses an option. Options may be of several kinds. They may be—1, *living* or *dead,* 2, *forced* or *avoidable;* 3, *momentous* or *trivial;* and for our purposes we may call an option a *genuine* option when it is of the forced, living, and momentous kind.

1. A living option is one in which both hypotheses are live ones. If I say to you: "Be a theosophist or be a Mohammedan," it is probably a dead option, because for you neither hypothesis is likely to be alive. But if I say: "Be an agnostic or be a Christian," it is otherwise: trained as you are, each hypothesis makes some appeal, however small, to your belief.

2. Next, if I say to you: "Choose between going out with your umbrella or without it," I do not offer you a genuine option, for it is not forced. You can easily avoid it by not going out at all. Similarly, if I say, "Either love me or hate me," "Either call my theory true or call it false," your option is avoidable. You may remain indifferent to me, neither loving nor hating, and you may decline to offer any judgment as to my theory. But if I say, "Either accept this truth or go without it," I put on you a forced option, for there is no standing place outside of the alternative. Every dilemma based on a complete logical disjunction, with no possibility of not choosing, is an option of this forced kind.

3. Finally, if I were Dr. Nansen and proposed to you to join my North Pole expedition, your option would be momentous; for this would probably be your only similar opportunity, and your choice now would either exclude you from the North Pole sort of immortality altogether or put at least the chance of it into your hands. He who refuses to embrace a unique opportunity loses the prize as surely as if he tried and failed. *Per contra,* the option is trivial when the opportunity is not unique, when the stake is insignificant, or when the decision is reversible if it later prove unwise. Such trivial options abound in the scientific life. A chemist finds an hypothesis live enough to spend a year in its verification: he believes in it to that extent. But if his experiments prove inconclusive either way, he is quit for his loss of time, no vital harm being done.

It will facilitate our discussion if we keep all these distinctions well in mind.

II.

The next matter to consider is the actual psychology of human opinion. When we look at certain facts, it seems as if our passional and volitional nature lay at the root of all our convictions. When we look at others, it seems as if they could do nothing when the intellect had once said its say. Let us take the latter facts up first.

Does it not seem preposterous on the very face of it to talk of our opinions being modifiable at will? Can our will either help or hinder our intellect in its perceptions of truth? Can we, by just willing it, believe that Abraham Lincoln's existence is a myth, and that the portraits of him in McClure's Magazine are all of some one else? Can we, by any effort of our will, or by any strength of wish that it were true, believe ourselves well and about when we are roaring with rheumatism in bed, or feel certain that the sum of the two one-dollar bills in our pocket must be a hundred dollars? We can *say* any of these things, but we are absolutely impotent to believe them; and of just such things is the whole fabric of the truths that we do believe in made up,—matters of fact, immediate or remote, as Hume said, and relations between ideas, which are either there or not there for us if we see them so, and which if not there cannot be put there by any action of our own.

In Pascal's Thoughts there is a celebrated passage known in literature as Pascal's wager. In it he tries to force us into Christianity by reasoning as if our concern with truth resembled our concern with the stakes in a game of chance. Translated freely his words are these: You must either believe or not believe that God is—which will you do? Your human reason cannot say. A game is going on between you and the nature of things which at the day of judgment will bring out either heads or tails. Weigh what your gains and your losses would be if you should stake all you have on heads, or God's existence: if you win in such case, you gain eternal beatitude; if you lose, you lose nothing at all. If there were an infinity of chances, and only one for God in this wager, still you ought to stake your all on God; for though you surely risk a finite loss by this procedure, any finite loss is reasonable, even a certain one is reasonable, if there is but the possibility of infinite gain. Go, then, and take holy water, and have masses said; belief will come and stupefy your scruples,—*Cela vous fera croire et vous abêtira* [That will make you believe and make you stupid]. Why should you not? At bottom, what have you to lose?

You probably feel that when religious faith expresses itself thus, in the language of the gaming-table, it is put to its last trumps. Surely Pascal's own personal belief in masses and holy water had far other springs; and this celebrated page of his is but an argument for others, a last desperate snatch at a weapon against the hardness of the unbelieving heart. We feel that a faith in masses and holy water adopted wilfully after such a mechanical calculation would lack the inner soul of faith's reality; and if we were ourselves in the place of the Deity, we should probably take particular pleasure in cutting off believers of this pattern from their infinite reward. It is evident that unless there be some pre-existing tendency to believe in masses and holy water, the option offered to the will by Pascal is not a living option. Certainly no Turk ever took to masses and holy water on its account; and even to us Protestants these means of salvation seem such foregone impossibilities that Pascal's logic, invoked for them specifically, leaves us unmoved. As well might the Mahdi write to us, saying, "I am the Expected One whom God has created in his effulgence. You shall be infinitely happy if you confess me; otherwise you shall be cut off from the light of the sun. Weigh, then, your infinite gain if I am genuine against your finite sacrifice if I am not!" His logic would be that of Pascal; but he would vainly use it on us, for the hypothesis he offers us is dead. No tendency to act on it exists in us to any degree.

The talk of believing by our volition seems, then, from one point of view, simply silly. From another point of view it is worse than silly, it is vile. When one turns to the magnificent edifice of the physical sciences, and sees how it was reared; what thousands of disinterested moral lives of men lie buried in its mere foundations; what patience and postponement, what choking down of preference, what submission to the icy laws of outer fact are wrought into its very stones and mortar; how absolutely impersonal it stands in its vast augustness,—then how besotted and contemptible seems every little sentimentalist who comes blowing his voluntary smoke-wreaths, and pretending to decide things from out of his private dream! Can we wonder if those bred in the rugged and manly school of science should feel like spewing such subjectivism out of their mouths? The whole system of loyalties which grow up in the schools of science go dead against its toleration; so that it is only natural that those who have caught the scientific fever should pass over to the opposite extreme, and write sometimes as if the incorruptibly truthful intellect ought positively to prefer bitterness and unacceptableness to the heart in its cup.

> It fortifies my soul to know
> That, though I perish, Truth is so—

sings Clough, while Huxley exclaims: "My only consolation lies in the reflection that, however bad our posterity may become, so far as they hold by the plain rule of not pretending to believe what they have no reason to believe, because it may be to their advantage so to pretend [the word 'pretend' is surely here redundant], they will not have reached the lowest depth of immorality." And that delicious *enfant terrible* Clifford writes: "Belief is desecrated when given to unproved and unquestioned statements for the solace and private pleasure of the believer. . . . Whoso would deserve well of his fellows in this matter will guard the purity of his belief with a very fanaticism of jealous care, lest at any time it should rest on an unworthy object, and catch a stain which can never be wiped away. . . . If [a] belief has been accepted on insufficient evidence [even though the belief be true, as Clifford on the same page explains] the pleasure is a stolen one. . . . It is sinful because it is stolen in defiance of our duty to mankind. That duty is to guard ourselves from such beliefs as from a pestilence which may shortly master our own body and then spread to the rest of the town. . . . It is wrong always, everywhere, and for every one, to believe anything upon insufficient evidence."

III.

All this strikes one as healthy, even when expressed, as by Clifford, with somewhat too much of robustious pathos in the voice. Free-will and simple wishing do seem, in the matter of our credences, to be only fifth wheels to the coach. Yet if any one should thereupon assume that intellectual insight is what remains after wish and will and sentimental preference have taken wing, or that pure reason is what then settles our opinions, he would fly quite as directly in the teeth of the facts.

It is only our already dead hypotheses that our willing nature is unable to bring to life again. But what has made them dead for us is for the most part a previous action of our willing nature of an antagonistic kind. When I say "willing nature," I do not mean only such deliberate volitions as may have set up habits of belief that we cannot now escape from,—I mean all such factors of belief as fear and hope, prejudice and passion, imitation and partisanship, the circumpressure of our caste and set. As a matter of fact we find ourselves believing, we hardly know how or why. Mr. Balfour gives the name of "authority" to all those influences, born of the intellectual climate, that make hypotheses possible or impossible for us, alive or dead. Here in this room, we all of us believe in molecules and the conservation of energy, in democracy and necessary progress, in Protestant Christianity and the duty of fighting for "the doctrine of the immortal Monroe," all for no reasons worthy of the name. We see into these matters with no more inner clearness, and probably with much less, than any disbeliever in them might possess. His unconventionality would probably have some grounds to show for its conclusions; but for us, not insight, but the *prestige* of the opinions, is what makes the spark shoot from them and light up our sleeping magazines of faith. Our reason is quite satisfied, in nine hundred and ninety-nine cases out of every thousand of us, if it can find a few arguments that will do to recite in case our credulity is criticised by some one else. Our faith is faith in some one else's faith, and in the greatest matters this is most the case. Our belief in truth itself, for instance, that there is a truth, and that our minds and it are made for each other,—what is it but a passionate affirmation of desire, in which our social system backs us up? We want to have a truth; we want to believe that our experiments and studies and discussions must put us in a continually better and better position towards it; and on this line we agree to fight out our thinking lives. But if a pyrrhonistic sceptic asks us *how we know* all this, can our logic find a reply? No! certainly it cannot. It is just one volition against another,—we are willing to go in for life upon a trust or assumption which he, for his part, does not care to make.

As a rule we disbelieve all facts and theories for which we have no use. Clifford's cosmic emotions find no use for Christian feelings. Huxley belabors the bishops because there is no use for sacerdotalism in his scheme of life. Newman, on the contrary, goes over to Romanism, and finds all sorts of reasons good for staying there, because a priestly system is for him an organic need and delight. Why do so few "scientists" even look at the evidence for telepathy, so called? Because they think, as a leading biologist, now dead, once said to me, that even if such a thing were true, scientists ought to band together to keep it suppressed and concealed. It would undo the uniformity of Nature and all sorts of other things without which scientists cannot carry on their pursuits. But if this very man had been shown something which as a scientist he might do with telepathy, he might not only have examined the evidence, but even have found it good enough. This very law which the logicians would impose upon us—if I may give the name of logicians to those who would rule out our willing nature here—is based on nothing but their own natural wish to exclude all elements for which they, in their professional quality of logicians, can find no use.

Evidently, then, our non-intellectual nature does influence our convictions. There are passional tendencies and volitions which run before and others which come after belief, and it is only the latter that are too late for the fair; and they are not too late when the previous passional work has been already in their own direction. Pascal's argument, instead of being powerless, then seems a regular clincher, and is the last stroke needed to make our faith in masses and holy water complete. The state of things is evidently far from simple; and pure insight and logic, whatever they might do ideally, are not the only things that really do produce our creeds.

IV.

Our next duty, having recognized this mixed-up state of affairs, is to ask whether it be simply reprehensible and pathological, or whether, on the contrary, we must treat it as a normal element in making up our minds. The thesis I defend is, briefly stated, this: *Our passional nature not only lawfully may, but must, decide an option between propositions, whenever it is a genuine option that cannot by its nature be decided on intellectual grounds; for to say, under such circumstances, "Do not decide, but leave the question open," is itself a passional decision,—just like deciding yes or no,—and is attended with the same risk of losing the truth.* The thesis thus abstractly expressed will, I trust, soon become quite clear. But I must first indulge in a bit more of preliminary work.

V.

It will be observed that for the purposes of this discussion we are on "dogmatic" ground,—ground, I mean, which leaves systematic philosophical scepticism altogether out of account. The postulate that there is truth, and that it is the destiny of our minds to attain it, we are deliberately resolving to make, though the sceptic will not make it. We part company with him, therefore, absolutely, at this point. But the faith that truth exists, and that our minds can find it, may be held in two ways. We may talk of the *empiricist* way and of the *absolutist* way of believing in truth. The absolutists in this matter say that we not only can attain to knowing truth, but we can *know when* we have attained to knowing it; while the empiricists think that although we may attain it, we cannot infallibly know when. To *know* is one thing, and to know for certain *that* we know is another. One may hold to the first being possible without the second; hence the empiricists and the absolutists, although neither of them is a sceptic in the usual philosophic sense of the term, show very different degrees of dogmatism in their lives.

If we look at the history of opinions, we see that the empiricist tendency has largely prevailed in science, while in philosophy the absolutist tendency has had everything its own way. The characteristic sort of happiness, indeed, which philosophies yield has mainly consisted in the conviction felt by each successive school or system that by it bottom-certitude had been attained. "Other philosophies are collections of opinions, mostly false; *my* philosophy gives standing-ground forever,"—who does not recognize in this the key-note of every system worthy of the name? A system, to be a system at all, must come as a *closed* system, reversible in this or that detail, perchance, but in its essential features never!

Scholastic orthodoxy, to which one must always go when one wishes to find perfectly clear statement, has beautifully elaborated this absolutist conviction in a doctrine which it calls that of "objective evidence." If, for example, I am unable to doubt that I now exist before you, that two is less than three, or that if all men are mortal then I am mortal too, it is because these things illumine my intellect irresistibly. The final ground of this objective evidence possessed by certain propositions is the *adæquatio intellectûs nostri cum rê.* The certitude it brings involves an *aptitudinem ad extorquendum certum assensum* on the part of the truth envisaged, and on the side of the subject a *quietem in cognitione,* when once the object is mentally received, that leaves no possibility of doubt behind; and in the whole transaction nothing operates but the *entitas ipsa* of the object and the *entitas ipsa* of the mind. We slouchy modern thinkers dislike to talk in Latin,—indeed, we dislike to talk in set terms at all; but at bottom our own state of mind is very much like this whenever we uncritically abandon ourselves: You believe in objective evidence, and I do. Of some things we feel that we are certain: we know, and we know that we do know. There is something that gives a click inside of us, a bell that strikes twelve, when the hands of our mental clock have swept the dial and meet over the meridian hour. The greatest empiricists among us are only empiricists on reflection: when left to their instincts, they dogmatize like Infallible popes. When the Cliffords tell us how sinful it is to be Christians on such "insufficient evidence," insufficiency is really the last thing they have in mind. For them the evidence is absolutely sufficient, only it makes the other way. They believe so completely in an anti-christian order of the universe that there is no living option: Christianity is a dead hypothesis from the start.

VI.

But now, since we are all such absolutists by instinct, what in our quality of students of philosophy ought we to do about the fact? Shall we espouse and indorse it? Or shall we treat it as a weakness of our nature from which we must free ourselves, if we can?

I sincerely believe that the latter course is the only one we can follow as reflective men. Objective evidence and certitude are doubtless very fine ideals to play with, but where on this moonlit and dream-visited planet are they found? I am, therefore, myself a complete empiricist so far as my theory of human knowledge goes. I live, to be sure, by the practical faith that we must go on experiencing and thinking over our experience, for only thus can our opinions grow more true; but to hold any one of them—I absolutely do not care which—as if it never could be reinterpretable or corrigible, I believe to be a tremendously mistaken attitude, and I think that the whole history of philosophy will bear me out. There is but one indefectibly certain truth, and that is the truth that pyrrhonistic scepticism itself leaves standing,—the truth that the present phenomenon of consciousness exists. That, however, is the bare starting-point of knowledge, the mere admission of a stuff to be philosophized about. The various philosophies are but so many attempts at expressing what this stuff really is. And if we repair to our libraries what disagreement do we discover! Where is a certainly true answer found? Apart from abstract propositions of comparison (such as two and two are the same as four), propositions which tell us nothing by themselves about concrete reality, we find no proposition ever regarded by any one as evidently certain that has not either been called a falsehood, or at least had its truth sincerely questioned by some one else. The transcending of the axioms of geometry, not in play but in earnest, by certain of our contemporaries (as Zöllner and Charles H. Hinton), and the rejection of the whole Aristotelian logic by the Hegelians, are striking instances in point.

No concrete test of what is really true has ever been agreed upon. Some make the criterion external to the moment of perception, putting it either in revelation, the *consensus gentium* [agreement of the people], the instincts of the heart, or the systematized experience of the race. Others make the perceptive moment its own test,—Descartes, for instance, with his clear and distinct ideas guaranteed by the veracity of God; Reid with his "common-sense"; and Kant with his forms of synthetic judgment *a priori*. The inconceivability of the opposite; the capacity to be verified by sense; the possession of complete organic unity or self-relation, realized when a thing is its own other,—are standards which, in turn, have been used. The much lauded objective evidence is never triumphantly there; it is a mere aspiration or *Grenzbegriff,* marking the infinitely remote ideal of our thinking life. To claim that certain truths now possess it, is simply to say that when you think them true and they *are* true, then their evidence is objective, otherwise it is not. But practically one's conviction that the evidence one goes by is of the real objective brand, is only one more subjective opinion added to the lot. For what a contradictory array of opinions have objective evidence and absolute certitude been claimed! The world is rational through and through,—its existence is an ultimate brute fact; there is a personal God,—a personal God is inconceivable; there is an extra-mental physical world immediately known,—the mind can only know its own ideas; a moral imperative exists,—obligation is only the resultant of desires; a permanent spiritual principle is in every one,—there are only shifting states of mind; there is an endless chain of causes,—there is an absolute first cause; an eternal necessity,—a freedom; a purpose,—no purpose; a primal One,—a primal Many; a universal continuity,—an essential discontinuity in things; an infinity,—no infinity. There is this,—there is that;

there is indeed nothing which some one has not thought absolutely true, while his neighbor deemed it absolutely false; and not an absolutist among them seems ever to have considered that the trouble may all the time be essential, and that the intellect, even with truth directly in its grasp, may have no infallible signal for knowing whether it be truth or no. When, indeed, one remembers that the most striking practical application to life of the doctrine of objective certitude has been the conscientious labors of the Holy Office of the Inquisition, one feels less tempted than ever to lend the doctrine a respectful ear.

But please observe, now, that when as empiricists we give up the doctrine of objective certitude, we do not thereby give up the quest or hope of truth itself. We still pin our faith on its existence, and still believe that we gain an ever better position towards it by systematically continuing to roll up experiences and think. Our great difference from the scholastic lies in the way we face. The strength of his system lies in the principles, the origin, the *terminus a quo* [starting point] of his thought; for us the strength is in the outcome, the upshot, the *terminus ad quem* [conclusion]. Not where it comes from but what it leads to is to decide. It matters not to an empiricist from what quarter an hypothesis may come to him: he may have acquired it by fair means or by foul; passion may have whispered or accident suggested it; but if the total drift of thinking continues to confirm it, that is what he means by its being true.

VII.

One more point, small but important, and our preliminaries are done. There are two ways of looking at our duty in the matter of opinion,—ways entirely different, and yet ways about whose difference the theory of knowledge seems hitherto to have shown very little concern. *We must know the truth, and we must avoid error,*—these are our first and great commandments as would-be knowers; but they are not two ways of stating an identical commandment, they are two separable laws. Although it may indeed happen that when we believe the truth *A,* we escape as an incidental consequence from believing the falsehood *B,* it hardly ever happens that by merely disbelieving *B* we necessarily believe *A.* We may in escaping *B* fall into believing other falsehoods, *C* or *D,* just as bad as *B,* or we may escape *B* by not believing anything at all, not even *A.*

Believe truth! Shun error!—these, we see, are two materially different laws; and by choosing between them we may end by coloring differently our whole intellectual life. We may regard the chase for truth as paramount, and the avoidance of error as secondary; or we may, on the other hand, treat the avoidance of error as more imperative, and let truth take its chance. Clifford, in the instructive passage which I have quoted, exhorts us to the latter course. Believe nothing, he tells us, keep your mind in suspense forever, rather than by closing it on insufficient evidence incur the awful risk of believing lies. You, on the other hand, may think that the risk of being in error is a very small matter when compared with the blessings of real knowledge, and be ready to be duped many times in your investigation rather than postpone indefinitely the chance of guessing true. I myself find it impossible to go with Clifford. We must remember that these feelings of our duty about either truth or error are in any case only expressions of our passional life. Biologically considered, our minds are as ready to grind out falsehood as veracity, and he who says, "Better go without belief forever than believe a lie!" merely shows his own preponderant private horror of becoming a dupe. He may be critical of many of his desires and fears, but this fear he slavishly obeys. He cannot imagine any one questioning its binding force. For my own part, I have also a horror of being duped; but I can believe that worse things than being duped may happen to a man in this world: so Clifford's exhortation has to my ears a thoroughly fantastic sound. It is like a general informing his soldiers that it is better to keep out of battle forever than to risk a single wound. Not so are victories either over enemies or over nature gained. Our errors are surely not such awfully solemn things. In a world where we are so certain to incur them in spite of all our caution, a certain lightness of heart seems healthier than this excessive nervousness on their behalf. At any rate, it seems the fittest thing for the empiricist philosopher.

VIII.

And now, after all this introduction, let us go straight at our question. I have said, and now repeat it, that not only as a matter of fact do we find our passional nature influencing us in our opinions, but that there are some options between opinions in which this influence must be regarded both as an inevitable and as a lawful determinant of our choice.

I fear here that some of you my hearers will begin to scent danger, and lend an inhospitable ear. Two first steps of passion you have indeed had to admit as necessary,—we must think so as to avoid dupery, and we must think so as to gain truth; but the surest path to those ideal consummations, you will probably consider, is from now onwards to take no further passional step.

Well, of course, I agree as far as the facts will allow. Wherever the option between losing truth and gaining it is not momentous, we can throw the chance of *gaining truth* away, and at any rate save ourselves from any chance of *believing falsehood,* by not making up our minds at all till objective evidence has come. In scientific questions, this is almost always the case; and even in human affairs in general, the need of acting is seldom so urgent that a false belief to act on is better than no belief at all. Law courts, indeed, have to decide on the best evidence attainable for the moment, because a judge's duty is to make law as well as to ascertain it, and (as a learned judge once said to me) few cases are worth spending much time over: the great thing is to have them decided on *any* acceptable principle, and got out of the way. But in our dealings with objective nature we obviously are recorders, not makers, of the truth; and decisions for the mere sake of deciding promptly and getting on to the next business would be wholly out of place. Throughout the breadth of physical nature facts are what they are quite independently of us, and seldom is there any such hurry about them that the risks of being duped by believing a premature theory need be faced. The questions here are always trivial options, the hypotheses are hardly living (at any rate not living for us spectators), the choice between believing truth or falsehood is seldom forced. The attitude of sceptical balance is therefore the absolutely wise one if we would escape mistakes. What difference, indeed, does it make to most of us whether we have or have not a theory of the Rontgen rays, whether we believe or not in mind-stuff, or have a conviction about the causality of conscious states? It makes no difference. Such options are not forced on us. On every account it is better not to make them, but still keep weighing reasons *pro et contra* with an indifferent hand.

I speak, of course, here of the purely judging mind. For purposes of discovery such indifference is to be less highly recommended, and science would be far less advanced than she is if the passionate desires of individuals to get their own faiths confirmed had been kept out of the game. See for example the sagacity which Spencer and Weismann now display. On the other hand, if you want an absolute duffer in an investigation, you must, after all, take the man who has no interest whatever in its results: he is the warranted incapable, the positive fool. The most useful investigator, because the most sensitive observer, is always he whose eager interest in one side of the question is balanced by an equally keen nervousness lest he become deceived.* Science has organized this nervousness into a regular *technique,* her so-called method of verification; and she has fallen so deeply in love with the method that one may even say she has ceased to care for truth by itself at all. It is only truth as technically verified that interests her. The truth of truths might come in merely affirmative form, and she would decline to touch it. Such truth as that, she might repeat with Clifford, would be stolen in defiance of her duty to mankind. Human passions, however, are stronger than technical rules. "Le coeur a ses raisons," as Pascal says, "que la raison ne connait pas"; ["The heart has reasons which reason does not know"] and however indifferent to all but the bare rules of the game the umpire, the abstract intellect, may be, the concrete players who furnish him the materials to judge of are usually, each one of them, in love with some pet "live hypothesis" of his own. Let us agree, however, that wherever there is no forced option, the dispassionately judicial intellect with no pet hypothesis, saving us, as it does, from dupery at any rate, ought to be our ideal.

The question next arises: Are there not somewhere forced options in our speculative questions, and can we (as men who may be interested at least as much in positively gaining truth as in merely escaping dupery) always wait with impunity till the coercive evidence shall have arrived? It seems a *priori* improbable that the truth should be so nicely adjusted to our needs and powers as that. In the great boarding-house of nature, the cakes and the butter and the syrup seldom come out so even and leave the plates so clean. Indeed, we should view them with scientific suspicion if they did.

IX.

Moral questions immediately present themselves as questions whose solution cannot wait for sensible proof. A moral question is a question not of what sensibly exists, but of what is good, or would be good if it did exist. Science can tell us what exists; but to compare the *worths,* both of what exists and of what does not exist, we must consult not science, but what Pascal calls our heart. Science herself consults her heart when she lays it down that the infinite ascertainment of fact and correction of false belief are the supreme goods for man. Challenge the statement, and science can only repeat it oracularly, or else prove it by showing that such ascertainment and correction bring man all sorts of other goods which man's heart in turn declares. The question of having moral beliefs at all or not having them is decided by our will. Are our moral preferences true or false, or are they only odd biological phenomena, making things good or bad for *us,* but in themselves indifferent? How can your pure intellect decide? If your heart does not *want* a world of moral reality, your head will assuredly never make you believe in one. Mephistophelian scepticism, indeed, will satisfy the head's play-instincts much better than any rigorous idealism can. Some men (even at the student age) are so naturally cool-hearted that the moralistic hypothesis never has for them any pungent life,

*Compare Wilfrid Ward's Essay, "The Wish to Believe," in his *Witness to the Unseen,* Macmillan & Co., 1893.

and in their supercilious presence the hot young moralist always feels strangely ill at ease. The appearance of knowingness is on their side, of *naïveté* and gullibility on his. Yet, in the inarticulate heart of him, he clings to it that he is not a dupe, and that there is a realm in which (as Emerson says) all their wit and intellectual superiority is no better than the cunning of a fox. Moral scepticism can no more be refuted or proved by logic than intellectual scepticism can. When we stick to it that there *is* truth (be it of either kind), we do so with our whole nature, and resolve to stand or fall by the results. The sceptic with his whole nature adopts the doubting attitude; but which of us is the wiser, Omniscience only knows.

Turn now from these wide questions of good to a certain class of questions of fact, questions concerning personal relations, states of mind between one man and another. *Do you like me or not?*—for example. Whether you do or not depends, in countless instances, on whether I meet you half-way, am willing to assume that you must like me, and show you trust, and expectation. The previous faith on my part in your liking's existence is in such cases what makes your liking come. But if I stand aloof, and refuse to budge an inch until I have objective evidence, until you shall have done something apt, as the absolutists say, *ad extorquendum assensum meum* [to extort my consent], ten to one your liking never comes. How many women's hearts are vanquished by the mere sanguine insistence of some man that they *must* love him! He will not consent to the hypothesis that they cannot. The desire for a certain kind of truth here brings about that special truth's existence; and so it is in innumerable cases of other sorts. Who gains promotions, boons, appointments, but the man in whose life they are seen to play the part of live hypotheses, who discounts them, sacrifices other things for their sake before they have come, and takes risks for them in advance? His faith acts on the powers above him as a claim, and creates its own verification.

A social organism of any sort whatever, large or small, is what it is because each member proceeds to his own duty with a trust that the other members will simultaneously do theirs. Wherever a desired result is achieved by the co-operation of many independent persons, its existence as a fact is a pure consequence of the precursive faith in one another of those immediately concerned. A government, an army, a commercial system, a ship, a college, an athletic team, all exist on this condition, without which not only is nothing achieved, but nothing is even attempted. A whole train of passengers (individually brave enough) will be looted by a few highwaymen, simply because the latter can count on one another, while each passenger fears that if he makes a movement of resistance, he will be shot before any one else backs him up. If we believed that the whole car-full would rise at once with us, we should each severally rise, and train-robbing would never even be attempted. There are, then, cases where a fact cannot come at all unless a preliminary faith exists in its coming. *And where faith in a fact can help create the fact,* that would be an insane logic which should say that faith running ahead of scientific evidence is the "lowest kind of immorality" into which a thinking being can fall. Yet such is the logic by which our scientific absolutists pretend to regulate our lives!

X.

In truths dependent on our personal action, then, faith based on desire is certainly a lawful and possibly an indispensable thing.

But now, it will be said, these are all childish human cases, and have nothing to do with great cosmical matters, like the question of religious faith. Let us then pass on to that. Religions differ so much in their accidents that in discussing the religious question we must make it very generic and broad. What then do we now mean by the religious hypothesis? Science says things are; morality says some things are better than other things; and religion says essentially two things.

First, she says that the best things are the more eternal things, the overlapping things, the things in the universe that throw the last stone, so to speak, and say the final word. "Perfection is eternal,"—this phrase of Charles Secrétan seems a good way of putting this first affirmation of religion, an affirmation which obviously cannot yet be verified scientifically at all.

The second affirmation of religion is that we are better off even now if we believe her first affirmation to be true.

Now, let us consider what the logical elements of this situation are *in case the religious hypothesis in both its branches be really true.* (Of course, we must admit that possibility at the outset. If we are to discuss the question at all, it must involve a living option. If for any of you religion be a hypothesis that cannot, by any living possibility be true, then you need go no farther. I speak to the "saving remnant" alone.) So proceeding, we see, first, that religion offers itself as a *momentous* option. We are supposed to gain, even now, by our belief, and to lose by our non-belief, a certain vital good. Secondly, religion is a *forced* option, so far as that good goes. We cannot escape the issue by remaining sceptical and waiting for more light, because, although we do avoid error in that way *if religion be untrue,* we lose the good, *if it be true,* just as certainly as if we positively chose to disbelieve. It is as if a man should hesitate indefinitely to ask a certain woman to marry him because he was not perfectly sure that she would prove an angel after he brought her home. Would he not cut himself off from that particular angel-possibility as decisively as if he went and married some one else? Scepticism, then, is not avoidance of option; it is option of a certain particular kind of risk. *Better risk loss of truth than chance of error,*—that is your faith-vetoer's exact position. He is actively playing his stake as much as the believer is; he is backing the field against the religious hypothesis, just as the believer is backing the religious hypothesis against the field. To preach scepticism to us as a duty until "sufficient evidence" for religion be found, is tantamount therefore to telling us, when in presence of the religious hypothesis, that to yield to our fear of its being error is wiser and better than to yield to our hope that it may be true. It is not intellect against all passions, then; it is only intellect with one passion laying down its law. And by what, forsooth, is the supreme wisdom of this passion warranted? Dupery for dupery, what proof is there that dupery through hope is so much worse than dupery through fear? I, for one, can see no proof; and I simply refuse obedience to the scientist's command to imitate his kind of option, in a case where my own stake is important enough to give me the right to choose my own form of risk. If religion be true and the evidence for it be still insufficient, I do not wish, by putting your extinguisher upon my nature (which feels to me as if it had after all some business in this matter), to forfeit my sole chance in life of getting upon the winning side,—that chance depending, of course, on my willingness to run the risk of acting as if my passional need of taking the world religiously might be prophetic and right.

All this is on the supposition that it really may be prophetic and right, and that, even to us who are discussing the matter, religion is a live hypothesis which may be true. Now, to most of us religion comes in a still further way that makes a veto on our active faith even more illogical. The more perfect and more eternal aspect of the universe is represented in our religions as having personal form. The universe is no longer a mere *It* to us, but a *Thou,* if we are religious; and any relation that may be possible from person to person might be possible here. For instance, although in one sense we are passive portions of the universe, in another we show a curious autonomy, as if we were small active centres on our own account. We feel, too, as if the appeal of religion to us were made to our own active good-will, as if evidence might be forever withheld from us unless we met the hypothesis half-way. To take a trivial illustration: just as a man who in a company of gentlemen made no advances, asked a warrant for every concession, and believed no one's word without proof, would cut himself off by such churlishness from all the social rewards that a more trusting spirit would earn,—so here, one who should shut himself up in snarling logicality and try to make the gods extort his recognition willy-nilly, or not get it at all, might cut himself off forever from his only opportunity of making the gods' acquaintance. This feeling, forced on us we know not whence, that by obstinately believing that there are gods (although not to do so would be so easy both for our logic and our life) we are doing the universe the deepest service we can, seems part of the living essence of the religious hypothesis. If the hypothesis were true in all its parts, including this one, then pure intellectualism, with its veto on our making willing advances, would be an absurdity; and some participation of our sympathetic nature would be logically required. I, therefore, for one, cannot see my way to accepting the agnostic rules for truth-seeking, or wilfully agree to keep my willing nature out of the game. I cannot do so for this plain reason, that *a rule of thinking which would absolutely prevent me from acknowledging certain kinds of truth if those kinds of truth were really there, would be an irrational rule.* That for me is the long and short of the formal logic of the situation, no matter what the kinds of truth might materially be.

I confess I do not see how this logic can be escaped. But sad experience makes me fear that some of you may still shrink from radically saying with me, *in abstracto,* that we have the right to believe at our own risk any hypothesis that is live enough to tempt our will. I suspect, however, that if this is so, it is because you have got away from the abstract logical point of view altogether, and are thinking (perhaps without realizing it) of some particular religious hypothesis which for you is dead. The freedom to "believe what we will" you apply to the case of some patent superstition; and the faith you think of is the faith defined by the schoolboy when he said, "Faith is when you believe something that you know ain't true." I can only repeat that this is misapprehension. *In concreto,* the freedom to believe can only cover living options which the intellect of the individual cannot by itself resolve; and living options never seem absurdities to him who has them to consider. When I look at the religious question as it really puts itself to concrete men, and when I think of all the possibilities which both practically and theoretically it involves, then this command that we shall put a stopper on our heart, instincts, and courage, and *wait*—acting of course meanwhile more or less as if religion were not true*—till doomsday, or till such time as our intellect and senses working together may have raked in evidence enough,—this command, I say, seems to me the queerest idol ever manufactured in the philosophic cave. Were we scholastic absolutists, there might be more excuse. If we had an infallible intellect with its objective certitudes, we might feel ourselves disloyal to such a perfect organ of knowledge in not trusting to it exclusively, in not waiting for its releasing word. But if we are empiricists, if we believe that no bell in us tolls to let us know for certain when truth is in our grasp, then it seems a piece of idle fantasticality to preach so solemnly our duty of waiting for the bell. Indeed

---

*Since belief is measured by action, he who forbids us to believe religion to be true, necessarily also forbids us to act as we should if we did believe it to be true. The whole defence of religious faith hinges upon action. If the action required or inspired by the religious hypothesis is in no way different from that dictated by the naturalistic hypothesis, then religious faith is a pure superfluity, better pruned away, and controversy about its legitimacy is a piece of idle trifling, unworthy of serious minds. I myself believe, of course, that the religious hypothesis gives to the world an expression which specifically determines our reactions, and makes them in a large part unlike what they might be on a purely naturalistic scheme of belief.

we *may* wait if we will,—I hope you do not think that I am denying that,—but if we do so, we do so at our peril as much as if we believed. In either case we *act,* taking our life in our hands. No one of us ought to issue vetoes to the other, nor should we bandy words of abuse. We ought, on the contrary, delicately and profoundly to respect one another's mental freedom: then only shall we bring about the intellectual republic; then only shall we have that spirit of inner tolerance without which all our outer tolerance is soulless, and which is empiricism's glory; then only shall we live and let live, in speculative as well as in practical things.

I began by a reference to Fitz James Stephen; let me end by a quotation from him. "What do you think of yourself? What do you think of the world? . . . These are questions with which all must deal as it seems good to them. They are riddles of the Sphinx, and in some way or other we must deal with them. . . . In all important transactions of life we have to take a leap in the dark. . . . If we decide to leave the riddles unanswered, that is a choice; if we waver in our answer, that, too, is a choice: but whatever choice we make, we make it at our peril. If a man chooses to turn his back altogether on God and the future, no one can prevent him; no one can show beyond reasonable doubt that he is mistaken. If a man thinks otherwise and acts as he thinks, I do not see that any one can prove that *he* is mistaken. Each must act as he thinks best; and if he is wrong, so much the worse for him. We stand on a mountain pass in the midst of whirling snow and blinding mist, through which we get glimpses now and then of paths which may be deceptive. If we stand still we shall be frozen to death. If we take the wrong road we shall be dashed to pieces. We do not certainly know whether there is any right one. What must we do? 'Be strong and of a good courage.' Act for the best, hope for the best, and take what comes. . . . If death ends all, we cannot meet death better."*

PRAGMATISM (in part)

LECTURE I: THE PRESENT DILEMMA
IN PHILOSOPHY

* * *

Philosophy is at once the most sublime and the most trivial of human pursuits. It works in the minutest crannies and it opens out the widest vistas. It "bakes no bread," as has been said, but it can inspire our souls with courage; and repugnant as its manners, its doubting and challenging, its quibbling and dialectics, often are to common people, no one of us can get along without the far-flashing beams of light it sends over the world's perspectives. These illuminations at least, and the contrast-effects of darkness and mystery that accompany them, give to what it says an interest that is much more than professional.

The history of philosophy is to a great extent that of a certain clash of human temperaments. Undignified as such a treatment may seem to some of my colleagues, I shall have to take account of this clash and explain a good many of the divergencies of

---

***Liberty, Equality, Fraternity,* p. 353, 2nd edition. London, 1874.

philosophers by it. Of whatever temperament a professional philosopher is, he tries, when philosophizing, to sink the fact of his temperament. Temperament is no conventionally recognized reason, so he urges impersonal reasons only for his conclusions. Yet his temperament really gives him a stronger bias than any of his more strictly objective premises. It loads the evidence for him one way or the other, making for a more sentimental or a more hard-hearted view of the universe, just as this fact or that principle would. He *trusts* his temperament. Wanting a universe that suits it, he believes in any representation of the universe that does suit it. He feels men of opposite temper to be out of key with the world's character, and in his heart considers them incompetent and "not in it," in the philosophic business, even though they may far excel him in dialectical ability.

Yet in the forum he can make no claim, on the bare ground of his temperament, to superior discernment or authority. There arises thus a certain insincerity in our philosophic discussions: the potentest of all our premises is never mentioned. I am sure it would contribute to clearness if in these lectures we should break this rule and mention it, and I accordingly feel free to do so.

Of course I am talking here of very positively marked men, men of radical idiosyncracy, who have set their stamp and likeness on philosophy and figure in its history. Plato, Locke, Hegel, Spencer, are such temperamental thinkers. Most of us have, of course, no very definite intellectual temperament, we are a mixture of opposite ingredients, each one present very moderately. We hardly know our own preferences in abstract matters; some of us are easily talked out of them, and end by following the fashion or taking up with the beliefs of the most impressive philosopher in our neighborhood, whoever he may be. But the one thing that has *counted* so far in philosophy is that a man should *see* things, see them straight in his own peculiar way, and be dissatisfied with any opposite way of seeing them. There is no reason to suppose that this strong temperamental vision is from now onward to count no longer in the history of man's beliefs.

Now the particular difference of temperament that I have in mind in making these remarks is one that has counted in literature, art, government, and manners as well as in philosophy. In manners we find formalists and free-and-easy persons. In government, authoritarians and anarchists. In literature, purists or academicals, and realists. In art, classics and romantics. You recognize these contrasts as familiar; well, in philosophy we have a very similar contrast expressed in the pair of terms "rationalist" and "empiricist," "empiricist" meaning your lover of facts in all their crude variety, "rationalist" meaning your devotee to abstract and eternal principles. No one can live an hour without both facts and principles, so it is a difference rather of emphasis; yet it breeds antipathies of the most pungent character between those who lay the emphasis differently; and we shall find it extraordinarily convenient to express a certain contrast in men's ways of taking their universe, by talking of the "empiricist" and of the "rationalist" temper. These terms make the contrast simple and massive.

More simple and massive than are usually the men of whom the terms are predicated. For every sort of permutation and combination is possible in human nature; and if I now proceed to define more fully what I have in mind when I speak of rationalists and empiricists, by adding to each of those titles some secondary qualifying characteristics, I beg you to regard my conduct as to a certain extent arbitrary. I select types of combination that nature offers very frequently, but by no means uniformly, and I select them solely for their convenience in helping me to my ulterior purpose of characterizing pragmatism. Historically we find the terms "intellectualism" and "sensationalism" used as synonyms of "rationalism" and "empiricism." Well, nature seems to combine most frequently with intellectualism an idealistic and optimistic tendency. Empiricists on the other hand are not uncommonly materialistic, and their optimism is apt to be decidedly conditional and tremulous. Rationalism is always monistic. It starts from wholes and universals, and makes much of the unity of things. Empiricism starts from the parts, and makes of the whole a collection—is not averse therefore to calling itself pluralistic. Rationalism usually considers itself more religious than empiricism, but there is much to say about this claim, so I merely mention it. It is a true claim when the individual rationalist is what is called a man of feeling, and when the individual empiricist prides himself on being hard-headed. In that case the rationalist will usually also be in favor of what is called free-will, and the empiricist will be a fatalist—I use the terms most popularly current. The rationalist finally will be of dogmatic temper in his affirmations, while the empiricist may be more sceptical and open to discussion.

I will write these traits down in two columns. I think you will practically recognize the two types of mental make-up that I mean if I head the columns by the titles "tender-minded" and "tough-minded" respectively.

The Tender-Minded	The Tough-Minded
Rationalistic (going by "principles"),	Empiricist (going by "facts"),
Intellectualistic,	Sensationalistic,
Idealistic,	Materialistic,
Optimistic,	Pessimistic,
Religious,	Irreligious,
Free-willist,	Fatalistic,
Monistic,	Pluralistic,
Dogmatical.	Skeptical.

Pray postpone for a moment the question whether the two contrasted mixtures which I have written down are each inwardly coherent and self-consistent or not. . . . It suffices for our immediate purpose that tender-minded and tough-minded people, characterized as I have written them down, do both exist. Each of you probably knows some well-marked example of each type, and you know what each example thinks of the example on the other side of the line. They have a low opinion of each other. Their antagonism, whenever as individuals their temperaments have been intense, has formed in all ages a part of the philosophic atmosphere of the time. It forms a part of the philosophic atmosphere to-day. The tough think of the tender as sentimentalists and softheads. The tender feel the tough to be unrefined, callous, or brutal. Their mutual reaction is very much like that that takes place when Bostonian tourists mingle with a population like that of Cripple Creek. Each type believes the other to be inferior to itself; but disdain in the one case is mingled with amusement, in the other it has a dash of fear.

Now, as I have already insisted, few of us are tender-foot Bostonians pure and simple, and few are typical Rocky Mountain toughs, in philosophy. Most of us have a hankering for the good things on both sides of the line. Facts are good, of course—give us lots of facts. Principles are good—give us plenty of principles. The world is indubitably one if you look at it in one way, but as indubitably is it many, if you look at it in another. It is both one and many—let us adopt a sort of pluralistic monism. Everything of course is necessarily determined, and yet of course our wills are free: a sort of free-will determinism is the true philosophy. The evil of the parts is undeniable, but the whole can't be evil: so practical pessimism may be combined with metaphysical optimism. And so forth—your ordinary philosophic layman never being a radical, never straightening out his system, but living vaguely in one plausible compartment of it or another to suit the temptations of successive hours.

But some of us are more than mere laymen in philosophy. We are worthy of the name of amateur athletes, and are vexed by too much inconsistency and vacillation in our creed. We cannot preserve a good intellectual conscience so long as we keep mixing incompatibles from opposite sides of the line. . . .

LECTURE II: WHAT PRAGMATISM MEANS

Some years ago, being with a camping party in the mountains, I returned from a solitary ramble to find every one engaged in a ferocious metaphysical dispute. The *corpus* of the dispute was a squirrel—a live squirrel supposed to be clinging to one side of a tree-trunk; while over against the tree's opposite side a human being was imagined to stand. This human witness tries to get sight of the squirrel by moving rapidly round the tree, but no matter how fast he goes, the squirrel moves as fast in the opposite direction, and always keeps the tree between himself and the man, so that never a glimpse of him is caught. The resultant metaphysical problem now is this: *Does the man go round the squirrel or not?* He goes round the tree, sure enough, and the squirrel is on the tree; but does he go round the squirrel? In the unlimited leisure of the wilderness, discussion had been worn threadbare. Everyone had taken sides, and was obstinate; and the numbers on both sides were even. Each side, when I appeared therefore appealed to me to make it a majority. Mindful of the scholastic adage that whenever you meet a contradiction you must make a distinction, I immediately sought and found one, as follows: "Which party is right," I said, "depends on what you *practically mean* by 'going round' the squirrel. If you mean passing from the north of him to the east, then to the south, then to the west, and then to the north of him again, obviously the man does go round him, for he occupies these successive positions. But if on the contrary you mean being first in front of him, then on the right of him, then behind him, then on his left, and finally in front again, it is quite as obvious that the man fails to go round him, for by the compensating movements the squirrel makes, he keeps his belly turned towards the man all the time, and his back turned away. Make the distinction, and there is no occasion for any farther dispute. You are both right and both wrong according as you conceive the verb 'to go round' in one practical fashion or the other."

Although one or two of the hotter disputants called my speech a shuffling evasion, saying they wanted no quibbling or scholastic hair-splitting, but meant just plain honest English "round," the majority seemed to think that the distinction had assuaged the dispute.

I tell this trivial anecdote because it is a peculiarly simple example of what I wish now to speak of as *the pragmatic method*. The pragmatic method is primarily a method of settling metaphysical disputes that otherwise might be interminable. Is the world one or many?—fated or free?—material or spiritual?—here are notions either of which may or may not hold good of the world; and disputes over such notions are unending. The pragmatic method in such cases is to try to interpret each notion by tracing its respective practical consequences. What difference would it practically make to any one if this notion rather than that notion were true? If no practical difference whatever can be traced, then the alternatives mean practically the same thing, and all dispute is idle. Whenever a dispute is serious, we ought to be able to show some practical difference that must follow from one side or the other's being right.

A glance at the history of the idea will show you still better what pragmatism means. The term is derived from the same Greek word ⟨*pragma*⟩, meaning action, from which our words "practice" and "practical" come. It was first introduced into philosophy by Mr. Charles Peirce in 1878. In an article entitled "How to Make Our Ideas Clear," in the "Popular Science Monthly" for January of that year. Mr. Peirce, after pointing out that our beliefs are really rules for action, said that, to develop a thought's meaning, we need only determine what conduct it is fitted to produce: that conduct is for us its sole significance. And the tangible fact at the root of all our thought-distinctions, however subtle, is that there is no one of them so fine as to consist in anything but a possible difference of practice. To attain perfect clearness in our thoughts of an object, then, we need only consider what conceivable effects of a practical kind the object may involve—what sensations we are to expect from it, and what reactions we must prepare. Our conception of these effects, whether immediate or remote, is then for us the whole of our conception of the object, so far as that conception has positive significance at all.

This is the principle of Peirce, the principle of pragmatism. It lay entirely unnoticed by any one for twenty years, until I, in an address before Professor Howison's philosophical union at the university of California, brought it forward again and made a special application of it to religion. By that date (1898) the times seemed ripe for its reception. The word "pragmatism" spread, and at present it fairly spots the pages of the philosophic journals. On all hands we find the "pragmatic movement" spoken of, sometimes with respect, sometimes with contumely, seldom with clear understanding. It is evident that the term applies itself conveniently to a number of tendencies that hitherto have lacked a collective name, and that it has "come to stay."

To take in the importance of Peirce's principle, one must get accustomed to applying it to concrete cases. I found a few years ago that Ostwald, the illustrious Leipzig chemist, had been making perfectly distinct use of the principle of pragmatism in his lectures on the philosophy of science, though he had not called it by that name.

"All realities influence our practice," he wrote me, "and that influence is their meaning for us. I am accustomed to put questions to my classes in this way: In what respects would the world be different if this alternative or that were true? If I can find nothing that would become different, then the alternative has no sense."

That is, the rival views mean practically the same thing, and meaning, other than practical, there is for us none. Ostwald in a published lecture gives this example of what he means. Chemists have long wrangled over the inner constitution of certain bodies called "tautomerous." Their properties seemed equally consistent with the notion that an instable hydrogen atom oscillates inside of them, or that they are instable mixtures of two bodies. Controversy raged, but never was decided. "It would never have begun," says Ostwald, "if the combatants had asked themselves what particular experimental fact could have been made different by one or the other view being correct. For it would then have appeared that no difference of fact could possibly ensue; and the quarrel was as unreal as if, theorizing in primitive times about the raising of dough by yeast, one party should have invoked a 'brownie,' while another insisted on an 'elf' as the true cause of the phenomenon."*

---

*"Theorie und Praxis," *Zeitsch. des Oesterreichischen Ingenieur u. Architecten-Vereines,* 1905, Nr. 4 u. 6. I find a still more radical pragmatism than Ostwald's in an address by Professor W.S. Franklin: "I think that the sickliest notion of physics, even if a student gets it, is that it is 'the science of masses, molecules, and the ether.' And I think that the healthiest notion, even if a student does not wholly get it, is that physics is the science of the ways of taking hold of bodies and pushing them!" (*Science,* January 2, 1903.)

It is astonishing to see how many philosophical disputes collapse into insignificance the moment you subject them to this simple test of tracing a concrete consequence. There can *be* no difference anywhere that doesn't *make* a difference elsewhere—no difference in abstract truth that doesn't express itself in a difference in concrete fact and in conduct consequent upon that fact, imposed on somebody, somehow, somewhere, and somewhen. The whole function of philosophy ought to be to find out what definite difference it will make to you and me, at definite instants of our life, if this world-formula or that world-formula be the true one.

There is absolutely nothing new in the pragmatic method. Socrates was an adept at it. Aristotle used it methodically. Locke, Berkeley, and Hume made momentous contributions to truth by its means. Shadworth Hodgson keeps insisting that realities are only what they are "known as." But these forerunners of pragmatism used it in fragments: they were preluders only. Not until in our time has it generalized itself, become conscious of a universal mission, pretended to a conquering destiny. I believe in that destiny, and I hope I may end by inspiring you with my belief.

Pragmatism represents a perfectly familiar attitude in philosophy, the empiricist attitude, but it represents it, as it seems to me, both in a more radical and in a less objectionable form than it has ever yet assumed. A pragmatist turns his back resolutely and once for all upon a lot of inveterate habits dear to professional philosophers. He turns away from abstraction and insufficiency, from verbal solutions, from bad *a priori* reasons, from fixed principles, closed systems, and pretended absolutes and origins. He turns towards concreteness and adequacy, towards facts, towards action and towards power. That means the empiricist temper regnant and the rationalist temper sincerely given up. It means the open air and possibilities of nature, as against dogma, artificiality, and the pretence of finality in truth.

At the same time it does not stand for any special results. It is a method only. But the general triumph of that method would mean an enormous change in what I called in my last lecture the "temperament" of philosophy. Teachers of the ultra-rationalistic type would be frozen out, much as the courtier type is frozen out in republics, as the ultramontane type of priest is frozen out in protestant lands. Science and metaphysics would come much nearer together, would in fact work absolutely hand in hand.

Metaphysics has usually followed a very primitive kind of quest. You know how men have always hankered after unlawful magic, and you know what a great part in magic *words* have always played. If you have his name, or the formula of incantation that binds him, you can control the spirit, genie, afrite, or whatever the power may be. Solomon knew the names of all the spirits, and having their names, he held them subject to his will. So the universe has always appeared to the natural mind as a kind of enigma, of which the key must be sought in the shape of some illuminating or power-bringing word or name. That word names the universe's *principle,* and to possess it is after a fashion to possess the universe itself. "God," "Matter," "Reason," "the Absolute," "Energy," are so many solving names. You can rest when you have them. You are at the end of your metaphysical quest.

But if you follow the pragmatic method, you cannot look on any such word as closing your quest. You must bring out of each word its practical cash-value, set it at work within the stream of your experience. It appears less as a solution, then, than as a program for more work, and more particularly as an indication of the ways in which existing realities may be *changed.*

Theories thus become instruments, not answers to enigmas, in which we can rest. We don't lie back upon them, we move forward, and, on occasion, make nature over again by their aid. Pragmatism unstiffens all our theories, limbers them up and sets each one at work. Being nothing essentially new, it harmonizes with many ancient philosophic tendencies. It agrees with nominalism for instance, in always appealing to particulars; with utilitarianism in emphasizing practical aspects; with positivism in its disdain for verbal solutions, useless questions and metaphysical abstractions.

All these, you see, are *anti-intellectualist* tendencies. Against rationalism as a pretension and a method pragmatism is fully armed and militant. But, at the outset, at least, it stands for no particular results. It has no dogmas, and no doctrines save its method. As the young Italian pragmatist Papini has well said, it lies in the midst of our theories, like a corridor in a hotel. Innumerable chambers open out of it. In one you may find a man writing an atheistic volume; in the next some one on his knees praying for faith and strength; in a third a chemist investigating a body's properties. In a fourth a system of idealistic metaphysics is being excogitated; in a fifth the impossibility of metaphysics is being shown. But they all own the corridor, and all must pass through it if they want a practicable way of getting into or out of their respective rooms.

No particular results then, so far, but only an attitude of orientation, is what the pragmatic method means. *The attitude of looking away from first things, principles, "categories," supposed necessities; and of looking towards last things, fruits, consequences, facts.*

So much for the pragmatic method! You may say that I have been praising it rather than explaining it to you, but I shall presently explain it abundantly enough by showing how it works on some familiar problems. Meanwhile the word pragmatism has come to be used in a still wider sense, as meaning also a certain *theory of truth*. I mean to give a whole lecture to the statement of that theory, after first paving the way, so I can be very brief now. But brevity is hard to follow, so I ask for your redoubled attention for a quarter of an hour. If much remains obscure, I hope to make it clearer in the later lectures.

One of the most successfully cultivated branches of philosophy in our time is what is called inductive logic, the study of the conditions under which our sciences have evolved. Writers on this subject have begun to show a singular unanimity as to what the laws of nature and elements of fact mean, when formulated by mathematicians, physicists and chemists. When the first mathematical, logical, and natural uniformities, the first *laws,* were discovered, men were so carried away by the clearness, beauty and simplification that resulted, that they believed themselves to have deciphered authentically the eternal thoughts of the Almighty. His mind also thundered and reverberated in syllogisms. He also thought in conic sections, squares and roots and ratios, and geometrized like Euclid. He made Kepler's laws for the planets to follow; he made velocity increase proportionally to the time in falling bodies; he made the law of the sines for light to obey when refracted; he established the classes, orders, families and genera of plants and animals, and fixed the distances between them. He thought the archetypes of all things, and devised their variations; and when we rediscover any one of these his wondrous institutions, we seize his mind in its very literal intention.

But as the sciences have developed farther, the notion has gained ground that most, perhaps all, of our laws are only approximations. The laws themselves, moreover, have grown so numerous that there is no counting them; and so many rival formulations are proposed in all the branches of science that investigators have become accustomed to the notion that no theory is absolutely a transcript of reality, but that any one of them may from some point of view be useful. Their great use is to summarize old facts and to lead to new ones. They are only a man-made language, a conceptual shorthand, as some one calls them, in which we write our reports of nature; and languages, as is well known, tolerate much choice of expression and many dialects.

Thus human arbitrariness has driven divine necessity from scientific logic. If I mention the names of Sigwart, Mach, Ostwald, Pearson, Milhaud, Poincare, Duhem, Ruyssen, those of you who are students will easily identify the tendency I speak of, and will think of additional names.

Riding now on the front of this wave of scientific logic Messrs. Schiller and Dewey appear with their pragmatistic account of what truth everywhere signifies. Everywhere, these teachers say, "truth" in our ideas and beliefs means the same thing that it means in science. It means, they say, nothing but this, *that ideas (which themselves are but parts of our experience) become true just in so far as they help us to get into satisfactory relation with other parts of our experience,* to summarize them and get about among them by conceptual short-cuts instead of following the interminable succession of particular phenomena. Any idea upon which we can ride, so to speak; any idea that will carry us prosperously from any one part of our experience to any other part, linking things satisfactorily, working securely, simplifying, saving labor; is true for just so much, true in so far forth, true *instrumentally.* This is the "instrumental" view of truth taught so successfully at Chicago, the view that truth in our ideas means their power to "work," promulgated so brilliantly at Oxford.

Messrs. Dewey, Schiller and their allies, in reaching this general conception of all truth, have only followed the example of geologists, biologists and philologists. In the establishment of these other sciences, the successful stroke was always to take some simple process actually observable in operation—as denudation by weather, say, or variation from parental type, or change of dialect by incorporation of new words and pronunciations—and then to generalize it, making it apply to all times, and produce great results by summating its effects through the ages.

The observable process which Schiller and Dewey particularly singled out for generalization is the familiar one by which any individual settles into *new opinions.* The process here is always the same. The individual has a stock of old opinions already, but he meets a new experience that puts them to a strain. Somebody contradicts them; or in a reflective moment he discovers that they contradict each other; or he hears of facts with which they are incompatible; or desires arise in him which they cease to satisfy. The result is an inward trouble to which his mind till then had been a stranger, and from which he seeks to escape by modifying his previous mass of opinions. He saves as much of it as he can, for in this matter of belief we are all extreme conservatives. So he tries to change first this opinion, and then that (for they resist change very variously), until at last some new idea comes up which he can graft upon the ancient stock with a minimum of disturbance of the latter, some idea that mediates between the stock and the new experience and runs them into one another most felicitously and expediently.

This new idea is then adopted as the true one. It preserves the older stock of truths with a minimum of modification, stretching them just enough to make them admit the novelty, but conceiving that in ways as familiar as the case leaves possible. An *outrée* [exaggerated] explanation, violating all our preconceptions, would never pass for a true account of a novelty. We should scratch round industriously till we found something less excentric. The most violent revolutions in an individual's beliefs leave most of his old order standing. Time and space, cause and effect, nature and history, and one's own biography remain untouched. New truth is always a go-between, a smoother-over of transitions. It marries old opinion to new fact so as ever to show a minimum of jolt, a maximum of continuity. We hold a theory true just in proportion to its success in solving this "problem of maxima and minima." But success in solving this problem is eminently a matter of approximation. We say this theory solves it on the whole more satisfactorily than that theory; but that means more satisfactorily to ourselves, and individuals will emphasize their points of satisfaction differently. To a certain degree, therefore, everything here is plastic.

The point I now urge you to observe particularly is the part played by the older truths. Failure to take account of it is the source of much of the unjust criticism levelled against pragmatism. Their influence is absolutely controlling. Loyalty to them is the first principle—in most cases it is the only principle; for by far the most usual way of handling phenomena so novel that they would make for a serious rearrangement of our preconception is to ignore them altogether, or to abuse those who bear witness for them.

You doubtless wish examples of this process of truth's growth, and the only trouble is their superabundance. The simplest case of new truth is of course the mere numerical addition of new kinds of facts, or of new single facts of old kinds, to our experience—an addition that involves no alteration in the old beliefs. Day follows day, and its contents are simply added. The new contents themselves are not true, they simply *come* and *are*. Truth is *what we say about them,* and when we say that they have come, truth is satisfied by the plain additive formula.

But often the day's contents oblige a rearrangement. If I should now utter piercing shrieks and act like a maniac on this platform, it would make many of you revise your ideas as to the probable worth of my philosophy. "Radium" came the other day as part of the day's content, and seemed for a moment to contradict our ideas of the whole order of nature, that order having come to be identified with what is called the conservation of energy. The mere sight of radium paying heat away indefinitely out of its own pocket seemed to violate that conservation. What to think? If the radiations from it were nothing but an escape of unsuspected "potential" energy, pre-existent inside of the atoms, the principle of conservation would be saved. The discovery of "helium" as the radiation's outcome, opened a way to this belief. So Ramsay's view is generally held to be true, because, although it extends our old ideas of energy, it causes a minimum of alteration in their nature.

I need not multiply instances. A new opinion counts as "true" just in proportion as it gratifies the individual's desire to assimilate the novel in his experience to his beliefs in stock. It must both lean on old truth and grasp new fact; and its success (as I said a moment ago) in doing this, is a matter for the individual's appreciation. When old truth grows, then, by new truth's addition, it is for subjective reasons. We are in the process and obey the reasons. That new idea is truest which performs most felicitously its function of satisfying our double urgency. It makes itself true, gets itself classed as true, by the way it works; grafting itself then upon the ancient body of truth, which thus grows much as a tree grows by the activity of a new layer of cambium.

Now Dewey and Schiller proceed to generalize this observation and to apply it to the most ancient parts of truth. They also once were plastic. They also were called true for human reasons. They also mediated between still earlier truths and what in those days were novel observations. Purely objective truth, truth in whose establishment the function of giving human satisfaction in marrying previous parts of experience with newer parts played no role whatever, is nowhere to be found. The reasons why we call things true is the reason why they *are* true, for "to be true" *means* only to perform this marriage-function.

The trail of the human serpent is thus over everything. Truth independent; truth that we *find* merely; truth no longer malleable to human need; truth incorrigible, in a word; such truth exists indeed superabundantly—or is supposed to exist by rationalistically minded thinkers; but then it means only the dead heart of the living tree, and its being there means only that truth also has its paleontology, and its "prescription," and may grow stiff with years of veteran service and petrified in men's regard by sheer antiquity. But how plastic even the oldest truths nevertheless really are has been vividly shown in our day by the transformation of logical and mathematical ideas, a transformation which seems even to be invading physics. The ancient formulas are reinterpreted as special expressions of much wider principles, principles that our ancestors never got a glimpse of in their present shape and formulation.

Mr. Schiller still gives to all this view of truth the name of "Humanism," but, for this doctrine too, the name of pragmatism seems fairly to be in the ascendant, so I will treat it under the name of pragmatism in these lectures.

Such then would be the scope of pragmatism—first, a method; and second, a genetic theory of what is meant by truth. And these two things must be our future topics.

What I have said of the theory of truth will, I am sure, have appeared obscure and unsatisfactory to most of you by reason of its brevity. I shall make amends for that hereafter. In a lecture on "common sense" I shall try to show what I mean by truths grown petrified by antiquity. In another lecture I shall expatiate on the idea that our thoughts become true in proportion as they successfully exert their go between function. In a third I shall show how hard it is to discriminate subjective from objective factors in Truth's development. You may not follow me wholly in these lectures; and if you do, you may not wholly agree with me. But you will, I know, regard me at least as serious, and treat my effort with respectful consideration.

You will probably be surprised to learn, then, that Messrs. Schiller's and Dewey's theories have suffered a hailstorm of contempt and ridicule. All rationalism has risen against them. In influential quarters Mr. Schiller, in particular, has been treated like an impudent schoolboy who deserves a spanking. I should not mention this, but for the fact that it throws so much sidelight upon that rationalistic temper to which I have opposed the temper of pragmatism. Pragmatism is uncomfortable away from facts. Rationalism is comfortable only in the presence of abstractions. This pragmatist talk about truths in the plural, about their utility and satisfactoriness, about the success with which they "work," etc., suggests to the typical intellectualist mind a sort of coarse lame second-rate makeshift article of truth. Such truths are not real truth. Such tests are merely subjective. As against this, objective truth must be something non-utilitarian, haughty, refined, remote, august, exalted. It must be an absolute correspondence of our thoughts with an equally absolute reality. It must be what we *ought* to think unconditionally. The conditioned ways in which we *do* think are so much irrelevance and matter for psychology. Down with psychology, up with logic, in all this question!

See the exquisite contrast of the types of mind! The pragmatist clings to facts and concreteness, observes truth at its work in particular cases, and generalizes. Truth, for him, becomes a class-name for all sorts of definite working-values in experience. For the rationalist it remains a pure abstraction, to the bare name of which we must defer. When the pragmatist undertakes to show in detail just *why* we must defer, the rationalist is unable to recognize the concretes from which his own abstraction is taken. He accuses us of *denying* truth; whereas we have only sought to trace exactly why people follow it and always ought to follow it. Your typical ultra-abstractionist fairly shudders at concreteness: other things equal, he positively prefers the pale and spectral. If the two universes were offered, he would always choose the skinny outline rather than the rich thicket of reality. It is so much purer, clearer, nobler.

I hope that as these lectures go on, the concreteness and closeness to facts of the pragmatism which they advocate may be what approves itself to you as its most satisfactory peculiarity. It only follows here the example of the sister-sciences, interpreting the unobserved by the observed. It brings old and new harmoniously together. It converts the absolutely empty notion of a static relation of "correspondence" (what that may mean we must ask later) between our minds and reality, into that of a rich and active commerce (that any one may follow in detail and understand) between particular thoughts of ours, and the great universe of other experiences in which they play their parts and have their uses.

But enough of this at present? The justification of what I say must be postponed. I wish now to add a word in further explanation of the claim I made at our last meeting, that pragmatism may be a happy harmonizer of empiricist ways of thinking with the more religious demands of human beings.

Men who are strongly of the fact-loving temperament, you may remember me to have said, are liable to be kept at a distance by the small sympathy with facts which that philosophy from the present-day fashion of idealism offers them. It is far too intellectualistic. Old fashioned theism was bad enough, with its notion of God as an exalted monarch, made up of a lot of unintelligible or preposterous "attributes"; but, so long as it held strongly by the argument from design, it kept some touch with concrete realities. Since, however, Darwinism has once for all displaced design from the minds of the "scientific," theism has lost that foothold; and some kind of an immanent or pantheistic deity working in things rather than above them is, if any, the kind recommended to our contemporary imagination. Aspirants to a philosophic religion turn, as a rule, more hopefully nowadays towards idealistic pantheism than towards the older dualistic theism, in spite of the fact that the latter still counts able defenders.

But, as I said in my first lecture, the brand of pantheism offered is hard for them to assimilate if they are lovers of facts, or empirically minded. It is the absolutistic brand, spurning the dust and reared upon pure logic. It keeps no connexion whatever with concreteness. Affirming the Absolute Mind, which is its substitute for God, to be the rational presupposition of all particulars of fact, whatever they may be, it remains supremely indifferent to what the particular facts in our world actually are. Be they what they may, the Absolute will father them. Like the sick lion in Esop's fable, all footprints lead into his den, but *nulla vestigia retrorsum.* You cannot redescend into the world of particulars by the Absolute's aid, or deduce any necessary consequences of detail important for your life from your idea of his nature. He gives you indeed the assurance that all is well with *Him,* and for his eternal way of thinking; but thereupon he leaves you to be finitely saved by your own temporal devices.

Far be it from me to deny the majesty of this conception, or its capacity to yield religious comfort to a most respectable class of minds. But from the human point of view, no one can pretend that it doesn't suffer from the faults of remoteness and abstractness. It is eminently a product of what I have ventured to call the rationalistic temper. It disdains empiricism's needs. It substitutes a pallid outline for the real world's richness. It is dapper, it is noble in the bad sense, in the sense in which to be noble is to be inapt for humble service. In this real world of sweat and dirt, it seems to me that when a view of things is "noble," that ought to count as a presumption against its truth, and as a philosophic disqualification. The prince of darkness may be a gentleman, as we are told he is, but whatever the God of earth and heaven is, he can surely be no gentleman. His menial services are needed in the dust of our human trials, even more than his dignity is needed in the empyrean.

Now pragmatism, devoted though she be to facts, has no such materialistic bias as ordinary empiricism labors under. Moreover, she has no objection whatever to the realizing of abstractions, so long as you get about among particulars with their aid and they actually carry you somewhere. Interested in no conclusions but those which our minds and our experiences work out together, she has no a priori prejudices against theology. *If theological ideas prove to have a value for concrete life, they will be true, for pragmatism, in the sense of being good for so much. For how much more they are true, will depend entirely on their relations to the other truths that also have to be acknowledged.*

What I said just now about the Absolute, of transcendental idealism, is a case in point. First, I called it majestic and said it yielded religious comfort to a class of minds, and then I accused it of remoteness and sterility. But so far as it affords such comfort, it surely is not sterile; it has that amount of value; it performs a concrete function. As a good pragmatist, I myself ought to call the Absolute true "in so far forth," then; and I unhesitatingly now do so.

But what does *true in so far forth* mean in this case? To answer, we need only apply the pragmatic method. What do believers in the Absolute mean by saying that their belief affords them comfort? They mean that since, in the Absolute finite evil is "over-ruled" already, we may, therefore, whenever we wish, treat the temporal as if it were potentially the eternal, be sure that we can trust its outcome, and, without sin, dismiss our fear and drop the worry of our finite responsibility. In short, they mean that we have a right ever and anon to take a moral holiday, to let the world wag in its own way, feeling that its issues are in better hands than ours and are none of our business.

The universe is a system of which the individual members may relax their anxieties occasionally, in which the don't-care mood is also right for men, and moral holidays in order,—that, if I mistake not, is part, at least, of what the Absolute is "known-as," that is the great difference in our particular experiences which his being true makes, for us, that is his cash-value when he is pragmatically interpreted. Farther than that the ordinary lay-reader in philosophy who thinks favorably of absolute idealism does not venture to sharpen his conceptions. He can use the Absolute for so much, and so much is very precious. He is pained at hearing you speak incredulously of the Absolute, therefore, and disregards your criticisms because they deal with aspects of the conception that he fails to follow.

If the Absolute means this, and means no more than this, who can possibly deny the truth of it? To deny it would be to insist that men should never relax, and that holidays are never in order.

I am well aware how odd it must seem to some of you to hear me say that an idea is "true" so long as to believe it is profitable to our lives. That it is *good,* for as much as it profits, you will gladly admit. If what we do by its aid is good, you will allow the idea itself to be good in so far forth, for we are the better for possessing it. But is it not a strange misuse of the word "truth," you will say, to call ideas also "true" for this reason?

To answer this difficulty fully is impossible at this stage of my account. You touch here upon the very central point of Messrs. Schiller's, Dewey's and my own doctrine of truth, which I can not discuss with detail until my sixth lecture. Let me now say only this, that truth is *one species of good,* and not, as is usually supposed, a category distinct from good, and co-ordinate with it. *The true is the name of whatever proves itself to be good in the way of belief, and good, too, for definite, assignable reasons.* Surely you must admit this, that if there were *no* good for life in true ideas, or if the knowledge of them were positively disadvantageous and false ideas the only useful ones, then the current notion that truth is divine and precious, and its pursuit a duty, could never have grown up or become a dogma. In a world like that, our duty would be to *shun* truth, rather. But in this world, just as certain foods are not only agreeable to our taste, but good for our teeth, our stomach, and our tissues; so certain ideas are not only agreeable to think about, or agreeable as supporting other ideas that we are fond of, but they are also helpful in life's practical struggles. If there be any life that it is really better we should lead, and if there be any idea which, if believed in, would help us to lead that life, then it would be really *better for us* to believe in that idea, *unless, indeed, belief in it incidentally clashed with other greater vital benefits.*

"What would be better for us to believe!" This sounds very like a definition of truth. It comes very near to saying "what we *ought* to believe": and in *that* definition none of you would find any oddity. Ought we ever not to believe what it is *better for us* to believe? And can we then keep the notion of what is better for us, and what is true for us, permanently apart?

Pragmatism says no, and I fully agree with her. Probably you also agree, so far as the abstract statement goes, but with a suspicion that if we practically did believe everything that made for good in our own personal lives, we should be found indulging all kinds of fancies about this world's affairs, and all kinds of sentimental superstitions about a world hereafter. Your suspicion here is undoubtedly well founded, and it is evident that something happens when you pass from the abstract to the concrete that complicates the situation.

I said just now that what is better for us to believe is true *unless the belief incidentally clashes with some other vital benefit.* Now in real life what vital benefits is any particular belief of ours most liable to clash with? What indeed except the vital benefits yielded by *other beliefs* when these prove incompatible with the first ones? In other words, the greatest enemy of any one of our truths may be the rest of our truths. Truths have once for all this desperate instinct of self-preservation and of desire to extinguish whatever contradicts them. My belief in the Absolute, based on the good it does me, must run the gauntlet of all my other beliefs. Grant that it may be true in giving me a moral holiday. Nevertheless, as I conceive it,—and let me speak now confidentially, as it were, and merely in my own private person,—it clashes with other truths of mine whose benefits I hate to give up on its account. It happens to be associated with a kind of logic of which I am the enemy, I find that it entangles me in metaphysical paradoxes that are inacceptable, etc., etc. But as I have enough trouble in life already without adding the trouble of carrying these intellectual inconsistencies, I personally just give up the Absolute. I just *take* my moral holidays; or else as a professional philosopher, I try to justify them by some other principle.

If I could restrict my notion of the Absolute to its bare holiday-giving value, it wouldn't clash with my other truths. But we can not easily thus restrict our hypotheses. They carry supernumerary features, and these it is that clash so. My disbelief in the Absolute means then disbelief in those other supernumerary features, for I fully believe in the legitimacy of taking moral holidays.

You see by this what I meant when I called pragmatism a mediator and reconciler and said, borrowing the word from Papini, that she "unstiffens" our theories. She has in fact no prejudices whatever, no obstructive dogmas, no rigid canons of what shall count as proof. She is completely genial. She will entertain any hypothesis, she will consider any evidence. It follows that in the religious field she is at a great advantage both over positivistic empiricism, with its anti-theological bias, and over religious rationalism, with its exclusive interest in the remote, the noble, the simple, and the abstract in the way of conception.

In short, she widens the field of search for God. Rationalism sticks to logic and the empyrean. Empiricism sticks to the external senses. Pragmatism is willing to take anything, to follow either logic or the senses and to count the humblest and most personal experiences. She will count mystical experiences if they have practical consequences. She will take a God who lives in the very dirt of private fact—if that should seem a likely place to find him.

Her only test of probable truth is what works best in the way of leading us, what fits every part of life best and combines with the collectivity of experience's demands, nothing being omitted. If theological ideas should do this, if the notion of God, in particular, should prove to do it, how could pragmatism possibly deny God's existence? She could see no meaning in treating as "not true" a notion that was pragmatically so successful. What other kind of truth could there be, for her, than all this agreement with concrete reality?

In my last lecture I shall return again to the relations of pragmatism with religion. But you see already how democratic she is. Her manners are as various and flexible, her resources as rich and endless, and her conclusions as friendly as those of mother nature.

Friedrich Nietzsche
1844–1900

$\mathbf{F}$riedrich Wilhelm Nietzsche was born in Röcken, Prussia, in 1844. He was named in honor of the Prussian king, Friedrich Wilhelm IV, whose birthday, October 15, he shared. Nietzsche's father, Ludwig Nietzsche, was a Lutheran minister and his mother, Franziska Oehler Nietzsche, was the daughter of a Lutheran minister. When Nietzsche was only five years old, his father died from what was then called "softening of the brain" after a year of mental instability. The rest of Nietzsche's childhood was spent in a household of women, including his widowed mother, his sister, his anxious paternal grandmother, and two maiden aunts.

Following grade school, Nietzsche attended a famous boarding school at Pforta where he did outstanding work. However, while there, Nietzsche suffered migraine headaches, which afflicted him until he experienced a mental breakdown in 1889. The medicine he took to relieve the headaches would upset his stomach and leave him nauseous. For much of his adult life, he would alternate between the extremes of headaches and nausea with only short periods of health in between.

In 1864 he enrolled at the University of Bonn to study theology and classical philology (linguistics), but he left within a year. By this time he had given up whatever religious faith he had and was no longer interested in theology. He moved to the University of Leipzig to continue his studies in philology. His professor at Leipzig, Friedrich Ritschl, was so impressed with Nietzsche's work that he published some of his papers and later recommended him for a chair of classical philology at the University of Basel. In 1869, at the unusual age of only twenty-four, Nietzsche was given the chair as an associate professor. He had produced neither a doctoral dissertation nor the additional book normally required of an associate professor. Leipzig immediately awarded him a doctorate without examination or thesis and within a year he was promoted to full professor at Basel.

In 1872 Nietzsche published his first book, *The Birth of Tragedy,* which included a laudatory section on Richard Wagner's music. Over the next four years Nietzsche wrote four meditations (published collectively in English as *Thoughts out of Season*), the last of which was another tribute to Wagner. During this period Nietzsche and Wagner were close friends and Nietzsche often visited Wagner's villa on Lake Lucerne. But by 1878 they had broken relations over Wagner's nationalism and anti-Semitism.

Nietzsche's health began to deteriorate, and he was forced to resign from the university in 1879. Over the next ten years, Nietzsche travelled and devoted all his remaining energy to writing, publishing such books as *The Gay Science* (1882), *Thus Spoke Zarathustra* (1883-1885), *Beyond Good and Evil* (1886), *Towards a Genealogy of Morals* (1887), and his final denunciation of his former friend, *The Case of Wagner* (1888).

By the end of 1888, Nietzsche was showing signs of oncoming madness and in January of 1889 he collapsed in the street of Turin, Italy, while hugging the neck of a horse. For the next eleven years until his death in 1900, he lived in the care of his mother and sister. Works that he had written in 1888, including *The Will to Power, The Twilight of the Idols, The Anti-Christ,* and his outrageous autobiography *Ecco Homo* (which includes chapter headings such as "Why I Am So Clever"), were published after distorted editing by his sister. Only in the twentieth century have unedited versions of these works become available.

The cause of Nietzsche's insanity has been vigorously debated. Critics have held that his ideas caused it and claim to have found evidence of insanity in many of his writings. His sister romanticized that he went mad because Germany spurned him. More likely explanations are that he contracted syphilis during a rare sexual escapade while a young man or that he simply inherited a brain disease from his father.

* * *

Nietzsche's style of writing in epigrams, aphorisms, stories, poetry, and essays virtually defies an editor to systematically summarize his thought. But while Nietzsche never sought to build a system, there are recurring, interwoven themes represented by the selections given here.

In *The Birth of Tragedy,* translated by Francis Golffing, Nietzsche presents a distinction between Apollonian and Dionysian tendencies in art. The Apollonian tendency (named for the Greek god of the sun, Apollo) represents the harmony and restraint exemplified by Greek sculpture and architecture. The Dionysian tendency (named for the Greek god of wine and revelry, Dionysos) represents wild abandonment as exemplified by the drunken sexual frenzies of the Dionysian cult festivals or the music of Beethoven's Ninth Symphony. Greek tragedy arises as a synthesis of Apollonian form and Dionysian urges. But Greek tragedy is in turn superseded by Greek rationalism as exemplified by Socrates: the theoretical man who optimistically sees knowledge as the panacea to the problems of life. What is needed now, Nietzsche argues, is a new synthesis of these Dionysian and Apollonian tendencies by an "artistic" Socrates. Such a Socratic figure would be a creative genius who would honestly face the harshness of life without losing a clear rational analytic perspective.

In order to produce new values, such a creative genius must be free from all constraints, including moral constraints that would limit creativity by imposing "universal" standards. In the first essay of *Genealogy of Morals,* also given here in the Francis Golffing translation, Nietzsche shows how such a limiting morality developed as he distinguishes between "master morality" and "slave morality." Master morality is basically affirmative and defines itself on its own terms. In this morality "good" means that which is noble, powerful, and beautiful and belongs to the highest rank; and "bad" signifies that which is base, low-minded, and unworthy of greatness. On the other hand, slave morality is basically negative and claims to find values "out there," ordained by God. It is born out of resentment and identifies the "good" with such base sentiments as humility and pity. Instead of "bad," this morality uses the vindictive term "evil" to castigate all who would stand against it. Nietzsche claims that beginning with the Jews, and completed by the Christians, this slave morality had infected all of Europe with its life-denying poison. What is now needed is a "transvaluation of all values," which would move us "beyond good and evil."

In affirming the master morality, the creative genius must begin by proclaiming the death of God. With the death of God, slave morality—and all values dependent on God—collapses and the individual is free to create self-defined values. The brief selection here from *The Gay Science,* translated by Walter Kaufmann, is one of several passages in which Nietzsche announces the death of God.

Once freed from the constraints of slave morality and the external values imposed by God, the genius could become an *Übermensch* ("overman" or "superman"). Such an overman would be a this-world antithesis to God and would affirm life without any resentment. The overman would be to humans as humans are to apes. But, most importantly, the overman would be one who acknowledges and celebrates the will to power.

According to Nietzsche, all human behavior can be understood in terms of the will to power and every relationship between persons is a power relationship. In master morality the hero asserts the will to power by taking direct action. In slave morality, as explained in our final selection from Walter Kaufmann's translation of *The Anti-Christ,* the will to power is perverted into resentment in order to gain the imaginary powers of revenge and pity.

But the will to power can also be expressed *within* the person. That is, more than gaining power over others, the will to power can lead to power over the self. The overman will be the one who uses power in this way to "overcome his animal nature, organize the chaos of his passions, sublimate his impulses, and give style to his character,"* becoming completely free and self-created.

Ironically, despite his distaste for anti-Semitism and his emphasis on the *self-*overcoming aspects of the will to power, Nietzsche was hailed as a hero by the Nazis. They used his emphases on the master morality and the will to power as a justification for their atrocities. Nietzsche's sister, Elisabeth, married a German anti-Semite and in her old age eagerly received Adolph Hitler at the Nietzsche Archives. Yet despite its unfortunate association with the Nazis, Nietzsche's

---

*Walter Kaufmann, *Nietzsche: Philosopher, Psychologist, Antichrist* (Princeton, NJ: Princeton University Press, 1950), p. 316.

thought has continued to be influential as his insights have been developed by existentialists, phenomenologists, psychoanalysts, poststructuralists, and deconstructionists, as well as poets and novelists.

* * *

A representative sampling of Neitzsche's thought can be found in *The Portable Nietzsche,* edited by Walter A. Kaufmann (New York: Viking Press, 1968). The best general introduction to Nietzsche's thought remains Walter A. Kaufmann, *Nietzsche: Philosopher, Psychologist, Antichrist* (Princeton, NJ: Princeton University Press, 1968), while other helpful overviews include Arthur C. Danto, *Nietzsche as Philosopher* (New York: Macmillan, 1965); R.J. Hollingdale, *Nietzsche* (London: Routledge & Kegan Paul, 1973); Frederick Copleston, *Friedrich Nietzsche: Philosopher of Culture* (London: Burns and Oates, 1978); and Alexander Nehamas, *Nietzsche: Life as Literature* (Cambridge, MA: Harvard University Press, 1985). Ivo Frenzel, *Friedrich Nietzsche: An Illustrated Biography,* translated by Joachim Neugroschel (New York: Pegasus, 1967), and Sander L. Gilman, ed., *Conversations with Nietzsche: A Life in the Words of His Contemporaries,* translated by David J. Parent (New York: Oxford University Press, 1987), provide general biographies, while H.F. Peters, *Zarathustra's Sister: The Case of Elisabeth and Friedrich Nietzsche* (New York: Crown, 1977), presents a fascinating history of the expropriation of Nietzsche's thought in the service of German anti-Semitism. Walter A. Kaufmann, *Nietzsche, Heidegger, and Buber* (New York: McGraw-Hill, 1980); Allan Megill, *Prophets of Extremity: Nietzsche, Heidegger, Foucault, Derrida* (Berkeley: University of California Press, 1985); and William Lloyd Newell, *The Secular Magi: Marx, Freud, and Nietzsche on Religion* (New York: Pilgrim Press, 1986), show the connections between Nietzsche and other important thinkers. For collections of critical essays, see Robert C. Solomon, ed., *Nietzsche: A Collection of Critical Essays* (Garden City, NY: Anchor Doubleday, 1973), and Harold Bloom, ed., *Friedrich Nietzsche* (New York: Chelsea House Publishers, 1987). Finally, Robert C. Solomon and Kathleen M. Higgins, eds., *Reading Nietzsche* (New York: Oxford University Press, 1988), provide helpful introductory essays on several of Nietzsche's works.

THE BIRTH OF TRAGEDY (in part)

I

Much will have been gained for esthetics once we have succeeded in apprehending directly—rather than merely *ascertaining*—that art owes its continuous evolution to the Apollonian-Dionysiac duality, even as the propagation of the species depends on

The Birth of Tragedy, translated by Francis Golffing from *The Birth of Tragedy and The Genealogy of Morals,* by Friedrich Nietzsche. Copyright © 1956 by Doubleday, a division of Bantam Doubleday Dell Publishing Group, Inc. Used by permission of Doubleday, a division of Bantam Doubleday Dell Publishing Group, Inc.

the duality of the sexes, their constant conflicts and periodic acts of reconciliation. I have borrowed my adjectives from the Greeks, who developed their mystical doctrines of art through plausible *embodiments,* not through purely conceptual means. It is by those two art-sponsoring deities, Apollo and Dionysos, that we are made to recognize the tremendous split, as regards both origins and objectives, between the plastic, Apollonian arts and the non-visual art of music inspired by Dionysos. The two creative tendencies developed alongside one another, usually in fierce opposition, each by its taunts forcing the other to more energetic production, both perpetuating in a discordant concord that agon which the term art but feebly denominates: until at last, by the thaumaturgy of an Hellenic act of will, the pair accepted the yoke of marriage and, in this condition, begot Attic tragedy, which exhibits the salient features of both parents.

To reach a closer understanding of both these tendencies, let us begin by viewing them as the separate art realms of *dream* and *intoxication,* two physiological phenomena standing toward one another in much the same relationship as the Apollonian and Dionysiac. It was in a dream, according to Lucretius, that the marvelous gods and goddesses first presented themselves to the minds of men. That great sculptor, Phidias, beheld in a dream the entrancing bodies of more-than-human beings, and likewise, if anyone had asked the Greek poets about the mystery of poetic creation, they too would have referred him to dreams and instructed him much as Hans Sachs instructs us in *Die Meistersinger:*

> My friend, it is the poet's work
> Dreams to interpret and to mark.
> Believe me that man's true conceit
> In a dream becomes complete:
> All poetry we ever read
> Is but true dreams interpreted.

The fair illusion of the dream sphere, in the production of which every man proves himself an accomplished artist, is a precondition not only of all plastic art, but even, as we shall see presently, of a wide range of poetry. Here we enjoy an immediate apprehension of form, all shapes speak to us directly, nothing seems indifferent or redundant. Despite the high intensity with which these dream realities exist for us, we still have a residual sensation that they are illusions; at least such has been my experience—and the frequency, not to say normality, of the experience is borne out in many passages of the poets. Men of philosophical disposition are known for their constant premonition that our everyday reality, too, is an illusion, hiding another, totally different kind of reality. It was Schopenhauer who considered the ability to view at certain times all men and things as mere phantoms or dream images to be the true mark of philosophic talent. The person who is responsive to the stimuli of art behaves toward the reality of dream much the way the philosopher behaves toward the reality of existence: he observes exactly and enjoys his observations, for it is by these images that he interprets life, by these processes that he rehearses it. Nor is it by pleasant images only that such plausible connections are made: the whole divine comedy of life, including its somber aspects, its sudden balkings, impish accidents, anxious expectations, moves past him, not quite like a shadow play—for it is he himself, after all, who lives and suffers through these scenes—yet never without giving a fleeting sense of illusion; and I imagine that many persons have reassured themselves amidst the perils of dream by calling out, "It is a dream! I want it to go on." I have even heard of people spinning out the causality of one and the same dream over three or more successive nights. All these facts clearly bear witness that our innermost being, the common substratum of humanity, experiences dreams with deep delight and a sense of real necessity. This deep and happy sense of the necessity of dream experiences was expressed by the Greeks in the image of Apollo. Apollo is at once the god of all plastic powers and the soothsaying god. He who is etymologically the "lucent" one, the god of light, reigns also over the fair illusion of our inner world of fantasy. The perfection of these conditions in contrast to our imperfectly understood waking reality, as well as our profound awareness of nature's healing powers during the interval of sleep and dream, furnishes a symbolic analogue to the soothsaying faculty and quite generally to the arts, which make life possible and worth living. But the image of Apollo must incorporate that thin line which the dream image may not cross, under penalty of becoming pathological, of imposing itself on us as crass reality: a discreet limitation, a freedom from all extravagant urges, the sapient tranquillity of the plastic god. His eye must be sunlike, in keeping with his origin. Even at those moments when he is angry and ill-tempered there lies upon him the consecration of fair illusion. In an eccentric way one might say of Apollo what Schopenhauer says, in the first part of *The World as Will and Idea,* of man caught in the veil of Maya: "Even as on an immense, raging sea, assailed by huge wave crests, a man sits in a little rowboat trusting his frail craft, so, amidst the furious torments of this world, the individual sits tranquilly, supported by the *principium individuationis* and relying on it." One might say that the unshakable confidence in that principle has received its most magnificent expression in Apollo, and that Apollo himself may be regarded as the marvelous divine image of the *principium individuationis,* whose looks and gestures radiate the full delight, wisdom, and beauty of "illusion."

In the same context Schopenhauer has described for us the tremendous awe which seizes man when he suddenly begins to doubt the cognitive modes of experience, in other words, when in a given instance the law of causation seems to suspend itself. If we add to this awe the glorious transport which arises in man, even from the very depths of nature, at the shattering of the *principium individuationis,* then we are in a position to apprehend the essence of Dionysiac rapture, whose closest analogy is furnished by physical intoxication. Dionysiac stirrings arise either through the influence of those narcotic potions of which all primitive races speak in their hymns, or through the powerful approach of spring, which penetrates with joy the whole frame of nature. So stirred, the individual forgets himself completely. It is the Same Dionysiac power which in medieval Germany drove ever increasing crowds of people singing and dancing from place to place; we recognize in these St. John's and St. Vitus' dancers the bacchic choruses of the Greeks, who had their precursors in Asia Minor and as far back as Babylon and the orgiastic Sacaea. There are people who, either from lack of experience or out of sheer stupidity, turn away from such phenomena, and, strong in the sense of their own sanity, label them either mockingly or pityingly "endemic diseases." These benighted souls have no idea how cadaverous and ghostly their "sanity" appears as the intense throng of Dionysiac revelers sweeps past them.

Not only does the bond between man and man come to be forged once more by the magic of the Dionysiac rite, but nature itself, long alienated or subjugated, rises again to celebrate the reconciliation with her prodigal son, man. The earth offers its gifts voluntarily, and the savage beasts of mountain and desert approach in peace. The chariot of Dionysos is bedecked with flowers and garlands; panthers and tigers stride beneath his yoke. If one were to convert Beethoven's "Paean to Joy" into a painting, and refuse to curb the imagination when that multitude prostrates itself reverently in the dust, one might form some apprehension of Dionysiac ritual. Now the slave emerges as

Starry Night, 1889, by Vincent Van Gogh (1853–1890). It is hard not to think of the paintings of Nietzsche's contemporary Vincent Van Gogh when reading Nietzsche's words: "If one were to convert Beethoven's 'Paean to Joy' into a painting, and refuse to curb the imagination when that multitude prostrates itself reverently in the dust, one might form some apprehension of Dionysiac ritual." *(Museum of Modern Art, New York)*

a freeman; all the rigid, hostile walls which either necessity or despotism has erected between men are shattered. Now that the gospel of universal harmony is sounded, each individual becomes not only reconciled to his fellow but actually at one with him—as though the veil of Maya had been torn apart and there remained only shreds floating before the vision of mystical Oneness. Man now expresses himself through song and dance as the member of a higher community; he has forgotten how to walk, how to speak, and is on the brink of taking wing as he dances. Each of his gestures betokens enchantment; through him sounds a supernatural power, the same power which makes the animals speak and the earth render up milk and honey. He feels himself to be godlike and strides with the same elation and ecstasy as the gods he has seen in his dreams. No longer the *artist,* he has himself become a *work of art:* the productive power of the whole universe is now manifest in his transport, to the glorious satisfaction of the primordial One. The finest clay, the most precious marble—man—is here kneaded and hewn, and the chisel blows of the Dionysiac world artist are accompanied by the cry of the Eleusinian mystagogues: "Do you fall on your knees, multitudes, do you divine your creator?"

II

So far we have examined the Apollonian and Dionysiac states as the product of formative forces arising directly from nature without the mediation of the human artist. At this stage artistic urges are satisfied directly, on the one hand through the imagery of dreams, whose perfection is quite independent of the intellectual rank, the artistic development of the individual; on the other hand, through an ecstatic reality which once again takes no account of the individual and may even destroy him, or else redeem him through a mystical experience of the collective. In relation to these immediate creative conditions of nature every artist must appear as "imitator," either as the Apollonian dream artist or the Dionysiac ecstatic artist, or, finally (as in Greek tragedy, for example) as dream and ecstatic artist in one. We might picture to ourselves how the last of these, in a state of Dionysiac intoxication and mystical self-abrogation, wandering apart from the reveling throng, sinks upon the ground, and how there is then revealed to him his own condition—complete oneness with the essence of the universe—in a dream similitude.

Having set down these general premises and distinctions, we now turn to the Greeks in order to realize to what degree the formative forces of nature were developed in them. Such an inquiry will enable us to assess properly the relation of the Greek artist to his prototypes or, to use Aristotle's expression, his "imitation of nature." Of the dreams the Greeks dreamed it is not possible to speak with any certainty, despite the extant dream literature and the large number of dream anecdotes. But considering the incredible accuracy of their eyes, their keen and unabashed delight in colors, one can hardly be wrong in assuming that their dreams too showed a strict consequence of lines and contours, hues and groupings, a progression of scenes similar to their best bas-reliefs. The perfection of these dream scenes might almost tempt us to consider the dreaming Greek as a Homer and Homer as a dreaming Greek; which would be as though the modern man were to compare himself in his dreaming to Shakespeare.

Yet there is another point about which we do not have to conjecture at all: I mean the profound gap separating the Dionysiac Greeks from the Dionysiac barbarians. Throughout the range of ancient civilization (leaving the newer civilizations out of account for the moment) we find evidence of Dionysiac celebrations which stand to the Greek type in much the same relation as the bearded satyr, whose name and attributes are derived from the he-goat, stands to the god Dionysos. The central concern of such celebrations was, almost universally, a complete sexual promiscuity overriding every form of established tribal law; all the savage urges of the mind were unleashed on those occasions until they reached that paroxysm of lust and cruelty which has always struck me as the "witches' cauldron" *par excellence*. It would appear that the Greeks were for a while quite immune from these feverish excesses which must have reached them by every known land or sea route. What kept Greece safe was the proud, imposing image of Apollo, who in holding up the head of the Gorgon to those brutal and grotesque Dionysiac forces subdued them. Doric art has immortalized Apollo's majestic rejection of all license. But resistance became difficult, even impossible, as soon as similar urges began to break forth from the deep substratum of Hellenism itself. Soon the function of the Delphic god developed into something quite different and much more limited: all he could hope to accomplish now was to wrest the destructive weapon, by a timely gesture of pacification, from his opponent's hand. That act of pacification represents the most important event in the history of Greek ritual; every department of life now shows symptoms of a revolutionary change. The two great antagonists have been reconciled.

Each feels obliged henceforth to keep to his bounds, each will honor the other by the bestowal of periodic gifts, while the cleavage remains fundamentally the same. And yet, if we examine what happened to the Dionysiac powers under the pressure of that treaty we notice a great difference: in the place of the Babylonian Sacaea, with their throwback of men to the condition of apes and tigers, we now see entirely new rites celebrated: rites of universal redemption, of glorious transfiguration. Only now has it become possible to speak of nature's celebrating an aesthetic triumph; only now has the abrogation of the principium individuationis become an aesthetic event. That terrible witches' brew concocted of lust and cruelty has lost all power under the new conditions. Yet the peculiar blending of emotions in the heart of the Dionysiac reveler—his ambiguity if you will—seems still to hark back (as the medicinal drug harks back to the deadly poison) to the days when the infliction of pain was experienced as joy while a sense of supreme triumph elicited cries of anguish from the heart. For now in every exuberant joy there is heard an undertone of terror, or else a wistful lament over an irrecoverable loss. It is as though in these Greek festivals a sentimental trait of nature were coming to the fore, as though nature were bemoaning the fact of her fragmentation, her decomposition into separate individuals. The chants and gestures of these revelers, so ambiguous in their motivation, represented an absolute *novum* in the world of the Homeric Greeks; their Dionysiac music, in especial, spread abroad terror and a deep shudder. It is true: music had long been familiar to the Greeks as an Apollonian art, as a regular beat like that of waves lapping the shore, a plastic rhythm expressly developed for the portrayal of Apollonian conditions. Apollo's music was a Doric architecture of sound—of barely hinted sounds such as are proper to the cithara. Those very elements which characterize Dionysiac music and, after it, music quite generally: the heart-shaking power of tone, the uniform stream of melody, the incomparable resources of harmony—all those elements had been carefully kept at a distance as being inconsonant with the Apollonian norm. In the Dionysiac dithyramb man is incited to strain his symbolic faculties to the utmost; something quite unheard of is now clamoring to be heard: the desire to tear asunder the veil of Maya, to sink back into the original oneness of nature; the desire to express the very essence of nature symbolically. Thus an entirely new set of symbols springs into being. First all the symbols pertaining to physical features: mouth, face, the spoken word, the dance movement which coordinates the limbs and bends them to its rhythm. Then suddenly all the rest of the symbolic forces—music and rhythm as such, dynamics, harmony—assert themselves with great energy. In order to comprehend this total emancipation of all the symbolic powers one must have reached the same measure of inner freedom those powers themselves were making manifest; which is to say that the votary of Dionysos could not be understood except by his own kind. It is not difficult to imagine the awed surprise with which the Apollonian Greek must have looked on him. And that surprise would be further increased as the latter realized, with a shudder, that all this was not so alien to him after all, that his Apollonian consciousness was but a thin veil hiding from him the whole Dionysiac realm.

III

In order to comprehend this we must take down the elaborate edifice of Apollonian culture stone by stone until we discover its foundations. At first the eye is struck by the marvelous shapes of the Olympian gods who stand upon its pediments, and whose exploits, in shining bas-relief, adorn its friezes. The fact that among them we find Apollo as one god among many, making no claim to a privileged position, should not mislead us. The same drive that found its most complete representation in Apollo generated the whole Olympian world, and in this sense we may consider Apollo the father of that world. But what was the radical need out of which that illustrious society of Olympian beings sprang?

Whoever approaches the Olympians with a different religion in his heart, seeking moral elevation, sanctity, spirituality, loving-kindness, will presently be forced to turn away from them in ill-humored disappointment. Nothing in these deities reminds us of asceticism, high intellect, or duty: we are confronted by luxuriant, triumphant *existence,* which deifies the good and the bad indifferently. And the beholder may find himself dismayed in the presence of such overflowing life and ask himself what potion these heady people must have drunk in order to behold, in whatever direction they looked, Helen laughing back at them, the beguiling image of their own existence. But we shall call out to this beholder, who has already turned his back: Don't go! Listen first to what the Greeks themselves have to say of this life, which spreads itself before you with such puzzling serenity. An old legend has it that King Midas hunted a long time in the woods for the wise Silenus, companion of Dionysos, without being able to catch him. When he had finally caught him the king asked him what he considered man's greatest good. The daemon remained sullen and uncommunicative until finally, forced by the king, he broke into a shrill laugh and spoke: "Ephemeral wretch, begotten by accident and toil, why do you force me to tell you what it would be your greatest boon not to hear? What would be best for you is quite beyond your reach: not to have been born, not to be, to be *nothing.* But the second best is to die soon."

What is the relation of the Olympian gods to this popular wisdom? It is that of the entranced vision of the martyr to his torment.

Now the Olympian magic mountain opens itself before us, showing us its very roots. The Greeks were keenly aware of the terrors and horrors of existence; in order to be able to live at all they had to place before them the shining fantasy of the Olympians. Their tremendous distrust of the titanic forces of nature: *Moira,* mercilessly enthroned beyond the knowable world; the vulture which fed upon the great philanthropist Prometheus; the terrible lot drawn by wise Oedipus; the curse on the house of Atreus which brought Orestes to the murder of his mother: that whole Panic philosophy, in short, with its mythic examples, by which the gloomy Etruscans perished, the Greeks conquered—or at least hid from view—again and again by means of this artificial Olympus. In order to live at all the Greeks had to construct these deities. The Apollonian need for beauty had to develop the Olympian hierarchy of joy by slow degrees from the original titanic hierarchy of terror, as roses are seen to break from a thorny thicket. How else could life have been borne by a race so hypersensitive, so emotionally intense, so equipped for suffering? The same drive which called art into being as a completion and consummation of existence, and as a guarantee of further existence, gave rise also to that Olympian realm which acted as a transfiguring mirror to the Hellenic will. The gods justified human life by living it themselves—the only satisfactory theodicy ever invented. To exist in the clear sunlight of such deities was now felt to be the highest good, and the only real grief suffered by Homeric man was inspired by the thought of leaving that sunlight, especially when the departure seemed imminent. Now it became possible to stand the wisdom of Silenus on its head and proclaim that it was the worst evil for man to die soon, and second worst for him to die at all. Such laments as arise now arise over short-lived Achilles, over the generations ephemeral as leaves, the decline of the heroic age. It is not unbecoming to even the greatest hero to yearn for an afterlife, though it be as a day laborer. So impetuously, during the Apollonian phase, does man's will desire to remain on earth, so identified does he become with existence, that even his lament turns to a song of praise.

It should have become apparent by now that the harmony with nature which we late-comers regard with such nostalgia, and for which Schiller has coined the cant term naive, is by no means a simple and inevitable condition to be found at the gateway to every culture, a kind of paradise. Such a belief could have been endorsed only by a period for which Rousseau's Emile was an artist and Homer just such an artist nurtured in the bosom of nature. Whenever we encounter "naïveté" in art, we are face to face with the ripest fruit of Apollonian culture—which must always triumph first over titans, kill monsters, and overcome the somber contemplation of actuality, the intense susceptibility to suffering, by means of illusions strenuously and zestfully entertained. But how rare are the instances of true naïveté, of that complete identification with the beauty of appearance! It is this achievement which makes Homer so magnificent—Homer, who, as a single individual, stood to Apollonian popular culture in the same relation as the individual dream artist to the oneiric capacity of a race and of nature generally. The naïveté of Homer must be viewed as a complete victory of Apollonian illusion. Nature often uses illusions of this sort in order to accomplish its secret purposes. The true goal is covered over by a phantasm. We stretch out our hands to the latter, while nature, aided by our deception, attains the former. In the case of the Greeks it was the will wishing to behold itself in the work of art, in the transcendence of genius; but in order so to behold itself its creatures had first to view themselves as glorious, to transpose themselves to a higher sphere, without having that sphere of pure contemplation either challenge them or upbraid them with insufficiency. It was in that sphere of beauty that the Greeks saw the Olympians as their mirror images; it was by means of that aesthetic mirror that the Greek will opposed suffering and the somber wisdom of suffering which always accompanies artistic talent. As a monument to its victory stands Homer, the naive artist.

*   *   *

XV

. . . The influence of Socrates (like a shadow cast by the evening sun, ever lengthening into the future) has prompted generation after generation to reconsider the foundations of its art—art taken in its deepest and broadest sense—and as that influence is eternal it also guarantees the eternity of artistic endeavor. But before people were able to realize that all art is intimately dependent on the Greeks from Homer to Socrates, they had necessarily toward the Greeks the same attitude that the Athenians had toward Socrates. Practically every era of Western civilization has at one time or another tried to liberate itself from the Greeks, in deep dissatisfaction because whatever they themselves achieved, seemingly quite original and sincerely admired, lost color and life when held against the Greek model and shrank to a botched copy, a caricature. Time and again a hearty anger has been felt against that presumptuous little nation which had the nerve to brand, for all time, whatever was not created on its own soil as "barbaric." Who are these people, whose historical splendor was ephemeral, their institutions ridiculously narrow, their mores dubious and sometimes objectionable, who yet pretend to the special place among the nations which genius claims among the crowd? None of the later detractors was fortunate enough to find the cup of hemlock with which such a being could be disposed of once and for all: all the poisons of envy, slander, and rage have proved insufficient to destroy that complacent magnificence. And so people have continued to be both ashamed and fearful of the Greeks—though now and again someone has come along who has acknowledged the full truth: that the Greeks are the chariot drivers of every subsequent culture, but that, almost always, chariot and horses are of too poor a quality for the drivers, who then make sport of driving the chariot into the abyss—which they themselves clear with the bold leap of Achilles.

In order to see Socrates as one of these charioteers, it is necessary only to view him as the prototype of an entirely new mode of existence. He is the great exemplar of that theoretical man whose significance and aims we must now attempt to understand. Like the artist, *theoretical* man takes infinite pleasure in all that exists and is thus saved from the practical ethics of pessimism, with its lynx eyes that shine only in the dark. But while the artist, having unveiled the truth garment by garment, remains with his gaze fixed on what is still hidden, theoretical man takes delight in the cast garments and finds his highest satisfaction in the unveiling process itself, which proves to him his own power. Science could not have developed as it has done if its sole concern had been that one naked goddess. For then the adepts of science would have felt like people trying to dig a hole through the earth, each of whom soon realizes that though he toil in lifelong labor he will excavate only an infinitesimal fraction of the great distance and that even this fraction will be covered over before his eyes by another's efforts, so that a third man would do well to find a new spot for his tunneling. Moreover, once it has been proved beyond question that the Antipodes can never be reached by such a direct method, what person in his right mind would want to go on digging—unless it were for the accidental benefit of striking some precious metal or hitting upon a law of nature? For this reason Lessing, most honest of theoretical men, dared to say that the search for truth was more important to him than truth itself and thereby revealed the innermost secret of inquiry, to the surprise and annoyance of his fellows. Yet, sure enough, alongside sporadic perceptions such as this one of Lessing's, which represented an act of honesty as well as high-spirited defiance, we find a type of deep-seated illusion, first manifested in Socrates: the illusion that thought, guided by the thread of causation, might plumb the farthest abysses of being and even *correct* it. This grand metaphysical illusion has become integral to the scientific endeavor and again and again leads science to those far limits of its inquiry where it becomes art—*which, in this mechanism, is what is really intended.*

If we examine Socrates in the light of this idea, he strikes us as the first who was able not only to live under the guidance of that instinctive scientific certainty but to die by it, which is much more difficult. For this reason the image of the dying Socrates—mortal man freed by knowledge and argument from the fear of death—is the emblem which, hanging above the portal of every science, reminds the adept that his mission is to make existence appear intelligible and thereby justified. If arguments prove insufficient, the element of myth may be used to strengthen them—that myth which I have described as the necessary consequence, and ultimate intention, of all science.

Once we have fully realized how, after Socrates, the mystagogue of science, one school of philosophers after another came upon the scene and departed; how generation after generation of inquirers, spurred by an insatiable thirst for knowledge, explored every aspect of the universe; and how by that ecumenical concern a common net of knowledge was spread over the whole globe, affording glimpses into the workings of an entire solar system—once we have realized all this, and the monumental pyramid of present-day knowledge, we cannot help viewing Socrates as the vortex and turning point of Western civilization. For if we imagine that immense store of energy used, not for the purposes of knowledge, but for the practical, egotistical ends of individuals and nations, we may readily see the consequence: universal wars of extermination and constant migrations of peoples would have weakened man's instinctive zest for life to such an extent that, suicide having become a matter of course, duty might have commanded the son to kill his parents, the friend his friend, as among the Fiji islanders. We know that such wholesale slaughter prevails wherever art in some form or other—especially as religion or science—has not served as antidote to barbarism.

As against this practical pessimism, Socrates represents the archetype of the theoretical optimist, who, strong in the belief that nature can be fathomed, considers knowledge to be the true panacea and error to be radical evil. To Socratic man the one noble and truly human occupation was that of laying bare the workings of nature, of separating true knowledge from illusion and error. So it happened that ever since Socrates the mechanism of concepts, judgments, and syllogisms has come to be regarded as the highest exercise of man's powers, nature's most admirable gift. Socrates and his successors, down to our own day, have considered all moral and sentimental accomplishments—noble deeds, compassion, self-sacrifice, heroism, even that spiritual calm, so difficult of attainment, which the Apollonian Greek called *sophrosyne*—to be ultimately derived from the dialectic of knowledge, and therefore teachable. Whoever has tasted the delight of a Socratic perception, experienced how it moves to encompass the whole world of phenomena in ever widening circles, knows no sharper incentive to life than his desire to complete the conquest, to weave the net absolutely tight. To such a person the Platonic Socrates appears as the teacher of an entirely new form of "Greek serenity" and affirmation. This positive attitude toward existence must release itself in actions for the most part pedagogic, exercised upon noble youths, to the end of producing genius. But science, spurred on by its energetic notions, approaches irresistibly those outer limits where the optimism implicit in logic must collapse. For the periphery of science has an infinite number of points. Every noble and gifted man has, before reaching the midpoint of his career, come up against some point of the periphery that defied his understanding, quite apart from the fact that we have no way of knowing how the area of the circle is ever to be fully charted. When the inquirer, having pushed to the circumference, realizes how logic in that place curls about itself and bites its own tail, he is struck with a new kind of perception: a tragic perception, which requires, to make it tolerable, the remedy of art.

If we look about us today, with eyes refreshed and fortified by the spectacle of the Greeks, we shall see how the insatiable zest for knowledge, prefigured in Socrates, has been transformed into tragic resignation and the need for art; while, to be sure, on a lower level that same zest appears as hostile to all art and especially to the truly tragic, Dionysiac art, as I have tried to show paradigmatically in the subversion of Aeschylean art by Socratism.

At this point we find ourselves, not without trepidation, knocking at the gates of present and future. Will this dialectic inversion lead to ever new configurations of genius, above all to that of Socrates as the practitioner of music? Will the all-encompassing net of art (whether under the name of religion or science) be woven ever more tightly and delicately? Or will it be torn to shreds by the restless and barbaric activities of our present day? Deeply concerned, yet not unhopeful, we stand aside for a little while as spectators privileged to witness these tremendous struggles and transitions. Alas, it is the spell inherent in such battles that he who watches them must also fight them.

*   *   *

XXV

Music and tragic myth are equally expressive of the Dionysiac talent of a nation and cannot be divorced from one another. Both have their origin in a realm of art which lies beyond the Apollonian; both shed their transfiguring light on a region in whose rapt harmony dissonance and the horror of existence fade away in enchantment. Confident of their supreme powers, they both toy with the sting of displeasure, and by their toying they both justify the existence of even the "worst possible world." Thus the Dionysiac element, as against the Apollonian, proves itself to be the eternal and original power of art, since it calls into being the entire world of phenomena. Yet in the midst of that world a new transfiguring light is needed to catch and hold in life the stream of individual forms. If we could imagine an incarnation of dissonance—and what is man if not that?—that dissonance, in order to endure life, would need a marvelous illusion to cover it with a veil of beauty. This is the proper artistic intention of Apollo, in whose name are gathered together all those countless illusions of fair semblance which at any moment make life worth living and whet our appetite for the next moment.

But only so much of the Dionysiac substratum of the universe may enter an individual consciousness as can be dealt with by that Apollonian transfiguration; so that these two prime agencies must develop in strict proportion, conformable to the laws of eternal justice. Whenever the Dionysiac forces become too obstreperous, as is the case today, we are safe in assuming that Apollo is close at hand, though wrapped in a cloud, and that the rich effects of his beauty will be witnessed by a later generation.

The reader may intuit these effects if he has ever, though only in a dream, been carried back to the ancient Hellenic way of life. Walking beneath high Ionic peristyles, looking toward a horizon defined by pure and noble lines, seeing on either hand the glorified reflections of his shape in gleaming marble and all about him men moving solemnly or delicately, with harmonious sounds and rhythmic gestures: would he not then, overwhelmed by this steady stream of beauty, be forced to raise his hands to Apollo and call out: "Blessed Greeks! how great must be your Dionysos, if the Delic god thinks such enchantments necessary to cure you of your dithyrambic madness!" To one so moved, an ancient Athenian with the august countenance of Aeschylus might reply: "But you should add, extraordinary stranger, what suffering must this race have endured in order to achieve such beauty! Now come with me to the tragedy and let us sacrifice in the temple of both gods."

THE GENEALOGY OF MORALS (in part)

"GOOD AND EVIL," "GOOD AND BAD"

I

The English psychologists to whom we owe the only attempts that have thus far been made to write a genealogy of morals are no mean posers of riddles, but the riddles they pose are themselves, and being incarnate have one advantage over their books—they are interesting. What are these English psychologists really after? One finds them always, whether intentionally or not, engaged in the same task of pushing into the foreground the nasty part of the psyche, looking for the effective motive forces of human development in the very last place we would wish to have them found, e.g., in the inertia of habit, in forgetfulness, in the blind and fortuitous association of ideas: always in something that is purely passive, automatic, reflexive, molecular, and, moreover, profoundly stupid. What drives these psychologists forever in the same direction? A secret, malicious desire to belittle humanity, which they do not acknowledge even to themselves? A pessimistic distrust, the suspiciousness of the soured idealist? Some petty resentment of Christianity (and Plato) which does not rise above the threshold of consciousness? Or could it be a prurient taste for whatever is embarrassing, painfully paradoxical, dubious and absurd in existence? Or is it, perhaps, a kind of stew—a little meanness, a little bitterness, a bit of anti-Christianity, a touch of prurience and desire for condiments? . . . But, again, people tell me that these men are simply dull old frogs who hop and creep in and around man as in their own element—as though man were a bog. However, I am reluctant to listen to this, in fact I refuse to believe it; and if I may express a wish where I cannot express a conviction, I do wish wholeheartedly that things may be otherwise with these men—that these microscopic examiners of the soul may be really courageous, magnanimous, and proud animals, who know how to contain their emotions and have trained themselves to subordinate all wishful thinking to the truth—any truth, even a homespun, severe, ugly, obnoxious, un-Christian, unmoral truth. For such truths do exist.

II

All honor to the beneficent spirits that may motivate these historians of ethics! One thing is certain, however, they have been quite deserted by the true spirit of history. They all, to a man, think unhistorically, as is the age-old custom among philosophers. The amateurishness of their procedure is made plain from the very beginning, when it is a question of explaining the provenance of the concept and judgment good. "Originally," they decree, "altruistic actions were praised and approved by their recipients, that is, by those to whom they were useful. Later on, the origin of that praise having been forgotten, such actions were felt to be good simply because it was the habit to

Genealogy of Morals, First Essay: "'Good and Evil,' 'Good and Bad'" (complete), translated by Francis Golffing from *The Birth of Tragedy and The Genealogy of Morals*, by Friedrich Nietzsche. Copyright © 1956 by Doubleday, a division of Bantam Doubleday Dell Publishing Group, Inc. Used by permission of Doubleday, a division of Bantam Doubleday Dell Publishing Group, Inc.

commend them." We notice at once that this first derivation has all the earmarks of the English psychologists' work. Here are the key ideas of utility, forgetfulness, habit, and, finally, error, seen as lying at the root of that value system which civilized man had hitherto regarded with pride as the prerogative of all men. This pride must now be humbled, these values devalued. Have the debunkers succeeded?

Now it is obvious to me, first of all, that their theory looks for the genesis of the concept *good* in the wrong place: the judgment *good* does not originate with those to whom the good has been done. Rather it was the "good" themselves, that is to say the noble, mighty, highly placed, and high-minded who decreed themselves and their actions to be good, i.e., belonging to the highest rank, in contradistinction to all that was base, low-minded and plebeian. It was only this *pathos of distance* that authorized them to create values and name them—what was utility to them? The notion of utility seems singularly inept to account for such a quick jetting forth of supreme value judgments. Here we come face to face with the exact opposite of that lukewarmness which every scheming prudence, every utilitarian calculus presupposes—and not for a time only, for the rare, exceptional hour, but permanently. The origin of the opposites *good* and *bad* is to be found in the pathos of nobility and distance, representing the dominant temper of a higher, ruling class in relation to a lower, dependent one. (The lordly right of bestowing names is such that one would almost be justified in seeing the origin of language itself as an expression of the rulers' power. They say, "This is that or that"; they seal off each thing and action with a sound and thereby take symbolic possession of it.) Such an origin would suggest that there is no *a priori* necessity for associating the word *good* with altruistic deeds, as those moral psychologists are fond of claiming. In fact, it is only after aristocratic values have begun to decline that the egotism-altruism dichotomy takes possession of the human conscience; to use my own terms, it is the herd instinct that now asserts itself. Yet it takes quite a while for this instinct to assume such sway that it can reduce all moral valuations to that dichotomy—as is currently happening throughout Europe, where the prejudice equating the terms *moral, altruistic,* and *disinterested* has assumed the obsessive force of an *idée fixe*.

III

Quite apart from the fact that this hypothesis about the origin of the value judgment *good* is historically untenable, its psychology is intrinsically unsound. Altruistic deeds were originally commended for their usefulness, but this original reason has now been forgotten—so the claim goes. How is such a forgetting conceivable? Has there ever been a point in history at which such deeds lost their usefulness? Quite the contrary, this usefulness has been apparent to every age, a thing that has been emphasized over and over again. Therefore, instead of being forgotten, it must have impressed itself on the consciousness with ever increasing clearness. The opposite theory is far more sensible, though this does not necessarily make it any the truer—the theory held by Herbert Spencer, for example, who considers the concept *good* qualitatively the same as the concepts *useful* or *practical;* so that in the judgments good and bad, humanity is said to have summed up and sanctioned precisely its unforgotten and unforgettable experiences of the *useful practical* and the *harmful impractical*. According to this theory, the *good* is that which all along has proved itself useful and which therefore may lay the highest claim to be considered valuable. As I have said, the derivation of this theory is suspect, but at least the explanation is self-consistent and psychologically tenable within its limits.

IV

The clue to the correct explanation was furnished me by the question "What does the etymology of the terms for good in various languages tell us?" I discovered that all these terms lead us back to the same conceptual transformation. The basic concept is always *noble* in the hierarchical, class sense, and from this has developed, by historical necessity, the concept good embracing nobility of mind, spiritual distinction. This development is strictly parallel to that other which eventually converted the notions common, *plebeian, base* into the notion *bad.** Here we have an important clue to the actual genealogy of morals; that it has not been hit upon earlier is due to the retarding influence which democratic prejudice has had upon all investigation of origins. This holds equally true with regard to the seemingly quite objective areas of natural science and physiology, though I cannot enlarge upon the question now. The amount of damage such prejudice is capable of doing in ethics and history, once it becomes inflamed with hatred, is clearly shown by the case of Buckle. Here we see the plebeian bias of the modern mind, which stems from England, erupt once again on its native soil with all the violence of a muddy volcano and all the vulgar and oversalted eloquence characteristic of volcanoes.

V

As for our own problem, which we may justly call a *quiet* one, addressing itself to a very restricted audience, it is of interest to note that many of the words and roots denominating *good* still, to this day, carry overtones of the meanings according to which the nobility regarded themselves as possessing the highest moral rank. It is true that, most often, they described themselves simply in terms of their superior power (as the rulers, lords, sovereigns) or else in terms of the visible signs of their superiority, as the rich, the possessors (this is the meaning of arya, and there are corresponding terms in the Iranian and Slavic languages); but also in terms of a typical character trait, and this is the case that concerns us here. They speak of themselves as "the truthful"; most resolute in doing this were members of the Greek aristocracy, whose mouthpiece is the Megarian poet Theognis. The word they used was *esthlos,* meaning one who *is,* who has true reality, who is true. By a subjective turn the true later became the *truthful.* During this phase the word provided the shibboleth of the nobility, describing the aristocrat, as Theognis saw and portrayed him, in distinction from the lying plebeian, until finally, after the decline of the aristocracy, the word came to stand for spiritual nobility, and ripened and sweetened. The words *kakos* and *deilos* (the plebeian, in contrast to the *agathos*) emphasize cowardice and provide a hint as to the direction in which we should look for the etymology of *agathos,* a word allowing of more than one interpretation. The Latin *malus* (beside which I place *melas*) might designate the common man as dark, especially black-haired ("hic niger est"), as the pre-Aryan settler of the Italian soil, notably distinguished from the new blond conqueror race by his color. At any rate, the Gaelic presented me with an exactly analogous case: *fin,* as in the name Fingal, the characteristic term for nobility, eventually the good, noble, pure, originally the fair-

---

*The most eloquent proof of this is the etymological relationship between the German words *schlecht* (bad) and *schlicht* (simple). For a long time the first term was used interchangeably with the second, without any contemptuous connotation as yet, merely to designate the commoner as opposed to the nobleman. About the time of the Thirty Years' War the meaning changed to the present one.

haired as opposed to the dark, black-haired native population. The Celts, by the way, were definitely a fair-haired race; and it is a mistake to try to relate the area of dark-haired people found on ethnographic maps of Germany to Celtic bloodlines, as Virchow does. These are the last vestiges of the pre-Aryan population of Germany. (The subject races are seen to prevail once more, throughout almost all of Europe: in color, shortness of skull, perhaps also in intellectual and social instincts. Who knows whether modern democracy, the even more fashionable anarchism, and especially that preference for the *commune,* the most primitive of all social forms, which is now shared by all European socialists—whether all these do not represent a throwback, and whether, even physiologically, the Aryan race of conquerors is not doomed?) The Latin *bonus* I venture to interpret as warrior; providing that I am justified in deriving *bonus* from an older *duonus* (c.f. *bellum* → *duellum* → *duen-lum,* which seems to preserve that *duonus*). *Bonus* would then spell the man of strife, of discord, the warrior: we can now form some idea of what, in ancient Rome, constituted a man's goodness. And might not our German *gut* signify *göttlich,* the man of divine race? And further be identical with the racial term, earlier also a term of rank, *Goth?* My arguments in support of this conjecture do not belong here.

VI

Granting that political supremacy always gives rise to notions of spiritual supremacy, it at first creates no difficulties (though difficulties might arise later) if the ruling caste is also the priestly caste and elects to characterize itself by a term which reminds us of its priestly function. In this context we encounter for the first time concepts of pure and *impure* opposing each other as signs of class, and here, too, *good* and *bad* as terms no longer referring to class, develop before long. The reader should be cautioned, however, against taking pure and impure in too large or profound or symbolic a sense: all the ideas of ancient man were understood in a sense much more crude, narrow, superficial and non-symbolic than we are able to imagine today. The pure man was originally one who washed himself, who refused to eat certain foods entailing skin diseases, who did not sleep with the unwashed plebeian women, who held blood in abomination—hardly more than that. At the same time, given the peculiar nature of a priestly aristocracy, it becomes clear why the value opposites would early turn inward and become dangerously exacerbated; and in fact the tension between such opposites has opened abysses between man and man, over which not even an Achilles of free thought would leap without a shudder. There is from the very start something unwholesome about such priestly aristocracies, about their way of life, which is turned away from action and swings between brooding and emotional explosions: a way of life which may be seen as responsible for the morbidity and neurasthenia of priests of all periods. Yet are we not right in maintaining that the cures which they have developed for their morbidities have proved a hundred times more dangerous than the ills themselves? Humanity is still suffering from the after-effects of those priestly cures. Think, for example, of certain forms of diet (abstinence from meat), fasting, sexual continence, escape "into the desert"; think further of the whole anti-sensual metaphysics of the priests, conducive to inertia and false refinement; of the self-hypnosis encouraged by the example of fakirs and Brahmans, where a glass knob and an *idée fixe* take the place of the god. And at last, supervening on all this, comes utter satiety, together with its radical remedy, nothingness—or God, for the desire for a mystical union with God is nothing other than the

Buddhist's desire to sink himself in nirvana. Among the priests everything becomes more dangerous, not cures and specifics alone but also arrogance, vindictiveness, acumen, profligacy, love, the desire for power, disease. In all fairness it should be added, however, that only on this soil, the precarious soil of priestly existence, has man been able to develop into an interesting creature; that only here has the human mind grown both profound and evil; and it is in these two respects, after all, that man has proved his superiority over the rest of creation.

VII

By now the reader will have got some notion how readily the priestly system of valuations can branch off from the aristocratic and develop into its opposite. An occasion for such a division is furnished whenever the priest caste and the warrior caste jealously clash with one another and find themselves unable to come to terms. The chivalrous and aristocratic valuations presuppose a strong physique, blooming, even exuberant health, together with all the conditions that guarantee its preservation: combat, adventure, the chase, the dance, war games, etc. The value system of the priestly aristocracy is founded on different presuppositions. So much the worse for them when it becomes a question of war! As we all know, priests are the most evil enemies to have—why should this be so? Because they are the most impotent. It is their impotence which makes their hate so violent and sinister, so cerebral and poisonous. The greatest haters in history— but also the most intelligent haters—have been priests. Beside the brilliance of priestly vengeance all other brilliance fades. Human history would be a dull and stupid thing without the intelligence furnished by its impotents. Let us begin with the most striking example. Whatever else has been done to damage the powerful and great of this earth seems trivial compared with what the Jews have done, that priestly people who succeeded in avenging themselves on their enemies and oppressors by radically inverting all their values, that is, by an act of the most spiritual vengeance. This was a strategy entirely appropriate to a priestly people in whom vindictiveness had gone most deeply underground. It was the Jew who, with frightening consistency, dared to invert the aristocratic value equations good/noble/powerful/beautiful/happy/favored-of-the-gods and maintain, with the furious hatred of the underprivileged and impotent, that "only the poor, the powerless, are good; only the suffering, sick, and ugly, truly blessed. But you noble and mighty ones of the earth will be, to all eternity, the evil, the cruel, the avaricious, the godless, and thus the cursed and damned!" . . . We know who has fallen heir to this Jewish inversion of values. . . . In reference to the grand and unspeakably disastrous initiative which the Jews have launched by this most radical of all declarations of war, I wish to repeat a statement I made in a different context *(Beyond Good and Evil)*, to wit, that it was the Jews who started the slave revolt in morals; a revolt with two millennia of history behind it, which we have lost sight of today simply because it has triumphed so completely.

VIII

You find that difficult to understand? You have no eyes for something that took two millennia to prevail? . . . There is nothing strange about this: all long developments are difficult to see in the round. From the tree trunk of Jewish vengeance and hatred—the deepest and sublimest hatred in human history, since it gave birth to ideals and a new set of values—grew a branch that was equally unique: a new love, the deepest and sublimest of loves. From what other trunk could this branch have sprung? But let no one surmise that this love represented a denial of the thirst for vengeance, that it contravened the Jewish hatred. Exactly the opposite is true. Love grew out of hatred as the tree's crown, spreading triumphantly in the purest sunlight, yet having, in its high and sunny realm, the same aims—victory, aggrandizement, temptation—which hatred pursued by digging its roots ever deeper into all that was profound and evil. Jesus of Nazareth, the gospel of love made flesh, the "redeemer," who brought blessing and victory to the poor, the sick, the sinners—what was he but temptation in its most sinister and irresistible form, bringing men by a roundabout way to precisely those Jewish values and renovations of the ideal? Has not Israel, precisely by the detour of this "redeemer," this seeming antagonist and destroyer of Israel, reached the final goal of its sublime vindictiveness? Was it not a necessary feature of a truly brilliant politics of vengeance, a farsighted, subterranean, slowly and carefully planned vengeance, that Israel had to deny its true instrument publicly and nail him to the cross like a mortal enemy, so that "the whole world" (meaning all the enemies of Israel) might naively swallow the bait? And could one, by straining every resource, hit upon a bait more dangerous than this? What could equal in debilitating narcotic power the symbol of the "holy cross," the ghastly paradox of a crucified god, the unspeakably cruel mystery of God's self-crucifixion for the benefit of mankind? One thing is certain, that in this sign Israel has by now triumphed over all other, nobler values.

IX

—"But what is all this talk about nobler values? Let us face facts: the people have triumphed—or the slaves, the mob, the herd, whatever you wish to call them—and if the Jews brought it about, then no nation ever had a more universal mission on this earth. The lords are a thing of the past, and the ethics of the common man is completely triumphant. I don't deny that this triumph might be looked upon as a kind of blood poisoning, since it has resulted in a mingling of the races, but there can be no doubt that the intoxication has succeeded. The 'redemption' of the human race (from the lords, that is) is well under way; everything is rapidly becoming Judaized, or Christianized, or mobized—the word makes no difference. The progress of this poison throughout the body of mankind cannot be stayed; as for its tempo, it can now afford to slow down, become finer, barely audible—there's all the time in the world. . . . Does the Church any longer have a necessary mission, or even a *raison d'être?* Or could it be done without? *Quaeritur.* It would almost seem that it retards rather than accelerates that progress. In which case we might consider it useful. But one thing is certain, it has gradually become something crude and lumpish, repugnant to a sensitive intelligence, a truly modern taste. Should it not, at least, be asked to refine itself a bit? . . . It alienates more people today than it seduces. . . . Who among us would be a freethinker, were it not for the Church? It is the Church which offends us, not its poison. . . . Apart from the Church we, too, like the poison. . . ." This was a "freethinker's" reaction to my argument—an honest fellow, as he has abundantly proved, and a democrat to boot. He had been listening to me until that moment, and could not stand to hear my silence. For I have a great deal to be silent about in this matter.

X

The slave revolt in morals begins by rancor turning creative and giving birth to values—the rancor of beings who, deprived of the direct outlet of action, compensate by an imaginary vengeance. All truly noble morality grows out of triumphant self-affirmation. Slave ethics, on the other hand, begins by saying no to an "outside," an "other," a non-self, and that no is its creative act. This reversal of direction of the evaluating look, this invariable looking outward instead of inward, is a fundamental feature of rancor. Slave ethics requires for its inception a sphere different from and hostile to its own. Physiologically speaking, it requires an outside stimulus in order to act at all; all its action is reaction. The opposite is true of aristocratic valuations: such values grow and act spontaneously, seeking out their contraries only in order to affirm themselves even more gratefully and delightedly. Here the negative concepts, *humble, base, bad,* are late, pallid counterparts of the positive, intense and passionate credo, "We noble, good, beautiful, happy ones." Aristocratic valuations may go amiss and do violence to reality, but this happens only with regard to spheres which they do not know well, or from the knowledge of which they austerely guard themselves: the aristocrat will, on occasion, misjudge a sphere which he holds in contempt, the sphere of the common man, the people. On the other hand we should remember that the emotion of contempt, of looking down, provided that it falsifies at all, is as nothing compared with the falsification which suppressed hatred, impotent vindictiveness, effects upon its opponent, though only in effigy. There is in all contempt too much casualness and nonchalance, too much blinking of facts and impatience, and too much inborn gaiety for it ever to make of its object a downright caricature and monster. Hear the almost benevolent nuances the Greek aristocracy, for example, puts into all its terms for the commoner; how emotions of compassion, consideration, indulgence, sugar-coat these words until, in the end, almost all terms referring to the common man survive as expressions for "unhappy," "pitiable" (cf. *deilos, deilaios, poneros, mochtheros,* the last two of which properly characterize the common man as a drudge and beast of burden); how, on the other hand, the words *bad, base, unhappy* have continued to strike a similar note for the Greek ear, with the timbre "unhappy" preponderating. The "wellborn" really felt that they were also the "happy." They did not have to construct their happiness factitiously by looking at their enemies, as all rancorous men are wont to do, and being fully active, energetic people they were incapable of divorcing happiness from action. They accounted activity a necessary part of happiness (which explains the origin of the phrase *eu prattein*).

All this stands in utter contrast to what is called happiness among the impotent and oppressed, who are full of bottled-up aggressions. Their happiness is purely passive and takes the form of drugged tranquillity, stretching and yawning, peace, "sabbath," emotional slackness. Whereas the noble lives before his own conscience with confidence and frankness (*gennaios* "nobly bred" emphasizes the nuance "truthful" and perhaps also "ingenuous"), the rancorous person is neither truthful nor ingenuous nor honest and forthright with himself. His soul squints; his mind loves hide-outs, secret paths, and back doors; everything that is hidden seems to him his own world, his security, his comfort; he is expert in silence, in long memory, in waiting, in provisional self-depreciation, and in self-humiliation. A race of such men will, in the end, inevitably be cleverer than a race of aristocrats, and it will honor sharp-wittedness to a much greater degree, i.e., as an absolutely vital condition for its existence. Among the noble, mental acuteness always tends slightly to suggest luxury and overrefinement.

The fact is that with them it is much less important than is the perfect functioning of the ruling, unconscious instincts or even a certain temerity to follow sudden impulses, court danger, or indulge spurts of violent rage, love, worship, gratitude, or vengeance. When a noble man feels resentment, it is absorbed in his instantaneous reaction and therefore does not poison him. Moreover, in countless cases where we might expect it, it never arises, while with weak and impotent people it occurs without fail. It is a sign of strong, rich temperaments that they cannot for long take seriously their enemies, their misfortunes, their *misdeeds;* for such characters have in them an excess of plastic curative power, and also a power of oblivion. (A good modern example of the latter is Mirabeau, who lacked all memory for insults and meannesses done him, and who was unable to forgive because he had forgotten.) Such a man simply shakes off vermin which would get beneath another's skin—and only here, if anywhere on earth, is it possible to speak of "loving one's enemy." The noble person will respect his enemy, and respect is already a bridge to love. . . . Indeed he requires his enemy for himself, as his mark of distinction, nor could he tolerate any other enemy than one in whom he finds nothing to despise and much to esteem. Imagine, on the other hand, the "enemy" as conceived by the rancorous man! For this is his true creative achievement: he has conceived the "evil enemy," the Evil One, as a fundamental idea, and then as a pendant he has conceived a Good One—himself.

XI

The exact opposite is true of the noble-minded, who spontaneously creates the notion *good,* and later derives from it the conception of the *bad.* How ill-matched these two concepts look, placed side by side: the bad of noble origin, and the *evil* that has risen out of the cauldron of unquenched hatred! The first is a by-product, a complementary color, almost an afterthought; the second is the beginning, the original creative act of slave ethics. But neither is the conception of good the same in both cases, as we soon find out when we ask ourselves who it is that is really evil according to the code of rancor. The answer is: precisely the good one of the opposite code, that is the noble, the powerful—only colored, reinterpreted, reenvisaged by the poisonous eye of resentment. And we are the first to admit that anyone who knew these "good" ones only as enemies would find them evil enemies indeed. For these same men who, amongst themselves, are so strictly constrained by custom, worship, ritual, gratitude, and by mutual surveillance and jealousy, who are so resourceful in consideration, tenderness, loyalty, pride and friendship, when once they step outside their circle become little better than uncaged beasts of prey. Once abroad in the wilderness, they revel in the freedom from social constraint and compensate for their long confinement in the quietude of their own community. They revert to the innocence of wild animals: we can imagine them returning from an orgy of murder, arson, rape, and torture, jubilant and at peace with themselves as though they had committed a fraternity prank—convinced, moreover, that the poets for a long time to come will have something to sing about and to praise. Deep within all these noble races there lurks the beast of prey, bent on spoil and conquest. This hidden urge has to be satisfied from time to time, the beast let loose in the wilderness. This goes as well for the Roman, Arabian, German, Japanese nobility as for the Homeric heroes and the Scandinavian vikings. The noble races have everywhere left in their wake the catchword "barbarian." And even their highest culture shows an awareness of this trait and a certain pride in it (as we see, for

example, in Pericles' famous funeral oration, when he tells the Athenians: "Our boldness has gained us access to every land and sea, and erected monuments to itself *for
both good and evil*.") This "boldness" of noble races, so headstrong, absurd, incalculable, sudden, improbable (Pericles commends the Athenians especially for their
rathumia), their utter indifference to safety and comfort, their terrible pleasure in destruction, their taste for cruelty —all these traits are embodied by their victims in the
image of the "barbarian," the "evil enemy," the Goth or the Vandal. The profound and
icy suspicion which the German arouses as soon as he assumes power (we see it happening again today) harks back to the persistent horror with which Europe for many
centuries witnessed the raging of the blond Teutonic beast (although all racial connection between the old Teutonic tribes and ourselves has been lost). I once drew attention to the embarrassment Hesiod must have felt when he tried to embody the cultural
epochs of mankind in the gold, silver, and iron ages. He could cope with the contradictions inherent in Homer's world, so marvelous on the one hand, so ghastly and brutal on the other, only by making two ages out of one and presenting them in temporal
sequence; first, the age of the heroes and demigods of Troy and Thebes, as that world
was still remembered by the noble tribes who traced their ancestry to it; and second,
the iron age, which presented the same world as seen by the descendants of those who
had been crushed, despoiled, brutalized, sold into slavery. If it were true, as passes
current nowadays, that the real meaning of culture resides in its power to domesticate
man's savage instincts, then we might be justified in viewing all those rancorous
machinations by which the noble tribes, and their ideals, have been laid low as the
true instruments of culture. But this would still not amount to saying that the *organiz-
ers* themselves represent culture. Rather, the exact opposite would be true, as is
vividly shown by the current state of affairs. These carriers of the leveling and re-
tributive instincts, these descendants of every European and extra-European slavedom,
and especially of the pre-Aryan populations, represent human retrogression most fla-
grantly. Such "instruments of culture" are a disgrace to man and might make one sus-
picious of culture altogether. One might be justified in fearing the wild beast lurking
within all noble races and in being on one's guard against it, but who would not a
thousand times prefer fear when it is accompanied with admiration to security accompanied by the loathsome sight of perversion, dwarfishness, degeneracy? And is not the
latter our predicament today? What accounts for our repugnance to man—for there is
no question that he makes us suffer? Certainly not our fear of him, rather the fact that
there is no longer anything to be feared from him; that the vermin "man" occupies the
entire stage; that, tame, hopelessly mediocre, and savorless, he considers himself the
apex of historical evolution; and not entirely without justice, since he is still somewhat
removed from the mass of sickly and effete creatures whom Europe is beginning to
stink of today.

XII

Here I want to give vent to a sigh and a last hope. Exactly what is it that I, especially,
find intolerable; that I am unable to cope with; that asphyxiates me? A bad smell. The
smell of failure, of a soul that has gone stale. God knows it is possible to endure all
kinds of misery—vile weather, sickness, trouble, isolation. All this can be coped with,
if one is born to a life of anonymity and battle. There will always be moments of re-
emergence into the light, when one tastes the golden hour of victory and once again

stands foursquare, unshakable, ready to face even harder things, like a bowstring drawn taut against new perils. But, you divine patronesses—if there are any such in the realm beyond good and evil—grant me now and again the sight of something perfect, wholly achieved, happy, magnificently triumphant, something still capable of inspiring fear! Of a man who will justify the existence of mankind, for whose sake one may continue to believe in mankind! . . . The leveling and diminution of European man is our greatest danger; because the sight of him makes us despond. . . . We no longer see anything these days that aspires to grow greater; instead, we have a suspicion that things will continue to go downhill, becoming ever thinner, more placid, smarter, cosier, more ordinary, more indifferent, more Chinese, more Christian—without doubt man is getting "better" all the time. . . . This is Europe's true predicament: together with the fear of man we have also lost the love of man, reverence for man, confidence in man, indeed the *will to man*. Now the sight of man makes us despond. What is nihilism today if not that?

XIII

But to return to business: our inquiry into the origins of that other notion of goodness, as conceived by the resentful, demands to be completed. There is nothing very odd about lambs disliking birds of prey, but this is no reason for holding it against large birds of prey that they carry off lambs. And when the lambs whisper among themselves, "These birds of prey are evil, and does not this give us a right to say that whatever is the opposite of a bird of prey must be good?" there is nothing intrinsically wrong with such an argument—though the birds of prey will look somewhat quizzically and say, "*We* have nothing against these good lambs; in fact, we love them; nothing tastes better than a tender lamb."—To expect that strength will not manifest itself as strength, as the desire to overcome, to appropriate, to have enemies, obstacles, and triumphs, is every bit as absurd as to expect that weakness will manifest itself as strength. A quantum of strength is equivalent to a quantum of urge, will, activity, and it is only the snare of language (of the arch-fallacies of reason petrified in language), presenting all activity as conditioned by an agent—the "subject"—that blinds us to this fact. For, just as popular superstition divorces the lightning from its brilliance, viewing the latter as an activity whose subject is the lightning, so does popular morality divorce strength from its manifestations, as though there were behind the strong a neutral agent, free to manifest its strength or contain it. But no such agent exists; there is no "being" behind the doing, acting, becoming; the "doer" has simply been added to the deed by the imagination—the doing is everything. The common man actually doubles the doing by making the lightning flash; he states the same event once as cause and then again as effect. The natural scientists are no better when they say that "energy *moves*," "energy *causes*." For all its detachment and freedom from emotion, our science is still the dupe of linguistic habits; it has never yet got rid of those changelings called "subjects." The atom is one such changeling, another is the Kantian "thing-in-itself." Small wonder, then, that the repressed and smoldering emotions of vengeance and hatred have taken advantage of this superstition and in fact espouse no belief more ardently than that it is within the discretion of the strong to be weak, of the bird of prey to be a lamb. Thus they assume the right of calling the bird of prey to account for being a bird of prey. We can hear the oppressed, downtrodden, violated whispering among themselves with the wily vengefulness of the impotent, "Let us be unlike those evil ones. Let us be good. And the good shall be he who does not do violence, does not attack or retaliate, who leaves vengeance to God, who, like us, lives hidden, who shuns all that is evil, and altogether asks very little of life—like us, the patient, the humble, the just ones." Read in cold blood, this means nothing more than "We weak ones are, in fact, weak. It is a good thing that we do nothing for which we are not strong enough." But this plain fact, this basic prudence, which even the insects have (who, in circumstances of great danger, sham death in order not to have to "do" too much) has tricked itself out in the garb of quiet, virtuous resignation, thanks to the duplicity of impotence—as though the weakness of the weak, which is after all his essence, his natural way of being, his sole and inevitable reality, were a spontaneous act, a meritorious deed. This sort of person requires the belief in a "free subject" able to choose indifferently, out of that instinct of self-preservation which notoriously justifies every kind of lie. It may well be that to this day the subject, or in popular language the soul, has been the most viable of all articles of faith simply because it makes it possible for the majority of mankind—i.e., the weak and oppressed of every sort—to practice the sublime sleight of hand which gives weakness the appearance of free choice and one's natural disposition the distinction of merit.

XIV

Would anyone care to learn something about the way in which ideals are manufactured? Does anyone have the nerve? . . . Well then, go ahead! There's a chink through which you can peek into this murky shop. But wait just a moment, Mr. Foolhardy; your eyes must grow accustomed to the fickle light. . . . All right, tell me what's going on in there, audacious fellow; now I am the one who is listening.

"I can't see a thing, but I hear all the more. There's a low, cautious whispering in every nook and corner. I have a notion these people are lying. All the sounds are sugary and soft. No doubt you were right; they are transmuting weakness into merit."

"Go on."

"Impotence, which cannot retaliate, into kindness; pusillanimity into humility; submission before those one hates into obedience to One of whom they say that he has commanded this submission—they call him God. The inoffensiveness of the weak, his cowardice, his ineluctable standing and waiting at doors, are being given honorific titles such as patience; to be *unable* to avenge oneself is called to be *unwilling* to avenge oneself—even forgiveness ("for they know not what *they* do—we alone know what *they* do.") Also there's some talk of loving one's enemy—accompanied by much sweat."

"Go on."

"I'm sure they are quite miserable, all these whisperers and smalltime counterfeiters, even though they huddle close together for warmth. But they tell me that this very misery is the sign of their election by God, that one beats the dogs one loves best, that this misery is perhaps also a preparation, a test, a kind of training, perhaps even more than that: something for which eventually they will be compensated with tremendous interest—in gold? No, in happiness. They call this *bliss*."

"Go on."

"Now they tell me that not only are they better than the mighty of this earth, whose spittle they must lick (not from fear—by no means—but because God commands us to honor our superiors), but they are even better off, or at least they will be better off someday. But I've had all I can stand. The smell is too much for me. This shop where they manufacture ideals seems to me to stink of lies."

"But just a moment. You haven't told me anything about the greatest feat of these black magicians, who precipitate the white milk of loving-kindness out of every kind of blackness. Haven't you noticed their most consummate sleight of hand, their boldest, finest, most brilliant trick? Just watch! These vermin, full of vindictive hatred, what are they brewing out of their own poisons? Have you ever heard vengeance and hatred mentioned? Would you ever guess, if you only listened to their words, that these are men bursting with hatred?"

"I see what you mean. I'll open my ears again—and stop my nose. Now I can make out what they seem to have been saying all along: 'We, the good ones, are also the just ones.' They call the thing they seek not retribution but the triumph of justice; the thing they hate is not their enemy, by no means—they hate injustice, ungodliness; the thing they hope for and believe in is not vengeance, the sweet exultation of vengeance ('sweeter than honey' as Homer said) but 'the triumph of God, who is just, over the godless'; what remains to them to love on this earth is not their brothers in hatred, but what they call their 'brothers in love'—all who are good and just."

"And what do they call that which comforts them in all their sufferings—their phantasmagoria of future bliss?"

"Do I hear correctly? They call it Judgment Day, the coming of *their* kingdom, the 'Kingdom of God.' Meanwhile they live in 'faith,' in 'love,' in 'hope.'"

"Stop! I've heard enough."

XV

Faith in what? Love for what? Hope of what? There can be no doubt that these weaklings, too, want a chance to be strong, to have *their* kingdom come. They call it simply the Kingdom of God—what admirable humility! But in order to have that experience one must live a very long time, beyond death; one must have eternal life to indemnify oneself for that terrestrial life of faith, love, and hope. Indemnify for what and by what means? . . . It seems to me that Dante committed a grave blunder when, with disconcerting naïveté, he put over the gate of hell the inscription: "Me, too, eternal love created." At any rate, the inscription over the gate of the Christian paradise, with its "eternal bliss," would read more fittingly, "Me, too, eternal hate created"—provided that it is fitting to place a truth above the gateway to a lie. For in what, precisely, does the bliss of that paradise consist?

We may have guessed by now, but still it is well to have the thing certified for us by a competent authority in these matters, Thomas Aquinas, the great teacher and saint. *Beati in regno coelesti,* he says, meek as a lamb, *videbunt poenas damnatorum, ut beatitudo illis magis complaceat.* Or, if the reader prefers, here is the same sentiment more forcefully expressed by a triumphant Father of the Church (Tertullian) who wishes to dissuade his Christians from the cruel debauch of public spectacles—on what grounds? "Our faith offers us so much more," he writes in *De spectaculis,* ch. 29 ff., "and something so much stronger. Having been redeemed, joys of quite a different kind are ours. We have martyrs instead of athletes. If we crave blood, we have the blood of Christ. . . . But think what awaits us on the day of his triumph!" And the rapt visionary continues: "Yes, and there are still to come other spectacles—that last, that eternal Day of Judgment, that Day which the Gentiles never believed would come, that Day they laughed at, when this old world and all its generations shall be consumed in one fire. How vast the spectacle that day, and how wide! What sight shall wake my wonder, what my laughter, my joy and exultation as I see all those kings, those great kings, welcomed (we are told) in heaven, along with Jove, along with those who told of their ascent, groaning in the depths of darkness! And the magistrates who persecuted the name of Jesus, liquefying in fiercer flames than they kindled in their rage against the Christians! Those sages, too, the philosophers blushing before their disciples as they blaze together, the disciples whom they taught that God was concerned with nothing, that men have no souls at all, or that what souls they have shall never return to their former bodies! And, then, the poets trembling before the judgment seat, not of Rhadamanthus, not of Minos, but of Christ, whom they never looked to see! And then there will be the tragic actors to be heard, more vocal in their own tragedy; and the players to be seen, lither of limb by far in the fire; and then the charioteer to watch, red all over in the wheel of flame, and, next, the athletes to be gazed upon, not in their gymnasiums but hurled in the fire—unless it be that not even then would I wish to see them, in my desire rather to turn an insatiable gaze on them who vented their rage and fury on the Lord. 'This is he,' I shall say, 'the son of the carpenter or the harlot *(Tertullian here mimics Jewish diatribe, as is shown by what immediately follows as well as by his term for the mother of Jesus, which occurs in the Talmud),* the Sabbath-breaker, the Samaritan, who had a devil. This is he whom you bought from Judas; this is he who was struck with reed and fist, defiled with spittle, given gall and vinegar to drink. This is he whom the disciples secretly stole away, that it might be said he had risen—unless it was the gardener who removed him, lest his lettuces should be trampled by the throng of visitors!' Such sights, such exultation—what praetor, consul, quaestor, priest, will ever give you of his bounty? And yet all these, in some sort, are ours, pictured through faith in the imagination of the spirit. But what are those things which eye hath not seen nor ear heard, nor ever entered into the heart of man (I Cor. 2:9)? Things of greater joy than circus, theater, or amphitheater, or any stadium, I believe."* *Per fidem:* so it is written.

XVI

Let us conclude. The two sets of valuations, good/bad and good/evil, have waged a terrible battle on this earth, lasting many millennia; and just as surely as the second set has for a long time now been in the ascendant, so surely are there still places where the battle goes on and the issue remains in suspension. It might even be claimed that by being raised to a higher plane the battle has become much more profound. Perhaps there is today not a single intellectual worth his salt who is not divided on that issue, a battleground for those opposites. The watchwords of the battle, written in characters which have remained legible throughout human history, read: "Rome vs. Israel, Israel vs. Rome." No battle has ever been more momentous than this one. Rome viewed Israel as a monstrosity; the Romans regarded the Jews as *convicted* of hatred against the whole of mankind—and rightly so if one is justified in associating the welfare of the human species with absolute supremacy of aristocratic values. But how did the Jews, on their part, feel about Rome? A thousand indications point to the answer. It is enough to read once more the Revelations of St. John, the most rabid outburst of vindictiveness in all recorded history. (We ought to acknowledge the profound consistency of the Christian instinct in assigning this book of hatred and the most extravagantly doting of the Gospels to the same disciple. There is a piece of truth hidden here, no matter how much

---

*Translated by T.R. Glover.

literary skullduggery may have gone on.) The Romans were the strongest and most noble people who ever lived. Every vestige of them, every least inscription, is a sheer delight, provided we are able to read the spirit behind the writing. The Jews, on the
contrary, were the priestly, rancorous nation par excellence, though possessed of an un-
equaled ethical genius; we need only compare with them nations of comparable endowments, such as the Chinese or the Germans, to sense which occupies the first rank. Has
the victory so far been gained by the Romans or by the Jews? But this is really an idle
question. Remember who it is before whom one bows down, in Rome itself, as before
the essence of all supreme values—and not only in Rome but over half the globe, wherever man has grown tame or desires to grow tame: before three Jews and one Jewess
(Jesus of Nazareth, the fisherman Peter, the rug weaver Paul, and Maria, the mother of
that Jesus). This is very curious: Rome, without a doubt, has capitulated. It is true that
during the Renaissance men witnessed a strange and splendid awakening of the classical ideal; like one buried alive, Rome stirred under the weight of a new Judaic Rome
that looked like an ecumenical synagogue and was called the Church. But presently
Israel triumphed once again, thanks to the plebeian rancor of the German and English
Reformation, together with its natural corollary, the restoration of the Church—which
also meant the restoration of ancient Rome to the quiet of the tomb. In an even more
decisive sense did Israel triumph over the classical ideal through the French Revolution. For then the last political nobleness Europe had known, that of seventeenth- and
eighteenth-century France, collapsed under the weight of vindictive popular instincts.
A wilder enthusiasm was never seen. And yet, in the midst of it all, something
tremendous, something wholly unexpected happened: the ancient classical ideal appeared incarnate and in unprecedented splendor before the eyes and conscience of
mankind. Once again, stronger, simpler, more insistent than ever, over against the lying shibboleth of the rights of the majority, against the furious tendency toward leveling out and debasement, sounded the terrible yet exhilarating shibboleth of the "prerogative of the few." Like a last signpost to an *alternative* route Napoleon appeared,
most isolated and anachronistic of men, the embodiment of the noble ideal. It might
be well to ponder what exactly Napoleon, that synthesis of the brutish with the more
than human, did represent. . . .

XVII

Was it all over then? Had that greatest conflict of ideals been shelved for good? Or
had it only been indefinitely adjourned? Might not the smoldering fire start up again
one day, all the more terrible because longer and more secretly nourished? Moreover,
should we not wish for this event with all our hearts, and even help to promote it? If
the reader at this point begins to develop his own train of thought, he is not likely
soon to come to the end of it. All the more reason why I should conclude, assuming
that I have made sufficiently clear what I mean by the dangerous slogan on the title
page of my last book, *Beyond Good and Evil*. At all events, I do not mean "beyond
good and bad."

NOTE I want to take this opportunity to express publicly a wish which I have hitherto
expressed only in occasional conversations with scholars: that the philosophy department of some leading university might offer a series of prizes for essays on the evolution of moral ideas. Perhaps my present book will help to encourage such a plan. I

would propose the following question, which deserves the attention of philologists, historians, and philosophers alike, *What light does the science of linguistics, especially the study of etymology, throw on the evolution of moral ideas?* However, it would also be necessary for that purpose to enlist the assistance of physiologists and medical men. This can be most fittingly accomplished by the professional philosophers, who as a body have shown such remarkable skill in the past in bringing about amicable and productive relations between philosophy, on the one hand, and physiology and medicine, on the other. It should be stressed that all tables of values, all moral injunctions, with which history and anthropology concern themselves, require first and foremost a physiological investigation and interpretation and next a critique on the part of medical science. The question "What is this or that table of values really worth?" must be viewed under a variety of perspectives, for the question "valuable to what end?" is one of extraordinary complexity. For example, something obviously valuable in terms of the longest possible survival of a race (or of its best adaptation to a given climate, or of the preservation of its greatest numbers) would by no means have the same value if it were a question of developing a more powerful type. The welfare of the many and the welfare of the few are radically opposite ends. To consider the former *a priori* the higher value may be left to the naïveté of English biologists. All sciences are now under the obligation to prepare the ground for the future task of the philosopher, which is to solve the problem of value, to determine the true hierarchy of values.

THE GAY SCIENCE (in part)

The Madman. Have you not heard of that madman who lit a lantern in the bright morning hours, ran to the market place, and cried incessantly, "I seek God! I seek God!" As many of those who do not believe in God were standing around just then, he provoked much laughter. Why, did he get lost? said one. Did he lose his way like a child? said another. Or is he hiding? Is he afraid of us? Has he gone on a voyage? or emigrated? Thus they yelled and laughed. The madman jumped into their midst and pierced them with his glances.

"Whither is God" he cried. "I shall tell you. *We have killed him*—you and I. All of us are his murderers. But how have we done this? How were we able to drink up the sea? Who gave us the sponge to wipe away the entire horizon? What did we do when we unchained this earth from its sun? Whither is it moving now? Whither are we moving now? Away from all suns? Are we not plunging continually? Backward, sideward, forward, in all directions? Is there any up or down left? Are we not straying as through an infinite nothing? Do we not feel the breath of empty space? Has it not become colder? Is not night and more night coming on all the while? Must not lanterns be lit in the morning? Do we not hear anything yet of the noise of the gravediggers who are burying God? Do we not smell anything yet of God's decomposition? Gods too decom-

The Gay Science, from *The Portable Nietzsche* by Walter Kaufmann. Copyright 1954 by The Viking Press, renewed © 1982 by Viking Penguin Inc. Used by permission of Viking Penguin, a division of Penguin Books USA Inc.

pose. God is dead. God remains dead. And we have killed him. How shall we, the murderers of all murderers, comfort ourselves? What was holiest and most powerful of all that the world has yet owned has bled to death under our knives. Who will wipe this blood off us? What water is there for us to clean ourselves? What festivals of atonement, what sacred games shall we have to invent? Is not the greatness of this deed too great for us? Must not we ourselves become gods simply to seem worthy of it? There has never been a greater deed; and whoever will be born after us—for the sake of this deed he will be part of a higher history than all history hitherto."

Here the madman fell silent and looked again at his listeners; and they too were silent and stared at him in astonishment. At last he threw his lantern on the ground, and it broke and went out. "I come too early," he said then; "my time has not come yet. This tremendous event is still on its way, still wandering—it has not yet reached the ears of man. Lightning and thunder require time, the light of the stars requires time, deeds require time even after they are done, before they can be seen and heard. This deed is still more distant from them than the most distant stars—*and yet they have done it themselves*."

It has been related further that on that same day the madman entered divers churches and there sang his *requiem aeternam deo*. Led out and called to account, he is said to have replied each time, "What are these churches now if they are not the tombs and sepulchers of God?"

THE ANTI-CHRIST (in part)

PREFACE: REVALUATION OF ALL VALUES

This book belongs to the very few. Perhaps not one of them is even living yet. Maybe they will be the readers who understand my *Zarathustra:* how *could* I mistake myself for one of those for whom there are ears even now? Only the day after tomorrow belongs to me. Some are born posthumously.

The conditions under which I am understood, and then of *necessity*—I know them only too well. One must be honest in matters of the spirit to the point of hardness before one can even endure my seriousness and my passion. One must be skilled in living on mountains—seeing the wretched ephemeral babble of politics and national self-seeking, *beneath* oneself. One must have become indifferent; one must never ask if the truth is useful or if it may prove our undoing. The predilection of strength for questions for which no one today has the courage; the courage for the *forbidden;* the predestination to the labyrinth. An experience of seven solitudes. New ears for new music. New eyes for what is most distant. A new conscience for truths that I have so far remained mute. And the will to the economy of the great style: keeping our strength, our *enthusiasm* in harness. Reverence for oneself; love of oneself; unconditional freedom before oneself.

The Anti-Christ, from *The Portable Nietzsche* by Walter Kaufmann. Copyright 1954 by the Viking Press, renewed © 1982 by Viking Penguin Inc. Used by permission of Viking Penguin, a division of Penguin Books USA Inc.

Well then! Such men alone are my readers, my right readers, my predestined readers: what matter the *rest?* The rest—that is merely mankind. One must be above mankind in strength, in *loftiness* of soul—in contempt.

FIRST BOOK: ATTEMPT AT A CRITIQUE OF CHRISTIANITY

1. Let us face ourselves. We are Hyperboreans; we know very well how far off we live. "Neither by land nor by sea will you find the way to the Hyperboreans"—Pindar already knew this about us. Beyond the north, ice, and death—*our* life, *our* happiness. We have discovered happiness, we know the way, we have found the exit out of the labyrinth of thousands of years. Who else has found it? Modern man perhaps? "I have got lost; I am everything that has got lost," sighs modern man.

This modernity was our sickness: lazy peace, cowardly compromise, the whole virtuous uncleanliness of the modern Yes and No. This tolerance and *largeur* of the heart, which "forgives" all because it "understands" all, is *sirocco* for us. Rather live in the ice than among modern virtues and other south winds!

We were intrepid enough, we spared neither ourselves nor others; but for a long time we did not know where to turn with our intrepidity. We became gloomy, we were called fatalists. *Our fatum*—the abundance, the tension, the damming of strength. We thirsted for lightning and deeds and were most remote from the happiness of the weakling, "resignation." In our atmosphere was a thunderstorm; the nature we are became dark—*for we saw no way.* Formula for our happiness: a Yes, a No, a straight line, a goal.

2. What is good? Everything that heightens the feeling of power in man, the will to power, power itself.

What is bad? Everything that is born of weakness.

What is happiness? The feeling that power is *growing,* that resistance is overcome.

Not contentedness but more power; not peace but war; not virtue but fitness (Renaissance virtue, *virtù,* virtue that is moraline*-free).

The weak and the failures shall perish: first principle of our love of man. And they shall even be given every possible assistance.

What is more harmful than any vice? Active pity for all the failures and all the weak: Christianity.

3. The problem I thus pose is not what shall succeed mankind in the sequence of living beings (man is an *end*), but what type of man shall be *bred,* shall be *willed,* for being higher in value, worthier of life, more certain of a future.

Even in the past this higher type has appeared often—but as a fortunate accident, as an exception, never as something *willed.* In fact, this has been the type most dreaded—almost *the* dreadful—and from dread the opposite type was willed, bred, and *attained:* the domestic animal, the herd animal, the sick human animal—the Christian.

---

*The coinage of a man who neither smoked nor drank coffee.

4. Mankind does *not* represent a development toward something better or stronger or higher in the sense accepted today. "Progress" is merely a modern idea, that is, a false idea. The European of today is vastly inferior in value to the European of the Renaissance: further development is altogether *not* according to any necessity in the direction of elevation, enhancement, or strength.

In another sense, success in individual cases is constantly encountered in the most widely different places and cultures: here we really do find a *higher type,* which is, in relation to mankind as a whole, a kind of overman. Such fortunate accidents of great success have always been possible and will perhaps always be possible. And even whole families, tribes, or peoples may occasionally represent such a *bull's-eye.*

5. Christianity should not be beautified and embellished: it has waged deadly war against this higher type of man; it has placed all the basic instincts of this type under the ban; and out of these instincts it has distilled evil and the Evil One: the strong man as the typically reprehensible man, the "reprobate." Christianity has sided with all that is weak and base, with all failures; it has made an ideal of whatever *contradicts* the instinct of the strong life to preserve itself; it has corrupted the reason even of those strongest in spirit by teaching men to consider the supreme values of the spirit as something sinful, as something that leads into error—as temptations. The most pitiful example: the corruption of Pascal, who believed in the corruption of his reason through original sin when it had in fact been corrupted only by his Christianity.

6. It is a painful, horrible spectacle that has dawned on me: I have drawn back the curtain from the *corruption* of man. In my mouth, this word is at least free from one suspicion: that it might involve a moral accusation of man. It is meant—let me emphasize this once more—*moraline-free.* So much so that I experience this corruption most strongly precisely where men have so far aspired most deliberately to "virtue" and "godliness." I understand corruption, as you will guess, in the sense of decadence: it is my contention that all the values in which mankind now sums up its supreme desiderata are *decadence-values.*

I call an animal, a species, or an individual corrupt when it loses its instincts, when it chooses, when it prefers, what is disadvantageous for it. A history of "lofty sentiments," of the "ideals of mankind"—and it is possible that I shall have to write it— would almost explain too *why* man is so corrupt. Life itself is to my mind the instinct for growth, for durability, for an accumulation of forces, for *power:* where the will to power is lacking there is decline. It is my contention that all the supreme values of mankind *lack* this will—that the values which are symptomatic of decline, *nihilistic* values, are lording it under the holiest name.

7. Christianity is called the religion of *pity.* Pity stands opposed to the tonic emotions which heighten our vitality: it has a depressing effect. We are deprived of strength when we feel pity. That loss of strength which suffering as such inflicts on life is still further increased and multiplied by pity. Pity makes suffering contagious. Under certain circumstances, it may engender a total loss of life and vitality out of all proportion to the magnitude of the cause (as in the case of the death of the Nazarene). That is the first consideration, but there is a more important one.

Suppose we measure pity by the value of the reactions it usually produces; then its perilous nature appears in an even brighter light. Quite in general, pity crosses the law of development, which is the law of *selection.* It preserves what is ripe for destruction; it defends those who have been disinherited and condemned by life; and by the abundance of the failures of all kinds which it keeps alive, it gives life itself a gloomy and questionable aspect.

Some have dared to call pity a virtue (in every *noble* ethic it is considered a weakness); and as if this were not enough, it has been made *the* virtue, the basis and source of all virtues. To be sure—one should always keep this in mind—this was done by a philosophy that was nihilistic and had inscribed the *negation of life* upon its shield. Schopenhauer was consistent enough: pity negates life and renders it *more deserving of negation*.

Pity is the *practice* of nihilism. To repeat: this depressive and contagious instinct crosses those instincts which aim at the preservation of life and at the enhancement of its value. It multiplies misery and conserves all that is miserable, and is thus a prime instrument of the advancement of decadence: pity persuades men to *nothingness!* Of course, one does not say "nothingness" but "beyond" or "God," or "*true* life," or Nirvana, salvation, blessedness.

This innocent rhetoric from the realm of the religious-moral idiosyncrasy appears much less innocent as soon as we realize which tendency it is that here shrouds itself in sublime words: *hostility against life*. Schopenhauer was hostile to life; therefore pity became a virtue for him.

Aristotle, as is well known, considered pity a pathological and dangerous condition, which one would be well advised to attack now and then with a purge: he understood tragedy as a purge. From the standpoint of the instinct of life, a remedy certainly seems necessary for such a pathological and dangerous accumulation of pity as it is represented by the case of Schopenhauer (and unfortunately by our entire literary and artistic decadence from St. Petersburg to Paris, from Tolstoy to Wagner)—to puncture it and make it *burst*.

In our whole unhealthy modernity there is nothing more unhealthy than Christian pity. To be physicians *here,* to be inexorable here, to wield the scalpel *here*—that is *our* part, that is *our* love of man, that is how we are philosophers, we *Hyperboreans*.

*   *   *

62. With this I am at the end and I pronounce my judgment. I *condemn* Christianity. I raise against the Christian church the most terrible of all accusations that any accuser ever uttered. It is to me the highest of all conceivable corruptions. It has had the will to the last corruption that is even possible. The Christian church has left nothing untouched by its corruption; it has turned every value into an un-value, every truth into a lie, every integrity into a vileness of the soul. Let anyone dare to speak to me of its "humanitarian" blessings! To *abolish* any distress ran counter to its deepest advantages: it lived on distress, it *created* distress to eternalize *itself*.

The worm of sin, for example: with this distress the church first enriched mankind. The "equality of souls before God," this falsehood, this *pretext* for the rancor of all the base-minded, this explosive of a concept which eventually became revolution, modern idea, and the principle of decline of the whole order of society—is *Christian* dynamite. "Humanitarian" blessings of Christianity! To breed out of *humanitas* a self-contradiction, an art of self-violation, a will to lie at any price, a repugnance, a contempt for all good and honest instincts! Those are some of the blessings of Christianity!

Parasitism as the *only* practice of the church; with its ideal of anemia, of "holiness," draining all blood, all love, all hope for life; the beyond as the will to negate every reality; the cross as the mark of recognition for the most subterranean conspiracy that ever existed—against health, beauty, whatever has turned out well, courage, spirit, *graciousness* of the soul, *against life itself.*

This eternal indictment of Christianity I will write on all walls, wherever there are walls—I have letters to make even the blind see.

I call Christianity the one great curse, the one great innermost corruption, the one great instinct of revenge, for which no means is poisonous, stealthy, subterranean, *small* enough—I call it the one immortal blemish of mankind.

And time is reckoned from the *dies nefastus* with which this calamity began—after the *first* day of Christianity! *Why not rather after its last day? After today?* Revaluation of all values!

Henri Bergson
1859–1941

Henri Bergson was born in Paris of Jewish ancestry. His father was Polish and his mother English. He graduated from the Lycée Condorcet (the French equivalent of preparatory school) in 1878 where he distinguished himself in mathematics and letters. He then attended the École Normale Supérieure where he continued his studies in mathematics and philosophy.

Bergson began his teaching career at the lycée in Angers in 1881. Over the next two decades he also taught at institutions in Clermont-Ferrand and Paris. In 1900 he was appointed to the chair of modern philosophy at the Collège de France. For the next twenty-one years Bergson taught at this elite institution, acquiring a reputation as a scintillating teacher. According to some reports, his lectures were so popular that some students would sit through a preceding lecture in the same hall to insure getting a seat at his lecture. During this time Bergson published two of his most famous works, *An Introduction to Metaphysics* (1903) and *Creative Evolution* (1907). Mostly on the basis of these works, he was elected to the French Academy and received the Nobel Prize for literature (1928).

In 1921 poor health forced Bergson to cancel his public lectures, and in 1924 he formally resigned his chair of philosophy. For a time he chaired the Committee for Intellectual Cooperation of the League of Nations until, once again, ill health forced him into retirement. Despite failing health, he published his third major work, *The Two Sources of Morality,* in 1932.

The fall of France to the Nazis in 1940 led to laws requiring the registration of Jews. Though his international reputation and his enfeebled condition, which made it difficult for him to stand unassisted, exempted Bergson from this requirement, he insisted on taking his place in a registration line with the other Jews. He died shortly after this ordeal in early 1941.

*   *   *

Bergson's first major work, *An Introduction to Metaphysics,* reprinted here (complete) in the T.E. Hulme translation, begins by distinguishing two ways of knowing something: analysis (or intelligence) and intuition. Analysis looks at an object from many perspectives, creating a series of discrete appearances, and then uses symbols to express the common features of those perspectives. For example, one could take photographs of a town from every possible angle and develop some way of symbolizing all the common features from each of those angles. This is the method of most science: Science uses symbols dealing with classes of objects, noting similarities in form and function. But this approach remains external to the object known, reducing the object "to elements common both to it and other objects." Such a way of knowing is always relative and imperfect; it will never yield metaphysical knowledge of the object in question. No matter how many town photographs one takes, one can never capture the solidity of the *real* town.

By contrast, intuition is "the kind of *intellectual sympathy* by which one places oneself within an object in order to coincide with what is unique in it and consequently inexpressible." While the knowledge gained by analysis is necessarily partial and relative, intuitive knowledge is of a whole and absolute. To continue the analogy, once one has really entered the town and its life, all the partial perspectives of the photographs become a whole. By entering into an object one can grasp the essential nature of that object—one can do metaphysics. In Bergson's words:

> If there exists any means of possessing a reality absolutely instead of knowing it relatively, of placing oneself within it instead of looking at it from outside points of view, of having the intuition instead of making the analysis: in short, of seizing it without any expression, translation, or symbolic representation—metaphysics is that means. *Metaphysics, then, is the science which claims to dispense with symbols.*

According to Bergson there is one reality that we all "seize from within, by intuition and not by simple analysis": ourselves. Both empiricists and rationalists make the mistake of identifying the self with a series of discrete psychical states, or as some abstract entity found in the "gaps" between these psychical states. But the self as experienced "from within" is not coextensive with its states or manifestations. The self as actually lived exhibits both a multiplicity of states of consciousness and a unity that binds them together. While it is possible to analyze these two aspects of the self separately (multiplicity and unity), intuition knows that multiplicity and unity are only perspectives by means of which we get at the *essential* nature of the self's continuous existence.

This continuous existence Bergson calls "duration"—an essential quality not only of the self, but of all reality. By intuitively knowing duration from within (by knowing one's self), one can come to know that all reality is "tendency" or becoming. Instead of searching for the illusory permanence of "things made," intuitive knowing leads us to "things in the making." While analysis leads us to posit "states" and "things," which result in contradictions and skepticism, intuition seeks to grasp living reality "in some other way." This other way can be seen in mathematics. Infinitesimal calculus, says Bergson, illustrates the intuitive grasping of reality by its effort to "substitute the *being made* for the *ready made,* to follow the generation of magnitudes, to grasp motion no longer from without and in its displayed result, but from within and in its tendency to change."

In his later works Bergson applied the method of intuition to such issues as free will and determinism, time, evolution, God, morality, and the nature of society. In each case he used notions known by intuition, such as duration, to find new answers for old questions.

While critics claim Bergson's ideas suffer from a lack of logical coherence and there is no longer a clearly defined Bergsonian school, his attempt to resurrect metaphysics has been influential. The metaphysics of Alfred North Whitehead (1861–1947) and the world-view of Pierre Teilhard de Chardin (1881–1955) have also developed along the lines of evolving and becoming, and Chardin has directly used some of Bergson's ideas.

* * *

There are several good introductory studies of Bergson's thought, including A.D. Lindsay, *The Philosophy of Bergson* (New York: Dent, 1911); Herbert Wildon Carr, *The Philosophy of Change: A Study of the Fundamental Principle of the Philosophy of Bergson* (London: Macmillan and Co., 1914); Ian W. Alexander, *Bergson: Philosopher of Reflection* (London: Bowes & Bowes, 1957); A.R. Lindsay, *Bergson* (London: Routledge & Kegan Paul, 1989); and L. Kowakowski, *Bergson* (New York: Oxford University Press, 1985). Jacques Chevalier, *Henri Bergson,* translated by Lilian A. Clare (New York: Macmillan, 1928), focuses on the French intellectual climate from which Bergson's thought emerged. For comparisons of Bergson with other thinkers, see Jacques Maritain, *Bergsonian Philosophy and Thomism,* translated by Mabelle L. Andison and J. Gordon Andison (1955; reprinted New York: Greenwood Press, 1968), and A.E. Pilkington, *Bergson and His Influence: A Reassessment* (Cambridge: Cambridge University Press, 1976; this work assumes a knowledge of French). For essays, see Thomas Hanna, ed., *The Bergsonian Heritage* (New York: Columbia University Press, 1962). Finally, for a highly critical response to Bergson, see Bertrand Russell's books, *The Philosophy of Henri Bergson* (1914; reprinted Folcroft, PA: Folcroft Library Editions, 1971), and "Mysticism and Logic," in *Mysticism and Logic and Other Essays* (New York: Longmans, Green and Co., 1918), reprinted in this volume, especially pages 375–378.

AN INTRODUCTION TO METAPHYSICS

A comparison of the definitions of metaphysics and the various conceptions of the absolute leads to the discovery that philosophers, in spite of their apparent divergencies, agree in distinguishing two profoundly different ways of knowing a thing. The first implies that we move round the object; the second that we enter into it. The first depends on the point of view at which we are placed and on the symbols by which we express ourselves. The second neither depends on a point of view nor relies on any symbol. The first kind of knowledge may be said to stop at the relative; the second, in those cases where it is possible, to attain the *absolute*.

Consider, for example, the movement of an object in space. My perception of the motion will vary with the point of view, moving or stationary, from which I observe it. My expression of it will vary with the systems of axes, or the points of reference, to which I relate it; that is, with the symbols by which I translate it. For this double reason I call such motion *relative:* in the one case, as in the other, I am placed outside the object itself. But when I speak of an *absolute* movement, I am attributing to the moving object an interior and, so to speak, states of mind; I also imply that I am in sympathy with those states, and that I insert myself in them by an effort of imagination. Then, according as the object is moving or stationary, according as it adopts one movement or another, what I experience will vary. And what I experience will depend neither on the point of view I may take up in regard to the object, since I am inside the object itself, nor on the symbols by which I may translate the motion, since I have rejected all translations in order to possess the original. In short, I shall no longer grasp the movement from without, remaining where I am, but from where it is, from within, as it is in itself. I shall possess an absolute.

Consider, again, a character whose adventures are related to me in a novel. The author may multiply the traits of his hero's character, may make him speak and act as much as he pleases, but all this can never be equivalent to the simple and indivisible feeling which I should experience if I were able for an instant to identify myself with the person of the hero himself. Out of that indivisible feeling, as from a spring, all the words, gestures, and actions of the man would appear to me to flow naturally. They would no longer be accidents which, added to the idea I had already formed of the character, continually enriched that idea, without ever completing it. The character would be given to me all at once, in its entirety, and the thousand incidents which manifest it, instead of adding themselves to the idea and so enriching it, would seem to me, on the contrary, to detach themselves from it, without, however, exhausting it or impoverishing its essence. All the things I am told about the man provide me with so many points of view from which I can observe him. All the traits which describe him, and which can make him known to me only by so many comparisons with persons or things I know already, are signs by which he is expressed more or less symbolically. Symbols and points of view, therefore, place me outside him; they give me only what he has in common with others, and not what belongs to him and to him alone. But that which is properly himself, that which constitutes his essence, cannot be perceived from without, being internal by definition, nor be expressed by symbols, being incommensurable with everything else. Description, history, and analysis leave me here in the relative. Coincidence with the person himself would alone give me the absolute.

It is in this sense, and in this sense only, that *absolute* is synonymous with *perfection*. Were all the photographs of a town, taken from all possible points of view, to go on indefinitely completing one another, they would never be equivalent to the solid town in which we walk about. Were all the translations of a poem into all possible languages to add together their various shades of meaning and, correcting each other by a kind of mutual retouching, to give a more and more faithful image of the poem they translate, they would yet never succeed in rendering the inner meaning of the original. A representation taken from a certain point of view, a translation made with certain symbols, will always remain imperfect in comparison with the object of which a view has been taken, or which the symbols seek to express. But the absolute, which is the object and not its representation, the original and not its translation, is perfect, by being perfectly what it is.

It is doubtless for this reason that the *absolute* has often been identified with the *infinite*. Suppose that I wished to communicate to some one who did not know Greek the extraordinarily simple impression that a passage in Homer makes upon me; I should first give a translation of the lines, I should then comment on my translation, and then develop the commentary; in this way, by piling up explanation on explanation, I might approach nearer and nearer to what I wanted to express; but I should never quite reach it. When you raise your arm, you accomplish a movement of which you have, from within, a simple perception; but for me, watching it from the outside, your arm passes through one point, then through another, and between these two there will be still other points; so that, if I began to count, the operation would go on for ever. Viewed from the inside, then, an absolute is a simple thing; but looked at from the outside, that is to say, relatively to other things, it becomes, in relation to these signs which express it, the gold coin for which we never seem able to finish giving small change. Now, that which lends itself at the same time both to an indivisible apprehension and to an inexhaustible enumeration is, by the very definition of the word, an infinite.

It follows from this that an absolute could only be given in an *intuition,* whilst everything else falls within the province of *analysis.* By intuition is meant the kind of *intellectual sympathy* by which one places oneself within an object in order to coincide with what is unique in it and consequently inexpressible. Analysis, on the contrary, is the operation which reduces the object to elements already known, that is, to elements common both to it and other objects. To analyze, therefore, is to express a thing as a function of something other than itself. All analysis is thus a translation, a development into symbols, a representation taken from successive points of view from which we note as many resemblances as possible between the new object which we are studying and others which we believe we know already. In its eternally unsatisfied desire to embrace the object around which it is compelled to turn, analysis multiplies without end the number of its points of view in order to complete its always incomplete representation, and ceaselessly varies its symbols that it may perfect the always imperfect translation. It goes on, therefore, to infinity. But intuition, if intuition is possible, is a simple act.

Now it is easy to see that the ordinary function of positive science is analysis. Positive science works, then, above all, with symbols. Even the most concrete of the natural sciences, those concerned with life, confine themselves to the visible form of living beings, their organs and anatomical elements. They make comparisons between these forms, they reduce the more complex to the more simple; in short, they study the workings of life in what is, so to speak, only its visual symbol. If there exists any means of possessing a reality absolutely instead of knowing it relatively, of placing oneself within it instead of looking at it from outside points of view, of having the intuition instead of making the analysis: in short, of seizing it without any expression, translation, or symbolic representation—metaphysics is that means. *Metaphysics, then, is the science which claims to dispense with symbols.*

There is one reality, at least, which we all seize from within, by intuition and not by simple analysis. It is our own personality in its flowing through time—our self which endures. We may sympathize intellectually with nothing else, but we certainly sympathize with our own selves.

When I direct my attention inward to contemplate my own self (supposed for the moment to be inactive), I perceive at first, as a crust solidified on the surface, all the perceptions which come to it from the material world. These perceptions are clear, distinct, juxtaposed or juxtaposable one with another; they tend to group themselves into objects. Next, I notice the memories which more or less adhere to these perceptions and which serve to interpret them. These memories have been detached, as it were, from the depth of my personality, drawn to the surface by the perceptions which resemble them; they rest on the surface of my mind without being absolutely myself. Lastly, I feel the stir of tendencies and motor habits—a crowd of virtual actions, more or less firmly bound to these perceptions and memories. All these clearly defined elements appear more distinct from me, the more distinct they are from each other. Radiating, as they do, from within outwards, they form, collectively, the surface of a sphere which tends to grow larger and lose itself in the exterior world. But if I draw myself in from the periphery towards the centre, if I search in the depth of my being that which is most uniformly, most constantly, and most enduringly myself, I find an altogether different thing.

There is, beneath these sharply cut crystals and this frozen surface, a continuous flux which is not comparable to any flux I have ever seen. There is a succession of states, each of which announces that which follows and contains that which precedes it. They can, properly speaking, only be said to form multiple states when I have already passed them and turn back to observe their track. Whilst I was experiencing them they were so solidly organized, so profoundly animated with a common life, that I could not have said where any one of them finished or where another commenced. In reality no one of them begins or ends, but all extend into each other.

This inner life may be compared to the unrolling of a coil, for there is no living being who does not feel himself coming gradually to the end of his rôle; and to live is to grow old. But it may just as well be compared to a continual rolling up, like that of a thread on a ball, for our past follows us, it swells incessantly with the present that it picks up on its way; and consciousness means memory.

But actually it is neither an unrolling nor a rolling up, for these two similes evoke the idea of lines and surfaces whose parts are homogeneous and superposable on one another. Now, there are no two identical moments in the life of the same conscious being. Take the simplest sensation, suppose it constant, absorb in it the entire personality: the consciousness which will accompany this sensation cannot remain identical with itself for two consecutive moments, because the second moment always contains, over and above the first, the memory that the first has bequeathed to it. A consciousness which could experience two identical moments would be a consciousness without memory. It would die and be born again continually. In what other way could one represent unconsciousness?

It would be better, then, to use as a comparison the myriad-tinted spectrum, with its insensible gradations leading from one shade to another. A current of feeling which passed along the spectrum, assuming in turn the tint of each of its shades, would experience a series of gradual changes, each of which would announce the one to follow and would sum up those which preceded it. Yet even here the successive shades of the spectrum always remain external one to another. They are juxtaposed; they occupy space. But pure duration, on the contrary, excludes all idea of juxtaposition, reciprocal externality, and extension.

Let us, then, rather, imagine an infinitely small elastic body, contracted, if it were possible, to a mathematical point. Let this be drawn out gradually in such a manner that from the point comes a constantly lengthening line. Let us fix our attention not on the line as a line, but on the action by which it is traced. Let us bear in mind that this action, in spite of its duration, is indivisible if accomplished without stopping, that if a stopping-point is inserted, we have two actions instead of one, that each of these separate actions is then the indivisible operation of which we speak, and that it is not the moving action itself which is divisible, but, rather, the stationary line it leaves behind it as its track in space. Finally, let us free ourselves from the space which underlies the movement in order to consider only the movement itself, the act of tension or extension; in short, pure mobility. We shall have this time a more faithful image of the development of our self in duration.

However, even this image is incomplete, and, indeed, every comparison will be insufficient, because the unrolling of our duration resembles in some of its aspects the unity of an advancing movement and in others the multiplicity of expanding states; and, clearly, no metaphor can express one of these two aspects without sacrificing the other. If I use the comparison of the spectrum with its thousand shades, I have before me a thing already made, whilst duration is continually in the making. If I think of an elastic which is being stretched, or of a spring which is extended or relaxed, I forget the richness of color, characteristic of duration that is lived, to see only the simple movement by which consciousness passes from one shade to another. The inner life is all this at once: variety of qualities, continuity of progress, and unity of direction. It cannot be represented by images.

But it is even less possible to represent it by *concepts,* that is by abstract, general, or simple ideas. It is true that no image can reproduce exactly the original feeling I have of the flow of my own conscious life. But it is not even necessary that I should attempt to render it. If a man is incapable of getting for himself the intuition of the constitutive duration of his own being, nothing will ever give it to him, concepts no more than images. Here the single aim of the philosopher should be to promote a certain effort, which in most men is usually fettered by habits of mind more useful to life. Now the image has at least this advantage, that it keeps us in the concrete. No image can replace the intuition of duration, but many diverse images, borrowed from very different orders of things, may, by the convergence of their action, direct consciousness to the precise point where there is a certain intuition to be seized. By choosing images as dissimilar as possible, we shall prevent any one of them from usurping the place of the intuition it is intended to call up, since it would then be driven away at once by its rivals. By providing that, in spite of their differences of aspect, they all require from the mind the same kind of attention, and in some sort the same degree of tension, we shall gradually accustom consciousness to a particular and clearly-defined disposition—that precisely which it must adopt in order to appear to itself as it really is, without any veil. But, then, consciousness must at least consent to make the effort. For it will have been shown nothing: it will simply have been placed in the attitude it must take up in order to make the desired effort, and so come by itself to the intuition. Concepts on the contrary—especially if they are simple—have the disadvantage of being in reality symbols substituted for the object they symbolize, and demand no effort on our part. Examined closely, each of them, it would be seen, retains only that part of the object which is common to it and to others, and expresses, still more than the image does, a *comparison* between the object and others which resemble it. But as the comparison has made manifest a resemblance, as the resemblance is a property of the object, and as a property has every appearance of being a part of the object which possesses it, we easily persuade ourselves that by setting concept beside concept we are reconstructing the whole of the object with its parts, thus obtaining, so to speak, its intellectual equivalent. In this way we believe that we can form a faithful representation of duration by setting in line the concepts of unity, multiplicity, continuity, finite or infinite divisibility, etc. There precisely is the illusion. There also is the danger. Just in so far as abstract ideas can render

Rouen Cathedral, West Facade, Sunlight, 1894, by Claude Monet (1840–1926). Monet produced a series of paintings exploring the effect of light on the Rouen Cathedral. Each painting pushed the possibilities of the broken color impression at various times of day and different seasons to express the insubstantial, impermanent nature of the visual experience. While these paintings may direct us to an intuition of duration, none of them can capture the *solidity* of the real cathedral or the "richness of color, characteristic of duration that is lived." *(Chester Dale Collection/National Gallery of Art, Washington, DC)*

service to analysis, that is, to the scientific study of the object in its relations to other objects, so far are they incapable of replacing intuition, that is, the metaphysical investigation of what is essential and unique in the object. For on the one hand these concepts, laid side by side, never actually give us more than an artificial reconstruction of the object, of which they can only symbolize certain general, and, in a way, impersonal aspects; it is therefore useless to believe that with them we can seize a reality of which they present to us the shadow alone. And, on the other hand, besides the illusion there is also a very serious danger. For the concept generalizes at the same time as it abstracts. The concept can only symbolize a particular property by making it common to an infinity of things. It therefore always more or less deforms the property by the extension it gives to it. Replaced in the metaphysical object to which it belongs, a property coincides with the object, or at least moulds itself on it, and adopts the same outline. Extracted from the metaphysical object, and presented in a concept, it grows indefinitely larger, and goes beyond the object itself, since henceforth it has to contain it, along with a number of other objects. Thus the different concepts that we form of the properties of a thing inscribe round it so many circles, each much too large and none of them fitting it exactly. And yet, in the thing itself the properties coincided with the thing, and coincided consequently with one another. So that if we are bent on reconstructing the object with concepts, some artifice must be sought whereby this coincidence of the object and its properties can be brought about. For example, we may choose one of the concepts and try, starting from it, to get round to the others. But we shall then soon discover that according as we start from one concept or another, the meeting and combination of the concepts will take place in an altogether different way. According as we start, for example, from unity or from multiplicity, we shall have to conceive differently the multiple unity of duration. Everything will depend on the weight we attribute to this or that concept, and this weight will always be arbitrary, since the concept extracted from the object has no weight, being only the shadow of a body. In this way, as many different *systems* will spring up as there are external points of view from which the reality can be examined, or larger circles in which it can be enclosed. Simple concepts have, then, not only the inconvenience of dividing the concrete unity of the object into so many symbolical expressions; they also divide philosophy into distinct schools, each of which takes its seat, chooses its counters, and carries on with the others a game that will never end. Either metaphysics is only this play of ideas, or else, if it is a serious occupation of the mind, if it is a science and not simply an exercise, it must transcend concepts in order to reach intuition. Certainly, concepts are necessary to it, for all the other sciences work as a rule with concepts, and metaphysics cannot dispense with the other sciences. But it is only truly itself when it goes beyond the concept, or at least when it frees itself from rigid and ready-made concepts in order to create a kind very different from those which we habitually use; I mean supple, mobile, and almost fluid representations, always ready to mould themselves on the fleeting forms of intuition. We shall return later to this important point. Let it suffice us for the moment to have shown that our duration can be presented to us directly in an intuition, that it can be suggested to us indirectly by images, but that it can never—if we confine the word concept to its proper meaning—be enclosed in a conceptual representation.

Let us try for an instant to consider our duration as a multiplicity. It will then be necessary to add that the terms of this multiplicity, instead of being distinct, as they are in any other multiplicity, encroach on one another; and that while we can no doubt, by an effort of imagination, solidify duration once it has elapsed, divide it into juxtaposed portions and count all these portions, yet this operation is accomplished on the frozen memory of the duration, on the stationary trace which the mobility of duration leaves behind it, and not on the duration itself. We must admit, therefore, that if there is a multiplicity here, it bears no resemblance to any other multiplicity we know. Shall we say, then, that duration has unity? Doubtless, a continuity of elements which prolong themselves into one another participates in unity as much as in multiplicity, but this moving, changing, colored, living unity has hardly anything in common with the abstract, motionless, and empty unity which the concept of pure unity circumscribes. Shall we conclude from this that duration must be defined as unity and multiplicity at the same time? But singularly enough, however much I manipulate the two concepts, portion them out, combine them differently, practise on them the most subtle operations of mental chemistry, I never obtain anything which resembles the simple intuition that I have of duration; while, on the contrary, when I replace myself in duration by an effort of intuition, I immediately perceive how it is unity, multiplicity, and many other things besides. These different concepts, then, were only so many standpoints from which we could consider duration. Neither separated nor reunited have they made us penetrate into it.

We do penetrate into it, however, and that can only be by an effort of intuition. In this sense, an inner, absolute knowledge of the duration of the self by the self is possible. But if metaphysics here demands and can obtain an intuition, science has none the less need of an analysis. Now it is a confusion between the function of analysis and that of intuition which gives birth to the discussions between the schools and the conflicts between systems.

Psychology, in fact, proceeds like all the other sciences by analysis. It resolves the self, which has been given to it at first in a simple intuition, into sensations, feelings, ideas, etc., which it studies separately. It substitutes, then, for the self a series of elements which form the facts of psychology. But are these *elements* really *parts?* That is the whole question, and it is because it has been evaded that the problem of human personality has so often been stated in insoluble terms.

It is incontestable that every psychical state, simply because it belongs to a person, reflects the whole of a personality. Every feeling, however simple it may be, contains virtually within it the whole past and present of the being experiencing it, and, consequently, can only be separated and constituted into a "state" by an effort of abstraction or of analysis. But it is no less incontestable that without this effort of abstraction or analysis there would be no possible development of the science of psychology. What, then, exactly, is the operation by which a psychologist detaches a mental state in order to erect it into a more or less independent entity? He begins by neglecting that special coloring of the personality which cannot be expressed in known and common terms. Then he endeavors to isolate, in the person already thus simplified, some aspect which lends itself to an interesting inquiry. If he is considering inclination, for example, he will neglect the inexpressible shade which colors it, and which makes the inclination mine and not yours; he will fix his attention on the movement by which our personality *leans towards* a certain object: he will isolate this attitude, and it is this special aspect of the personality, this snapshot of the mobility of the inner life, this "diagram" of concrete inclination, that he will erect into an independent fact. There is in this something very like what an artist passing through Paris does when he makes, for example, a sketch of a tower of Notre Dame. The tower is inseparably united to the building, which is itself no less inseparably united to the ground, to its surroundings, to the whole of Paris, and so on. It is first necessary to detach it from all these; only one aspect of the whole is noted, that formed by the tower of Notre Dame. Moreover, the special form of this tower is due to the grouping of the stones of which it is composed; but the artist does not concern himself with these stones, he notes only the silhouette of the tower. For the real and internal organization of the thing he substitutes, then, an external and schematic representation. So that, on the whole, his sketch corresponds to an observation of the object from a certain point of view and to the choice of a certain means of representation. But exactly the same thing holds true of the operation by which the psychologist extracts a single mental state from the whole personality. This isolated psychical state is hardly anything but a sketch, the commencement of an artificial reconstruction; it is the whole considered under a certain elementary aspect in which we are specially interested and which we have carefully noted. It is not a part, but an element. It has not been obtained by a natural dismemberment, but by analysis.

Now beneath all the sketches he has made at Paris the visitor will probably, by way of memento, write the word "Paris." And as he has really seen Paris, he will be able, with the help of the original intuition he had of the whole, to place his sketches therein, and so join them up together. But there is no way of performing the inverse operation; it is impossible, even with an infinite number of accurate sketches, and even with the word "Paris" which indicates that they must be combined together, to get back to an intuition that one has never had, and to give oneself an impression of what Paris is like if one has never seen it. This is because we are not dealing here with real *parts,* but with mere *notes* of the total impression. To take a still more striking example, where the notation is more completely symbolic, suppose that I am shown, mixed together at random, the letters which make up a poem I am ignorant of. If the letters were *parts* of the poem, I could attempt to reconstitute the poem with them by trying the different possible arrangements, as a child does with the pieces of a Chinese puzzle. But I should never for a moment think of attempting such a thing in this case, because the letters are not *component* parts, but only *partial expressions,* which is quite a different thing. That is why, if I know the poem, I at once put each of the letters in its proper place and join them up without difficulty by a continuous connection, whilst the inverse operation is impossible. Even when I believe I am actually attempting this inverse operation, even when I put the letters end to end, I begin by thinking of some plausible meaning. I thereby give myself an intuition, and from this intuition I attempt to redescend to the elementary symbols which would reconstitute its expression. The very idea of reconstituting a thing by operations practised on symbolic elements alone implies such an absurdity that it would never occur to any one if they recollected that they were not dealing with fragments of the thing, but only, as it were, with fragments of its symbol.

Such is, however, the undertaking of the philosophers who try to reconstruct personality with psychical states, whether they confine themselves to those states alone, or whether they add a kind of thread for the purpose of joining the states together. Both empiricists and rationalists are victims of the same fallacy. Both of them mistake *partial notations* for *real parts,* thus confusing the point of view of analysis and of intuition, of science and of metaphysics.

The empiricists say quite rightly that psychological analysis discovers nothing more in personality than psychical states. Such is, in fact, the function, and the very definition of analysis. The psychologist has nothing else to do but analyze personality, that is, to note certain states; at the most he may put the label "ego" on these states in saying they are "states of the ego," just as the artist writes the word "Paris" on each of his sketches. On the level at which the psychologist places himself, and on which he must place himself, the "ego" is only a sign by which the primitive, and moreover very confused, intuition which has furnished the psychologist with his subject-matter is recalled; it is only a word, and the great error here lies in believing that while remaining on the same level we can find behind the word a thing. Such has been the error of those philosophers who have not been able to resign themselves to being only psychologists in psychology, Taine and Stuart Mill, for example. Psychologists in the method they apply, they have remained metaphysicians in the object they set before themselves. They desire an intuition, and by a strange inconsistency they seek this intuition in analysis, which is the very negation of it. They look for the ego, and they claim to find it in psychical states, though this diversity of states has itself only been obtained, and could only be obtained, by transporting oneself outside the ego altogether, so as to make a series of sketches, notes, and more or less symbolic and schematic diagrams. Thus, however much they place the states side by side, multiplying points of contact and exploring the intervals, the ego always escapes them, so that they finish by seeing in it nothing but a vain phantom. We might as well deny that the *Iliad* had a meaning, on the ground that we had looked in vain for that meaning in the intervals between the letters of which it is composed.

Philosophical empiricism is born here, then, of a confusion between the point of view of intuition and that of analysis. Seeking for the original in the translation, where naturally it cannot be, it denies the existence of the original on the ground that it is not found in the translation. It leads of necessity to negations; but on examining the matter closely, we perceive that these negations simply mean that analysis is not intuition, which is self-evident. From the original, and, one must add, very indistinct intuition which gives positive science its material, science passes immediately to analysis, which multiplies to infinity its observations of this material from outside points of view. It soon comes to believe that by putting together all these diagrams it can reconstitute the object itself. No wonder, then, that it sees this object fly before it, like a child that would like to make a solid plaything out of the shadows outlined along the wall!

But rationalism is the dupe of the same illusion. It starts out from the same confusion as empiricism, and remains equally powerless to reach the inner self. Like empiricism, it considers psychical states as so many fragments detached from an ego that binds them together. Like empiricism, it tries to join these fragments together in order to re-create the unity of the self. Like empiricism, finally, it sees this unity of the self, in the continually renewed effort it makes to clasp it, steal away indefinitely like a phantom. But whilst empiricism, weary of the struggle, ends by declaring that there is nothing else but the multiplicity of psychical states, rationalism persists in affirming the unity of the person. It is true that, seeking this unity on the level of the psychical states themselves, and obliged, besides, to put down to the account of these states all the qualities and determinations that it finds by analysis (since analysis by its very definition leads always to *states*), nothing is left to it, for the unity of personality, but something purely negative, the absence of all determination. The psychical states having necessarily in this analysis taken and kept for themselves everything that can serve as matter, the "unity of the ego" can never be more than a form without content. It will be absolutely indeterminate and absolutely void. To these detached psychical states, to these shadows of the ego, the sum of which was for the empiricists the equivalent of the self, rationalism, in order to reconstitute personality, adds something still more unreal, the void in which these shadows move—a place for shadows, one might say. How could this "form," which is in truth formless, serve to characterize a living, active, concrete personality, or to distinguish Peter from Paul? Is it astonishing that the philosophers who have isolated this "form" of personality should, then, find it insufficient to characterize a definite person, and that they should be gradually led to make their empty ego a kind of bottomless receptacle, which belongs no more to Peter than to Paul, and in which there is room, according to our preference, for entire humanity, for God, or for existence in general? I see in this matter only one difference between empiricism and rationalism. The former, seeking the unity of the ego in the gaps, as it were, between the psychical states, is led to fill the gaps with other states, and so on indefinitely, so that the ego, compressed in a constantly narrowing interval, tends towards zero, as analysis is pushed farther and farther; whilst rationalism, making the ego the place where mental states are lodged, is confronted with an empty space which we have no reason to limit here rather than there, which goes beyond each of the successive boundaries that we try to assign to it, which constantly grows larger, and which tends to lose itself no longer in zero, but in the infinite.

The distance, then, between a so-called "empiricism" like that of Taine and the most transcendental speculations of certain German pantheists is very much less than is generally supposed. The method is analogous in both cases; it consists in reasoning about the *elements* of a translation as if they were *parts* of the original. But a true empiricism is that which proposes to get as near to the original itself as possible, to search deeply into its life, and so, by a kind of *intellectual auscultation* [listening], to feel the throbbings of its soul; and this true empiricism is the true metaphysics. It is true that the task is an extremely difficult one, for none of the ready-made conceptions which thought employs in its daily operations can be of any use. Nothing is more easy than to say that the ego is multiplicity, or that it is unity, or that it is the synthesis of both. Unity and multiplicity are here representations that we have no need to cut out on the model of the object; they are found ready-made, and have only to be chosen from a heap. They are stocksize clothes which do just as well for Peter as for Paul, for they set off the form of neither. But an empiricism worthy of the name, an empiricism which works only to measure, is obliged for each new object that it studies to make an absolutely fresh effort. It cuts out for the object a concept which is appropriate to that object alone, a concept which can as yet hardly be called a concept, since it applies to this one thing. It does not proceed by combining current ideas like unity and multiplicity; but it leads us, on the contrary, to a simple, unique representation, which, however once formed, enables us to understand easily how it is that we can place it in the frames unity, multiplicity, etc., all much larger than itself. In short, philosophy thus defined does not consist in the choice of certain concepts, and in taking sides with a school, but in the search for a unique intuition from which we can descend with equal ease to different concepts, because we are placed above the divisions of the schools.

That personality has unity cannot be denied; but such an affirmation teaches one nothing about the extraordinary nature of the particular unity presented by personality. That our self is multiple I also agree, but then it must be understood that it is a multiplicity which has nothing in common with any other multiplicity. What is really important for philosophy is to know exactly what unity, what multiplicity, and what reality superior both to abstract unity and multiplicity the multiple unity of the self actually is. Now philosophy will know this only when it recovers possession of the simple intuition of the self by the self. Then, according to the direction it chooses for its descent from this summit, it will arrive at unity or multiplicity, or at any one of the concepts by which we try to define the moving life of the self. But no mingling of these concepts would give anything which at all resembles the self that endures.

If we are shown a solid cone, we see without any difficulty how it narrows towards the summit and tends to be lost in a mathematical point, and also how it enlarges in the direction of the base into an indefinitely increasing circle. But neither the point nor the circle, nor the juxtaposition of the two on a plane, would give us the least idea of a cone. The same thing holds true of the unity and multiplicity of mental life, and of the zero and the infinite towards which empiricism and rationalism conduct personality.

Concepts, as we shall show elsewhere, generally go together in couples and represent two contraries. There is hardly any concrete reality which cannot be observed from two opposing standpoints, which cannot consequently be subsumed under two antagonistic concepts. Hence a thesis and an antithesis which we endeavor in vain to reconcile logically, for the very simple reason that it is impossible, with concepts and observations taken from outside points of view, to make a thing. But from the object, seized by intuition, we pass easily in many cases to the two contrary concepts and as in that way thesis and antithesis can be seen to spring from reality, we grasp at the same time how it is that the two are opposed and how they are reconciled.

It is true that to accomplish this, it is necessary to proceed by a reversal of the usual work of the intellect. *Thinking* usually consists in passing from concepts to things, and not from things to concepts. To know a reality, in the usual sense of the word "know," is to take ready-made concepts, to portion them out and to mix them together until a practical equivalent of the reality is obtained. But it must be remembered that the normal work of the intellect is far from being disinterested. We do not aim generally at knowledge for the sake of knowledge, but in order to take sides, to draw profit—in short, to satisfy an interest. We inquire up to what point the object we seek to know is *this* or *that,* to what known class it belongs, and what kind of action, bearing, or attitude it should suggest to us. These different possible actions and attitudes are so many *conceptual directions* of our thought, determined once for all; it remains only to follow them: in that precisely consists the application of concepts to things. To try to fit a concept on an object is simply to ask what we can do with the object, and what it can do for us. To label an object with a certain concept is to mark in precise terms the kind of action or attitude the object should suggest to us. All knowledge, properly so called, is then oriented in a certain direction, or taken from a certain point of view. It is true that our interest is often complex. This is why it happens that our knowledge of the same object may face several successive directions and may be taken from various points of view. It is this which constitutes, in the usual meaning of the terms, a "broad" and "comprehensive" knowledge of the object; the object is then brought not under one single concept, but under several in which it is supposed to "participate." How does it participate in all these concepts at the same time? This is a question which does not concern our practical action and about which we need not trouble. It is, therefore, natural and legitimate in daily life to proceed by the juxtaposition and portioning out of concepts; no philosophical difficulty will arise from this procedure, since by a tacit agreement we shall abstain from philosophizing. But to carry this *modus operendi* into philosophy, to pass here also from concepts to the thing, to use in order to obtain a disinterested knowledge of an object (that this time we desire to grasp as it is in itself) a manner of knowing inspired by a determinate interest, consisting by definition in an externally-taken view of the object, is to go against the end that we have chosen, to condemn philosophy to an eternal skirmishing between the schools and to install contradiction in the very heart of the object and of the method. Either there is no philosophy possible, and all knowledge of things is a practical knowledge aimed at the profit to be drawn from them, or else philosophy consists in placing oneself within the object itself by an effort of intuition.

But in order to understand the nature of this intuition, in order to fix with precision where intuition ends and where analysis begins, it is necessary to return to what was said earlier about the flux of duration.

It will be noticed that an essential characteristic of the concepts and diagrams to which analysis leads is that, while being considered, they remain stationary. I isolate from the totality of interior life that psychical entity which I call a simple sensation; so long as I study it, I suppose that it remains constant. If I noticed any change in it, I should say that it was not a single sensation but several successive sensations, and I should then transfer to each of these successive sensations the immutability that I first attributed to the total sensation. In any case I can, by pushing the analysis far enough, always manage to arrive at elements which I agree to consider immutable. There, and there only, shall I find the solid basis of operations which science needs for its own proper development.

But, then, I cannot escape the objection that there is no state of mind, however simple, which does not change every moment, since there is no consciousness without memory, and no continuation of a state without the addition, to the present feeling, of the memory of past moments. It is this which constitutes duration. Inner duration is the continuous life of a memory which prolongs the past into the present, the present either containing within it in a distinct form the ceaselessly growing image of the past, or, more probably, showing by its continual change of quality the heavier and still heavier load we drag behind us as we grow older. Without this survival of the past into the present there would be no duration, but only instantaneity.

Probably if I am thus accused of taking the mental state out of duration by the mere fact that I analyze it, I shall reply, "Is not each of these elementary psychical states, to which my analysis leads, itself a state which occupies time? My analysis," I shall say, "does indeed resolve the inner life into states, each of which is homogeneous with itself; only, since the homogeneity extends over a definite number of minutes or of seconds, the elementary psychical state does not cease to endure, although it does not change."

But, in saying that, I fail to see that the definite number of minutes and of seconds, which I am attributing here to the elementary psychical state, has simply the value of a sign intended to remind me that the psychical state, supposed homogeneous, is in reality a state which changes and endures. The state, taken in itself, is a perpetual becoming. I have extracted from this becoming a certain average of quality, which I have supposed invariable; I have in this way constituted a stable and consequently schematic state. I have, on the other hand, extracted from it Becoming in general, i.e., a becoming which is not the becoming of any particular thing, and this is what I have called the *time* the state occupies. Were I to look at it closely, I should see that this abstract time is as immobile for me as the state which I localize in it, that it could flow only by a continual change of quality, and that if it is without quality, merely the theatre of the change, it thus becomes an immobile medium. I should see that the construction of this homogeneous time is simply designed to facilitate the comparison between the different concrete durations, to permit us to count simultaneities, and to measure one flux of duration in relation to another. And lastly I should understand that, in attaching the sign of a definite number of minutes and of seconds to the representation of an elementary psychical state, I am merely reminding myself and others that the state has been detached from an ego which endures, and merely marking out the place where it must again be set in movement in order to bring it back from the abstract schematic thing it has become to the concrete state it was at first. But I ignore all that, because it has nothing to do with analysis.

This means that analysis operates always on the immobile, whilst intuition places itself in mobility, or, what comes to the same thing, in duration. There lies the very distinct line of demarcation between intuition and analysis. The real, the experienced, and the concrete are recognized by the fact that they are variability itself, the element by the fact that it is invariable. And the element is invariable by definition, being a diagram, a simplified reconstruction, often a mere symbol, in any case a motionless view of the moving reality.

But the error consists in believing that we can reconstruct the real with these diagrams. As we have already said and may as well repeat here—from intuition one can pass to analysis, but not from analysis to intuition.

Out of variability we can make as many variations, qualities and modifications as we please, since these are so many static views, taken by analysis, of the mobility given to intuition. But these modifications, put end to end, will produce nothing which resembles variability, since they are not parts of it, but elements, which is quite a different thing.

Consider, for example, the variability which is nearest to homogeneity, that of movement in space. Along the whole of this movement we can imagine possible stoppages; these are what we call the positions of the moving body, or the points by which it passes. But with these positions, even with an infinite number of them, we shall never make movement. They are not parts of the movement, they are so many snapshots of it; they are, one might say, only supposed stopping-places. The moving body is never really *in* any of the points; the most we can say is that it passes through them. But passage, which is movement, has nothing in common with stoppage, which is immobility. A movement cannot be superposed on an immobility, or it would then coincide with it, which would be a contradiction. The points are not *in* the movement, as parts, nor even *beneath* it, as positions occupied by the moving body. They are simply projected by us under the movement, as so many places where a moving body, which by hypothesis does not stop, would be if it were to stop. They are not, therefore, properly speaking, positions, but "suppositions," aspects, or points of view of the mind. But how could we construct a thing with points of view?

Nevertheless, this is what we try to do whenever we reason about movement, and also about time, for which movement serves as a means of representation. As a result of an illusion deeply rooted in our mind, and because we cannot prevent ourselves from considering analysis as the equivalent of intuition, we begin by distinguishing along the whole extent of the movement, a certain number of possible stoppages or points, which we make, whether they like it or no, parts of the movement. Faced with our impotence to reconstruct the movement with these points, we insert other points, believing that we can in this way get nearer to the essential mobility in the movement. Then, as this mobility still escapes us, we substitute for a fixed and finite number of points an "indefinitely increasing" number—thus vainly trying to counterfeit, by the movement of a thought that goes on indefinitely adding points to points, the real and undivided motion of the moving body. Finally, we say that movement is composed of points, but that it comprises, in addition, the obscure and mysterious passage from one position to the next. As if the obscurity was not due entirely to the fact that we have supposed immobility to be clearer than mobility and rest anterior to movement! As if the mystery did not follow entirely from our attempting to pass from stoppages to movement by way of addition, which is impossible, when it is so easy to pass, by simple diminution, from movement to the slackening of movement, and so to immobility! It is movement that we must accustom ourselves to look upon as simplest and clearest, immobility being only the extreme limit of the slowing down of movement, a limit reached only, perhaps, in thought and never realized in nature. What we have done is to seek for the meaning of the poem in the form of the letters of which it is composed; we have believed that by considering an increasing number of letters we would grasp at last the ever-escaping meaning, and in desperation, seeing that it was useless to seek for a part of the sense in each of the letters, we have supposed that it was between each letter and the next that this long-sought fragment of the mysterious sense was lodged! But the letters, it must be pointed out once again, are not parts of the thing, but elements of the symbol. Again, the positions of the moving body are not parts of the movement; they are points of the space which is supposed to underlie the movement. This empty and immobile space which is merely conceived, never perceived, has the value of a symbol only. How could you ever manufacture reality by manipulating symbols?

But the symbol in this case responds to the most inveterate habits of our thought. We place ourselves as a rule in immobility, in which we find a point of support for practical purposes, and with this immobility we try to reconstruct motion. We only obtain in this way a clumsy imitation, a counterfeit of real movement, but this imitation is much more useful in life than the intuition of the thing itself would be. Now our mind has an irresistible tendency to consider that idea clearest which is most often useful to it. That is why immobility seems to it clearer than mobility, and rest anterior to movement.

The difficulties to which the problem of movement has given rise from the earliest antiquity have originated in this way. They result always from the fact that we insist on passing from space to movement, from the trajectory to the flight, from immobile positions to mobility, and on passing from one to the other by way of addition. But it is movement which is anterior to immobility, and the relation between positions and a displacement is not that of parts to a whole, but that of the diversity of possible points of view to the real indivisibility of the object.

Many other problems are born of the same illusion. What stationary points are to the movement of a moving body, concepts of different qualities are to the qualitative change of an object. The various concepts into which a change can be analyzed are therefore so many stable views of the instability of the real. And to think of an object— in the usual meaning of the word "think"—is to take one or more of these immobile views of its mobility. It consists, in short, in asking from time to time where the object is, in order that we may know what to do with it. Nothing could be more legitimate, moreover, than this method of procedure, so long as we are concerned only with a practical knowledge of reality. Knowledge, in so far as it is directed to practical matters, has only to enumerate the principal possible attitudes of the thing towards us, as well as our best possible attitude towards it. Therein lies the ordinary function of ready-made concepts, those stations with which we mark out the path of becoming. But to seek to penetrate with them into the inmost nature of things, is to apply to the mobility of the real a method created in order to give stationary points of observation on it. It is to forget that, if metaphysic is possible, it can only be a laborious, and even painful, effort to remount the natural slope of the work of thought, in order to place oneself directly, by a kind of intellectual expansion, within the thing studied: in short, a passage from reality to concepts and no longer from concepts to reality. Is it astonishing that, like children trying to catch smoke by closing their hands, philosophers so often see the object they would grasp fly before them? It is in this way that many of the quarrels between the schools are perpetuated, each of them reproaching the others with having allowed the real to slip away.

But if metaphysics is to proceed by intuition, if intuition has the mobility of duration as its object, and if duration is of a psychical nature, shall we not be confining the philosopher to the exclusive contemplation of himself? Will not philosophy come to consist in watching oneself merely live, "as a sleepy shepherd watches the water flow"? To talk in this way would be to return to the error which, since the beginning of this study, we have not ceased to point out. It would be to misconceive the singular nature of duration, and at the same time the essentially active, I might almost say violent, character of metaphysical intuition. It would be failing to see that the method we speak of alone permits us to go beyond idealism, as well as realism, to affirm the existence of objects inferior and superior (though in a certain sense interior) to us, to make them coexist together without difficulty, and to dissipate gradually the obscurities that analysis accumulates round these great problems. Without entering here upon the study of these different points, let us confine ourselves to showing how the intuition we speak of is not a single act, but an indefinite series of acts, all doubtless of the same kind, but each of a very particular species, and how this diversity of acts corresponds to all the degrees of being.

If I seek to *analyze* duration—that is, to resolve it into ready-made concepts—I am compelled, by the very nature of the concepts and of analysis, to take two opposing views of *duration in general,* with which I then attempt to reconstruct it. This combination, which will have, moreover, something miraculous about it—since one does not understand how two contraries would ever meet each other—can present neither a diversity of degrees nor a variety of forms; like all miracles, it is or it is not. I shall have to say, for example, that there is on the one hand a *multiplicity* of successive states of consciousness, and on the other a *unity* which binds them together. Duration will be the "synthesis" of this unity and this multiplicity, a mysterious operation which takes place in darkness, and in regard to which, I repeat, one does not see how it would admit of shades or of degrees. In this hypothesis there is, and can only be, one single duration, that in which our own consciousness habitually works. To express it more clearly—if we consider duration under the simple aspect of a movement accomplishing itself in space, and we seek to reduce to concepts movement considered as representative of time, we shall have, on the one hand, as great a number of points on the trajectory as we may desire, and, on the other hand, an abstract unity which holds them together as a thread holds together the pearls of a necklace. Between this abstract multiplicity and this abstract unity, the combination, when once it has been posited as possible, is something unique, which will no more admit of shades than does the addition of given numbers in arithmetic. But if, instead of professing to analyze duration (*i.e.,* at bottom, to make a synthesis of it with concepts), we at once place ourselves in it by an effort of intuition, we have the feeling of a certain very determinate tension, in which the determination itself appears as a choice between an infinity of possible durations. Henceforward we can picture to ourselves as many durations as we wish, all very different from each other, although each of them, on being reduced to concepts—that is, observed externally from two opposing points of view—always comes in the end to the same indefinable combination of the many and the one.

Let us express the same idea with more precision. If I consider duration as a multiplicity of moments bound to each other by a unity which goes through them like a thread, then, however short the chosen duration may be, these moments are unlimited in number. I can suppose them as close together as I please; there will always be between these mathematical points other mathematical points, and so on to infinity. Looked at from the point of view of multiplicity, then, duration disintegrates into a powder of moments, none of which endures, each being an instantaneity. If, on the other hand, I consider the unity which binds the moments together, this cannot endure either, since by hypothesis everything that is changing, and everything that is really durable in the duration, has been put to the account of the multiplicity of moments. As I probe more deeply into its essence, this unity will appear to me as some immobile substratum of that which is moving, as some intemporal essence of time; it is this that I shall call eternity; an eternity of death, since it is nothing else than the movement emptied of the mobility which made its life. Closely examined, the opinions of the opposing schools on the subject of duration would be seen to differ solely in this, that they attribute a capital importance to one or the other of these two concepts. Some adhere to the point of view of the multiple; they set up as concrete reality the distinct moments of a time which they have reduced to powder; the unity which enables us to call the grains a powder they hold to be much more artificial. Others, on the contrary, set up the unity of duration as concrete reality. They place themselves in the eternal. But as their eternity remains, notwithstanding, abstract, since it is empty, being the eternity of a concept which, by hypothesis, excludes from itself the opposing concept, one does not see how this eternity would permit of an indefinite number of moments coexisting in it. In the first hypothesis we have a world resting on nothing, which must end and begin again of its own accord at each instant. In the second we have an infinity of abstract eternity, about which also it is just as difficult to understand why it does not remain enveloped in itself and how it allows things to coexist with it. But in both cases, and whichever of the two metaphysics it be that one is switched into, time appears, from the psychological point of view, as a mixture of two abstractions, which admit of neither degrees nor shades. In one system as in the other, there is only one unique duration, which carries everything with it—a bottomless, bankless river, which flows without assignable force in a direction which could not be defined. Even then we can call it only a river, and the river only flows, because reality obtains from the two doctrines this concession, profiting by a moment of perplexity in their logic. As soon as they recover from this perplexity, they freeze this flux either into an immense solid sheet, or into an infinity of crystallized needles, always into a *thing* which necessarily partakes of the immobility of a *point of view*.

It is quite otherwise if we place ourselves from the first, by an effort of intuition, in the concrete flow of duration. Certainly, we shall then find no logical reason for positing multiple and diverse durations. Strictly, there might well be no other duration than our own, as, for example, there might be no other color in the world but orange. But just as a consciousness based on color, which sympathized internally with orange instead of perceiving it externally, would feel itself held between red and yellow, would even perhaps suspect beyond this last color a complete spectrum into which the continuity from red to yellow might expand naturally, so the intuition of our duration, far from leaving us suspended in the void as pure analysis would do, brings us into contact with a whole continuity of durations which we must try to follow, whether downwards or upwards; in both cases we can extend ourselves indefinitely by an increasingly violent effort, in both cases we transcend ourselves. In the first we advance towards a more and more attenuated duration, the pulsations of which, being rapider than ours, and dividing our simple sensation, dilute its quality into quantity; at the limit would be pure homogeneity, that pure *repetition* by which we define materiality. Advancing in the other direction, we approach a duration which *strains,* contracts, and intensifies itself more and more: at the limit would be eternity. No longer conceptual eternity, which is an eternity of death, but an eternity of life. A living, and therefore still moving eternity in which our own particular duration would be included as the vibrations are in light; an eternity which would be the concentration of all duration, as materiality is its dispersion. Between these two extreme limits intuition moves, and this movement is the very essence of metaphysics.

There can be no question of following here the various stages of this movement. But having presented a general view of the method and made a first application of it, it may not be amiss to formulate, as precisely as we can, the principles on which it rests. Most of the following propositions have already received in this essay some degree of proof. We hope to demonstrate them more completely when we come to deal with other problems.

I. *There is a reality that is external and yet given immediately to the mind.* Common-sense is right on this point, as against the idealism and realism of the philosophers.

II. This reality is mobility. Not *things* made, but things in the making, not self-maintaining *states,* but only changing states, exist. Rest is never more than apparent, or, rather, relative. The consciousness we have of our own self in its continual flux introduces us to the interior of a reality, on the model of which we must represent other realities. *All reality, therefore, is tendency, if we agree to mean by tendency an incipient change of direction.*

III. Our mind, which seeks for solid points of support, has for its main function in the ordinary course of life that of representing *states* and *things.* It takes, at long intervals, almost instantaneous views of the undivided mobility of the real. It thus obtains *sensations* and *ideas.* In this way it substitutes for the continuous the discontinuous, for motion stability, for tendency in process of change, fixed points marking a direction of change and tendency. This substitution is necessary to common-sense, to language, to practical life, and even, in a certain degree, which we shall endeavor to determine, to positive science. *Our intellect, when it follows its natural bent, proceeds on the one hand by solid perceptions, and on the other by stable conceptions.* It starts from the immobile, and only conceives and expresses movement as a function of immobility. It takes up its position in ready-made concepts, and endeavors to catch in them, as in a net, something of the reality which passes. This is certainly not done in order to obtain an internal and metaphysical knowledge of the real, but simply in order to utilize the real, each concept (as also each sensation) being a *practical question* which our activity puts to reality and to which reality replies, as must be done in business, by a Yes or a No. But, in doing that, it lets that which is its very essence escape from the real.

IV. The inherent difficulties of metaphysic, the antinomies which it gives rise to, and the contradictions into which it falls, the division into antagonistic schools, and the irreducible opposition between systems are largely the result of our applying, to the disinterested knowledge of the real, processes which we generally employ for practical ends. They arise from the fact that we place ourselves in the immobile in order to lie in wait for the moving thing as it passes, instead of replacing ourselves in the moving thing itself, in order to traverse with it the immobile positions. They arise from our professing to reconstruct reality—which is tendency and consequently mobility—with percepts and concepts whose function it is to make it stationary. With stoppages, however numerous they may be, we shall never make mobility; whereas, if mobility is given, we can, by means of diminution, obtain from it by thought as many stoppages as we desire. In other words, *it is clear that fixed concepts may be extracted by our thought from mobile reality; but there are no means of reconstructing the mobility of the real with fixed concepts.* Dogmatism, however, in so far as it has been a builder of systems, has always attempted this reconstruction.

V. In this it was bound to fail. It is on this impotence and on this impotence only that the sceptical, idealist, critical doctrines really dwell: in fact, all doctrines that deny to our intelligence the power of attaining the absolute. But because we fail to reconstruct the living reality with stiff and ready-made concepts, it does not follow that we cannot grasp it in some other way. *The demonstrations which have been given of the relativity of our knowledge are therefore tainted with an original vice; they imply, like the dogmatism they attack, that all knowledge must necessarily start from concepts with fixed outlines, in order to clasp with them the reality which flows.*

VI. But the truth is that our intelligence can follow the opposite method. It can place itself within the mobile reality, and adopt its ceaselessly changing direction; in short, can grasp it by means of that *intellectual sympathy* which we call intuition. This is extremely difficult. The mind has to do violence to itself, has to reverse the direction of the operation by which it habitually thinks, has perpetually to revise, or rather to recast, all its categories. But in this way it will attain to fluid concepts, capable of following reality in all its sinuosities and of adopting the very movement of the inward life of things. Only thus will a progressive philosophy be built up, freed from the disputes which arise between the various schools, and able to solve its problems naturally, because it will be released from the artificial expression in terms of which such problems are posited. *To philosophize, therefore, is to invert the habitual direction of the work of thought.*

VII. This inversion has never been practised in a methodical manner; but a profoundly considered history of human thought would show that we owe to it all that is greatest in the sciences, as well as all that is permanent in metaphysics. The most powerful of the methods of investigation at the disposal of the human mind, the infinitesimal calculus, originated from this very inversion. Modern mathematics is precisely an effort to substitute the *being made for the ready made,* to follow the generation of magnitudes, to grasp motion no longer from without and in its displayed result, but from within and in its tendency to change; in short, to adopt the mobile continuity of the outlines of things. It is true that it is confined to the outline, being only the science of magnitudes. It is true also that it has only been able to achieve its marvelous applications by the invention of certain symbols, and that if the intuition of which we have just spoken lies at the origin of invention, it is the symbol alone which is concerned in the application. But metaphysics, which aims at no application, can and usually must abstain from converting intuition into symbols. Liberated from the obligation of working for practically useful results, it will indefinitely enlarge the domain of its investigations. What it may lose in comparison with science in utility and exactitude, it will regain in range and extension. Though mathematics is only the science of magnitudes, though mathematical processes are applicable only to quantities, it must not be forgotten that quantity is always quality in a nascent state; it is, we might say, the limiting case of quality. It is natural, then, that metaphysics should adopt the generative idea of our mathematics in order to extend it to all qualities; that is, to reality in general. It will not, by doing this, in any way be moving towards universal mathematics, that chimera of modern philosophy. On the contrary, the farther it goes, the more untranslatable into symbols will be the objects it encounters. But it will at least have begun by getting into contact with the continuity and mobility of the real, just where this contact can be most marvelously utilized. It will have contemplated itself in a mirror which reflects an image of itself, much shrunken, no doubt, but for that reason very luminous. It will have seen with greater clearness what the mathematical processes borrow from concrete reality, and it will continue in the direction of concrete reality, and not in that of mathematical processes. Having then discounted beforehand what is too modest, and at the same time too ambitious, in the following formula, we may say that *the object of metaphysics is to perform qualitative differentiations and integrations.*

VIII. The reason why this object has been lost sight of, and why science itself has been mistaken in the origin of the processes it employs, is that intuition, once attained, must find a mode of expression and of application which conforms to the habits of our thought, and one which furnishes us, in the shape of well-defined concepts, with the solid points of support which we so greatly need. In that lies the condition of what we call exactitude and precision, and also the condition of the unlimited extension of a general method to particular cases. Now this extension and this work of logical improvement can be continued for centuries, whilst the act which creates the method lasts but for a moment. That is why we so often take the logical equipment of science for science itself, forgetting the metaphysical intuition from which all the rest has sprung.

From the overlooking of this intuition proceeds all that has been said by philosophers and by men of science themselves about the "relativity" of scientific knowledge. *What is relative is the symbolic knowledge by pre-existing concepts, which proceeds from the fixed to the moving, and not the intuitive knowledge which installs itself in that which is moving and adopts the very life of things.* This intuition attains the absolute.

Science and metaphysics therefore come together in intuition. A truly intuitive philosophy would realize the much-desired union of science and metaphysics. While it would make of metaphysics a positive science—that is, a progressive and indefinitely perfectible one—it would at the same time lead the positive sciences, properly socalled, to become conscious of their true scope, often far greater than they imagine. It would put more science into metaphysics, and more metaphysics into science. It would result in restoring the continuity between the intuitions which the various sciences have obtained here and there in the course of their history, and which they have obtained only by strokes of genius.

IX. That there are not two different ways of knowing things fundamentally, that the various sciences have their root in metaphysics, is what the ancient philosophers generally thought. Their error did not lie there. It consisted in their being always dominated by the belief, so natural to the human mind, that a variation can only be the expression and development of what is invariable. Whence it followed that action was an enfeebled contemplation, duration a deceptive and shifting image of immobile eternity, the Soul a fall from the Idea. The whole of the philosophy which begins with Plato and culminates in Plotinus is the development of a principle which may be formulated thus: "There is more in the immutable than in the moving, and we pass from the stable to the unstable by a mere diminution." Now it is the contrary which is true.

Modern science dates from the day when mobility was set up as an independent reality. It dates from the day when Galileo, setting a ball rolling down an inclined plane, firmly resolved to study this movement from top to bottom for itself, in itself, instead of seeking its principle in the concepts of *high* and *low,* two immobilities by which Aristotle believed he could adequately explain the mobility. And this is not an isolated fact in the history of science. Several of the great discoveries, of those at least which have transformed the positive sciences or which have created new ones, have been so many soundings in the depths of pure duration. The more living the reality touched, the deeper was the sounding.

But the lead-line sunk to the sea bottom brings up a fluid mass which the sun's heat quickly dries into solid and discontinuous grains of sand. And the intuition of duration, when it is exposed to the rays of the understanding, in like manner quickly turns into fixed, distinct, and immobile concepts. In the living mobility of things the understanding is bent on marking real or virtual stations, it notes departures and arrivals; for this is all that concerns the thought of man in so far as it is simply human. It is more than human to grasp what is happening in the interval. But philosophy can only be an effort to transcend the human condition.

Men of science have fixed their attention mainly on the concepts with which they have marked out the pathway of intuition. The more they laid stress on these residual products, which have turned into symbols, the more they attributed a symbolic character to every kind of science. And the more they believed in the symbolic character of science, the more did they indeed make science symbolical. Gradually they have blotted out all difference, in positive science, between the natural and the artificial, between the data of immediate intuition, and the enormous work of analysis which the understanding pursues round intuition. Thus they have prepared the way for a doctrine which affirms the relativity of all our knowledge.

But metaphysics has also labored to the same end.

How could the masters of modern philosophy, who have been renovators of science as well as of metaphysics, have had no sense of the moving continuity of reality? How could they have abstained from placing themselves in what we call concrete duration? They have done so to a greater extent than they were aware; above all, much more than they said. If we endeavor to link together, by a continuous connection, the intuitions about which systems have become organized, we find, together with other convergent and divergent lines, one very determinate direction of thought and of feeling. What is this latent thought? How shall we express the feeling? To borrow once more the language of the Platonists, we will say—depriving the words of their psychological sense, and giving the name of Idea to a certain settling down into easy intelligibility, and that of Soul to a certain longing after the restlessness of life that an invisible current causes modern philosophy to place the Soul above the Idea. It thus tends, like modern science, and even more so than modern science, to advance in an opposite direction to ancient thought.

But this metaphysics, like this science, has enfolded its deeper life in a rich tissue of symbols, forgetting something that, while science needs symbols for its analytical development, the main object of metaphysics is to do away with symbols. Here, again, the understanding has pursued its work of fixing, dividing, and reconstructing. It has pursued this, it is true, under a rather different form. Without insisting on a point which we propose to develop elsewhere, it is enough here to say that the understanding, whose function it is to operate on stable elements, may look for stability either in *relations* or in *things*. In so far as it works on concepts of relations, it culminates in *scientific* symbolism. In so far as it works on concepts of things, it culminates in *metaphysical* symbolism. But in both cases the arrangement comes from the understanding. Hence, it would fain believe itself independent. Rather than recognize at once what it owes to an intuition of the depths of reality, it prefers exposing itself to the danger that its whole work may be looked upon as nothing but an artificial arrangement of symbols. So that if we were to hold on to the letter of what metaphysicians and scientists say, and also to the material aspect of what they do, we might believe that the metaphysicians have dug a deep tunnel beneath reality, that the scientists have thrown an elegant bridge over it, but that the moving stream of things passes between these two artificial constructions without touching them.

One of the principal artifices of the Kantian criticism consisted in taking the metaphysician and the scientist literally, forcing both metaphysics and science to the extreme limit of symbolism to which they could go, and to which, moreover, they make their way of their own accord as soon as the understanding claims an independence full of perils. Having once overlooked the ties that bind science and metaphysics to intellectual intuition, Kant has no difficulty in showing that our science is wholly relative, and our metaphysics entirely artificial. Since he has exaggerated the independence of the understanding in both cases, since he has relieved both metaphysics and science of the intellectual intuition which served them as inward ballast, science with its relations presents to him no more than a film of form, and metaphysics, with its things, no more than a film of matter. Is it surprising that the first, then, reveals to him only frames packed within frames, and the second only phantoms chasing phantoms?

He has struck such telling blows at our science and our metaphysic that they have not even yet quite recovered from their bewilderment. Our mind would readily resign itself to seeing in science a knowledge that is wholly relative, and in metaphysics a speculation that is entirely empty. It seems to us, even at this present date, that the Kantian criticism applies to all metaphysics and to all science. In reality, it applies more especially to the philosophy of the ancients, as also to the form—itself borrowed from the ancients—in which the moderns have most often left their thought. It is valid against a metaphysic which claims to give us a *single* and completed system of things, against a science professing to be a *single* system of relations; in short, against a science and a metaphysic presenting themselves with the architectural simplicity of the Platonic theory of ideas or of a Greek temple. If metaphysics claims to be made up of concepts which were ours before its advent, if it consists in an ingenious arrangement of preexisting ideas which we utilize as building material for an edifice, if, in short, it is anything else but the constant expansion of our mind, the ever-renewed effort to transcend our actual ideas and perhaps also our elementary logic, it is but too evident that, like all the works of pure understanding, it becomes artificial. And if science is wholly and entirely a work of analysis or of conceptual representation, if experience is only to serve therein as a verification for "clear ideas," if, instead of starting from multiple and diverse intuition—which insert themselves in the particular movement of each reality, but do not always dovetail into each other,—it professes to be a vast mathematic, a single and closed-in system of relations, imprisoning the whole of reality in a network prepared in advance,—it becomes a knowledge purely relative to human understanding. If we look carefully into the *Critique of Pure Reason,* we see that science for Kant did indeed mean this kind of *universal mathematic,* and metaphysics this practically unaltered *Platonism.* In truth, the dream of a universal mathematic is itself but a survival of Platonism. Universal mathematic is what the world of ideas becomes when we suppose that the Idea consists in a relation or in a law, and no longer in a thing. Kant took this dream of a few modern philosophers for a reality; more than this, he believed that all scientific knowledge was only a detached fragment of, or rather a stepping-stone to, universal mathematics. Hence the main task of the *Critique* was to lay the foundation of this mathematic—that is, to determine what the intellect must be, and what the object, in order that an uninterrupted mathematic may bind them together. And of necessity, if all possible experience can be made to enter thus into the rigid and already formed framework of our understanding, it is (unless we assume a pre-established harmony) because our understanding itself organizes nature, and finds itself again therein as in a mirror. Hence the possibility of science, which owes all its efficacy to its relativity, and the impossibility of metaphysics, since the latter finds nothing more to do than to parody with phantoms of things the work of conceptual arrangement which science practises seriously on relations. Briefly, *the whole* Critique of Pure Reason *ends in establishing that Platonism, illegitimate if Ideas are things, becomes legitimate if Ideas are relations, and that the ready-made idea, once brought down in this way from heaven to earth, is in fact, as Plato held, the common basis alike of thought and of nature. But the whole of the* Critique of Pure Reason *also rests on this postulate, that our intellect is incapable of anything but Platonizing*—that is, of pouring all possible experience into pre-existing moulds.

On this the whole question depends. If scientific knowledge is indeed what Kant supposed, then there is one simple science, preformed and even preformulated in nature, as Aristotle believed; great discoveries, then, serve only to illuminate, point by point, the already drawn line of this logic, immanent in things, just as on the night of a fête we light up one by one the rows of gas-jets which already outline the shape of some building. And if metaphysical knowledge is really what Kant supposed, it is reduced to a *choice* between two attitudes of the mind before all the great problems, both equally possible; its manifestations are so many arbitrary and always ephemeral choices between two solutions, virtually formulated from all eternity: it lives and dies by anti-nomies. But the truth is that modern science does not present this unilinear simplicity, nor does modern metaphysics present these irreducible oppositions.

Modern science is neither one nor simple. It rests, I freely admit, on ideas which in the end we find clear; but these ideas have gradually become clear through the use made of them; they owe most of their clearness to the light which the facts, and the applications to which they led, have by reflection shed on them—the clearness of a concept being scarcely anything more at bottom than the certainty, at last obtained, of manipulating the concept profitably. At its origin, more than one of these concepts must have appeared obscure, not easily reconcilable with the concepts already admitted into science, and indeed very near the border-line of absurdity. This means that science does not proceed by an orderly dovetailing together of concepts predestined to fit each other exactly. True and fruitful ideas are so many close contacts with currents of reality, which do not necessarily converge on the same point. However, the concepts in which they lodge themselves manage somehow, by rubbing off each other's corners, to settle down well enough together.

On the other hand, modern metaphysics is not made up of solutions so radical that they can culminate in irreducible oppositions. It would be so, no doubt, if there were no means of accepting at the same time and on the same level the thesis and the antithesis of the antinomies. But philosophy consists precisely in this, that by an effort of intuition one places oneself within that concrete reality, of which the *Critique* takes from without the two opposed views, thesis and antithesis. I could never imagine how black and white interpenetrate if I had never seen gray; but once I have seen gray I easily understand how it can be considered from two points of view, that of white and that of black. Doctrines which have a certain basis of intuition escape the Kantian criticism exactly in so far as they are intuitive; and these doctrines are the whole of metaphysics, provided we ignore the metaphysics which is fixed and dead in *theses,* and consider only that which is living in *philosophers*. The divergencies between the schools—that is, broadly speaking, between the groups of disciples formed round a few great masters—are certainly striking. But would we find them as marked between the masters themselves? Something here dominates the diversity of systems, something, we repeat, which is simple and definite like a sounding, about which one feels that it has touched at greater or less depth the bottom of the same ocean, though each time it brings up to the surface very different materials. It is on these materials that the disciples usually work; in this lies the function of analysis. And the master, in so far as he formulates, develops, and translates into abstract ideas what he brings, is already in a way his own disciple. But the simple act which started the analysis, and which conceals itself behind the analysis, proceeds from a faculty quite different from the analytical. This is, by its very definition, intuition.

In conclusion, we may remark that there is nothing mysterious in this faculty. Every one of us has had occasion to exercise it to a certain extent. Any one of us, for instance, who has attempted literary composition, knows that when the subject has been studied at length, the materials all collected, and the notes all made, something more is needed in order to set about the work of composition itself, and that is an often very painful effort to place ourselves directly at the heart of the subject, and to seek as deeply as possible an impulse, after which we need only let ourselves go. This impulse, once received, starts the mind on a path where it rediscovers all the information it had collected, and a thousand other details besides; it develops and analyzes itself into terms which could be enumerated indefinitely. The farther we go, the more terms we discover; we shall never say all that could be said, and yet, if we turn back suddenly upon the impulse that we feel behind us, and try to seize it, it is gone; for it was not a thing, but the direction of a movement, and though indefinitely extensible, it is infinitely simple. Metaphysical intuition seems to be something of the same kind. What corresponds here to the documents and notes of literary composition is the sum of observations and experience gathered together by positive science. For we do not obtain an intuition from reality—that is, an intellectual sympathy with the most intimate part of it—unless we have won its confidence by a long fellowship with its superficial manifestations. And it is not merely a question of assimilating the most conspicuous facts; so immense a mass of facts must be accumulated and fused together, that in this fusion all the preconceived and premature ideas which observers may unwittingly have put into their observations will be certain to neutralize each other. In this way only can the bare materiality of the known facts be exposed to view. Even in the simple and privileged case which we have used as an example, even for the direct contact of the self with the self, the final effort of distinct intuition would be impossible to any one who had not combined and compared with each other a very large number of psychological analyses. The masters of modern philosophy were men who had assimilated all the scientific knowledge of their time, and the partial eclipse of metaphysics for the last half-century has evidently no other cause than the extraordinary difficulty which the philosopher finds to-day in getting into touch with positive science, which has become far too specialized. But metaphysical intuition, although it can be obtained only through material knowledge, is quite other than the mere summary or synthesis of that knowledge. It is distinct from these, we repeat, as the motor impulse is distinct from the path traversed by the moving body, as the tension of the spring is distinct from the visible movements of the pendulum. In this sense metaphysics has nothing in common with a generalization of facts, and nevertheless it might be defined as *integral experience*.

Edmund Husserl
1859–1938

Edmund Husserl was born in Prostêjov (Prossnitz), Moravia, in what is now the Czech Republic but was at that time part of the Austrian Empire. After elementary school there, he attended gymnasia (high schools) in Vienna and Olmütz before enrolling at the University of Leipzig in 1876. For two years he studied mathematics, physics, and astronomy, attending philosophy lectures only in his spare time. In 1878 he transferred to the Friedrich-Wilhelm University of Berlin, where he continued his study of mathematics (under the renowned Karl Weierstrass) as well as his hobby of philosophy. After three years he moved to the University of Vienna, where he received a Ph.D. in mathematics in 1883.

He was offered a teaching position in mathematics at Berlin, but Husserl decided to remain in Vienna so that he could continue studying philosophy. For two years he worked with the philosophical psychologist Franz Brentano (1838–1917). Following Brentano's advice, Husserl then moved to the University of Halle, where he published his first book, *Philosophy of Arithmetic* (1891). In 1901 he moved to the University of Göttingen, where he spent the next sixteen years and published a number of important works, including his *Ideas: General Introduction to Pure Phenomenology* (1913). His last post was at the University of Freiburg, where he taught until his retirement in 1928. Among his Freiburg associates was Martin Heidegger. Following retirement, Husserl wrote voluminously—though little was published during his lifetime. Toward the end of his life, the Nazis barred him from formal academic activities because of his Jewish ancestry.

After his death in 1938, the Husserl Archive was established in Louvain, Belgium. The Archive has preserved, transcribed, and over the decades published Husserl's shorthand notes as the *Husserliana* series. The Archive has also hosted congresses on, and published essays in, phenomenology.

*   *   *

Franz Brentano, Husserl's teacher, criticized British empiricism for its tendency to present consciousness in terms of ideas or representations. Brentano argued that the key constituent of mental states is intentionality—thought's correlation rather than its immobile state. In order to have consciousness, one must be conscious *of* something. One cannot just think, one must think *about* something; one cannot just desire, one must have desire *for* something; one cannot just be aware, one must be aware *of* something. In each case the "something" is the "intentional object" of consciousness. Contrary to Kant, Brentano held that consciousness does not *construct* these objects, it only *points to* them.

The end of the nineteenth century brought two quite different responses to Brentano. The analytic tradition, which tended to dominate English-speaking philosophy, focused almost exclusively on objects of consciousness, ignoring consciousness itself. The phenomenological tradition, dominant on the European continent, examined the nature of consciousness itself.

Husserl is the acknowledged father of this phenomenological response. Like Descartes, Husserl considered consciousness the main topic for philosophy. In examining the form of this consciousness, Husserl discovered what he called "the natural standpoint." He describes this standpoint in the section from *Ideas: General Introduction to Pure Phenomenology* reprinted here in the Boyce-Gibson translation:

> I am aware of a world, spread out in space endlessly, and in time becoming and become, without end. I am aware of it, that means, first of all, I discover it immediately, intuitively, I experience it. Through sight, touch, hearing, etc., . . . corporeal things somehow spatially distributed are *for me simply there,* . . . "present," whether or not I pay them special attention by busying myself with them, considering, thinking, feeling, willing.

This is the world as it is actually lived by an individual. While we can develop "worlds" of arithmetic or science by our knowledge of things from a particular standpoint, the natural standpoint—the world as actually lived by individuals—is always prior to, and conditioning of, any particular knowledge possible.

Yet according to Husserl it is possible to get behind this natural standpoint to identify an invariant intentional structure. Husserl developed a method of "bracketing," which he called ⟨*epochē*⟩ (from the Greek word for noncommitment or suspended judgment). For example, I may look with pleasure at a blossoming apple tree. From the natural standpoint I can see that the tree exists outside of me in space and time and that I am enjoying my psychical state of pleasure. From the natural standpoint, moreover, there is an assumed relation between me and the apple tree. But Descartes had shown that this perception could be mistaken—I could be hallucinating. As a result, my knowledge of the tree is uncertain. But I can suspend my judgments about the tree and perform an ⟨*epochē*⟩. This "bracketing" moves me from a natural to a phenomenological standpoint, where I now recognize "a nexus of exotic experiences of perception and pleasure valuation." Of this nexus of intending tree-experiences I *am* certain. By no longer referring to objective existence, by applying the phenomenological ⟨*epochē*⟩ instead, I have arrived at the pure datum of intending experience.

In the latter part of *Ideas* and in several other works, Husserl developed this method further, showing how to use the newly acquired phenomenological data. For example, in examining the experience of time, Husserl found that "lived time" is not the time of clocks and calendars but is always experienced as *now.* Similarly, in the experience of "lived space" one always finds oneself *here,* and everything else at different degrees of *there.* More importantly, Husserl believed it possible to apply the phenomenological method not only to the *objects* of consciousness but to consciousness itself. When we perform such an ⟨*epochē*⟩ on consciousness, we discover an invariant structure: the transcendental ego. "The 'I' and the 'we,' which apprehend, presuppose the hidden 'I' and 'we' to whom they are 'present.'"*

In *Philosophy and the Crisis of European Man* (1935), reprinted here (complete) in the Quentin Lauer translation, Husserl argues that Europe is in crisis because philosophy has lost its way. Writing two years after the accession to power of Hitler and the National Socialists in Germany, Husserl claimed that philosophy had lost sight of the "spiritual" nature of human beings. The Western philosophical ideal began with the Greeks' disinterested rationality, epitomized in the attitude of ⟨*thaumazein*⟩ or "wonder." But by the early twentieth century, disinterested rationality had identified with what Husserl called "naturalism": the belief that "the extraordinary successes of natural knowledge are now to be extended to knowledge of the spirit." But this extension of natural science to psychic life objectifies and so relativizes the unique "inner life of the spirit." Naturalism confuses the spiritual life of consciousness with the space–time material objects with which it works, and so misses the point. To overcome this crisis in thought, naturalism must be rejected and "European man" reborn in the spirit of Greek rationality:

> Only in . . . a supreme consciousness of self, which itself becomes a branch of the infinite task, can philosophy fulfill its function of putting itself, and therewith a genuine humanity, on the right track.

Martin Heidegger used the phenomenological method to develop his ontology, and Jean-Paul Sartre used the method to develop his own "existential" interpretation of consciousness. Husserl has lived on through his followers.

* * *

For works on phenomenology in general, see Herbert Speigelberg, *The Phenomenological Movement,* 2 vols. (The Hague, Netherlands: Martinus Nijhoff, 1960), and Joseph J. Kockelmans, ed., *Phenomenology* (Garden City, NY: Anchor Doubleday, 1967). For a clear and concise comparison of phenomenology and the analytic tradition, see W.T. Jones, *The Twentieth Century to Wittgenstein and Sartre,* 2nd ed. (New York: Harcourt Brace Jovanovich, 1975), chapters 7 and 8.

Marvin Farber, *The Foundations of Phenomenology* (Albany: State University

*Encyclopedia Britannica, 14th ed., "Phenomenology," by Edmund Husserl.

of New York Press, 1943), provides a standard study of Husserl's thought, while Joseph J. Kockelmans, *A First Introduction to Husserl's Phenomenology* (Pittsburgh: Duquesne University Press, 1967); David Bell, *Husserl* (New York: Routledge, 1990); and Rudolf Bernet, Iso Kern, and Eduard Marbach, *An Introduction to Husserlian Phenomenology* (Evanston, IL: Northwestern University Press, 1993), provide introductions. Paul Ricoeur, *Husserl: An Analysis of His Phenomenology,* translated by Edward G. Ballard and Lester E. Embree (Evanston, IL: Northwestern University Press, 1967), and Hans Georg Gadamer, *Philosophical Hermeneutics,* translated by David E. Linge (Berkeley: University of California Press, 1976), have written studies of Husserl as well as important works of philosophy in themselves. Among the many studies of particular areas of Husserl's thought, see David Carr, *Phenomenology and the Problem of History: A Study of Husserl's Transcendental Philosophy* (Evanston, IL: Northwestern University Press, 1974); Erazim V. Kohák, *Idea and Experience: Edmund Husserl's Project of Phenomenology in "Ideas I"* (Chicago: University of Chicago Press, 1978); Timothy J. Stapleton, *Husserl and Heidegger: The Question of a Phenomenological Beginning* (Albany: State University of New York Press, 1983); and James M. Edie, *Edmund Husserl's Phenomenology: A Critical Commentary* (Bloomington: Indiana University Press, 1987). For a collections of essays, see R.O. Elveton, ed., *The Phenomenology of Husserl* (Chicago: Quadrangle Books, 1970); Frederick Elliston and Peter McCormick, eds., *Husserl: Expositions and Appraisals* (Notre Dame, IN: University of Notre Dame Press, 1977); Robert Sokolowski, ed., *Edmund Husserl and the Phenomenological Tradition* (Washington, DC: Catholic University of America Press, 1988); and *Husserl Studies,* an ongoing journal published by Kluwer Academic Publishers, Hingham, MA.

IDEAS: GENERAL INTRODUCTION TO PURE PHENOMENOLOGY (in part)

SECOND SECTION: THE FUNDAMENTAL PHENOMENOLOGICAL OUTLOOK

Chapter 1: The Thesis of the Natural Standpoint and Its Suspension

§27. The world of the natural standpoint: I and my world about me

Our first outlook upon life is that of natural human beings, imaging, judging, feeling, willing, *"from the natural standpoint."* Let us make clear to ourselves what this means in the form of simple meditations which we can best carry on in the first person.

Reprinted with the permission of The Humanities Press, a Division of Macmillan, Inc. from Edmund Husserl: *Ideas: General Introduction to Pure Phenomenology,* translated by W.R. Boyce Gibson. Copyright © 1931 by the Humanities Press, Inc.

I am aware of a world, spread out in space endlessly, and in time becoming and become, without end. I am aware of it, that means, first of all, I discover it immediately, intuitively, I experience it. Through sight, touch, hearing, etc., in the different ways of sensory perception, corporeal things somehow spatially distributed are *for me simply there,* in verbal or figurative sense "present," whether or not I pay them special attention by busying myself with them, considering, thinking, feeling, willing. Animal beings also, perhaps man, are immediately there for me; I look up, I see them, I hear them coming towards me, I grasp them by the hand; speaking with them, I understand immediately what they are sensing and thinking, the feelings that stir them, what they wish or will. They too are present as realities in my field of intuition, even when I pay them no attention. But it is not necessary that they and other objects likewise should be present precisely in my *field of perception.* For me real objects are there, definite, more or less familiar, agreeing with what is actually perceived without being themselves perceived or even intuitively present. I can let my attention wander from the writing-table I have just seen and observed, through the unseen portions of the room behind my back to the verandah, into the garden, to the children in the summer-house, and so forth, to all the objects concerning which I precisely "know" that they are there and yonder in my immediate co-perceived surroundings—a knowledge which has nothing of conceptual thinking in it, and first changes into clear intuiting with the bestowing of attention, and even then only partially and for the most part very imperfectly.

But not even with the added reach of this intuitively clear or dark, distinct or indistinct *co-present* margin, which forms a continuous ring around the actual field of perception, does that world exhaust itself which in every waking moment is in some conscious measure "present" before me. It reaches rather in a fixed order of being into the limitless beyond. What is actually perceived, and what is more or less clearly co-present and determinate (to some extent at least), is partly pervaded, partly girt about with a *dimly apprehended depth or fringe of indeterminate reality.* I can pierce it with rays from the illuminating focus of attention with varying success. Determining representations, dim at first, then livelier, fetch me something out, a chain of such recollections takes shape, the circle of determinacy extends ever farther, and eventually so far that the connexion with the actual field of perception as the *immediate* environment is established. But in general the issue is a different one: an empty mist of dim indeterminacy gets studded over with intuitive possibilities or presumptions, and only the "form" of the world as "world" is foretokened. Moreover, the zone of indeterminacy is infinite. The misty horizon that can never be completely outlined remains necessarily there.

As it is with the world in its ordered being as a spatial present —the aspect I have so far been considering—so likewise is it with the world in respect to *its ordered being in the succession of time.* This world now present to me, and in every waking 'now' obviously so, has its temporal horizon, infinite in both directions, its known and unknown, its intimately alive and its unalive past and future. Moving freely within the moment of experience which brings what is present into my intuitional grasp, I can follow up these connexions of the reality which immediately surrounds me. I can shift my standpoint in space and time, look this way and that, turn temporally forwards and backwards; I can provide for myself constantly new and more or less clear and meaningful perceptions and representations, and images also more or less clear, in which I make intuitable to myself whatever can possibly exist really or supposedly in the steadfast order of space and time.

In this way, when consciously awake, I find myself at all times, and without my ever being able to change this, set in relation to a world which, through its constant changes, remains one and ever the same. It is continually "present" for me, and I myself am a member of it. Therefore this world is not there for me as a mere *world of facts and affairs,* but, with the same immediacy, as a *world of values,* a *world of goods,* a *practical world.* Without further effort on my part I find the things before me furnished not only with the qualities that befit their positive nature, but with value-characters such as beautiful or ugly, agreeable or disagreeable, pleasant or unpleasant, and so forth. Things in their immediacy stand there as objects to be used, the "table" with its "books," the "glass to drink from," the "vase," the "piano," and so forth. These values and practicalities, they too belong to *the constitution of the "actually present" objects as such,* irrespective of my turning or not turning to consider them or indeed any other objects. The same considerations apply of course just as well to the men and beasts in my surroundings as to "mere things." They are my "friends" or my "foes," my "servants" or "superiors," "strangers" or "relatives," and so forth.

§28. The "cogito." My natural world-about-me and the ideal worlds-about-me

It is then to this world, *the world in which I find myself and which is also my world-about-me,* that the complex forms of my manifold and shifting *spontaneities* of consciousness stand related: observing in the interests of research the bringing of meaning into conceptual form through description; comparing and distinguishing, collecting and counting, presupposing and inferring, the theorizing activity of consciousness, in short, in its different forms and stages. Related to it likewise are the diverse acts and states of sentiment and will: approval and disapproval, joy and sorrow, desire and aversion, hope and fear, decision and action. All these, together with the sheer acts of the Ego, in which I become acquainted with the world as *immediately* given me, through spontaneous tendencies to turn towards it and to grasp it, are included under the one Cartesian expression: *Cogito.* In the natural urge of life I live continually in *this fundamental form of all "wakeful" living,* whether in addition I do or do not assert the *cogito,* and whether I am or am not "reflectively" concerned with the Ego and the *cogitare.* If I am so concerned, a new *cogito* has become livingly active, which for its part is not reflected upon, and so not objective for me.

I am present to myself continually as someone who perceives, represents, thinks, feels, desires, and so forth; and *for the most part* herein I find myself related in present experience to the fact-world which is constantly about me. But I am not always so related, not every *cogito* in which I live has for its *cogitatum* things, men, objects or contents of one kind or another. Perhaps I am busied with pure numbers and the laws they symbolize: nothing of this sort is present in the world about me, this world of "real fact." And yet the world of numbers also is there for me, as the field of objects with which I am arithmetically busied; while I am thus occupied some numbers or constructions of a numerical kind will be at the focus of vision, girt by an arithmetical horizon partly defined, partly not; but obviously this being-there-for-me, like the being there at all, is something very different from this. *The arithmetical world is there for me only when and so long as I occupy the arithmetical standpoint.* But the *natural* world, the world in the ordinary sense of the word, is *constantly there for me,* so long as I live naturally and look in its direction. I am then at the *"natural standpoint,"* which is just another way of stating the same thing. And there is no need to modify these conclusions when I proceed to appropriate to myself the arithmetical world, and other similar "worlds," by adopting the corresponding standpoint. The nat-

ural world *still remains "present,"* I am at the natural standpoint after as well as before, and in this respect *undisturbed by the adoption of new standpoints.* If my *cogito*
is active *only* in the worlds proper to the new standpoints, the natural world remains
unconsidered; it is now the background for my consciousness as act, but it is *not the
encircling sphere within which an arithmetical world finds its true and proper place.*
The two worlds are present together but *disconnected,* apart, that is, from their relation
to the Ego, in virtue of which I can freely direct my glance or my acts to the one or to
the other.

§29. The "other" ego-subject and the intersubjective natural world-about-me

Whatever holds good for me personally, also holds good, as I know, for all other
men whom I find present in my world-about-me. Experiencing them as men, I understand and take them as Ego-subjects, units like myself, and related to their natural surroundings. But this in such wise that I apprehend the world-about-them and the world-
about-me objectively as one and the same world, which differs in each case only
through affecting consciousness differently. Each has his place whence he sees the
things that are present, and each enjoys accordingly different appearances of the things.
For each, again, the fields of perception and memory actually present are different, quite
apart from the fact that even that which is here intersubjectively known in common is
known in different ways, is differently apprehended, shows different grades of clearness, and so forth. Despite all this, we come to understandings with our neighbours, and
set up in common an objective spatio-temporal fact-world as *the world about us that is
there for us all, and to which we ourselves none the less belong.*

§30. The general thesis of the natural standpoint

That which we have submitted towards the characterization of what is given to us
from the natural standpoint, and thereby of the natural standpoint itself, was a piece of
pure description *prior to all "theory."* In these studies we stand bodily aloof from all
theories, and by 'theories' we here mean anticipatory ideas of every kind. Only as facts
of our environment, not as agencies for uniting facts validly together, do theories concern us at all. But we do not set ourselves the task of continuing the pure description and
raising it to a systematically inclusive and exhaustive characterization of the data, in
their full length and breadth, discoverable from the natural standpoint (or from any
standpoint, we might add, that can be knit up with the same in a common consent). A
task such as this can and must—as scientific—be undertaken, and it is one of extraordinary importance, although so far scarcely noticed. Here it is not ours to attempt. For us
who are striving towards the entrance-gate of phenomenology all the necessary work in
this direction has already been carried out; the few features pertaining to the natural
standpoint which we need are of a quite general character, and have already figured in
our descriptions, and been sufficiently *and fully clarified.* We even made a special point
of securing this full measure of clearness.

We emphasize a most important point once again in the sentences that follow:
I find continually present and standing over against me the one spatio-temporal fact-
world to which I myself belong, as do all other men found in it and related in the
same way to it. This "fact-world," as the word already tells us, I find to *be out there,*
and also *take it just as it gives itself to me as something that exists out there.* All
doubting and rejecting of the data of the natural world leaves standing the *general*

thesis of the natural standpoint. "The" world is as fact-world always there; at the most it is at odd points "other" than I supposed, this or that under such names as "illusion," "hallucination," and the like, must be *struck out of it,* so to speak; but the "it" remains ever, in the sense of the general thesis, a world that has its being out there. To know it more comprehensively, more trustworthily, more perfectly than the naive lore of experience is able to do, and to solve all the problems of scientific knowledge which offer themselves upon its ground, that is the goal of the *sciences of the natural standpoint.*

§31. Radical alteration of the natural thesis "disconnexion," "bracketing"

Instead now of remaining at this standpoint, we propose to alter it radically. Our aim must be to convince ourselves of the possibility of this alteration on grounds of principle.

The General Thesis according to which the real world about me is at all times known not merely in a general way as something apprehended, but as a fact-world *that has its being out there,* does *not* consist of course *in an act proper,* in an articulated judgment about existence. It is and remains something all the time the standpoint is adopted, that is, it endures persistently during the whole course of our life of natural endeavour. What has been at any time perceived clearly, or obscurely made present, in short everything out of the world of nature known through experience and prior to any thinking, bears in its totality and in all its articulated sections the character "present" "out there," a character which can function essentially as the ground of support for an explicit (predicative) existential judgment which is in agreement with the character it is grounded upon. If we express that same judgment, we know quite well that in so doing we have simply put into the form of a statement and grasped as a predication what already lay somehow in the original experience, or lay there as the character of something "present to one's hand."

We can treat the potential and unexpressed thesis exactly as we do the thesis of the explicit judgment. A procedure of this sort, *possible at any time,* is, for instance, *the attempt to doubt everything* which Descartes, with an entirely different end in view, with the purpose of setting up an absolutely indubitable sphere of Being, undertook to carry through. We link on here, but add directly and emphatically that this attempt to doubt everything should serve us *only as a device of method,* helping us to stress certain points which by its means, as though secluded in its essence, must be brought clearly to light.

The attempt to doubt everything has its place in the realm of our *perfect freedom.* We can *attempt to doubt* anything and everything, however convinced we may be concerning what we doubt, even though the evidence which seals our assurance is completely adequate.

Let us consider what is essentially involved in an act of this kind. He who attempts to doubt is attempting to doubt "Being" of some form or other, or it may be Being expanded into such predicative forms as "It is," "It is this or thus," and the like. The attempt does not affect the form of Being itself. He who doubts, for instance, whether an object, whose Being he does not doubt, is constituted in such and such a way, doubts *the way it is constituted.* We can obviously transfer this way of speaking from the doubting to the *attempt* at doubting. It is clear that we cannot doubt the Being of anything, and in the same act of consciousness (under the unifying form of simultaneity) bring what is substantive to this Being under the terms of the Natural Thesis, and so confer upon it the character of "being actually there" *(vorhanden)*. Or to put the same in another way: we cannot at once doubt and hold for certain one and the same quality of Being. It is likewise clear that the *attempt* to doubt any object of awareness in respect of its *being actually there necessarily conditions a certain suspension (Aufhebung) of the thesis;* and it is precisely this that interests us. It is not a transformation of the thesis into its antithesis, of positive into negative; it is also not a transformation into presumption, suggestion, indecision, doubt (in one or another sense of the word); such shifting indeed is not at our free pleasure. *Rather is it something quite unique. We do not abandon the thesis we have adopted, we make no change in our conviction,* which remains in itself what it is so long as we do not introduce new motives of judgment, which we precisely refrain from doing. And yet the thesis undergoes a modification—whilst remaining in itself what it is, *we set it as it were "out of action,"* we *"disconnect it," "bracket it."* It still remains there like the bracketed in the bracket, like the disconnected outside the connexional system. We can also say: The thesis is experience as lived *(Erlebnis), but we make "no use" of it,* and by that, of course, we do not indicate privation (as when we say of the ignorant that he makes no use of a certain thesis); in this case rather, as with all parallel expressions, we are dealing with indicators that point to a definite but *unique form of consciousness,* which clamps on to the original simple thesis (whether it actually or even predicatively *posits* existence or not), and transvalues it in a quite peculiar way. *This transvaluing is a concern of our full freedom, and is opposed to all cognitive attitudes* that would set themselves up as co-ordinate with *the thesis,* and yet within the unity of "simultaneity" remain incompatible with it, as indeed it is in general with all attitudes whatsoever in the strict sense of the word.

In the attempt *to doubt* applied to a thesis which, as we presuppose, is certain and tenaciously held, the "disconnexion" takes place in and with a modification of the antithesis, namely, with the *"supposition" (Ansetzung) of Non-Being,* which is thus the partial basis of the attempt to doubt. With Descartes this is so markedly the case that one can say that his universal attempt at doubt is just an attempt at universal denial. We disregard this possibility here, we are not interested in every analytic component of the attempt to doubt, nor therefore in its exact and completely sufficing analysis. *We extract only the phenomenon of "bracketing" or "disconnecting,"* which is obviously not limited to that of the attempt to doubt, although it can be detached from it with special ease, but can appear *in other contexts also,* and with no less ease *independently.* In relation to every thesis and wholly uncoerced we can use this *peculiar ⟨epochē⟩, a certain refraining from judgment which is compatible with the unshaken and unshakable because self-evidencing conviction of Truth.* The thesis is "put out of action," bracketed, it passes off into the modified status of a "bracketed thesis," and the judgment *simpliciter* into *"bracketed judgment."*

Naturally one should not simply identify this consciousness with that of "mere supposal," that nymphs, for instance, are dancing in a ring; for thereby *no disconnecting* of a living conviction that goes on living takes place, although from another side the close relation of the two forms of consciousness lies clear. Again, we are not concerned here with supposal in the sense of *"assuming"* or *taking for granted,* which in the equivocal speech of current usage may also be expressed in the words: "I suppose (I make the assumption) that it is so and so."

Let us add further that nothing hinders us *from speaking of bracketing correlatively* also, in respect of *an objectivity to be posited,* whatever be the region or category to which it belongs. What is meant in this case is that *every thesis related to this objectivity* must be *disconnected* and changed into its bracketed counterpart. On closer view, moreover, the 'bracketing' image is from the outset better suited to the sphere of the object, just as the expression 'to put out of action' better suits the sphere of the Act or of Consciousness.

§32. The phenomenological ⟨epochē⟩

We can now let the universal ⟨epochē⟩ in the sharply defined and novel sense we have given to it step into the place of the Cartesian attempt at universal doubt. But on good grounds we *limit* the universality of this ⟨epochē⟩. For were it as inclusive as it is in general capable of being, then since every thesis and every judgment can be modified freely to any extent, and every objectivity that we can judge or criticize can be bracketed, no field would be left over for unmodified judgments, to say nothing of a science. But our design is just to discover a new scientific domain, such as might be won precisely *through the method of bracketing,* though only through a definitely limited form of it.

The limiting consideration can be indicated in a word.

We put out of action the general thesis which belongs to the essence of the natural standpoint, we place in brackets whatever it includes respecting the nature of Being: *this entire natural world therefore* which is continually "there for us," "present to our hand," and will ever remain there, is a "fact-world" of which we continue to be conscious, even though it pleases us to put it in brackets.

If I do this, as I am fully free to do, I do *not* then *deny* this "world," as though I were a sophist, *I do not doubt that it is there* as though I were a sceptic; but I use the "phenomenological" ⟨epochē⟩, which *completely bars me from using any judgment that concerns spatio-temporal existence (Dasein).*

Thus *all sciences which relate to this natural world,* though they stand never so firm to me, though they fill me with wondering admiration, though I am far from any thought of objecting to them in the least degree, *I disconnect them* all, *I make absolutely no use of their standards, I do not appropriate a single one of the propositions that enter into their systems, even though their evidential value is perfect, I take none of them, no one of them serves me for a foundation*—so long, that is, as it is understood, in the way these sciences themselves understand it, as a truth *concerning the realities* of this world. *I may accept it only after I have placed it in the bracket.* That means: only in the modified consciousness of the judgment as it appears in disconnexion, and *not as it figures within the science as its proposition, a proposition which claims to be valid and whose validity I recognize and make use of.*

The ⟨epochē⟩ here in question will not be confused with that which positivism demands, and against which, as we were compelled to admit, it is itself an offender. We are not concerned at present with removing the preconceptions which trouble the pure positivity *(Sachlichkeit)* of research, with the constituting of a science "free from theory" and "free from metaphysics" by bringing all the grounding back to the immediate data, nor with the means of reaching such ends, concerning whose value there is indeed no question. What *we* demand lies along another line. The whole world as placed within the nature-setting and presented in experience as real, taken completely "free from all theory," just as it is in reality experienced, and made clearly manifest in and through the linkings of our experiences, has now no validity for us, it must be set in brackets, untested indeed but also uncontested. Similarly all theories and sciences, positivistic or otherwise, which relate to this world, however good they may be, succumb to the same fate.

Nude Descending a Staircase, Number 2, 1912, by Marcel Duchamp
(1887–1968). Duchamp's shattered and reassembled nude figure
descending the staircase in robotic rhythm purposely challenges the
viewer to derive a personal interpretation of the image—to move
beyond the natural standpoint with its judgments concerning spacio-
temporal existence. *(Philadelphia Museum of Art: Louise and Walter
Arensberg Collection)*

PHILOSOPHY AND THE CRISIS
OF EUROPEAN MAN

I

In this lecture I will venture an attempt to awaken new interest in the oft-treated theme of the European crisis by developing the philosophico-historical idea (or the teleological sense) of European man. In so far as in thus developing the topic I bring out the essential function that philosophy and its ramifications in our sciences have to perform in this process, the European crisis will also be given added clarification.

We can illustrate this in terms of the well-known distinction between scientific medicine and "naturopathy." Just as in the common life of peoples the latter derives from naïve experience and tradition, so scientific medicine results from the utilization of insights belonging to purely theoretical sciences concerned with the human body, primarily anatomy and physiology. These in turn are based on those fundamental sciences that seek a universal explanation of nature as such, physics and chemistry.

Now let us turn our gaze from man's body to his spirit, the theme of the so-called humanistic sciences. In these sciences theoretical interest is directed exclusively to human beings as persons, to their personal life and activity, as also correlatively to the concrete results of this activity. To live as a person is to live in a social framework, wherein I and we live together in community and have the community as a horizon.* Now, communities are structured in various simple or complex forms, such as family, nation, or international community. Here the word "live" is not to be taken in a physiological sense but rather as signifying purposeful living, manifesting spiritual creativity—in the broadest sense, creating culture within historical continuity. It is this that forms the theme of various humanistic sciences. Now, there is an obvious difference between healthy growth and decline, or to put it another way, between health and sickness, even for societies, for peoples, for states. In consequence there arises the not so farfetched question: how is it that in this connection there has never arisen a medical science concerned with nations and with international communities? The European nations are sick; Europe itself, they say, is in critical condition. Nor in this situation are there lacking all sorts of nature therapies. We are, in fact, quite overwhelmed with a torrent of naïve and extravagant suggestions for reform. But why is it that so luxuriantly developed humanistic sciences here fail to perform the service that in their own sphere the natural sciences perform so competently?

Those who are familiar with the spirit of modern science will not be embarrassed for an answer. The greatness of the natural sciences consists in their refusal to be content with an observational empiricism, since for them all descriptions of nature are but

---

*The notion of "horizon," which played such an important part in Husserl's earlier writings, has here taken on a somewhat broader connotation. Formerly it signified primarily those concomitant elements in consciousness that are given, without being the direct object of the act of consciousness under consideration. In every act of consciousness there are aspects of the object that are not directly intended but which are recognized, either by recall or anticipation, as belonging to the object intended. These aspects constitute its horizon. In the present essay "the community as a horizon" signifies the framework in which experience occurs, conditioning that experience and supplying the diverse aspects of objectivity that are not directly intended in any one act of consciousness. [Translator's note.]

"Philosophy and the Crisis of European Man" from *Phenomenology and the Crisis of Philosophy* by Edmund Husserl, translated by Quentin Lauer. Copyright © 1965 by Quentin Lauer. Reprinted by permission of HarperCollins Publishers.

methodical procedures for arriving at exact explanations, ultimately physico-chemical explanations. They are of the opinion that "merely descriptive" sciences tie us to the finitudes of our earthly environing world. Mathematically exact natural science, however, embraces with its method the infinities contained in its actualities and real possibilities. It sees in the intuitively given a merely subjective appearance, and it teaches how to investigate intersubjective ("objective") nature itself with systematic approximation on the basis of elements and laws that are unconditionally universal. At the same time, such exact science teaches how to explain all intuitively pre-given concretions, whether men, or animals, or heavenly bodies, by an appeal to what is ultimate, i.e., how to induce from the appearances, which are the data in any factual case, future possibilities and probabilities, and to do this with a universality and exactitude that surpasses any empiricism limited to intuition. The consistent development of exact sciences in modern times has been a true revolution in the technical mastery of nature.

In the humanistic sciences the methodological situation (in the sense already quite intelligible to us) is unfortunately quite different, and this for internal reasons. Human spirituality is, it is true, based on the human *physis,* each individually human soul-life is founded on corporeality, and thus too each community on the bodies of the individual human beings who are its members. If, then, as is done in the sphere of nature, a really exact explanation and consequently a similarly extensive scientific practical application is to become possible for the phenomena belonging to the humanistic sciences, then must the practitioners of the humanistic sciences consider not only the spirit as spirit but must also go back to its bodily foundations, and by employing the exact sciences of physics and chemistry, carry through their explanations. The attempt to do this, however, has been unsuccessful (and in the foreseeable future there is no remedy to be had) due to the complexity of the exact psycho-physical research needed in the case of individual human beings, to say nothing of the great historical communities. If the world were constructed of two, so to speak, equal spheres of reality—nature and spirit—neither with a preferential position methodologically and factually, the situation would be different. But only nature can be handled as a self-contained world; only natural science can with complete consistency abstract from all that is spirit and consider nature purely as nature. On the other side such a consistent abstraction from nature does not, for the practitioner of humanistic science who is interested purely in the spiritual, lead to a self-contained "world," a world whose interrelationships are purely spiritual, that could be the theme of a pure and universal humanistic science, parallel to pure natural science. Animal spirituality,* that of the human and animal "souls," to which all other spirituality is referred, is in each individual instance causally based on corporeality. It is thus understandable that the practitioner of humanistic science, interested solely in the spiritual as such, gets no further than the descriptive, than a historical record of spirit, and thus remains tied to intuitive finitudes. Every example manifests this. A historian, for example, cannot, after all, treat the history of ancient Greece without taking into consideration the physical geography of ancient Greece; he cannot treat its architecture without considering the materiality of its buildings, etc., etc. That seems clear enough.

What is to be said, then, if the whole mode of thought that reveals itself in this presentation rests on fatal prejudices and is in its results partly responsible for Europe's sickness? I am convinced that this is the case, and in this way I hope to make under-

---

*Where there is consciousness, there is spirit, and in animals there is consciousness. For Husserl, self-consciousness is a mark of "personality" rather than "spirituality." [Translator's note.]

standable that herein lies an essential source for the conviction which the modern scientist has that the possibility of grounding a purely self-contained and universal science of the spirit is not even worth mentioning, with the result that he flatly rejects it.

It is in the interests of our Europe-problem to penetrate a bit more deeply into this question and to expose the above, at first glance lucidly clear, argumentation. The historian, the investigator of spirit, of culture, constantly has of course physical nature too among the phenomena with which he is concerned; in our example, nature in ancient Greece. But this is not nature in the sense understood by natural science; rather it is nature as it was for the ancient Greeks, natural reality present to their eyes in the world that surrounded them. To state it more fully; the historical environing world of the Greeks is not the objective world in our sense; rather it is their "representation of the world," i.e., their own subjective evaluation, with all the realities therein that were valid for them, for example the gods, the daemons, etc.

Environing world is a concept that has its place exclusively in the spiritual sphere. That we live in our own particular environing world, to which all our concerns and efforts are directed, points to an event that takes place purely in the spiritual order. Our environing world is a spiritual structure in us and in our historical life. Here, then, there is no reason for one who makes his theme the spirit as spirit to demand for it any but a purely spiritual explanation. And this has general validity: to look upon environing nature as in itself alien to spirit, and consequently to desire to support humanistic science with natural science and thus presumably to make the former exact, is nonsense.

Obviously, too, it is forgotten that natural science (like all sciences as such) is a title for spiritual activities, those of natural scientists in cooperation with each other; as such these activities belong, as do all spiritual occurrences, to the realm of what should be explained by means of a science of the spirit. Is it not, then, nonsensical and circular, to desire to explain by means of natural science the historical event "natural science," to explain it by invoking natural science and its laws of nature, both of which, as produced by spirit, are themselves part of the problem?

Blinded by naturalism (no matter how much they themselves may verbally oppose it), the practitioners of humanistic science have completely neglected even to pose the problem of a universal and pure science of the spirit and to seek a theory of the essence of spirit as spirit, a theory that pursues what is unconditionally universal in the spiritual order with its own elements and its own laws. Yet this last should be done with a view to gaining thereby scientific explanations in an absolutely conclusive sense.

The preceding reflections proper to a science of the spirit provide us with the right attitude for grasping and handling our theme of spiritual Europe as a problem belonging purely to science of the spirit, first of all from the point of view of spirit's history. As has already been stated in the introductory remarks, in following this path we should reveal an extraordinary teleology, which is, so to speak, innate only in our Europe. This, moreover, is most intimately connected with the eruption (or the invasion) of philosophy and of its ramifications, the sciences, in the ancient Greek spirit. We already suspect that there will be question of clarifying the profoundest reasons for the origin of fatal naturalism, or—and this is of equal importance—of modern dualism in interpreting the world. Ultimately the proper sense of European man's crisis should thereby come to light.

We may ask, "How is the spiritual image of Europe to be characterized?" This does not mean Europe geographically, as it appears on maps, as though European man were to be in this way confined to the circle of those who live together in this territory. In the spiritual sense it is clear that to Europe belong the English dominions, the United States, etc., but not, however, the Eskimos or Indians of the country fairs, or the Gypsies, who are constantly wandering about Europe. Clearly the title Europe designates the unity of a spiritual life and a creative activity—with all its aims, interests, cares, and troubles, with its plans, its establishments, its institutions. Therein individual human beings work in a variety of societies, on different levels, in families, races, nations, all intimately joined together in spirit and, as I said, in the unity of one spiritual image. This should stamp on persons, groups, and all their cultural accomplishments an all-unifying character.

"The spiritual image of Europe"—what is it? It is exhibiting the philosophical idea immanent in the history of Europe (of spiritual Europe). To put it another way, it is its immanent teleology, which, if we consider mankind in general, manifests itself as a new human epoch emerging and beginning to grow, the epoch of a humanity that from now on will and can live only in the free fashioning of its being and its historical life out of rational ideas and infinite tasks.

Every spiritual image has its place essentially in a universal historical space or in a particular unity of historical time in terms of coexistence or succession—it has its history. If, then, we follow historical connections, beginning as we must with ourselves and our own nation, historical continuity leads us ever further away from our own to neighboring nations, and so from nation to nation, from age to age. Ultimately we come to ancient times and go from the Romans to the Greeks, to the Egyptians, the Persians, etc.; in this there is clearly no end. We go back to primeval times, and we must perforce turn to Menghin's significant and genial work *The History of the Stone Age*. To an investigation of this type mankind manifests itself as a single life of men and of peoples, bound together by spiritual relationships alone, filled with all types of human beings and of cultures, but constantly flowing each into the other. It is like a sea in which human beings, peoples, are the waves constantly forming, changing, and disappearing, some more richly, more complexly involved, others more simply.

In this process consistent, penetrating observation reveals new, characteristic compositions and distinctions. No matter how inimical the European nations may be toward each other, still they have a special inner affinity of spirit that permeates all of them and transcends their national differences. It is a sort of fraternal relationship that gives us the consciousness of being at home in this circle. This becomes immediately evident as soon as, for example, we penetrate sympathetically into the historical process of India, with its many peoples and cultural forms. In this circle there is again the unity of a family-like relationship, but one that is strange to us. On the other hand, Indians find us strangers and find only in each other their fellows. Still, this essential distinction between fellowship and strangeness, which is relativized on many levels and is a basic category of all historicity, cannot suffice. Historical humanity does not always divide itself in the same way according to this category. We get a hint of that right in our own Europe. Therein lies something unique, which all other human groups, too, feel with regard to us, something that, apart from all considerations of expediency, becomes a motivation for them—despite their determination to retain their spiritual autonomy constantly to Europeanize themselves, whereas we, if we understand ourselves properly, will never, for example, Indianize ourselves. I mean we feel (and with all its vagueness this feeling is correct) that in our European humanity there is an innate entelechy that thoroughly controls the changes in the European image and gives to it the sense of a development in the direction of an ideal image of life and of being, as moving toward an eternal pole. It is not as though there were question here of one of those known orientations that give to the physical realm of organic beings its character; not a question, therefore, of something like biological development in stages from seminal form up to maturity followed by aging and dying out. There is essentially no zoology of peoples.

They are spiritual unities. They have not, and above all the supernationality Europe has not, a mature form that has been or can be reached, no form of regular repetition. From the point of view of soul, humanity has never been a finished product, nor will it be, nor can it ever repeat itself. The spiritual *telos* of European Man, in which is included the particular *telos* of separate nations and of individual human beings, lies in infinity; it is an infinite idea, toward which in secret the collective spiritual becoming, so to speak, strives. Just as in the development it becomes a conscious *telos,* so too it becomes necessarily practical as a goal of the will, and thereby is introduced a new, a higher stage of development that is guided by norms, by normative ideas.

All of this, however, is not intended as a speculative interpretation of our historicity but rather as the expression of a vital anticipation arising out of unprejudiced reflection. But this anticipation serves as intentional guidance toward seeing in European history extraordinarily significant connections, in the pursuit of which the anticipated becomes for us guaranteed certainty. Anticipation is the emotional guide to all discoveries.

Let us develop this. Spiritually Europe has a birthplace. By this I do not mean a geographical place, in some one land, though this too is true. I refer, rather, to a spiritual birthplace in a nation or in certain men or groups of men belonging to this nation. It is the ancient Greek nation in the seventh and sixth centuries B.C. In it there grows up a new kind of attitude of individuals toward their environing world. Consequent upon this emerges a completely new type of spiritual structure, rapidly growing into a systematically rounded *(geschlossen)* cultural form that the Greeks called philosophy. Correctly translated, in its original sense, this bespeaks nothing but universal science, science of the world as a whole, of the universal unity of all being. Very soon the interest in the totality and, by the same token, the question regarding the all-embracing becoming and the resulting being begin to particularize themselves in accord with the general forms and regions of being. Thus philosophy, the one science, is ramified into the various particular sciences.

In the emergence of philosophy in this sense, a sense, that is, which includes all sciences, I see—no matter how paradoxical this may seem—the original phenomenon of spiritual Europe. The elucidations that follow, however brief they must be kept, will soon eliminate the seeming paradox.

Philosophy-science is the title for a special class of cultural structures. The historical movement that has taken on the form of European supernationality goes back to an ideal image whose dimension is the infinite; not, however, to an image that could be recognized in a merely external morphological examination of changing forms. To have a norm constantly in view is something intimately a part of the intentional life of individual persons and consequently of nations and of particular societies within the latter, and ultimately of the organism formed by the nations united together as Europe. This, of course, is not true of all persons and, therefore, is not fully developed in the higher-level personalities constituted by intersubjective acts. Still, it is present in them in the form of a necessary progressive development and extension in the spirit of universally valid norms. This spirit, however, signifies at the same time the progressive transformation of collective humanity beginning with the effective formation of ideas in small and even in the smallest circles. Ideas, conceived within individual persons as sense-structures that in a wonderfully new manner secrete within themselves intentional infinities, are not in space like real things, which latter, entering as they do into the field of human experiences, do not by that very fact as yet signify anything for the human being as a person. With the first conception of ideas man gradually becomes a new man. His spiritual being enters into the movement of a progressive reformation. This movement from the very beginning involves communication and awakens a new style of personal existence in its vital circle by a better understanding of a correspondingly new becoming. In this movement first of all (and subsequently even beyond it) a special type of humanity spreads out, living in finitude but oriented toward poles of infinity. By the very same token there grows up a new mode of sociality and a new form of enduring society, whose spiritual life, cemented together by a common love of and creation of ideas and by the setting of ideal norms for life, carries within itself a horizon of infinity for the future—an infinity of generations finding constant spiritual renewal in ideas. This takes place first of all in the spiritual territory of a single nation, the Greeks, as a development of philosophy and of philosophical communities. Along with this there grows, first in this nation, a general cultural spirit that draws the whole of mankind under its sway and is therefore a progressive transformation in the shape of a new historicity.

This rough sketch will gain in completeness and intelligibility as we examine more closely the historical origin of philosophical and scientific man and thereby clarify the sense of Europe and, consequently, the new type of historicity that through this sort of development distinguishes itself from history in general.

First, let us elucidate the remarkable character of philosophy as it unfolds in ever-new special sciences. Let us contrast it with other forms of culture already present in pre-scientific man, in his artefacts, his agriculture, his architecture, etc. All manifest classes of cultural products along with the proper methods for insuring their successful production. Still, they have a transitory existence in their environing world. Scientific achievements, on the other hand, once the method of insuring their successful creation has been attained, have an entirely different mode of being, an entirely different temporality. They do not wear out, they are imperishable. Repeated creation does not produce something similar, at best something similarly useful. Rather, no matter how many times the same person or any number of persons repeat these achievements, they remain exactly identical, identical in sense and in value. Persons united together in actual mutual understanding can only experience what their respective fellows have produced in the same manner as identical with what they have produced themselves. In a word, what scientific activity achieves is not real but ideal.

What is more, however, whatever validity or truth has been gained in this way serves as material for the production of higher-level idealities; and this goes on and on. Now, in the developed theoretical interest, each interest receives ahead of time the sense of a merely relative goal; it becomes a transition to constantly new, higher-level goals in an infinity pre-indicated as science's universal field of endeavor, its "domain." Thus science designates the idea of an infinity of tasks, of which at any time a finite number have already been accomplished and are retained in their enduring validity. These constitute at the same time the fund of premises for an endless horizon of tasks united into one all-embracing task.

Here, however, an important supplementary remark should be made. In science the ideality of what is produced in any particular instance means more than the mere capacity for repetition based on a sense that has been guaranteed as identical; the idea of truth in the scientific sense is set apart (and of this we have still to speak) from the truth proper to pre-scientific life. Scientific truth claims to be unconditioned truth, which involves infinity, giving to each factually guaranteed truth a merely relative character, making it only an approach oriented, in fact, toward the infinite horizon, wherein the truth in itself is, so to speak, looked on as an infinitely distant point. By the same token this infinity belongs also to what in the scientific sense "really is." A fortiori, there is infinity involved in "universal" validity for "everyone," as the subject of whatever rational foundations are to be secured; nor is this any longer everyone in the finite sense the term has in pre-scientific life.

Having thus characterized the ideality peculiar to science, with the ideal infinities variously implied in the very sense of science, we are faced, as we survey the historical situation, with a contrast that we express in the following proposition: no other cultural form in the pre-philosophical historical horizon is a culture of ideas in the above-mentioned sense; none knows any infinite tasks—none knows of such universes of idealities that as wholes and in all their details, as also in their methods of production, bear within themselves an essential infinity.

Extra-scientific culture, not yet touched by science, is a task accomplished by man in finitude. The openly endless horizon around him is not made available to him. His aims and activities, his commerce and his travel, his personal, social, national, mythical motivation—all this moves about in an environing world whose finite dimensions can be viewed. Here there are no infinite tasks, no ideal attainments whose very infinity is man's field of endeavor—a field of endeavor such that those who work in it are conscious that it has the mode of being proper to such an infinite sphere of tasks.

With the appearance of Greek philosophy, however, and with its first definitive formulation in a consistent idealizing of the new sense of infinity, there occurs, from this point of view, a progressive transformation that ultimately draws into its orbit all ideas proper to finitude and with them the entire spiritual culture of mankind. For us Europeans there are, consequently, even outside the philosophico-scientific sphere, any number of infinite ideas (if we may use the expression), but the analogous character of infinity that they have (infinite tasks, goals, verifications, truths, "true values," "genuine goods," "absolutely" valid norms) is due primarily to the transformation of man through philosophy and its idealities. Scientific culture in accord with ideas of infinity means, then, a revolutionizing of all culture, a revolution that affects man's whole manner of being as a creator of culture. It means also a revolutionizing of historicity, which is now the history of finite humanity's disappearance, to the extent that it grows into a humanity with infinite tasks.

Here we meet the obvious objection that philosophy, the science of the Greeks, is not, after all, distinctive of them, something which with them first came into the world. They themselves tell of the wise Egyptians, Babylonians, etc.; and they did in fact learn much from these latter. Today we possess all sorts of studies on Indian, Chinese, and other philosophies, studies that place these philosophies on the same level with Greek philosophy, considering them merely as different historical formulations of one and the same cultural idea. Of course, there is not lacking something in common. Still, one must not allow intentional depths to be covered over by what is merely morphologically common and be blind to the most essential differences of principle.

Before anything else, the attitude of these two kinds of "philosophers," the overall orientation of their interests, is thoroughly different. Here and there one may observe a world-embracing interest that on both sides (including, therefore, the Indian, Chinese, and other like "philosophies") leads to universal cognition of the world, everywhere developing after the manner of a sort of practical vocational interest and for quite intelligible reasons leading to vocational groups, in which from generation to generation common results are transmitted and even developed. Only with the Greeks, however, do we find a universal ("cosmological") vital interest in the essentially new form of a purely "theoretical" attitude. This is true, too, of the communal form in which the interest works itself out, the corresponding, essentially new attitude of the philosophers and the scientists (mathematicians, astronomers, etc.). These are the men who, not isolated but with each other and for each other, i.e., bound together in a common interpersonal endeavor, strive for and carry into effect *theoria* and only *theoria*. These are the ones whose growth and constant improvement ultimately, as the circle of cooperators extends and the generations of investigators succeed each other, become a will oriented in the direction of an infinite and completely universal task. The theoretical attitude has its historical origin in the Greeks.

Speaking generally, attitude bespeaks a habitually determined manner of vital willing, wherein the will's directions or interests, its aims and its cultural accomplishments, are pre-indicated and thus the overall orientation determined. In this enduring orientation taken as a norm, the individual life is lived. The concrete cultural contents change in a relatively enclosed historicity. In its historical situation mankind (or the closed community, such as a nation, a race, etc.) always lives within the framework of some sort of attitude. Its life always has a normative orientation and within this a steady historicity or development.

Thus if the theoretical attitude in its newness is referred back to a previous, more primitive normative attitude, the theoretical is characterized as a transformed attitude. Looking at the historicity of human existence universally in all its communal forms and in its historical stages, we find, then, that essentially a certain style of human existence (taken in formal universality) points to a primary historicity, within which the actual normative style of culture-creating existence at any time, no matter what its rise or fall or stagnation, remains formally the same. In this regard we are speaking of the natural, the native attitude, of originally natural life, of the first primitively natural form of cultures—be they higher or lower, uninhibitedly developing or stagnating. All other attitudes, then, refer back to these natural ones as transformations of them. To put it more concretely, in an attitude natural to one of the actual human groups in history there must arise at a point in time motives that for the first time impel individual men and groups having this attitude to transform it.

How are we, then, to characterize the essentially primitive attitude, the fundamental historical mode of human existence? The answer: on the basis of generation men naturally live in communities—in a family, a race, a nation—and these communities are in themselves more or less abundantly subdivided into particular social units. Now, life on the level of nature is characterized as a naïvely direct living immersed in the world, in the world that in a certain sense is constantly there consciously as a universal horizon but is not, merely by that fact, thematic. Thematic is that toward which man's attention is turned. Being genuinely alive is always having one's attention turned to this or that, turned to something as to an end or a means, as relevant or irrelevant, interesting or indifferent, private or public, to something that is in daily demand or to something that is startlingly new. All this belongs to the world horizon, but there is need of special motives if the one who is caught up in such a life in the world is to transform himself and is to come to the point where he somehow makes this world itself his theme, where he conceives an enduring interest in it.

But here more detailed explanations are needed. Individual human beings who change their attitudes as human beings belonging to their own general vital community (their nation), have their particular natural interests (each his own). These they can by no change in attitude simply lose; that would mean for each ceasing to be the individual he is, the one he has been since birth. No matter what the circumstances, then, the transformed attitude can only be a temporary one. It can take on a lasting character that will endure as a habit throughout an entire life only in the form of an unconditional determination of will to take up again the selfsame attitudes in a series of periods that are temporary but intimately bound together. It will mean that by virtue of a continuity that bridges intentionally the discreteness involved, men will hold on to the new type of interests as worth being realized and will embody them in corresponding cultural forms.

We are familiar with this sort of thing in the occupations that make their appearance even in a naturally primitive form of cultural life, where there are temporary periods devoted to the occupation, periods that interrupt the rest of life with its concrete temporality (e.g., the working hours of a functionary, etc.).

Now, there are two possibilities. On the one hand, the interests of the new attitude will be made subservient to the natural interests of life, or what is essentially the same, to natural practicality. In this case the new attitude is itself a practical one. This, then, can have a sense similar to the practical attitude of the politician, who as a state functionary is attentive to the common good and whose attitude, therefore, is to serve the practical interests of all (and incidentally his own). This sort of thing admittedly still belongs to the domain of the natural attitude, which is, of course, different for different types of community members and is in fact one thing for the leaders of the community and another for the "citizens"—both obviously understood in the broadest sense. In any event, the analogy makes it clear that the universality of a practical attitude, in this case one that embraces a whole world, need in no way signify being interested in and occupied with all the details and particularities of that world—it would obviously be unthinkable.

In contrast to the higher-level practical attitude there exists, however, still another essential possibility of a change in the universal natural attitude (with which we shall soon become acquainted in its type, the mythical-religious attitude), which is to say, the theoretical attitude—a name being given to it, of course, only provisionally, because in this attitude philosophical *theoria* must undergo a development and so become its proper aim or field of interest. The theoretical attitude, even though it too is a professional attitude, is thoroughly unpractical. Thus it is based on a deliberate ⟨*epoché*⟩ from all practical interests,* and consequently even those of a higher level, that serve natural needs within the framework of a life's occupation governed by such practical interests.

Still, it must at the same time be said that there is no question here of a definitive "cutting off" of the theoretical life from the practical. We are not saying that the concrete life of the theoretical thinker falls into two disconnected vital continuities partitioned off from each other, which would mean, socially speaking, that two spiritually unconnected spheres would come into existence. For there is still a third form of universal attitude possible (in contrast both to the mythical-religious, which is based on the natural, and to the theoretical attitudes). It is the synthesis of opposing interests that occurs in the transition from the theoretical to the practical attitude. In this way *theoria* (the universal science), whose growth has manifested a tight unity through an ⟨*epoché*⟩ from all practical considerations, is called upon (and even proves in a theoretical insight that it is called upon) to serve humanity in a new way, first of all in its concrete existence as it continues to live naturally. This takes place in the form of a new kind of practical outlook, a universal critique of all life and of its goals, of all the forms and systems of culture that have already grown up in the life of mankind. This brings with it a critique of mankind itself and of those values that explicitly or implicitly guide it. Carrying it to a further consequence, it is a practical outlook whose aim is to elevate mankind

---

*In a somewhat different context the meaning of ⟨*epoché*⟩ here parallels its technical meaning as employed, for example, in *Ideen I* [*Ideas: General Introduction to Pure Phenomenology*. See page 312 in this volume—FB.] It is neither an elimination of nor a prescinding from other interests. Rather, it simply "puts them in brackets," thus retaining them, but allowing them in no way to influence theoretical considerations. [Translator's note.]

through universal scientific reason in accord with norms of truth in every form, and thus to transform it into a radically new humanity made capable of an absolute responsibility to itself on the basis of absolute theoretical insights. Still, prior to this synthesis of theoretical universality and a practical outlook with universal interests, there is obviously another synthesis of theory and practice—the utilization of the limited results of theory, of those special sciences that are limited to the practical aspects of natural life, having relinquished by their very specialization the universality of theoretical interest. Here the primitively natural attitude and the theoretical are joined together in an orientation toward finite goals.

For a profounder understanding of Greco-European science (universally speaking, this means philosophy) in its fundamental difference from the equally notable oriental "philosophies," it is now necessary to consider in more detail the practically universal attitude, and to explain it as mythical-religious, an attitude that, prior to European science, brings those other philosophies into being. It is a well-known fact, to say nothing of an essentially obvious necessity, that mythical-religious motives and a mythical-religious practice together belong to a humanity living naturally—before Greek philosophy, and with it a scientific world view, entered on the scene and matured. A mythical-religious attitude is one that takes as its theme the world as a totality—a practical theme. The world in this case is, of course, one that has a concrete, traditional significance for the men in question (let us say, a nation) and is thus mythically apperceived. This sort of mythical-natural attitude embraces from the very first not only men and animals and other infrahuman and infra-animal beings *(Wesen)* but also the suprahuman. The view that embraces them as a totality is a practical one; not, however, as though man, whose natural life, after all, is such that he is actually interested only in certain realities, could ever have come to the point where everything together would suddenly and in equal degree take on practical relevance. Rather, to the extent that the whole world is looked upon as dominated by mythical powers and to the extent that human destiny depends immediately or mediately on the way these powers rule in the world, a universally mythical world view may have its source in practicality and is, then, itself a world view whose interests are practical. It is understandable that priests belonging to a priesthood in charge of both mythical-religious interests and of the traditions belonging to them should have motives for such a mythical-religious attitude. With this priesthood there arises and spreads the linguistically solidified "knowledge" of these mythical powers (in the broadest sense thought of as personal). This knowledge quasi-automatically takes on the form of a mystical speculation which, by setting itself up as a naïvely convincing interpretation, transforms the mythos itself. At the same time, obviously, attention is constantly directed also to the ordinary world ruled by these mythical powers and to the human and infrahuman beings belonging to it (these, incidentally, unsettled in their own essential being, are also open to the influence of mythical factors). This attention looks to the ways in which the powers control the events of this world, the manner in which they themselves must be subject to a unified supreme order of power, the manner in which they with regard to individual functions and functioners intervene by initiating and carrying out, by handing down decrees of fate. All this speculative knowledge, however, has as its purpose to serve man toward his human aims, to enable him to live the happiest possible life on earth, to protect that life from sickness, from misfortune, need, and death. It is understandable that in this mythico-practical approach to knowing the world there can arise not a little knowledge of the actual world, of the world known in a sort of scientific experience, a knowledge subsequently to be subjected to a scientific evaluation. Still, this sort of knowledge is and remains mythico-practical in its logical connections, and it is a mistake for someone brought up in the scientific modes of thought initiated in Greece and progressively developed in modern times to speak of Indian and Chinese philosophy (astronomy, mathematics) and thus to interpret India, Babylonia, and China in a European way.

There is a sharp cleavage, then, between the universal but mythico-practical attitude and the "theoretical," which by every previous standard is unpractical, the attitude of ⟨*thaumazein*⟩ [Gr. = to wonder], to which the great men of Greek philosophy's first culminating period, Plato and Aristotle, trace the origin of philosophy. Men are gripped by a passion for observing and knowing the world, a passion that turns from all practical interests and in the closed circle of its own knowing activities, in the time devoted to this sort of investigation, accomplishes and wants to accomplish only pure ⟨*theoria*⟩. In other words, man becomes the disinterested spectator, overseer of the world, he becomes a philosopher. More than that, from this point forward his life gains a sensitivity for motives which are possible only to this attitude, for novel goals and methods of thought, in the framework of which philosophy finally comes into being and man becomes philosopher.

Like everything that occurs in history, of course, the introduction of the theoretical attitude has its factual motivation in the concrete circumstances of historical events. Therefore it is worthwhile to explain in this connection how, considering the manner of life and the horizon of Greek man in the seventh century B.C., in his intercourse with the great and already highly cultivated nations surrounding him, that ⟨*thaumazein*⟩ could introduce itself and at first become established in individuals. Regarding this we shall not enter into greater detail; it is more important for us to understand the path of motivation, with its sense-giving and sense-creating, which leads from mere conversion (or from mere ⟨*thaumazein*⟩) to ⟨*theoria*⟩—a historical fact, that nevertheless must have in it something essential. It is important to explain the change from original ⟨*theoria*⟩, from the completely "disinterested" (consequent upon the ⟨*epochē*⟩ from all practical interests) world view (knowledge of the world based only on universal contemplation) to the ⟨*theoria*⟩ proper to science—both stages exemplifying the contrast between ⟨*doxa*⟩ [Gr. = opinion] and ⟨*episteme*⟩ [Gr. = knowledge]. The theoretical interest that comes on the scene as that ⟨*thaumazein*⟩, is clearly a modification of curiosity that has its original place in natural life as an interruption in the course of "earnest living," as a working out of originally effected vital interests, or as a playful looking about when the specific needs of actual life have been satisfied or working hours are past. Curiosity, too (not in the sense of an habitual "vice"), is a modification, an interest raised above merely vital interests and prescinding from them.

With an attitude such as this, man observes first of all the variety of nations, his own and others, each with its own environing world, which with its traditions, its gods and demigods, with its mythical powers, constitutes for each nation the self-evident, real world. In the face of this extraordinary contrast there arises the distinction between the represented and the real world, and a new question is raised concerning the truth—not everyday truth bound as it is to tradition but a truth that for all those who are not blinded by attachment to tradition is identical and universally valid, a truth in itself. Thus it is proper to the theoretical attitude of the philosopher that he is more and more pre-determined to devote his whole future life, in the sense of a universal life, to the task of ⟨*theoria*⟩, to build theoretical knowledge upon theoretical knowledge *in infinitum.*

In isolated personalities, like Thales, et al., there thus grows up a new humanity—men whose profession it is to create a philosophical life, philosophy as a novel form of culture. Understandably there grows up at the same time a correspondingly novel form of community living. These ideal forms are, as others understand them and make them their own, simply taken up and made part of life. In like manner they lead to coopera-

tive endeavor and to mutual help through criticism. Even the outsiders, the nonphiloso-
phers, have their attention drawn to the unusual activity that is going on. As they come
to understand, they either become philosophers themselves, or if they are too much
taken up with their own work, they become pupils. Thus philosophy spreads in a
twofold manner, as a widening community of professional philosophers and as a common educational movement growing along with the former. Here also, however, lies the
origin of the subsequent, so unfortunate internal split in the unity of the people into educated and uneducated. Still, it is clear that this tendency to spread is not confined to the
limits of the originating nation. Unlike all other cultural products, this is not a movement of interests bound to the soil of national traditions. Even foreigners learn in their
turn to understand and in general to share in the gigantic cultural change which streams
forth from philosophy. Now precisely this must be further characterized.

As philosophy spreads in the form of research and training, it produces a twofold
effect. On the one hand, most essential to the theoretical attitude of philosophical man
is the characteristic universality of the critical standpoint, which its determination not to
accept without question any pre-given opinion, any tradition, and thus to seek out, with
regard to the entire universe handed down in tradition, the true in itself—which is ideal.
Yet this is not merely a new way of looking at knowledge. By virtue of the demand to
subject the whole of experience to ideal norms, i.e., those of unconditional truth, there
results at the same time an all-embracing change in the practical order of human existence and thus of cultural life in its entirety. The practical must no longer take its norms
from naïve everyday experience and from tradition but from the objective truth. In this
way ideal truth becomes an absolute value that in the movement of education and in its
constant application in the training of children carries with it a universal revision of
practice. If we consider somewhat more in detail the manner of this transformation, we
shall immediately understand the inevitable: if the general idea of truth in itself becomes the universal norm of all the relative truths that play a role in human life—actual
and conjectural situation truths—then this fact affects all traditional norms, those of
right, of beauty, of purpose, of dominant values in persons, values having a personal
character, etc.

Thus there grows up a special type of man and a special vocation in life correlative to the attainment of a new culture. Philosophical knowledge of the world produces
not only these special types of result but also a human conduct that immediately influences the rest of practical living with all its demands and its aims, aims of the historical
tradition according to which one is educated, thus giving these aims their own validity.
A new and intimate community, we might say a community of ideal interests, is cultivated among men—men who live for philosophy, united in their dedication to ideas,
which ideas are not only of use to all but are identically the property of all. Inevitably
there develops a particular kind of cooperation whereby men work with each other and
for each other, helping each other by mutual criticism, with the result that the pure and
unconditioned validity of truth grows as a common possession. In addition there is the
necessary tendency toward the promotion of interest, because others understand what is
herein desired and accomplished; and this is a tendency to include more and more as yet
unphilosophical persons in the community of those who philosophize. This occurs first
of all among members of the same nation. Nor can this expansion be confined to professional scientific research; rather its success goes far beyond the professional circle,
becoming an educational movement.

Now, if this educational movement spreads to ever wider circles of the people,
and naturally to the superior, dominant types, to those who are less involved in the cares
of life, the results are of what sort? Obviously it does not simply bring about a homoge-

neous change in the normal, on the whole satisfactory national life; rather in all probability it leads to great cleavages, wherein the national life and the entire national culture go into an upheaval. The conservatives, content with tradition, and the philosophical circle will struggle against each other, and without doubt the battle will carry over into the sphere of political power. At the very beginning of philosophy, persecution sets in. The men dedicated to those ideas are outlawed. And yet ideas are stronger than any forces rooted in experience.

A further point to be taken into consideration here is that philosophy, having grown out of a critical attitude to each and every traditional predisposition, is limited in its spread by no national boundaries. All that must be present is the capacity for a universal critical attitude, which too, of course, presupposes a certain level of pre-scientific culture. Thus can the upheaval in the national culture propagate itself, first of all because the progressing universal science becomes a common possession of nations that were at first strangers to each other, and then because a unified community, both scientific and educational, extends to the majority of nations.

Still another important point must be adduced; it concerns philosophy's position in regard to traditions. There are in fact two possibilities to observe here. Either the traditionally accepted is completely rejected, or its content is taken over philosophically, and thereby it too is reformed in the spirit of philosophical ideality. An outstanding case in point is that of religion—from which I should like to exclude the "polytheistic religions." Gods in the plural, mythical powers of every kind, are objects belonging to the environing world, on the same level of reality as animal or man. In the concept of God, the singular is essential. Looking at this from the side of man, moreover, it is proper that the reality of God, both as being and as value, should be experienced as binding man interiorly. There results, then, an understandable blending of this absoluteness with that of philosophical ideality. In the overall process of idealization that philosophy undertakes, God is, so to speak, logicized and becomes even the bearer of the absolute logos. I should like, moreover, to see a logic in the very fact that theologically religion invokes faith itself as evidence and thus as a proper and most profound mode of grounding true being. National gods, however, are simply there as real facts of the environing world, without anyone confronting philosophy with questions stemming from a critique of cognition, with questions of evidence.

Substantially, though in a somewhat sketchy fashion, we have now described the historical movement that makes understandable how, beginning with a few Greek exceptions, a transformation of human existence and of man's entire cultural life could be set in motion, beginning in Greece and its nearest neighbors. Moreover, now it is also discernible how, following upon this, a supernationality of a completely new kind could arise. I am referring, of course, to the spiritual form of Europe. It is now no longer a number of different nations bordering on each other, influencing each other only by commercial competition and war. Rather a new spirit stemming from philosophy and the sciences based on it, a spirit of free criticism providing norms for infinite tasks, dominates man, creating new, infinite ideals. These are ideals for individual men of each nation and for the nations themselves. Ultimately, however, the expanding synthesis of nations too has its infinite ideals, wherein each of these nations, by the very fact that it strives to accomplish its own ideal task in the spirit of infinity, contributes its best to the community of nations. In this give and take the supernational totality with its graded structure of societies grows apace, filled with the spirit of one all-inclusive task, infinite in the variety of its branches yet unique in its infinity. In this total society with its ideal orientation, philosophy itself retains the role of guide, which is its special infinite task. Philosophy has the role of a free and universal theoretical disposition that embraces at once all ideals and the one overall ideal—in short, the universe of all norms. Philosophy has constantly to exercise through European man its role of leadership for the whole of mankind.

II

It is now time that there be voiced misunderstandings and doubts that are certainly very importunate and which, it seems to me, derive their suggestive force from the language of popular prejudice.

Is not what is here being advocated something rather out of place in our times—saving the honor of rationalism, of enlightenment, of an intellectualism that, lost in theory, is isolated from the world, with the necessarily bad result that the quest for learning becomes empty, becomes intellectual snobbishness? Does it not mean falling back into the fatal error of thinking that science makes men wise, that science is called upon to create a genuine humanity, superior to destiny and finding satisfaction in itself? Who is going to take such thoughts seriously today?

This objection certainly is relatively justified in regard to the state of development in Europe from the seventeenth up to the end of the nineteenth century. But it does not touch the precise sense of what I am saying. I should like to think that I, seemingly a reactionary, am far more revolutionary than those who today in word strike so radical a pose.

I, too, am quite sure that the European crisis has its roots in a mistaken rationalism. That, however, must not be interpreted as meaning that rationality as such is an evil or that in the totality of human existence it is of minor importance. The rationality of which alone we are speaking is rationality in that noble and genuine sense, the original Greek sense, that became an ideal in the classical period of Greek philosophy—though of course it still needed considerable clarification through self-examination. It is its vocation, however, to serve as a guide to mature development. On the other hand, we readily grant (and in this regard German idealism has spoken long before us) that the form of development given to *ratio* in the rationalism of the Enlightenment was an aberration, but nevertheless an understandable aberration.

Reason is a broad title. According to the good old definition, man is the rational living being, a sense in which even the Papuan is man and not beast. He has his aims, and he acts with reflection, considering practical possibilities. As products and methods grow, they enter into a tradition that is ever intelligible in its rationality. Still, just as man (and even the Papuan) represents a new level of animality in comparison with the beast—so with regard to humanity and its reason does philosophical reason represent a new level. The level of human existence with its ideal norms for infinite tasks, the level of existence *sub specie aeternitatis,* is, however, possible only in the form of absolute universality, precisely that which is a priori included in the idea of philosophy. It is true that universal philosophy, along with all the particular sciences, constitutes only a partial manifestation of European culture. Contained, however, in the sense of my entire presentation is the claim that this part is, so to speak, the functioning brain upon whose normal functioning the genuine, healthy spirit of Europe depends. The humanity of higher man, of reason, demands, therefore, a genuine philosophy.

But at this very point there lurks a danger. "Philosophy"—in that we must certainly distinguish philosophy as a historical fact belonging to this or that time from philosophy as idea, idea of an infinite task. The philosophy that at any particular time is historically actual is the more or less successful attempt to realize the guiding idea of the infinity, and thereby the totality, of truths. Practical ideals, viewed as external poles from the line of which one cannot stray during the whole of life without regret, without being untrue to oneself and thus unhappy, are in this view by no means yet clear and determined; they are anticipated in an equivocal generality. Determination comes only with concrete pursuit and with at least relatively successful action. Here the constant danger is that of falling into one-sidedness and premature satisfaction, which are punished in subsequent contradictions. Thence the contrast between the grand claims of philosophical systems, that are all the while incompatible with each other. Added to this are the necessity and yet the danger of specialization.

In this way, of course, one-sided rationality can become an evil. It can also be said that it belongs to the very essence of reason that philosophers can at first understand and accomplish their infinite task only on the basis of an absolutely necessary one-sidedness. In itself there is no absurdity here, no error. Rather, as has been remarked, the direct and necessary path for reason allows it initially to grasp only one aspect of the task, at first without recognizing that a thorough knowledge of the entire infinite task, the totality of being, involves still other aspects. When inadequacy reveals itself in obscurities and contradiction, then this becomes a motive to engage in a universal reflection. Thus the philosopher must always have as his purpose to master the true and full sense of philosophy, the totality of its infinite horizons. No one line of knowledge, no individual truth must be absolutized. Only in such a supreme consciousness of self, which itself becomes a branch of the infinite task, can philosophy fulfill its function of putting itself, and therewith a genuine humanity, on the right track. To know that this is the case, however, also involves once more entering the field of knowledge proper to philosophy on the highest level of reflection upon itself. Only on the basis of this constant reflectiveness is a philosophy a universal knowledge.

I have said that the course of philosophy goes through a period of naïveté. This, then, is the place for a critique of the so renowned irrationalism, or it is the place to uncover the naïveté of that rationalism that passes as genuine philosophical rationality, and that admittedly is characteristic of philosophy in the whole modern period since the Renaissance, looking upon itself as the real and hence universal rationalism. Now, as they begin, all the sciences, even those whose beginnings go back to ancient times, are unavoidably caught up in this naïveté. To put it more exactly, the most general title for this naïveté is objectivism, which is given a structure in the various types of naturalism, wherein the spirit is naturalized. Old and new philosophies were and remain naïvely objectivistic. It is only right, however, to add that German idealism, beginning with Kant, was passionately concerned with overcoming the naïveté that had already become very sensitive. Still, it was incapable of really attaining to the level of superior reflectiveness that is decisive for the new image of philosophy and of European man.

What I have just said I can make intelligible only by a few sketchy indications. Natural man (let us assume, in the pre-philosophical period) is oriented toward the world in all his concerns and activities. The area in which he lives and works is the environing world which in its spatio-temporal dimensions surrounds him and of which he considers himself a part. This continues to be true in the theoretical attitude, which at first can be nothing but that of the disinterested spectator of a world that is demythologized before his eyes. Philosophy sees in the world the universe of what is, and world becomes objective world over against representations of the world—which latter change subjectively, whether on a national or an individual scale—and thus truth becomes objective truth. Thus philosophy begins as cosmology. At first, as is self-evident, it is oriented in its theoretical interest to corporeal nature, since in fact all spatio-temporal data do have, at least basically, the form of corporeality. Men and beasts are not merely bodies, but to the view oriented to the environing world they appear as some sort of corporeal being and thus as realities included in the universal spatio-temporality. In this way all psychic events, those of this or that ego, such as experience, thinking, willing, have a certain objectivity. Community life, that of families, of peoples, and the like, seems then to resolve itself into the life of particular individuals, who are psychophysical objects. In the light of psychophysical causality there is no purely spiritual continuity in spiritual grouping; physical nature envelops everything.

The historical process of development is definitively marked out through this focus on the environing world. Even the hastiest glance at the corporeality present in the environing world shows that nature is a homogeneous, unified totality, a world for itself, so to speak, surrounded by a homogeneous spatio-temporality and divided into individual things, all similar in being *res extensae* and each determining the other causally. Very quickly comes a first and greatest step in the process of discovery: overcoming the finitude of nature that has been thought of as objective-in-itself, finitude in spite of the open infinity of it. Infinity is discovered, and first of all in form of idealized quantities, masses, numbers, figures, straight lines, poles, surfaces, etc. Nature, space, and time become capable of stretching ideally into infinity and also of being infinitely divided ideally. From the art of surveying develops geometry; from counting, arithmetic; from everyday mechanics, mathematical mechanics; etc. Now, without anyone forming a hypothesis in this regard, the world of perceived nature is changed into a mathematical world, the world of mathematical natural sciences. As ancient times moved forward, with the mathematics proper to that stage, the first discovery of infinite ideals and of infinite tasks was accomplished simultaneously. That discovery becomes for all subsequent times the guiding star of the sciences.

How, then, did the intoxicating success of this discovery of physical infinity affect the scientific mastery of the realm of spirit? In the focus on the environing world, a constantly objective attitude, everything spiritual appeared to be based on physical corporeality. Thus an application of the mode of thought proper to natural science was obvious. For this reason we already find in the early stages Democritean materialism and determinism. However, the greatest minds recoiled from this and also from any newer style of psychophysics. Since Socrates, man is made thematic precisely as human, man with his spiritual life in society. Man retains an orientation to the objective world, but with the advent of Plato and Aristotle this world becomes the great theme of investigations. At this point a remarkable cleavage makes itself felt: the human belongs to the universe of objective facts, but as persons, as egos, men have goals, aims. They have norms for tradition, truth norms—eternal norms. Though the development proceeded haltingly in ancient times, still it was not lost. Let us make the leap to so-called "modern" times. With glowing enthusiasm the infinite task of a mathematical knowledge of nature and in general of a world knowledge is undertaken. The extraordinary successes of natural knowledge are now to be extended to knowledge of the spirit. Reason had proved its power in nature. "As the sun is one all-illuminating and warming sun, so too is reason one" (Descartes). The method of natural science must also embrace the mysteries of spirit. The spirit is real and objectively in the world, founded as such in corporeality. With this the interpretation of the world immediately takes on a predominantly dualistic, i.e., psychophysical, form. The same causality—only split in two—embraces the one world; the sense of rational explanation is everywhere the same, but in such a way that all explanation of spirit, in the only way in which it can be universal, involves the physical. There can be no pure, self-contained search for an explanation of the spiritual, no purely inner-oriented psychology or theory of spirit beginning with the ego in psychical self-experience and extending to the other psyche. The way that must be traveled is the external one, the path of physics and chemistry. All the fond talk of common spirit, of the common will of a people, of nations' ideal political goals, and the like, are romanticism and mythology, derived from an analogous application of concepts that have a proper sense only in the individual personal sphere. Spiritual being is fragmentary. To the question regarding the source of all these difficulties the following answer is to be given: this objectivism or this psychophysical interpretation of the world, despite its seeming self-evidence, is a naïve one-sidedness that never was understood to be such. To speak of the spirit as reality *(Realität)*, presumably a real *(realen)* annex to bodies and having its supposedly spatio-temporal being within nature, is an absurdity.

At this point, however, it is important for our problem of the crisis to show how it is that the "modern age," that has for centuries been so proud of its successes in theory and practice, has itself finally fallen into a growing dissatisfaction and must even look upon its own situation as distressful. Want has invaded all the sciences, most recently as a want of method. Moreover, the want that grips us Europeans, even though it is not understood, involves very many persons.

There are all sorts of problems that stem from naïveté, according to which objectivistic science holds what it calls the objective world to be the totality of what is, without paying any attention to the fact that no objective science can do justice to the subjectivity that achieves science. One who has been trained in the natural sciences finds it self-evident that whatever is merely subjective must be eliminated and that the method of natural science, formulated according to a subjective mode of representation, is objectively determined. In the same manner he seeks what is objectively true for the psychic too. By the same token, it is taken for granted that the subjective, eliminated by the physical scientist, is, precisely as psychic, to be investigated in psychology and of course in psychophysical psychology. The investigator of nature, however, does not make it clear to himself that the constant foundation of his admittedly subjective thinking activity is the environing world of life. This latter is constantly presupposed as the basic working area, in which alone his questions and his methodology make sense. Where, at the present time, is that powerful bit of method that leads from the intuitive environing world to the idealizing of mathematics and its interpretation as objective being, subjected to criticism and clarification? Einstein's revolutionary changes concern the formulas wherein idealized and naïvely objectivized nature *(physis)* is treated. But regarding the question of how formulas or mathematical objectification in general are given a sense based on life and the intuitive environing world, of this we hear nothing. Thus Einstein does nothing to reformulate the space and time in which our actual life takes place.

Mathematical science of nature is a technical marvel for the purpose of accomplishing inductions whose fruitfulness, probability, exactitude, and calculability could previously not even be suspected. As an accomplishment it is a triumph of the human spirit. With regard to the rationality of its methods and theories, however, it is a thoroughly relative science. It presupposes as data principles that are themselves thoroughly lacking in actual rationality. In so far as the intuitive environing world, purely subjective as it is, is forgotten in the scientific thematic, the working subject is also forgotten, and the scientist is not studied. (Thus from this point of view the rationality of the exact sciences is on a level with the rationality of the Egyptian pyramids.)

It is true, of course, that since Kant we have a special theory of knowledge, and on the other hand there is psychology, which with its claims to scientific exactitude wants to be the universal fundamental science of the spirit. Still, our hope for real rationality, i.e., for real insight, is disappointed here as elsewhere. The psychologists simply fail to see that they too study neither themselves nor the scientists who are doing the investigating nor their own vital environing world. They do not see that from the very beginning they necessarily presuppose themselves as a group of men belonging to their own environing world and historical period. By the same token, they do not see that in pursuing their aims they are seeking a truth in itself, universally valid for everyone. By its objectivism psychology simply cannot make a study of the soul in its properly essential sense, which is to say, the ego that acts and is acted upon. Though by determining the bodily function involved in an experience of evaluating or willing, it may objectify the experience and handle it inductively, can it do the same for purposes, values, norms? Can it study reason as some sort of "disposition"? Completely ignored is the fact that objectivism, as the genuine work of the investigator intent upon finding true norms, presupposes just such norms; that objectivism refuses to be inferred from facts, since in the process facts are already intended as truths and not as illusions. It is true, of course, that there exists a feeling for the difficulties present here, with the result that the dispute over psychologism is fanned into a flame. Nothing is accomplished, however, by rejecting a psychological grounding of norms, above all of norms for truth in itself. More and more perceptible becomes the overall need for a reform of modern psychology in its entirety. As yet, however, it is not understood that psychology through its objectivism has been found wanting; that it simply fails to get at the proper essence of spirit; that in isolating the soul and making it an object of thought, that in reinterpreting psychophysically being-in-community, it is being absurd. True, it has not labored in vain, and it has established many empirical rules, even practically worthwhile ones. Yet it is no more a real psychology than moral statistics with its no less worthwhile knowledge is a moral science.

In our time we everywhere meet the burning need for an understanding of spirit, while the unclarity of the methodological and factual connection between the natural sciences and the sciences of the spirit has become almost unbearable. Dilthey, one of the greatest scientists of the spirit, has directed his whole vital energy to clarifying the connection between nature and spirit, to clarifying the role of psychophysical psychology, which he thinks is to be complemented by a new, descriptive and analytic psychology. Efforts by Windelband and Rickert have likewise, unfortunately, not brought the desired insight. Like everyone else, these men are still committed to objectivism. Worst of all are the new psychological reformers, who are of the opinion that the entire fault lies in the long-dominant atomistic prejudice, that a new era has been introduced with wholistic psychology *(Ganzheitspsychologie)*. There can, however, never be any improvement so long as an objectivism based on a naturalistic focusing on the environing world is not seen in all its naïveté, until men recognize thoroughly the absurdity of the dualistic interpretation of the world, according to which nature and spirit are to be looked upon as realities *(Realitäten)* in the same sense. In all seriousness my opinion is this: there never has nor ever will be an objective science of spirit, an objective theory of the soul, objective in the sense that it permits the attribution of an existence under the forms of spatio-temporality to souls or to communities of persons.

The spirit and in fact only the spirit is a being in itself and for itself; it is autonomous and is capable of being handled in a genuinely rational, genuinely and thoroughly scientific way only in this autonomy. In regard to nature and scientific truth concerning it, however, the natural sciences give merely the appearance of having brought nature to a point where for itself it is rationally known. For true nature in its proper scientific sense is a product of the spirit that investigates nature, and thus the science of nature presupposes the science of the spirit. The spirit is essentially qualified to exercise self-knowledge, and as scientific spirit to exercise scientific self-knowledge, and that over and over again. Only in the kind of pure knowledge proper to science of the spirit is the scientist unaffected by the objection that his accomplishment is self-concealing. As a consequence, it is absurd for the sciences of the spirit to dispute with the sciences of nature for equal rights. To the extent that the former concede to the latter that their objectivity is an autonomy, they are themselves victims of objectivism. Moreover, in the way the sciences of the spirit are at present developed, with their manifold disciplines, they forfeit the ultimate, actual rationality which the spiritual *Weltanschauung* [world-view] makes possible. Precisely this lack of genuine rationality on all sides is the source of what has become for man an unbearable unclarity regarding his own existence and his infinite tasks. These last are inseparably united in one task: only if the spirit returns to itself from its naïve exteriorization, clinging to itself and purely to itself, can it be adequate to itself.

Now, how did the beginning of such a self-examination come about? A beginning was impossible so long as sensualism, or better, a psychology of data, a *tabula rasa* psychology, held the field. Only when Brentano promoted psychology to being a science of vital intentional experiences was an impulse given that could lead further—though Brentano himself had not yet overcome objectivism and psychological naturalism. The development of a real method of grasping the fundamental essence of spirit in its intentionalities and consequently of instituting an analysis of spirit with a consistency reaching to the infinite, led to transcendental phenomenology. It was this that overcame naturalistic objectivism, and for that matter any form of objectivism, in the only possible way, by beginning one's philosophizing from one's own ego; and that purely as the author of all one accepts, becoming in this regard a purely theoretical spectator. This attitude brings about the successful institution of an absolutely autonomous science of spirit in the form of a consistent understanding of self and of the world as a spiritual accomplishment. Spirit is not looked upon here as part of nature or parallel to it; rather nature belongs to the sphere of spirit. Then, too, the ego is no longer an isolated thing alongside other such things in a pre-given world. The serious problem of personal egos external to or alongside of each other comes to an end in favor of an intimate relation of beings in each other and for each other.

Regarding this question of interpersonal relations, nothing can be said here; no one lecture could exhaust the topic. I do hope, however, to have shown that we are not renewing here the old rationalism, which was an absurd naturalism, utterly incapable of grasping the problems of spirit that concern us most. The ratio now in question is none other than spirit understanding itself in a really universal, really radical manner, in the form of a science whose scope is universal, wherein an entirely new scientific thinking is established in which every conceivable question, whether of being, of norm, or of so-called "existence," finds its place. It is my conviction that intentional phenomenology has for the first time made spirit as spirit the field of systematic, scientific experience, thus effecting a total transformation of the task of knowledge. The universality of the absolute spirit embraces all being in an absolute historicity, into which nature fits as a product of spirit. It is intentional, which is to say transcendental, phenomenology that sheds light on the subject by virtue of its point of departure and its methods. Only when seen from the phenomenological point of view is naturalistic objectivism, along with the profoundest reasons for it, to be understood. Above all, phenomenology makes clear that, because of its naturalism, psychology simply could not come to terms with the activity and the properly radical problem of spirit's life.

III

Let us summarize the fundamental notions of what we have sketched here. The "crisis of European existence," which manifests itself in countless symptoms of a corrupted life, is no obscure fate, no impenetrable destiny. Instead, it becomes manifestly understandable against the background of the philosophically discoverable "teleology of European history." As a presupposition of this understanding, however, the phenomenon "Europe" is to be grasped in its essential core. To get the concept of what is contra-essential in the present "crisis," the concept "Europe" would have to be developed as the historical teleology of infinite goals of reason; it would have to be shown how the European "world" was born from ideas of reason, i.e., from the spirit of philosophy. The "crisis" could then become clear as the "seeming collapse of rationalism." Still, as we said, the reason for the downfall of a rational culture does not lie in the essence of rationalism itself but only in its exteriorization, its absorption in "naturalism" and "objectivism."

The crisis of European existence can end in only one of two ways: in the ruin of a Europe alienated from its rational sense of life, fallen into a barbarian hatred of spirit; or in the rebirth of Europe from the spirit of philosophy, through a heroism of reason that will definitively overcome naturalism. Europe's greatest danger is weariness. Let us as "good Europeans" do battle with this danger of dangers with the sort of courage that does not shirk even the endless battle. If we do, then from the annihilating conflagration of disbelief, from the fiery torrent of despair regarding the West's mission to humanity, from the ashes of the great weariness, the phoenix of a new inner life of the spirit will arise as the underpinning of a great and distant human future, for the spirit alone is immortal.

John Dewey
1859–1952

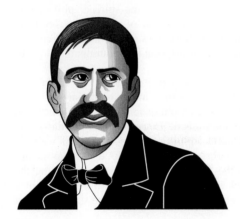

Charles Sanders Peirce, William James, and John Dewey were the great American pragmatists. The youngest of the three, John Dewey, was born and raised in Burlington, Vermont. His father, Archibald Dewey, was a successful grocer. Dewey's mother, Lucina Artemisia Rich Dewey, was deeply involved in philanthropic work, through which Dewey and his brother came into contact with the poor. The New England traditions of hard work, modesty, and honesty and the American belief in democracy combined with his family's concern for social justice to create Dewey's unique *persona*.

Following an adequate but unexceptional career in the local schools, Dewey attended the University of Vermont, after which he taught classics, algebra, and science at a high school in Pennsylvania. After two years of teaching, he returned to Burlington to continue his studies in philosophy. Encouraged by his former philosophy professor and by the editor of a philosophy journal, he borrowed five hundred dollars and enrolled in graduate school at the newly formed Johns Hopkins University. Peirce was one of his teachers at the university, though at the time Dewey was more influenced by the Hegelian idealism of G.S. Morris.

After completing his dissertation on Kant's psychology and receiving a Ph.D. in 1884, Dewey joined the faculty of the University of Michigan. During his ten years there, Dewey began to move in more practical directions. For example, he began to work with the education department on issues in teacher training, and he wrote books on psychology, including *Psychology* (1887) and *The Psychology of Number and Its Application to Methods of Teaching Arithmetic* (1895). At Michigan, Dewey met and married one of his students, Alice Chipman, and together they had five children and adopted a sixth.

In 1894 Dewey moved to the University of Chicago to become the head of the Department of Philosophy, Psychology, and Pedagogy—his three major interests by this time. In this position he set up a laboratory school, the "Dewey School," where his theories of education and teacher training were tested and refined. The school was student centered and emphasized learning by doing—rather than by rote memory—and had a profound effect on American education. Dewey's most influential books, *School and Society* (1900) and *The Child and the Curriculum* (1902), came out of his work at the lab school. In Chicago Dewey was also involved in a number of social causes, including the famous Hull House where he worked with those affected by urbanization.

Disputes with the administration of the university over the Dewey school reached a peak in 1904 with a controversy about Alice Dewey's appointment as principal of the school. The Deweys left Chicago and John Dewey, by now acknowledged as one of the leading educators in the country, accepted a position at Columbia University, where, for the next twenty-five years, he taught and wrote and from which he travelled extensively. He lectured on education in Japan, China, and the Soviet Union. Throughout his Columbia period and even after his retirement in 1929, Dewey continued his involvement with social issues. He was a founder of the American Civil Liberties Union and the American Association of University Professors, and he chaired a tribunal to investigate Stalin's charges against Trotsky. Dewey also wrote prolifically (the bibliography of his works is over 150 pages long) in philosophy and education and on a variety of social issues.

* * *

While Husserl called for a return to the disinterested rationality of the Greeks, Dewey called all such spectator knowledge disastrous. While Husserl condemned "naturalism," Dewey called on philosophers to adapt the method of the natural sciences to resolve practical problems, particularly the problem of human values. In fact, Dewey saw his philosophy, which he called "instrumentalism," as a bridge between science and ethics.

According to Dewey, genuine inquiry begins with an "indeterminate situation"—with confusion or perplexity. Articulating the nature of the problem is the first stage of inquiry: "To see that a situation requires inquiry is the initial step in inquiry." Next, one creates hypotheses to resolve the difficulty. These hypothetical solutions are then clarified and refined still further by reasoning and by clarifying meanings. These stages of hypothesis-creation and meaning-clarification will use concepts as their tools or "instruments" (hence the name "instrumentalism"). Finally, one is ready for the final stage of testing the reasoned solution. If successful, the inquiry will result in "a cleared-up, unified, resolved situation at the close." In such a cleared-up situation, the original elements of the problem will be converted into a "unified whole."

The knowledge gained by a successful inquiry is expressed in propositions that are "warrantedly assertible." Dewey purposely avoided the word "true" in order to eliminate the false notion of "truth" as a metaphysical absolute. He used the word "truth" only to refer to those "processes of change so directed that they achieve an intended consummation."

Dewey's minimalist definition of truth flies in the face of the Western philosophy inherited from the Greeks, which is one long search for a larger truth. In *Quest for Certainty* (1929), for example, Dewey explains that "man has a fundamental urge to seek security"; and it is this "insecurity [that] generates the quest for certainty." The Greeks sought to overcome this insecurity by exalting pure intellect over practical issues. Knowledge became the office by which one "uncovers the antecedently real"—a conception that endured long after the Greeks.

In "Construction of the Good" from *Quest for Certainty,* reprinted here (complete), Dewey explains how this Greek conception of knowledge and certainty led to a bifurcation between science and values, and he offers instead a way to reintegrate the two realities. After reviewing Western philosophy's decline, Dewey presents his main thesis concerning values:

> *Judgments about values are judgments about the conditions and the results of experienced objects; judgments about that which should regulate the formation of our desires, affections and enjoyments.*

By making values a type of judgment—"value judgments"—Dewey puts values back into philosophy. The instrumental method used sucessfully in science can be used with values as well. Such value-inquiry begins with a problem—what ought I to do?—and then uses the instruments of concepts to lead to solutions—to value judgments. Such a value inquiry would require understanding the nature of an experienced object in order to know if that object will naturally and repeatedly yield satisfaction, that is, if it is capable of being valued. But like all judgments in science, value judgments too will never be final. Just as initial judgments about physical objects may later prove deceptive, so also our initial enjoyment of an object may later be regretted. This view removes values from the domain of absolute truth, on the one hand, but it also removes them from the subjective realm of mere emotion.

* * *

For general works on pragmatism, see the introduction to Peirce (page 198).

A good place to begin the study of Dewey is Sidney Hook, *John Dewey: An Intellectual Portrait* (Westport, CT: Greenwood Press, 1971). Other general introductions include George R. Geiger, *John Dewey in Perspective* (New York: Oxford University Press, 1958), which emphasizes Dewey's aesthetics; Richard Bernstein, *John Dewey* (New York: Washington Square Press, 1966); and J.E. Tiles, *Dewey* (New York: Routledge, 1988). For a highly critical examination of Dewey's philosophy, see W.T. Feldman, *The Philosophy of John Dewey: A Critical Analysis* (1934; reprinted New York: Greenwood Press, 1968). For collections of essays, see Sidney Hook, ed., *John Dewey: Philosopher of Science and Freedom* (New York: Barnes & Noble, 1950); Paul A. Schlipp, ed., *The Philosophy of John Dewey,* 2nd ed. (New York: Tudor Publishing Company, 1951); C.W. Hendel, ed., *John Dewey and the Experimental Spirit in Philosophy* (New York: Bobbs-Merrill, 1959); and Sidney Morganbesser, ed., *Dewey & His Critics: Essays from "The Journal of Philosophy"* (Indianapolis, IN: Hackett, 1977).

THE QUEST FOR CERTAINTY (in part)

CHAPTER 10: THE CONSTRUCTION OF GOOD

We saw at the outset of our discussion that insecurity generates the quest for certainty. Consequences issue from every experience, and they are the source of our interest in what is present. Absence of arts of regulation diverted the search for security into irrelevant modes of practice, into rite and cult; thought was devoted to discovery of omens rather than of signs of what is to occur. Gradually there was differentiation of two realms, one higher, consisting of the powers which determine human destiny in all important affairs. With this religion was concerned. The other consisted of the prosaic matters in which man relied upon his own skill and his matter-of-fact insight. Philosophy inherited the idea of this division. Meanwhile in Greece many of the arts had attained a state of development which raised them above a merely routine state; there were intimations of measure, order and regularity in materials dealt with which give intimations of underlying rationality. Because of the growth of mathematics, there arose also the ideal of a purely rational knowledge, intrinsically solid and worthy and the means by which the intimations of rationality within changing phenomena could be comprehended within science. For the intellectual class the stay and consolation, the warrant of certainty, provided by religion was henceforth found in intellectual demonstration of the reality of the objects of an ideal realm.

With the expansion of Christianity, ethico-religious traits came to dominate the purely rational ones. The ultimate authoritative standards for regulation of the dispositions and purposes of the human will were fused with those which satisfied the demands for necessary and universal truth. The authority of ultimate Being was, moreover, represented on earth by the Church; that which in its nature transcended intellect was made known by a revelation of which the Church was the interpreter and guardian. The system endured for centuries. While it endured, it provided an integration of belief and conduct for the western world. Unity of thought and practice extended down to every detail of the management of life; efficacy of its operation did not depend upon thought. It was guaranteed by the most powerful and authoritative of all social institutions.

Its seemingly solid foundation was, however, undermined by the conclusions of modern science. They effected, both in themselves and even more in the new interests and activities they generated, a breach between what man is concerned with here and now and the faith concerning ultimate reality which, in determining his ultimate and eternal destiny, had previously given regulation to his present life. The problem of restoring integration and cooperation between man's beliefs about the world in which he lives and his beliefs about the values and purposes that should direct his conduct is the deepest problem of modern life. It is the problem of any philosophy that is not isolated from that life.

The attention which has been given to the fact that in its experimental procedure science has surrendered the separation between knowing and doing has its source in the fact that there is now provided within a limited, specialized and technical field the possibility and earnest, as far as theory is concerned, of effecting the needed integration in the wider field of collective human experience. Philosophy is called upon to be the the-

Reprinted by permission of The Putnam Publishing Group from *The Quest for Certainty* by John Dewey. Copyright © 1929, 1957. Renewed by Frederick A. Dewey.

ory of the practice, through ideas sufficiently definite to be operative in experimental endeavor, by which the integration may be made secure in actual experience. Its central problem is the relation that exists between the beliefs about the nature of things due to natural science to beliefs about values—using that word to designate whatever is taken to have rightful authority in the direction of conduct. A philosophy which should take up this problem is struck first of all by the fact that beliefs about values are pretty much in the position in which beliefs about nature were before the scientific revolution. There is either a basic distrust of the capacity of experience to develop its own regulative standards, and an appeal to what philosophers call eternal values, in order to ensure regulation of belief and action; or there is acceptance of enjoyments actually experienced irrespective of the method or operation by which they are brought into existence. Complete bifurcation between rationalistic method and an empirical method has its final and most deeply human significance in the ways in which good and bad are thought of and acted for and upon.

As far as technical philosophy reflects this situation, there is division of theories of values into two kinds. On the one hand, goods and evils, in every region of life, as they are concretely experienced, are regarded as characteristic of an inferior order of Being—intrinsically inferior. Just because they are things of human experience, their worth must be estimated by reference to standards and ideals derived from ultimate reality. Their defects and perversion are attributed to the same fact; they are to be corrected and controlled through adoption of methods of conduct derived from loyalty to the requirements of Supreme Being. This philosophic formulation gets actuality and force from the fact that it is a rendering of the beliefs of men in general as far as they have come under the influence of institutional religion. Just as rational conceptions were once superimposed upon observed and temporal phenomena, so eternal values are superimposed upon experienced goods. In one case as in the other, the alternative is supposed to be confusion and lawlessness. Philosophers suppose these eternal values are known by reason; the mass of persons that they are divinely revealed.

Nevertheless, with the expansion of secular interests, temporal values have enormously multiplied; they absorb more and more attention and energy. The sense of transcendent values has become enfeebled; instead of permeating all things in life, it is more and more restricted to special times and acts. The authority of the church to declare and impose divine will and purpose has narrowed. Whatever men say and profess, their tendency in the presence of actual evils is to resort to natural and empirical means to remedy them. But in formal belief, the old doctrine of the inherently disturbed and unworthy character of the goods and standards of ordinary experience persists. This divergence between what men do and what they nominally profess is closely connected with the confusions and conflicts of modern thought.

It is not meant to assert that no attempts have been made to replace the older theory regarding the authority of immutable and transcendent values by conceptions more congruous with the practices of daily life. The contrary is the case. The utilitarian theory, to take one instance, has had great power. The idealistic school is the only one in contemporary philosophies, with the exception of one form of neo-realism, that makes much of the notion of a reality which is all one with ultimate moral and religious values. But this school is also the one most concerned with the conservation of "spiritual" life. Equally significant is the fact that empirical theories retain the notion that thought and judgment are concerned with values that are experienced independently of them. For these theories, emotional satisfactions occupy the same place that sensations hold in traditional empiricism. Values are constituted by liking and enjoyment; to be enjoyed and to be a value are two names for one and the same fact. Since science has extruded values from its objects, these empirical theories do everything possible to emphasize their purely subjective character of value. A psychological theory of desire and liking is supposed to cover the whole ground of the theory of values; in it, immediate feeling is the counterpart of immediate sensation.

I shall not object to this empirical theory as far as it connects the theory of values with concrete experiences of desire and satisfaction. The idea that there is such a connection is the only way known to me by which the pallid remoteness of the rationalistic theory, and the only too glaring presence of the institutional theory of transcendental values can be escaped. The objection is that the theory in question holds down value to objects *antecedently* enjoyed, apart from reference to the method by which they come into existence; it takes enjoyments which are causal because unregulated by intelligent operations to be values in and of themselves. Operational thinking needs to be applied to the judgment of values just as it has now finally been applied in conceptions of physical objects. Experimental empiricism in the field of ideas of good and bad is demanded to meet the conditions of the present situation.

The scientific revolution came about when material of direct and uncontrolled experience was taken as problematic; as supplying material to be transformed by reflective operations into known objects. The contrast between experienced and known objects was found to be a temporal one; namely, one between empirical subject-matters which were had or "given" prior to the acts of experimental variation and redisposition and those which succeeded these acts and issued from them. The notion of an act whether of sense or thought which supplied a valid measure of thought in immediate knowledge was discredited. Consequences of operations became the important thing. The suggestion almost imperatively follows that escape from the defects of transcendental absolutism is not to be had by setting up as values enjoyments that happen anyhow, but in defining value by enjoyments which are the consequences of intelligent action. Without the intervention of thought, enjoyments are not values but problematic goods, becoming values when they re-issue in a changed form from intelligent behavior. The fundamental trouble with the current empirical theory of values is that it merely formulates and justifies the socially prevailing habit of regarding enjoyments as they are actually experienced as values in and of themselves. It completely side-steps the question of regulation of these enjoyments. This issue involves nothing less than the problem of the directed reconstruction of economic, political and religious institutions.

There was seemingly a paradox involved in the notion that if we turned our backs upon the immediately perceived qualities of things, we should be enabled to form valid conceptions of objects, and that these conceptions could be used to bring about a more secure and more significant experience of them. But the method terminated in disclosing the connections or interactions upon which perceived objects, viewed as events, depend. Formal analogy suggests that we regard our direct and original experience of things liked and enjoyed as only *possibilities* of values to be achieved; that enjoyment becomes a value when we discover the relations upon which its presence depends. Such a causal and operational definition gives only a conception of a value, not a value itself. But the utilization of the conception in action results in an object having secure and significant value.

The formal statement may be given concrete content by pointing to the difference between the enjoyed and the enjoyable, the desired and the desirable, the satis*fying* and the satis*factory*. To say that something is enjoyed is to make a statement about a fact, something already in existence; it is not to judge the value of that fact. There is no difference between such a proposition and one which says that something is sweet or sour, red or black. It is just correct or incorrect and that is the end of the matter. But to call an object a value is to assert that it satisfies or fulfills certain conditions. Function and status in meeting conditions is a different matter from bare existence. The fact that something is desired only raises the *question* of its desirability; it does not settle it. Only a child in the degree of his immaturity thinks to settle the question of desirability by reiterated proclamation: "I want it, I want it, I want it." What is objected to in the current empirical theory of values is not connection of them with desire and enjoyment but failure to distinguish between enjoyments of radically different sorts. There are many common expressions in which the difference of the two kinds is clearly recognized. Take for example the difference between the ideas of "satisfying" and "satisfactory." To say that something satisfies is to report something as an isolated finality. To assert that it is sat-is*factory* is to define it in its connections and interactions. The fact that it pleases or is immediately congenial poses a problem to judgment. How shall the satisfaction be rated? Is it a value or is it not? Is it something to be prized and cherished, *to be* enjoyed? Not stern moralists alone but everyday experience informs us that finding satisfaction in a thing may be a warning, a summons to be on the lookout for consequences. To declare something satis*factory* is to assert that it meets specifiable conditions. It is, in effect, a judgment that the thing "will do." It involves a prediction; it contemplates a future in which the thing will continue to serve; it *will* do. It asserts a consequence the thing will actively institute; it will *do*. That it is satisfying is the content of a proposition of fact; that it is satisfactory is a judgment, an estimate, an appraisal. It denotes an attitude *to be* taken, that of striving to perpetuate and to make secure.

It is worth notice that besides the instances given, there are many other recognitions in ordinary speech of the distinction. The endings "able," "worthy" and "ful" are cases in point. Noted and notable, noteworthy; remarked and remarkable; advised and advisable; wondered at and wonderful; pleasing and beautiful; loved and lovable; blamed and blameable, blameworthy; objected to and objectionable; esteemed and estimable; admired and admirable; shamed and shameful; honored and honorable; approved and approvable, worthy of approbation, etc. The multiplication of words adds nothing to the force of the distinction. But it aids in conveying a sense of the fundamental character of the distinction; of the difference between mere report of an already existent fact and judgment as to the importance and need of bringing a fact into existence; or, if it is already there, of sustaining it in existence. The latter is a genuine practical judgment, and marks the only type of judgment that has to do with the direction of action. Whether or no we reserve the term "value" for the latter (as seems to me proper) is a minor matter; that the distinction be acknowledged as the key to understanding the relation of values to the direction of conduct is the important thing.

This element of direction by an idea of value applies to science as well as anywhere else. For in every scientific undertaking, there is passed a constant succession of estimates; such as "it is worth treating these facts as data or evidence; it is advisable to try this experiment; to make that observation; to entertain such and such a hypothesis; to perform this calculation," etc.

The word "taste" has perhaps got too completely associated with arbitrary liking to express the nature of judgments of value. But if the word be used in the sense of an appreciation at once cultivated and active, one may say that the formation of taste is the chief matter wherever values enter in, whether intellectual, esthetic or moral. Relatively immediate judgments, which we call tact or to which we give the name of intuition, do not precede reflective inquiry, but are the funded products of much thoughtful experience. Expertness of taste is at once the result and the reward of constant exercise of thinking. Instead of there being no disputing about tastes, they are the one thing worth disputing about, if by "dispute" is signified discussion involving reflective inquiry.

Taste, if we use the word in its best sense, is the outcome of experience brought cumulatively to bear on the intelligent appreciation of the real worth of likings and enjoyments. There is nothing in which a person so completely reveals himself as in the things which he judges enjoyable and desirable. Such judgments are the sole alternative to the domination of belief by impulse, chance, blind habit and self-interest. The formation of a cultivated and effectively operative good judgment or taste with respect to what is esthetically admirable, intellectually acceptable and morally approvable is the supreme task set to human beings by the incidents of experience.

Propositions about what is or has been liked are of instrumental value in reaching judgments of value, in as far as the conditions and consequences of the thing liked are thought about. In themselves they make no claims; they put forth no demand upon subsequent attitudes and acts; they profess no authority to direct. If one likes a thing he likes it; that *is* a point about which there can be no dispute:—although it is not so easy to state just *what* is liked as is frequently assumed. A judgment about what is *to be* desired and enjoyed is, on the other hand, a claim on future action; it possesses *de jure* and not merely *de facto* quality. It is a matter of frequent experience that likings and enjoyments are of all kinds, and that many are such as reflective judgments condemn. By way of self-justification and "rationalization," an enjoyment creates a tendency to assert that the thing enjoyed is a value. This assertion of validity adds authority to the fact. It is a decision that the object has a right to exist and hence a claim upon action to further its existence.

The analogy between the status of the theory of values and the theory of ideas about natural objects before the rise of experimental inquiry may be carried further. The sensationalistic theory of the origin and test of thought evoked, by way of reaction, the transcendental theory of a *priori* ideas. For it failed utterly to account for objective connection, order and regularity in objects observed. Similarly, any doctrine that identifies the mere fact of being liked with the value of the object liked so fails to give direction to conduct when direction is needed that it automatically calls forth the assertion that there are values eternally in Being that are the standards of all judgments and the obligatory ends of all action. Without the introduction of operational thinking, we oscillate between a theory that, in order to save the objectivity of judgments of values, isolates them from experience and nature, and a theory that, in order to save their concrete and human significance, reduces them to mere statements about our own feelings.

Not even the most devoted adherents of the notion that enjoyment and value are equivalent facts would venture to assert that because we have once liked a thing we should go on liking it; they are compelled to introduce the idea that *some* tastes are to be cultivated. Logically, there is no ground for introducing the idea of cultivation; liking is liking, and one is as good as another. If enjoyments *are* values, the judgment of value cannot regulate the form which liking takes; it cannot regulate its own conditions. Desire and purpose, and hence action, are left without guidance, although the question of regulation of their formation is the supreme problem of practical life. Values (to sum up) may be connected inherently with liking, and yet not with every liking but only with those that judgment has approved, after examination of the relation upon which the object liked depends. A casual liking is one that happens without knowledge of how it occurs nor to what effect. The difference between it and one which is sought because of a judgment that it is worth having and is to be striven for, makes just the difference between enjoyments which are accidental and enjoyments that have value and hence a claim upon our attitude and conduct.

In any case, the alternative rationalistic theory does not afford the guidance for the sake of which eternal and immutable norms are appealed to. The scientist finds no help in determining the probable truth of some proposed theory by comparing it with a standard of absolute truth and immutable being. He has to rely upon definite operations undertaken under definite conditions—upon method. We can hardly imagine an architect getting aid in the construction of a building from an ideal at large, though we can understand his framing an ideal on the basis of knowledge of actual conditions and needs. Nor does the ideal of perfect beauty in antecedent Being give direction to a painter in producing a particular work of art. In morals, absolute perfection does not seem to be more than a generalized hypostatization of the recognition that there is a good to be sought, an obligation to be met—both being concrete matters. Nor is the defect in this respect merely negative. An examination of history would reveal, I am confident, that these general and remote schemes of value actually obtain a content definite enough and near enough to concrete situations as to afford guidance in action only by consecrating some institution or dogma already having social currency. Concreteness is gained, but it is by protecting from inquiry some accepted standard which perhaps is outworn and in need of criticism.

When theories of values do not afford intellectual assistance in framing ideas and beliefs about values that are adequate to direct action, the gap must be filled by other means. If intelligent method is lacking, prejudice, the pressure of immediate circumstance, self-interest and class-interest, traditional customs, institutions of accidental historic origin, are *not* lacking, and they tend to take the place of intelligence. Thus we are led to our main proposition: *Judgments about values are judgments about the conditions and the results of experienced objects; judgments about that which should regulate the formation of our desires, affections and enjoyments.* For whatever decides their formation will determine the main course of our conduct, personal and social.

If it sounds strange to hear that we should frame our judgments as to what has value by considering the connections in existence of what we like and enjoy, the reply is not far to seek. As long as we do not engage in this inquiry enjoyments (values if we choose to apply that term) are casual; they are given by "nature," not constructed by art. Like natural objects in their qualitative existence, they at most only supply material for elaboration in rational discourse. A *feeling* of good or excellence is as far removed from goodness in fact as a feeling that objects are intellectually thus and so is removed from their being actually so. To recognize that the truth of natural objects can be reached only by the greatest care in selecting and arranging directed operations, and then to suppose that values can be truly determined by the mere fact of liking seems to leave us in an incredible position. All the serious perplexities of life come back to the genuine difficulty of forming a judgment as to the values of the situation; they come back to a conflict of goods. Only dogmatism can suppose that serious moral conflict is between something clearly bad and something known to be good, and that uncertainty lies wholly in the will of the one choosing. Most conflicts of importance are conflicts between things which are or have been satisfying, not between good and evil. And to suppose that we can make a hierarchical table of values at large once for all, a kind of catalogue in which they are arranged in an order of ascending or descending worth, is to indulge in a gloss on our inability to frame intelligent judgments in the concrete. Or else it is to dignify customary choice and prejudice by a title of honor.

The alternative to definition, classification and systematization of satisfactions just as they happen to occur is judgment of them by means of the relations under which they occur. If we know the conditions under which the act of liking, of desire and enjoyment, takes place, we are in a position to know what are the consequences of that act. The difference between the desired and the desirable, admired and the admirable, becomes effective at just this point. Consider the difference between the proposition "That thing has been eaten," and the judgment "That thing is edible." The former statement involves no knowledge of any relation except the one stated; while we are able to judge of the edibility of anything only when we have a knowledge of its interactions with other things sufficient to enable us to foresee its probable effects when it is taken into the organism and produces effects there.

To assume that anything can be known in isolation from its connections with other things is to identify knowing with merely having some object before perception or in feeling, and is thus to lose the key to the traits that distinguish an object as known. It is futile, even silly, to suppose that some quality that is directly present constitutes the whole of the thing presenting the quality. It does not do so when the quality is that of being hot or fluid or heavy, and it does not when the quality is that of giving pleasure, or being enjoyed. Such qualities are, once more, effects, ends in the sense of closing termini of processes involving causal connections. They are something to be investigated, challenges to inquiry and judgment. The more connections and interactions we ascertain, the more we *know* the object in question. Thinking is search for these connections. Heat experienced as a consequence of directed operations has a meaning quite different from the heat that is casually experienced without knowledge of how it came about. The same is true of enjoyments. Enjoyments that issue from conduct directed by insight into relations have a meaning and a validity due to the way in which they are experienced. Such enjoyments are not repented of; they generate no after-taste of bitterness. Even in the midst of direct enjoyment, there is a sense of validity, of authorization, which intensifies the enjoyment. There is solicitude for perpetuation of the *object* having value which is radically different from mere anxiety to perpetuate the *feeling* of enjoyment.

Such statements as we have been making are, therefore, far from implying that there are values apart from things actually enjoyed as good. To find a thing *enjoyable* is, so to say, a *plus* enjoyment. We saw that it was foolish to treat the scientific object as a rival to or substitute for the perceived object, since the former is intermediate between uncertain and settled situations and those experienced under conditions of greater control. In the same way, judgment of the value of an object to be experienced is instrumental to appreciation of it when it is realized. But the notion that every object that happens to satisfy has an equal claim with every other to be a value is like supposing that every object of perception has the same cognitive force as every other. There is no knowledge without perception; but objects perceived are *known* only when they are determined as consequences of connective operations. There is no value except where there is satisfaction, but there have to be certain conditions fulfilled to transform a satisfaction into a value.

The time will come when it will be found passing strange that we of this age should take such pains to control by every means at command the formation of ideas of physical things, even those most remote from human concern, and yet are content with haphazard beliefs about the qualities of objects that regulate our deepest interests; that we are scrupulous as to methods of forming ideas of natural objects, and either dogmatic or else driven by immediate conditions in framing those about values. There is, by implication, if not explicitly, a prevalent notion that values are already well known and that all which is lacking is the will to cultivate them in the order of their worth. In fact the most profound lack is not the will to act upon goods already known but the will to know what they are.

It is not a dream that it is possible to exercise some degree of regulation of the occurrence of enjoyments which are of value. Realization of the possibility is exemplified, for example, in the technologies and arts of industrial life—that is, up to a definite limit. Men desired heat, light, and speed of transit and of communication beyond what nature provides of itself. These things have been attained not by lauding the enjoyment of these things and preaching their desirability, but by study of the conditions of their manifestation. Knowledge of relations having been obtained, ability to produce followed, and enjoyment ensued as a matter of course. It is, however, an old story that enjoyment of these things as goods is no warrant of their bringing only good in their train. As Plato was given to pointing out, the physician may know to heal and the orator to persuade, but the ulterior knowledge of whether it is better for a man to be healed or to be persuaded to the orator's opinion remains unsettled. Here there appears the split between what are traditionally and conventionally called the values of the baser arts and the higher values of the truly personal and humane arts.

With respect to the former, there is no assumption that they can be had and enjoyed without definite operative knowledge. With respect to them it is also clear that the degree in which we value them is measurable by the pains taken to control the conditions of their occurrence. With respect to the latter, it is assumed that no one who is honest can be in doubt what they are; that by revelation, or conscience, or the instruction of others, or immediate feeling, they are clear beyond question. And instead of action in their behalf being taken to be a measure of the extent in which things *are* values to us, it is assumed that the difficulty is to persuade men to act upon what they already know to be good. Knowledge of conditions and consequences is regarded as wholly indifferent to judging what is of serious value, though it is useful in a prudential way in trying to actualize it. In consequence, the existence of values that are by common consent of a secondary and technical sort are under a fair degree of control, while those denominated supreme and imperative are subject to all the winds of impulse, custom and arbitrary authority.

This distinction between higher and lower types of value is itself something to be looked into. Why should there be a sharp division made between some goods as physical and material and others as ideal and "spiritual"? The question touches the whole dualism of the material and the ideal at its root. To denominate anything "matter" or "material" is not in truth to disparage it. It is, if the designation is correctly applied, a way of indicating that the thing in question is a condition or means of the existence of something else. And disparagement of effective means is practically synonymous with disregard of the things that are termed, in eulogistic fashion, ideal and spiritual. For the latter terms if they have any concrete application at all signify something which is a desirable consummation of conditions, a cherished fulfillment of means. The sharp separation between material and ideal good thus deprives the latter of the underpinning of effective support while it opens the way for treating things which should be employed as means as ends in themselves. For since men cannot after all live without some measure of possession of such matters as health and wealth, the latter things will be viewed as values and ends in isolation unless they are treated as integral constituents of the goods that are deemed supreme and final.

The relations that determine the occurrence of what human beings experience, especially when social connections are taken into account, are indefinitely wider and more complex than those that determine the events termed physical; the latter are the outcome of definite selective operations. This is the reason why we know something about remote objects like the stars better than we know significantly characteristic things about our own bodies and minds. We forget the infinite number of things we do not know about the stars, or rather that what we call a star is itself the product of the elimination, enforced and deliberate, of most of the traits that belong to an actual existence. The amount of knowledge we possess about stars would not seem very great or very important if it were carried over to human beings and exhausted our knowledge of them. It is inevitable that genuine knowledge of man and society should lag far behind physical knowledge.

But this difference is not a ground for making a sharp division between the two, nor does it account for the fact that we make so little use of the experimental method of forming our ideas and beliefs about the concerns of man in his characteristic social relations. For this separation religions and philosophies must admit some responsibility. They have erected a distinction between a narrower scope of relations and a wider and fuller one into a difference of kind, naming one kind material, and the other mental and moral. They have charged themselves gratuitously with the office of diffusing belief in the necessity of the division, and with instilling contempt for the material as something inferior in kind in its intrinsic nature and worth. Formal philosophies undergo evaporation of their technical solid contents; in a thinner and more viable form they find their way into the minds of those who know nothing of their original forms. When these diffuse and, so to say, airy emanations re-crystallize in the popular mind they form a hard deposit of opinion that alters slowly and with great difficulty.

What difference would it actually make in the arts of conduct, personal and social, if the experimental theory were adopted not as a mere theory, but as a part of the working equipment of habitual attitudes on the part of everyone? It would be impossible, even were time given, to answer the question in adequate detail, just as men could not foretell in advance the consequences for knowledge of adopting the experimental method. It is the nature of the method that it has to be tried. But there are generic lines of difference which, within the limits of time at disposal, may be sketched.

Change from forming ideas and judgments of value on the basis of conformity to antecedent objects, to constructing enjoyable objects directed by knowledge of consequences, is a change from looking to the past to looking to the future. I do not for a moment suppose that the experiences of the past, personal and social, are of no importance. For without them we should not be able to frame any ideas whatever of the conditions under which objects are enjoyed nor any estimate of the consequences of esteeming and liking them. But past experiences are significant in giving us intellectual instrumentalities of judging just these points. They are tools, not finalities. Reflection upon what we have liked and have enjoyed is a necessity. But it tells us nothing about the *value* of these things until enjoyments are themselves reflectively controlled, or, until, as they now recalled, we form the best judgment possible about what led us to like this sort of thing and what has issued from the fact that we liked it.

We are not, then, to get away from enjoyments experienced in the past and from recall of them, but from the notion that they are the arbiters of things to be further enjoyed. At present, the arbiter is found in the past, although there are many ways of interpreting what in the past is authoritative. Nominally, the most influential conception doubtless is that of a revelation once had or a perfect life once lived. Reliance upon precedent, upon institutions created in the past, especially in law, upon rules of morals that have come to us through unexamined customs, upon uncriticized tradition, are other forms of dependence. It is not for a moment suggested that we can get away from customs and established institutions. A mere break would doubtless result simply in chaos. But there is no danger of such a break. Mankind is too inertly conservative both by constitution and by education to give the idea of this danger actuality. What there is genuine danger of is that the force of new conditions will produce disruption externally and mechanically: this is an ever present danger. The prospect is increased, not mitigated, by that conservatism which insists upon the adequacy of old standards to meet new conditions. What is needed is intelligent examination of the consequences that are actually effected by inherited institutions and customs, in order that there may be intelligent consideration of the ways in which they are to be intentionally modified in behalf of generation of different consequences.

This is the significant meaning of transfer of experimental method from the technical field of physical experience to the wider field of human life. We trust the method in forming our beliefs about things not directly connected with human life. In effect, we distrust it in moral, political and economic affairs. In the fine arts, there are many signs of a change. In the past, such a change has often been an omen and precursor of changes in other human attitudes. But, generally speaking, the idea of actively adopting experimental method in social affairs, in the matters deemed of most enduring and ultimate worth, strikes most persons as a surrender of all standards and regulative authority. But in principle, experimental method does not signify random and aimless action; it implies direction by ideas and knowledge. The question at issue is a practical one. Are there in existence the ideas and the knowledge that permit experimental method to be effectively used in social interests and affairs?

Where will regulation come from if we surrender familiar and traditionally prized values as our directive standards? Very largely from the findings of the natural sciences. For one of the effects of the separation drawn between knowledge and action is to deprive scientific knowledge of its proper service as a guide of conduct—except once more in those technological fields which have been degraded to an inferior rank. Of course, the complexity of the conditions upon which objects of human and liberal value depend is a great obstacle, and it would be too optimistic to say that we have as yet enough knowledge of the scientific type to enable us to regulate our judgments of value very extensively. But we have more knowledge than we try to put to use, and until we try more systematically we shall not know what are the important gaps in our sciences judged from the point of view of their moral and humane use.

For moralists usually draw a sharp line between the field of the natural sciences and the conduct that is regarded as moral. But a moral that frames its judgments of value on the basis of consequences must depend in a most intimate manner upon the conclusions of science. For the knowledge of the relations between changes which enable us to connect things as antecedents and consequences *is* science. The narrow scope which moralists often give to morals, their isolation of some conduct as virtuous and vicious from other large ranges of conduct, those having to do with health and vigor, business, education, with all the affairs in which desires and affection are implicated, is perpetuated by this habit of exclusion of the subject-matter of natural science from a rôle in formation of moral standards and ideals. The same attitude operates in the other direction to keep natural science a technical specialty, and it works unconsciously to encourage its use exclusively in regions where it can be turned to personal and class advantage, as in war and trade.

Another great difference to be made by carrying the experimental habit into all matter of practice is that it cuts the roots of what is often called subjectivism, but which is better termed egoism. The subjective attitude is much more widespread than would be inferred from the philosophies which have that label attached. It is as rampant in realistic philosophies as in any others, sometimes even more so, although disguised from those who hold these philosophies under the cover of reverence of and enjoyment of ultimate values. For the implication of placing the standard of thought and knowledge in antecedent existence is that our thought makes no difference in what is significantly real. It then affects only our own attitude toward it.

This constant throwing of emphasis back upon a change made in ourselves instead of one made in the world in which we live seems to me the essence of what is objectionable in "subjectivism." Its taint hangs about even Platonic realism with its insistent evangelical dwelling upon the change made within the mind by contemplation of the realm of essence, and its depreciation of action as transient and all but sordid—a concession to the necessities of organic existence. All the theories which put conversion "of the eye of the soul" in the place of a conversion of natural and social objects that modifies goods actually experienced, [are] a retreat and escape from existence—and this retraction into self is, once more, the heart of subjective egoisms. The typical example is perhaps the other-worldliness found in religions whose chief concern is with the salvation of the personal soul. But other-worldliness is found as well in estheticism and in all seclusion within ivory towers.

It is not in the least implied that change in personal attitudes, in the disposition of the "subject," is not of great importance. Such change, on the contrary, is involved in any attempt to modify the conditions of the environment. But there is a radical difference between a change in the self that is cultivated and valued as an end, and one that is a means to alteration, through action, of objective conditions. The Aristotelian-medieval conviction that highest bliss is found in contemplative possession of ultimate Being presents an ideal attractive to some types of mind; it sets forth a refined sort of enjoyment. It is a doctrine congenial to minds that despair of the effort involved in creation of a better world of daily experience. It is, apart from theological attachments, a doctrine sure to recur when social conditions are so troubled as to make actual endeavor seem hopeless. But the subjectivism so externally marked in modern thought as compared with ancient is either a development of the old doctrine under new conditions or is of merely technical import. The medieval version of the doctrine at least had the active support of a great social institution by means of which man could be brought into the state of mind that prepared him for ultimate enjoyment of eternal Being. It had a certain solidity and depth which is lacking in modern theories that would attain the result by merely emotional or speculative procedures, or by any means not demanding a change in objective existence so as to render objects of value more empirically secure.

The nature in detail of the revolution that would be wrought by carrying into the region of values the principle now embodied in scientific practice cannot be told; to attempt it would violate the fundamental idea that we know only after we have acted and in consequences of the outcome of action. But it would surely effect a transfer of attention and energy from the subjective to the objective. Men would think of themselves as agents not as ends; ends would be found in experienced enjoyment of the fruits of a transforming activity. In as far as the subjectivity of modern thought represents a discovery of the part played by personal responses, organic and acquired, in the causal production of the qualities and values of objects, it marks the possibility of a decisive gain. It puts us in possession of some of the conditions that control the occurrence of experienced objects, and thereby it supplies us with an instrument of regulation. There is something querulous in the sweeping denial that things as experienced, as perceived and enjoyed, in any way depend upon interaction with human selves. The error of doctrines that have exploited the part played by personal and subjective reactions in determining what is perceived and enjoyed lies either in exaggerating this factor of constitution into the sole condition—as happens in subjective idealism—or else in treating it as a finality instead of, as with all knowledge, an instrument in direction of further action.

A third significant change that would issue from carrying over experimental method from physics to man concerns the import of standards, principles, rules. With the transfer, these, and all tenets and creeds about good and goods, would be recognized to be hypotheses. Instead of being rigidly fixed, they would be treated as intellectual instruments to be tested and confirmed—and altered—through consequences effected by acting upon them. They would lose all pretense of finality—the ulterior source of dogmatism. It is both astonishing and depressing that so much of the energy of mankind has gone into fighting for (with weapons of the flesh as well as of the spirit) the truth of creeds, religious, moral and political, as distinct from what has gone into efforts to try creeds by putting them to the test of acting upon them. The change would do away with the intolerance and fanaticism that attend the notion that beliefs and judgments are capable of inherent truth and authority; inherent in the sense of being independent of what they lead to when used as directive principles. The transformation does not imply merely that men are responsible for acting upon what they profess to believe; that is an old doctrine. It goes much further. Any belief as such is tentative, hypothetical; it is not just to be acted upon, but is to be *framed* with reference to its office as a guide to action. Consequently, it should be the last thing in the world to be picked up casually and then clung to rigidly. When it is apprehended as a tool and only a tool, an instrumentality of direction, the same scrupulous attention will go to its formation as now goes into the making of instruments of precision in technical fields. Men, instead of being proud of accepting and asserting beliefs and "principles" on the ground of loyalty, will be as ashamed of that procedure as they would now be to confess their assent to a scientific theory out of reverence for Newton or Helmholz or whomever, without regard to evidence.

If one stops to consider the matter, is there not something strange in the fact that men should consider loyalty to "laws," principles, standards, ideals to be an inherent virtue, accounted unto them for righteousness? It is as if they were making up for some secret sense of weakness by rigidity and intensity of insistent attachment. A moral law, like a law in physics, is not something to swear by and stick to at all hazards; it is a formula of the way to respond when specified conditions present themselves. Its soundness and pertinence are tested by what happens when it is acted upon. Its claim or authority rests finally upon the imperativeness of the situation that has to be dealt with, not upon its own intrinsic nature—as any tool achieves dignity in the measure of needs served by it. The idea that adherence to standards external to experienced objects is the only alternative to confusion and lawlessness was once held in science. But knowledge became steadily progressive when it was abandoned, and clues and tests found within concrete acts and objects were employed. The test of consequences is more exacting than that afforded by fixed general rules. In addition, it secures constant development, for when new acts are tried new results are experienced, while the lauded immutability of eternal ideals and norms is in itself a denial of the possibility of development and improvement.

The various modifications that would result from adoption in social and humane subjects of the experimental way of thinking are perhaps summed up in saying that it would place *method and means* upon the level of importance that has, in the past, been imputed exclusively to ends. Means have been regarded as menial, and the useful as the servile. Means have been treated as poor relations to be endured, but not inherently welcome. The very meaning of the word "ideals" is significant of the divorce which has obtained between means and ends. "Ideals" are thought to be remote and inaccessible of attainment; they are too high and fine to be sullied by realization. They serve vaguely to arouse "aspiration," but they do not evoke and direct strivings for embodiment in actual existence. They hover in an indefinite way over the actual scene; they are expiring ghosts of a once significant kingdom of divine reality whose rule penetrated to every detail of life.

It is impossible to form a just estimate of the paralysis of effort that has been produced by indifference to means. Logically, it is truistic that lack of consideration for means signifies that so-called ends are not taken seriously. It is as if one professed devotion to painting pictures conjoined with contempt for canvas, brush and paints; or love of music on condition that no instruments, whether the voice or something external, be used to make sounds. The good workman in the arts is known by his respect for his tools and by his interest in perfecting his technique. The glorification in the arts of ends at the expense of means would be taken to be a sign of complete insincerity or even insanity. Ends separated from means are either sentimental indulgences or if they happen to exist are merely accidental. The ineffectiveness in action of "ideals" is due precisely to the supposition that means and ends are not on exactly the same level with respect to the attention and care they demand.

It is, however, much easier to point out the formal contradiction implied in ideals that are professed without equal regard for the instruments and techniques of their realization, than it is to appreciate the concrete ways in which belief in their separation has found its way into life and borne corrupt and poisonous fruits. The separation marks the form in which the traditional divorce of theory and practice has expressed itself in actual life. It accounts for the relative impotency of arts concerned with enduring human welfare. Sentimental attachment and subjective eulogy take the place of action. For there is no art without tools and instrumental agencies. But it also explains the fact that in actual behavior, energies devoted to matters nominally thought to be inferior, material and sordid, engross attention and interest. After a polite and pious deference has been paid to "ideals," men feel free to devote themselves to matters which are more immediate and pressing.

It is usual to condemn the amount of attention paid by people in general to material ease, comfort, wealth, and success gained by competition, on the ground that they give to mere means the attention that ought to be given to ends, or that they have taken for ends things which in reality are only means. Criticisms of the place which economic interest and action occupy in present life are full of complaints that men allow lower aims to usurp the place that belongs to higher and ideal values. The final source of the trouble is, however, that moral and spiritual "leaders" have propagated the notion that ideal ends may be cultivated in isolation from "material" means, as if means and material were not synonymous. While they condemn men for giving to means the thought and energy that ought to go to ends, the condemnation should go to them. For they have not taught their followers to think of material and economic activities as *really* means. They have been unwilling to frame their conception of the values that should be regulative of human conduct on the basis of the actual conditions and operations by which alone values can be actualized.

Practical needs are imminent; with the mass of mankind they are imperative. Moreover, speaking generally, men are formed to act rather than to theorize. Since the ideal ends are so remotely and accidentally connected with immediate and urgent conditions that need attention, after lip service is given to them, men naturally devote themselves to the latter. If a bird in the hand is worth two in a neighboring bush, an actuality in hand is worth, for the direction of conduct, many ideals that are so remote as to be invisible and inaccessible. Men hoist the banner of the ideal, and then march in the direction that concrete conditions suggest and reward.

Deliberate insincerity and hypocrisy are rare. But the notion that action and sentiment are inherently unified in the constitution of human nature has nothing to justify it. Integration is something to be achieved. Division of attitudes and responses, compartmentalizing of interests, is easily acquired. It goes deep just because the acquisition is unconscious, a matter of habitual adaptation to conditions. Theory separated from concrete doing and making is empty and futile; practice then becomes an immediate seizure of opportunities and enjoyments which conditions afford without the direction which theory—knowledge and ideas—has power to supply. The problem of the relation of theory and practice is not a problem of theory alone; it is that, but it is also the most practical problem of life. For it is the question of how intelligence may inform action, and how action may bear the fruit of increased insight into meaning: a clear view of the values that are worth while and of the means by which they are to be made secure in experienced objects. Construction of ideals in general and their sentimental glorification are easy; the responsibilities both of studious thought and of action are shirked. Persons having the advantage of positions of leisure and who find pleasure in abstract theorizing—a most delightful indulgence to those to whom it appeals—have a large measure of liability for a cultivated diffusion of ideals and aims that are separated from the conditions which are the means of actualization. Then other persons who find themselves in positions of social power and authority readily claim to be the bearers and defenders of ideal ends in church and state. They then use the prestige and authority their representative capacity as guardians of the highest ends confers on them to cover actions taken in behalf of the harshest and narrowest of material ends.

The present state of industrial life seems to give a fair index of the existing separation of means and ends. Isolation of economics from ideal ends, whether of morals or of organized social life, was proclaimed by Aristotle. Certain things, he said, are conditions of a worthy life, personal and social, but are not constituents of it. The economic life of man, concerned with satisfaction of wants, is of this nature. Men have wants and they must be satisfied. But they are only prerequisites of a good life, not intrinsic elements in it. Most philosophers have not been so frank nor perhaps so logical. But upon the whole, economics has been treated as on a lower level than either morals or politics. Yet the life which men, women and children actually lead, the opportunities open to them, the values they are capable of enjoying, their education, their share in all the things of art and science, are mainly determined by economic conditions. Hence we can hardly expect a moral system which ignores economic conditions to be other than remote and empty.

Industrial life is correspondingly brutalized by failure to equate it as the means by which social and cultural values are realized. That the economic life, thus exiled from the pale of higher values, takes revenge by declaring that it is the only social reality, and by means of the doctrine of materialistic determination of institutions and conduct in all fields, denies to deliberate morals and politics any share of causal regulation, is not surprising.

When economists were told that their subject-matter was merely material, they naturally thought they could be "scientific" only by excluding all reference to distinctively human values. Material wants, efforts to satisfy them, even the scientifically regulated technologies highly developed in industrial activity, are then taken to form a complete and closed field. If any reference to social ends and values is introduced it is by way of an external addition, mainly hortatory. That economic life largely determines the conditions under which mankind has access to concrete values may be recognized or it may not be. In either case, the notion that it is the means to be utilized in order to secure significant values as the common and shared possession of mankind is alien and inoperative. To many persons, the idea that the ends professed by morals are impotent save as they are connected with the working machinery of economic life seems like deflowering the purity of moral values and obligations.

The social and moral effects of the separation of theory and practice have been merely hinted at. They are so manifold and so pervasive that an adequate consideration of them would involve nothing less than a survey of the whole field of morals, economics and politics. It cannot be justly stated that these effects are in fact direct consequences of the quest for certainty by thought and knowledge isolated from action. For, as we have seen, this quest was itself a reflex product of actual conditions. But it may be truly asserted that this quest, undertaken in religion and philosophy, has had results which have reinforced the conditions which originally brought it about. Moreover, search for safety and consolation amid the perils of life by means other than intelligent action, by feeling and thought alone, began when actual means of control were lacking, when arts were undeveloped. It had then a relative historic justification that is now lacking. The primary problem for thinking which lays claim to be philosophic in its breadth and depth is to assist in bringing about a reconstruction of all beliefs rooted in a basic separation of knowledge and action; to develop a system of operative ideas congruous with present knowledge and with present facilities of control over natural events and energies.

We have noted more than once how modern philosophy has been absorbed in the problem of affecting an adjustment between the conclusions of natural science and the beliefs and values that have authority in the direction of life. The genuine and poignant issue does not reside where philosophers for the most part have placed it. It does not consist in accommodation to each other of two realms, one physical and the other ideal and spiritual, nor in the reconciliation of the "categories" of theoretical and practical reason. It is found in that isolation of executive means and ideal interests which has grown up under the influence of the separation of theory and practice. For this, by nature, involves the separation of the material and the spiritual. Its solution, therefore, can be found only in action wherein the phenomena of material and economic life are equated with the purposes that command the loyalties of affection and purpose, and in which ends and ideals are framed in terms of the possibilities of actually experienced situations. But while the solution cannot be found in "thought" alone, it can be furthered by thinking which is operative—which frames and defines ideas in terms of what may be done, and which uses the conclusions of science as instrumentalities. William James was well within the bounds of moderation when he said that looking forward instead of backward, looking to what the world and life might become instead of to what they have been, is an alteration in the "seat of authority."

It was incidentally remarked earlier in our discussion that the serious defect in the current empirical philosophy of values, the one which identifies them with things actually enjoyed irrespective of the conditions upon which they depend, is that it formulates and in so far consecrates the conditions of our present social experience. Throughout these chapters, primary attention has perforce been given to the methods and statements of philosophic theories. But these statements are technical and specialized in formulation only. In origin, content and import they are reflections of some condition or some phase of concrete human experience. Just as the theory of the separation of theory and practice has a practical origin and a momentous practical consequence, so the empirical theory that values are identical with whatever men actually enjoy, no matter how or what, formulates an aspect, and an undesirable one, of the present social situation.

For while our discussion has given more attention to the other type of philosophical doctrine, that which holds that regulative and authoritative standards are found in transcendent eternal values, it has not passed in silence over the fact that actually the greater part of the activities of the greater number of human beings is spent in effort to seize upon and hold onto such enjoyments as the actual scene permits. Their energies and their enjoyments are controlled in fact, but they are controlled by external conditions rather than by intelligent judgment and endeavor. If philosophies have any influence over the thoughts and acts of men, it is a serious matter that the most widely held empirical theory should in effect justify this state of things by identifying values with the objects of any interest as such. As long as the only theories of value placed before us for intellectual assent alternate between sending us to a realm of eternal and fixed values and sending us to enjoyments such as actually obtain, the formulation, even as only a theory, of an experimental empiricism which finds values to be identical with goods that are the fruit of intelligently directed activity has its measure of practical significance.

Bertrand Russell
1872–1970

Bertrand Arthur William Russell was born into a prestigious family in Trelleck, Wales. His parents, Lord and Lady Amberley, were close friends with John Stuart Mill, and Russell's grandfather, Lord John Russell, had been prime minister to Queen Victoria. Both of Russell's parents died by the time he was three, and so, with his brother, he was sent to live with his grandparents, Lord and Lady Russell. When his grandfather died a few years later, his grandmother took responsibility for his education. Unlike most privileged English boys, Russell did not attend a boarding school—Lady Russell did not approve of them. Instead, she arranged for a series of Swiss and German governesses followed by English tutors to educate her grandsons. While Russell thus enjoyed virtually every privilege, he later reported that his adolescent life seemed so bleak that he would have committed suicide had he not been "restrained by the desire to know more mathematics."

In 1890 Russell entered Cambridge University, where he was finally able to study his beloved mathematics on his own. His years at the university were the happiest of his life. He quickly established himself as one of the brightest students and formed several close friendships, including a lifelong one with G.E. Moore (1873–1958). Following graduation Russell served briefly with the British ambassador to France before moving to Berlin to study economics and political theory. In 1895 Russell was elected a fellow of Trinity College, Cambridge, and worked extensively on the foundations of mathematics. He published *Principles of Mathematics* (1903) and, together with Alfred North Whitehead, the epoch-making *Principia Mathematica* (1910–1913). During this time Russell also made the first of three unsuccessful runs for Parliament.

Russell was appointed lecturer in philosophy at Cambridge in 1910—a position he held until 1916 when he was dismissed for his opposition to the continued fighting of World War I. He also spent six months in jail for alleging that U.S. troops were used for strikebreaking in America. He was reinstated in his Cambridge position in 1919 but soon resigned and never again assumed permanent teaching duties. During his years as a lecturer, Russell also produced some of his most important works of philosophy and logic, including *The Problems of Philosophy* (1912), *Our Knowledge of the External World* (1914), and *Introduction to Mathematical Philosophy* (written while in prison and published in 1919).

In Russell's post-teaching period, he wrote and lectured widely—often taking controversial positions on social and political issues. For example, he alienated many of his socialist friends when, after a visit to the Soviet Union in 1920, he published his observations in *The Theory and Practice of Bolshevism:*

> [Russia is] one vast prison in which the jailors were cruel bigots. When I found my friends applauding these men as liberators and regarding the regime that they were creating as a paradise, I wondered . . . whether it was my friends or I that were mad.

His book *Marriage and Morals* (1929) caused a stir by minimizing the seriousness of extramarital affairs and by advocating informal trial marriages. His works on religion, *What I Believe* (1925), *Religion and Science* (1935), and the later *Why I Am Not a Christian* (1957) made Russell's atheism explicit. Russell also tried his hand at practical social reform. With his second wife, Dora, he started a school in 1927 to implement the educational theories of his books *On Education, Especially Early Childhood* (1926) and *Education and the Social Order* (1932).

In 1938 Russell accepted a visiting professorship at the University of Chicago and later at the University of California at Los Angeles. He declined a permanent offer from UCLA in order to accept an invitation from the College of the City of New York; however, before he could begin a judge ruled him unfit, claiming, among other things, that Russell's appointment would constitute "a chair of indecency." Russell mocked the decision on the title page of his *An Inquiry into Meaning and Truth*, published the next year, by listing his many honors, then adding "Judicially pronounced unworthy to be Professor of Philosophy at the College of the City of New York (1940)." To that long list of honors he would be able to add the Nobel Prize for literature in 1950.

In his later years Russell continued to write on a variety of topics—and to get into trouble with authorities. At age eighty-nine he served another jail sentence—this time for his part in a nuclear-disarmament rally in London. By the time of his death, in 1970, Russell was acknowledged as the leading British philosopher of the century.

*   *   *

It is difficult to summarize Russell's thought, partly because he developed and abandoned several philosophical theories during his long lifetime. Philosopher

C.D. Broad once commented, "As we all know, Mr. Russell produces a different system of philosophy every few years." But while the specifics of Russell's philosophic enterprise evolved, reflecting his fertile and inventive mind, there were at least two basic assumptions that remained within his mature philosophy.

First, Russell believed philosophy should be scientific and analytical. As he wrote in "Logical Atomism" (1924):

> Although . . . comprehensive construction is part of the business of philosophy, I do not believe it is the most important part. The most important part, to my mind, consists in criticizing and clarifying notions which are apt to be regarded as fundamental and accepted uncritically. As instances I might mention: mind, matter, consciousness, knowledge, experience, causality, will, time. I believe all these notions to be inexact and approximate, essentially infected with vagueness, incapable of forming part of any exact science.

Second, in "criticizing and clarifying notions" Russell was committed to the principle of parsimony known as "Ockham's Razor" (after the medieval thinker, William of Ockham). Ockham's injunction asserted that "entities are not to be multiplied beyond necessity," meaning one should always seek the simplest explanation. Russell's version of this principle, articulated in several of his works, states that "Whenever possible, substitute constructions out of known entities for inferences to unknown entities."

In the selection from *The Problems of Philosophy* reprinted here, Russell wields this razor in an analysis of the common objects of our sensory perception and our language about such objects. Russell points out that sense-data are the only "known entities" actually given in experience:

> What the senses *immediately* tell us is not the truth about the object as it is apart from us, but only the truth about certain sense-data which, so far as we can see, depend upon the relations between us and the object.

Rather than inferring some "unknown entity" (such as "being" or "substance") as the cause of our sense-data, we can consider a given object to be the class or collection of all sense-data we normally associate with that object. Our knowledge of physical objects is not direct but is gained by "acquaintance" with the sense-data that make up the appearance of an object.

The language used to make propositions about such objects is also dependent upon acquaintance. If we are to use language in a meaningful manner, "the meaning we attach to our words must be something with which we are acquainted" either in terms of a thing or a description. Using Russell's example, a statement about Julius Caesar can be meaningful because, although we have no acquaintance with the "thing" (i.e., we have not met Caesar), we do have in mind some *description* of Caesar.

Our second selection, "Mysticism and Logic," given here complete, represents Russell at his nontechnical best. In the essay, Russell defines mysticism as "little more than a certain intensity and depth of feeling in regard to what is believed about the universe." He goes on to argue that mysticism is mistaken in its understanding of knowledge, unity, time, and the nature of evil. Russell singles out Bergson's philosophy for special criticism as an example of muddle-headed mystical thinking. Despite his scathing attack on mystical beliefs, Russell finds "an element of wisdom" in the mystical attitude and claims that all the greatest philosophers have felt a need for mysticism.

These two selections include some of Russell's major themes and give some sense of his style, but his contributions to philosophy go beyond what can be included here. His work in mathematics and logic changed both of those disciplines; his theory of logical atomism represented an important step in the philosophy of language; his theories of descriptions and of types helped to clear up a number of logical puzzles; and in addition there are his writings on education, sociology, politics, and religion. In short, Russell touched on virtually all areas of human existence, and even those who differ with his conclusions cannot help but be impressed with the breadth and depth of his thought.

*   *   *

For biographical information, see Ronald William Clark, *The Life of Bertrand Russell* (New York: Knopf, 1976), or Russell's autobiography, Bertrand Russell, *The Autobiography of Bertrand Russell* (Boston: Little, Brown, 1967). A.J. Ayer, *Russell and Moore: The Analytic Heritage* (Cambridge, MA: Harvard University Press, 1971), puts Russell's thought in the context of analytic philosophy, while J. Watling, *Bertrand Russell* (New York: British Book Center, 1971), and A.J. Ayer, *Bertrand Russell* (Chicago: University of Chicago Press, 1988), provide good general introductions. Studies on specific areas of Russell's thought include Lillian Woodworth Aiken, *Bertrand Russell's Philosophy of Morals* (New York: Humanities Press, 1963); Robert J. Clack, *Bertrand Russell's Philosophy of Language* (The Hague, Netherlands: Martinus Nijhoff, 1969); and Elizabeth R. Eames, *Bertrand Russell's Theory of Knowledge* (New York: George Braziller, 1969). For collections of essays, see Paul A. Schilpp, ed., *The Philosophy of Bertrand Russell* (New York: Tudor Publishing Company, 1951)—part of the Library of Living Philosophers; Ralph Schoenman, ed., *Bertrand Russell: Philosopher of the Century* (Boston: Little, Brown, 1967); E.D. Klernke, ed., *Essays on Bertrand Russell* (Urbana: University of Illinois Press, 1970); and D.F. Pears, ed., *Bertrand Russell* (Garden City, NY: Anchor Doubleday, 1972).

THE PROBLEMS OF PHILOSOPHY
(in part)

CHAPTER 1: APPEARANCE AND REALITY

Is there any knowledge in the world which is so certain that no reasonable man could doubt it? This question, which at first sight might not seem difficult, is really one of the most difficult that can be asked. When we have realized the obstacles in the way of a straightforward and confident answer, we shall be well launched on the study of philosophy—for philosophy is merely the attempt to answer such ultimate questions, not

Bertrand Russell, *The Problems of Philosophy* (Oxford: Oxford University Press, 1912). Reprinted by permission.

carelessly and dogmatically, as we do in ordinary life and even in the sciences, but critically, after exploring all that makes such questions puzzling, and after realizing all the vagueness and confusion that underlie our ordinary ideas.

In daily life, we assume as certain many things which, on a closer scrutiny, are found to be so full of apparent contradictions that only a great amount of thought enables us to know what it is that we really may believe. In the search for certainty, it is natural to begin with our present experiences, and in some sense, no doubt, knowledge is to be derived from them. But any statement as to what it is that our immediate experiences make us know is very likely to be wrong. It seems to me that I am now sitting in a chair, at a table of a certain shape, on which I see sheets of paper with writing or print. By turning my head I see out of the window buildings and clouds and the sun. I believe that the sun is about ninety-three million miles from the earth; that it is a hot globe many times bigger than the earth; that, owing to the earth's rotation, it rises every morning, and will continue to do so for an indefinite time in the future. I believe that, if any other normal person comes into my room, he will see the same chairs and tables and books and papers as I see, and that the table which I see is the same as the table which I feel pressing against my arm. All this seems to be so evident as to be hardly worth stating, except in answer to a man who doubts whether I know anything. Yet all this may be reasonably doubted, and all of it requires much careful discussion before we can be sure that we have stated it in a form that is wholly true.

To make our difficulties plain, let us concentrate attention on the table. To the eye it is oblong, brown, and shiny, to the touch it is smooth and cool and hard; when I tap it, it gives out a wooden sound. Any one else who sees and feels and hears the table will agree with this description, so that it might seem as if no difficulty would arise; but as soon as we try to be more precise our troubles begin. Although I believe that the table is "really" of the same colour all over, the parts that reflect the light look much brighter than the other parts, and some parts look white because of reflected light. I know that, if I move, the parts that reflect the light will be different, so that the apparent distribution of colours on the table will change. It follows that if several people are looking at the table at the same moment, no two of them will see exactly the same distribution of colours, because no two can see it from exactly the same point of view, and any change in the point of view makes some change in the way the light is reflected.

For most practical purposes these differences are unimportant, but to the painter they are all-important: the painter has to unlearn the habit of thinking that things seem to have the colour which common sense says they "really" have, and to learn the habit of seeing things as they appear. Here we have already the beginning of one of the distinctions that cause most trouble in philosophy—the distinction between "appearance" and "reality," between what things seem to be and what they are. The painter wants to know what things seem to be, the practical man and the philosopher want to know what they are; but the philosopher's wish to know this is stronger than the practical man's, and is more troubled by knowledge as to the difficulties of answering the question.

To return to the table. It is evident from what we have found, that there is no colour which pre-eminently appears to be *the* colour of the table, or even of any one particular part of the table—it appears to be of different colours from different points of view, and there is no reason for regarding some of these as more really its colour than others. And we know that even from a given point of view the colour will seem different by artificial light, or to a colour-blind man, or to a man wearing blue spectacles, while in the dark there will be no colour at all, though to touch and hearing the table will be unchanged. This colour is not something which is inherent in the table, but something depending upon the table and the spectator and the way the light falls on the table. When, in ordinary life, we speak of *the* colour of the table, we only mean the sort of colour which it will seem to have to a normal spectator from an ordinary point of view under usual conditions of light. But the other colours which appear under other conditions have just as good a right to be considered real; and therefore, to avoid favouritism, we are compelled to deny that, in itself, the table has any one particular colour.

The same thing applies to the texture. With the naked eye one can see the grain, but otherwise the table looks smooth and even. If we looked at it through a microscope, we should see roughnesses and hills and valleys, and all sorts of differences that are imperceptible to the naked eye. Which of these is the "real" table? We are naturally tempted to say that what we see through the microscope is more real, but that in turn would be changed by a still more powerful microscope. If, then, we cannot trust what we see with the naked eye, why should we trust what we see through a microscope? Thus, again, the confidence in our senses with which we began deserts us.

The *shape* of the table is no better. We are all in the habit of judging as to the "real" shapes of things, and we do this so unreflectingly that we come to think we actually see the real shapes. But, in fact, as we all have to learn if we try to draw, a given thing looks different in shape from every different point of view. If our table is "really" rectangular, it will look, from almost all points of view, as if it had two acute angles and two obtuse angles. If opposite sides are parallel, they will look as if they converged to a point away from the spectator; if they are of equal length, they will look as if the nearer side were longer. All these things are not commonly noticed in looking at a table, because experience has taught us to construct the "real" shape from the apparent shape, and the "real" shape is what interests us as practical men. But the "real" shape is not what we see, it is something inferred from what we see. And what we see is constantly changing in shape as we move about the room; so that here again the senses seem not to give us the truth about the table itself, but only about the appearance of the table.

Similar difficulties arise when we consider the sense of touch. It is true that the table always gives us a sensation of hardness, and we feel that it resists pressure. But the sensation we obtain depends upon how hard we press the table and also upon what part of the body we press with; thus the various sensations due to various pressures or various parts of the body cannot be supposed to reveal *directly* any definite property of the table, but at most to be *signs* of some property which perhaps *causes* all the sensations, but is not actually apparent in any of them. And the same applies still more obviously to the sounds which can be elicited by rapping the table.

Thus it becomes evident that the real table, if there is one, is not the same as what we immediately experience by sight or touch or hearing. The real table, if there is one, is not *immediately* known to us all, but must be an inference from what is immediately known. Hence, two very difficult questions at once arise; namely, (1) Is there a real table at all? (2) If so, what sort of object can it be?

It will help us in considering these questions to have a few simple terms of which the meaning is definite and clear. Let us give the name of "sense-data" to the things that are immediately known in sensation: such things as colours, sounds, smells, hardnesses, roughnesses, and so on. We shall give the name "sensation" to the experience of being immediately aware of these things. Thus, whenever we see a colour, we have a sensation of the colour, but the colour itself is a sense-datum, not a sensation. The colour is that *of* which we are immediately aware, and the awareness itself is the sensation. It is plain that if we are to know anything about the table, it must be by means of the sense-data—brown colour, oblong shape, smoothness, etc.—which we associate with the table; but, for the reasons which have been given, we cannot say that the table *is* the sense-data, or even that the sense-data are directly properties of the table. Thus a problem arises as to the relation of the sense-data to the real table, supposing there is such a thing.

The real table, if it exists, we will call a "physical object." Thus we have to consider the relation of sense-data to physical objects. The collection of all physical objects is called "matter." Thus our two questions may be re-stated as follows: (1) Is there any such thing as matter? (2) If so, what is its nature?

The philosopher who first brought prominently forward the reasons for regarding the immediate objects of our senses as not existing independently of us was Bishop Berkeley (1685-1753). His *Three Dialogues between Hylas and Philonous, in Opposition to Sceptics and Atheists,* undertake to prove that there is no such thing as matter at all, and that the world consists of nothing but minds and their ideas. Hylas has hitherto believed in matter, but he is no match for Philonous, who mercilessly drives him into contradictions and paradoxes, and makes his own denial of matter seem, in the end, as if it were almost common sense. The arguments employed are of very different value: some are important and sound, others are confused or quibbling. But Berkeley retains the merit of having shown that the existence of matter is capable of being denied without absurdity, and that if there are any things that exist independently of us they cannot be the immediate objects of our sensations.

There are two different questions involved when we ask whether matter exists, and it is important to keep them clear. We commonly mean by "matter" something which is opposed to "mind," something which we think of as occupying space and as radically incapable of any sort of thought or consciousness. It is chiefly in this sense that Berkeley denies matter; that is to say, he does not deny that the sense-data which we commonly take as signs of the existence of the table are really signs of the existence of *something* independent of us, but he does deny that this something is, non-mental, that it is neither mind nor ideas entertained by some mind. He admits that there must be something which continues to exist when we go out of the room or shut our eyes, and that what we call seeing the table does really give us reason for believing in something which persists even when we are not seeing it. But he thinks that this something cannot be radically different in nature from what we see, and cannot be independent of seeing altogether, though it must be independent of *our* seeing. He is thus led to regard the "real" table as an idea in the mind of God. Such an idea has the required permanence and independence of ourselves, without being—as matter would otherwise be—something quite unknowable, in the sense that we can only infer it, and can never be directly and immediately aware of it.

Other philosophers since Berkeley have also held that, although the table does not depend for its existence upon being seen by me, it does depend upon being seen (or otherwise apprehended in sensation) by *some* mind—not necessarily the mind of God, but more often the whole collective mind of the universe. This they hold, as Berkeley does, chiefly because they think there can be nothing real—or at any rate nothing known to be real—except minds and their thoughts and feelings. We might state the argument by which they support their view in some such way as this: "Whatever can be thought of is an idea in the mind of the person thinking of it; therefore nothing can be thought of except ideas in minds; therefore anything else is inconceivable, and what is inconceivable cannot exist."

Such an argument, in my opinion, is fallacious; and of course those who advance it do not put it so shortly or so crudely. But whether valid or not, the argument has been very widely advanced in one form or another; and very many philosophers, perhaps a majority, have held that there is nothing real except minds and their ideas. Such philosophers are called "idealists." When they come to explaining matter, they either say, like Berkeley, that matter is really nothing but a collection of ideas, or they say, like Leibniz (1646–1716), that what appears as matter is really a collection of more or less rudimentary minds.

But these philosophers, though they deny matter as opposed to mind, nevertheless, in another sense, admit matter. It will be remembered that we asked two questions; namely, (1) Is there a real table at all? (2) If so, what sort of object can it be? Now both Berkeley and Leibniz admit that there is a real table, but Berkeley says it is certain ideas in the mind of God, and Leibniz says it is a colony of souls. Thus both of them answer our first question in the affirmative, and only diverge from the views of ordinary mortals in their answer to our second question. In fact, almost all philosophers seem to be agreed that there is a real table: they almost all agree that, however much our sense-data—colour, shape, smoothness, etc.—may depend upon us, yet their occurrence is a sign of something existing independently of us, something differing, perhaps, completely from our sense-data, and yet to be regarded as causing those sense-data whenever we are in a suitable relation to the real table.

Now obviously this point in which the philosophers are agreed—the view that there *is* a real table, whatever its nature may be—is vitally important, and it will be worth while to consider what reasons there are for accepting this view before we go on to the further question as to the nature of the real table. Our next chapter, therefore, will be concerned with the reasons for supposing that there is a real table at all.

Before we go farther it will be well to consider for a moment what it is that we have discovered so far. It has appeared that, if we take any common object of the sort that is supposed to be known by the senses, what the senses *immediately* tell us is not the truth about the object as it is apart from us, but only the truth about certain sense-data which, so far as we can see, depend upon the relations between us and the object. Thus what we directly see and feel is merely "appearance," which we believe to be a sign of some "reality" behind. But if the reality is not what appears, have we any means of knowing whether there is any reality at all? And if so, have we any means of finding out what it is like?

Such questions are bewildering, and it is difficult to know that even the strangest hypotheses may not be true. Thus our familiar table, which has roused but the slightest thoughts in us hitherto, has become a problem full of surprising possibilities. The one thing we know about it is that it is not what it seems. Beyond this modest result, so far, we have the most complete liberty of conjecture. Leibniz tells us it is a community of souls; Berkeley tells us it is an idea in the mind of God; sober science, scarcely less wonderful, tells us it is a vast collection of electric charges in violent motion.

Among these surprising possibilities, doubt suggests that perhaps there is no table at all. Philosophy, if it cannot *answer* so many questions as we could wish, has at least the power of *asking* questions which increase the interest of the world, and show the strangeness and wonder lying just below the surface even in the commonest things of daily life.

* * *

CHAPTER 5: KNOWLEDGE BY ACQUAINTANCE
AND KNOWLEDGE BY DESCRIPTION

In the preceding chapter [on "Idealism"] we saw that there are two sorts of knowledge: knowledge of things, and knowledge of truths. In this chapter we shall be concerned exclusively with knowledge of things, of which in turn we shall have to distinguish two kinds. Knowledge of things, when it is of the kind we call knowledge by *acquaintance,* is essentially simpler than any knowledge of truths, and logically independent of knowledge of truths, though it would be rash to assume that human beings ever, in fact, have acquaintance with things without at the same time knowing some truth about them. Knowledge of things by *description,* on the contrary, always involves, as we shall find in the course of the present chapter, some knowledge of truths as its source and ground. But first of all we must make clear what we mean by "acquaintance" and what we mean by "description."

We shall say that we have *acquaintance* with anything of which we are directly aware, without the intermediary of any process of inference or any knowledge of truths. Thus in the presence of my table I am acquainted with the sense-data that make up the appearance of my table—its colour, shape, hardness, smoothness, etc.; all these are things of which I am immediately conscious when I am seeing and touching my table. The particular shade of colour that I am seeing may have many things said about it—I may say that it is brown, that it is rather dark, and so on. But such statements, though they make me know truths *about* the colour, do not make me know the colour itself any better than I did before: so far as concerns knowledge of the colour itself, as opposed to knowledge of truths about it, I know the colour perfectly and completely when I see it, and no further knowledge of it itself is even theoretically possible. Thus the sense-data which make up the appearance of my table are things with which I have acquaintance, things immediately known to me just as they are.

My knowledge of the table as a physical object, on the contrary, is not direct knowledge. Such as it is, it is obtained through acquaintance with the sense-data that make up the appearance of the table. We have seen that it is possible, without absurdity, to doubt whether there is a table at all, whereas it is not possible to doubt the sense-data. My knowledge of the table is of the kind which we shall call "knowledge by description." The table is "the physical object which causes such-and-such sense-data." This *describes* the table by means of the sense-data. In order to know anything at all about the table, we must know truths connecting it with things with which we have acquaintance: we must know that "such-and-such sense-data are caused by a physical object." There is no state of mind in which we are directly aware of the table; all our knowledge of the table is really knowledge of *truths,* and the actual thing which is the table is not, strictly speaking, known to us at all. We know a description, and we know that there is just one object to which this description applies, though the object itself is not directly known to us. In such a case, we say that our knowledge of the object is knowledge by description.

All our knowledge, both knowledge of things and knowledge of truths, rests upon acquaintance as its foundation. It is therefore important to consider what kinds of things there are with which we have acquaintance.

Sense-data, as we have already seen, are among the things with which we are acquainted; in fact, they supply the most obvious and striking example of knowledge by acquaintance. But if they were the sole example, our knowledge would be very much more restricted than it is. We should only know what is now present to our senses: we could not know anything about the past—not even that there was a past—nor could we know any truths about our sense-data, for all knowledge of truths, as we shall show, demands acquaintance with things which are of an essentially different character from sense-data, the things which are sometimes called "abstract ideas," but which we shall call "universals." We have therefore to consider acquaintance with other things besides sense-data if we are to obtain any tolerably adequate analysis of our knowledge.

The first extension beyond sense-data to be considered is acquaintance by *memory*. It is obvious that we often remember what we have seen or heard or had otherwise present to our senses, and that in such cases we are still immediately aware of what we remember, in spite of the fact that it appears as past and not as present. This immediate knowledge by memory is the source of all our knowledge concerning the past: without it, there could be no knowledge of the past by inference, since we should never know that there was anything past to be inferred.

The next extension to be considered is acquaintance by *introspection*. We are not only aware of things, but we are often aware of being aware of them. When I see the sun, I am often aware of my seeing the sun; thus "my seeing the sun" is an object with which I have acquaintance. When I desire food, I may be aware of my desire for food; thus "my desiring food" is an object with which I am acquainted. Similarly we may be aware of our feeling pleasure or pain, and generally of the events which happen in our minds. This kind of acquaintance, which may be called self-consciousness, is the source of all our knowledge of mental things. It is obvious that it is only what goes on in our own minds that can be thus known immediately. What goes on in the minds of others is known to us through our perception of their bodies, that is, through the sense-data in us which are associated with their bodies. But for our acquaintance with the contents of our own minds, we should be unable to imagine the minds of others, and therefore we could never arrive at the knowledge that they have minds. It seems natural to suppose that self-consciousness is one of the things that distinguish men from animals: animals, we may suppose, though they have acquaintance with sense-data, never become aware of this acquaintance. I do not mean that they *doubt* whether they exist, but that they have never become conscious of the fact that they have sensations and feelings, nor therefore of the fact that they, the subjects of their sensations and feelings, exist.

We have spoken of acquaintance with the contents of our minds as *self-consciousness*, but it is not, of course, consciousness of our *self*: it is consciousness of particular thoughts and feelings. The question whether we are also acquainted with our bare selves, as opposed to particular thoughts and feelings, is a very difficult one, upon which it would be rash to speak positively. When we try to look into ourselves we always seem to come upon some particular thought or feeling, and not upon the "I" which has the thought or feeling. Nevertheless there are some reasons for thinking that we are acquainted with the "I," though the acquaintance is hard to disentangle from other things. To make clear what sort of reason there is, let us consider for a moment what our acquaintance with particular thoughts really involves.

When I am acquainted with "my seeing the sun," it seems plain that I am acquainted with two different things in relation to each other. On the one hand there is the sense-datum which represents the sun to me, on the other hand there is that which sees this sense-datum. All acquaintance, such as my acquaintance with the sense-datum which represents the sun, seems obviously a relation between the person acquainted and the object with which the person is acquainted. When a case of acquaintance is one with which I can be acquainted (as I am acquainted with my acquaintance with the sense-datum representing the sun), it is plain that the person acquainted is myself. Thus, when

I am acquainted with my seeing the sun, the whole fact with which I am acquainted is "Self-acquainted-with-sense-datum."

Further, we know the truth "I am acquainted with this sense-datum." It is hard to see how we could know this truth, or even understand what is meant by it, unless we were acquainted with something which we call "I." It does not seem necessary to suppose that we are acquainted with a more or less permanent person, the same today as yesterday, but it does seem as though we must be acquainted with that thing, whatever its nature, which sees the sun and has acquaintance with sense-data. Thus, in some sense it would seem we must be acquainted with our Selves as opposed to our particular experiences. But the question is difficult, and complicated arguments can be adduced on either side. Hence, although acquaintance with ourselves seems *probably* to occur, it is not wise to assert that it undoubtedly does occur.

We may therefore sum up as follows what has been said concerning acquaintance with things that exist. We have acquaintance in sensation with the data of the outer senses, and in introspection with the data of what may be called the inner sense— thoughts, feelings, desires, etc.; we have acquaintance in memory with things which have been data either of the outer senses or of the inner sense. Further, it is probable, though not certain, that we have acquaintance with Self, as that which is aware of things or has desires towards things.

In addition to our acquaintance with particular existing things, we also have acquaintance with what we shall call universals, that is to say, general ideas, such as *whiteness, diversity, brotherhood,* and so on. Every complete sentence must contain at least one word which stands for a universal, since all verbs have a meaning which is universal. . . . It is only necessary [at this point] to guard against the supposition that whatever we can be acquainted with must be something particular and existent. Awareness of universals is called conceiving, and a universal of which we are aware is called a *concept.*

It will be seen that among the objects with which we are acquainted are not included physical objects (as opposed to sense-data), nor other people's minds. These things are known to us by what I call "knowledge by description," which we must now consider.

By a "description" I mean any phrase of the form "a so-and-so" or "the so-and-so." A phrase of the form "a so-and-so" I shall call an "ambiguous" description; a phrase of the form "the so-and-so" (in the singular) I shall call a "definite" description. Thus "a man" is an ambiguous description, and "the man with the iron mask" is a definite description. There are various problems connected with ambiguous descriptions, but I pass them by, since they do not directly concern the matter we are discussing, which is the nature of our knowledge concerning objects in cases where we know that there is an object answering to a definite description, though we are not *acquainted* with any such object. This is a matter which is concerned exclusively with *definite* descriptions. I shall therefore, in the sequel, speak simply of "descriptions" when I mean "definite descriptions." Thus a description will mean any phrase of the form "the so-and-so" in the singular.

We shall say that an object is "known by description" when we know that it is "the so-and-so," i.e. when we know that there is one object, and no more, having a certain property; and it will generally be implied that we do not have knowledge of the same object by acquaintance. We know that the man with the iron mask existed, and many propositions are known about him; but we do not know who he was. We know that the candidate who gets the most votes will be elected, and in this case we are very likely also acquainted (in the only sense in which one can be acquainted with some one else) with the man who is, in fact, the candidate who will get most votes; but we do not know which of the candidates he is, i.e. we do not know any proposition of the form "A is the candidate who will get most votes" where A is one of the candidates by name. We shall say that we have "merely descriptive knowledge" of the so-and-so when, although we know that the so-and-so exists, and although we may possibly be acquainted with the object which is, in fact, the so-and-so, yet we do not know any proposition "a is the so-and-so," where a is something with which we are acquainted.

When we say "the so-and-so exists," we mean that there is just one object which is the so-and-so. The proposition "a is the so-and-so" means that a has the property so-and-so, and nothing else has. "Mr. A. is the Unionist candidate for this constituency" means "Mr. A. is a Unionist candidate for this constituency, and no one else is." "The Unionist candidate for this constituency exists" means "some one is a Unionist candidate for this constituency, and no one else is." Thus, when we are acquainted with an object which is the so-and-so, we know that the so-and-so exists; but we may know that the so-and-so exists when we are not acquainted with any object which we know to be the so-and-so, and even when we are not acquainted with any object which, in fact, is the so-and-so.

Common words, even proper names, are usually really descriptions. That is to say, the thought in the mind of a person using a proper name correctly can generally only be expressed explicitly if we replace the proper name by a description. Moreover, the description required to express the thought will vary for different people, or for the same person at different times. The only thing constant (so long as the name is rightly used) is the object to which the name applies. But so long as this remains constant, the particular description involved usually makes no difference to the truth or falsehood of the proposition in which the name appears.

Let us take some illustrations. Suppose some statement made about Bismarck. Assuming that there is such a thing as direct acquaintance with oneself, Bismarck himself might have used his name directly to designate the particular person with whom he was acquainted. In this case, if he made a judgement about himself, he himself might be a constituent of the judgement. Here the proper name has the direct use which it always wishes to have, as simply standing for a certain object, and not for a description of the object. But if a person who knew Bismarck made a judgement about him, the case is different. What this person was acquainted with were certain sense-data which he connected (rightly, we will suppose) with Bismarck's body. His body, as a physical object, and still more his mind, were only known as the body and the mind connected with these sense-data. That is, they were known by description. It is, of course, very much a matter of chance which characteristics of a man's appearance will come into a friend's mind when he thinks of him; thus the description actually in the friend's mind is accidental. The essential point is that he knows that the various descriptions all apply to the same entity, in spite of not being acquainted with the entity in question.

When we, who did not know Bismarck, make a judgement about him, the description in our minds will probably be some more or less vague mass of historical knowledge—far more, in most cases, than is required to identify him. But, for the sake of illustration, let us assume that we think of him as "the first Chancellor of the German Empire." Here all the words are abstract except "German." The word "German" will, again, have different meanings for different people. To some it will recall travels in Germany, to some the look of Germany on the map, and so on. But if we are to obtain a description which we know to be applicable, we shall be compelled, at some point, to bring in a reference to a particular with which we are acquainted. Such reference is involved in any mention of past, present, and future (as opposed to definite dates), or of here and there, or of what others have told us. Thus it would seem that, in some way or other, a description known to be applicable to a particular must involve some reference to a particular with which we are acquainted, if our knowledge about the thing described is not to be merely what follows *logically* from the description. For example, "the most long-lived of men" is a description involving only universals, which must apply to some man, but we can make no judgements concerning this man which involve knowledge about him beyond what the description gives. If, however, we say, "The first Chancellor of the German Empire was an astute diplomatist," we can only be assured of the truth of our judgement in virtue of something with which we are acquainted—usually a testimony heard or read. Apart from the information we convey to others, apart from the fact about the actual Bismarck, which gives importance to our judgement, the thought we really have contains the one or more particulars involved, and otherwise consists wholly of concepts.

All names of places—London, England, Europe, the Earth, the Solar System—similarly involve, when used, descriptions which start from some one or more particulars with which we are acquainted. I suspect that even the Universe, as considered by metaphysics, involves such a connexion with particulars. In logic, on the contrary, where we are concerned not merely with what does exist, but with whatever might or could exist or be, no reference to actual particulars is involved.

It would seem that, when we make a statement about something only known by description, we often *intend* to make our statement, not in the form involving the description, but about the actual thing described. That is to say, when we say anything about Bismarck, we should like, if we could, to make the judgement which Bismarck alone can make, namely, the judgement of which he himself is a constituent. In this we are necessarily defeated, since the actual Bismarck is unknown to us. But we know that there is an object B, called Bismarck, and that B was an astute diplomatist. We can thus *describe* the proposition we should like to affirm, namely, "B was an astute diplomatist," where B is the object which was Bismarck. If we are describing Bismarck as "the first Chancellor of the German Empire," the proposition we should like to affirm may be described as "the proposition asserting, concerning the actual object which was the first Chancellor of the German Empire, that this object was an astute diplomatist." What enables us to communicate in spite of the varying descriptions we employ is that we know there is a true proposition concerning the actual Bismarck, and that however we may vary the description (so long as the description is correct) the proposition described is still the same. This proposition, which is described and is known to be true, is what interests us; but we are not acquainted with the proposition itself, and do not know *it,* though we know it is true.

It will be seen that there are various stages in the removal from acquaintance with particulars: there is Bismarck to people who knew him; Bismarck to those who only know of him through history; the man with the iron mask; the longest-lived of men. These are progressively further removed from acquaintance with particulars; the first comes as near to acquaintance as is possible in regard to another person; in the second, we shall still be said to know "who Bismarck was"; in the third, we do not know who was the man with the iron mask, though we can know many propositions about him which are not logically deducible from the fact that he wore an iron mask; in the fourth, finally, we know nothing beyond what is logically deducible from the definition of the man. There is a similar hierarchy in the region of universals. Many universals, like many particulars, are only known to us by description. But here, as in the case of particulars, knowledge concerning what is known by description is ultimately reducible to knowledge concerning what is known by acquaintance.

The fundamental principle in the analysis of prepositions containing descriptions is this: *Every proposition which we can understand must be composed wholly of constituents with which we are acquainted.*

We shall not at this stage attempt to answer all the objections which may be urged against this fundamental principle. For the present, we shall merely point out that, in some way or other, it must be possible to meet these objections, for it is scarcely conceivable that we can make a judgement or entertain a supposition without knowing what it is that we are judging or supposing about. We must attach *some* meaning to the words we use, if we are to speak significantly and not utter mere noise; and the meaning we attach to our words must be something with which we are acquainted. Thus when, for example, we make a statement about Julius Caesar, it is plain that Julius Caesar himself is not before our minds, since we are not acquainted with him. We have in mind some *description* of Julius Caesar: "the man who was assassinated on the Ides of March," "the founder of the Roman Empire," or, perhaps, merely "the man whose name was *Julius Caesar*." (In this last description, *Julius Caesar* is a noise or shape with which we are acquainted.) Thus our statement does not mean quite what it seems to mean, but means something involving, instead of Julius Caesar, some description of him which is composed wholly of particulars and universals with which we are acquainted.

The chief importance of knowledge by description is that it enables us to pass beyond the limits of our private experience. In spite of the fact that we can only know truths which are wholly composed of terms which we have experienced in acquaintance, we can yet have knowledge by description of things which we have never experienced. In view of the very narrow range of our immediate experience, this result is vital, and until it is understood, much of our knowledge must remain mysterious and therefore doubtful.

* * *

CHAPTER 15: THE VALUE OF PHILOSOPHY

Having now come to the end of our brief and very incomplete review of the problems of philosophy, it will be well to consider, in conclusion, what is the value of philosophy and why it ought to be studied. It is the more necessary to consider this question, in view of the fact that many men, under the influence of science or of practical affairs, are inclined to doubt whether philosophy is anything better than innocent but useless trifling, hair-splitting distinctions, and controversies on matters concerning which knowledge is impossible.

This view of philosophy appears to result, partly from a wrong conception of the ends of life, partly from a wrong conception of the kind of goods which philosophy strives to achieve. Physical science, through the medium of inventions, is useful to innumerable people who are wholly ignorant of it; thus the study of physical science is to be recommended, not only, or primarily, because of the effect on the student, but rather because of the effect on mankind in general. Thus utility does not belong to philosophy. If the study of philosophy has any value at all for others than students of philosophy, it must be only indirectly, through its effects upon the lives of those who study it. It is in these effects, therefore, if anywhere, that the value of philosophy must be primarily sought.

But further, if we are not to fail in our endeavour to determine the value of philosophy, we must first free our minds from the prejudices of what are wrongly called "practical" men. The "practical" man, as this word is often used, is one who recognizes only material needs, who realizes that men must have food for the body, but is oblivious of the necessity of providing food for the mind. If all men were well off, if poverty and disease had been reduced to their lowest possible point, there would still remain much to be done to produce a valuable society; and even in the existing world the goods of the mind are at least as important as the goods of the body. It is exclusively among the goods of the mind that the value of philosophy is to be found; and only those who are not indifferent to these goods can be persuaded that the study of philosophy is not a waste of time.

Philosophy, like all other studies, aims primarily at knowledge. The knowledge it aims at is the kind of knowledge which gives unity and system to the body of sciences, and the kind which results from a critical examination of the grounds of our convictions, prejudices, and beliefs. But it cannot be maintained that philosophy has had any very great measure of success in its attempts to provide definite answers to its questions. If you ask a mathematician, a mineralogist, a historian, or any other man of learning, what definite body of truths has been ascertained by his science, his answer will last as long as you are willing to listen. But if you put the same question to a philosopher, he will, if he is candid, have to confess that his study has not achieved positive results such as have been achieved by other sciences. It is true that this is partly accounted for by the fact that, as soon as definite knowledge concerning any subject becomes possible, this subject ceases to be called philosophy, and now becomes a separate science. The whole study of the heavens, which now belongs to astronomy, was once included in philosophy; Newton's great work was called "the mathematical principles of natural philosophy." Similarly, the study of the human mind, which was a part of philosophy, has now been separated from philosophy and has become the science of psychology. Thus, to a great extent, the uncertainty of philosophy is more apparent than real: those questions which are already capable of definite answers are placed in the sciences, while those only to which, at present, no definite answer can be given, remain to form the residue which is called philosophy.

This is, however, only a part of the truth concerning the uncertainty of philosophy. There are many questions—and among them those that are of the profoundest interest to our spiritual life—which, so far as we can see, must remain insoluble to the human intellect unless its powers become of quite a different order from what they are now. Has the universe any unity of plan or purpose, or is it a fortuitous concourse of atoms? Is consciousness a permanent part of the universe, giving hope of indefinite growth in wisdom, or is it a transitory accident on a small planet on which life must ultimately become impossible? Are good and evil of importance to the universe or only to man? Such questions are asked by philosophy, and variously answered by various philosophers. But it would seem that, whether answers be otherwise discoverable or not, the answers suggested by philosophy are none of them demonstrably true. Yet, however slight may be the hope of discovering an answer, it is part of the business of philosophy to continue the consideration of such questions, to make us aware of their importance, to examine all the approaches to them, and to keep alive that speculative interest in the universe which is apt to be killed by confining ourselves to definitely ascertainable knowledge.

Many philosophers, it is true, have held that philosophy could establish the truth of certain answers to such fundamental questions. They have supposed that what is of most importance in religious beliefs could be proved by strict demonstration to be true. In order to judge of such attempts, it is necessary to take a survey of human knowledge, and to form an opinion as to its methods and its limitations. On such a subject it would be unwise to pronounce dogmatically; but if the investigations of our previous chapters have not led us astray, we shall be compelled to renounce the hope of finding philosophical proofs of religious beliefs. We cannot, therefore, include as part of the value of philosophy any definite set of answers to such questions. Hence, once more, the value of philosophy must not depend upon any supposed body of definitely ascertainable knowledge to be acquired by those who study it.

The value of philosophy is, in fact, to be sought largely in its very uncertainty. The man who has not tincture of philosophy goes through life imprisoned in the prejudices derived from common sense, from the habitual beliefs of his age or his nation, and from convictions which have grown up in his mind without the co-operation or consent of his deliberate reason. To such a man the world tends to become definite, finite, obvious; common objects rouse no questions, and unfamiliar possibilities are contemptuously rejected. As soon as we begin to philosophize, on the contrary, we find, as we saw in our opening chapters, that even the most everyday things lead to problems to which only very incomplete answers can be given. Philosophy, though unable to tell us with certainty what is the true answer to the doubts which it raises, is able to suggest many possibilities which enlarge our thoughts and free them from the tyranny of custom. Thus, while diminishing our feeling of certainty as to what things are, it greatly increases our knowledge as to what they may be; it removes the somewhat arrogant dogmatism of those who have never travelled into the region of liberating doubt, and it keeps alive our sense of wonder by showing familiar things in an unfamiliar aspect.

Apart from its utility in showing unsuspected possibilities, philosophy has a value—perhaps its chief value—through the greatness of the objects which it contemplates, and the freedom from narrow and personal aims resulting from this contemplation. The life of the instinctive man is shut up within the circle of his private interests: family and friends may be included, but the outer world is not regarded except as it may help or hinder what comes within the circle of instinctive wishes. In such a life there is something feverish and confined, in comparison with which the philosophic life is calm and free. The private world of instinctive interests is a small one, set in the midst of a great and powerful world which must, sooner or later, lay our private world in ruins. Unless we can so enlarge our interests as to include the whole outer world, we remain like a garrison in a beleaguered fortress, knowing that the enemy prevents escape and that ultimate surrender is inevitable. In such a life there is no peace, but a constant strife between the insistence of desire and the powerlessness of will. In one way or another, if our life is to be great and free, we must escape this prison and this strife.

One way of escape is by philosophic contemplation. Philosophic contemplation does not, in its widest survey, divide the universe into two hostile camps—friends and foes, helpful and hostile, good and bad—it views the whole impartially. Philosophic contemplation, when it is unalloyed, does not aim at proving that the rest of the universe is akin to man. All acquisition of knowledge is an enlargement of the Self, but this enlargement is best attained when it is not directly sought. It is obtained when the desire for knowledge is alone operative, by a study which does not wish in advance that its objects should have this or that character, but adapts the Self to the characters which it finds in its objects. This enlargement of Self is not obtained when, taking the Self as it is, we try to show that the world is so similar to this Self that knowledge of it is possible without any admission of what seems alien. The desire to prove this is a form of self-assertion and, like all self-assertion, it is an obstacle to the growth of Self which it desires, and of which the Self knows that it is capable. Self-assertion, in philosophic speculation as elsewhere, views the world as a means to its own ends; thus it makes the world of less account than Self, and the Self sets bounds to the greatness of its goods. In contemplation, on the contrary, we start from the not-Self, and through its greatness the boundaries of Self are enlarged; through the infinity of the universe the mind which contemplates it achieves some share in infinity.

For this reason greatness of soul is not fostered by those philosophies which assimilate the universe to Man. Knowledge is a form of union of Self and not-Self; like all union, it is impaired by dominion, and therefore by any attempt to force the universe into conformity with what we find in ourselves. There is a widespread philosophical tendency towards the view which tells us that Man is the measure of all things, that truth is man-made, that space and time and the world of universals are properties of the mind, and that, if there be anything not created by the mind, it is unknowable and of no account for us. This view, if our previous discussions were correct, is untrue; but in addition to being untrue, it has the effect of robbing philosophic contemplation of all that gives it value, since it fetters contemplation to Self. What it calls knowledge is not a union with the not-Self, but a set of prejudices, habits, and desires, making an impenetrable veil between us and the world beyond. The man who finds pleasure in such a theory of knowledge is like the man who never leaves the domestic circle for fear his word might not be law.

The true philosophic contemplation, on the contrary, finds its satisfaction in every enlargement of the not-Self, in everything that magnifies the objects contemplated, and thereby the subject contemplating. Everything, in contemplation, that is personal or private, everything that depends upon habit, self-interest, or desire, distorts the object, and hence impairs the union which the intellect seeks. By thus making a barrier between subject and object, such personal and private things become a prison to the intellect. The free intellect will see as God might see, without a *here* and *now,* without hopes and fears, without the trammels of customary beliefs and traditional prejudices, calmly, dispassionately, in the sole and exclusive desire of knowledge—knowledge as impersonal, as purely contemplative, as it is possible for man to attain. Hence also the free intellect will value more the abstract and universal knowledge into which the accidents of private history do not enter, than the knowledge brought by the senses, and dependent, as such knowledge must be, upon an exclusive and personal point of view and a body whose sense-organs distort as much as they reveal.

The mind which has become accustomed to the freedom and impartiality of philosophic contemplation will preserve something of the same freedom and impartiality in the world of action and emotion. It will view its purposes and desires as parts of the whole, with the absence of insistence that results from seeing them as infinitesimal fragments in a world of which all the rest is unaffected by any one man's deeds. The impartiality which, in contemplation, is the unalloyed desire for truth, is the very same quality of mind which, in action, is justice, and in emotion is that universal love which can be given to all, and not only to those who are judged useful or admirable. Thus contemplation enlarges not only the objects of our thoughts, but also the objects of our actions and our affections: it makes us citizens of the universe, not only of one walled city at war with all the rest. In this citizenship of the universe consists man's true freedom, and his liberation from the thraldom of narrow hopes and fears.

Thus, to sum up our discussion of the value of philosophy; philosophy is to be studied, not for the sake of any definite answers to its questions, since no definite answers can, as a rule, be known to be true, but rather for the sake of the questions themselves; because these questions enlarge our conception of what is possible, enrich our intellectual imagination and diminish the dogmatic assurance which closes the mind against speculation; but above all because, through the greatness of the universe which philosophy contemplates, the mind also is rendered great, and becomes capable of that union with the universe which constitutes its highest good.

MYSTICISM AND LOGIC

Metaphysics, or the attempt to conceive the world as a whole by means of thought, has been developed, from the first, by the union and conflict of two very different human impulses, the one urging men towards mysticism, the other urging them towards science. Some men have achieved greatness through one of these impulses alone, others through the other alone: in Hume, for example, the scientific impulse reigns quite unchecked, while in Blake a strong hostility to science co-exists with profound mystic insight. But the greatest men who have been philosophers have felt the need both of science and of mysticism: the attempt to harmonise the two was what made their life, and what always must, for all its arduous uncertainty, make philosophy, to some minds, a greater thing than either science or religion.

Before attempting an explicit characterisation of the scientific and the mystical impulses, I will illustrate them by examples from two philosophers whose greatness lies in the very intimate blending which they achieved. The two philosophers I mean are Heraclitus and Plato.

Heraclitus, as every one knows, was a believer in universal flux: time builds and destroys all things. From the few fragments that remain, it is not easy to discover how he arrived at his opinions, but there are some sayings that strongly suggest scientific observation as the source.

"The things that can be seen, heard, and learned," he says, "are what I prize the most." This is the language of the empiricist, to whom observation is the sole guarantee of truth. "The sun is new every day," is another fragment; and this opinion, in spite of its paradoxical character, is obviously inspired by scientific reflection, and no doubt seemed to him to obviate the difficulty of understanding how the sun can work its way underground from west to east during the night. Actual observation must also have suggested to him his central doctrine, that Fire is the one permanent substance, of which all visible things are passing phases. In combustion we see things change utterly, while their flame and heat rise up into the air and vanish.

"This world, which is the same for all," he says, "no one of gods or men has made; but it was ever, is now, and ever shall be, an ever-living Fire, with measures kindling, and measures going out."

"The transformations of Fire are, first of all, sea; and half of the sea is earth, half whirlwind."

This theory, though no longer one which science can accept, is nevertheless scientific in spirit. Science, too, might have inspired the famous saying to which Plato alludes: "You cannot step twice into the same rivers; for fresh waters are ever flowing in

Bertrand Russell, *Mysticism and Logic and Other Essays*. New York: Longmans, Green and Co., 1918. Reprinted by permission.

upon you." But we find also another statement among the extant fragments: "We step and do not step into the same rivers; we are and are not."

The comparison of this statement, which is mystical, with the one quoted by Plato, which is scientific, shows how intimately the two tendencies are blended in the system of Heraclitus. Mysticism is, in essence, little more than a certain intensity and depth of feeling in regard to what is believed about the universe; and this kind of feeling leads Heraclitus, on the basis of his science, to strangely poignant sayings concerning life and the world, such as:

"Time is a child playing draughts, the kingly power is a child's."

It is poetic imagination, not science, which presents Time as despotic lord of the world, with all the irresponsible frivolity of a child. It is mysticism, too, which leads Heraclitus to assert the identity of opposites: "Good and ill are one," he says; and again: "To God all things are fair and good and right, but men hold some things wrong and some right."

Much of mysticism underlies the ethics of Heraclitus. It is true that a scientific determinism alone might have inspired the statement: "Man's character is his fate"; but only a mystic would have said:

"Every beast is driven to the pasture with blows"; and again:

"It is hard to fight with one's heart's desire. Whatever it wishes to get, it purchases at the cost of soul"; and again:

"Wisdom is one thing. It is to know the thought by which all things are steered through all things."

Examples might be multiplied, but those that have been given are enough to show the character of the man: the facts of science, as they appeared to him, fed the flame in his soul, and in its light he saw into the depths of the world by the reflection of his own dancing swiftly penetrating fire. In such a nature we see the true union of the mystic and the man of science—the highest eminence, as I think, that it is possible to achieve in the world of thought.

In Plato, the same twofold impulse exists, though the mystic impulse is distinctly the stronger of the two, and secures ultimate victory whenever the conflict is sharp. His description of the cave is the classical statement of belief in a knowledge and reality truer and more real than that of the senses:

> Imagine a number of men living in an underground cavernous chamber, with an entrance open to the light, extending along the entire length of the cavern, in which they have been confined, from their childhood, with their legs and necks so shackled that they are obliged to sit still and look straight forwards, because their chains render it impossible for them to turn their heads round: and imagine a bright fire burning some way off, above and behind them, and an elevated roadway passing between the fire and the prisoners, with a low wall built along it, like the screens which conjurors put up in front of their audience, and above which they exhibit their wonders.
>
> I have it, he replied.
>
> Also figure to yourself a number of persons walking behind this wall, and carrying with them statues of men, and images of other animals, wrought in wood and stone and all kinds of materials, together with various other articles, which overtop the wall; and, as you might expect, let some of the passers-by be talking, and others silent.
>
> You are describing a strange scene, and strange prisoners.
>
> They resemble us, I replied.
>
> Now consider what would happen if the course of nature brought them a release from their fetters, and a remedy for their foolishness, in the following manner. Let us suppose that one of them has been released, and compelled suddenly to stand up, and turn his neck

round and walk with open eyes towards the light; and let us suppose that he goes through all these actions with pain, and that the dazzling splendour renders him incapable of discerning those objects of which he used formerly to see the shadows. What answer should you expect him to make, if some one were to tell him that in those days he was watching foolish phantoms, but that now he is somewhat nearer to reality, and is turned towards things more real, and sees more correctly; above all, if he were to point out to him the several objects that are passing by, and question him, and compel him to answer what they are? Should you not expect him to be puzzled, and to regard his old visions as truer than the objects now forced upon his notice?

Yes, much truer. . . .

Hence, I suppose, habit will be necessary to enable him to perceive objects in that upper world. At first he will be most successful in distinguishing shadows; then he will discern the reflections of men and other things in water, and afterwards the realities; and after this he will raise his eyes to encounter the light of the moon and stars, finding it less difficult to study the heavenly bodies and the heaven itself by night, than the sun and the sun's light by day.

Doubtless.

Last of all, I imagine, he will be able to observe and contemplate the nature of the sun, not as it *appears* in water or on alien ground, but as it is in itself in its own territory.

Of course.

His next step will be to draw the conclusion, that the sun is the author of the seasons and the years, and the guardian of all things in the visible world, and in a manner the cause of all those things which he and his companions used to see.

Obviously, this will be his next step. . . .

Now this imaginary case, my dear Glaucon, you must apply in all its parts to our former statements, by comparing the region which the eye reveals, to the prison house, and the light of the fire therein to the power of the sun: and if, by the upward ascent and the contemplation of the upper world, you understand the mounting of the soul into the intellectual region, you will hit the tendency of my own surmises, since you desire to be told what they are; though, indeed, God only knows whether they are correct. But, be that as it may, the view which I take of the subject is to the following effect. In the world of knowledge, the essential Form of Good is the limit of our enquiries, and can barely be perceived; but, when perceived, we cannot help concluding that it is in every case the source of all that is bright and beautiful,—in the visible world giving birth to light and its master, and in the intellectual world dispensing, immediately and with full authority, truth and reason;—and that whosoever would act wisely, either in private or in public, must set this Form of Good before his eyes. [*Republic,* 514, translated by Davies and Vaughan]

But in this passage, as throughout most of Plato's teaching, there is an identification of the good with the truly real, which became embodied in the philosophical tradition, and is still largely operative in our own day. In thus allowing a legislative function to the good, Plato produced a divorce between philosophy and science, from which, in my opinion, both have suffered ever since and are still suffering. The man of science, whatever his hopes may be, must lay them aside while he studies nature; and the philosopher, if he is to achieve truth must do the same. Ethical considerations can only legitimately appear when the truth has been ascertained: they can and should appear as determining our feeling towards the truth, and our manner of ordering our lives in view of the truth, but not as themselves dictating what the truth is to be.

There are passages in Plato—among those which illustrate the scientific side of his mind—where he seems clearly aware of this. The most noteworthy is the one in which Socrates, as a young man, is explaining the theory of ideas to Parmenides.

After Socrates has explained that there is an idea of the good, but not of such things as hair and mud and dirt, Parmenides advises him "not to despise even the meanest things," and this advice shows the genuine scientific temper. It is with this impartial temper that the mystic's apparent insight into a higher reality and a hidden good has to be combined if philosophy is to realise its greatest possibilities. And it is failure in this respect that has made so much of idealistic philosophy thin, lifeless, and insubstantial. It is only in marriage with the world that our ideals can bear fruit: divorced from it, they remain barren. But marriage with the world is not to be achieved by an ideal which shrinks from fact, or demands in advance that the world shall conform to its desires.

Parmenides himself is the source of a peculiarly interesting strain of mysticism which pervades Plato's thought—the mysticism which may be called "logical" because it is embodied in theories on logic. This form of mysticism, which appears, so far as the West is concerned, to have originated with Parmenides, dominates the reasonings of all the great mystical metaphysicians from his day to that of Hegel and his modern disciples. Reality, he says, is uncreated, indestructible, unchanging, indivisible; it is "immovable in the bonds of mighty chains, without beginning and without end; since coming into being and passing away have been driven afar, and true belief has cast them away." The fundamental principle of his inquiry is stated in a sentence which would not be out of place in Hegel: "Thou canst not know what is not—that is impossible—nor utter it; for it is the same thing that can be thought and that can be." And again: "It needs must be that what can be thought and spoken of is; for it is possible for it to be, and it is not possible for what is nothing to be." The impossibility of change follows from this principle; for what is past can be spoken of, and therefore, by the principle, still is.

Mystical philosophy, in all ages and in all parts of the world, is characterised by certain beliefs which are illustrated by the doctrines we have been considering.

There is, first, the belief in insight as against discursive analytic knowledge: the belief in a way of wisdom, sudden, penetrating, coercive, which is contrasted with the slow and fallible study of outward appearance by a science relying wholly upon the senses. All who are capable of absorption in an inward passion must have experienced at times the strange feeling of unreality in common objects, the loss of contact with daily things, in which the solidity of the outer world is lost, and the soul seems, in utter loneliness, to bring forth, out of its own depths, the mad dance of fantastic phantoms which have hitherto appeared as independently real and living. This is the negative side of the mystic's initiation: the doubt concerning common knowledge, preparing the way for the reception of what seems a higher wisdom. Many men to whom this negative experience is familiar do not pass beyond it, but for the mystic it is merely the gateway to an ampler world.

The mystic insight begins with the sense of a mystery unveiled, of a hidden wisdom now suddenly become certain beyond the possibility of a doubt. The sense of certainty and revelation comes earlier than any definite belief. The definite beliefs at which mystics arrive are the result of reflection upon the inarticulate experience gained in the moment of insight. Often, beliefs which have no real connection with this moment become subsequently attracted into the central nucleus; thus in addition to the convictions which all mystics share, we find, in many of them, other convictions of a more local and temporary character, which no doubt become amalgamated with what was essentially mystical in virtue of their subjective certainty. We may ignore such inessential accretions, and confine ourselves to the beliefs which all mystics share.

The first and most direct outcome of the moment of illumination is belief in the possibility of a way of knowledge which may be called revelation or insight or intuition, as contrasted with sense, reason, and analysis, which are regarded as blind guides leading to the morass of illusion. Closely connected with this belief is the conception of a Reality behind the world of appearance and utterly different from it. This Reality is regarded with an admiration often amounting to worship; it is felt to be always and everywhere close at hand, thinly veiled by the shows of sense, ready, for the receptive mind, to shine in its glory even through the apparent folly and wickedness of Man. The poet, the artist, and the lover are seekers after that glory: the haunting beauty that they pursue is the faint reflection of its sun. But the mystic lives in the full light of the vision: what others dimly seek he knows, with a knowledge beside which all other knowledge is ignorance.

The second characteristic of mysticism is its belief in unity, and its refusal to admit opposition or division anywhere. We found Heraclitus saying "good and ill are one"; and again he says, "the way up and the way down is one and the same." The same attitude appears in the simultaneous assertion of contradictory propositions, such as: "We step and do not step into the same rivers; we are and are not." The assertion of Parmenides, that reality is one and indivisible, comes from the same impulse towards unity. In Plato, this impulse is less prominent, being held in check by his theory of ideas; but it reappears, so far as his logic permits, in the doctrine of the primacy of the Good.

A third mark of almost all mystical metaphysics is the denial of the reality of Time. This is an outcome of the denial of division; if all is one, the distinction of past and future must be illusory. We have seen this doctrine prominent in Parmenides; and among moderns it is fundamental in the systems of Spinoza and Hegel.

The last of the doctrines of mysticism which we have to consider is its belief that all evil is mere appearance, an illusion produced by the divisions and oppositions of the analytic intellect. Mysticism does not maintain that such things as cruelty, for example, are good, but it denies that they are real: they belong to that lower world of phantoms from which we are to be liberated by the insight of the vision. Sometimes—for example in Hegel, and at least verbally in Spinoza—not only evil, but good also, is regarded as illusory, though nevertheless the emotional attitude towards what is held to be Reality is such as would naturally be associated with the belief that Reality is good. What is, in all cases, ethically characteristic of mysticism is absence of indignation or protest, acceptance with joy, disbelief in the ultimate truth of the division into two hostile camps, the good and the bad. This attitude is a direct outcome of the nature of the mystical experience: with its sense of unity is associated a feeling of infinite peace. Indeed it may be suspected that the feeling of peace produces, as feelings do in dreams, the whole system of associated beliefs which make up the body of mystic doctrine. But this is a difficult question, and one on which it cannot be hoped that mankind will reach agreement.

Four questions thus arise in considering the truth or falsehood of mysticism, namely:

I. Are there two ways of knowing, which may be called respectively reason and intuition? And if so, is either to be preferred to the other?

II. Is all plurality and division illusory?

III. Is time unreal?

IV. What kind of reality belongs to good and evil?

On all four of these questions, while fully developed mysticism seems to me mistaken, I yet believe that, by sufficient restraint, there is an element of wisdom to be learned from the mystical way of feeling, which does not seem to be attainable in any other manner. If this is the truth, mysticism is to be commended as an attitude towards life, not as a creed about the world. The metaphysical creed, I shall maintain, is a mistaken outcome of the emotion, although this emotion, as colouring and informing all other thoughts and feelings, is the inspirer of whatever is best in Man. Even the cautious and patient investigation of truth by science, which seems the very antithesis of the mystic's swift certainty, may be fostered and nourished by that very spirit of reverence in which mysticism lives and moves.

I. REASON AND INTUITION*

Of the reality or unreality of the mystic's world I know nothing. I have no wish to deny it, nor even to declare that the insight which reveals it is not a genuine insight.

What I do wish to maintain—and it is here that the scientific attitude becomes imperative—is that insight, untested and unsupported, is an insufficient guarantee of truth, in spite of the fact that much of the most important truth is first suggested by its means. It is common to speak of an opposition between instinct and reason; in the eighteenth century, the opposition was drawn in favour of reason, but under the influence of Rousseau and the romantic movement instinct was given the preference, first by those who rebelled against artificial forms of government and thought, and then, as the purely rationalistic defence of traditional theology became increasingly difficult, by all who felt in science a menace to creeds which they associated with a spiritual outlook on life and the world. Bergson, under the name of "intuition," has raised instinct to the position of sole arbiter of metaphysical truth. But in fact the opposition of instinct and reason is mainly illusory. Instinct, intuition, or insight is what first leads to the beliefs which subsequent reason confirms or confutes; but the confirmation, where it is possible, consists, in the last analysis, of agreement with other beliefs no less instinctive. Reason is a harmonising, controlling force rather than a creative one. Even in the most purely logical realm, it is insight that first arrives at what is new.

Where instinct and reason do sometimes conflict is in regard to single beliefs, held instinctively, and held with such determination that no degree of inconsistency with other beliefs leads to their abandonment. Instinct, like all human faculties, is liable to error. Those in whom reason is weak are often unwilling to admit this as regards themselves, though all admit it in regard to others. Where instinct is least liable to error is in practical matters as to which right judgment is a help to survival: friendship and hostility in others, for instance, are often felt with extraordinary discrimination through very careful disguises. But even in such matters a wrong impression may be given by reserve or flattery; and in matters less directly practical, such as philosophy deals with, very strong instinctive beliefs are sometimes wholly mistaken, as we may come to know through their perceived inconsistency with other equally strong beliefs. It is such considerations that necessitate the harmonising mediation of reason, which tests our beliefs by their mutual compatibility, and examines, in doubtful cases, the possible sources of error on the one side and on the other. In this there is no opposition to instinct as a whole, but only to blind reliance upon some one interesting aspect of instinct to the exclusion of other more commonplace but not less trustworthy aspects. It is such one-sidedness, not instinct itself, that reason aims at correcting.

These more or less trite maxims may be illustrated by application to Bergson's advocacy of "intuition" as against "intellect." There are, he says, "two profoundly dif-

*This section, and also one or two pages in later sections, have been printed in a course of Lowell lectures *On Our Knowledge of the External World,* published by the Open Court Publishing Company. But I have left them here, as this is the context for which they were originally written. [Russell's note.]

ferent ways of knowing a thing. The first implies that we move round the object: the second that we enter into it. The first depends on the point of view at which we are placed and on the symbols by which we express ourselves. The second neither depends on a point of view nor relies on any symbol. The first kind of knowledge may be said to stop at the *relative;* the second, in those cases where it is possible, to attain the *absolute.*"* The second of these, which is intuition, is, he says, "the kind of *intellectual sympathy* by which one places oneself within an object in order to coincide with what is unique in it and therefore inexpressible." In illustration, he mentions self-knowledge: "there is one reality, at least, which we all seize from within, by intuition and not by simple analysis. It is our own personality in its flowing through time—our self which endures." The rest of Bergson's philosophy consists in reporting, through the imperfect medium of words, the knowledge gained by intuition, and the consequent complete condemnation of all the pretended knowledge derived from science and common sense.

This procedure, since it takes sides in a conflict of instinctive beliefs, stands in need of justification by proving the greater trustworthiness of the beliefs on one side than of those on the other. Bergson attempts this justification in two ways, first by explaining that intellect is a purely practical faculty to secure biological success, secondly by mentioning remarkable feats of instinct in animals and by pointing out characteristics of the world which, though intuition can apprehend them, are baffling to intellect as he interprets it.

Of Bergson's theory that intellect is a purely practical faculty, developed in the struggle for survival, and not a source of true beliefs, we may say, first, that it is only through intellect that we know of the struggle for survival and of the biological ancestry of man: if the intellect is misleading, the whole of this merely inferred history is presumably untrue. If, on the other hand, we agree with him in thinking that evolution took place as Darwin believed, then it is not only intellect, but all our faculties, that have been developed under the stress of practical utility. Intuition is seen at its best where it is directly useful, for example in regard to other people's characters and dispositions. Bergson apparently holds that capacity, for this kind of knowledge is less explicable by the struggle for existence than, for example, capacity for pure mathematics. Yet the savage deceived by false friendship is likely to pay for his mistake with his life; whereas even in the most civilised societies men are not put to death for mathematical incompetence. All the most striking of his instances of intuition in animals have a very direct survival value. The fact is, of course, that both intuition and intellect have been developed because they are useful, and that, speaking broadly, they are useful when they give truth and become harmful when they give falsehood. Intellect, in civilised man, like artistic capacity, has occasionally been developed beyond the point where it is useful to the individual; intuition, on the other hand, seems on the whole to diminish as civilisation increases. It is greater, as a rule, in children than in adults, in the uneducated than in the educated. Probably in dogs it exceeds anything to be found in human beings. But those who see in these facts a recommendation of intuition ought to return to running wild in the woods, dyeing themselves with woad and living on hips and haws.**

Let us next examine whether intuition possesses any such infallibility as Bergson claims for it. The best instance of it, according to him, is our acquaintance with ourselves; yet self-knowledge is proverbially rare and difficult. Most men, for example,

---

Introduction to Metaphysics [reprinted in this volume].
**[A "woad" is an herbal dye; "hips" are the fruits of a rose bush; and "haws" are hawthorn berries.]

have in their nature meannesses, vanities, and envies of which they are quite unconscious, though even their best friends can perceive them without any difficulty. It is true
that intuition has a convincingness which is lacking to intellect: while it is present, it is
almost impossible to doubt its truth. But if it should appear, on examination, to be at
least as fallible as intellect, its greater subjective certainty becomes a demerit, making it
only the more irresistibly deceptive. Apart from self-knowledge, one of the most notable examples of intuition is the knowledge people believe themselves to possess of
those with whom they are in love: the wall between different personalities seems to become transparent, and people think they see into another soul as into their own. Yet deception in such cases is constantly practised with success; and even where there is no
intentional deception, experience gradually proves, as a rule, that the supposed insight
was illusory, and that the slower more groping methods of the intellect are in the long
run more reliable.

Bergson maintains that intellect can only deal with things in so far as they resemble what has been experienced in the past, while intuition has the power of apprehending the uniqueness and novelty that always belong to each fresh moment. That there is
something unique and new at every moment, is certainly true; it is also true that this
cannot be fully expressed by means of intellectual concepts. Only direct acquaintance
can give knowledge of what is unique and new. But direct acquaintance of this kind is
given fully in sensation, and does not require, so far as I can see, any special faculty of
intuition for its apprehension. It is neither intellect nor intuition, but sensation, that supplies new data; but when the data are new in any remarkable manner, intellect is much
more capable of dealing with them than intuition would be. The hen with a brood of
ducklings no doubt has intuition which seems to place her inside them, and not merely
to know them analytically; but when the ducklings take to the water, the whole apparent
intuition is seen to be illusory, and the hen is left helpless on the shore. Intuition, in fact,
is an aspect and development of instinct, and, like all instinct, is admirable in those customary surroundings which have moulded the habits of the animal in question, but totally incompetent as soon as the surroundings are changed in a way which demands
some non-habitual mode of action.

The theoretical understanding of the world, which is the aim of philosophy, is not
a matter of great practical importance to animals, or to savages, or even to most
civilised men. It is hardly to be supposed, therefore, that the rapid, rough and ready
methods of instinct or intuition will find in this field a favourable ground for their application. It is the older kinds of activity, which bring out our kinship with remote generations of animal and semi-human ancestors, that show intuition at its best. In such matters as self-preservation and love, intuition will act sometimes (though not always) with
a swiftness and precision which are astonishing to the critical intellect. But philosophy
is not one of the pursuits which illustrate our affinity with the past: it is a highly refined,
highly civilised pursuit, demanding, for its success, a certain liberation from the life of
instinct, and even, at times, a certain aloofness from all mundane hopes and fears. It is
not in philosophy, therefore, that we can hope to see intuition at its best. On the contrary, since the true objects of philosophy, and the habit of thought demanded for their
apprehension, are strange, unusual, and remote, it is here, more almost than anywhere
else, that intellect proves superior to intuition, and that quick unanalysed convictions
are least deserving of uncritical acceptance.

In advocating the scientific restraint and balance, as against the self-assertion of a
confident reliance upon intuition, we are only urging, in the sphere of knowledge, that
largeness of contemplation, that impersonal disinterestedness, and that freedom from
practical preoccupations which have been inculcated by all the great religions of the

world. Thus our conclusion, however it may conflict with the explicit beliefs of many mystics, is, in essence, not contrary to the spirit which inspires those beliefs, but rather the outcome of this very spirit as applied in the realm of thought.

II. UNITY AND PLURALITY

One of the most convincing aspects of the mystic illumination is the apparent revelation of the oneness of all things, giving rise to pantheism in religion and to monism in philosophy. An elaborate logic, beginning with Parmenides, and culminating in Hegel and his followers, has been gradually developed, to prove that the universe is one indivisible Whole, and that what seem to be its parts, if considered as substantial and self existing, are mere illusion. The conception of a Reality quite other than the world of appearance, a reality one, indivisible, and unchanging, was introduced into Western philosophy by Parmenides, not, nominally at least, for mystical or religious reasons, but on the basis of a logical argument as to the impossibility of not-being, and most subsequent metaphysical systems are the outcome of this fundamental idea.

The logic used in defence of mysticism seems to be faulty as logic, and open to technical criticisms, which I have explained elsewhere. I shall not here repeat these criticisms, since they are lengthy and difficult, but shall instead attempt an analysis of the state of mind from which mystical logic has arisen.

Belief in a reality quite different from what appears to the senses arises with irresistible force in certain moods, which are the source of most mysticism, and of most metaphysics. While such a mood is dominant, the need of logic is not felt, and accordingly the more thoroughgoing mystics do not employ logic, but appeal directly to the immediate deliverance of their insight. But such fully developed mysticism is rare in the West. When the intensity of emotional conviction subsides, a man who is in the habit of reasoning will search for logical grounds in favour of the belief which he finds in himself. But since the belief already exists, he will be very hospitable to any ground that suggests itself. The paradoxes apparently proved by his logic are really the paradoxes of mysticism, and are the goal which he feels his logic must reach if it is to be in accordance with insight. The resulting logic has rendered most philosophers incapable of giving any account of the world of science and daily life. If they had been anxious to give such an account, they would probably have discovered the errors of their logic; but most of them were less anxious to understand the world of science and daily life than to convict it of unreality in the interests of a super-sensible "real" world.

It is in this way that logic has been pursued by those of the great philosophers who were mystics. But since they usually took for granted the supposed insight of the mystic emotion, their logical doctrines were presented with a certain dryness, and were believed by their disciples to be quite independent of the sudden illumination from which they sprang. Nevertheless their origin clung to them, and they remained—to borrow a useful word from Mr. Santayana— "malicious" in regard to the world of science and common sense. It is only so that we can account for the complacency with which philosophers have accepted the inconsistency of their doctrines with all the common and scientific facts which seem best established and most worthy of belief.

The logic of mysticism shows, as is natural, the defects which are inherent in anything malicious. The impulse to logic, not felt while the mystic mood is dominant, reasserts itself as the mood fades, but with a desire to retain the vanishing insight, or at least to prove that it *was* insight, and that what seems to contradict it is illusion. The logic which thus arises is not quite disinterested or candid, and is inspired by a certain hatred of the daily world to which it is to be applied. Such an attitude naturally does not tend to the best results. Everyone knows that to read an author simply in order to refute him is not the way to understand him; and to read the book of Nature with a conviction that it is all illusion is just as unlikely to lead to understanding. If our logic is to find the common world intelligible, it must not be hostile, but must be inspired by a genuine acceptance such as is not usually to be found among metaphysicians.

III. TIME

The unreality of time is a cardinal doctrine of many metaphysical systems, often nominally based, as already by Parmenides, upon logical arguments, but originally derived, at any rate in the founders of new systems, from the certainty which is born in the moment of mystic insight. As a Persian Sufi poet says:

> Past and future are what veil God from our sight.
> Burn up both of them with fire! How long
> Wilt thou be partitioned by these segments as a reed?

The belief that what is ultimately real must be immutable is a very common one: it gave rise to the metaphysical notion of substance, and finds, even now, a wholly illegitimate satisfaction in such scientific doctrines as the conservation of energy and mass.

It is difficult to disentangle the truth and the error in this view. The arguments for the contention that time is unreal and that the world of sense is illusory must, I think, be regarded as fallacious. Nevertheless there is some sense—easier to feel than to state—in which time is an unimportant and superficial characteristic of reality. Past and future must be acknowledged to be as real as the present, and a certain emancipation from slavery to time is essential to philosophic thought. The importance of time is rather practical than theoretical, rather in relation to our desires than in relation to truth. A truer image of the world, I think, is obtained by picturing things as entering into the stream of time from an eternal world outside, than from a view which regards time as the devouring tyrant of all that is. Both in thought and in feeling, even though time be real, to realise the unimportance of time is the gate of wisdom.

That this is the case may be seen at once by asking ourselves why our feelings towards the past are so different from our feelings towards the future. The reason for this difference is wholly practical: our wishes can affect the future but not the past, the future is to some extent subject to our power, while the past is unalterably fixed. But every future will some day be past: if we see the past truly now, it must, when it was still future, have been just what we now see it to be, and what is now future must be just what we shall see it to be when it has become past. The felt difference of quality between past and future, therefore, is not an intrinsic difference, but only a difference in relation to us: to impartial contemplation, it ceases to exist. And impartiality of contemplation is, in the intellectual sphere, that very same virtue of disinterestedness which, in the sphere of action, appears as justice and unselfishness. Whoever wishes to see the world truly, to rise in thought above the tyranny of practical desires, must learn to overcome the difference of attitude towards past and future, and to survey the whole stream of time in one comprehensive vision.

The kind of way in which, as it seems to me, time ought not to enter into our theoretic philosophical thought, may be illustrated by the philosophy which has become associated with the idea of evolution, and which is exemplified by Nietzsche, pragmatism, and Bergson. This philosophy, on the basis of the development which has led from the lowest forms of life up to man, sees in *progress* the fundamental law of the universe, and thus admits the difference between *earlier* and *later* into the very citadel of its contemplative outlook. With its past and future history of the world, conjectural as it is, I do not wish to quarrel. But I think that, in the intoxication of a quick success, much that is required for a true understanding of the universe has been forgotten. Something of Hellenism, something, too, of Oriental resignation, must be combined with its hurrying Western self-assertion before it can emerge from the ardour of youth into the mature wisdom of manhood. In spite of its appeals to science, the true scientific philosophy, I think, is something more arduous and more aloof, appealing to less mundane hopes, and requiring a severer discipline for its successful practice.

Darwin's *Origin of Species* persuaded the world that the difference between different species of animals and plants is not the fixed immutable difference that it appears to be. The doctrine of natural kinds, which had rendered classification easy and definite, which was enshrined in the Aristotelian tradition, and protected by its supposed necessity for orthodox dogma, was suddenly swept away for ever out of the biological world. The difference between man and the lower animals, which to our human conceit appears enormous, was shown to be a gradual achievement, involving intermediate beings who could not with certainty be placed either within or without the human family. The sun and the planets had already been shown by Laplace to be very probably derived from a primitive more or less undifferentiated nebula. Thus the old fixed landmarks became wavering and indistinct, and all sharp outlines were blurred. Things and species lost their boundaries, and none could say where they began or where they ended.

But if human conceit was staggered for a moment by its kinship with the ape, it soon found a way to reassert itself, and that way is the "philosophy" of evolution. A process which led from the amoeba to Man appeared to the philosophers to be obviously a progress—though whether the amoeba would agree with this opinion is not known. Hence the cycle of changes which science had shown to be the probable history of the past was welcomed as revealing a law of development towards good in the universe—an evolution or unfolding of an idea slowly embodying itself in the actual. But such a view, though it might satisfy Spencer and those whom we may call Hegelian evolutionists, could not be accepted as adequate by the more whole-hearted votaries of change. An ideal to which the world continuously approaches is, to these minds, too dead and static to be inspiring. Not only the aspiration, but the ideal too, must change and develop with the course of evolution: there must be no fixed goal, but a continual fashioning of fresh needs by the impulse which is life and which alone gives unity to the process.

Life, in this philosophy, is a continuous stream, in which all divisions are artificial and unreal. Separate things, beginnings and endings, are mere convenient fictions: there is only smooth unbroken transition. The beliefs of to-day may count as true to-day, if they carry us along the stream; but to-morrow they will be false, and must be replaced by new beliefs to meet the new situation. All our thinking consists of convenient fictions, imaginary congealings of the stream: reality flows on in spite of all our fictions, and though it can be lived, it cannot be conceived in thought. Somehow, without explicit statement, the assurance is slipped in that the future, though we cannot foresee it, will be better than the past or the present: the reader is like the child which expects a sweet because it has been told to open its mouth and shut its eyes. Logic, mathematics, physics disappear in this philosophy, because they are too "static"; what is real is no impulse and movement towards a goal which, like the rainbow, recedes as we advance, and makes every place different when it reaches it from what it appeared to be at a distance.

I do not propose to enter upon a technical examination of this philosophy. I wish only to maintain that the motives and interests which inspire it are so exclusively practical, and the problems with which it deals are so special, that it can hardly be regarded as touching any of the questions that, to my mind, constitute genuine philosophy.

The predominant interest of evolutionism is in the question of human destiny, or at least of the destiny of Life. It is more interested in morality and happiness than in knowledge for its own sake. It must be admitted that the same may be said of many other philosophies, and that a desire for the kind of knowledge which philosophy can give is very rare. But if philosophy is to attain truth, it is necessary first and foremost that philosophers should acquire the disinterested intellectual curiosity which characterises the genuine man of science. Knowledge concerning the future—which is the kind of knowledge that must be sought if we are to know about human destiny—is possible within certain narrow limits. It is impossible to say how much the limits may be enlarged with the progress of science. But what is evident is that any proposition about the future belongs by its subject-matter to some particular science, and is to be ascertained, if at all, by the methods of that science. Philosophy is not a short cut to the same kind of results as those of the other sciences: if it is to be a genuine study, it must have a province of its own, and aim at results which the other sciences can neither prove nor disprove.

Evolutionism, in basing itself upon the notion of *progress,* which is change from the worse to the better, allows the notion of time, as it seems to me, to become its tyrant rather than its servant, and thereby loses that impartiality of contemplation which is the source of all that is best in philosophic thought and feeling. Metaphysicians, as we saw, have frequently denied altogether the reality of time. I do not wish to do this; I wish only to preserve the mental outlook which inspired the denial, the attitude which, in thought, regards the past as having the same reality as the present and the same importance as the future. "In so far," says Spinoza,* "as the mind conceives a thing according to the dictate of reason, it will be equally affected whether the idea is that of a future, past, or present thing." It is this "conceiving according to the dictate of reason" that I find lacking in the philosophy which is based on evolution.

IV. GOOD AND EVIL

Mysticism maintains that all evil is illusory, and sometimes maintains the same view as regards good, but more often holds that all Reality is good. Both views are to be found in Heraclitus: "Good and ill are one," he says, but again, "To God all things are fair and good and right, but men hold some things wrong and some right." A similar twofold position is to be found in Spinoza, but he uses the word "perfection" when he means to speak of the good that is not merely human. "By reality and perfection I mean the same thing," he says; but elsewhere we find the definition: "By good I shall mean that which we certainly know to be useful to us." Thus perfection belongs to Reality in its own nature, but goodness is relative to ourselves and our needs, and disappears in an impartial survey. Some such distinction, I think, is necessary in order to understand the ethical outlook of mysticism: there is a lower mundane kind of good and evil, which divides

*Quotations here are all from Spinoza's *Ethics.*

the world of appearance into what seem to be conflicting parts; but there is also a higher, mystical kind of good, which belongs to Reality and is not opposed by any correlative kind of evil.

It is difficult to give a logically tenable account of this position without recognising that good and evil are subjective, that what is good is merely that towards which we have one kind of feeling, and what is evil is merely that towards which we have another kind of feeling. In our active life, where we have to exercise choice, and to prefer this to that of two possible acts, it is necessary to have a distinction of good and evil, or at least of better and worse. But this distinction, like everything pertaining to action, belongs to what mysticism regards as the world of illusion, if only because it is essentially concerned with time. In our contemplative life, where action is not called for, it is possible to be impartial, and to overcome the ethical dualism which action requires. So long as we remain *merely* impartial, we may be content to say that both the good and the evil of action are illusions. But if, as we must do if we have the mystic vision, we find the whole world worthy of love and worship, if we see

> The earth, and every common sight . . .
> Apparell'd in celestial light,

we shall say that there is a higher good than that of action, and that this higher good belongs to the whole world as it is in reality. In this way the twofold attitude and the apparent vacillation of mysticism are explained and justified.

The possibility of this universal love and joy in all that exists is of supreme importance for the conduct and happiness of life, and gives inestimable value to the mystic emotion, apart from any creeds which may be built upon it. But if we are not to be led into false beliefs, it is necessary to realise exactly what the mystic emotion reveals. It reveals a possibility of human nature—a possibility of a nobler, happier, freer life than any that can be otherwise achieved. But it does not reveal anything about the non-human, or about the nature of the universe in general. Good and bad, and even the higher good that mysticism finds everywhere, are the reflections of our own emotions on other things, not part of the substance of things as they are in themselves. And therefore an impartial contemplation, freed from all pre-occupation with Self, will not judge things good or bad, although it is very easily combined with that feeling of universal love which leads the mystic to say that the whole world is good.

The philosophy of evolution, through the notion of progress, is bound up with the ethical dualism of the worse and the better, and is thus shut out, not only from the kind of survey which discards good and evil altogether from its view, but also from the mystical belief in the goodness of everything. In this way the distinction of good and evil, like time, becomes a tyrant in this philosophy, and introduces into thought the restless selectiveness of action. Good and evil, like time, are, it would seem, not general or fundamental in the world of thought, but late and highly specialised members of the intellectual hierarchy.

Although, as we saw, mysticism can be interpreted so as to agree with the view that good and evil are not intellectually fundamental, it must be admitted that here we are no longer in verbal agreement with most of the great philosophers and religious teachers of the past. I believe, however, that the elimination of ethical considerations from philosophy is both scientifically necessary and—though this may seem a paradox—an ethical advance. Both these contentions must be briefly defended.

The hope of satisfaction to our more human desires—the hope of demonstrating that the world has this or that desirable ethical characteristic—is not one which, so far as I can see, a scientific philosophy can do anything whatever to satisfy. The difference between a good world and a bad one is a difference in the particular characteristics of the particular things that exist in these worlds: it is not a sufficiently abstract difference to come within the province of philosophy. Love and hate, for example, are ethical opposites, but to philosophy they are closely analogous attitudes towards objects. The general form and structure of those attitudes towards objects which constitute mental phenomena is a problem for philosophy, but the difference between love and hate is not a difference of form or structure, and therefore belongs rather to the special science of psychology than to philosophy. Thus the ethical interests which have often inspired philosophers must remain in the background: some kind of ethical interest may inspire the whole study, but none must obtrude in the detail or be expected in the special results which are sought.

If this view seems at first sight disappointing, we may remind ourselves that a similar change has been found necessary in all the other sciences. The physicist or chemist is not now required to prove the ethical importance of his ions or atoms; the biologist is not expected to prove the utility of the plants or animals which he dissects. In pre-scientific ages this was not the case. Astronomy, for example, was studied because men believed in astrology: it was thought that the movements of the planets had the most direct and important bearing upon the lives of human beings. Presumably, when this belief decayed and the disinterested study of astronomy began, many who had found astrology absorbingly interesting decided that astronomy had too little human interest to be worthy of study. Physics, as it appears in Plato's *Timaeus* for example, is full of ethical notions: it is an essential part of its purpose to show that the earth is worthy of admiration. The modern physicist, on the contrary, though he has no wish to deny that the earth is admirable, is not concerned, as physicist, with its ethical attributes: he is merely concerned to find out facts, not to consider whether they are good or bad. In psychology, the scientific attitude is even more recent and more difficult than in the physical sciences: it is natural to consider that human nature is either good or bad, and to suppose that the difference between good and bad, so all-important in practice, must be important in theory also. It is only during the last century that an ethically neutral psychology has grown up; and here too, ethical neutrality has been essential to scientific success.

In philosophy, hitherto, ethical neutrality has been seldom sought and hardly ever achieved. Men have remembered their wishes, and have judged philosophies in relation to their wishes. Driven from the particular sciences, the belief that the notions of good and evil must afford a key to the understanding of the world has sought a refuge in philosophy. But even from this last refuge, if philosophy is not to remain a set of pleasing dreams, this belief must be driven forth. It is a commonplace that happiness is not best achieved by those who seek it directly; and it would seem that the same is true of the good. In thought, at any rate, those who forget good and evil and seek only to know the facts are more likely to achieve good than those who view the world through the distorting medium of their own desires.

We are thus brought back to our seeming paradox, that a philosophy which does not seek to impose upon the world its own conceptions of good and evil is not only more likely to achieve truth, but is also the outcome of a higher ethical standpoint than one which, like evolutionism and most traditional systems, is perpetually appraising the universe and seeking to find in it an embodiment of present ideals. In religion, and in every deeply serious view of the world and of human destiny, there is an element of submission, a realisation of the limits of human power, which is somewhat lacking in the modern world, with its quick material successes and its insolent belief in the boundless possibilities of progress. "He that loveth his life shall lose it"; and there is danger lest, through a too confident love of life, life itself should lose much of what gives it its highest worth. The submission which religion inculcates in action is essentially the same in spirit as that which science teaches in thought; and the ethical neutrality by which its victories have been achieved is the outcome of that submission.

The good which it concerns us to remember is the good which it lies in our power to create—the good in our own lives and in our attitude towards the world. Insistence on belief in an external realisation of the good is a form of self-assertion, which, while it cannot secure the external good which it desires, can seriously impair the inward good which lies within our power, and destroy that reverence towards fact which constitutes both what is valuable in humility and what is fruitful in the scientific temper.

Human beings cannot, of course, wholly transcend human nature; something subjective, if only the interest that determines the direction of our attention, must remain in all our thought. But scientific philosophy comes nearer to objectivity than any other human pursuit, and gives us, therefore, the closest constant and the most intimate relation with the outer world that it is possible to achieve. To the primitive mind, everything is either friendly or hostile; but experience has shown that friendliness and hostility are not the conceptions by which the world is to be understood. Scientific philosophy thus represents, though as yet only in a nascent condition, a higher form of thought than any pre-scientific belief or imagination, and, like every approach to self-transcendence, it brings with it a rich reward in increase of scope and breadth and comprehension. Evolutionism, in spite of its appeals to particular scientific facts, fails to be a truly scientific philosophy because of its slavery to time, its ethical preoccupations, and its predominant interest in our mundane concerns and destiny. A truly scientific philosophy will be more humble, more piecemeal, more arduous, offering less glitter of outward mirage to flatter fallacious hopes, but more indifferent to fate, and more capable of accepting the world without the tyrannous imposition of our human and temporary demands.

Martin Heidegger
1889–1976

Martin Heidegger was born and died in the small German town of Messkirch in the Black Forest region of Baden-Württemberg. His father was the caretaker of the local Catholic church. Heidegger was reared as a Catholic and attended local secondary schools, where he was particularly interested in the ancient Greeks and the classics; this classical heritage remained the bedrock of his intellectual life. As a teenager in a Jesuit seminary he was captivated by Franz Brentano's work on Aristotle's understanding of "Being." He made the study of Being his life's work and never wavered from that goal.

After a brief period as a Jesuit novice, Heidegger studied philosophy at the University of Freiburg. Excused from World War I for health reasons, he finished his studies in 1916 with a thesis on the medieval thinker John Duns Scotus. For the next seven years he taught at the university, the last three years as the assistant to Edmund Husserl. During this period of time, Heidegger apprenticed himself to Husserl's phenomenological method, using it on his own special study of Being. In 1923 Heidegger moved to the University of Marburg where, in 1927, he published his *magnum opus, Being and Time,* dedicated to his teacher and friend, Husserl. When Husserl retired from Freiburg in 1928, Heidegger assumed Husserl's chair of philosophy there.

What followed is one of the most controversial episodes in recent philosophy. When the Nazis came to power in 1933, the rector of the University of Freiburg was ousted and Heidegger was elected to replace him. In the course of his inaugural lecture as rector, Heidegger made the following remarks:

"Academic Freedom," celebrated so often, is banished from the German university; . . . this freedom was not genuine because it was only negative. . . . The concept of freedom [for] the German student is now brought back to its truth. From this truth the bond and service of the German student will unfold in [the] future.*

Later that same year Heidegger wrote in the student newspaper:

Doctrine and "ideas" shall no longer govern your existence. The *Führer* himself, and only he, is the current and future reality of Germany, and his word is your law. Learn to know ever more deeply within you: "From now on every matter demands determination and every action demands responsibility."
Heil Hitler!
MARTIN HEIDEGGER**

Critics claim that Heidegger had always been sympathetic to the Nazi cause and that he apparently disowned his teacher Husserl (who was Jewish). As late as 1953 Heidegger affirmed the "inner truth and greatness" of the Nazi movement. He once said that philosophy could only be done properly in either the German or the Greek language and that among the moderns, the Germans alone, as a people placed by history between the barbarians of America to the west and Russia to the east, could save Western thought.

Heidegger's supporters point to his refusal to endorse the firing of two anti-Nazi deans, which led to his resignation as rector within a year. Furthermore, say some, it is unfair to judge Heidegger's early support for the Nazis from a post–World War II point of view. Heidegger in 1933 could not be expected to know the unspeakable horrors of 1939–1945. Finally, supporters ask philosophers especially to avoid the *argumentum ad hominem:* Even if Heidegger were partially compromised, that is not sufficient reason to dismiss a whole body of thought.

Whatever the truth in this debate, Allied occupation powers considered the evidence of Nazi collaboration sufficient to bar Heidegger from teaching between 1945 and 1951. Hence after the war, Heidegger spent much of his time in his simple hut at Todtnauberg in the Black Forest. He retired permanently from teaching in 1959. Late in life he visited Greece and France but lived his final years largely in quiet seclusion.

* * *

In his major work, *Being and Time,* Heidegger announced the interest that would dominate his writings throughout his life: "The question of the meaning of Being." According to Heidegger, the Pre-Socratics had understood Being, but sub-

---

Die Selbstbehauptung der Deutschen Universität (The Self-Affirmation of the German University, 1933) as quoted in Walter Kaufmann, *Discovering the Mind: Volume Two, Nietzsche, Heidegger, and Buber* (New York: McGraw-Hill, 1980), p. 221.

**Freiburger Studentenzeitung,* November 3, 1933, p. 1, quoted in Martin Heidegger, *German Existentialism,* translated with an introduction by Dagobert D. Runes (New York: Philosophical Library, 1965), pp. 27–28.

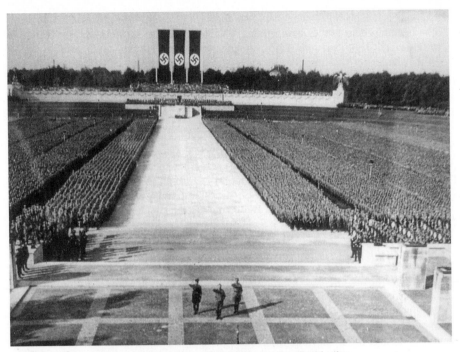

Nazi Party Congress at Nuremberg, 1934 (Hitler is standing in the center). The lives of an entire generation of philosophers were directly influenced by Hitler's rise to power in 1934. Bergson and Husserl both died as outcasts because of their Jewish ancestry; Heidegger was an early Nazi sympathizer (though there is a great deal of debate about his later feelings toward and involvement with the party); Sartre was a German prisoner-of-war and later a member of the resistance; Wittgenstein volunteered as a hospital orderly in England; and Quine and Ayer both served in the Allied war effort. *(National Archive)*

sequent Western thinkers had forgotten Being itself by focusing too intently on individual being*s*. As a result, contemporary metaphysics no longer recalled the seminal question of Being. This question of Being can be put in stark terms: "Why is there any Being at all and not rather Nothing?" This might seem an odd question to us, but it is odd (asserts Heidegger) only because we have lost our original amazement in the very presence of Being itself.

In order to gain some understanding of Being, Heidegger suggests we examine the one being with which we are intimately acquainted: human being. The phenomenological method (Husserl), which "unconceals" the data of experience by allowing these data to "show themselves," provides the way to such an examination. Using this method to examine the self, one discovers one's self as a "being-in-the-world" or *Dasein* ("being-there").

Dasein is different from other realities. First, "in its very Being, that Being is an *issue* for it"; that is, *Dasein* is aware of Being. Second, the kind of Being of which *Dasein* is aware is called "existence." Human existence is not to be grasped the way one understands the existence of rocks or planets, but in the special ways of anticipation of, and decision for, possibilities. As the self confronts its choices, it especially recognizes that with death, "being-in-the-world" eventually becomes "no-longer-being-there." This awareness of *Dasein* as "being-toward-death" is filled with *Angst* (dread). Borrowing Kierkegaard's analysis of dread, Heidegger says that the self can try to avoid this *Angst* by losing the "I" in the "they"—that is, by ignoring its individuality and becoming part of the crowd. But a "they" existence is "inauthentic" and removed from Being. Instead, authentic being—"being-toward-death"—can reveal to *Dasein* a "freedom" that releases it from the "Illusions of the 'they'" and allows it to embrace *Angst*.

Our first selection, "The Way Back into the Ground of Metaphysics," translated by Walter Kaufmann, was selected by Heidegger himself for an anthology edited by Kaufmann. Heidegger originally wrote the piece as an introduction to a collection of articles based on his inaugural lecture at Freiburg in 1929. Though this introduction was written in 1949, it still summarizes several of the early Heidegger's key convictions about Being and has the added virtue of being one of his more accessible works.

In "The Question Concerning Technology," given here (complete) in the William Lovitt translation, Heidegger argues that modern technology has led us to the brink of disaster because it induces the awful forgetfulness of Being. He explains that for the Greeks, ⟨technē⟩, from which we get the word "technology," referred to all ⟨poiēsis⟩ or "bringing-forth." Furthermore, ⟨technē⟩ was wholesomely connected with ⟨epistēmē⟩, both of which were originally "terms for knowing in the widest sense." In this older way ⟨technē⟩ led to a kind of "revealing" of Being. But beginning with Plato, ⟨technē⟩ has undergone a long debasement until it is now cut off almost entirely from creative ⟨poiēsis⟩ and only means "manufacturing." The only "revealing" that occurs in modern technology "is a challenging [*Herausfordern*], which puts to nature the unreasonable demand that it supply energy which can be extracted and stored as such." As a result, *"nowhere does man today any longer encounter himself, i.e., his essence"* and so his Being, at least his *Dasein,* is forgotten. To restore technology to its rightful place, concludes Heidegger, we must restore the link between ⟨technē⟩ and ⟨poiēsis⟩ through art and poetry:

> Essential reflection upon technology and decisive confrontation with it must happen in a realm that is, on the one hand, akin to the essence of technology and, on the other, fundamentally different from it.
> Such a realm is art.

Heidegger has had more than his share of critics. Analytic philosophers have been particularly critical of his use of language. One such philosopher concluded that "Heidegger's account of human life, where it is not vacuous, is transparently false."* However, despite the criticisms of his life and thought, Heidegger has had a profound effect on philosophy—especially in the field he originated: philosophical hermeneutics. Further, his insights have been developed in psychoanalysis and literary theory and in phenomenology and theology and continue to shape contemporary views.

* * *

*Alasdair MacIntyre, "Existentialism," in D.J. O'Connor, *A Critical History of Western Philosophy* (New York: Free Press, 1964), p. 518.

General introductions to Heidegger's thought include Marjorie Grene, *Martin Heidegger* (New York: Hillary House, 1957); W.J. Richardson, *Heidegger: Through Phenomenology to Thought* (New York: Humanities Press, 1963); J.A. Kockelman, *Heidegger: A First Introduction to His Philosophy,* translated by T. Schrynemakers (Pittsburgh: Duquesne University Press, 1965); J.L. Mehta, *Martin Heidegger: The Way and the Vision* (Honolulu: University Press of Hawaii, 1976); and George Steiner, *Martin Heidegger* (New York: Viking Press, 1978). For a criticism of Heidegger's thought, see Walter Kaufmann, *Discovering the Mind: Volume Two, Nietzsche, Heidegger, and Buber* (New York: McGraw-Hill, 1980). Michael Gelven, *A Commentary on Heidegger's* Being and Time (New York: Harper & Row, 1970), and E.F. Kaelin, *Heidegger's "Being and Time": A Reading for Readers* (Tallahassee: University Presses of Florida, 1988), provide guides to Heidegger's major work. For comparative studies, see Arne Naess, *Four Modern Philosophers: Carnap, Wittgenstein, Heidegger, Sartre,* translated by Alastair Hannay (Chicago: University of Chicago Press, 1968); Timothy J. Stapleton, *Husserl and Heidegger* (Albany: State University of New York Press, 1983); and Allan Megill, *Prophets of Extremity: Nietzsche, Heidegger, Foucault, Derrida* (Berkeley: University of California Press, 1985). Collections of essays include Thomas Sheehan, ed., *Heidegger: The Man and the Thinker* (Chicago: Precedent Publishing, 1981), and John Sallis, ed., *Reading Heidegger* (Bloomington: Indiana University Press, 1992).

Finally, out of the large number of recent books on the controversy surrounding Heidegger's Nazi ties, one may consult Victor Farías, *Heidegger and Nazism,* edited by Joseph Margolis and Tom Rockmore (Philadelphia: Temple University Press, 1989); Joseph Margolis and Tom Rockmore, eds., *The Heidegger Case* (Philadelphia: Temple University Press, 1992); Tom Rockmore, *On Heidegger's Nazism and Philosophy* (Berkeley: University of California Press, 1992); and Heinrich Wiegrand Petzet, *Encounters and Dialogues with Martin Heidegger 1929–1976,* translated by Parvis Emad and Kenneth Malz (Chicago: University of Chicago Press, 1993).

THE WAY BACK INTO THE GROUND OF METAPHYSICS

Descartes, writing to Picot, who translated the *Principia Philosophiae* into French, observed: "Thus the whole of philosophy is like a tree: the roots are metaphysics, the trunk is physics, and the branches that issue from the trunk are all the other sciences. . . ." *(Opp. ed. Ad. et Ta.IX,14.)*

Sticking to this image, we ask: In what soil do the roots of the tree of philosophy have their hold? Out of what ground do the roots—and through them the whole tree— receive their nourishing juices and strength? What element, concealed in the ground,

"The Way Back into the Ground of Metaphysics" by Martin Heidegger, from *Existentialism from Dostoevsky to Sartre* by Walter Kaufmann. Copyright © 1975 by NAL. Used by permission of Dutton Signet, a division of Penguin Books USA Inc.

enters and lives in the roots that support and nourish the tree? What is the basis and element of metaphysics? What is metaphysics, viewed from its ground? What is metaphysics itself, at bottom?

Metaphysics thinks about beings as beings. Wherever the question is asked what beings are, beings as such are in sight. Metaphysical representation owes this sight to the light of Being. The light itself, i.e., that which such thinking experiences as light, does not come within the range of metaphysical thinking; for metaphysics always represents beings only as beings. Within this perspective, metaphysical thinking does, of course, inquire about the being which is the source and originator of this light. But the light itself is considered sufficiently illuminated as soon as we recognize that we look through it whenever we look at beings.

In whatever manner beings are interpreted—whether as spirit, after the fashion of spiritualism; or as matter and force, after the fashion of materialism; or as becoming and life, or idea, will, substance, subject, or *energeia;* or as the eternal recurrence of the same events—every time, beings as beings appear in the light of Being. Wherever metaphysics represents beings, Being has entered into the light. Being has arrived in a state of unconcealedness (⟨*alēthia*⟩). But whether and how Being itself involves such unconcealedness, whether and how it manifests itself in, and as, metaphysics, remains obscure. Being in its revelatory essence, i.e., in its truth, is not recalled. Nevertheless, when metaphysics gives answers to its question concerning beings as such, metaphysics speaks out of the unnoticed revealedness of Being. The truth of Being may thus be called the ground in which metaphysics, as the root of the tree of philosophy, is kept and from which it is nourished.

Because metaphysics inquires about beings as beings, it remains concerned with beings and does not devote itself to Being as Being. As the root of the tree, it sends all nourishment and all strength into the trunk and its branches. The root branches out in the soil to enable the tree to grow out of the ground and thus to leave it. The tree of philosophy grows out of the soil in which metaphysics is rooted. The ground is the element in which the root of the tree lives, but the growth of the tree is never able to absorb this soil in such a way that it disappears in the tree as part of the tree. Instead, the roots, down to the subtlest tendrils, lose themselves in the soil. The ground is ground for the roots, and in the ground the roots forget themselves for the sake of the tree. The roots still belong to the tree even when they abandon themselves, after a fashion, to the element of the soil. They squander themselves and their element on the tree. As roots, they do not devote themselves to the soil—at least not as if it were their life to grow only into this element and to spread out in it. Presumably, the element would not be the same element either if the roots did not live in it.

Metaphysics, insofar as it always represents only beings as beings, does not recall Being itself. Philosophy does not concentrate on its ground. It always leaves its ground—leaves it by means of metaphysics. And yet it never escapes its ground.

Insofar as a thinker sets out to experience the ground of metaphysics, insofar as the attempts to recall the truth of Being itself instead of merely representing beings as beings, his thinking has in a sense left metaphysics. From the point of view of metaphysics, such thinking goes back into the ground of metaphysics. But what still appears as ground from this point of view is presumably something else, once it is experienced in its own terms—something as yet unsaid, according to which the essence of metaphysics, too, is something else and not metaphysics.

Such thinking, which recalls the truth of Being, is no longer satisfied with mere metaphysics, to be sure; but it does not oppose and think against metaphysics either. To return to our image, it does not tear up the root of philosophy. It tills the ground and plows the soil for this root. Metaphysics remains the basis of philosophy. The basis of thinking, however, it does not reach. When we think of the truth of Being, metaphysics is overcome. We can no longer accept the claim of metaphysics that it takes care of the fundamental involvement in "Being" and that it decisively determines all relations to beings as such. But this "overcoming of metaphysics" does not abolish metaphysics. As long as man remains the *animal rationale* he is also the *animal metaphysicum*. As long as man understands himself as the rational animal, metaphysics belongs, as Kant said, to the nature of man. But if our thinking should succeed in its efforts to go back into the ground of metaphysics, it might well help to bring about a change in human nature, accompanied by a transformation of metaphysics.

If, as we unfold the question concerning the truth of Being, we speak of overcoming metaphysics, this means: recalling Being itself. Such recalling goes beyond the tradition of forgetting the ground of the root of philosophy. The thinking attempted in *Being and Time* (1927) sets out on the way to prepare an overcoming of metaphysics, so understood. That, however, which prompts such thinking can only be that which is to be recalled. That Being itself and how Being itself concerns our thinking does not depend upon our thinking alone. That Being itself, and the manner in which Being itself, strikes a man's thinking, that rouses his thinking and stirs it to rise from Being itself to respond and correspond to Being as such.

Why, however, should such an overcoming of metaphysics be necessary? Is the point merely to underpin that discipline of philosophy which was the root hitherto, or to supplant it with a yet more basic discipline? Is it a question of changing the philosophic system of instruction? No. Or are we trying to go back into the ground of metaphysics in order to uncover a hitherto overlooked presupposition of philosophy, and thereby to show that philosophy does not yet stand on an unshakable foundation and therefore cannot yet be the absolute science? No.

It is something else that is at stake with the arrival of the truth of Being or its failure to arrive: it is neither the state of philosophy nor philosophy itself alone, but rather the proximity or remoteness of that from which philosophy, insofar as it means the representation of beings as such, receives its nature and its necessity. What is to be decided is nothing less than this: can Being itself, out of its own unique truth, bring about its involvement in human nature; or shall metaphysics, which turns its back to its ground, prevent further that the involvement of Being in man may generate a radiance out of the very essence of this involvement itself—a radiance which might lead man to belong to Being?

In its answers to the question concerning beings as such, metaphysics operates with a prior conception of Being. It speaks of Being necessarily and hence continually. But metaphysics does not induce Being itself to speak, for metaphysics does not recall Being in its truth, nor does it recall truth as unconcealedness, nor does it recall the nature of unconcealedness. To metaphysics the nature of truth always appears only in the derivative form of the truth of knowledge and the truth of propositions which formulate our knowledge. Unconcealedness, however, might be prior to all truth in the sense of *veritas*. ⟨*Alēthia*⟩ might be the word that offers a hitherto unnoticed hint concerning the nature of *esse* which has not yet been recalled. If this should be so, then the representational thinking of metaphysics could certainly never reach this nature of truth, however zealously it might devote itself to historical studies of pre-Socratic philosophy; for what is at stake here is not some renaissance of pre-Socratic thinking: any such attempt would be vain and absurd. What is wanted is rather some regard for the arrival of the hitherto unexpressed nature of unconcealedness, for it is in this form that Being has announced itself. Meanwhile the truth of Being has remained concealed from metaphysics during its long history from Anaximander to Nietzsche. Why does metaphysics not recall it? Is the failure to recall it merely a function of some kinds of metaphysical thinking? Or is it an essential feature of the fate of metaphysics that its own ground eludes it because in the rise of unconcealedness its very core, namely concealedness, stays away in favor of the unconcealed which appears in the form of beings?

Metaphysics, however, speaks continually and in the most various ways of Being. Metaphysics gives, and seems to confirm, the appearance that it asks and answers the question concerning Being. In fact, metaphysics never answers the question concerning the truth of Being, for it never asks this question. Metaphysics does not ask this question because it thinks of Being only by representing beings as beings. It means all beings as a whole, although it speaks of Being. It refers to Being and means beings as beings. From its beginning to its completion, the propositions of metaphysics have been strangely involved in a persistent confusion of beings and Being. This confusion, to be sure, must be considered an event and not a mere mistake. It cannot by any means be charged to a mere negligence of thought or a carelessness of expression. Owing to this persistent confusion, the claim that metaphysics poses the question of Being lands us in utter error.

Due to the manner in which it thinks of beings, metaphysics almost seems to be, without knowing it, the barrier which keeps man from the original involvement of Being in human nature.

What if the absence of this involvement and the oblivion of this absence determined the entire modern age? What if the absence of Being abandoned man more and more exclusively to beings, leaving him forsaken and far from any involvement of Being in his nature, while this forsakenness itself remained veiled? What if this were the case—and had been the case for a long time now? What if there were signs that this oblivion will become still more decisive in the future?

Would there still be occasion for a thoughtful person to give himself arrogant airs in view of this fateful withdrawal with which Being presents us? Would there still be occasion, if this should be our situation, to deceive ourselves with pleasant phantasms and to indulge, of all things, in an artificially induced elation? If the oblivion of Being which has been described here should be real, would there not be occasion enough for a thinker who recalls Being to experience a genuine horror? What more can his thinking do than to endure in dread this fateful withdrawal while first of all facing up to the oblivion of Being? But how could thought achieve this as long as its fatefully granted dread seems to it no more than a mood of depression? What does such dread, which is fated by Being, have to do with psychology or psychoanalysis?

Suppose that the overcoming of metaphysics involved the endeavor to commence with a regard for the oblivion of Being—the attempt to learn to develop such a regard, in order to experience this oblivion and to absorb this experience into the involvement of Being in man, and to preserve it there: then, in the distress of the oblivion of Being, the question "What is metaphysics?" might well become the most necessary necessity for thought.

Thus everything depends on this: that our thinking should become more thoughtful in its season. This is achieved when our thinking, instead of implementing a higher degree of exertion, is directed toward a different point of origin. The thinking which is posited by beings as such, and therefore representational and illuminating in that way, must be supplanted by a different kind of thinking which is brought to pass by Being itself and, therefore, responsive to Being.

All attempts are futile which seek to make representational thinking which remains metaphysical, and only metaphysical, effective and useful for immediate action in everyday public life. The more thoughtful our thinking becomes and the more adequate it is to the involvement of Being in it, the purer our thinking will stand *eo ipso* in the one action appropriate to it: recalling what is meant for it and thus, in a sense, what is already meant.

But who still recalls what is meant? One makes inventions. To lead our thinking on the way on which it may find the involvement of the truth of Being in human nature, to open up a path for our thinking on which it may recall Being itself in its truth—to do that the thinking attempted in *Being and Time* is "on its way." On this way—that is, in the service of the question concerning the truth of Being—it becomes necessary to stop and think about human nature; for the experience of the oblivion of Being, which is not specifically mentioned because it still had to be demonstrated, involves the crucial conjecture that in view of the unconcealedness of Being the involvement of Being in human nature is an essential feature of Being. But how could this conjecture, which is experienced here, become an explicit question before every attempt had been made to liberate the determination of human nature from the concept of subjectivity and from the concept of the *animal rationale?* To characterize with a single term both the involvement of Being in human nature and the essential relation of man to the openness ("there") of Being as such, the name of "being there [*Dasein*]" was chosen for that sphere of being in which man stands as man. This term was employed, even though in metaphysics it is used interchangeably with *existentia,* actuality, reality, and objectivity, and although this metaphysical usage is further supported by the common [German] expression *"menschliches Dasein."* Any attempt, therefore, to re-think *Being and Time* is thwarted as long as one is satisfied with the observation that, in this study, the term "being there" is used in place of "consciousness." As if this were simply a matter of using different words! As if it were not the one and only thing at stake here: namely, to get men to think about the involvement of Being in human nature and thus, from our point of view, to present first of all an experience of human nature which may prove sufficient to direct our inquiry. The term "being there" neither takes the place of the term "consciousness" nor does the "object" designated as "being there" take the place of what we think of when we speak of "consciousness." "Being there" names that which should first of all be experienced, and subsequently thought of, as a place—namely, the location of the truth of Being.

What the term "being there" means throughout the treatise on *Being and Time* is indicated immediately by its introductory key sentence: *"The 'essence' of being there lies in its existence."* [Das *"Wesen" des Daseins liegt in seiner Existenz.*]

To be sure, in the language of metaphysics the word "existence" is a synonym of "being there": both refer to the reality of anything at all that is real, from God to a grain of sand. As long, therefore, as the quoted sentence is understood only superficially, the difficulty is merely transferred from one word to another, from "being there" to "existence." In *B.&T.* the term "existence" is used exclusively for the being of man. Once "existence" is understood rightly, the "essence" of being there can be recalled: in its openness, Being itself manifests and conceals itself, yields itself and withdraws; at the same time, this truth of Being does not exhaust itself in being there, nor can it by any means simply be identified with it after the fashion of the metaphysical proposition: all objectivity is as such also subjectivity.

What does "existence" mean in *B.&T.?* The word designates a mode of Being; specifically, the Being of those beings who stand open for the openness of Being in which they stand, by standing it. This "standing it," this enduring, is experienced under the name of "care." The ecstatic essence of being there is approached by way of care, and, conversely, care is experienced adequately only in its ecstatic essence. "Standing it," experienced in this manner, is the essence of the *ekstasis* which must be grasped by thought. The ecstatic essence of existence is therefore still understood inadequately as long as one thinks of it as merely "standing out," while interpreting the "out" as meaning "away from" the inside of an immanence of consciousness and spirit. For in this manner, existence would still be understood in terms of "subjectivity" and "substance"; while, in fact, the "out" ought to be understood in terms of the openness of Being itself. The *stasis* of the ecstatic consists—strange as it may sound—in standing in the "out" and "there" of unconcealedness in which Being itself is present. What is meant by "existence" in the context of an inquiry that is prompted by, and directed toward, the truth of Being, can be most beautifully designated by the word "instancy [*Instandigkeit*]." We must think at the same time, however, of standing in the openness of Being, of enduring and outstanding this standing-in (care), and of out-braving the utmost (being toward death); for it is only together that they constitute the full essence of existence.

The being that exists is man. Man alone exists. Rocks are, but they do not exist. Trees are, but they do not exist. Horses are, but they do not exist. Angels are, but they do not exist. God is, but he does not exist. The proposition "man alone exists" does not mean by any means that man alone is a real being while all other beings are unreal and mere appearances or human ideas. The proposition "man exists" means: man is that being whose Being is distinguished by the open-standing standing-in in the unconcealedness of Being, from Being, in Being. The existential nature of man is the reason why man can represent beings as such, and why he can be conscious of them. All consciousness presupposes ecstatically understood existence as the *essentia* of man—*essentia* meaning that as which man is present insofar as he is man. But consciousness does not itself create the openness of beings, nor is it consciousness that makes it possible for man to stand open for beings. Whither and whence and in what free dimension could the intentionality of consciousness move, if instancy were not the essence of man in the first instance? What else could be the meaning—if anybody has ever seriously thought about this—of the word *sein* in the [German] words *Bewusstsein* ["consciousness"; literally: "being conscious"] and *Selbstbewusstsein* ["self-consciousness"] if it did not designate the existential nature of that which is in the mode of existence? To be a self is admittedly one feature of the nature of that being which exists; but existence does not consist in being a self, nor can it be defined in such terms. We are faced with the fact that metaphysical thinking understands man's selfhood in terms of substance or—and at bottom this amounts to the same—in terms of the subject. It is for this reason that the first way which leads away from metaphysics to the ecstatic existential nature of man must lead through the metaphysical conception of human selfhood (*B.&T.*, §§63 and 64).

The question concerning existence, however, is always subservient to that question which is nothing less than the only question of thought. This question, yet to be unfolded, concerns the truth of Being as the concealed ground of all metaphysics. For this reason the treatise which sought to point the way back into the ground of metaphysics did not bear the title "Existence and Time," nor "Consciousness and Time," but *Being and Time*. Nor can this title be understood as if it were parallel to the customary juxtapositions of Being and Becoming, Being and Seeming, Being and Thinking, or Being and Ought. For in all these cases Being is limited, as if Becoming, Seeming, Thinking, and Ought did not belong to Being, although it is obvious that they are not nothing and thus belong to Being. In *Being and Time,* Being is not something other than Time: "Time" is called the first name of the truth of Being, and this truth is the presence of Being and thus Being itself. But why "Time" and "Being"?

By recalling the beginnings of history when Being unveiled itself in the thinking of the Greeks, it can be shown that the Greeks from the very beginning experienced the Being of beings as the presence of the present. When we translate ⟨*einai*⟩ as "being," our translation is linguistically correct. Yet we merely substitute one set of sounds for another. As soon as we examine ourselves it becomes obvious that we neither think ⟨*einai*⟩, as it were, in Greek nor have in mind a correspondingly clear and univocal concept when we speak of "being." What, then, are we saying when instead of ⟨*einai*⟩ we say "being," and instead of "being," ⟨*einai*⟩ and *esse?* We are saying nothing. The Greek, Latin, and German word all remain equally obtuse. As long as we adhere to the customary usage we merely betray ourselves as the pacemakers of the greatest thoughtlessness which has ever gained currency in human thought and which has remained dominant until this moment. This ⟨*einai*⟩, however, means: to be present [*anwesen;* this verb form, in place of the idiomatic *"anwesend sein,"* is Heidegger's neology]. The true being of this being present [*das Wesen dieses Anwesens*] is deeply concealed in the earliest names of Being. But for us ⟨*einai*⟩ and ⟨*ousia*⟩ as ⟨*par*⟩ and ⟨*apousia*⟩ means this first of all: in being present there moves, unrecognized and concealed, present time and duration—in one word, Time. Being as such is thus unconcealed owing to Time. Thus Time points to unconcealedness, i.e., the truth of Being. But the Time of which we should think here is not experienced through the changeful career of beings. Time is evidently of an altogether different nature which neither has been recalled by way of the time concept of metaphysics nor ever can be recalled in this way. Thus Time becomes the first name, which is yet to be heeded, of the truth of Being, which is yet to be experienced.

A concealed hint of Time speaks not only out of the earliest metaphysical names of Being but also out of its last name, which is "the eternal recurrence of the same events." Through the entire epoch of metaphysics, Time is decisively present in the history of Being, without being recognized or thought about. To this Time, space is neither co-ordinated nor merely subordinated.

Suppose one attempts to make a transition from the representation of beings as such to recalling the truth of Being: such an attempt, which starts from this representation, must still represent, in a certain sense, the truth of Being, too; and any such representation must of necessity be heterogeneous and ultimately, insofar as it is a representation, inadequate for that which is to be thought. This relation, which comes out of metaphysics and tries to enter into the involvement of the truth of Being in human nature, is called understanding. But here understanding is viewed, at the same time, from the point of view of the unconcealedness of Being. Understanding is a project thrust forth and ecstatic, which means that it stands in the sphere of the open. The sphere which opens up as we project, in order that something (Being in this case) may prove itself as something (in this case, Being as itself in its unconcealedness), is called the sense. (Cf. *B.&T.,* p. 151) "The sense of Being" and "the truth of Being" mean the same.

Let us suppose that Time belongs to the truth of Being in a way that is still concealed: then every project that holds open the truth of Being, representing a way of understanding Being, must look out into Time as the horizon of any possible understanding of Being. (Cf. *B.&T.,* §§31–34 and 68.)

The preface to *Being and Time,* on the first page of the treatise, ends with these sentences: "To furnish a concrete elaboration of the question concerning the sense of 'Being' is the intention of the following treatise. The interpretation of Time as the horizon of every possible attempt to understand Being is its provisional goal."

All philosophy has fallen into the oblivion of Being which has, at the same time, become and remained the fateful demand on thought in *B.&T.;* and philosophy could hardly have given a clearer demonstration of the power of this oblivion of Being than it has furnished us by the somnambulistic assurance with which it has passed by the real and only question of *B.&T.* What is at stake here is, therefore, not a series of misunderstandings of a book but our abandonment by Being.

Metaphysics states what beings are as beings. It offers a ⟨*logos*⟩ (statement) about the ⟨*onta*⟩ (beings). The later title "ontology" characterizes its nature, provided, of course, that we understand it in accordance with its true significance and not through its narrow scholastic meaning. Metaphysics moves in the sphere of the ⟨*on hā on*⟩: it deals with beings as beings. In this manner, metaphysics always represents beings as such in their totality; it deals with the beingness of beings (the ⟨*ousia*⟩ of the ⟨*on*⟩). But metaphysics represents the beingness of beings [*die Seiendheit des Seienden*] in a twofold manner: in the first place, the totality of beings as such with an eye to their most universal traits (⟨*on kapsolou, koinon*⟩); but at the same time also the totality of beings as such in the sense of the highest and therefore divine being (⟨*on kapsolon akrotaton pseion*⟩). In the metaphysics of Aristotle, the unconcealedness of beings as such has specifically developed in this twofold manner. (Cf. Met. Γ, E, K.)

Because metaphysics represents beings as beings, it is, two-in-one, the truth of beings in their universality and in the highest being. According to its nature, it is at the same time ontology in the narrower sense and theology. This ontotheological nature of philosophy proper (⟨*prōtā philosophia*⟩) is, no doubt, due to the way in which the ⟨*on*⟩ opens up in it, namely as ⟨*on*⟩. Thus the theological character of ontology is not merely due to the fact that Greek metaphysics was later taken up and transformed by the ecclesiastic theology of Christianity. Rather it is due to the manner in which beings as beings have from the very beginning disconcealed themselves. It was this unconcealedness of beings that provided the possibility for Christian theology to take possession of Greek philosophy—whether for better or for worse may be decided by the theologians, on the basis of their experience of what is Christian; only they should keep in mind what is written in the First Epistle of Paul the Apostle to the Corinthians: "⟨*ouxi emōranen ho theos tān sophian tou kosmou*⟩; Has not God let the wisdom of this world become foolishness?" (I Cor. 1:20). The ⟨*sophia tou kosmou*⟩ [wisdom of this world], however, is that which, according to 1:22, the "⟨*Hellānes philosophia*⟩, the Greeks seek. Aristotle even calls the ⟨*prōtā philosophia*⟩ (philosophy proper) quite specifically ⟨*zātoumenā*⟩— what is sought. Will Christian theology make up its mind one day to take seriously the word of the apostle and thus also the conception of philosophy as foolishness?

As the truth of beings as such, metaphysics has a twofold character. The reason for this twofoldness, however, let alone its origin, remains unknown to metaphysics; and this is no accident, nor due to mere neglect. Metaphysics has this twofold character because it is what it is: the representation of beings as beings. Metaphysics has no choice. Being metaphysics, it is by its very nature excluded from the experience of Being; for it always represents beings (⟨*on*⟩) only with an eye to what of Being has already manifested itself as beings (⟨*hā on*⟩). But metaphysics never pays attention to what has concealed itself in this very ⟨*on*⟩ insofar as it became unconcealed.

Thus the time came when it became necessary to make a fresh attempt to grasp by thought what precisely is said when we speak of ⟨*on*⟩ or use the word "being" [*seiend*]. Accordingly, the question concerning the ⟨*on*⟩ was reintroduced into human thinking. (Cf. *B.&T.,* Preface.) But this reintroduction is no mere repetition of the Platonic-Aristotelian question; instead it asks about that which conceals itself in the ⟨*on*⟩.

Metaphysics is founded upon that which conceals itself here as long as metaphysics studies the ⟨*on hā on*⟩. The attempt to inquire back into what conceals itself here seeks, from the point of view of metaphysics, the fundament of ontology. Therefore this attempt is called, in *Being and Time* (page 13) "fundamental ontology" [*Fundamen-*

talontologie]. Yet this title, like any title, is soon seen to be inappropriate. From the point of view of metaphysics, to be sure, it says something that is correct; but precisely for that reason it is misleading, for what matters is success in the transition from metaphysics to recalling the truth of Being. As long as this thinking calls itself "fundamental ontology" it blocks and obscures its own way with this title. For what the title "fundamental ontology" suggests is, of course, that the attempt to recall the truth of Being— and not, like all ontology, the truth of beings—is itself (seeing that it is called "fundamental ontology") still a kind of ontology. In fact, the attempt to recall the truth of Being sets out on the way back into the ground of metaphysics, and with its first step it immediately leaves the realm of all ontology. On the other hand, every philosophy which revolves around an indirect or direct conception of "transcendence" remains of necessity essentially an ontology, whether it achieves a new foundation of ontology or whether it assures us that it repudiates ontology as a conceptual freezing of experience.

Coming from the ancient custom of representing beings as such, the very thinking that attempted to recall the truth of Being became entangled in these customary conceptions. Under these circumstances it would seem that both for a preliminary orientation and in order to prepare the transition from representational thinking to a new kind of thinking that recalls [*das andenkende Denken*], nothing could be more necessary than the question: What is metaphysics?

The unfolding of this question in the following lecture culminates in another question. This is called the basic question of metaphysics: Why is there any being at all and not rather Nothing? Meanwhile [since this lecture was first published in 1929], to be sure, people have talked back and forth a great deal about dread and the Nothing, both of which are spoken of in this lecture. But one has never yet deigned to ask oneself why a lecture which moves from thinking of the truth of Being to the Nothing, and then tries from there to think into the nature of metaphysics, should claim that this question is the basic question of metaphysics. How can an attentive reader help feeling on the tip of his tongue an objection which is far more weighty than all protests against dread and the Nothing? The final question provokes the objection that an inquiry which attempts to recall Being by way of the Nothing returns in the end to a question concerning beings. On top of that, the question even proceeds in the customary manner of metaphysics by beginning with a causal "Why?" To this extent, then, the attempt to recall Being is repudiated in favor of representational knowledge of beings on the basis of beings. And to make matters still worse, the final question is obviously the question which the metaphysician Leibniz posed in his *Principes de la nature et de la grace:* "*Pourquoi il y a plutot quelque chose que rien?*" (Opp. ed. Gerh. tom. VI, 602.n. 7).

Does the lecture, then, fall short of its intention? After all, this would be quite possible in view of the difficulty of effecting a transition from metaphysics to another kind of thinking. Does the lecture end up by asking Leibniz' metaphysical question about the supreme cause of all things that have being? Why, then, is Leibniz' name not mentioned, as decency would seem to require?

Or is the question asked in an altogether different sense? If it does not concern itself with beings and inquire about their first cause among all beings, then the question must begin from that which is not a being. And this is precisely what the question names, and it capitalizes the word: the Nothing. This is the sole topic of the lecture. The demand seems obvious that the end of the lecture should be thought through, for once, in its own perspective which determines the whole lecture. What has been called the basic question of metaphysics would then have to be understood and asked in terms of fundamental ontology as the question that comes out of the ground of metaphysics and as the question about this ground.

But if we grant this lecture that in the end it thinks in the direction of its own distinctive concern, how are we to understand this question?

The question is: Why is there any being at all and not rather Nothing? Suppose that we do not remain within metaphysics to ask metaphysically in the customary manner; suppose we recall the truth of Being out of the nature and the truth of metaphysics; then this might be asked as well: How did it come about that beings take precedence everywhere and lay claim to every "is" while that which is not a being is understood as Nothing, though it is Being itself, and remains forgotten? How did it come about that with Being It really is nothing and that the Nothing really is not? Is it perhaps from this that the as yet unshaken presumption has entered into all metaphysics that "Being" may simply be taken for granted and that Nothing is therefore made more easily than beings? That is indeed the situation regarding Being and Nothing. If it were different, then Leibniz could not have said in the same place by way of an explanation: *"Car le rien est plus simple et plus facile que quelque chose* [For the nothing is simpler and easier than any thing]."

What is more enigmatic: that beings are, or that Being is? Or does even this reflection fail to bring us close to that enigma which has occurred with the Being of beings?

Whatever the answer may be, the time should have ripened meanwhile for thinking through the lecture "What is Metaphysics?" which has been subjected to so many attacks, from its end, for once—from *its* end and not from an imaginary end.

THE QUESTION CONCERNING TECHNOLOGY

In what follows we shall be *questioning* concerning technology. Questioning builds a way. We would be advised, therefore, above all to pay heed to the way, and not to fix our attention on isolated sentences and topics. The way is one of thinking. All ways of thinking, more or less perceptibly, lead through language in a manner that is extraordinary. We shall be questioning concerning *technology,* and in so doing we should like to prepare a free relationship to it. The relationship will be free if it opens our human existence to the essence of technology. When we can respond to this essence, we shall be able to experience the technological within its own bounds.

Technology is not equivalent to the essence of technology. When we are seeking the essence of "tree," we have to become aware that what pervades every tree, as tree, is not itself a tree that can be encountered among all the other trees.

Likewise, the essence of technology is by no means anything technological. Thus we shall never experience our relationship to the essence of technology so long as we merely conceive and push forward the technological, put up with it, or evade it. Everywhere we remain unfree and chained to technology, whether we passionately affirm or deny it. But we are delivered over to it in the worst possible way when we regard it as something neutral; for this conception of it, to which today we particularly like to do homage, makes us utterly blind to the essence of technology.

Martin Heidegger, *The Question Concerning Technology and Other Essays.* Translated by William Lovitt. New York: Harper Torchbooks, 1977. Reprinted by permission.

According to ancient doctrine, the essence of a thing is considered to be *what* the thing is. We ask the question concerning technology when we ask what it is. Everyone knows the two statements that answer our question. One says: Technology is a means to an end. The other says: Technology is a human activity. The two definitions of technology belong together. For to posit ends and procure and utilize the means to them is a human activity. The manufacture and utilization of equipment, tools, and machines, the manufactured and used things themselves, and the needs and ends that they serve, all belong to what technology is. The whole complex of these contrivances is technology. Technology itself is a contrivance—in Latin, an *instrumentum.*

The current conception of technology, according to which it is a means and a human activity, can therefore be called the instrumental and anthropological definition of technology.

Who would ever deny that it is correct? It is in obvious conformity with what we are envisioning when we talk about technology. The instrumental definition of technology is indeed so uncannily correct that it even holds for modern technology, of which, in other respects, we maintain with some justification that it is, in contrast to the older handwork technology, something completely different and therefore new. Even the power plant with its turbines and generators is a man-made means to an end established by man. Even the jet aircraft and the high-frequency apparatus are means to ends. A radar station is of course less simple than a weather vane. To be sure, the construction of a high-frequency apparatus requires the interlocking of various processes of technical-industrial production. And certainly a sawmill in a secluded valley of the Black Forest is a primitive means compared with the hydroelectric plant on the Rhine River.

But this much remains correct: modern technology too is a means to an end. This is why the instrumental conception of technology conditions every attempt to bring man into the right relation to technology. Everything depends on our manipulating technology in the proper manner as a means. We will, as we say, "get" technology "spiritually in hand." We will master it. The will to mastery becomes all the more urgent the more technology threatens to slip from human control.

But suppose now that technology were no mere means, how would it stand with the will to master it? Yet we said, did we not, that the instrumental definition of technology is correct? To be sure. The correct always fixes upon something pertinent in whatever is under consideration. However, in order to be correct, this fixing by no means needs to uncover the thing in question in its essence. Only at the point where such an uncovering happens does the true come to pass. For that reason the merely correct is not yet the true. Only the true brings us into a free relationship with that which concerns us from its essence. Accordingly, the correct instrumental definition of technology still does not show us technology's essence. In order that we may arrive at this, or at least come close to it, we must seek the true by way of the correct. We must ask: What is the instrumental itself? Within what do such things as means and end belong? A means is that whereby something is effected and thus attained. Whatever has an effect as its consequence is called a cause. But not only that by means of which something else is effected is a cause. The end in keeping with which the kind of means to be used is determined is also considered a cause. Wherever ends are pursued and means are employed, wherever instrumentality reigns, there reigns causality.

For centuries philosophy has taught that there are four causes: (1) the *causa materialis,* the material, the matter out of which, for example, a silver chalice is made; (2) the *causa formalis,* the form, the shape into which the material enters; (3) the *causa finalis,* the end, for example, the sacrificial rite in relation to which the chalice required is determined as to its form and matter; (4) the *causa efficiens,* which brings about the effect that is the finished, actual chalice, in this instance, the silversmith. What technology is, when represented as a means, discloses itself when we trace instrumentality back to fourfold causality.

But suppose that causality, for its part, is veiled in darkness with respect to what it is? Certainly for centuries we have acted as though the doctrine of the four causes had fallen from heaven as a truth as clear as daylight. But it might be that the time has come to ask, why are there just four causes? In relation to the aforementioned four, what does "cause" really mean? From whence does it come that the causal character of the four causes is so unifiedly determined that they belong together?

So long as we do not allow ourselves to go into these questions, causality, and with it instrumentality, and with this the accepted definition of technology, remain obscure and groundless.

For a long time we have been accustomed to representing cause as that which brings something about. In this connection, to bring about means to obtain results, effects. The *causa efficiens,* but one among the four causes, sets the standard for all causality. This goes so far that we no longer even count the *causa finalis,* telic finality, as causality. *Causa, casus,* belongs to the verb *cadere,* to fall, and means that which brings it about that something turns out as a result in such and such a way. The doctrine of the four causes goes back to Aristotle. But everything that later ages seek in Greek thought under the conception and rubric "causality," in the realm of Greek thought and for Greek thought per se has simply nothing at all to do with bringing about and effecting. What we call cause [*Ursache*] and the Romans call *causa* is called *aition* by the Greeks, that to which something else is indebted [*das, was ein anderes verschuldet*]. The four causes are the ways, all belonging at once to each other, of being responsible for something else. An example can clarify this.

Silver is that out of which the silver chalice is made. As this matter *(hyle),* it is co-responsible for the chalice. The chalice is indebted to, i.e., owes thanks to, the silver for that of which it consists. But the sacrificial vessel is indebted not only to the silver. As a chalice, that which is indebted to the silver appears in the aspect of a chalice, and not in that of a brooch or a ring. Thus the sacred vessel is at the same time indebted to the aspect *(eidos)* of chaliceness. Both the silver into which the aspect is admitted as chalice and the aspect in which the silver appears are in their respective ways co-responsible for the sacrificial vessel.

But there remains yet a third that is above all responsible for the sacrificial vessel. It is that which in advance confines the chalice within the realm of consecration and bestowal. Through this the chalice is circumscribed as sacrificial vessel. Circumscribing gives bounds to the thing. With the bounds the thing does not stop; rather, from within them it begins to be what after production it will be. That which gives bounds, that which completes, in this sense is called in Greek *telos,* which is all too often translated as "aim" and "purpose," and so misinterpreted. The *telos* is responsible for what as matter and what as aspect are together co-responsible for the sacrificial vessel.

Finally there is a fourth participant in the responsibility for the finished sacrificial vessel's lying before us ready for use, i.e., the silversmith—but not at all because he, in working, brings about the finished sacrificial chalice as if it were the effect of a making; the silversmith is not a *causa efficiens.*

The Aristotelian doctrine neither knows the cause that is named by this term, nor uses a Greek word that would correspond to it.

The silversmith considers carefully and gathers together the three aforementioned ways of being responsible and indebted. To consider carefully [*überlegen*] is in Greek *legein, logos. Legein* is rooted in *apophainesthai,* to bring forward into appearance. The silversmith is co-responsible as that from whence the sacred vessel's bringing-forth and subsistence take and retain their first departure. The three previously mentioned ways of being responsible owe thanks to the pondering of the silversmith for the "that" and the "how" of their coming into appearance and into play for the production of the sacrificial vessel.

Thus four ways of owing hold sway in the sacrificial vessel that lies ready before us. They differ from one another, yet they belong together. What unites them from the beginning? In what does this playing in unison of the four ways of being responsible play? What is the source of the unity of the four causes? What, after all, does this owing and being responsible mean, thought as the Greeks thought it?

Today we are too easily inclined either to understand being responsible and being indebted moralistically as a lapse, or else to construe them in terms of effecting. In either case we bar to ourselves the way to the primal meaning of that which is later called causality. So long as this way is not opened up to us we shall also fail to see what instrumentality, which is based on causality, actually is.

In order to guard against such misinterpretations of being responsible and being indebted, let us clarify the four ways of being responsible in terms of that for which they are responsible. According to our example, they are responsible for the silver chalice's lying ready before us as a sacrificial vessel. Lying before and lying ready *(hypokeisthai)* characterize the presencing of something that is present. The four ways of being responsible bring something into appearance. They let it come forth into presencing [*Anwesen*]. They set it free to that place and so start it on its way, namely, into its complete arrival. The principal characteristic of being responsible is this starting something on its way into arrival. It is in the sense of such a starting something on its way into arrival that being responsible is an occasioning or an inducing to go forward [*Ver-an-lassen*]. On the basis of a look at what the Greeks experienced in being responsible, in *aitia,* we now give this verb "to occasion" a more inclusive meaning, so that it now is the name for the essence of causality thought as the Greeks thought it. The common and narrower meaning of "occasion," in contrast, is nothing more than striking against and releasing, and means a kind of secondary cause within the whole of causality.

But in what, then, does the playing in unison of the four ways of occasioning play? These let what is not yet present arrive into presencing. Accordingly, they are unifiedly governed by a bringing that brings what presences into appearance. Plato tells us what this bringing is in a sentence from the Symposium (205b): "Every occasion for whatever passes beyond the nonpresent and goes forward into presencing is *poiēsis,* bringing-forth [*Her-vorbringen*]."

It is of utmost importance that we think bringing-forth in its full scope and at the same time in the sense in which the Greeks thought it. Not only handicraft manufacture, not only artistic and poetical bringing into appearance and concrete imagery, is a bringing-forth, *poiēsis.* Physis also, the arising of something from out of itself, is a bringing-forth, *poiēsis.* Physis is indeed *poiēsis* in the highest sense. For what presences by means of physis has the bursting open belonging to bringing-forth, e.g., the bursting of a blossom into bloom, in itself *(en heautoi).* In contrast, what is brought forth by the artisan or the artist, e.g., the silver chalice, has the bursting open belonging to bringing-forth, not in itself, but in another *(en allōi),* in the craftsman or artist.

The modes of occasioning, the four causes, are at play, then, within bringing-forth. Through bringing-forth the growing things of nature as well as whatever is completed through the crafts and the arts come at any given time to their appearance.

But how does bringing-forth happen, be it in nature or in handwork and art? What is the bringing-forth in which the fourfold way of occasioning plays? Occasioning has to do with the presencing [*Anwesen*] of that which at any given time comes to appearance in bringing-forth. Bringing-forth brings out of concealment into unconcealment. Bringing-forth comes to pass only insofar as something concealed comes into unconcealment. This coming rests and moves freely within what we call revealing [*das Entbergen*]. The Greeks have the word *alētheia* for revealing. The Romans translate this with *veritas*. We say "truth" and usually understand it as correctness of representation.

But where have we strayed to? We are questioning concerning technology, and we have arrived now at alētheia, at revealing. What has the essence of technology to do with revealing? The answer: everything. For every bringing-forth is grounded in revealing. Bringing-forth, indeed, gathers within itself the four modes of occasioning—causality—and rules them throughout. Within its domain belong end and means as well as instrumentality. Instrumentality is considered to be the fundamental characteristic of technology. If we inquire step by step into what technology, represented as means, actually is, then we shall arrive at revealing. The possibility of all productive manufacturing lies in revealing.

Technology is therefore no mere means. Technology is a way of revealing. If we give heed to this, then another whole realm for the essence of technology will open itself up to us. It is the realm of revealing, i.e., of truth.

This prospect strikes us as strange. Indeed, it should do so, as persistently as possible and with so much urgency that we will finally take seriously the simple question of what the name "technology" means. The word stems from the Greek. *Technikon* means that which belongs to *technē*. We must observe two things with respect to the meaning of this word. One is that *technē* is the name not only for the activities and skills of the craftsman, but also for the arts of the mind and the fine arts. *Technē* belongs to bringing-forth, to *poiēsis;* it is something poetic.

The other thing that we should observe with regard to *technē* is even more important. From earliest times until Plato the word *technē* is linked with the word *epistēmē*. Both words are terms for knowing in the widest sense. They mean to be entirely at home in something, to understand and be expert in it. Such knowing provides an opening up. As an opening up it is a revealing. Aristotle, in a discussion of special importance (*Nicomachean Ethics,* Bk. VI, chaps. 3 and 4), distinguishes between *epistēmē* and *technē* and indeed with respect to what and how they reveal *technē* is a mode of *alētheuein*. It reveals whatever does not bring itself forth and does not yet lie here before us, whatever can look and turn out now one way and now another. Whoever builds a house or a ship or forges a sacrificial chalice reveals what is to be brought forth, according to the terms of the four modes of occasioning. This revealing gathers together in advance the aspect and the matter of ship or house, with a view to the finished thing envisioned as completed, and from this gathering determines the manner of its construction. Thus what is decisive in *technē* does not lie at all in making and manipulating nor in the using of means, but rather in the revealing mentioned before. It is as revealing, and not as manufacturing, that *technē* is a bringing-forth.

Thus the clue to what the word *technē* means and to how the Greeks defined it leads us into the same context that opened itself to us when we pursued the question of what instrumentality as such in truth might be.

Technology is a mode of revealing. Technology comes to presence in the realm where revealing and unconcealment take place, where *alētheia,* truth, happens.

In opposition to this definition of the essential domain of technology, one can object that it indeed holds for Greek thought and that at best it might apply to the techniques of the handcraftsman, but that it simply does not fit modern machine-powered technology. And it is precisely the latter and it alone that is the disturbing thing, that moves us to ask the question concerning technology per se. It is said that modern technology is something incomparably different from all earlier technologies because it is based on modern physics as an exact science. Meanwhile we have come to understand more clearly that the reverse holds true as well: modern physics, as experimental, is dependent upon technical apparatus and upon progress in the building of apparatus. The establishing of this mutual relationship between technology and physics is correct. But it remains a merely historiographical establishing of facts and says nothing about that in which this mutual relationship is grounded. The decisive question still remains: Of what essence is modern technology that it thinks of putting exact science to use?

What is modern technology? It too is a revealing. Only when we allow our attention to rest on this fundamental characteristic does that which is new in modern technology show itself to us.

And yet, the revealing that holds sway throughout modern technology does not unfold into a bringing-forth in the sense of *poiēsis*. The revealing that rules in modern technology is a challenging [*Herausfordern*], which puts to nature the unreasonable demand that it supply energy which can be extracted and stored as such. But does this not hold true for the old windmill as well? No. Its sails do indeed turn in the wind; they are left entirely to the wind's blowing. But the windmill does not unlock energy from the air currents in order to store it.

In contrast, a tract of land is challenged in the hauling out of coal and ore. The earth now reveals itself as a coal mining district, the soil as a mineral deposit. The field that the peasant formerly cultivated and set in order appears different from how it did when to set in order still meant to take care of and maintain. The work of the peasant does not challenge the soil of the field. In sowing grain it places seed in the keeping of the forces of growth and watches over its increase. But meanwhile even the cultivation of the field has come under the grip of another kind of setting-in-order, which sets upon nature. It sets upon it in the sense of challenging it. Agriculture is now the mechanized food industry. Air is now set upon to yield nitrogen, the earth to yield ore, ore to yield uranium, for example; uranium is set upon to yield atomic energy, which can be released either for destruction or for peaceful use.

This setting-upon that challenges the energies of nature is an expediting, and in two ways. It expedites in that it unlocks and exposes. Yet that expediting is always itself directed from the beginning toward furthering something else, i.e., toward driving on to the maximum yield at the minimum expense. The coal that has been hauled out in some mining district has not been produced in order that it may simply be at hand somewhere or other. It is being stored; that is, it is on call, ready to deliver the sun's warmth that is stored in it. The sun's warmth is challenged forth for heat, which in turn is ordered to deliver steam whose pressure turns the wheels that keep a factory running.

The hydroelectric plant is set into the current of the Rhine. It sets the Rhine to supplying its hydraulic pressure, which then sets the turbines turning. This turning sets those machines in motion whose thrust sets going the electric current for which the long-distance power station and its network of cables are set up to dispatch electricity. In the context of the interlocking processes pertaining to the orderly disposition of electrical energy, even the Rhine itself appears to be something at our command. The hydro-electric plant is not built into the Rhine River as was the old wooden bridge that joined bank with bank for hundreds of years. Rather, the river is dammed up into the power plant. What the river is now, namely, a water-power supplier, derives from the essence of the power station. In order that we may even remotely consider the monstrousness that reigns here, let us ponder for a moment the contrast that is spoken by the two titles: "The Rhine," as dammed up into the *power* works, and "The Rhine," as uttered by the *art* work, in Hölderlin's hymn by that name. But, it will be replied, the Rhine is still a river in the landscape, is it not? Perhaps. But how? In no other way than as an object on call for inspection by a tour group ordered there by the vacation industry.

The revealing that rules throughout modern technology has the character of a setting-upon, in the sense of a challenging-forth. Such challenging happens in that the energy concealed in nature is unlocked, what is unlocked is transformed, what is transformed is stored up, what is stored up is, in turn, distributed, and what is distributed is switched about ever anew. Unlocking, transforming, storing, distributing, and switching about are ways of revealing. But the revealing never simply comes to an end. Neither does it run off into the indeterminate. The revealing reveals to itself its own manifoldly interlocking paths, through regulating their course. This regulating itself is, for its part, everywhere secured. Regulating and securing even become the chief characteristics of the revealing that challenges.

What kind of unconcealment is it, then, that is peculiar to that which results from this setting-upon that challenges? Everywhere everything is ordered to stand by, to be immediately on hand, indeed to stand there just so that it may be on call for a further ordering. Whatever is ordered about in this way has its own standing. We call it the standing-reserve [*Bestand*]. The word expresses here something more, and something more essential, than mere "stock." The word "standing-reserve" assumes the rank of an inclusive rubric. It designates nothing less than the way in which everything presences that is wrought upon by the revealing that challenges. Whatever stands by in the sense of standing-reserve no longer stands over against us as object.

Yet an airliner that stands on the runway is surely an object. Certainly. We can represent the machine so. But then it conceals itself as to what and how it is. Revealed, it stands on the taxi strip only as standing-reserve, inasmuch as it is ordered to insure the possibility of transportation. For this it must be in its whole structure and in every one of its constituent parts itself on call for duty, i.e., ready for takeoff. (Here it would be appropriate to discuss Hegel's definition of the machine as an autonomous tool. When applied to the tools of the craftsman, his characterization is correct. Characterized in this way, however, the machine is not thought at all from the essence of technology within which it belongs. Seen in terms of the standing-reserve, the machine is completely unautonomous, for it has its standing only from the ordering of the orderable.)

The fact that now, wherever we try to point to modern technology as the revealing that challenges, the words "setting-upon," "ordering," "standing-reserve," obtrude and accumulate in a dry, monotonous, and therefore oppressive way, has its basis in what is now coming to utterance.

Who accomplishes the challenging setting-upon through which what we call the real is revealed as standing-reserve? Obviously, man. To what extent is man capable of such a revealing? Man can, indeed, conceive, fashion, and carry through this or that in one way or another. But man does not have control over unconcealment itself, in which at any given time the real shows itself or withdraws. The fact that the real has been showing itself in the light of Ideas ever since the time of Plato, Plato did not bring about. The thinker only responded to what addressed itself to him.

Only to the extent that man for his part is already challenged to exploit the energies of nature can this revealing which orders happen. If man is challenged, ordered, to do this, then does not man himself belong even more originally than nature within the standing-reserve? The current talk about human resources, about the supply of patients for a clinic, gives evidence of this. The forester who measures the felled timber in the woods and who to all appearances walks the forest path in the same way his grandfather did is today ordered by the industry that produces commercial woods, whether he knows it or not. He is made subordinate to the orderability of cellulose, which for its part is challenged forth by the need for paper, which is then delivered to newspapers and illustrated magazines. The latter, in their turn, set public opinion to swallowing what is printed, so that a set configuration of opinion becomes available on demand. Yet precisely because man is challenged more originally than are the energies of nature, i.e., into the process of ordering, he never is transformed into mere standing-reserve. Since man drives technology forward, he takes part in ordering as a way of revealing. But the unconcealment itself, within which ordering unfolds, is never a human handiwork, any more than is the realm man traverses every time he as a subject relates to an object.

Where and how does this revealing happen if it is no mere handiwork of man? We need not look far. We need only apprehend in an unbiased way that which has already claimed man so decisively that he can only be man at any given time as the one so claimed. Wherever man opens his eyes and ears, unlocks his heart, and gives himself over to meditating and striving, shaping and working, entreating and thanking, he finds himself everywhere already brought into the unconcealed. The unconcealment of the unconcealed has already come to pass whenever it calls man forth into the modes of re-vealing allotted to him. When man, in his way, from within unconcealment reveals that which presences, he merely responds to the call of unconcealment even when he con-tradicts it. Thus when man, investigating, observing, pursues nature as an area of his own conceiving, he has already been claimed by a way of revealing that challenges him to approach nature as an object of research, until even the object disappears into the ob-jectlessness of standing-reserve.

Modern technology, as a revealing which orders, is thus no mere human doing. Therefore we must take that challenging, which sets upon man to order the real as standing-reserve, in accordance with the way it shows itself. That challenging gathers man into ordering. This gathering concentrates man upon ordering the real as standing-reserve.

That which primordially unfolds the mountains into mountain ranges and courses through them in their folded togetherness is the gathering that we call *"Gebirg"* [moun-tain chain].

That original gathering from which unfold the ways in which we have feelings of one kind or another we name *"Gemut"* [disposition].

We now name that challenging claim which gathers man thither to order the self-revealing as standing-reserve: *"Ge-stell"* [enframing].

We dare to use this word in a sense that has been thoroughly unfamiliar up to now.

According to ordinary usage, the word *Gestell* [frame] means some kind of appa-ratus, e.g., a bookrack. *Gestell* is also the name for a skeleton. And the employment of the word *Gestell* [enframing] that is now required of us seems equally eerie, not to speak of the arbitrariness with which words of a mature language are so misused. Can anything be more strange? Surely not. Yet this strangeness is an old custom of thought. And indeed thinkers follow this custom precisely at the point where it is a matter of thinking that which is highest. We, late born, are no longer in a position to appreciate the significance of Plato's daring to use the word *eidos* for that which in everything and in each particular thing endures as present. For *eidos,* in the common speech, meant the outward aspect [*Ansicht*] that a visible thing offers to the physical eye. Plato exacts of this word, however, something utterly extraordinary: that it name what precisely is not and never will be perceivable with physical eyes. But even this is by no means the full extent of what is extraordinary here. For *idea* names not only the nonsensuous aspect of what is physically visible. Aspect *(idea)* names and also is that which constitutes the essence in the audible, the tasteable, the tactile, in everything that is in any way accessible. Compared with the demands that Plato makes on language and thought in this and in other instances, the use of the word *Gestell* as the name for the essence of modern technology, which we are venturing, is almost harmless. Even so, the usage now required remains something exacting and is open to misinterpretation.

Enframing means the gathering together of that setting-upon that sets upon man, i.e., challenges him forth, to reveal the real, in the mode of ordering, as standing-reserve. Enframing means that way of revealing that holds sway in the essence of modern technology and that is itself nothing technological. On the other hand, all those things that are so familiar to us and are standard parts of assembly, such as rods, pistons, and chassis, belong to the technological. The assembly itself, however, together with the aforementioned stockparts, falls within the sphere of technological activity. Such activity always merely responds to the challenge of enframing, but it never comprises enframing itself or brings it about.

The word *stellen* [to set upon] in the name *Ge-stell* [enframing] not only means challenging. At the same time it should preserve the suggestion of another *Stellen* from which it stems, namely that producing and presenting [*Her-und Dar-stellen*], which, in the sense of *poiēsis,* lets what presences come forth into unconcealment. This producing that brings forth, e.g., erecting a statue in the temple precinct, and the ordering that challenges now under consideration are indeed fundamentally different, and yet they remain related in their essence. Both are ways of revealing, of *alētheia.* In enframing that unconcealment comes to pass in conformity with which the work of modern technology reveals the real as standing-reserve. This work is therefore neither only a human activity nor a mere means within such activity. The merely instrumental, merely anthropological definition of technology is therefore in principle untenable. And it may not be rounded out by being referred back to some metaphysical or religious explanation that undergirds it.

It remains true, nonetheless, that man in the technological age is, in a particularly striking way, challenged forth into revealing. That revealing concerns nature, above all, as the chief storehouse of the standing energy reserve. Accordingly, man's ordering attitude and behavior display themselves first in the rise of modern physics as an exact science. Modern science's way of representing pursues and entraps nature as a calculable coherence of forces. Modern physics is not experimental physics because it applies apparatus to the questioning of nature. The reverse is true. Because physics, indeed already as pure theory, sets nature up to exhibit itself as a coherence of forces calculable in advance, it orders its experiments precisely for the purpose of asking whether and how nature reports itself when set up in this way.

But after all, mathematical science arose almost two centuries before technology. How, then, could it have already been set upon by modern technology and placed in its service? The facts testify to the contrary. Surely technology got underway only when it could be supported by exact physical science. Reckoned chronologically, this is correct. Thought historically, it does not hit upon the truth.

The modern physical theory of nature prepares the way not simply for technology but for the essence of modern technology. For such gathering-together, which challenges man to reveal by way of ordering, already holds sway in physics. But in it that gathering does not yet come expressly to the fore. Modern physics is the herald of enframing, a herald whose origin is still unknown. The essence of modern technology has for a long time been concealed, even where power machinery has been invented, where electrical technology is in full swing, and where atomic technology is well underway.

All coming to presence, not only modern technology, keeps itself everywhere concealed to the last. Nevertheless, it remains, with respect to its holding sway, that which precedes all: the earliest. The Greek thinkers already knew of this when they said: That which is earlier with regard to its rise into dominance becomes manifest to us men only later. That which is primally early shows itself only ultimately to men. Therefore, in the realm of thinking, a painstaking effort to think through still more primally what was primally thought is not the absurd wish to revive what is past, but rather the sober readiness to be astounded before the coming of the dawn.

Chronologically speaking, modern physical science begins in the seventeenth century. In contrast, machine-power technology develops only in the second half of the eighteenth century. But modern technology, which for chronological reckoning is the later, is, from the point of view of the essence holding sway within it, historically earlier.

If modern physics must resign itself ever increasingly to the fact that its realm of representation remains inscrutable and incapable of being visualized, this resignation is not dictated by any committee of researchers. It is challenged forth by the rule of enframing, which demands that nature be orderable as standing-reserve. Hence physics, in its retreat from the kind of representation that turns only to objects, which has been the sole standard until recently, will never be able to renounce this one thing: that nature reports itself in some way or other that is identifiable through calculation and that it remains orderable as a system of information. This system is then determined by a causality that has changed once again. Causality now displays neither the character of the occasioning that brings forth nor the nature of the *causa efficiens,* let alone that of the *causa formalis.* It seems as though causality is shrinking into a reporting—a reporting challenged forth—of standing-reserves that must be guaranteed either simultaneously or in sequence. To this shrinking would correspond the process of growing resignation that Heisenberg's lecture depicts in so impressive a manner.

Because the essence of modern technology lies in enframing, modern technology must employ exact physical science. Through its so doing the deceptive illusion arises that modern technology is applied physical science. This illusion can maintain itself only so long as neither the essential origin of modern science nor indeed the essence of modern technology is adequately found out through questioning.

We are questioning concerning technology in order to bring to light our relationship to its essence. The essence of modern technology shows itself in what we call enframing. But simply to point to this is still in no way to answer the question concerning technology, if to answer means to respond, in the sense of correspond, to the essence of what is being asked about.

Where do we find ourselves if now we think one step further regarding what enframing itself actually is? It is nothing technological, nothing on the order of a machine. It is the way in which the real reveals itself as standing-reserve. Again we ask: Does such revealing happen somewhere beyond all human doing? No. But neither does it happen exclusively *in* man, or definitively *through* man.

Enframing is the gathering together which belongs to that setting-upon which challenges man and puts him in position to reveal the real, in the mode of ordering, as standing-reserve. As the one who is challenged forth in this way, man stands within the essential realm of enframing. He can never take up a relationship to it only subsequently. Thus the question as to how we are to arrive at a relationship to the essence of technology, asked in this way, always comes too late. But never too late comes the question as to whether we actually experience ourselves as the ones whose activities everywhere, public and private, are challenged forth by enframing. Above all, never too late comes the question as to whether and how we actually admit ourselves into that wherein enframing itself comes to presence.

The essence of modern technology starts man upon the way of that revealing through which the real everywhere, more or less distinctly, becomes standing-reserve. "To start upon a way" means "to send" in our ordinary language. We shall call the sending that gathers [*versammelnde Schicken*], that first starts man upon a way of revealing, *destining* [*Geschick*]. It is from this destining that the essence of all history [*Geschichte*] is determined. History is neither simply the object of written chronicle nor merely the process of human activity. That activity first becomes history as something destined. And it is only the destining into objectifying representation that makes the historical accessible as an object for historiography, i.e., for a science, and on this basis makes possible the current equating of the historical with that which is chronicled.

Enframing, as a challenging-forth into ordering, sends into a way of revealing. Enframing is an ordaining of destining, as is every way of revealing. Bringing-forth, *poiēsis,* is also a destining in this sense.

Always the unconcealment of that which is goes upon a way of revealing. Always the destining of revealing holds complete sway over men. But that destining is never a fate that compels. For man becomes truly free only insofar as he belongs to the realm of destining and so becomes one who listens, though not one who simply obeys.

The essence of freedom is *originally* not connected with the will or even with the causality of human willing.

Freedom governs the open in the sense of the cleared and lighted up, i.e., the revealed. To the occurrence of revealing, i.e., of truth, freedom stands in the closest and most intimate kinship. All revealing belongs within a harboring and a concealing. But that which frees—the mystery—is concealed and always concealing itself. All revealing comes out of the open, goes into the open, and brings into the open. The freedom of the open consists neither in unfettered arbitrariness nor in the constraint of mere laws. Freedom is that which conceals in a way that opens to light, in whose lighting shimmers that veil that hides the essential occurrence of all truth and lets the veil appear as what veils. Freedom is the realm of the destining that at any given time starts a revealing on its way.

The essence of modern technology lies in enframing. Enframing belongs within the destining of revealing. These sentences express something different from the talk that we hear more frequently, to the effect that technology is the fate of our age, where "fate" means the inevitableness of an unalterable course.

But when we consider the essence of technology we experience enframing as a destining of revealing. In this way we are already sojourning within the open space of destining, a destining that in no way confines us to a stultified compulsion to push on blindly with technology or, what comes to the same, to rebel helplessly against it and curse it as the work of the devil. Quite to the contrary, when we once open ourselves expressly to the essence of technology we find ourselves unexpectedly taken into a freeing claim.

The essence of technology lies in enframing. Its holding sway belongs within destining. Since destining at any given time starts man on a way of revealing, man, thus underway, is continually approaching the brink of the possibility of pursuing and pushing forward nothing but what is revealed in ordering, and of deriving all his standards on this basis. Through this the other possibility is blocked, that man might be admitted more and sooner and ever more primally to the essence of what is unconcealed and to its unconcealment, in order that he might experience as his essence the requisite belonging to revealing.

Placed between these possibilities, man is endangered by destining. The destining of revealing is as such, in every one of its modes, and therefore necessarily, *danger*.

In whatever way the destining of revealing may hold sway, the unconcealment in which everything that is shows itself at any given time harbors the danger that man may misconstrue the unconcealed and misinterpret it. Thus where everything that presences exhibits itself in the light of a cause-effect coherence, even God, for representational thinking, can lose all that is exalted and holy, the mysteriousness of his distance. In the light of causality, God can sink to the level of a cause, of *causa efficiens*. He then becomes even in theology the God of the philosophers, namely of those who define the unconcealed and the concealed in terms of the causality of making, without ever considering the essential origin of this causality.

In a similar way the unconcealment in accordance with which nature presents itself as a calculable complex of the effects of forces can indeed permit correct determinations; but precisely through these successes the danger may remain that in the midst of all that is correct the true will withdraw.

The destining of revealing is in itself not just any danger, but *the* danger.

Yet when destining reigns in the mode of enframing, it is the supreme danger. This danger attests itself to us in two ways. As soon as what is unconcealed no longer concerns man even as object, but exclusively as standing-reserve, and man in the midst of objectlessness is nothing but the orderer of the standing-reserve, then he comes to the very brink of a precipitous fall, that is, he comes to the point where he himself will have to be taken as standing-reserve. Meanwhile, man, precisely as the one so threatened, exalts himself to the posture of lord of the earth. In this way the illusion comes to prevail that everything man encounters exists only insofar as it is his construct. This illusion gives rise in turn to one final delusion: it seems as though man everywhere and always encounters only himself. Heisenberg has with complete correctness pointed out that the real must present itself to contemporary man in this way. *In truth, however, precisely nowhere does man today any longer encounter himself, i.e., his essence.* Man stands so decisively in attendance on the challenging-forth of enframing that he does not grasp enframing as a claim, that he fails to see himself as the one spoken to, and hence also fails in every way to hear in what respect he ek-sists, from out of his essence, in the realm of an exhortation or address, so that he *can never* encounter only himself.

But enframing does not simply endanger man in his relationship to himself and to everything that is. As a destining, it banishes man into that kind of revealing that is an ordering. Where this ordering holds sway, it drives out every other possibility of revealing. Above all, enframing conceals that revealing which, in the sense of *poiēsis,* lets what presences come forth into appearance. As compared with that other revealing, the setting-upon that challenges forth thrusts man into a relation to whatever is that is at once antithetical and rigorously ordered. Where enframing holds sway, regulating and securing of the standing-reserve mark all revealing. They no longer even let their own fundamental characteristic appear, namely, this revealing as such.

Thus the challenging-enframing not only conceals a former way of revealing, bringing-forth, but it conceals revealing itself and with it that wherein unconcealment, i.e., truth, comes to pass.

Enframing blocks the shining-forth and holding sway of truth. The destining that sends into ordering is consequently the extreme danger. What is dangerous is not technology. Technology is not demonic; but its essence is mysterious. The essence of technology, as a destining of revealing, is the danger. The transformed meaning of the word "enframing" will perhaps become somewhat more familiar to us now if we think enframing in the sense of destining and danger.

The threat to man does not come in the first instance from the potentially lethal machines and apparatus of technology. The actual threat has already afflicted man in his essence. The rule of enframing threatens man with the possibility that it could be denied to him to enter into a more original revealing and hence to experience the call of a more primal truth.

Thus where enframing reigns, there is *danger* in the highest sense.

> But where danger is, grows
> The saving power also.

Let us think carefully about these words of Hölderlin. What does it mean to "save"? Usually we think that it means only to seize hold of a thing threatened by ruin in order to secure it in its former continuance. But the verb "to save" says more. "To save" is to fetch something home into its essence, in order to bring the essence for the first time into its genuine appearing. If the essence of technology, enframing, is the extreme danger, if there is truth in Hölderlin's words, then the rule of enframing cannot exhaust itself solely in blocking all lighting-up of every revealing, all appearing of truth. Rather, precisely the essence of technology must harbor in itself the growth of the saving power. But in that case, might not an adequate look into what enframing is, as a destining of revealing, bring the upsurgence of the saving power into appearance?

In what respect does the saving power grow also there where the danger is? Where something grows, there it takes root, from thence it thrives. Both happen concealedly and quietly and in their own time. But according to the words of the poet we have no right whatsoever to expect that there where the danger is we should be able to lay hold of the saving power immediately and without preparation. Therefore we must consider now, in advance, in what respect the saving power does most profoundly take root and thence thrive even where the extreme danger lies—in the holding sway of enframing. In order to consider this, it is necessary, as a last step upon our way, to look with yet clearer eyes into the danger. Accordingly, we must once more question concerning technology. For we have said that in technology's essence roots and thrives the saving power.

But how shall we behold the saving power in the essence of technology so long as we do not consider in what sense of "essence" it is that enframing is actually the essence of technology?

Thus far we have understood "essence" in its current meaning. In the academic language of philosophy "essence" means what something is; in Latin, *quid. Quidditas, whatness,* provides the answer to the question concerning essence. For example, what pertains to all kinds of trees—oaks, beeches, birches, firs—is the same "treeness." Under this inclusive genus—the "universal"—fall all real and possible trees. Is then the essence of technology, enframing, the common genus for everything technological? If this were the case then the steam turbine, the radio transmitter, and the cyclotron would each be an enframing. But the word "enframing" does not mean here a tool or any kind of apparatus. Still less does it mean the general concept of such resources. The machines and apparatus are no more cases and kinds of enframing than are the man at the switchboard and the engineer in the drafting room. Each of these in its own way indeed belongs as stockpart, available resource, or executor, within enframing; but enframing is never the essence of technology in the sense of a genus. Enframing is a way of revealing which is a destining, namely the way that challenges forth. The revealing that brings forth *(poiēsis)* is also a way that has the character of destining. But these ways are not kinds that, arrayed beside one another, fall under the concept of revealing. Revealing is that destining which, ever suddenly and inexplicably to all thinking, apportions itself into the revealing that brings forth and the revealing that challenges, and which allots itself to man. The revealing that challenges has its origin as a destining in bringing-forth. But at the same time enframing, in a way characteristic of a destining, blocks *poiēsis.*

Thus enframing, as a destining of revealing, is indeed the essence of technology, but never in the sense of genus and *essentia.* If we pay heed to this, something astounding strikes us: it is technology itself that makes the demand on us to think in another way what is usually understood by "essence." But in what way?

If we speak of the "essence of a house" and the "essence of a state" we do not mean a generic type; rather we mean the ways in which house and state hold sway, administer themselves, develop, and decay—the way in which they "develop" [*wesen*]. Johann Peter Hebel in a poem, "Ghost on Kanderer Street," for which Goethe had a special fondness, uses the old word *die Weserei.* It means the city hall, inasmuch as there the life of the community gathers and village existence is constantly in play, i.e., comes to presence. It is from the verb *wesen* that the noun is derived. *Wesen* understood as a verb is the same as *währen* [to last or endure], not only in terms of meaning, but also in terms of the phonetic formation of the word. Socrates and Plato already think the essence of something as what essences, what comes to presence, in the sense of what endures. But they think what endures as what remains permanently *(aei on).* And they find what endures permanently in what persists throughout all that happens in what remains. That which remains they discover, in turn, in the aspect *(eidos, idea),* for example the Idea "house."

The Idea "house" displays what anything is that is fashioned as a house. Particular, real, and possible houses, in contrast, are changing and transitory derivatives of the Idea and thus belong to what does not endure.

But it can never in any way be established that enduring is based solely on what Plato thinks as *idea* and Aristotle thinks as to *ti ēn einai* (that which any particular thing has always been), or what metaphysics in its most varied interpretations thinks as *essentia.*

All essencing endures. But is enduring only permanent enduring? Does the essence of technology endure in the sense of the permanent enduring of an Idea that hovers over everything technological, thus making it seem that by technology we mean some mythological abstraction? The way in which technology essences lets itself be seen only on the basis of that permanent enduring in which enframing comes to pass as a destining of revealing. Goethe once uses the mysterious word *fortgewähren* [to grant permanently] in place of *fortwähren* [to endure permanently]. He hears *währen* [to endure] and *gëwahren* [to grant] here in one unarticulated accord. And if we now ponder more carefully than we did before what it is that actually endures and perhaps alone endures, we may venture to say: *Only what is granted endures. What endures primally out of the earliest beginning is what grants.*

As the essencing of technology, enframing is what endures. Does enframing hold sway at all in the sense of granting? No doubt the question seems a horrendous blunder. For according to everything that has been said, enframing is, rather, a destining that gathers together into the revealing that challenges forth. Challenging is anything but a granting. So it seems, so long as we do not notice that the challenging-forth into the ordering of the real as standing-reserve still remains a destining that starts man upon a way of revealing. As this destining, the coming to presence of technology gives man entry into something which, of himself, he can neither invent nor in any way make. For there is no such thing as a man who exists singly and solely on his own.

But if this destining, enframing, is the extreme danger, not only for man's coming to presence, but for all revealing as such, should this destining still be called a granting? Yes, most emphatically, if in this destining the saving power is said to grow. Every destining of revealing comes to pass from a granting and as such a granting. For it is granting that first conveys to man that share in revealing that the coming-to-pass of revealing needs. So needed and used, man is given to belong to the coming-to-pass of truth. The granting that sends one way or another into revealing is as such the saving power. For the saving power lets man see and enter into the highest dignity of his essence. This dignity lies in keeping watch over the unconcealment—and with it, from the first, the concealment—of all coming to presence on this earth. It is precisely in enframing, which threatens to sweep man away into ordering as the supposed single way of revealing, and so thrusts man into the danger of the surrender of his free essence—it is precisely in this extreme danger that the innermost indestructible belongingness of man within granting may come to light, provided that we, for our part, begin to pay heed to the essence of technology.

Thus the coming to presence of technology harbors in itself what we least suspect, the possible upsurgence of the saving power.

Everything, then, depends upon this: that we ponder this arising and that we, recollecting, watch over it. How can this happen? Above all through our catching sight of what comes to presence in technology, instead of merely gaping at the technological. So long as we represent technology as an instrument, we remain transfixed in the will to master it. We press on past the essence of technology.

When, however, we ask how the instrumental comes to presence as a kind of causality, then we experience this coming to presence as the destining of a revealing.

When we consider, finally, that the coming to presence of the essence of technology comes to pass in the granting that needs and uses man so that he may share in revealing, then the following becomes clear:

The essence of technology is in a lofty sense ambiguous. Such ambiguity points to the mystery of all revealing, i.e., of truth.

On the one hand, enframing challenges forth into the frenziedness of ordering that blocks every view into the coming-to-pass of revealing and so radically endangers the relation to the essence of truth.

On the other hand, enframing comes to pass for its part in the granting that lets man endure—as yet inexperienced, but perhaps more experienced in the future—that he may be the one who is needed and used for the safekeeping of the essence of truth. Thus does the arising of the saving power appear.

The irresistibility of ordering and the restraint of the saving power draw past each other like the paths of two stars in the course of the heavens. But precisely this, their passing by, is the hidden side of their nearness.

When we look into the ambiguous essence of technology, we behold the constellation, the stellar course of the mystery.

The question concerning technology is the question concerning the constellation in which revealing and concealing, in which the coming to presence of truth comes to pass.

But what help is it to us to look into the constellation of truth? We look into the danger and see the growth of the saving power.

Through this we are not yet saved. But we are thereupon summoned to hope in the growing light of the saving power. How can this happen? Here and now and in little things, that we may foster the saving power in its increase. This includes holding always before our eyes the extreme danger.

The coming to presence of technology threatens revealing, threatens it with the possibility that all revealing will be consumed in ordering and that everything will present itself only in the unconcealedness of standing-reserve. Human activity can never directly counter this danger. Human achievement alone can never banish it. But human reflection can ponder the fact that all saving power must be of a higher essence than what is endangered, though at the same time kindred to it.

But might there not perhaps be a more primally granted revealing that could bring the saving power into its first shining-forth in the midst of the danger that in the technological age rather conceals than shows itself?

There was a time when it was not technology alone that bore the name *technē.* Once that revealing which brings forth truth into the splendor of radiant appearance was also called *technē.*

Once there was a time when the bringing-forth of the true into the beautiful was called *technē.* The *poiēsis* of the fine arts was also called *technē.*

At the outset of the destining of the West, in Greece, the arts soared to the supreme height of the revealing granted them. They illuminated the presence [*Gegenwart*] of the gods and the dialogue of divine and human destinings. And art was simply called *technē.* It was a single, manifold revealing. It was pious, *promos,* i.e., yielding to the holding sway and the safekeeping of truth.

The arts were not derived from the artistic. Art works were not enjoyed aesthetically. Art was not a sector of cultural activity.

What was art—perhaps only for that brief but magnificent age? Why did art bear the modest name *technē?* Because it was a revealing that brought forth and made present, and therefore belonged within *poiēsis.* It was finally that revealing which holds complete sway in all the fine arts, in poetry, and in everything poetical that obtained *poiēsis* as its proper name.

The same poet from whom we heard the words

> But where danger is, grows
> The saving power also . . .

says to us:

> . . . poetically dwells man upon this earth.

The poetical brings the true into the splendor of what Plato in the *Phaedrus* calls to *ekphanestaton,* that which shines forth most purely. The poetical thoroughly pervades every art, every revealing of coming to presence into the beautiful.

Could it be that the fine arts are called to poetic revealing? Could it be that revealing lays claim to the arts most primally, so that they for their part may expressly foster the growth of the saving power, may awaken and found anew our vision of that which grants and our trust in it?

Whether art may be granted this highest possibility of its essence in the midst of the extreme danger, no one can tell. Yet we can be astounded. Before what? Before this other possibility: that the frenziedness of technology may entrench itself everywhere to such an extent that someday, throughout everything technological, the essence of technology may come to presence in the coming-to-pass of truth.

Because the essence of technology is nothing technological, essential reflection upon technology and decisive confrontation with it must happen in a realm that is, on the one hand, akin to the essence of technology and, on the other, fundamentally different from it.

Such a realm is art. But certainly only if reflection upon art for its part, does not shut its eyes to the constellation of truth concerning which we are *questioning*.

Thus questioning, we bear witness to the crisis that in our sheer preoccupation with technology we do not yet experience the coming to presence of technology, that in our sheer aesthetic-mindedness we no longer guard and preserve the coming to presence of art. Yet the more questioningly we ponder the essence of technology, the more mysterious the essence of art becomes.

The closer we come to the danger, the more brightly do the ways into the saving power begin to shine and the more questioning we become. For questioning is the piety of thought.

Ludwig Wittgenstein
1889–1951

Ludwig Wittgenstein was born into one of Vienna's leading families. His father, Karl, was a wealthy steel industrialist and his mother, Leopoldine, a concert pianist. Johannes Brahams, Gustaf Mahler, and Pablo Casals were frequent houseguests of the Wittgensteins. Educated at home by tutors, Wittgenstein showed great promise in mathematics and engineering. According to one report, he built a working sewing machine from matchsticks at age ten.

Wittgenstein remained home until age fifteen, when he enrolled at the *Linz Realschule,* where he studied engineering for two years before transferring to Berlin. In 1908 Wittgenstein enrolled at the University of Manchester, England, for aerodynamics studies. While designing a propeller, Wittgenstein developed an interest in mathematics, which led him to Cambridge. There, from 1912–1913, he studied with Bertrand Russell. Russell later recalled one of his first encounters with Wittgenstein:

> At the end of his first term at Cambridge he came to me and said, "Will you please tell me whether I am a complete idiot or not?" I replied, "My dear fellow, I don't know. Why are you asking me?" He said, "Because if I am a complete idiot, I shall become an aeronaut; but, if not, I shall become a philosopher." I told him to write me something during the vacation on some philosophical subject and I would then tell him whether he was a complete idiot or not. At the beginning of the following term

he brought me the fulfillment of this suggestion. After reading only one sentence, I said to him, "No, you must not become an aeronaut."*

Wittgenstein immersed himself in philosophical studies, filling notebooks with ideas. When World War I began in 1914, he enlisted as a machine-gunner in the Austrian army. While in the army he continued his philosophical work, writing a short treatise in 1918 based on his notebooks. That same year he was captured by the Italian army. In captivity, he managed to send a copy of this treatise to Russell, who considered it a work of genius and arranged for its publication as the *Tractatus Logico-Philosophicus* (1921). This was the only philosophical book Wittgenstein published during his lifetime.

Wittgenstein believed his *Tractatus* gave the definitive answer to all philosophical problems. Following the war, therefore, he left philosophy completely. After a course at a teacher's training college, he spent the next six years as a schoolteacher in remote Austrian villages. But teaching did not suit his temperament and he was desperately unhappy. He resigned in 1926 and worked as a monastery gardener before moving back to Vienna to design a house for his sister. While in Vienna, Wittgenstein began talking philosophy again with Moritz Schlick, professor of philosophy at the University of Vienna, and other professors who admired his *Tractatus*.

Philosophically revived, Wittgenstein returned to Cambridge in 1929, and, after submitting his now famous *Tractatus* as a doctoral dissertation, he became a research fellow of Trinity College. Again, Wittgenstein filled notebooks with philosophical reflections and prepared them for publication. But, with the exception of one paper, Wittgenstein never saw any of his new ideas in print; he always considered his newest thoughts incomplete or not yet adequately formulated.

For the rest of his life, Wittgenstein continued his association with Cambridge—though he never felt completely comfortable with academic life. On several occasions he left the university, sometimes living in isolation in his Norwegian hut. In 1939 he was appointed professor of philosophy at Cambridge, succeeding G.E. Moore. But before he could take the chair, World War II began, and he volunteered as a hospital orderly in London. He returned to Cambridge following the war, but he found his job so dreadful he resigned after two years. Living alone in Ireland he completed his second major work, *Philosophical Investigations,* though again he could not bring himself to publish it. (It appeared posthumously in 1953.)

During a visit to the United States in 1949 his health began to deteriorate. On his return to Cambridge, doctors discovered prostate cancer and he died eighteen months later, in 1951. Since his death, his literary executors have published over a dozen books of uncompleted manuscripts, notes, lectures, and letters.

*   *   *

Throughout his adult life, Wittgenstein was interested in philosophy as an activity rather than a set of theories. The goal of philosophy is to remove or "dissolve"

---

*Bertrand Russell, *Portraits from Memory* (London: Allen & Unwin, 1957), pp. 26–27.

problems, and the primary means for doing this is analysis of language. According to Wittgenstein, most philosophical problems can be traced to a misuse of language. In one of his early notebooks he wrote:

> Philosophy gives no pictures of reality and can neither confirm nor confute scientific investigations. Philosophy teaches us the logical form of propositions: that is its fundamental task.*

Thirty-five years later he still maintained this philosophical position: "Philosophy is a battle against the bewitchment of our intelligence by means of language."**

But despite this theme, Wittgenstein developed two different ways to understand language. The early Wittgenstein created a "picture theory of meaning" that held that language consists of statements or propositions that picture the world. Just as a picture has something in common with that which it pictures, so language has a logical form in common with the world it pictures. This logical form is usually obscured by ordinary language, so the philosopher's job is to clear up ordinary language by crafting a language that more perfectly pictures the world. This perfected language will have to exclude many propositions (such as those in ethics, metaphysics, or religion), consigning them to silence. Our selection from the *Tractatus,* translated by D.F. Pears and B.F. McGuiness, presents this early theory.

Wittgenstein's early theory was adopted and modified by Moritz Schlick and his "Vienna Circle." This group developed a philosophy that came to be called "logical positivism." Like Wittgenstein, they worked on an ideal language, free from the ambiguities of ordinary discourse, that would clearly exhibit its logical form. They also held that such a language would exclude the propositions of ethics, metaphysics, and religion. (For more on logical positivism, see the introduction to A.J. Ayer, pages 441–443.)

The early Wittgenstein, and the logical positivism that adapted many of his ideas, had a profound impact on the philosophy of the middle twentieth century. But Wittgenstein himself moved to a different understanding of language: a "language game" theory. This theory found the earlier picture theory too narrow; a perfected language is neither possible nor desirable. As he explains in our selection from the *Investigations,* given here in the G.E.M. Anscombe translation, there are many kinds of meaningful sentences that share certain characteristics, but not others. Just as there is no one characteristic common to all games, so there is no one theory to explain all language uses. The proper way to understand a sentence is not to break it down into its constituent parts and analyze its logical form. Instead, we should examine the "forms of life" out of which the sentence arises, to see what "game" it is playing. "The meaning of a word," Wittgenstein wrote, "is its use in the language."

The later Wittgenstein was not interested in creating a perfect language. He sought rather to expose the underlying assumptions of language and the forms of life out of which our sentences arise. By understanding language in terms of the social environment that gives it birth, the later Wittgenstein encouraged a socio-

---

*Ludwig Wittgenstein, *Notebooks 1914–1916* (London: Basil Blackwell, 1961), p. 93.
**Ludwig Wittgenstein, *Philosophical Investigations* (New York: Macmillan, 1958), no. 109, p. 47.

logical understanding of language. Accordingly, Wittgenstein argued against the idea of a private language—a language apart from communal interactions.

The influence of Wittgenstein's early work peaked in the 1950s. But his later understanding of philosophy, and his lifelong conception of philosophy as activity, is still influential, particularly in the English-speaking world. For example, feminist philosophers have used Wittgenstein's insights to show how patriarchal language both influences and is influenced by social structures, while theologians have tried to understand the language of sacred texts by explorations of their historical contexts. Wittgenstein's belief that the aim of philosophy is to dissolve problems—"To shew the fly the way out of the fly-bottle"—has continued to impress, or, as critics would say, to depress, philosophy.

*   *   *

Among the many general introductions to Wittgenstein's life and thought, Anthony Kenney, *Wittgenstein* (Cambridge, MA: Harvard University Press, 1973), still provides one of the best. Also helpful are George Pitcher, *The Philosophy of Wittgenstein* (Englewood Cliffs, NJ: Prentice Hall, 1964); David Pears, *Ludwig Wittgenstein* (New York: Viking Press, 1970); A.J. Ayer, *Wittgenstein* (Chicago: University of Chicago Press, 1985); Ray Monk, *Ludwig Wittgenstein: The Duty of Genius* (New York: Penguin Books, 1990); and Joachim Schulte, *Wittgenstein: An Introduction,* translated by William H. Brenner and John F. Holley (Albany: State University of New York Press, 1992). Both Norman Malcolm, *Ludwig Wittgenstein: A Memoir* (London: Oxford University Press, 1958), and K.T. Fann, ed., *Wittgenstein: The Man and His Philosophy* (New York: Delta, 1967), provide personal memoirs, while Allan Janik and Stephen Toulmin, *Wittgenstein's Vienna* (New York: Simon & Schuster, 1973), and Ray Monk, *Ludwig Wittgenstein: The Duty of Genius* (New York: Penguin, 1992), give biographies. For guides to Wittgenstein's two major works, see G.E.M. Anscombe, *An Introduction to Wittgenstein's "Tractatus"* (London: Hillary House, 1959); H.O. Mounce, *Wittgenstein's "Tractatus"* (Chicago: University of Chicago Press, 1981); Garth Hallett, *A Companion to Wittgenstein's "Philosophical Investigations"* (Ithaca, NY: Cornell University Press, 1977); and G.P. Baker and P.M.S. Hacker, *Wittgenstein: Understanding and Meaning* (Chicago: University of Chicago Press, 1979). Collections of essays include Irving Copi, ed., *Essays on Wittgenstein's "Tractatus"* (New York: Macmillan, 1966); George Pitcher, ed., *Wittgenstein's "Investigations"* (Garden City, NY: Anchor Doubleday, 1966); and Peter A. French, Theodore E. Uehling, Jr., and Howard K. Wettstein, eds., *The Wittgenstein Legacy* (Notre Dame, IN: University of Notre Dame Press, 1992).

TRACTATUS LOGICO-PHILOSOPHICUS
(in part)

PREFACE

Perhaps this book will be understood only by someone who has himself already had the thoughts that are expressed in it—or at least similar thoughts.—So it is not a text-book.—Its purpose would be achieved if it gave pleasure to one person who read and understood it.

The book deals with the problems of philosophy, and shows, I believe, that the reason why these problems are posed is that the logic of our language is misunderstood. The whole sense of the book might be summed up in the following words: what can be said at all can be said clearly, and what we cannot talk about we must consign to silence.

Thus the aim of the book is to set a limit to thought, or rather—not to thought, but to the expression of thoughts: for in order to be able to set a limit to thought, we should have to find both sides of the limit thinkable (i.e. we should have to be able to think what cannot be thought).

It will therefore only be in language that the limit can be set, and what lies on the other side of the limit will simply be nonsense.

I do not wish to judge how far my efforts coincide with those of other philosophers. Indeed, what I have written here makes no claim to novelty in detail, and the reason why I give no sources is that it is a matter of indifference to me whether the thoughts that I have had have been anticipated by someone else.

I will only mention that I am indebted to Frege's great works and to the writings of my friend Mr. Bertrand Russell for much of the stimulation of my thoughts.

If this work has any value, it consists in two things: the first is that thoughts are expressed in it, and on this score the better the thoughts are expressed—the more the nail has been hit on the head—the greater will be its value.—Here I am conscious of having fallen a long way short of what is possible. Simply because my powers are too slight for the accomplishment of the task.—May others come and do it better.

On the other hand the *truth* of the thoughts that are here set forth seems to me unassailable and definitive. I therefore believe myself to have found, on all essential points, the final solution of the problems. And if I am not mistaken in this belief, then the second thing in which the value of this work consists is that it shows how little is achieved when these problems are solved.

Ludwig Wittgenstein, *Tractatus Logico-Philosophicus*. Translated by D.F. Pears and B.F. McGuiness. London: Routledge & Kegan Paul PLC, 1972. New York: Humanities Press, 1972. Reprinted by permission of Routledge & Kegan Paul.

TRACTATUS LOGICO-PHILOSOPHICUS

1*   The world is all that is the case.

1.1   The world is the totality of facts, not of things.

1.11   The world is determined by the facts, and by their being *all* the facts.

1.12   For the totality of facts determines what is the case, and also whatever is not the case.

1.13   The facts in logical space are the world.

1.2   The world divides into facts.

1.21   Each item can be the case or not the case while everything else remains the same.

2   What is the case—a fact—is the existence of states of affairs.

2.01   A state of affairs (a state of things) is a combination of objects (things).

2.011   It is essential to things that they should be possible constituents of states of affairs.

2.012   In logic nothing is accidental: if a thing *can* occur in a state of affairs, the possibility of the state of affairs must be written into the thing itself.

2.0121   It would seem to be a sort of accident, if it turned out that a situation would fit a thing that could already exist entirely on its own.

    If things can occur in states of affairs, this possibility must be in them from the beginning.

    (Nothing in the province of logic can be merely possible. Logic deals with every possibility and all possibilities are its facts.)

    Just as we are quite unable to imagine spatial objects outside space or temporal objects outside time, so too there is *no* object that we can imagine excluded from the possibility of combining with others.

    If I can imagine objects combined in states of affairs, I cannot imagine them excluded from the *possibility* of such combinations.

2.0122   Things are independent in so far as they can occur in all *possible* situations, but this form of independence is a form of connexion with states of affairs, a form of dependence. (It is impossible for words to appear in two different roles: by themselves, and in propositions.)

2.0123   If I know an object I also know all its possible occurrences in states of affairs.

    (Every one of these possibilities must be part of the nature of the object.)

    A new possibility cannot be discovered later.

2.01231 If I am to know an object, though I need not know its external properties, I must know all its internal properties.

2.0124   If all objects are given, then at the same time all *possible* states of affairs are also given.

2.013   Each thing is, as it were, in a space of possible states of affairs. This space I can imagine empty, but I cannot imagine the thing without the space.

2.0131   A spatial object must be situated in infinite space. (A spatial point is an argument-place.)

    A speck in the visual field, though it need not be red, must have some colour: it is, so to speak, surrounded by colour-space. Tones must have *some* pitch, objects of the sense of touch *some* degree of hardness, and so on.

---

*The decimal numbers assigned to the individual propositions indicate the logical importance of the propositions, the stress laid on them in my exposition. The propositions *n*.1, *n*.2, *n*.3, etc. are comments on proposition no. *n*; the propositions *n.m*1, *n.m*2, etc. are comments on proposition no. *n.m;* and so on.

2.014   Objects contain the possibility of all situations.

2.0141   The possibility of its occurring in states of affairs is the form of an object.

2.02   Objects are simple.

2.0201   Every statement about complexes can be resolved into a statement about their constituents and into the propositions that describe the complexes completely.

2.021   Objects make up the substance of the world. That is why they cannot be composite.

2.0211   If the world had no substance, then whether a proposition had sense would depend on whether another proposition was true.

2.0212   In that case we could not sketch out any picture of the world (true or false).

2.022   It is obvious that an imagined world, however different it may be from the real one, must have *something*—a form—in common with it.

2.023   Objects are just what constitute this unalterable form.

2.0231   The substance of the world *can* only determine a form, and not any material properties. For it is only by means of propositions that material properties are represented—only by the configuration of objects that they are produced.

2.0232   In a manner of speaking, objects are colourless.

2.0233   If two objects have the same logical form, the only distinction between them, apart from their external properties, is that they are different.

2.02331 Either a thing has properties that nothing else has, in which case we can immediately use a description to distinguish it from the others and refer to it; or, on the other hand, there are several things that have the whole set of their properties in common, in which case it is quite impossible to indicate one of them.
      For if there is nothing to distinguish a thing, I cannot distinguish it, since if I do it will be distinguished after all.

2.024   Substance is what subsists independently of what is the case.

2.025   It is form and content.

2.0251   Space, time, and colour (being coloured) are forms of objects.

2.026   There must be objects, if the world is to have an unalterable form.

2.027   Objects, the unalterable, and the subsistent are one and the same.

2.0271   Objects are what is unalterable and subsistent; their configuration is what is changing and unstable.

2.0272   The configuration of objects produces states of affairs.

2.03   In a state of affairs objects fit into one another like the links of a chain.

2.031   In a state of affairs objects stand in a determinate relation to one another.

2.032   The determinate way in which objects are connected in a state of affairs is the structure of the state of affairs.

2.033   Its form is the possibility of its structure.

2.034   The structure of a fact consists of the structures of states of affairs.

2.04   The totality of existing states of affairs is the world.

2.05   The totality of existing states of affairs also determines which states of affairs do not exist.

2.06   The existence and non-existence of states of affairs is reality.
      (We also call the existence of states of affairs a positive fact, and their non-existence a negative fact.)

2.061   States of affairs are independent of one another.

2.062   From the existence or non-existence of one state of affairs it is impossible to infer the existence or non-existence of another.

2.063   The sum-total of reality is the world.

2.1   We picture facts to ourselves.

Composition in Yellow, Red, Blue and Black, 1921, by Piet Mondrian (1872–1944). The painter/draftsman Mondrian constructed nonobjective paintings with mathematical precision. The clarity of form and structure, together with the lack of any ornamentation, provides a visual metaphor for the precision and austerity of Wittgenstein's *Tractatus. (Giraudon/Art Resource, NY)*

2.11   A picture presents a situation in logical space, the existence and non-existence of states of affairs.

2.12   A picture is a model of reality.

2.13   In a picture objects have the elements of the picture corresponding to them.

2.131   In a picture the elements of the picture are the representatives of objects.

2.14   What constitutes a picture is that its elements are related to one another in a determinate way.

2.141   A picture is a fact.

2.15   The fact that the elements of a picture are related to one another in a determinate way represents that things are related to one another in the same way.

Let us call this connexion of its elements the structure of the picture, and let us call the possibility of this structure the pictorial form of the picture.

2.151   Pictorial form is the possibility that things are related to one another in the same way as the elements of the picture.

2.1511 *That* is how a picture is attached to reality; it reaches right out to it.

2.1512 It is laid against reality like a ruler.

2.15121 Only the end-points of the graduating lines actually *touch* the object that is to be measured.

2.1513 So a picture, conceived in this way, also includes the pictorial relationship, which makes it into a picture.

2.1514 The pictorial relationship consists of the correlations of the picture's elements with things.

2.1515 These correlations are, as it were, the feelers of the picture's elements, with which the picture touches reality.

2.16   If a fact is to be a picture, it must have something in common with what it depicts.

2.161   There must be something identical in a picture and what it depicts, to enable the one to be a picture of the other at all.

2.17   What a picture must have in common with reality, in order to be able to depict it—correctly or incorrectly—in the way it does, is its pictorial form.

2.171   A picture can depict any reality whose form it has.

A spatial picture can depict anything spatial, a coloured one anything coloured, etc.

2.172   A picture cannot, however, depict its pictorial form: it displays it.

2.173   A picture represents its subject from a position outside it. (Its standpoint is its representational form.) That is why a picture represents its subject correctly or incorrectly.

2.174   A picture cannot, however, place itself outside its representational form.

2.18   What any picture, of whatever form, must have in common with reality, in order to be able to depict it—correctly or incorrectly—in any way at all, is logical form, i.e. the form of reality.

2.181   A picture whose pictorial form is logical form is called a logical picture.

2.182   Every picture is *at the same time* a logical one. (On the other hand, not every picture is, for example, a spatial one.)

2.19   Logical pictures can depict the world.

2.2   A picture has logico-pictorial form in common with what it depicts.

2.201   A picture depicts reality by representing a possibility of existence and non-existence of states of affairs.

2.202   A picture represents a possible situation in logical space.

2.203   A picture contains the possibility of the situation that it represents.

2.21   A picture agrees with reality or fails to agree; it is correct or incorrect, true or false.

2.22   What a picture represents it represents independently of its truth or falsity, by means of its pictorial form.

2.221   What a picture represents is its sense.

2.222   The agreement or disagreement of its sense with reality constitutes its truth or falsity.

2.223   In order to tell whether a picture is true or false we must compare it with reality.

2.224   It is impossible to tell from the picture alone whether it is true or false.

2.225   There are no pictures that are true *a priori*.

3   A logical picture of facts is a thought.

3.001   "A state of affairs is thinkable"—this means that we can picture it to ourselves.

3.01   The totality of true thoughts is a picture of the world.

3.02   A thought contains the possibility of the situation of which it is the thought. What is thinkable is possible too.

3.03   Thought can never be of anything illogical, since, if it were, we should have to think illogically.

3.031   It used to be said that God could create anything except what would be contrary to the laws of logic.—The reason being that we could not *say* what an "illogical" world would look like.

3.032   It is as impossible to represent in language anything that "contradicts logic" as it is in geometry to represent by its co-ordinates a figure that contradicts the laws of space, or to give the co-ordinates of a point that does not exist.

3.0321   Though a state of affairs that would contravene the laws of physics can be represented by us spatially, one that would contravene the laws of geometry cannot.

3.04   If a thought were correct *a priori,* it would be a thought whose possibility ensured its truth.

3.05   *A priori* knowledge that a thought was true would be possible only if its truth were recognizable from the thought itself (without anything to compare it with).

3.1   In a proposition a thought finds an expression that can be perceived by the senses.

3.11   We use the perceptible sign of a proposition (spoken or written, etc.) as a projection of a possible situation.
    The method of projection is to think out the sense of the proposition.

3.12   I call the sign with which we express a thought a propositional sign.—And a proposition is a propositional sign in its projective relation to the world.

3.13   A proposition includes all that the projection includes, but not what is projected.
    Therefore, though what is projected is not itself included, its possibility is.
    A proposition does not actually contain its sense, but does contain the possibility of expressing it.
    ("The content of a proposition" means the content of a proposition that has sense.)
    A proposition contains the form, but not the content, of its sense.

3.14   What constitutes a propositional sign is that in it its elements (the words) stand in a determinate relation to one another.
    A propositional sign is a fact.

3.141   A proposition is not a medley of words.—(Just as a theme in music is not a medley of notes.)
A proposition is articulated.

3.142   Only facts can express a sense, a set of names cannot.

3.143   Although a propositional sign is a fact, this is obscured by the usual form of expression in writing or print.
For in a printed proposition, for example, no essential difference is apparent between a propositional sign and a word.
(That is what made it possible for Frege to call a proposition a composite name.)

3.1431   The essence of a propositional sign is very clearly seen if we imagine one composed of spatial objects (such as tables, chairs, and books) instead of written signs.
Then the spatial arrangement of these things will express the sense of the proposition.

*   *   *

6.4   All propositions are of equal value.

6.41   The sense of the world must lie outside the world. In the world everything is as it is, and everything happens as it does happen: *in* it no value exists—and if it did, it would have no value.
If there is any value that does have value, it must lie outside the whole sphere of what happens and is the case. For all that happens and is the case is accidental.
What makes it non-accidental cannot lie *within* the world, since if it did it would itself be accidental.
It must lie outside the world.

6.42   And so it is impossible for there to be propositions of ethics.
Propositions can express nothing of what is higher.

6.421   It is clear that ethics cannot be put into words. Ethics is transcendental.
(Ethics and aesthetics are one and the same.)

6.422   When an ethical law of the form, "Thou shalt . . .," is laid down, one's first thought is, "And what if I do not do it?" It is clear, however, that ethics has nothing to do with punishment and reward in the usual sense of the terms. So our question about the *consequences* of an action must be unimportant.— At least those consequences should not be events. For there must be some- thing right about the question we posed. There must indeed be some kind of ethical reward and ethical punishment, but they must reside in the action itself.
(And it is also clear that the reward must be something pleasant and the punishment something unpleasant.)

6.423   It is impossible to speak about the will in so far as it is the subject of ethical attributes.
And the will as a phenomenon is of interest only to psychology.

6.43   If good or bad acts of will do alter the world, it can only be the limits of the world that they alter, not the facts, not what can be expressed by means of lan- guage.
In short their effect must be that it becomes an altogether different world. It must, so to speak, wax and wane as a whole.

The world of the happy man is a different one from that of the unhappy man.

6.431   So too at death the world does not alter, but comes to an end.

6.4311   Death is not an event in life: we do not live to experience death.

If we take eternity to mean not infinite temporal duration but timelessness, then eternal life belongs to those who live in the present.

Our life has no end in just the way in which our visual field has no limits.

6.4312   Not only is there no guarantee of the temporal immortality of the human soul, that is to say of its eternal survival after death; but, in any case, this assumption completely fails to accomplish the purpose for which it has always been intended. Or is some riddle solved by my surviving for ever? Is not this eternal life itself as much of a riddle as our present life? The solution of the riddle of life in space and time lies *outside* space and time.

(It is certainly not the solution of any problems of natural science that is required.)

6.432   *How* things are in the world is a matter of complete indifference for what is higher. God does not reveal himself *in* the world.

6.4321   The facts all contribute only to setting the problem, not to its solution.

6.44   It is not *how* things are in the world that is mystical, but *that* it exists.

6.45   To view the world *sub specie aeterni* is to view it as a whole—a limited whole.

Feeling the world as a limited whole—it is this that is mystical.

6.5   When the answer cannot be put into words, neither can the question be put into words.

The riddle does not exist.

If a question can be framed at all, it is also *possible* to answer it.

6.51   Scepticism is *not* irrefutable, but obviously nonsensical, when it tries to raise doubts where no questions can be asked.

For doubt can exist only where a question exists, a question only where an answer exists, and an answer only where something *can be said.*

6.52   We feel that even when *all possible* scientific questions have been answered, the problems of life remain completely untouched. Of course there are then no questions left, and this itself is the answer.

6.521   The solution of the problem of life is seen in the vanishing of the problem.

(Is not this the reason why those who have found after a long period of doubt that the sense of life became clear to them have then been unable to say what constituted that sense?)

6.522   There are, indeed, things that cannot be put into words. They *make themselves manifest.* They are what is mystical.

6.53   The correct method in philosophy would really be the following: to say nothing except what can be said, i.e. propositions of natural science—i.e. something that has nothing to do with philosophy—and then, whenever someone else wanted to say something metaphysical, to demonstrate to him that he had failed to give a meaning to certain signs in his propositions. Although it would not be satisfying to the other person—he would not have the feeling that we were teaching him philosophy—*this* method would be the only strictly correct one.

6.54   My propositions serve as elucidations in the following way: anyone who understands me eventually recognizes them as nonsensical, when he has used them—as steps—to climb up beyond them. (He must, so to speak, throw away the ladder after he has climbed up it.)

He must transcend these propositions, and then he will see the world aright.

7   What we cannot speak about we must consign to silence.

PHILOSOPHICAL INVESTIGATIONS
(in part)

1. "When they (my elders) named some object, and accordingly moved towards something, I saw this and I grasped that the thing was called by the sound they uttered when they meant to point it out. Their intention was shewn by their bodily movements, as it were the natural language of all peoples: the expression of the face, the play of the eyes, the movement of other parts of the body, and the tone of voice which expresses our state of mind in seeking, having, rejecting, or avoiding something. Thus, as I heard words repeatedly used in their proper places in various sentences, I gradually learnt to understand what objects they signifed; and after I had trained my mouth to form these signs, I used them to express my own desires." (Augustine, *Confessions*, I. 8.)

These words, it seems to me, give us a particular picture of the essence of human language. It is this: the individual words in language name objects—sentences are combinations of such names. In this picture of language we find the roots of the following idea: Every word has a meaning. This meaning is correlated with the word. It is the object for which the word stands.

Augustine does not speak of there being any difference between kinds of word. If you describe the learning of language in this way you are, I believe, thinking primarily of nouns like "table," "chair," "bread," and of people's names, and only secondarily of the names of certain actions and properties; and of the remaining kinds of word as something that will take care of itself.

Now think of the following use of language: I send someone shopping. I give him a slip marked "five red apples." He takes the slip to the shopkeeper, who opens the drawer marked "apples"; then he looks up the word "red" in a table and finds a colour sample opposite it; then he says the series of cardinal numbers—I assume that he knows them by heart—up to the word "five" and for each number he takes an apple of the same colour as the sample out of the drawer. It is in this and similar ways that one operates with words. "But how does he know where and how he is to look up the word 'red' and what he is to do with the word 'five'?" Well, I assume that he *acts* as I have described. Explanations come to an end somewhere.—But what is the meaning of the word "five"?—No such thing was in question here, only how the word "five" is used.

2. That philosophical concept of meaning has its place in a primitive idea of the way language functions. But one can also say that it is the idea of a language more primitive than ours.

Let us imagine a language for which the description given by Augustine is right. The language is meant to serve for communication between a builder A and an assistant B. A is building with building-stones: there are blocks, pillars, slabs and beams. B has to pass the stones, and that in the order in which A needs them. For this purpose they use a language consisting of the words "block," "pillar," "slab," "beam." A calls them out;—B brings the stone which he has learnt to bring at such-and-such a call.—Conceive this as a complete primitive language.

Reprinted with permission of Macmillan Publishing Company from Ludwig Wittgenstein: *Philosophical Investigations*, Third Edition translated by G.E.M. Anscombe. Copyright © 1953 by Macmillan Publishing Company.

3. Augustine, we might say, does describe a system of communication; only not everything that we call language is this system. And one has to say this in many cases where the question arises "Is this an appropriate description or not?" The answer is: "Yes, it is appropriate, but only for this narrowly circumscribed region, not for the whole of what you were claiming to describe."

It is as if someone were to say: "A game consists in moving objects about on a surface according to certain rules . . ."—and we replied: You seem to be thinking of board games, but there are others. You can make your definition correct by expressly restricting it to those games.

4. Imagine a script in which the letters were used to stand for sounds, and also as signs of emphasis and punctuation. (A script can be conceived as a language for describing sound-patterns.) Now imagine someone interpreting that script as if there were simply a correspondence of letters to sounds and as if the letters had not also completely different functions. Augustine's conception of language is like such an over-simple conception of the script.

5. If we look at the example in ¶1, we may perhaps get an inkling how much this general notion of the meaning of a word surrounds the working of language with a haze which makes clear vision impossible. It disperses the fog to study the phenomena of language in primitive kinds of application in which one can command a clear view of the aim and functioning of the words.

A child uses such primitive forms of language when it learns to talk. Here the teaching of language is not explanation, but training.

6. We could imagine that the language of ¶2 was the *whole* language of A and B; even the whole language of a tribe. The children are brought up to perform *these* actions, to use *these* words as they do so, and to react in *this* way to the words of others.

An important part of the training will consist in the teacher's pointing to the objects, directing the child's attention to them, and at the same time uttering a word; for instance, the word "slab" as he points to that shape. (I do not want to call this "ostensive definition," because the child cannot as yet *ask* what the name is. I will call it "ostensive teaching of words." I say that it will form an important part of the training, because it is so with human beings; not because it could not be imagined otherwise.) This ostensive teaching of words can be said to establish an association between the word and the thing. But what does this mean? Well, it may mean various things; but one very likely thinks first of all that a picture of the object comes before the child's mind when it hears the word. But now, if this does happen—is it the purpose of the word?—Yes, it *may* be the purpose.—I can imagine such a use of words (of series of sounds). (Uttering a word is like striking a note on the keyboard of the imagination.) But in the language of ¶2 it is *not* the purpose of the words to evoke images. (It may, of course, be discovered that that helps to attain the actual purpose.)

But if the ostensive teaching has this effect,—am I to say that it effects an understanding of the word? Don't you understand the call "Slab!" if you act upon it in such-and-such a way?—Doubtless the ostensive teaching helped to bring this about; but only together with a particular training. With different training the same ostensive teaching of these words would have effected a quite different understanding.

"I set the brake up by connecting up rod and lever."—Yes, given the whole of the rest of the mechanism. Only in conjunction with that is it a brake-lever, and separated from its support it is not even a lever; it may be anything, or nothing.

7. In the practice of the use of language (2) one party calls out the words, the other acts on them. In instruction in the language the following process will occur: the learner *names* the objects; that is, he utters the word when the teacher points to the stone.—And there will be this still simpler exercise: the pupil repeats the words after the teacher—both of these being processes resembling language.

We can also think of the whole process of using words in (2) as one of those games by means of which children learn their native language. I will call these games "language-games" and will sometimes speak of a primitive language as a language-game.

And the processes of naming the stones and of repeating words after someone might also be called language-games. Think of much of the use of words in games like ring-a-ring-a-roses.

I shall also call the whole, consisting of language and the actions into which it is woven, the "language-game."

8. Let us now look at an expansion of language (2). Besides the four words "block," "pillar," etc., let it contain a series of words used as the shopkeeper in (I) used the numerals (it can be the series of letters of the alphabet); further, let there be two words, which may as well be "there" and "this" (because this roughly indicates their purpose), that are used in connexion with a pointing gesture; and finally a number of colour samples. A gives an order like: "d—slab—there." At the same time he shews the assistant a colour sample, and when he says "there" he points to a place on the building site. From the stock of slabs B takes one for each letter of the alphabet up to "d," of the same colour as the sample, and brings them to the place indicated by A.— On other occasions A gives the order "this—there." At "this" he points to a building stone. And so on.

9. When a child learns this language, it has to learn the series of 'numerals' a, b, c, . . . by heart. And it has to learn their use.—Will this training include ostensive teaching of the words?—Well, people will, for example, point to slabs and count: "a, b, c slabs."—Something more like the ostensive teaching of the words "block," "pillar," etc. would be the ostensive teaching of numerals that serve not to count but to refer to groups of objects that can be taken in at a glance. Children do learn the use of the first five or six cardinal numerals in this way.

Are "there" and "this" also taught ostensively?—Imagine how one might perhaps teach their use. One will point to places and things—but in this case the pointing occurs in the *use* of the words too and not merely in learning the use.—

10. Now what do the words of this language *signify?*—What is supposed to shew what they signify, if not the kind of use they have? And we have already described that. So we are asking for the expression "This word signifies *this*" to be made a part of the description. In other words the description ought to take the form: "The word . . . . signifies . . . . ."

Of course, one can reduce the description of the use of the word "slab" to the statement that this word signifies this object. This will be done when, for example, it is merely a matter of removing the mistaken idea that the word "slab" refers to the shape of building-stone that we in fact call a "block"—but the kind of *'referring'* this is, that is to say the use of these words for the rest, is already known.

Equally one can say that the signs "a," "b," etc. signify numbers; when for example this removes the mistaken idea that "a," "b," "c," play the part actually played in language by "block," "slab," "pillar." And one can also say that "c" means this number and not that one; when for example this serves to explain that the letters are to be used in the order a, b, c, d, etc. and not in the order a, b, d, c.

But assimilating the descriptions of the uses of words in this way cannot make the uses themselves any more like one another. For, as we see, they are absolutely unlike.

11. Think of the tools in a toolbox: there is a hammer, pliers, a saw, a screwdriver, a rule, a glue-pot, glue, nails and screws.—The functions of words are as diverse as the functions of these objects. (And in both cases there are similarities.)

Of course, what confuses us is the uniform appearance of words when we hear them spoken or meet them in script and print. For their *application* is not presented to us so clearly. Especially when we are doing philosophy!

12. It is like looking into the cabin of a locomotive. We see handles all looking more or less alike. (Naturally, since they are all supposed to be handled.) But one is the handle of a crank which can be moved continuously (it regulates the opening of a valve); another is the handle of a switch, which has only two effective positions, it is either off or on; a third is the handle of a brake-lever, the harder one pulls on it, the harder it brakes; a fourth, the handle of a pump: it has an effect only so long as it is moved to and fro.

13. When we say: "Every word in language signifies something" we have so far said *nothing whatever;* unless we have explained exactly what distinction we wish to make. (It might be, of course, that we wanted to distinguish the words of language (8) from words 'without meaning' such as occur in Lewis Carroll's poems, or words like "Lilliburlero" in songs.)

14. Imagine someone's saying: "*All* tools serve to modify something. Thus the hammer modifies the position of the nail, the saw the shape of the board, and so on."— And what is modified by the rule, the glue-pot, the nails?—"Our knowledge of a thing's length, the temperature of the glue, and the solidity of the box." Would anything be gained by this assimilation of expressions?—

15. The word "to signify" is perhaps used in the most straightforward way when the object signified is marked with the sign. Suppose that the tools A uses in building bear certain marks. When A shews his assistant such a mark, he brings the tool that has that mark on it.

It is in this and more or less similar ways that a name means and is given to a thing.—It will often prove useful in philosophy to say to ourselves: naming something is like attaching a label to a thing.

16. What about the colour samples that A shews to B: are they part of the *language?* Well, it is as you please. They do not belong among the words; yet when I say to someone: "Pronounce the word 'the,' " you will count the second "the" as part of the sentence. Yet it has a role just like that of a colour-sample in language-game (8); that is, it is a sample of what the other is meant to say.

It is most natural, and causes least confusion, to reckon the samples among the instruments of the language.

((Remark on the reflexive pronoun "*this* sentence."))

17. It will be possible to say: In language (8) we have different kinds *of word*. For the functions of the word "slab" and the word "block" are more alike than those of "slab" and "d." But how we group words into kinds will depend on the aim of the classification,—and on our own inclination.

Think of the different points of view from which one can classify tools or chessmen.

18. Do not be troubled by the fact that languages (2) and (8) consist only of orders. If you want to say that this shews them to be incomplete, ask yourself whether our language is complete;—whether it was so before the symbolism of chemistry and the notation of the infinitesimal calculus were incorporated in it; for these are, so to speak, suburbs of our language. (And how many houses or streets does it take before a town begins to be a town?) Our language can be seen as an ancient city: a maze of little streets and squares, of old and new houses, and of houses with additions from various periods; and this surrounded by a multitude of new boroughs with straight regular streets and uniform houses.

19. It is easy to imagine a language consisting only of orders and reports in battle.—Or a language consisting only of questions and expressions for answering yes and no. And innumerable others.—And to imagine a language means to imagine a form of life.

But what about this: is the call "Slab!" in example (2) a sentence or a word?—If a word, surely it has not the same meaning as the like-sounding word of our ordinary language, for in ¶2 it is a call. But if a sentence, it is surely not the elliptical sentence: "Slab!" of our language. As far as the first question goes you can call "Slab!" a word and also a sentence; perhaps it could be appropriately called a 'degenerate sentence' (as one speaks of a degenerate hyperbola); in fact it is our 'elliptical' sentence.—But that is surely only a shortened form of the sentence "Bring me a slab," and there is no such sentence in example (2).—But why should I not on the contrary have called the sentence "Bring me a slab" a *lengthening* of the sentence "Slab!"?—Because if you shout "Slab!" you really mean: "Bring me a slab."—But how do you do this: how do you *mean that* while you say "Slab!"? Do you say the unshortened sentence to yourself? And why should I translate the call "Slab!" into a different expression in order to say what someone means by it? And if they mean the same thing—why should I not say: "When he says 'Slab!' he means 'Slab!' "? Again, if you can mean "Bring me the slab," why should you not be able to mean "Slab!"? But when I call "Slab!," then what I want is, *that he should bring me a slab!*—Certainly, but does 'wanting this' consist in thinking in some form or other a different sentence from the one you utter?—

20. But now it looks as if when someone says "Bring me a slab" he could mean this expression as *one* long word corresponding to the single word "Slab!" Then can one mean it sometimes as one word and sometimes as four? And how does one usually mean it? I think we shall be inclined to say: we mean the sentence as four words when we use it in contrast with other sentences such as "*Hand* me a slab," "Bring *him* a slab," "Bring *two* slabs," etc.; that is, in contrast with sentences containing the separate words of our command in other combinations.—But what does using one sentence in contrast with others consist in? Do the others, perhaps, hover before one's mind? *All* of them? And *while* one is saying the one sentence, or before, or afterwards?—No. Even if such an explanation rather tempts us, we need only think for a moment of what actually hap-

pens in order to see that we are going astray here. We say that we use the command in contrast with other sentences because *our language* contains the possibility of those other sentences. Someone who did not understand our language, a foreigner, who had fairly often heard someone giving the order: "Bring me a slab!," might believe that this whole series of sounds was one word corresponding perhaps to the word for "building-stone" in his language. If he himself had then given this order perhaps he would have pronounced it differently, and we should say: he pronounces it so oddly because he takes it for a *single* word.—But then, is there not also something different going on in him when he pronounces it,—something corresponding to the fact that he conceives the sentence as a *single* word?—Either the same thing may go on in him, or something different. For what goes on in you when you give such an order? Are you conscious of its consisting of four words *while* you are uttering it? Of course you have a *mastery* of this language—which contains those other sentences as well—but is this having a mastery something that *happens* while you are uttering the sentence?—And I have admitted that the foreigner will probably pronounce a sentence differently if he conceives it differently; but what we call his wrong conception *need* not lie in anything that accompanies the utterance of the command.

The sentence is 'elliptical', not because it leaves out something that we think when we utter it, but because it is shortened—in comparison with a particular paradigm of our grammar.—Of course one might object here: "You grant that the shortened and the unshortened sentence have the same sense.—What is this sense, then? Isn't there a verbal expression for this sense?" But doesn't the fact that sentences have the same sense consist in their having the same *use?*—(In Russian one says "stone red" instead of "the stone is red"; do they feel the copula to be missing in the sense, or attach it in *thought?*)

21.   Imagine a language-game in which A asks and B reports the number of slabs or blocks in a pile, or the colours and shapes of the building-stones that are stacked in such-and-such a place.—Such a report might run: "Five slabs." Now what is the difference between the report or statement "Five slabs" and the order "Five slabs!"?—Well, it is the part which uttering these words plays in the language-game. No doubt the tone of voice and the look with which they are uttered, and much else besides, will also be different. But we could also imagine the tone's being the same—for an order and a report can be spoken in a *variety* of tones of voice and with various expressions of face—the difference being only in the application. (Of course, we might use the words "statement" and "command" to stand for grammatical forms of sentence and intonations; we do in fact call "Isn't the weather glorious to-day?" a question, although it is used as a statement.) We could imagine a language in which *all* statements had the form and tone of rhetorical questions; or every command the form of the question "Would you like to . . . ?." Perhaps it will then be said: "What he says has the form of a question but is really a command,"—that is, has the function of a command in the technique of using the language. (Similarly one says "You will do this" not as a prophecy but as a command. What makes it the one or the other?)

22.   Frege's idea that every assertion contains an assumption, which is the thing that is asserted, really rests on the possibility found in our language of writing every statement in the form: "It is asserted that such-and-such is the case."—But "that such-and-such is the case" is not a sentence in our language—so far it is not a *move* in the language-game. And if I write, not "It is asserted that . . . .," but "It is asserted: such-and-such is the case," the words "It is asserted" simply become superfluous.

We might very well also write every statement in the form of a question followed by a "Yes"; for instance: "Is it raining? Yes!" Would this shew that every statement contained a question?

Of course we have the right to use an assertion sign in contrast with a question-mark, for example, or if we want to distinguish an assertion from a fiction or a supposition. It is only a mistake if one thinks that the assertion consists of two actions, entertaining and asserting (assigning the truth-value, or something of the kind), and that in performing these actions we follow the propositional sign roughly as we sing from the musical score. Reading the written sentence loud or soft is indeed comparable with singing from a musical score, but *'meaning'* (thinking) the sentence that is read is not.

Frege's assertion sign marks the *beginning of the sentence*. Thus its function is like that of the full-stop. It distinguishes the whole period from a clause *within* the period. If I hear someone say "it's raining" but do not know whether I have heard the beginning and end of the period, so far this sentence does not serve to tell me anything.

23. But how many kinds of sentence are there? Say assertion, question, and command?—There are *countless* kinds: countless different kinds of use of what we call "symbols," "words," "sentences." And this multiplicity is not something fixed, given once for all; but new types of language, new language-games, as we may say, come into existence, and others become obsolete and get forgotten. (We can get a *rough picture* of this from the changes in mathematics.)

Here the term "language-*game*" is meant to bring into prominence the fact that the *speaking* of language is part of an activity, or of a form of life.

Review the multiplicity of language-games in the following examples, and in others:

> Giving orders, and obeying them—
> Describing the appearance of an object, or giving its measurements—
> Constructing an object from a description (a drawing)—
> Reporting an event—
> Speculating about an event—
> Forming and testing a hypothesis—
> Presenting the results of an experiment in tables and diagrams—
> Making up a story; and reading it—
> Play-acting—
> Singing catches—
> Guessing riddles—
> Making a joke; telling it—
> Solving a problem in practical arithmetic—
> Translating from one language into another—
> Asking, thanking, cursing, greeting, praying.

Imagine a picture representing a boxer in a particular stance. Now, this picture can be used to tell someone how he should stand, should hold himself; or how he should not hold himself; or how a particular man did stand in such-and-such a place; and so on. One might (using the language of chemistry) call this picture a proposition-radical. This will be how Frege thought of the "assumption." [Note added by Wittgenstein]

—It is interesting to compare the multiplicity of the tools in language and of the ways they are used, the multiplicity of kinds of word and sentence, with what logicians have said about the structure of language. (Including the author of the *Tractatus Logico-Philosophicus*.)

24. If you do not keep the multiplicity of language-games in view you will per-haps be inclined to ask questions like: "What is a question?"—Is it the statement that I do not know such-and-such, or the statement that I wish the other person would tell me . . . .? Or is it the description of my mental state of uncertainty?—And is the cry "Help!" such a description?

Think how many different kinds of thing are called "description": description of a body's position by means of its co-ordinates; description of a facial expression; de-scription of a sensation of touch; of a mood.

Of course it is possible to substitute the form of statement or description for the usual form of question: "I want to know whether . . . ." or "I am in doubt whether . . . ."—but this does not bring the different language-games any closer to-gether.

The significance of such possibilities of transformation, for example of turning all statements into sentences beginning "I think" or "I believe" (and thus, as it were, into descriptions of *my* inner life) will become clearer in another place. (Solipsism.)

25. It is sometimes said that animals do not talk because they lack the mental ca-pacity. And this means: "they do not think, and that is why they do not talk." But—they simply do not talk. Or to put it better: they do not use language—if we except the most primitive forms of language.—Commanding, questioning, recounting, chatting, are as much a part of our natural history as walking, eating, drinking, playing.

26. One thinks that learning language consists in giving names to objects. Viz., to human beings, to shapes, to colours, to pains, to moods, to numbers, etc. To repeat—naming is something like attaching a label to a thing. One can say that this is prepara-tory to the use of a word. But *what* is it a preparation *for?*

27. "We name things and then we can talk about them: can refer to them in talk."—As if what we did next were given with the mere act of naming. As if there were only one thing called "talking about a thing." Whereas in fact we do the most various things with our sentences. Think of exclamations alone, with their completely different functions.

Water!
Away!
Ow!
Help!
Fine!
No!

Are you inclined still to call these words "names of objects"?

In languages (2) and (8) there was no such thing as asking something's name. This, with its correlate, ostensive definition, is, we might say, a language-game on its own. That is really to say: we are brought up, trained, to ask: "What is that called?"—

upon which the name is given. And there is also a language-game of inventing a name for something, and hence of saying, "This is . . . ." and then using the new name. (Thus, for example, children give names to their dolls and then talk about them and to them. Think in this connexion how singular is the use of a person's name to *call* him!)

* * *

43. For a *large* class of cases—though not for all—in which we employ the word "meaning" it can be defined thus: the meaning of a word is its use in the language.

And the *meaning* of a name is sometimes explained by pointing to its *bearer*.

44. We said that the sentence "Excalibur has a sharp blade" made sense even when Excalibur was broken in pieces. Now this is so because in this language-game a name is also used in the absence of its bearer. But we can imagine a language-game with names (that is, with signs which we should certainly include among names) in which they are used only in the presence of the bearer; and so could *always* be replaced by a demonstrative pronoun and the gesture of pointing.

45. The demonstrative "this" can never be without a bearer. It might be said: "so long as there is a *this,* the word 'this' has a meaning too, whether *this* is simple or complex." But that does not make the word into a name. On the contrary: for a name is not used with, but only explained by means of, the gesture of pointing.

46. What lies behind the idea that names really signify simples?—

Socrates says in the Theaetetus: "If I make no mistake, I have heard some people say this: there is no definition of the primary elements—so to speak—out of which we and everything else are composed; for everything that exists in its own right can only be *named,* no other determination is possible, neither that it *is* nor that it *is not.* . . . . But what exists in its own right has to be . . . . . named without any other determination. In consequence it is impossible to give an account of any primary element; for it, nothing is possible but the bare name; its name is all it has. But just as what consists of these primary elements is itself complex, so the names of the elements become descriptive language by being compounded together. For the essence of speech is the composition of names."

Both Russell's 'individuals' and my 'objects' *(Tractatus Logico-Philosophicus)* were such primary elements.

47. But what are the simple constituent parts of which reality is composed?— What are the simple constituent parts of a chair?—The bits of wood of which it is made? Or the molecules, or the atoms?—"Simple" means: not composite. And here the point is: in what sense 'composite'? It makes no sense at all to speak absolutely of the 'simple parts of a chair.'

Again: Does my visual image of this tree, of this chair, consist of parts? And what are its simple component parts? Multi-colouredness is one kind of complexity; another is, for example, that of a broken outline composed of straight bits. And a curve can be said to be composed of an ascending and a descending segment.

If I tell someone without any further explanation: "What I see before me now is composite," he will have the right to ask: "What do you mean by 'composite'? For there are all sorts of things that that can mean!"—The question "Is what you see composite?" makes good sense if it is already established what kind of complexity—that is, which particular use of the word—is in question. If it had been laid down that the visual image of a tree was to be called "composite" if one saw not just a single trunk, but also branches, then the question "Is the visual image of this tree simple or composite?," and the question "What are its simple component parts?," would have a clear sense—a clear use. And of course the answer to the second question is not "The branches" (that would be an answer to the *grammatical* question: "What are here called 'simple component parts'?") but rather a description of the individual branches.

But isn't a chessboard, for instance, obviously, and absolutely, composite?—You are probably thinking of the composition out of thirty-two white and thirty-two black squares. But could we not also say, for instance, that it was composed of the colours black and white and the schema of squares? And if there are quite different ways of looking at it, do you still want to say that the chessboard is absolutely 'composite'?— Asking "Is this object composite?" *outside* a particular language-game is like what a boy once did, who had to say whether the verbs in certain sentences were in the active or passive voice, and who racked his brains over the question whether the verb "to sleep" meant something active or passive.

We use the word "composite" (and therefore the word "simple") in an enormous number of different and differently related ways. (Is the colour of a square on a chessboard simple, or does it consist of pure white and pure yellow? And is white simple, or does it consist of the colours of the rainbow?—Is this length of 2 cm. simple, or does it consist of two parts, each 1 cm. long? But why not of one bit 3 cm. long, and one bit 1 cm. long measured in the opposite direction?)

To the *philosophical* question: "Is the visual image of this tree composite, and what are its component parts?" the correct answer is: "That depends on what you understand by 'composite'." (And that is of course not an answer but a rejection of the question.)

*   *   *

65. Here we come up against the great question that lies behind all these considerations.—For someone might object against me: "You take the easy way out! You talk about all sorts of language-games, but have nowhere said what the essence of a language-game, and hence of language, is: what is common to all these activities, and what makes them into language or parts of language. So you let yourself off the very part of the investigation that once gave you yourself most headache, the part about the *general form of propositions* and of language."

And this is true.—Instead of producing something common to all that we call language, I am saying that these phenomena have no one thing in common which makes us use the same word for all,—but that they are *related* to one another in many different ways. And it is because of this relationship, or these relationships, that we call them all "language." I will try to explain this.

66. Consider for example the proceedings that we call "games." I mean board-games, card-games, ball-games, Olympic games, and so on. What is common to them all?—Don't say: "There *must* be something common, or they would not be called 'games'"—but *look and see* whether there is anything common to all.—For if you look at them you will not see something that is common to *all,* but similarities, relationships, and a whole series of them at that. To repeat: don't think, but look!—Look for example at board-games, with their multifarious relationships. Now pass to card-games; here you find many correspondences with the first group, but many common features drop

out, and others appear. When we pass next to ball-games, much that is common is retained, but much is lost.—Are they all 'amusing'? Compare chess with noughts and crosses. Or is there always winning and losing, or competition between players? Think of patience. In ball games there is winning and losing; but when a child throws his ball at the wall and catches it again, this feature has disappeared. Look at the parts played by skill and luck; and at the difference between skill in chess and skill in tennis. Think now of games like ring-a-ring-a-roses; here is the element of amusement, but how many other characteristic features have disappeared! And we can go through the many, many other groups of games in the same way; can see how similarities crop up and disappear.

And the result of this examination is: we see a complicated network of similarities overlapping and criss-crossing: sometimes overall similarities, sometimes similarities of detail.

67. I can think of no better expression to characterize these similarities than "family resemblances"; for the various resemblances between members of a family: build, features, colour of eyes, gait, temperament, etc., etc. overlap and criss-cross in the same way.—And I shall say: "games" form a family.

And for instance the kinds of number form a family in the same way. Why do we call something a "number"? Well, perhaps because it has a—direct—relationship with several things that have hitherto been called number; and this can be said to give it an indirect relationship to other things we call the same name. And we extend our concept of number as in spinning a thread we twist fibre on fibre. And the strength of the thread does not reside in the fact that some one fibre runs through its whole length, but in the overlapping of many fibres.

But if someone wished to say: "There is something common to all these constructions—namely the disjunction of all their common properties"—I should reply: Now you are only playing with words. One might as well say: "Something runs through the whole thread—namely the continuous overlapping of those fibres."

68. "All right: the concept of number is defined for you as the logical sum of these individual interrelated concepts: cardinal numbers, rational numbers, real numbers, etc.; and in the same way the concept of a game as the logical sum of a corresponding set of sub-concepts."—It need not be so. For I *can* give the concept 'number' rigid limits in this way, that is, use the word "number" for a rigidly limited concept, but I can also use it so that the extension of the concept is *not* closed by a frontier. And this is how we do use the word "game." For how is the concept of a game bounded? What still counts as a game and what no longer does? Can you give the boundary? No. You can *draw* one; for none has so far been drawn. (But that never troubled you before when you used the word "game.")

"But then the use of the word is unregulated, the 'game' we play with it is unregulated."—It is not everywhere circumscribed by rules; but no more are there any rules for how high one throws the ball in tennis, or how hard; yet tennis is a game for all that and has rules too.

69. How should we explain to someone what a game is? I imagine that we should describe *games* to him, and we might add: "This *and similar things* are called 'games'." And do we know any more about it ourselves? Is it only other people whom we cannot tell exactly what a game is?—But this is not ignorance. We do not know the boundaries because none have been drawn. To repeat, we can draw a boundary—for a special purpose. Does it take that to make the concept usable? Not at all! (Except for that special

purpose.) No more than it took the definition: 1 pace = 75 cm. to make the measure of length 'one pace' usable. And if you want to say "But still, before that it wasn't an exact measure," then I reply: very well, it was an inexact one.—Though you still owe me a definition of exactness.

70. "But if the concept 'game' is uncircumscribed like that, you don't really know what you mean by a 'game'."—When I give the description: "The ground was quite covered with plants"—do you want to say I don't know what I am talking about until I can give a definition of a plant?

My meaning would be explained by, say, a drawing and the words "The ground looked roughly like this." Perhaps I even say "it looked *exactly* like this."—Then were just *this* grass and *these* leaves there, arranged just like this? No, that is not what it means. And I should not accept any picture as exact in *this* sense.

Someone says to me: "Shew the children a game." I teach them gaming with dice, and the other says "I didn't mean that sort of game." Must the exclusion of the game with dice have come before his mind when he gave me the order?

---

71. One might say that the concept 'game' is a concept with blurred edges.— "But is a blurred concept a concept at all?"—Is an indistinct photograph a picture of a person at all? Is it even always an advantage to replace an indistinct picture by a sharp one? Isn't the indistinct one often exactly what we need?

Frege compares a concept to an area and says that an area with vague boundaries cannot be called an area at all. This presumably means that we cannot do anything with it.—But is it senseless to say: "Stand roughly there"? Suppose that I were standing with someone in a city square and said that. As I say it I do not draw any kind of boundary, but perhaps point with my hand—as if I were indicating a particular *spot*. And this is just how one might explain to someone what a game is. One gives examples and intends them to be taken in a particular way.—I do not, however, mean by this that he is supposed to see in those examples that common thing which I—for some reason—was unable to express; but that he is now to *employ* those examples in a particular way. Here giving examples is not an *indirect* means of explaining—in default of a better. For any general definition can be misunderstood too. The point is that *this* is how we play the game. (I mean the language-game with the word "game.")

*   *   *

241. "So you are saying that human agreement decides what is true and what is false?"—It is what human beings *say* that is true and false; and they agree in the *language* they use. That is not agreement in opinions but in form of life.

*   *   *

257. "What would it be like if human beings shewed no outward signs of pain (did not groan, grimace, etc.)? Then it would be impossible to teach a child the use of the word 'tooth-ache.'"—Well, let's assume the child is a genius and itself invents a name for the sensation!—But then, of course, he couldn't make himself understood when he used the word.—So does he understand the name, without being able to explain its meaning to anyone?—But what does it mean to say that he has 'named his pain'?—How has he

done this naming of pain?! And whatever he did, what was its purpose?—When one says "He gave a name to his sensation" one forgets that a great deal of stage-setting in the language is presupposed if the mere act of naming is to make sense. And when we speak of someone's having given a name to pain, what is presupposed is the existence of the grammar of the word "pain"; it shews the post where the new word is stationed.

258. Let us imagine the following case. I want to keep a diary about the recurrence of a certain sensation. To this end I associate it with the sign "S" and write this sign in a calendar for every day on which I have the sensation. I will remark first of all that a definition of the sign cannot be formulated.—But still I can give myself a kind of ostensive definition.—How? Can I point to the sensation? Not in the ordinary sense. But I speak, or write the sign down, and at the same time I concentrate my attention on the sensation—and so, as it were, point to it inwardly.—But what is this ceremony for? for that is all it seems to be! A definition surely serves to establish the meaning of a sign.—Well, that is done precisely by the concentrating of my attention; for in this way I impress on myself the connexion between the sign and the sensation.—But "I impress it on myself" can only mean: this process brings it about that I remember the connexion *right* in the future. But in the present case I have no criterion of correctness. One would like to say: whatever is going to seem right to me is right. And that only means that here we can't talk about 'right.'

*   *   *

305. "But you surely cannot deny that, for example, in remembering, an inner process takes place."—What gives the impression that we want to deny anything? When one says "Still, an inner process does take place here"—one wants to go on: "After all, you *see* it." And it is this inner process that one means by the word "remembering."—The impression that we wanted to deny something arises from our setting our faces against the picture of the 'inner process.' What we deny is that the picture of the inner process gives us the correct idea of the use of the word "to remember." We say that this picture with its ramifications stands in the way of our seeing the use of the word as it is.

*   *   *

309. What is your aim in philosophy?—To shew the fly the way out of the fly-bottle.

A.J. Ayer
1910–1989

Alfred Jules Ayer was born in London, the only child of immigrant parents. His father, Jules Ayer, was a Swiss-born businessman, and his mother, Reine Citroen Ayer, was a Dutch Jew whose distant cousin had founded the well-known Citroen automobile company. At age seven Ayer was sent to boarding school at Eastbourne and at age twelve he won an academic scholarship to prestigious Eton College. For the next six years he studied the classics, enjoyed the theater, and participated actively in sports (he was quite good at tennis and fantasized about becoming a professional cricket player). During this time he also gave up all religious belief.

In 1928 Ayer won a scholarship in classics to Christ Church College, Oxford. There he studied philosophy as well as Greek and Roman history. He was fascinated by the philosophy of the early Wittgenstein and spent time in Cambridge with the philosopher. After graduation he became a lecturer at Christ Church; but the college had over-hired, and he was given a two-term leave. He used this time to visit Austria, where he met Moritz Schlick and became an enthusiastic member of the "Vienna Circle" of logical positivists. Returning to Oxford full of zeal for the new philosophy, he wrote his most famous book, *Language, Truth, and Logic* (1936). The twenty-six-year-old Ayer immediately became the leading apologist for logical positivism in the English-speaking world.

After five years as a research student at Christ Church and after service in the Welsh Guards during World War II, Ayer became Fellow and Dean of Wadham, Oxford. In 1946 he was elected Grote Professor of Philosophy of Mind and Logic at University College, London. During this time he wrote extensively, modifying some of the brasher statements of his earlier writings. His major work from this period was his theory of knowledge, *The Problem of Knowledge* (1956). In addition to writing, Ayer served as editor of the Pelican Philosophy Series and president of the Aristotelian Society, was an activist in liberal political causes, and appeared as a regular guest on the BBC television program "The Brains Trust." In 1960 he returned to Oxford as Wykeham Professor of Logic. While at Oxford, he also lectured throughout the world. Though obliged to retire from his chair at Oxford at age sixty-seven, Ayer continued to write and teach until his death in 1989.

A year before his death Ayer had a "somewhat agonising but very astonishing experience" when his heart stopped beating for four minutes. In an article entitled "What I Saw When I Was Dead . . .," Ayer described the incident:

> I was confronted by a red light, exceedingly bright, and also very painful, even when I turned away from it. I was aware that this light was responsible for the government of the universe.*

In the same article Ayer made it clear that this event in no way shook his atheistic convictions.

* * *

Logical positivism has its roots in the empiricism of David Hume and the language theory of the early Wittgenstein. Hume had divided all meaningful ideas into two classes—those concerned with "relations of ideas" and those concerned with "matters of fact." The *a priori* propositions of logic and pure mathematics (known as "analytic" propositions) comprise the former class and propositions that depend on observation and experimentation (known as "synthetic") comprise the latter. But metaphysical ideas did not fit either class and hence were considered vacuous or meaningless. Wittgenstein's early *Tractatus* called for a philosophical language stripped of such meaningless statements:

> The correct method in philosophy would really be the following: to say nothing except what can be said, i.e. propositions of natural science—i.e. something that has nothing to do with philosophy—and then, whenever someone else wanted to say something metaphysical, to demonstrate to him that he had failed to give a meaning to certain signs in his propositions. . . . [T]his method would be the only strictly correct one.

Ayer, together with Moritz Schlick and the rest of the Vienna Circle, sought to develop this "correct" philosophy. The members of the circle called themselves "positivists" because they wanted to eliminate all metaphysical pseudo-propositions and to show that only logic, mathematics, and the natural sciences provide genuine knowledge. They were "logical" positivists because they claimed that the

---

*Spectator, 16 July 1988, as quoted in A.J. Ayer, *The Philosophy of A.J. Ayer,* edited by Lewis E. Hahn (LaSalle, IL: Open Court, 1992), p. 48.

logical analysis of supposed metaphysical assertions will not show them to be *false* but rather *meaningless.*

To determine which propositions were meaningful and which were not, logical positivists such as Ayer developed a verification criterion of meaning. In our selection from *Language, Truth, and Logic,* Ayer gives this version of the criterion for synthetic propositions:

> We say that a sentence is factually significant to any given person, if, and only if, he knows how to verify the proposition which it purports to express—that is, if he knows what observations would lead him, under certain conditions, to accept the proposition as being true, or reject it as being false.

Ayer immediately makes three qualifications to this principle. In the first place, he points out that he is only talking about "verifiability in principle." It might not be practically possible for me at this time, for example, to verify or falsify the existence of Tasmanian Devils on the island of Tasmania, but there is nothing in *principle* to keep me from doing so. Second, he distinguishes between "strong" and "weak" verification. A proposition is verifiable in the strong sense "if, and only if, its truth could be conclusively established in experience." But this "strong" verification would eliminate all general propositions such as "a body tends to expand when it is heated" since such truths cannot be "conclusively" established by a finite number of observations. Instead, Ayer opted for a weaker sense of verification: "Would any observations be relevant to the determination of its truth or falsehood?" Finally, Ayer made it clear that his criterion applies only to *synthetic* propositions. The propositions of philosophy, including the verification criterion itself, are "held to be linguistically necessary, and so analytic."

This last qualification points to a problem that was to vex the logical positivists: How does one verify the verification criterion? What observations would lead one to accept the proposition previously given ("We say that a sentence is factually significant . . .") as true, or reject it as false? In the *Tractatus,* Wittgenstein had noticed this problem with self-reference and concluded that the propositions that made up the *Tractatus* itself were "nonsense"—but that one could still use them to "see the world aright." Ayer sought to avoid the problem by claiming that the verification criterion was analytic, a mere tautology, and so not subject to the criterion. But if the criterion is only a tautology it would tell us nothing about the world. How could it then function as a test of meaning and what prevents it from being completely arbitrary?

In his later writings Ayer tried different ways of grounding the verification criterion, as did other positivists, but none of these attempts has satisfied contemporary philosophers. Partially as a result of the problems involved in developing a credible verification criterion, logical positivism no longer exists as a movement. But the spirit of hard-nosed positivistic empiricism is still with us.

*   *   *

For works on logical positivism, see R.W. Ashby, "Logical Positivism," in D.J. O'Connor, ed., *A Critical History of Western Philosophy* (New York: The Free Press, 1964); Peter Achinstein and Stephen F. Barker, *The Legacy of Logical Positivism* (Baltimore: The Johns Hopkins University Press, 1969); Barry R. Gross, *Analytic Philosophy: An Historical Introduction* (New York: Pegasus, 1970);

Frederick C. Copleston, *Contemporary Philosophy: Studies of Logical Positivism and Existentialism* (New York: Barnes & Noble, 1979); and Oswald Hanfling, *Logical Positivism* (New York: Columbia University Press, 1981). For a collection of primary source readings, see Oswald Hanfling, ed., *Essential Readings in Logical Positivism* (Oxford: Blackwell, 1981).

A good text for specific aspects of Ayer's thought is A.J. Ayer, *The Philosophy of A.J. Ayer,* edited by Lewis E. Hahn (La Salle, IL: Open Court, 1992), another volume in the outstanding Library of Living Philosophers Series. John Foster, *Ayer* (London: Routledge, 1985), gives a detailed discussion of Ayer's ideas, while Graham Macdonald and Crispin Wright, eds., *Fact, Science, and Morality: Essays on A.J. Ayer's "Language, Truth, and Logic"* (New York: Blackwell, 1987), and Barry Gower, ed., *Logical Positivism in Perspective: Essays on "Language, Truth and Logic"* (London: Croom Helm, 1987), gather essays on Ayer's most important work. A general collection of essays is A. Phillips Griffiths, ed., *A.J. Ayer Memorial Essays* (Cambridge: Cambridge University Press, 1991).

LANGUAGE, TRUTH AND LOGIC
(in part)

PREFACE TO FIRST EDITION

The views which are put forward in this treatise derive from the doctrines of Bertrand Russell and Wittgenstein, which are themselves the logical outcome of the empiricism of Berkeley and David Hume. Like Hume, I divide all genuine propositions into two classes: those which, in his terminology, concern "relations of ideas," and those which concern "matters of fact." The former class comprises the *a priori* propositions of logic and pure mathematics, and these I allow to be necessary and certain only because they are analytic. That is, I maintain that the reason why these propositions cannot be confuted in experience is that they do not make any assertion about the empirical world, but simply record our determination to use symbols in a certain fashion. Propositions concerning empirical matters of fact, on the other hand, I hold to be hypotheses, which can be probable but never certain. And in giving an account of the method of their validation I claim also to have explained the nature of truth.

To test whether a sentence expresses a genuine empirical hypothesis, I adopt what may be called a modified verification principle. For I require of an empirical hypothesis, not indeed that it should be conclusively verifiable, but that some possible sense-experience should be relevant to the determination of its truth or falsehood. If a putative proposition fails to satisfy this principle, and is not a tautology, then I hold that it is metaphysical, and that, being metaphysical, it is neither true nor false but literally senseless. It will be found that much of what ordinarily passes for philosophy is metaphysical according to this criterion, and, in particular, that it can not be significantly as-

A.J. Ayer, *Language, Truth and Logic.* New York: Dover Publications, 1936. Reprinted by permission.

serted that there is a non-empirical world of values, or that men have immortal souls, or that there is a transcendent God.

As for the propositions of philosophy themselves, they are held to be linguistically necessary, and so analytic. And with regard to the relationship of philosophy and empirical science, it is shown that the philosopher is not in a position to furnish speculative truths, which would, as it were, compete with the hypotheses of science, nor yet to pass *a priori* judgements upon the validity of scientific theories, but that his function is to clarify the propositions of science by exhibiting their logical relationships, and by defining the symbols which occur in them. Consequently I maintain that there is nothing in the nature of philosophy to warrant the existence of conflicting philosophical "schools." And I attempt to substantiate this by providing a definitive solution of the problems which have been the chief sources of controversy between philosophers in the past.

The view that philosophizing is an activity of analysis is associated in England with the work of G.E. Moore and his disciples. But while I have learned a great deal from Professor Moore, I have reason to believe that he and his followers are not prepared to adopt such a thoroughgoing phenomenalism as I do, and that they take a rather different view of the nature of philosophical analysis. The philosophers with whom I am in the closest agreement are those who compose the "Viennese circle," under the leadership of Moritz Schlick, and are commonly known as logical positivists. And of these I owe most to Rudolf Carnap. Further, I wish to acknowledge my indebtedness to Gilbert Ryle, my original tutor in philosophy, and to Isaiah Berlin, who have discussed with me every point in the argument of this treatise, and made many valuable suggestions, although they both disagree with much of what I assert. . . .

CHAPTER 1: THE ELIMINATION OF METAPHYSICS

The traditional disputes of philosophers are, for the most part, as unwarranted as they are unfruitful. The surest way to end them is to establish beyond question what should be the purpose and method of a philosophical enquiry. And this is by no means so difficult a task as the history of philosophy would lead one to suppose. For if there are any questions which science leaves it to philosophy to answer, a straightforward process of elimination must lead to their discovery.

We may begin by criticising the metaphysical thesis that philosophy affords us knowledge of a reality transcending the world of science and common sense. Later on, when we come to define metaphysics and account for its existence, we shall find that it is possible to be a metaphysician without believing in a transcendent reality; for we shall see that many metaphysical utterances are due to the commission of logical errors, rather than to a conscious desire on the part of their authors to go beyond the limits of experience. But it is convenient for us to take the case of those who believe that it is possible to have knowledge of a transcendent reality as a starting-point for our discussion. The arguments which we use to refute them will subsequently be found to apply to the whole of metaphysics.

One way of attacking a metaphysician who claimed to have knowledge of a reality which transcended the phenomenal world would be to enquire from what premises his propositions were deduced. Must he not begin, as other men do, with the evidence of his senses? And if so, what valid process of reasoning can possibly lead him to the conception of a transcendent reality? Surely from empirical premises nothing whatsoever concerning the properties, or even the existence, of anything super-empirical can legitimately be inferred. But this objection would be met by a denial on the part of the metaphysician that his assertions were ultimately based on the evidence of his senses. He would say that he was endowed with a faculty of intellectual intuition which enabled him to know facts that could not be known through sense-experience. And even if it could be shown that he was relying on empirical premises, and that his venture into a non-empirical world was therefore logically unjustified, it would not follow that the assertions which he made concerning this non-empirical world could not be true. For the fact that a conclusion does not follow from its putative premise is not sufficient to show that it is false. Consequently one cannot overthrow a system of transcendent metaphysics merely by criticising the way in which it comes into being. What is required is rather a criticism of the nature of the actual statements which comprise it. And this is the line of argument which we shall, in fact, pursue. For we shall maintain that no statement which refers to a "reality" transcending the limits of all possible sense-experience can possibly have any literal significance; from which it must follow that the labours of those who have striven to describe such a reality have all been devoted to the production of nonsense.

It may be suggested that this is a proposition which has already been proved by Kant. But although Kant also condemned transcendent metaphysics, he did so on different grounds. For he said that the human understanding was so constituted that it lost itself in contradictions when it ventured out beyond the limits of possible experience and attempted to deal with things in themselves. And thus he made the impossibility of a transcendent metaphysic not, as we do, a matter of logic, but a matter of fact. He asserted, not that our minds could not conceivably have had the power of penetrating beyond the phenomenal world, but merely that they were in fact devoid of it. And this leads the critic to ask how, if it is possible to know only what lies within the bounds of sense-experience, the author can be justified in asserting that real things do exist beyond, and how he can tell what are the boundaries beyond which the human understanding may not venture, unless he succeeds in passing them himself. As Wittgenstein says, "in order to draw a limit to thinking, we should have to think both sides of this limit,"* a truth to which Bradley gives a special twist in maintaining that the man who is ready to prove that metaphysics is impossible is a brother metaphysician with a rival theory of his own.**

Whatever force these objections may have against the Kantian doctrine, they have none whatsoever against the thesis that I am about to set forth. It cannot here be said that the author is himself overstepping the barrier he maintains to be impassable. For the fruitlessness of attempting to transcend the limits of possible sense-experience will be deduced, not from a psychological hypothesis concerning the actual constitution of the human mind, but from the rule which determines the literal significance of language. Our charge against the metaphysician is not that he attempts to employ the understanding in a field where it cannot profitably venture, but that he produces sentences which fail to conform to the conditions under which alone a sentence can be literally significant. Nor are we ourselves obliged to talk nonsense in order to show that all sentences of a certain type are necessarily devoid of literal significance. We need only formulate the criterion which enables us to test whether a sentence expresses a genuine proposition about a matter of fact, and then point out that the sentences under consideration fail

---

Tractatus Logico-Philosophicus, Preface.
**Bradley, *Appearance and Reality,* 2nd ed., p. 1.

to satisfy it. And this we shall now proceed to do. We shall first of all formulate the criterion in somewhat vague terms, and then give the explanations which are necessary to render it precise.

The criterion which we use to test the genuineness of apparent statements of fact is the criterion of verifiability. We say that a sentence is factually significant to any given person, if, and only if, he knows how to verify the proposition which it purports to express—that is, if he knows what observations would lead him, under certain conditions, to accept the proposition as being true, or reject it as being false. If, on the other hand, the putative proposition is of such a character that the assumption of its truth, or falsehood, is consistent with any assumption whatsoever concerning the nature of his future experience, then, as far as he is concerned, it is, if not a tautology, a mere pseudo-proposition. The sentence expressing it may be emotionally significant to him; but it is not literally significant. And with regard to questions the procedure is the same. We enquire in every case what observations would lead us to answer the question, one way or the other; and, if none can be discovered, we must conclude that the sentence under consideration does not, as far as we are concerned, express a genuine question, however strongly its grammatical appearance may suggest that it does.

As the adoption of this procedure is an essential factor in the argument of this book, it needs to be examined in detail.

In the first place, it is necessary to draw a distinction between practical verifiability, and verifiability in principle. Plainly we all understand, in many cases believe, propositions which we have not in fact taken steps to verify. Many of these are propositions which we could verify if we took enough trouble. But there remain a number of significant propositions, concerning matters of fact, which we could not verify even if we chose; simply because we lack the practical means of placing ourselves in the situation where the relevant observations could be made. A simple and familiar example of such a proposition is the proposition that there are mountains on the farther side of the moon. No rocket has yet been invented which would enable me to go and look at the farther side of the moon, so that I am unable to decide the matter by actual observation. But I do know what observations would decide it for me, if, as is theoretically conceivable, I were once in a position to make them. And therefore I say that the proposition is verifiable in principle, if not in practice, and is accordingly significant. On the other hand, such a metaphysical pseudo-proposition as "the Absolute enters into, but is itself incapable of, evolution and progress," is not even in principle verifiable. For one cannot conceive of an observation which would enable one to determine whether the Absolute did, or did not, enter into evolution and progress. Of course it is possible that the author of such a remark is using English words in a way in which they are not commonly used by English-speaking people, and that he does, in fact, intend to assert something which could be empirically verified. But until he makes us understand how the proposition that he wishes to express would be verified, he fails to communicate anything to us. And if he admits, as I think the author of the remark in question would have admitted, that his words were not intended to express either a tautology or a proposition which was capable, at least in principle, of being verified, then it follows that he has made an utterance which has no literal significance even for himself.

A further distinction which we must make is the distinction between the "strong" and the "weak" sense of the term "verifiable." A proposition is said to be verifiable, in the strong sense of the term, if, and only if, its truth could be conclusively established in experience. But it is verifiable, in the weak sense, if it is possible for experience to render it probable. In which sense are we using the term when we say that a putative proposition is genuine only if it is verifiable?

It seems to me that if we adopt conclusive verifiability as our criterion of signifi-cance, as some positivists have proposed, our argument will prove too much. Consider, for example, the case of general propositions of law—such propositions, namely, as "arsenic is poisonous"; "all men are mortal"; "a body tends to expand when it is heated." It is of the very nature of these propositions that their truth cannot be estab-lished with certainty by any finite series of observations. But if it is recognised that such general propositions of law are designed to cover an infinite number of cases, then it must be admitted that they cannot, even in principle, be verified conclusively. And then, if we adopt conclusive verifiability as our criterion of significance, we are logically obliged to treat these general propositions of law in the same fashion as we treat the statements of the metaphysician.

In face of this difficulty, some positivists have adopted the heroic course of say-ing that these general propositions are indeed pieces of nonsense, albeit an essentially important type of nonsense. But here the introduction of the term "important" is simply an attempt to hedge. It serves only to mark the authors' recognition that their view is somewhat too paradoxical, without in any way removing the paradox. Besides, the dif-ficulty is not confined to the case of general propositions of law, though it is there re-vealed most plainly. It is hardly less obvious in the case of propositions about the re-mote past. For it must surely be admitted that, however strong the evidence in favour of historical statements may be, their truth can never become more than highly probable. And to maintain that they also constituted an important, or unimportant, type of non-sense would be unplausible, to say the very least. Indeed, it will be our contention that no proposition, other than a tautology, can possibly be anything more than a probable hypothesis. And if this is correct, the principle that a sentence can be factually signifi-cant only if it expresses what is conclusively verifiable is self-stultifying as a criterion of significance. For it leads to the conclusion that it is impossible to make a significant statement of fact at all.

Nor can we accept the suggestion that a sentence should be allowed to be factu-ally significant if, and only if, it expresses something which is definitely confutable by experience. Those who adopt this course assume that, although no finite series of obser-vations is ever sufficient to establish the truth of a hypothesis beyond all possibility of doubt, there are crucial cases in which a single observation, or series of observations, can definitely confute it. But, as we shall show later on, this assumption is false. A hy-pothesis cannot be conclusively confuted any more than it can be conclusively verified. For when we take the occurrence of certain observations as proof that a given hypothe-sis is false, we presuppose the existence of certain conditions. And though, in any given case, it may be extremely improbable that this assumption is false, it is not logically im-possible. We shall see that there need be no self-contradiction in holding that some of the relevant circumstances are other than we have taken them to be, and consequently that the hypothesis has not really broken down. And if it is not the case that any hy-pothesis can be definitely confuted, we cannot hold that the genuineness of a proposi-tion depends on the possibility of its definite confutation.

Accordingly, we fall back on the weaker sense of verification. We say that the question that must be asked about any putative statement of fact is not, Would any ob-servations make its truth or falsehood logically certain? but simply, Would any obser-vations be relevant to the determination of its truth or falsehood? And it is only if a neg-ative answer is given to this second question that we conclude that the statement under consideration is nonsensical.

To make our position clearer, we may formulate it in another way. Let us call a proposition which records an actual or possible observation an experiential proposition.

Then we may say that it is the mark of a genuine factual proposition, not that it should be equivalent to an experiential proposition, or any finite number of experiential propositions, but simply that some experiential propositions can be deduced from it in conjunction with certain other premises without being deducible from those other premises alone.

This criterion seems liberal enough. In contrast to the principle of conclusive verifiability, it clearly does not deny significance to general propositions or to propositions about the past. Let us see what kinds of assertion it rules out.

A good example of the kind of utterance that is condemned by our criterion as being not even false but nonsensical would be the assertion that the world of sense-experience was altogether unreal. It must, of course, be admitted that our senses do sometimes deceive us. We may, as the result of having certain sensations, expect certain other sensations to be obtainable which are, in fact, not obtainable. But, in all such cases, it is further sense-experience that informs us of the mistakes that arise out of sense-experience. We say that the senses sometimes deceive us, just because the expectations to which our sense-experiences give rise do not always accord with what we subsequently experience. That is, we rely on our senses to substantiate or confute the judgements which are based on our sensations. And therefore the fact that our perceptual judgements are sometimes found to be erroneous has not the slightest tendency to show that the world of sense-experience is unreal. And, indeed, it is plain that no conceivable observation, or series of observations, could have any tendency to show that the world revealed to us by sense-experience was unreal. Consequently, anyone who condemns the sensible world as a world of mere appearance, as opposed to reality, is saying something which, according to our criterion of significance, is literally nonsensical.

An example of a controversy which the application of our criterion obliges us to condemn as fictitious is provided by those who dispute concerning the number of substances that there are in the world. For it is admitted both by monists, who maintain that reality is one substance, and by pluralists, who maintain that reality is many, that it is impossible to imagine any empirical situation which would be relevant to the solution of their dispute. But if we are told that no possible observation could give any probability either to the assertion that reality was one substance or to the assertion that it was many, then we must conclude that neither assertion is significant. We shall see later on that there are genuine logical and empirical questions involved in the dispute between monists and pluralists. But the metaphysical question concerning "substance" is ruled out by our criterion as spurious.

A similar treatment must be accorded to the controversy between realists and idealists, in its metaphysical aspect. A simple illustration, which I have made use of in a similar argument elsewhere, will help to demonstrate this. Let us suppose that a picture is discovered and the suggestion made that it was painted by Goya. There is a definite procedure for dealing with such a question. The experts examine the picture to see in what way it resembles the accredited works of Goya, and to see if it bears any marks which are characteristic of a forgery; they look up contemporary records for evidence of the existence of such a picture, and so on. In the end, they may still disagree, but each one knows what empirical evidence would go to confirm or discredit his opinion. Suppose, now, that these men have studied philosophy, and some of them proceed to maintain that this picture is a set of ideas in the perceiver's mind, or in God's mind, others that it is objectively real. What possible experience could any of them have which would be relevant to the solution of this dispute one way or the other? In the ordinary sense of the term "real," in which it is opposed to "illusory," the reality of the picture is not in doubt. The disputants have satisfied themselves that the picture is real, in this sense, by obtaining a correlated series of sensations of sight and sensations of touch. Is there any similar process by which they could discover whether the picture was real, in the sense in which the term "real" is opposed to "ideal"? Clearly there is none. But, if that is so, the problem is fictitious according to our criterion. This does not mean that the realist-idealist controversy may be dismissed without further ado. For it can legitimately be regarded as a dispute concerning the analysis of existential propositions, and so as involving a logical problem which, as we shall see, can be definitively solved. What we have just shown is that the question at issue between idealists and realists becomes fictitious when, as is often the case, it is given a metaphysical interpretation.

There is no need for us to give further examples of the operation of our criterion of significance. For our object is merely to show that philosophy, as a genuine branch of knowledge, must be distinguished from metaphysics. We are not now concerned with the historical question how much of what has traditionally passed for philosophy is actually metaphysical. We shall, however, point out later on that the majority of the "great philosophers" of the past were not essentially metaphysicians, and thus reassure those who would otherwise be prevented from adopting our criterion by considerations of piety.

As to the validity of the verification principle . . . it will be shown that all propositions which have factual content are empirical hypotheses; and that the function of an empirical hypothesis is to provide a rule for the anticipation of experience. And this means that every empirical hypothesis must be relevant to some actual, or possible, experience, so that a statement which is not relevant to any experience is not an empirical hypothesis, and accordingly has no factual content. But this is precisely what the principle of verifiability asserts.

It should be mentioned here that the fact that the utterances of the metaphysician are nonsensical does not follow simply from the fact that they are devoid of factual content. It follows from that fact, together with the fact that they are not *a priori* propositions. . . . *a priori* propositions, which have always been attractive to philosophers on account of their certainty, owe this certainty to the fact that they are tautologies. We may accordingly define a metaphysical sentence as a sentence which purports to express a genuine proposition, but does, in fact, express neither a tautology nor an empirical hypothesis. And as tautologies and empirical hypotheses form the entire class of significant propositions, we are justified in concluding that all metaphysical assertions are nonsensical. Our next task is to show how they come to be made.

The use of the term "substance," to which we have already referred, provides us with a good example of the way in which metaphysics mostly comes to be written. It happens to be the case that we cannot, in our language, refer to the sensible properties of a thing without introducing a word or phrase which appears to stand for the thing itself as opposed to anything which may be said about it. And, as a result of this, those who are infected by the primitive superstition that to every name a single real entity must correspond assume that it is necessary to distinguish logically between the thing itself and any, or all, of its sensible properties. And so they employ the term "substance" to refer to the thing itself. But from the fact that we happen to employ a single word to refer to a thing, and make that word the grammatical subject of the sentences in which we refer to the sensible appearances of the thing, it does not by any means follow that the thing itself is a "simple entity," or that it cannot be defined in terms of the totality of its appearances. It is true that in talking of "its" appearances we appear to distinguish the thing from the appearances, but that is simply an accident of linguistic usage. Logical analysis shows that what makes these "appearances" the "appearances of" the same thing is not their relationship to an entity other than themselves, but their relationship to one another. The metaphysician fails to see this because he is misled by a superficial grammatical feature of his language.

A simpler and clearer instance of the way in which a consideration of grammar leads to metaphysics is the case of the metaphysical concept of Being. The origin of our temptation to raise questions about Being, which no conceivable experience would enable us to answer, lies in the fact that, in our language, sentences which express existential propositions and sentences which express attributive propositions may be of the same grammatical form. For instance, the sentences "Martyrs exist" and "Martyrs suffer" both consist of a noun followed by an intransitive verb, and the fact that they have grammatically the same appearance leads one to assume that they are of the same logical type. It is seen that in the proposition "Martyrs suffer," the members of a certain species are credited with a certain attribute, and it is sometimes assumed that the same thing is true of such a proposition as "Martyrs exist." If this were actually the case, it would, indeed, be as legitimate to speculate about the Being of martyrs as it is to speculate about their suffering. But, as Kant pointed out, existence is not an attribute. For, when we ascribe an attribute to a thing, we covertly assert that it exists: so that if existence were itself an attribute, it would follow that all positive existential propositions were tautologies, and all negative existential propositions self-contradictory; and this is not the case. So that those who raise questions about Being which are based on the assumption that existence is an attribute are guilty of following grammar beyond the boundaries of sense.

A similar mistake has been made in connection with such propositions as "Unicorns are fictitious." Here again the fact that there is a superficial grammatical resemblance between the English sentences "Dogs are faithful" and "Unicorns are fictitious," and between the corresponding sentences in other languages, creates the assumption that they are of the same logical type. Dogs must exist in order to have the property of being faithful, and so it is held that unless unicorns in some way existed they could not have the property of being fictitious. But, as it is plainly self-contradictory to say that fictitious objects exist, the device is adopted of saying that they are real in some non-empirical sense—that they have a mode of real being which is different from the mode of being of existent things. But since there is no way of testing whether an object is real in this sense, as there is for testing whether it is real in the ordinary sense, the assertion that fictitious objects have a special non-empirical mode of real being is devoid of all literal significance. It comes to be made as a result of the assumption that being fictitious is an attribute. And this is a fallacy of the same order as the fallacy of supposing that existence is an attribute, and it can be exposed in the same way.

In general, the postulation of real non-existent entities results from the superstition, just now referred to, that, to every word or phrase that can be the grammatical subject of a sentence, there must somewhere be a real entity corresponding. For as there is no place in the empirical world for many of these "entities," a special non-empirical world is invoked to house them. To this error must be attributed, not only the utterances of a Heidegger, who bases his metaphysics on the assumption that "Nothing" is a name which is used to denote something peculiarly mysterious, but also the prevalence of such problems as those concerning the reality of propositions and universals whose senselessness, though less obvious, is no less complete.

These few examples afford a sufficient indication of the way in which most metaphysical assertions come to be formulated. They show how easy it is to write sentences which are literally nonsensical without seeing that they are nonsensical. And thus we see that the view that a number of the traditional "problems of philosophy" are metaphysical, and consequently fictitious, does not involve any incredible assumptions about the psychology of philosophers.

Among those who recognise that if philosophy is to be accounted a genuine branch of knowledge it must be defined in such a way as to distinguish it from metaphysics, it is fashionable to speak of the metaphysician as a kind of misplaced poet. As his statements have no literal meaning, they are not subject to any criteria of truth or falsehood: but they may still serve to express, or arouse, emotion, and thus be subject to ethical or aesthetic standards. And it is suggested that they may have considerable value, as means of moral inspiration, or even as works of art. In this way, an attempt is made to compensate the metaphysician for his extrusion from philosophy.

I am afraid that this compensation is hardly in accordance with his deserts. The view that the metaphysician is to be reckoned among the poets appears to rest on the assumption that both talk nonsense. But this assumption is false. In the vast majority of cases the sentences which are produced by poets do have literal meaning. The difference between the man who uses language scientifically and the man who uses it emotively is not that the one produces sentences which are incapable of arousing emotion, and the other sentences which have no sense, but that the one is primarily concerned with the expression of true propositions, the other with the creation of a work of art. Thus, if a work of science contains true and important propositions, its value as a work of science will hardly be diminished by the fact that they are inelegantly expressed. And similarly, a work of art is not necessarily the worse for the fact that all the propositions comprising it are literally false. But to say that many literary works are largely composed of falsehoods is not to say that they are composed of pseudo-propositions. It is, in fact, very rare for a literary artist to produce sentences which have no literal meaning. And where this does occur, the sentences are carefully chosen for their rhythm and balance. If the author writes nonsense, it is because he considers it most suitable for bringing about the effects for which his writing is designed.

The metaphysician, on the other hand, does not intend to write nonsense. He lapses into it through being deceived by grammar, or through committing errors of reasoning, such as that which leads to the view that the sensible world is unreal. But it is not the mark of a poet simply to make mistakes of this sort. There are some, indeed, who would see in the fact that the metaphysician's utterances are senseless a reason against the view that they have aesthetic value. And, without going so far as this, we may safely say that it does not constitute a reason for it.

It is true, however, that although the greater part of metaphysics is merely the embodiment of humdrum errors, there remain a number of metaphysical passages which are the work of genuine mystical feeling; and they may more plausibly be held to have moral or aesthetic value. But, as far as we are concerned, the distinction between the kind of metaphysics that is produced by a philosopher who has been duped by grammar, and the kind that is produced by a mystic who is trying to express the inexpressible, is of no great importance: what is important to us is to realise that even the utterances of the metaphysician who is attempting to expound a vision are literally senseless; so that henceforth we may pursue our philosophical researches with as little regard for them as for the more inglorious kind of metaphysics which comes from a failure to understand the workings of our language.

Jean-Paul Sartre
1905–1980

In addition to being one of the leading philosophers of the twentieth century, Jean-Paul Sartre was also an essayist, novelist, playwright, and editor. His name has become synonymous with existentialism, a movement that exploded beyond the boundaries of the academy to enter virtually every area of Western culture. Sartre himself became as famous as the philosophy he taught, and at his death in 1980 almost fifty thousand people accompanied his casket to Paris's Montparnasse Cemetery.

Jean-Paul-Charles-Aymard Sartre was born in Paris, the only child of naval officer Jean-Baptiste Sartre and his wife, Anne-Marie Schweitzer Sartre. Barely a year after his birth, his father died. Jean-Paul and his mother moved in with her parents. Sartre's maternal grandfather, a German-language teacher, had a study filled with books; this room fascinated the young Sartre. He taught himself to read, and by the age of eight he had read such French classics as *Madame Bovary*. While still a boy his devotion to books overwhelmed all other devotions—including that to religion. From about the age of twelve Sartre affirmed that he was a confirmed atheist. He did exceptionally well in his studies, exhibiting a clear independence of mind. One of his teachers noted on his report card: "Excellent student: mind already lively, good at discussing questions, but needs to depend a little less on himself."

In 1924 Sartre enrolled at the prestigious École Normale Supérieure. Over the next four years he studied for the *agrégation* in philosophy (the highest degree except for the doctorate in the French system) but surprisingly failed the written examination on his first attempt. A year later he retook the examination and placed first.

The person who took second in that 1929 examination was his study-partner, Simone de Beauvoir. The same year Sartre suggested to her that they take out "a two-year lease" on each other. Though neither believed in the bourgeois institution of marriage, and each had a variety of lovers, the two remained "companions" for life.

Over the next ten years Sartre served briefly in the army, studied in Berlin, taught at a number of lycées, and began writing. Among his early publications were the philosophical novel *Nausea* (1938) and the collection of short stories *The Wall* (1939).

In 1939 Sartre was called up for active duty by the French army. He was captured by the Germans in less than a year. Released a few months later, he seemed to return to a quiet life of teaching and writing. But Sartre was secretly a member of the French resistance. He was never involved in the armed resistance but worked with the intellectual resistance group "Socialism and Liberty." In 1943 Sartre published his most important philosophical text, *Being and Nothingness,* and three years later his most widely read philosophical work, *Existentialism Is a Humanism.*

After the war Sartre retired from teaching and with Maurice Merleau-Ponty and de Beauvoir founded the influential journal *Les Temps modernes.* In 1964 he was awarded the Nobel Prize for literature but refused to accept it. Together with de Beauvoir, he spent the rest of his life writing and promoting revolutionary po-

Guernica, 1937, by Pablo Picasso (1881–1973). In 1937 the city of Guernica was destroyed by German bombers simply for the purpose of testing their new weapons. Sartre's friend Picasso created this painting to memorialize the innocent sacrifice of the Spanish people. This representation of broken, fragmented pieces of humanity wrung by pain and anxiety captures well the reality of death and violence. Sartre insisted that to live fully one must squarely face such suffering. *(Museo del Prador, Madrid)*

litical causes. Frequently joining students or union workers in demonstrations, Sartre even served as president of the International War Crimes Tribunal, which condemned U.S. intervention in Vietnam. He was attracted to Marxist thought—though he frequently criticized the French Communist party for its inadequacies. The discrepancies between the determinism of Marxist theory and his existentialist emphasis on radical freedom have been the subject of many books. (See the suggested readings.)

Throughout his life, Sartre preferred the pleasures of the café over the joys of the hearth. For years he and de Beauvoir were fixtures at La Coupole, a restaurant on the Left Bank of Paris frequented by artists. But eventually his health deteriorated, exacerbated by his frequent use of amphetamines, and he was forced to retire to his apartment. After an agonizingly slow decline, Sartre died in 1980.

* * *

Like Heidegger before him, Sartre was fascinated with "being." According to Sartre, there are two categories of being: "being-in-itself" *(être en-soi)* and "being-for-itself" *(être pour-soi)*. Being-in-itself is complete in itself, "solid," fixed, and totally given: "Uncreated, without reason for being, without connection with any other being, being-in-itself is superfluous for all eternity." Like Parmenides' one, being-in-itself simply *is*. This is the being of rocks and trees. This being-in-itself has no sufficient reason for being, no purpose or meaning—it is "absurd."

Being-for-itself, on the other hand, is incomplete and fluid and without a determined structure. Being-for-itself is the being of human consciousness that at every moment is freely choosing its future. This consciousness arises by virtue of its power of negation, based on freedom: "[Consciousness] constitutes itself in its own flesh as the nihilation of a possibility which another human reality projects as its possibility. For that reason it must arise in the world as a Not." Individual consciousness constitutes itself by freely rejecting all roles that others try to force upon it. It is precisely in the act of saying "No" to all attempts to make me into a being-in-itself that I create myself as a being-for-itself.

In creating myself, I do not choose what I will become on the basis of preexisting values. There are no eternal values, no givens for me to use. Dostoevsky's character Ivan Karamazov had claimed, "If there is no God, all things are lawful." Sartre agreed and added that since there was no God, all things are, indeed, lawful. In fact, there is no possible justification for any choice I might make, since justification implies appeal to given values. I am free to choose my values without any external justification.

While this freedom is complete, it is not absolute. In the first place, as a free being, I encounter other free beings. My world is interrupted when the "other" gives me "the look." By looking at me, the other objectifies me, makes me a part of his or her world, part of his or her freedom: "Thus being-seen constitutes me as a being without defenses for a freedom which is not my freedom." But I can regain my freedom by looking back and by an act of will transforming the other into an object for me. (This world of people–objects led Sartre to exclaim, "Hell is other people.")

Second, I must acknowledge the "facticity" found in existence. I cannot change the fact that this tree is in front of me or that I cannot walk through it. But even here my freedom still prevails. I freely create the *meaning* of this tree as an object to climb or as a source of lumber or as a thing to be preserved or as a biological specimen. In creating these meanings, I create the world in which I live.

Some people are unwilling to face up to this radical freedom and turn their power of negation inward upon consciousness itself. In our selection from *Being and Nothingness,* translated by Hazel E. Barnes, Sartre calls this negative turn "bad faith." To live in bad faith is to deny oneself as a being-for-itself in order to become a being-in-itself; it is to blame others or circumstances for what one has become. This mode of being is *bad* faith because it refuses to acknowledge that only the individual determines the meanings of externals. Furthermore, one *always* has alternatives (no matter the circumstances, one could always commit suicide), and so one's choice is always free.

In *Existentialism Is a Humanism,* translated by Bernard Frechtman, Sartre expands on this freedom while defending the basic ideas of existentialism. He begins by discussing human artifacts, such as a book or a paper-cutter. An object like a paper-cutter begins as an essence, that is, as an "ensemble of both the production routines and the properties which enable it to be both produced and defined." One conceives of a paper-cutter (essentially) and how to make it and only *then* does one construct it. The essence of a paper-cutter precedes its existence. According to Sartre, theists believe that God does the same with human beings. First God conceives of humans and then creates them. But Sartre says that there is no God, and hence no preexisting human essence: "There is no human nature, since there is no God to conceive it." Instead, "Man is nothing else but what he makes of himself." For humans, existence precedes essence.

When one realizes the implications of this atheism and the primacy of freedom, one is brought to anguish and forlornness. But Sartre strongly denied that this state necessarily led to despair. While all my actions are indeed ultimately futile because of my eventual death, and while existence is in fact absurd, I can still *choose* my actions and so give my life meaning. As Sartre concluded, "In this sense existentialism is optimistic, a doctrine of action."

* * *

There are many studies of existentialism; see especially Gabriel Marcel, *The Philosophy of Existentialism,* translated by Manya Harari (New York: Citadel Press, 1956); Hazel E. Barnes, *An Existentialist Ethic* (Chicago: University of Chicago Press, 1967); and William Barrett's two books, *Irrational Man* (Garden City, NY: Doubleday, 1962) and *What Is Existentialism?* (New York: Grove Press, 1964). For primary source materials, see Walter Kaufmann, ed., *Existentialism from Dostoevsky to Sartre* (New York: Viking Press, 1956), and Charles Guignon and Derk Pereboom, *Existentialism: Basic Texts* (Indianapolis, IN: Hackett, 1994).

For biographies of Sartre, see Annie Cohen-Solal, *Sartre: A Life,* translated by Anna Cancogni (New York: Pantheon Books, 1987); John Gerassi, *Jean-Paul Sartre: Hated Conscience of His Century* (Chicago: University of Chicago Press, 1989); and Simone de Beauvoir's recounting of Sartre's final days, *Adieux: A Farewell to Sartre* (New York: Pantheon, 1984). For general introductions to Sartre's thought, see Mary Warnock, *The Philosophy of Sartre* (London: Hutchinson, 1965); Anthony Manser, *Sartre: A Philosophic Study* (London: Athlone Press, 1966); Arthur C. Danto, *Jean-Paul Sartre* (New York: Viking Press, 1975); and Peter Caws, *Sartre* (London: Routledge & Kegan Paul, 1979). Iris Murdoch, *Sartre: Romantic Rationalist* (New Haven, CT: Yale University

Press, 1959), explores the philosophical ideas in Sartre's novels. There are several discussions of Sartre's Marxism, including W. Desan, *The Marxism of Jean-Paul Sartre* (Garden City, NY: Doubleday, 1965); Mark Poster, *Sartre's Marxism* (Cambridge: Cambridge University Press, 1982); and Thomas R. Flynn, *Sartre and Marxist Existentialism: The Test Case of Collective Responsibility* (Chicago: University of Chicago Press, 1984). For essays, see Edith Kern, ed., *Sartre: A Collection of Critical Essays* (Englewood Cliffs, NJ: Prentice Hall, 1962); Mary Warnock, ed., *Sartre* (Garden City, NY: Anchor Doubleday, 1971); Hugh J. Silverman and Frederick A. Elliston, eds., *Jean-Paul Sartre: Contemporary Approaches to His Philosophy* (Pittsburgh: Duquesne University Press, 1980); Paul A. Schilpp, ed., *The Philosophy of Jean-Paul Sartre* (La Salle, IL: Open Court, 1981); and Christina Howells, ed., *The Cambridge Companion to Sartre* (Cambridge: Cambridge University Press, 1992).

BEING AND NOTHINGNESS (in part)

CHAPTER 2: BAD FAITH

I. Bad Faith and Falsehood

The human being is not only the being by whom *négatités* are disclosed in the world; he is also the one who can take negative attitudes with respect to himself. In our Introduction we defined consciousness as "a being such that in its being, its being is in question in so far as this being implies a being other than itself." But now that we have examined the meaning of "the question," we can at present also write the formula thus: "Consciousness is a being, the nature of which is to be conscious of the nothingness of its being." In a prohibition or a veto, for example, the human being denies a future transcendence. But this negation is not explicative. My consciousness is not restricted to *envisioning* a *négatité*. It constitutes itself in its own flesh as the nihilation of a possibility which another human reality projects as its possibility. For that reason it must arise in the world as a Not; it is as a Not that the slave first apprehends the master, or that the prisoner who is trying to escape sees the guard who is watching him. There are even men (e.g., caretakers, overseers, gaolers) whose social reality is uniquely that of the Not, who will live and die, having forever been only a Not upon the earth. Others so as to make the Not a part of their very subjectivity establish their human personality as a perpetual negation. This is the meaning and function of what Scheler calls "the man of resentment"—in reality, the Not. But there exist more subtle behaviors, the description of which will lead us further into the inwardness of consciousness. Irony is one of these. In irony a man annihilates what he posits within one and the same act; he leads us to believe in order not to be believed; he affirms to deny and denies to affirm; he creates a

Jean-Paul Sartre, *Being and Nothingness,* translated by Hazel E. Barnes. New York: Philosophical Library, 1956. Reprinted by permission.

positive object but it has no being other than its nothingness. Thus attitudes of negation toward the self permit us to raise a new question: What are we to say is the being of man who has the possibility of denying himself? But it is out of the question to discuss the attitude of "self-negation" in its universality. The kinds of behavior which can be ranked under this heading are too diverse; we risk retaining only the abstract form of them. It is best to choose and to examine one determined attitude which is essential to human reality and which is such that consciousness instead of directing its negation outward turns it toward itself. This attitude, it seems to me, is *bad faith (mauvaise foi)*.

Frequently this is identified with falsehood. We say indifferently of a person that he shows signs of bad faith or that he lies to himself. We shall willingly grant that bad faith is a lie to oneself, on condition that we distinguish the lie to oneself from lying in general. Lying is a negative attitude we will agree to that. But this negation does not bear on consciousness itself, it aims only at the transcendent. The essence of the lie implies in fact that the liar actually is in complete possession of the truth which he is hiding. A man does not lie about what he is ignorant of; he does not lie when he spreads an error of which he himself is the dupe; he does not lie when he is mistaken. The ideal description of the liar would be a cynical consciousness, affirming truth within himself, denying it in his words, and denying that negation as such. Now this doubly negative attitude rests on the transcendent; the fact expressed is transcendent since it does not exist, and the original negation rests on a *truth;* that is, on a particular type of transcendence. As for the inner negation which I effect correlatively with the affirmation for myself of the truth, this rests on words, that is, on an event in the world. Furthermore the inner disposition of the liar is positive; it could be the object of an affirmative judgment. The liar intends to deceive and he does not seek to hide this intention from himself nor to disguise the translucency of consciousness; on the contrary, he has recourse to it when there is a question of deciding secondary behavior. It explicitly exercises a regulatory control over all attitudes. As for his flaunted intention of telling the truth ("I'd never want to deceive you! This is true! I swear it!")—all this, of course, is the object of an inner negation, but also it is not recognized by the liar as his intention. It is played, imitated, it is the intention of the character which he plays in the eyes of his questioner, but this character, precisely because he does not exist, is a transcendent. Thus the lie does not put into the play the inner structure of present consciousness; all the negations which constitute it bear on objects which by this fact are removed from consciousness. The lie then does not require special ontological foundation, and the explanations which the existence of negation in general requires are valid without change in the case of deceit. Of course we have described the ideal lie; doubtless it happens often enough that the liar is more or less the victim of his lie, that he half persuades himself of it. But these common, popular forms of the lie are also degenerate aspects of it; they represent intermediaries between falsehood and bad faith. The lie is a behavior of transcendence.

The lie is also a normal phenomenon of what Heidegger calls the *"Mit-sein"* ["being with" others]. It presupposes my existence, the existence of the *Other,* my existence *for* the Other, and the existence of the Other *for* me. Thus there is no difficulty in holding that the liar must make the project of the lie in entire clarity and that he must possess a complete comprehension of the lie and of the truth which he is altering. It is sufficient that an over-all opacity hide his intentions from the *Other;* it is sufficient that the Other can take the lie for truth. By the lie consciousness affirms that it exists by nature as *hidden from the Other;* it utilizes for its own profit the ontological duality of myself and myself in the eyes of the Other.

The situation can not be the same for bad faith if this, as we have said, is indeed a lie to oneself. To be sure, the one who practices bad faith is hiding a displeasing truth or presenting as truth a pleasing untruth. Bad faith then has in appearance the structure of falsehood. Only what changes everything is the fact that in bad faith it is from myself that I am hiding the truth. Thus the duality of the deceiver and the deceived does not exist here. Bad faith on the contrary implies in essence the unity of a *single* consciousness. This does not mean that it can not be conditioned by the *Mit-sein* like all other phenomena of human reality, but the *Mit-sein* can call forth bad faith only by presenting itself as a *situation* which bad faith permits surpassing; bad faith does not come from outside to human reality. One does not undergo his bad faith; one is not infected with it; it is not a state. But consciousness affects itself with bad faith. There must be an original intention and a project of bad faith; this project implies a comprehension of bad faith as such and a pre-reflective apprehension (of) consciousness as affecting itself with bad faith. It follows first that the one to whom the lie is told and the one who lies are one and the same person, which means that I must know in my capacity as deceiver the truth which is hidden from me in my capacity as the one deceived. Better yet I must know the truth very exactly *in order* to conceal it more carefully—and this not at two different moments, which at a pinch would allow us to reestablish a semblance of duality—but in the unitary structure of a single project. How then can the lie subsist if the duality which conditions it is suppressed?

To this difficulty is added another which is derived from the total translucency of consciousness. That which affects itself with bad faith must be conscious (of) its bad faith since the being of consciousness is consciousness of being. It appears then that I must be in good faith, at least to the extent that I am conscious of my bad faith. But then this whole psychic system is annihilated. We must agree in fact that if I deliberately and cynically attempt to lie to myself, I fail completely in this undertaking; the lie falls back and collapses beneath my look; it is ruined *from behind* by the very consciousness of lying to myself which pitilessly constitutes itself well within my project as its very condition. We have here an evanescent phenomenon which exists only in and through its own differentiation. To be sure, these phenomena are frequent and we shall see that there is in fact an "evanescence" of bad faith, which, it is evident, vacillates continually between good faith and cynicism: Even though the existence of bad faith is very precarious, and though it belongs to the kind of psychic structures which we might call "metastable," [Sartre's word for subject to sudden changes] it presents nonetheless an autonomous and durable form. It can even be the normal aspect of life for a very great number of people. A person can *live* in bad faith, which does not mean that he does not have abrupt awakenings to cynicism or to good faith, but which implies a constant and particular style of life. Our embarrassment then appears extreme since we can neither reject nor comprehend bad faith.

To escape from these difficulties people gladly have recourse to the unconscious. In the psychoanalytical interpretation, for example, they use the hypothesis of a censor, conceived as a line of demarcation with customs, passport division, currency control, *etc.,* to reestablish the duality of the deceiver and the deceived. Here instinct or, if you prefer, original drives and complexes of drives constituted by our individual history, make up *reality*. It is neither true nor false since it does not *exist for itself*. It simply is, exactly like this table, which is neither true nor false *in itself* but simply real. As for the conscious symbols of the instinct, this interpretation takes them not for appearances but for real psychic facts. Fear, forgetting, dreams exist really in the capacity of concrete facts of consciousness in the same way as the words and the attitudes of the liar are concrete, really existing patterns of behavior. The subject has the same relation to these phenomena as the deceived to the behavior of the deceiver. He establishes them in their reality and must interpret them. There is a *truth* in the activities of the deceiver; if the deceived could reattach them to the situation where the deceiver establishes himself and to his project of the lie, they would become integral parts of truth, by virtue of being lying conduct. Similarly there is a truth in the symbolic acts; it is what the psychoanalyst discovers when he reattaches them to the historical situation of the patient, to the unconscious complexes which they express, to the blocking of the censor. Thus the subject deceives himself about the *meaning* of his conduct, he apprehends it in its concrete existence but not in its *truth,* simply because he cannot derive it from an original situation and from a psychic constitution which remain alien to him.

By the distinction between the "id" and the "ego," Freud has cut the psychic whole into two. I *am* the ego but I *am not* the id. I hold no privileged position in relation to my unconscious psyche. I *am* my own psychic phenomena in so far as I establish them in their conscious reality. For example I am the impulse to steal this or that book from this bookstall. I am an integral part of the impulse; I bring it to light and I determine myself hand-in-hand with it to commit the theft. But I am not those psychic facts, in so far as I receive them passively and am obliged to resort to hypotheses about their origin and their true meaning, just as the scholar makes conjectures about the nature and essence of an external phenomenon. This theft, for example, which I interpret as an immediate impulse determined by the rarity, the interest, or the price of the volume which I am going to steal—it is in truth a process derived from self-punishment, which is attached more or less directly to an Oedipus complex. The impulse toward the theft contains a truth which can be reached only by more or less probable hypotheses. The criterion of this truth will be the number of conscious psychic facts which it explains; from a more pragmatic point of view it will be also the success of the psychiatric cure which it allows. Finally the discovery of this truth will necessitate the cooperation of the psychoanalyst, who appears as the *mediator* between my unconscious drives and my conscious life. The Other appears as being able to effect the synthesis between the unconscious thesis and the conscious antithesis. I can know myself only through the mediation of the other, which means that I stand in relation to my "id," in the position of the Other. If I have a little knowledge of psychoanalysis, I can, under circumstances particularly favorable, try to psychoanalyze myself. But this attempt can succeed only if I distrust every kind of intuition, only if I apply to my case *from the outside,* abstract schemes and rules already learned. As for the results, whether they are obtained by my efforts alone or with the cooperation of a technician, they will never have the certainty which intuition confers; they will possess simply the always increasing probability of scientific hypotheses. The hypothesis of the Oedipus complex, like the atomic theory, is nothing but an "experimental idea"; as Pierce said, it is not to be distinguished from the totality of experiences which it allows to be realized and the results which it enables us to foresee. Thus psychoanalysis substitutes for the notion of bad faith, the idea of a lie without a liar; it allows me to understand how it is possible for me to be lied to without lying to myself since it places me in the same relation to myself that the Other is in respect to me; it replaces the duality of the deceiver and the deceived, the essential condition of the lie, by that of the "id" and the "ego." It introduces into my subjectivity the deepest intersubjective structure of the *Mit-sein.* Can this explanation satisfy us?

Considered more closely the psychoanalytic theory is not as simple as it first appears. It is not accurate to hold that the "id" is presented as a thing in relation to the hypothesis of the psychoanalyst, for a thing is indifferent to the conjectures which we make concerning it, while the "id" on the contrary is sensitive to them when we approach the truth. Freud in fact reports resistance when at the end of the first period the doctor is approaching the truth. This resistance is objective behavior apprehended from without: the patient shows defiance, refuses to speak, gives fantastic accounts of his dreams, sometimes even removes himself completely from the psychoanalytic treatment. It is a fair question to ask what part of himself can thus resist. It can not be the "Ego," envisaged as a psychic totality of the facts of consciousness; this could not suspect that the psychiatrist is approaching the end since the ego's relation to the *meaning* of its own reactions is exactly like that of the psychiatrist himself. At the very most it is possible for the ego to appreciate objectively the degree of probability in the hypotheses set forth, as a witness of the psychoanalysis might be able to do, according to the number of subjective facts which they explain. Furthermore, this probability would appear to the ego to border on certainty, which he could not take offence at since most of the time it is he who by a *conscious* decision is in pursuit of the psychoanalytic therapy. Are we to say that the patient is disturbed by the daily revelations which the psychoanalyst makes to him and that he seeks to remove himself, at the same time pretending in his own eyes to wish to continue the treatment? In this case it is no longer possible to resort to the unconscious to explain bad faith; it is there in full consciousness, with all its contradictions. But this is not the way that the psychoanalyst means to explain this resistance; for him it is secret and deep, it comes from afar; it has its roots in the very thing which the psychoanalyst is trying to make clear.

Furthermore it is equally impossible to explain the resistance as emanating from the complex which the psychoanalyst wishes to bring to light. The complex as such is rather the collaborator of the psychoanalyst since it aims at expressing itself in clear consciousness, since it plays tricks on the censor and seeks to elude it. The only level on which we can locate the refusal of the subject is that of the censor. It alone can comprehend the questions or the revelations of the psychoanalyst as approaching more or less near to the real drives which it strives to repress—it alone because it alone *knows* what it is repressing.

If we reject the language and the materialistic mythology of psychoanalysis, we perceive that the censor in order to apply its activity with discernment must know what it is repressing. In fact if we abandon all the metaphors representing the repression as the impact of blind forces, we are compelled to admit that the censor must choose and in order to choose must be aware of so doing. How could it happen otherwise that the censor allows lawful sexual impulses to pass through, that it permits needs (hunger, thirst, sleep) to be expressed in clear consciousness? And how are we to explain that it can relax its surveillance, that it can even be deceived by the disguises of the instinct? But it is not sufficient that it discern the condemned drives; it must also apprehend them *as to be repressed,* which implies in it at the very least an awareness of its activity. In a word, how could the censor discern the impulses needing to be repressed without being conscious of discerning them? How can we conceive of a knowledge which is ignorant of itself? To know is to know that one knows, said Alain. Let us say rather: All knowing is consciousness of knowing. Thus the resistance of the patient implies on the level of the censor an awareness of the thing repressed as such, a comprehension of the end toward which the questions of the psychoanalyst are leading, and an act of synthetic connection by which it compares the *truth* of the repressed complex to the psychoanalytic hypothesis which aims at it. These various operations in their turn imply that the censor is conscious (of) itself. But what type of selfconsciousness can the censor have? It must be the consciousness (of) being conscious of the drive to be repressed, but precisely *in order not to be conscious of it.* What does this mean if not that the censor is in bad faith?

Psychoanalysis has not gained anything for us since in order to overcome bad faith, it has established between the unconscious and consciousness an autonomous consciousness in bad faith. The effort to establish a veritable duality and even a trinity

(*Es, Ich, Ueberich* expressing themselves through the censor) has resulted in a mere verbal terminology. The very essence of the reflexive idea of hiding something from oneself implies the unity of one and the same psychic mechanism and consequently a double activity in the heart of unity, tending on the one hand to maintain and locate the thing to be concealed and on the other hand to repress and disguise it. Each of the two aspects of this activity is complementary to the other; that is, it implies the other in its being. By separating consciousness from the unconscious by means of the censor, psychoanalysis has not succeeded in dissociating the two phases of the act, since the libido is a blind conatus [striving] toward conscious expression and since the conscious phenomenon is a passive, faked result. Psychoanalysis has merely localized this double activity of repulsion and attraction on the level of the censor.

Furthermore the problem still remains of accounting for the unity of the total phenomenon (repression of the drive which disguises itself and "passes" in symbolic form), to establish comprehensible connections among its different phases. How can the repressed drive "disguise itself" if it does not include (1) the consciousness of being repressed, (2) the consciousness of having been pushed back because it is what it is, (3) a project of disguise? No mechanistic theory of condensation or of transference can explain these modifications by which the drive itself is affected, for the description of the process of disguise implies a veiled appeal to finality. And similarly how are we to account for the pleasure or the anguish which accompanies the symbolic and conscious satisfaction of the drive if consciousness does not include—beyond the censor—an obscure comprehension of the end to be attained as simultaneously desired and forbidden. By rejecting the conscious unity of the psyche, Freud is obliged to imply everywhere a magic unity linking distant phenomena across obstacles, just as sympathetic magic unites the spellbound person and the wax image fashioned in his likeness. The unconscious drive *(Trieb)* through magic is endowed with the character "repressed" or "condemned," which completely pervades it, colors it, and magically provokes its symbolism. Similarly the conscious phenomenon is entirely colored by its symbolic meaning although it can not apprehend this meaning by itself in clear consciousness.

Aside from its inferiority in principle, the explanation by magic does not avoid the coexistence—on the level of the unconscious, on that of the censor, and on that of consciousness—of two contradictory, complementary structures which reciprocally imply and destroy each other. Proponents of the theory have hypostasized and "reified" bad faith; they have not escaped it. This is what has inspired a Viennese psychiatrist, Steckel, to depart from the psychoanalytical tradition and to write in *La femme frigide:* "Every time that I have been able to carry my investigations far enough, I have established that the crux of the psychosis was conscious." In addition the cases which he reports in his work bear witness to a pathological bad faith which the Freudian doctrine can not account for. There is the question, for example, of women whom marital infidelity has made frigid; that is, they succeed in hiding from themselves not complexes deeply sunk in half physiological darkness, but acts of conduct which are objectively discoverable, which they can not fail to record at the moment when they perform them. Frequently in fact the husband reveals to Steckel that his wife has given objective signs of pleasure, but the woman when questioned will fiercely deny them. Here we find a pattern of *distraction.* Admissions which Steckel was able to draw out inform us that these pathologically frigid women apply themselves to becoming distracted in advance from the pleasure which they dread; many for example at the time of the sexual act turn their thoughts away toward their daily occupations, make up their household accounts. Will anyone speak of an unconscious here? Yet if the frigid woman thus distracts her consciousness from the pleasure which she experiences, it is by no means cynically and in full agreement with herself; *it is in order to prove to herself* that she is frigid. We have in fact to deal with a phenomenon of bad faith since the efforts taken in order not to be present to the experienced pleasure imply the recognition that the pleasure is experienced; they imply it *in order to deny it*. But we are no longer on the ground of psychoanalysis. Thus on the one hand the explanation by means of the unconscious, due to the fact that it breaks the psychic unity, can not account for the facts which at first sight it appeared to explain. And on the other hand, there exists an infinity of types of behavior in bad faith which explicitly reject this kind of explanation because their essence implies that they can appear only in the translucency of consciousness. We find that the problem which we had attempted to resolve is still untouched.

II. Patterns of Bad Faith

If we wish to get out of this difficulty, we should examine more closely the patterns of bad faith and attempt a description of them. This description will permit us perhaps to fix more exactly the conditions for the possibility of bad faith; that is, to reply to the question we raised at the outset: "What must be the being of man if he is to be capable of bad faith?"

Take the example of a woman who has consented to go out with a particular man for the first time. She knows very well the intentions which the man who is speaking to her cherishes regarding her. She knows also that it will be necessary sooner or later for her to make a decision. But she does not want to realize the urgency; she concerns herself only with what is respectful and discreet in the attitude of her companion. She does not apprehend this conduct as an attempt to achieve what we call "the first approach"; that is, she does not want to see possibilities of temporal development which his conduct presents. She restricts this behavior to what is in the present; she does not wish to read in the phrases which he addresses to her anything other than their explicit meaning. If he says to her, "I find you so attractive!" she disarms this phrase of its sexual background; she attaches to the conversation and to the behavior of the speaker, the immediate meanings, which she imagines as objective qualities. The man who is speaking to her appears to her sincere and respectful as the table is round or square, as the wall coloring is blue or gray. The qualities thus attached to the person she is listening to are in this way fixed in a permanence like that of things, which is no other than the projection of the strict present of the qualities into the temporal flux. This is because she does not quite know what she wants. She is profoundly aware of the desire which she inspires, but the desire cruel and naked would humiliate and horrify her. Yet she would find no charm in a respect which would be only respect. In order to satisfy her, there must be a feeling which is addressed wholly to her *personality*—i.e., to her full freedom—and which would be a recognition of her freedom. But at the same time this feeling must be wholly desire; that is, it must address itself to her body as object. This time then she refuses to apprehend the desire for what it is; she does not even give it a name; she recognizes it only to the extent that it transcends itself toward admiration, esteem, respect and that it is wholly absorbed in the more refined forms which it produces, to the extent of no longer figuring anymore as a sort of warmth and density. But then suppose he takes her hand. This act of her companion risks changing the situation by calling for an immediate decision. To leave the hand there is to consent in herself to flirt, to engage herself. To withdraw it is to break the troubled and unstable harmony which gives the hour its charm. The aim is to postpone the moment of decision as long as possible. We know what happens next; the young woman leaves her hand there, but she *does not notice* that she is leaving it. She does not notice because it happens by chance that she is at this moment all intellect. She draws her companion up to the most lofty regions of sentimental speculation; she speaks of Life, of her life, she shows herself in her essential aspect—a personality, a consciousness. And during this time the divorce of the body from the soul is accomplished; the hand rests inert between the warm hands of her companion—neither consenting nor resisting—a thing.

We shall say that this woman is in bad faith. But we see immediately that she uses various procedures in order to maintain herself in this bad faith. She has disarmed the actions of her companion by reducing them to being only what they are; that is, to existing in the mode of the in-itself. But she permits herself to enjoy his desire, to the extent that she will apprehend it as not being what it is, will recognize its transcendence. Finally, while sensing profoundly the presence of her own body—to the degree of being disturbed perhaps—she realizes herself as *not being* her own body, and she contemplates it as though from above as a passive object to which events can *happen* but which can neither provoke them nor avoid them because all its possibilities are outside of it. What unity do we find in these various aspects of bad faith? It is a certain art of forming contradictory concepts which unite in themselves both an idea and the negation of that idea. The basic concept which is thus engendered utilizes the double property of the human being, who is at once a *facticity* and a *transcendence*. These two aspects of human reality are and ought to be capable of a valid coordination. But bad faith does not wish either to coordinate them nor to surmount them in a synthesis. Bad faith seeks to affirm their identity while preserving their differences. It must affirm facticity as *being* transcendence and transcendence as *being* facticity, in such a way that at the instant when a person apprehends the one, he can find himself abruptly faced with the other.

We can find the prototype of formulae of bad faith in certain famous expressions which have been rightly conceived to produce their whole effect in a spirit of bad faith. Take for example the title of a work by Jacques Chardonne, *Love Is Much More than Love*.* We see here how unity is established between *present* love in its facticity—"the contact of two skins," sensuality, egoism, Proust's mechanism of jealousy, Adler's battle of the sexes, *etc.*—and love as transcendence—Mauriac's "river of fire," the longing for the infinite, Plato's *eros,* Lawrence's deep cosmic intuition, *etc.* Here we leave facticity to find ourselves suddenly beyond the present and the factual condition of man, beyond the psychological, in the heart of metaphysics. On the other hand, the title of a play by Sarment, *I Am Too Great for Myself,*** which also presents characters in bad faith, throws us first into full transcendence in order suddenly to imprison us within the narrow limits of our factual essence. We will discover this structure again in the famous sentence: "He has become what he was" or in its no less famous opposite: "Eternity at last changes each man into himself."† It is well understood that these various formulae have only the appearance of bad faith; they have been conceived in this paradoxical form explicitly to shock the mind and discountenance it by an enigma. But it is precisely this appearance which is of concern to us. What counts here is that the formulae do not constitute new, solidly structured ideas; on the contrary, they are formed so as to remain in perpetual disintegration and so that we may slide at any time from naturalistic present to transcendence and vice versa.

*L'amour, c'est beaucoup plus que l'amour.
**Je suis trop grand pour moi.
†Il est devenu ce qu'il était.
  Tel qu'en lui-même enfin l'éternité le change.

We can see the use which bad faith can make of these judgments which all aim at establishing that I am not what I am. If I were only what I am, I could, for example, seriously consider an adverse criticism which someone makes of me, question myself scrupulously, and perhaps be compelled to recognize the truth in it. But thanks to transcendence, I am not subject to all that I am. I do not even have to discuss the justice of the reproach. As Suzanne says to Figaro, "To prove that I am right would be to recognize that I can be wrong." I am on a plane where no reproach can touch me since what I really am is my transcendence. I flee from myself, I escape myself, I leave my tattered garment in the hands of the fault-finder. But the ambiguity necessary for bad faith comes from the fact that I affirm here that I am my transcendence in the mode of being of a thing. It is only thus, in fact, that I can feel that I escape all reproaches. It is in the sense that our young woman purifies the desire of anything humiliating by being willing to consider it only as pure transcendence, which she avoids even naming. But inversely "I Am Too Great for Myself," while showing our transcendence changed into facticity, is the source of an infinity of excuses for our failures or our weaknesses. Similarly the young coquette maintains transcendence to the extent that the respect, the esteem manifested by the actions of her admirer are already on the plane of the transcendent. But she arrests this transcendence, she glues it down with all the facticity of the present; respect is nothing other than respect, it is an arrested surpassing which no longer surpasses itself toward anything.

But although this *metastable* concept of "transcendence-facticity" is one of the most basic instruments of bad faith, it is not the only one of its kind. We can equally well use another kind of duplicity derived from human reality which we will express roughly by saying that its being-for-itself implies complementarily a being-for-others. Upon any one of my conducts it is always possible to converge two looks, mine and that of the Other. The conduct will not present exactly the same structure in each case. But as we shall see later, as each look perceives it, there is between these two aspects of my being, no difference between appearance and being—as if I were to myself the truth of myself and as if the Other possessed only a deformed image of me. The equal dignity of being, possessed by my being-for-others and by my being-for-myself permits a perpetually disintegrating synthesis and a perpetual game of escape from the for-itself to the for-others and from the for-others to the for-itself. We have seen also the use which our young lady made of our being-in-the-midst-of-the-world—*i.e.,* of our inert presence as a passive object among other objects—in order to relieve herself suddenly from the functions of her being-in-the-world—that is, from the being which causes there to be a world by projecting itself beyond the world toward its own possibilities. Let us note finally the confusing syntheses which play on the nihilating ambiguity of these temporal *ekstases,* affirming at once that I am what I have been (the man who deliberately arrests *himself* at one period in his life and refuses to take into consideration the later changes) and that I am not what I have been (the man who in the face of reproaches or rancor dissociates himself from his past by insisting on his freedom and on his perpetual recreation). In all these concepts, which have only a transitive role in the reasoning and which are eliminated from the conclusion (like hypochondriacs in the calculations of physicians), we find again the same structure. We have to deal with human reality as a being which is what it is not and which is not what it is.

But what exactly is necessary in order for these concepts of disintegration to be able to receive even a pretence of existence, in order for them to be able to appear for an instant to consciousness, even in a process of evanescence? A quick examination of the idea of sincerity, the antithesis of bad faith, will be very instructive in this connection. Actually sincerity presents itself as a demand and consequently is not a state. Now what is the ideal to be attained in this case? It is necessary that a man be *for himself* only what he *is*. But is this not precisely the definition of the in-itself—or if you prefer—the principle of identity? To posit as an ideal the being of things, is this not to assert by the same stroke that this being does not belong to human reality and that the principle of identity, far from being a universal axiom universally applied, is only a synthetic principle enjoying a merely regional universality? Thus in order that the concepts of bad faith can put us under illusion at least for an instant, in order that the candor of "pure hearts" (cf. Gide, Kessel) can have validity for human reality as an ideal, the principle of identity must not represent a constitutive principle of human reality and human reality must not be necessarily what it is but must be able to be what it is not. What does this mean?

If man is what he is, bad faith is for ever impossible and candor ceases to be his ideal and becomes instead his being. But is man what he is? And more generally, how can he *be* what he is when he exists as consciousness of being? If candor or sincerity is a universal value, it is evident that the maxim "one must be what one is" does not serve solely as a regulating principle for judgments and concepts by which I express what I am. It posits not merely an ideal of knowing but an ideal of being; it proposes for us an absolute equivalence of being with itself as a prototype of being. In this sense it is necessary that we *make ourselves* what we are. But what are we then if we have the constant obligation to make ourselves what we are, if our mode of being is having the obligation to be what we are?

Let us consider this waiter in the café. His movement is quick and forward, a little too precise, a little too rapid. He comes toward the patrons with a step a little too quick. He bends forward a little too eagerly; his voice, his eyes express an interest a little too solicitous for the order of the customer. Finally there he returns, trying to imitate in his walk the inflexible stiffness of some kind of automaton while carrying his tray with the recklessness of a tight-rope-walker by putting it in a perpetually unstable, perpetually broken equilibrium which he perpetually reestablishes by a light movement of the arm and hand. All his behavior seems to us a game. He applies himself to chaining his movements as if they were mechanisms, the one regulating the other; his gestures and even his voice seem to be mechanisms; he gives himself the quickness and pitiless rapidity of things. He is playing, he is amusing himself. But what is he playing? We need not watch long before we can explain it: he is playing *at being* a waiter in a café. There is nothing there to surprise us. The game is a kind of marking out and investigation. The child plays with his body in order to explore it, to take inventory of it; the waiter in the café plays with his condition in order to *realize* it. This obligation is not different from that which is imposed on all tradesmen. Their condition is wholly one of ceremony. The public demands of them that they realize it as a ceremony; there is the dance of the grocer, of the tailor, of the auctioneer, by which they endeavour to persuade their clientele that they are nothing but a grocer, an auctioneer, a tailor. A grocer who dreams is offensive to the buyer, because such a grocer is not wholly a grocer. Society demands that he limit himself to his function as a grocer, just as the soldier at attention makes himself into a soldier-thing with a direct regard which does not see at all, which is no longer meant to see, since it is the rule and not the interest of the moment which determines the point he must fix his eyes on (the sight "fixed at ten paces"). There are indeed many precautions to imprison a man in what he is, as if we lived in perpetual fear that he might escape from it, that he might break away and suddenly elude his condition.

In a parallel situation, from within, the waiter in the café can not be immediately a café waiter in the sense that this inkwell *is* an inkwell, or the glass is a glass. It is by no means that he can not form reflective judgments or concepts concerning his condition. He knows well what it "means": the obligation of getting up at five o'clock, of sweeping the floor of the shop before the restaurant opens, of starting the coffee pot going, *etc*. He knows the rights which it allows: the right to the tips, the right to belong to a union, *etc*. But all these concepts, all these judgments refer to the transcendent. It is a matter of abstract possibilities, of rights and duties conferred on a "person possessing rights." And it is precisely this person *who I have to be* (if I am the waiter in question) and who I am not. It is not that I do not wish to be this person or that I want this person to be different. But rather there is no common measure between his being and mine. It is a "representation" for others and for myself, which means that I can be he only in *representation*. But if I represent myself as him, I am not he; I am separated from him as the object from the subject, separated by *nothing*, but this nothing isolates me from him. I can not be he, I can only play *at being* him; that is, imagine to myself that I am he. And thereby I affect him with nothingness. In vain do I fulfill the functions of a café waiter. I can be he only in the neutralized mode, as the actor is Hamlet, by mechanically making the *typical gestures* of my state and by aiming at myself as an imaginary café waiter through those gestures taken as an "analogue."* What I attempt to realize is a being-in-itself of the café waiter, as if it were not just in my power to confer their value and their urgency upon my duties and the rights of my position, as if it were not my free choice to get up each morning at five o'clock or to remain in bed, even though it meant getting fired. As if from the very fact that I sustain this role in existence I did not transcend it on every side, as if I did not constitute myself as one *beyond* my condition. Yet there is no doubt that I am in a sense a café waiter—otherwise could I not just as well call myself a diplomat or a reporter? But if I am one, this can not be in the mode of being in-itself. I am a waiter in the mode of *being what I am not*.

Furthermore we are dealing with more than mere social positions; I am never any one of my attitudes, any one of my actions. The good speaker is the one who *plays* at speaking, because he can not *be speaking*. The attentive pupil who wishes to *be* attentive, his eyes riveted on the teacher, his ears open wide, so exhausts himself in playing the attentive role that he ends up by no longer hearing anything. Perpetually absent to my body, to my acts, I am despite myself that "divine absence" of which Valery speaks. I can not say either that I *am* here or that I *am* not here, in the sense that we say "that box of matches *is* on the table"; this would be to confuse my "being-in-the-world" with a "being-in the midst of the world." Nor that I *am* standing, nor that I *am* seated; this would be to confuse my body with the idiosyncratic totality of which it is only one of the structures. On all sides I escape being and yet—I am.

But take a mode of being which concerns only myself: I am sad. One might think that surely I am the sadness in the mode of being what I am. What is the sadness, however, if not the intentional unity which comes to reassemble and animate the totality of my conduct? It is the meaning of this dull look with which I view the world, of my bowed shoulders, of my lowered head, of the listlessness in my whole body. But at the very moment when I adopt each of these attitudes, do I not know that I shall not be able to hold on to it? Let a stranger suddenly appear and I will lift up my head, I will assume a lively cheerfulness. What will remain of my sadness except that I obligingly promise it an appointment for later after the departure of the visitor? Moreover is not this sadness itself a *conduct*? Is it not consciousness which affects itself with sadness as a magical recourse against a situation too urgent?** And in this case even, should we not say

*Cf. *L'Imaginaire*. Conclusion.
**Esquisse d'une théorie des émotions*. Hermann Paul. In English. *The Emotions: Outline of a Theory*. Philosophical Library. 1948.

that being sad means first to make oneself sad? That may be, someone will say, but after all doesn't giving oneself the being of sadness mean to receive this being? It makes no difference from where I receive it. The fact is that a consciousness which affects itself with sadness *is* sad precisely for this reason. But it is difficult to comprehend the nature of consciousness; the being-sad is not a ready-made being which I give to myself as I can give this book to my friend. I do not possess the property of *affecting myself with being.* If I make myself sad, I must continue to make myself sad from beginning to end. I can not treat my sadness as an impulse finally achieved and put it on file without recreating it, nor can I carry it in the manner of an inert body which continues its movement after the initial shock. There is no inertia in consciousness. If I make myself sad, it is because I *am* not sad—the being of the sadness escapes me by and in the very act by which I affect myself with it. The being-in-itself of sadness perpetually haunts my consciousness (of) being sad, but it is as a value which I can not realize; it stands as a regulative meaning of my sadness, not as its constitutive modality.

Someone may say that my consciousness at least *is,* whatever may be the object or the state of which it makes itself consciousness. But how do we distinguish my consciousness (of) being sad from sadness? Is it not all one? It is true in a way that my consciousness *is,* if one means by this that for another it is a part of the totality of being on which judgments can be brought to bear. But it should be noted, as Husserl clearly understood, that my consciousness appears originally to the Other as an absence. It is the object always present as the *meaning* of all my attitudes and all my conduct—and always absent, for it gives itself to the intuition of another as a perpetual question—still better, as a perpetual freedom. When Pierre looks at me, I know of course that he is looking at me. His eyes, things in the world, are fixed on my body, a thing in the world—that is the objective fact of which I can say: it *is.* But it is also a fact *in the world.* The meaning of this look is not a fact in the world, and this is what makes me uncomfortable. Although I make smiles, promises, threats, nothing can get hold of the approbation, the free judgment which I seek; I know that it is always beyond. I sense it in my very attitude, which is no longer like that of the worker toward the things he uses as instruments. My reactions, to the extent that I project myself toward the Other, are no longer for myself but are rather mere *presentations;* they await being constituted as graceful or uncouth, sincere or insincere, *etc.,* by an apprehension which is always beyond my efforts to provoke, an apprehension which will be provoked by my efforts only if of itself it lends them force (that is, only in so far as it causes itself to be provoked from the outside), *which is its own mediator with the transcendent.* Thus the objective fact of the being-in-itself of the consciousness of the Other is posited in order to disappear in negativity and in freedom: consciousness of the Other is as not-being; its being-in-itself "here and now" is not-to-be.

Consciousness of the *Other is what it is not.*

Furthermore the being of my own consciousness does not appear to me as the consciousness of the Other. It is because it makes itself, since its being is consciousness of being. But this means that making sustains being; consciousness has to be its own being, it is never sustained by being; it sustains being in the heart of subjectivity, which means once again that it is inhabited by being but that it is not being: *consciousness is not what it is.*

Under these conditions what can be the significance of the ideal of sincerity except as a task impossible to achieve, of which the very meaning is in contradiction with the structure of my consciousness. To be sincere, we said, is to be what one is. That supposes that I am not originally what I am. But here naturally Kant's "You ought, therefore you can" is implicitly understood. I can *become* sincere; this is what my duty and my effort-to achieve sincerity imply. But we definitely establish that the original structure of "not being what one is" renders impossible in advance all movement toward being in itself or "being what one is." And this impossibility is not hidden from consciousness; on the contrary, it is the very stuff of consciousness; it is the embarrassing constraint which we constantly experience; it is our very incapacity to recognize ourselves, to constitute ourselves as being what we are. It is this necessity which means that, as soon as we posit ourselves as a certain being, by a legitimate judgment, based on inner experience or correctly deduced from *a priori* or empirical premises, then by that very positing we surpass this being—and that not toward another being but toward emptiness, toward nothing.

How then can we blame another for not being sincere or rejoice in our own sincerity since this sincerity appears to us at the same time to be impossible? How can we in conversation, in confession, in introspection, even attempt sincerity since the effort will by its very nature be doomed to failure and since at the very time when we announce it we have a prejudicative comprehension of its futility? In introspection I try to determine exactly what I am, to make up my mind to be my true self without delay—even though it means consequently to set about searching for ways to change myself. But what does this mean if not that I am constituting myself as a thing? Shall I determine the ensemble of purposes and motivations which have pushed me to do this or that action? But this is already to postulate a causal determinism which constitutes the flow of my states of consciousness as a succession of physical states. Shall I uncover in myself "drives," even though it be to affirm them in shame? But is this not deliberately to forget that these drives are realized with my consent, that they are not forces of nature but that I lend them their efficacy by a perpetually renewed decision concerning their value. Shall I pass judgment on my character, on my nature? Is this not to veil from myself at that moment what I know only too well, that I thus judge a past to which by definition my present is not subject? The proof of this is that the same man who in sincerity posits that he is what in actuality he was, is indignant at the reproach of another and tries to disarm it by asserting that he can no longer be what he was. We are readily astonished and upset when the penalties of the court affect a man who in his new freedom is no longer the guilty person he was. But at the same time we require of this man that he recognize himself as being this guilty one. What then is sincerity except precisely a phenomenon of bad faith? Have we not shown indeed that in bad faith human reality is constituted as a being which is what it is not and which is not what it is?

Let us take an example: A homosexual frequently has an intolerable feeling of guilt, and his whole existence is determined in relation to this feeling. One will readily foresee that he is in bad faith. In fact it frequently happens that this man, while recognizing his homosexual inclination, while avowing each and every particular misdeed which he has committed, refuses with all his strength to consider himself *"a paederast."* His case is always "different," peculiar; there enters into it something of a game, of chance, of bad luck; the mistakes are all in the past; they are explained by a certain conception of the beautiful which women can not satisfy; we should see in them the results of a restless search, rather than the manifestations of a deeply rooted tendency, *etc., etc.* Here is assuredly a man in bad faith who borders on the comic since, acknowledging all the facts which are imputed to him, he refuses to draw from them the conclusion which they impose. His friend, who is his most severe critic, becomes irritated with this duplicity. The critic asks only one thing—and perhaps then he will show himself indulgent: that the guilty one recognize himself as guilty, that the homosexual declare frankly—whether humbly or boastfully matters little—"I am a paederast." We ask here: Who is in bad faith? The homosexual or the champion of sincerity?

The homosexual recognizes his faults, but he struggles with all his strength against the crushing view that his mistakes constitute for him a destiny. He does not wish to let himself be considered as a thing. He has an obscure but strong feeling that an homosexual is not an homosexual as this table is a table or as this red-haired man is red-haired. It seems to him that he has escaped from each mistake as soon as he has posited it and recognized it; he even feels that the psychic duration by itself cleanses him from each misdeed, constitutes for him an undetermined future, causes him to be born anew. Is he wrong? Does he not recognize in himself the peculiar, irreducible character of human reality? His attitude includes then an undeniable comprehension of truth. But at the same time he needs this perpetual rebirth, this constant escape in order to live; he must constantly put himself beyond reach in order to avoid the terrible judgment of collectivity. Thus he plays on the word *being*. He would be right actually if he understood the phrase, "I am not a paederast" in the sense of "I am not what I am." That is, if he declared to himself, "To the extent that a pattern of conduct is defined as the conduct of a paederast and to the extent that I have adopted this conduct, I am a paederast. But to the extent that human reality can not be finally defined by patterns of conduct, I am not one." But instead he slides surreptitiously towards a different connotation of the word "being." He understands "not being" in the sense of "not-being-in-itself." He lays claim to "not being a paederast" in the sense in which this table is not an inkwell. He is in bad faith.

But the champion of sincerity is not ignorant of the transcendence of human reality, and he knows how at need to appeal to it for his own advantage. He makes use of it even and brings it up in the present argument. Does he not wish, first in the name of sincerity, then of freedom, that the homosexual reflect on himself and acknowledge himself as an homosexual? Does he not let the other understand that such a confession will win indulgence for him? What does this mean if not that the man who will acknowledge himself as an homosexual will no longer be the same as the homosexual whom he acknowledges being and that he will escape into the region of freedom and of good will? The critic asks the man then to be what he is in order no longer to be what he is. It is the profound meaning of the saying, "A sin confessed is half pardoned." The critic demands of the guilty one that he constitute himself as a thing, precisely in order no longer to treat him as a thing. And this contradiction is constitutive of the demand of sincerity. Who can not see how offensive to the Other and how reassuring for me is a statement such as, "He's just a paederast," which removes a disturbing freedom from a trait and which aims at henceforth constituting all the acts of the Other as consequences following strictly from his essence. That is actually what the critic is demanding of his victim—that he constitute himself as a thing, that he should entrust his freedom to his friend as a fief, in order that the friend should return it to him subsequently—like a suzerain to his vassal. The champion of sincerity is in bad faith to the degree that in order to reassure himself, he pretends to judge, to the extent that he demands that freedom as freedom constitute itself as a thing. We have here only one episode in that battle to the death of consciousnesses which Hegel calls "the relation of the master and the slave." A person appeals to another and demands that in the name of his nature as consciousness he should radically destroy himself as consciousness, but while making this appeal he leads the other to hope for a rebirth beyond this destruction.

Very well, someone will say, but our man is abusing sincerity, playing one side against the other. We should not look for sincerity in the relation of the *Mit-sein* but rather where it is pure—in the relations of a person with himself. But who can not see that objective sincerity is constituted in the same way? Who can not see that the sincere man constitutes himself as a thing in order to escape the condition of a thing by the same act of sincerity? The man who confesses that he is evil has exchanged his disturbing "freedom-for-evil" for an inanimate character of evil; he *is* evil, he clings to himself, he is what he is. But by the same stroke, he escapes from that *thing,* since it is he who contemplates it, since it depends on him to maintain it under his glance or to let it collapse in an infinity of particular acts. He derives a *merit* from his sincerity, and the deserving man is not the evil man as he is evil but as he is beyond his evilness. At the same time the evil is disarmed since it is nothing, save on the plane of determinism, and since in confessing it, I posit my freedom in respect to it; my future is virgin; everything is allowed to me.

Thus the essential structure of sincerity does not differ from that of bad faith since the sincere man constitutes himself as what he is *in order not to be it.* This explains the truth recognized by all that one can fall into bad faith through being sincere. As Valéry pointed out, this is the case with Stendhal. Total, constant sincerity as a constant effort to adhere to oneself is by nature a constant effort to dissociate oneself from oneself. A person frees himself from himself by the very act by which he makes himself an object for himself. To draw up a perpetual inventory of what one is means constantly to re-deny oneself and to take refuge in a sphere where one is no longer anything but a pure, free regard. The goal of bad faith, as we said, is to put oneself out of reach; it is an escape. Now we see that we must use the same terms to define sincerity. What does this mean?

In the final analysis the goal of sincerity and the goal of bad faith are not so different. To be sure, there is a sincerity which bears on the past and which does not concern us here; I am sincere if I confess *having had* this pleasure or that intention. We shall see that if this sincerity is possible, it is because in his fall into the past, the being of man is constituted as a being-in-itself. But here our concern is only with the sincerity which aims at itself in present immanence. What is its goal? To bring me to confess to myself what I am in order that I may finally coincide with my being; in a word, to cause myself to be, in the mode of the in-itself, what I am in the mode of "not being what I am." Its assumption is that fundamentally I am already, in the mode of the in-itself, what I have to be. Thus we find at the base of sincerity a continual game of mirror and reflection, a perpetual passage from the being which is what it is, to the being which is not what it is and inversely from the being which is not what it is to the being which is what it is. And what is the goal of bad faith? To cause me to be what I am, in the mode of "not being what one is," or not to be what I am in the mode of "being what one is." We find here the same game of mirrors. In fact in order for me to have an intention of sincerity, I must at the outset simultaneously be and not be what I am. Sincerity does not assign to me a mode of being or a particular quality, but in relation to that quality it aims at making me pass from one mode of being to another mode of being. This second mode of being, the ideal of sincerity, I am prevented by nature from attaining; and at the very moment when I struggle to attain it, I have a vague prejudicative comprehension that I shall not attain it. But all the same, in order for me to be able to conceive an intention in bad faith, I must have such a nature that within my being I escape from my being. If I were sad or cowardly in the way in which this inkwell is an inkwell, the possibility of bad faith could not even be conceived. Not only should I be unable to escape from my being; I could not even imagine that I could escape from it. But if bad faith is possible by virtue of a simple project, it is because so far as my being is concerned, there is no difference between being and non-being if I am cut off from my project.

Bad faith is possible only because sincerity is conscious of missing its goal inevitably, due to its very nature. I can try to apprehend myself as *"not being cowardly,"* when I *am* so, only on condition that the "being cowardly" is itself "in question" at the very moment when it exists, on condition that it is itself *one* question, that at the very moment when I wish to apprehend it, it escapes me on all sides and annihilates itself. The condition under which I can attempt an effort in bad faith is that in one sense, I *am not* this coward which I do not wish to be. But if I were not cowardly in the simple mode of not-being-what-one-is-not, I would be "in good faith" by declaring that I am not cowardly. Thus this inapprehensible coward is evanescent; in order for me not to be cowardly, I must in some way also be cowardly. That does not mean that I must be "a little" cowardly, in the sense that "a little" signifies "to a certain degree cowardly—and not cowardly to a certain degree." No. I must at once both be and not be totally and in all respects a coward. Thus in this case bad faith requires that I should not be what I am; that is, that there be an imponderable difference separating being from non-being in the mode of being of human reality.

But bad faith is not restricted to denying the qualities which I possess, to not seeing the being which I am. It attempts also to constitute myself as being what I am not. It apprehends me positively as courageous when I am not so. And that is possible, once again, only if I am what I am not; that is, if non-being in me does not have being even as non-being. Of course necessarily I am not courageous; otherwise bad faith would not be bad faith. But in addition my effort in bad faith must include the ontological comprehension that even in my usual being what I am, I am not it really and that there is no such difference between the being of "being-sad," for example—which I am in the mode of not being what I am—and the "non-being" of not-being-courageous which I wish to hide from myself. Moreover it is particularly requisite that the very negation of being should be itself the object of a perpetual nihilation, that the very meaning of "non-being" be perpetually in question in human reality. If I were *not* courageous in the way in which this inkwell is not a table; that is, if I were isolated in my cowardice, propped firmly against it, incapable of putting it in relation to its opposite, if I were not capable of *determining* myself as cowardly—that is, to deny courage to myself and thereby to escape my cowardice in the very moment that I posit it—if it were not on principle *impossible* for me to coincide with my *not-being-courageous* as well as with my being—courageous—then any project of bad faith would be prohibited me. Thus in order for bad faith to be possible, sincerity itself must be in bad faith. The condition of the possibility for bad faith is that human reality, in its most immediate being, in the intrastructure of the pre-reflective *cogito,* must be what it is not and not be what it is.

III. The "Faith" of Bad Faith

We have indicated for the moment only those conditions which render bad faith conceivable, the structures of being which permit us to form concepts of bad faith. We can not limit ourselves to these considerations; we have not yet distinguished bad faith from falsehood. The two-faced concepts which we have described would without a doubt be utilized by a liar to discountenance his questioner, although their two-faced quality being established on the being of man and not on some empirical circumstance can and ought to be evident to all. The true problem of bad faith stems evidently from the fact that bad faith is *faith.* It can not be either a cynical lie or certainty—if certainty is the intuitive possession of the object. But if we take belief as meaning the adherence of being to its object when the object is not given or is given indistinctly, then bad faith is belief; and the essential problem of bad faith is a problem of belief.

How can we believe by bad faith in the concepts which we forge expressly to persuade ourselves? We must note in fact that the project of bad faith must be itself in bad faith. I am not only in bad faith at the end of my effort when I have constructed my two-faced concepts and when I have persuaded myself. In truth, I have not persuaded my-self; to the extent that I could be so persuaded, I have always been so. And at the very moment when I was disposed to put myself in bad faith, I of necessity was in bad faith with respect to this same disposition. For me to have represented it to myself as bad faith would have been cynicism; to believe it sincerely innocent would have been in good faith. The decision to be in bad faith does not dare to speak its name; it believes it-self and does not believe itself in bad faith; it believes itself and does not believe itself in good faith. It is this which from the upsurge of bad faith, determines the later attitude and, as it were, the *Weltanschauung* of bad faith.

Bad faith does not hold the norms and criteria of truth as they are accepted by the critical thought of good faith. What it decides first, in fact, is the nature of truth. With bad faith a truth appears, a method of thinking, a type of being which is like that of ob-jects; the ontological characteristic of the world of bad faith with which the subject sud-denly surrounds himself is this: that here being is what it is not, and is not what it is. Consequently a peculiar type of evidence appears: *non-persuasive* evidence. Bad faith apprehends evidence but it is resigned in advance to not being fulfilled by this evidence, to not being persuaded and transformed into good faith. It makes itself humble and modest; it is not ignorant, it says, that faith is decision and that after each intuition, it must decide and will what it is. Thus bad faith in its primitive project and in its coming into the world decides on the exact nature of its requirements. It stands forth in the firm resolution *not to demand too much,* to count itself satisfied when it is barely persuaded, to force itself in decisions to adhere to uncertain truths. This original project of bad faith is a decision in bad faith on the nature of faith. Let us understand clearly that there is no question of a reflective, voluntary decision, but of a spontaneous determination of our being. One *puts oneself* in bad faith as one goes to sleep and one is in bad faith as one dreams. Once this mode of being has been realized, it is as difficult to get out of it as to wake oneself up; bad faith is a type of being in the world, like waking or dreaming, which by itself tends to perpetuate itself, although its structure is of the *metastable* type. But bad faith is conscious of its structure, and it has taken precautions by deciding that the *metastable* structure is the structure of being and that non-persuasion is the structure of all convictions. It follows that if bad faith is faith and if it includes in its original proj-ect its own negation (it determines itself to be not quite convinced in order to convince itself that I am what I am not), then to start with, a faith which wishes itself to be not quite convinced must be possible. What are the conditions for the possibility of such a faith?

I believe that my friend Pierre feels friendship for me. I believe it in good *faith.* I believe it but I do not have for it any self-evident intuition, for the nature of the object does not lend itself to intuition. I *believe* it; that is, I allow myself to give in to all im-pulses to trust it; I decide to believe in it, and to maintain myself in this decision; I con-duct myself, finally, as if I were certain of it—and all this in the synthetic unity of one and the same attitude. This which I define as good faith is what Hegel would call the *im-mediate.* It is simple faith. Hegel would demonstrate at once that the immediate calls for mediation and that belief by becoming *belief for itself,* passes to the state of non-belief. If *I believe* that my friend Pierre likes me, this means that his friendship appears to me as the meaning of all his acts. Belief is a particular consciousness of *the meaning* of Pierre's acts. But if I know that I believe, the belief appears to me as pure subjective de-termination without external correlative. This is what makes the very word "to believe" a term utilized indifferently to indicate the unwavering firmness of belief ("My God, I believe in you") and its character as disarmed and strictly subjective. ("Is Pierre my friend? I do not know; I believe so.") But the nature of consciousness is such that in it the mediate and the immediate are one and the same being. To believe is to know that one believes, and to know that one believes is no longer to believe. Thus to believe is not to believe any longer because that is only to believe—this in the unity of one and the same non-thetic self-consciousness. To be sure, we have here forced the description of the phenomenon by designating it with the word *to know;* non-thetic consciousness is not to *know.* But it is in its very translucency at the origin of all knowing. Thus the non-thetic consciousness (of) believing is destructive of belief. But at the same time the very law of the pre-reflective *cogito* implies that the being of believing ought to be the consciousness of believing.

Thus belief is a being which questions its own being, which can realize itself only in its destruction, which can manifest itself to itself only by denying itself. It is a being for which to be is to appear and to appear is to deny itself. To believe is not-to-believe. We see the reason for it; the being of consciousness is to exist by itself, then to make itself be and thereby to pass beyond itself. In this sense consciousness is perpetually escaping itself, belief becomes non-belief, the immediate becomes mediation, the absolute becomes relative, and the relative becomes absolute. The ideal of good faith (to believe what one believes) is, like that of sincerity (to be what one is), an ideal of being-in-itself. Every belief is a belief that falls short; one never wholly believes what one believes. Consequently the primitive project of bad faith is only the utilization of this self-destruction of the fact of consciousness. If every belief in good faith is an impossible belief, then there is a place for every impossible belief. My inability to *believe* that I am courageous will not discourage me since every belief involves not quite believing. I shall define this impossible belief as *my* belief. To be sure, I shall not be able to hide from myself that I believe in order not to believe and that I do not believe *in order* to believe. But the subtle, total annihilation of bad faith by itself can not surprise me; it exists at the basis of all faith. What is it then? At the moment when I wish to believe myself courageous I know that I am a coward. And this certainly would come to destroy my belief. But *first,* I am not any more courageous than cowardly, if we are to understand this in the mode of being of the-in-itself. In the second place, I do not *know* that I am courageous; such a view of myself can be accompanied only by *belief,* for it surpasses pure reflective certitude. In the third place, it is very true that bad faith does not succeed in believing what it wishes to believe. But it is precisely as the acceptance of not believing what it believes that it is bad faith. Good faith wishes to flee the "not-believing-what-one-believes" by finding refuge in being. Bad faith flees being by taking refuge in "not-believing-what-one-believes." It has disarmed all beliefs in advance—those which it would like to take hold of and, by the same stroke, the others, those which it wishes to flee. In *willing* this self-destruction of belief, from which science escapes by searching for evidence, it ruins the beliefs which are opposed to it, which reveal themselves as *being only* belief. Thus we can better understand the original phenomenon of bad faith.

In bad faith there is no cynical lie nor knowing preparation for deceitful concepts. But the first act of bad faith is to flee what it can not flee, to flee what it is. The very project of flight reveals to bad faith an inner disintegration in the heart of being, and it is this disintegration which bad faith wishes to be. In truth, the two immediate attitudes which we can take in the face of our being are conditioned by the very nature of this being and its immediate relation with the in-itself. Good faith seeks to flee the inner disintegration of my being in the direction of the in-itself which it should be and is not. Bad faith seeks to flee the in-itself by means of the inner disintegration of my being. But it denies this very disintegration as it denies that it is itself bad faith. Bad faith seeks by means of "not-being-what-one-is" to escape from the in-itself which I am not in the mode of being what one is not. It denies itself as bad faith and aims at the in-itself which I am not in the mode of "not-being-what-one-is-not."* If bad faith is possible, it is because it is an immediate, permanent threat to every project of the human being; it is because consciousness conceals in its being a permanent risk of bad faith. The origin of this risk is the fact that the nature of consciousness simultaneously is to be what it is not and not to be what it is. In the light of these remarks we can now approach the ontological study of consciousness, not as the totality of the human being, but as the instantaneous nucleus of this being.

EXISTENTIALISM IS A HUMANISM

I should like on this occasion to defend existentialism against some charges which have been brought against it.

First, it has been charged with inviting people to remain in a kind of desperate quietism because, since no solutions are possible, we should have to consider action in this world as quite impossible. We should then end up in a philosophy of contemplation; and since contemplation is a luxury, we come in the end to a bourgeois philosophy. The communists in particular have made these charges.

On the other hand, we have been charged with dwelling on human degradation, with pointing up everywhere the sordid, shady, and slimy, and neglecting the gracious and beautiful, the bright side of human nature; for example, according to Mlle. Mercier, a Catholic critic, with forgetting the smile of the child. Both sides charge us with having ignored human solidarity, with considering man as an isolated being. The communists say that the main reason for this is that we take pure subjectivity, *the Cartesian I think,* as our starting point; in other words, the moment in which man becomes fully aware of what it means to him to be an isolated being; as a result, we are unable to return to a state of solidarity with the men who are not ourselves, a state which we can never reach in the *cogito.*

From the Christian standpoint, we are charged with denying the reality and seriousness of human undertakings, since, if we reject God's commandments and the eternal verities, there no longer remains anything but pure caprice, with everyone permitted to do as he pleases and incapable, from his own point of view, of condemning the points of view and acts of others.

I shall try today to answer these different charges. Many people are going to be surprised at what is said here about humanism. We shall try to see in what sense it is to be understood. In any case, what can be said from the very beginning is that by existentialism we mean a doctrine which makes human life possible and, in addition, declares that every truth and every action implies a human setting and a human subjectivity.

---

*If it is indifferent whether one is in good or in bad faith, because bad faith reapprehends good faith and slides to the very origin of the project of good faith, that does not mean that we can not radically escape bad faith. But this supposes a self-recovery of being which was previously corrupted. This self-recovery we shall call authenticity, the description of which has no place here.

Jean-Paul Satre, *Existentialism Is a Humanism,* translated by Bernard Frechtman. New York: Philosophical Library, 1947. Reprinted by permission.

As is generally known, the basic charge against us is that we put the emphasis on the dark side of human life. Someone recently told me of a lady who, when she let slip a vulgar word in a moment of irritation, excused herself by saying, "I guess I'm becoming an existentialist." Consequently, existentialism is regarded as something ugly; that is why we are said to be naturalists; and if we are, it is rather surprising that in this day and age we cause so much more alarm and scandal than does naturalism, properly so called. The kind of person who can take in his stride such a novel as Zola's *The Earth* is disgusted as soon as he starts reading an existentialist novel; the kind of person who is resigned to the wisdom of the ages—which is pretty sad—finds us even sadder. Yet, what can be more disillusioning than saying "true charity begins at home" or "a scoundrel will always return evil for good"?

We know the commonplace remarks made when this subject comes up, remarks which always add up to the same thing: we shouldn't struggle against the powers-that-be; we shouldn't resist authority; we shouldn't try to rise above our station; any action which doesn't conform to authority is romantic; any effort not based on past experience is doomed to failure; experience shows that man's bent is always toward trouble, that there must be a strong hand to hold him in check, if not, there will be anarchy. There are still people who go on mumbling these melancholy old saws, the people who say, "It's only human!" whenever a more or less repugnant act is pointed out to them, the people who glut themselves on *chansons réalistes;* these are the people who accuse existentialism of being too gloomy, and to such an extent that I wonder whether they are complaining about it, not for its pessimism, but much rather its optimism. Can it be that what really scares them in the doctrine I shall try to present here is that it leaves to man a possibility of choice? To answer this question, we must re-examine it on a strictly philosophical plane. What is meant by the term *existentialism?*

Most people who use the word would be rather embarrassed if they had to explain it, since, now that the word is all the rage, even the work of a musician or painter is being called existentialist. A gossip columnist in *Clartés* signs himself *The Existentialist,* so that by this time the word has been so stretched and has taken on so broad a meaning, that it no longer means anything at all. It seems that for want of an avant-garde doctrine analogous to surrealism, the kind of people who are eager for scandal and flurry turn to this philosophy which in other respects does not at all serve their purposes in this sphere.

Actually, it is the least scandalous, the most austere of doctrines. It is intended strictly for specialists and philosophers. Yet it can be defined easily. What complicates matters is that there are two kinds of existentialist; first, those who are Christian, among whom I would include Jaspers and Gabriel Marcel, both Catholic; and on the other hand the atheistic existentialists, among whom I class Heidegger, and then the French existentialists and myself. What they have in common is that they think that existence precedes essence, or, if you prefer, that subjectivity must be the starting point.

Just what does that mean? Let us consider some object that is manufactured, for example, a book or a paper-cutter: here is an object which has been made by an artisan whose inspiration came from a concept. He referred to the concept of what a paper-cutter is and likewise to a known method of production, which is part of the concept, something which is, by and large, a routine. Thus, the paper-cutter is at once an object produced in a certain way and, on the other hand, one having a specific use; and one cannot postulate a man who produces a paper-cutter but does not know what it is used for. Therefore, let us say that, for the paper-cutter, essence—that is, the ensemble of both the production routines and the properties which enable it to be both produced and defined—precedes existence. Thus, the presence of the paper-cutter or book in front of me is determined. Therefore, we have here a technical view of the world whereby it can be said that production precedes existence.

When we conceive God as the Creator, He is generally thought of as a superior sort of artisan. Whatever doctrine we may be considering, whether one like that of Descartes or that of Leibnitz, we always grant that will more or less follows understanding or, at the very least, accompanies it, and that when God creates He knows exactly what He is creating. Thus, the concept of man in the mind of God is comparable to the concept of paper-cutter in the mind of the manufacturer, and, following certain techniques and a conception, God produces man, just as the artisan, following a definition and a technique, makes a paper-cutter. Thus, the individual man is the realization of a certain concept in the divine intelligence.

In the eighteenth century, the atheism of the *philosophes* discarded the idea of God, but not so much for the notion that essence precedes existence. To a certain extent, this idea is found everywhere; we find it in Diderot, in Voltaire, and even in Kant. Man has a human nature; this human nature, which is the concept of the human, is found in all men, which means that each man is a particular example of a universal concept, man. In Kant, the result of this universality is that the wild-man, the natural man, as well as the bourgeois, are circumscribed by the same definition and have the same basic qualities. Thus, here too the essence of man precedes the historical existence that we find in nature.

Atheistic existentialism, which I represent, is more coherent. It states that if God does not exist, there is at least one being in whom existence precedes essence, a being who exists before he can be defined by any concept, and that this being is man, or, as Heidegger says, human reality. What is meant here by saying that existence precedes essence? It means that, first of all, man exists, turns up, appears on the scene, and, only afterwards, defines himself. If man, as the existentialist conceives him, is indefinable, it is because at first he is nothing. Only afterward will he be something, and he himself will have made what he will be. Thus, there is no human nature, since there is no God to conceive it. Not only is man what he conceives himself to be, but he is also only what he wills himself to be after this thrust toward existence.

Man is nothing else but what he makes of himself. Such is the first principle of existentialism. It is also what is called subjectivity, the name we are labeled with when charges are brought against us. But what do we mean by this, if not that man has a greater dignity than a stone or table? For we mean that man first exists, that is, that man first of all is the being who hurls himself toward a future and who is conscious of imagining himself as being in the future. Man is at the start a plan which is aware of itself, rather than a patch of moss, a piece of garbage, or a cauliflower; nothing exists prior to this plan; there is nothing in heaven; man will be what he will have planned to be. Not what he will want to be. Because by the word "will" we generally mean a conscious decision, which is subsequent to what we have already made of ourselves. I may want to belong to a political party, write a book, get married; but all that is only a manifestation of an earlier, more spontaneous choice that is called "will." But if existence really does precede essence, man is responsible for what he is. Thus, existentialism's first move is to make every man aware of what he is and to make the full responsibility of his existence rest on him. And when we say that a man is responsible for himself, we do not only mean that he is responsible for his own individuality, but that he is responsible for all men.

The word subjectivism has two meanings, and our opponents play on the two. Subjectivism means, on the one hand, that an individual chooses and makes himself; and, on the other, that it is impossible for man to transcend human subjectivity. The second of these is the essential meaning of existentialism. When we say that man chooses his own self, we mean that every one of us does likewise; but we also mean by that that in making this choice he also chooses all men. In fact, in creating the man that we want to be, there is not a single one of our acts which does not at the same time create an image of man as we think he ought to be. To choose to be this or that is to affirm at the same time the value of what we choose, because we can never choose evil. We always choose the good, and nothing can be good for us without being good for all.

If, on the other hand, existence precedes essence, and if we grant that we exist and fashion our image at one and the same time, the image is valid for everybody and for our whole age. Thus, our responsibility is much greater than we might have supposed, because it involves all mankind. If I am a workingman and choose to join a Christian trade-union rather than be a communist, and if by being a member I want to show that the best thing for man is resignation, that the kingdom of man is not of this world, I am not only involving my own case—I want to be resigned for everyone. As a result, my action has involved all humanity. To take a more individual matter, if I want to marry, to have children; even if this marriage depends solely on my own circumstances or passion or wish, I am involving all humanity in monogamy and not merely myself. Therefore, I am responsible for myself and for everyone else. I am creating a certain image of man of my own choosing. In choosing myself, I choose man.

This helps us understand what the actual content is of such rather grandiloquent words as anguish, forlornness, despair. As you will see, it's all quite simple.

First, what is meant by anguish? The existentialists say at once that man is in anguish. What that means is this: the man who involves himself and who realizes that he is not only the person he chooses to be, but also a law-maker who is, at the same time, choosing all mankind as well as himself, can not help escape the feeling of his total and deep responsibility. Of course, there are many people who are not anxious; but we claim that they are hiding their anxiety, that they are fleeing from it. Certainly, many people believe that when they do something, they themselves are the only ones involved, and when someone says to them, "What if everyone acted that way?" they shrug their shoulders and answer, "Everyone doesn't act that way." But really, one should always ask himself, "What would happen if everybody looked at things that way?" There is no escaping this disturbing thought except by a kind of double-dealing. A man who lies and makes excuses for himself by saying "not everybody does that," is someone with an uneasy conscience, because the act of lying implies that a universal value is conferred upon the lie.

Anguish is evident even when it conceals itself. This is the anguish that Kierkegaard called the anguish of Abraham. You know the story: an angel has ordered Abraham to sacrifice his son; if it really were an angel who has come and said, "You are Abraham, you shall sacrifice your son," everything would be all right. But everyone might first wonder, "Is it really an angel, and am I really Abraham? What proof do I have?"

There was a mad woman who had hallucinations; someone used to speak to her on the telephone and give her orders. Her doctor asked her, "Who is it who talks to you?" She answered, "He says it's God." What proof did she really have that it was God? If an angel comes to me, what proof is there that it's an angel? And if I hear voices, what proof is there that they come from heaven and not from hell, or from the subconscious, or a pathological condition? What proves that they are addressed to me? What proof is there that I have been appointed to impose my choice and my conception of man on humanity? I'll never find any proof or sign to convince me of that. If a voice addresses me, it is always for me to decide that this is the angel's voice; if

I consider that such an act is a good one, it is I who will choose to say that it is good rather than bad.

Now, I'm not being singled out as an Abraham, and yet at every moment I'm obliged to perform exemplary acts. For every man, everything happens as if all mankind had its eyes fixed on him and were guiding itself by what he does. And every man ought to say to himself, "Am I really the kind of man who has the right to act in such a way that humanity might guide itself by my actions?" And if he does not say that to himself, he is masking his anguish.

There is no question here of the kind of anguish which would lead to quietism, to inaction. It is a matter of a simple sort of anguish that anybody who has had responsibilities is familiar with. For example, when a military officer takes the responsibility for an attack and sends a number of men to death, he chooses to do so, and in the main he alone makes the choice. Doubtless, orders come from above, but they are too broad; he interprets them, and on this interpretation depend the lives of ten or fourteen or twenty men. In making a decision he can not help having a certain anguish. All leaders know this anguish. That doesn't keep them from acting; on the contrary, it is the very condition of their action. For it implies that they envisage a number of possibilities, and when they choose one, they realize that it has value only because it is chosen. We shall see that this kind of anguish, which is the kind that existentialism describes, is explained, in addition, by a direct responsibility to the other men whom it involves. It is not a curtain separating us from action, but is part of action itself.

When we speak of forlornness, a term Heidegger was fond of, we mean only that God does not exist and that we have to face all the consequences of this. The existentialist is strongly opposed to a certain kind of secular ethics which would like to abolish God with the least possible expense. About 1880, some French teachers tried to set up a secular ethic which went something like this: God is a useless and costly hypothesis; we are discarding it; but, meanwhile, in order for there to be an ethics, a society, a civilization, it is essential that certain values be taken seriously and that they be considered as having an *a priori* existence. It must be obligatory, *a priori*, to be honest, not to lie, not to beat your wife, to have children, etc., etc. So we're going to try a little device which will make it possible to show that values exist all the same, inscribed in a heaven of ideas, though otherwise God does not exist. In other words—and this, I believe, is the tendency of everything called reformism in France—nothing will be changed if God does not exist. We shall find ourselves with the same norms of honesty, progress, and humanism, and we shall have made of God an outdated hypothesis which will peacefully die off by itself.

The existentialist, on the contrary, thinks it very distressing that God does not exist, because all possibility of finding values in a heaven of ideas disappears along with Him; there can no longer be an *a priori* Good, since there is no infinite and perfect consciousness to think it. Nowhere is it written that the Good exists, that we must be honest, that we must not lie; because the fact is we are on a plane where there are only men. Dostoevski said, "If God didn't exist, everything would be possible." That is the very starting point of existentialism. Indeed, everything is permissible if God does not exist, and as a result man is forlorn, because neither within him nor without does he find anything to cling to. He can't start making excuses for himself.

If existence really does precede essence, there is no explaining things away by reference to a fixed and given human nature. In other words, there is not determinism, man is free, man is freedom. On the other hand, if God does not exist, we find no values or commands to turn to which legitimize our conduct. So, in the bright realm of values, we have no excuse behind us, nor justification before us. We are alone, with no excuses.

That is the idea I shall try to convey when I say that man is condemned to be free. Condemned, because he did not create himself, yet, in other respects is free; because, once thrown into the world, he is responsible for everything he does. The existentialist does not believe in the power of passion. He will never agree that a sweeping passion is a ravaging torrent which fatally leads a man to certain acts and is therefore an excuse. He thinks that man is responsible for his passion.

The existentialist does not think man is going to help himself by finding in the world some omen by which to orient himself. Because he thinks that man will interpret the omen to suit himself. Therefore, he thinks that man, with no support and no aid, is condemned every moment to invent man. Ponge, in a very fine article, has said, "Man is the future of man." That's exactly it. But if it is taken to mean that this future is recorded in heaven, that God sees it, then it is false, because it would really no longer be a future. If it is taken to mean that, whatever a man may be, there is a future to be forged, a virgin future before him, then this remark is sound. But then we are forlorn.

To give you an example which will enable you to understand forlornness better, I shall cite the case of one of my students who came to see me under the following circumstances: his father was on bad terms with his mother, and, moreover, was inclined to be a collaborationist; his older brother had been killed in the German offensive of 1940, and the young man, with somewhat immature but generous feelings, wanted to avenge him. His mother lived alone with him, very much upset by the half-treason of her husband and the death of her older son; the boy was her only consolation.

The boy was faced with the choice of leaving for England and joining the Free French Forces—that is, leaving his mother behind—or remaining with his mother and helping her to carry on. He was fully aware that the woman lived only for him and that his going-off—and perhaps his death—would plunge her into despair. He was also aware that every act that he did for his mother's sake was a sure thing, in the sense that it was helping her to carry on, whereas every effort he made toward going off and fighting was an uncertain move which might run aground and prove completely useless; for example, on his way to England he might, while passing through Spain, be detained indefinitely in a Spanish camp; he might reach England or Elgiers and be stuck in an office at a desk job. As a result, he was faced with two very different kinds of action: one, concrete, immediate, but concerning only one individual; the other concerned an incomparably vaster group, a national collectivity, but for that very reason was dubious, and might be interrupted en route. And, at the same time, he was wavering between two kinds of ethics. On the one hand, an ethics of sympathy, of personal devotion; on the other, a broader ethics, but one whose efficacy was more dubious. He had to choose between the two.

Who could help him choose? Christian doctrine? No. Christian doctrine says, "Be charitable, love your neighbor, take the more rugged path, etc., etc." But which is the more rugged path? Whom should he love as a brother? The fighting man or his mother? Which does the greater good, the vague act of fighting in a group, or the concrete one of helping a particular human being to go on living? Who can decide *a priori?* Nobody. No book of ethics can tell him. The Kantian ethics says, "Never treat any person as a means, but as an end." Very well, if I stay with my mother, I'll treat her as an end and not as a means; but by virtue of this very fact, I'm running the risk of treating the people around me who are fighting, as means; and, conversely, if I go to join those who are fighting, I'll be treating them as an end, and, by doing that, I run the risk of treating my mother as a means.

If values are vague, and if they are always too broad for the concrete and specific case that we are considering, the only thing left for us is to trust our instincts. That's what this young man tried to do; and when I saw him, he said, "In the end, feeling is what counts. I ought to choose whichever pushes me in one direction. If I feel that I love my mother enough to sacrifice everything else for her—my desire for vengeance, for action, for adventure—then I'll stay with her. If, on the contrary, I feel that my love for my mother isn't enough, I'll leave."

But how is the value of a feeling determined? What gives his feeling for his mother value? Precisely the fact that he remained with her. I may say that I like so-and-so well enough to sacrifice a certain amount of money for him, but I may say so only if I've done it. I may say "I love my mother well enough to remain with her" if I have remained with her. The only way to determine the value of this affection is, precisely, to perform an act which confirms and defines it. But, since I require this affection to justify my act, I find myself caught in a vicious circle.

On the other hand, Gide has well said that a mock feeling and a true feeling are almost indistinguishable; to decide that I love my mother and will remain with her, or to remain with her by putting on an act, amount somewhat to the same thing. In other words, the feeling is formed by the acts one performs; so, I can not refer to it in order to act upon it. Which means that I can neither seek within myself the true condition which will impel me to act, nor apply to a system of ethics for concepts which will permit me to act. You will say, "At least, he did go to a teacher for advice." But if you seek advice from a priest, for example, you have chosen this priest; you already knew, more or less, just about what advice he was going to give you. In other words, choosing your adviser is involving yourself. The proof of this is that if you are a Christian, you will say, "Consult a priest." But some priests are collaborating, some are just marking time, some are resisting. Which to choose? If the young man chooses a priest who is resisting or collaborating, he has already decided on the kind of advice he's going to get. Therefore, in coming to see me he knew the answer I was going to give him, and I had only one answer to give: "You're free, choose, that is, invent." No general ethics can show you what is to be done; there are no omens in the world. The Catholics will reply, "But there are." Granted—but, in any case, I myself choose the meaning they have.

When I was a prisoner, I knew a rather remarkable young man who was a Jesuit. He had entered the Jesuit order in the following way: he had a number of very bad breaks; in childhood, his father died, leaving him in poverty, and he was a scholarship student at a religious institution where he was constantly made to feel that he was being kept out of charity; then, he failed to get any of the honors and distinctions that children like; later on, at about eighteen, he bungled a love affair; finally, at twenty-two, he failed in military training, a childish enough matter, but it was the last straw.

This young fellow might well have felt that he had botched everything. It was a sign of something, but of what? He might have taken refuge in bitterness or despair. But he very wisely looked upon all this as a sign that he was not made for secular triumphs, and that only the triumphs of religion, holiness, and faith were open to him. He saw the hand of God in all this, and so he entered the order. Who can help seeing that he alone decided what the sign meant?

Some other interpretation might have been drawn from this series of setbacks; for example, that he might have done better to turn carpenter or revolutionist. Therefore, he is fully responsible for the interpretation. Forlornness implies that we ourselves choose our being. Forlornness and anguish go together.

As for despair, the term has a very simple meaning. It means that we shall confine ourselves to reckoning only with what depends upon our will, or on the ensemble of probabilities which make our action possible. When we want something, we always have to reckon with probabilities. I may be counting on the arrival of a friend. The friend is coming by rail or street-car; this supposes that the train will arrive on schedule, or that the street-car will not jump the track. I am left in the realm of possibility; but possibilities are to be reckoned with only to the point where my action comports with the ensemble of these possibilities, and no further. The moment the possibilities I am considering are not rigorously involved by my action, I ought to disengage myself from them, because no God, no scheme, can adapt the world and its possibilities to my will. When Descartes said, "Conquer yourself rather than the world," he meant essentially the same thing.

The Marxists to whom I have spoken reply, "You can rely on the support of others in your action, which obviously has certain limits because you're not going to live forever. That means: rely on both what others are doing elsewhere to help you, in China, in Russia, and what they will do later on, after your death, to carry on the action and lead it to its fulfillment, which will be the revolution. You even *have* to rely upon that, otherwise you're immoral." I reply at once that I will always rely on fellow-fighters insofar as these comrades are involved with me in a common struggle, in the unity of a party or a group in which I can more or less make my weight felt; that is, one whose ranks I am in as a fighter and whose movements I am aware of at every moment. In such a situation, relying on the unity and will of the party is exactly like counting on the fact that the train will arrive on time, or that the car won't jump the track. But, given that man is free and that there is no human nature for me to depend on, I can not count on men whom I do not know by relying on human goodness or man's concern for the good of society. I don't know what will become of the Russian revolution; I may make an example of it to the extent that at the present time it is apparent that the proletariat plays a part in Russia that it plays in no other nation. But I can't swear that this will inevitably lead to a triumph of the proletariat. I've got to limit myself to what I see.

Given that men are free and that tomorrow they will freely decide what man will be, I can not be sure that, after my death, fellow-fighters will carry on my work to bring it to its maximum perfection. Tomorrow, after my death, some men may decide to set up Fascism, and the others may be cowardly and muddled enough to let them do it. Fascism will then be the human reality, so much the worse for us.

Actually, things will be as man will have decided they are to be. Does that mean that I should abandon myself to quietism? No. First, I should involve myself; then, act on the old saw, "Nothing ventured, nothing gained." Nor does it mean that I shouldn't belong to a party, but rather that I shall have no illusions and shall do what I can. For example, suppose I ask myself, "Will socialization, as such, ever come about?" I know nothing about it. All I know is that I'm going to do everything in my power to bring it about. Beyond that, I can't count on anything. Quietism is the attitude of people who say, "Let others do what I can't do." The doctrine I am presenting is the very opposite of quietism, since it declares, "There is no reality except in action." Moreover, it goes further, since it adds, "Man is nothing else than his plan; he exists only to the extent that he fulfills himself; he is therefore nothing else than the ensemble of his acts, nothing else than his life."

According to this, we can understand why our doctrine horrifies certain people. Because often the only way they can bear their wretchedness is to think, "Circumstances have been against me. What I've been and done doesn't show my true worth. To be sure, I've had no great love, no great friendship, but that's because I haven't met a man or woman who was worthy. The books I've written haven't been very good because I haven't had the proper leisure. I haven't had children to devote myself to because I didn't find a man with whom I could have spent my life. So there remains within me, unused and quite viable, a host of propensities, inclinations, possibilities, that one wouldn't guess from the mere series of things I've done."

Now, for the existentialist there is really no love other than one which manifests itself in a person's being in love. There is no genius other than one which is expressed in works of art; the genius of Proust is the sum of Proust's works; the genius of Racine is his series of tragedies. Outside of that, there is nothing. Why say that Racine could have written another tragedy, when he didn't write it? A man is involved in life, leaves his impress on it, and outside of that there is nothing. To be sure, this may seem a harsh thought to someone whose life hasn't been a success. But, on the other hand, it prompts people to understand that reality alone is what counts, that dreams, expectations, and hopes warrant no more than to define a man as a disappointed dream, as miscarried hopes, as vain expectations. In other words, to define him negatively and not positively. However, when we say, "You are nothing else than your life," that does not imply that the artist will be judged solely on the basis of his works of art; a thousand other things will contribute toward summing him up. What we mean is that a man is nothing else than a series of undertakings, that he is the sum, the organization, the ensemble of the relationships which make up these undertakings.

When all is said and done, what we are accused of, at bottom, is not our pessimism, but an optimistic toughness. If people throw up to us our works of fiction in which we write about people who are soft, weak, cowardly, and sometimes even downright bad, it's not because these people are soft, weak, cowardly, or bad; because if we were to say, as Zola did, that they are that way because of heredity, the workings of environment, society, because of biological or psychological determinism, people would be reassured. They would say, "Well, that's what we're like, no one can do anything about it." But when the existentialist writes about a coward, he says that this coward is responsible for his cowardice. He's not like that because he has a cowardly heart or lung or brain; he's not like that on account of his physiological makeup; but he's like that because he has made himself a coward by his acts. There's no such thing as a cowardly constitution; there are nervous constitutions; there is poor blood, as the common people say, or strong constitutions. But the man whose blood is poor is not a coward on that account, for what makes cowardice is the act of renouncing or yielding. A constitution is not an act; the coward is defined on the basis of the acts he performs. People feel, in a vague sort of way, that this coward we're talking about is guilty of being a coward, and the thought frightens them. What people would like is that a coward or a hero be born that way.

One of the complaints most frequently made about *The Ways of Freedom** can be summed up as follows: "After all, these people are so spineless, how are you going to make heroes out of them?" This objection almost makes me laugh, for it assumes that people are born heroes. That's what people really want to think. If you're born cowardly, you may set your mind perfectly at rest; there's nothing you can do about it; you'll be cowardly all your life, whatever you may do. If you're born a hero, you may set your mind just as much at rest; you'll be a hero all your life; you'll drink like a hero and eat like a hero. What the existentialist says is that the coward makes himself cowardly, that the hero makes himself heroic. There's always a possibility for the coward not to be cowardly any more and for the hero to stop being heroic. What counts is total involvement; some one particular action or set of circumstances is not total involvement.

Thus, I think we have answered a number of the charges concerning existentialism. You see that it can not be taken for a philosophy of quietism, since it defines man

---

Les Chennus de la Liberté, A trilogy of novels of which two—*L'Age de Raison (The Age of Reason)* and *Le Sursis (The Reprieve)*—had been published at the time of this article.

in terms of action; nor for a pessimistic description of man—there is no doctrine more optimistic, since man's destiny is within himself; nor for an attempt to discourage man from acting, since it tells him that the only hope is in his acting and that action is the only thing that enables a man to live. Consequently, we are dealing here with an ethic of action and involvement.

Nevertheless, on the basis of a few notions like these, we are still charged with immuring man in his private subjectivity. There again we're very much misunderstood. Subjectivity of the individual is indeed our point of departure, and this for strictly philosophic reasons. Not because we are bourgeois, but because we want a doctrine based on truth and not a lot of fine theories, full of hope but with no real basis. There can be no other truth to take off from than this: *I think; therefore I exist.* There we have the absolute truth of consciousness becoming aware of itself. Every theory which takes man out of the moment in which he becomes aware of himself is, at its very beginning, a theory which confounds truth, for outside the Cartesian *cogito,* all views are only probable, and a doctrine of probability which is not bound to a truth dissolves into thin air. In order to describe the probable, you must have a firm hold on the true. Therefore, before there can be any truth whatsoever, there must be an absolute truth; and this one is simple and easily arrived at; it's on everyone's doorstep; it's a matter of grasping it directly.

Secondly, this theory is the only one which gives man dignity, the only one which does not reduce him to an object. The effect of all materialism is to treat all men, including the one philosophizing, as objects, that is, as an ensemble of determined reactions in no way distinguished from the ensemble of qualities and phenomena which constitute a table or a chair or a stone. We definitely wish to establish the human realm as an ensemble of values distinct from the material realm. But the subjectivity that we have thus arrived at, and which we have claimed to be truth, is not a strictly individual subjectivity, for we have demonstrated that one discovers in the cogito not only himself, but others as well.

The philosophies of Descartes and Kant to the contrary, through the *I think* we reach our own self in the presence of others, and the others are just as real to us as our own self. Thus, the man who becomes aware of himself through the *cogito* also perceives all others, and he perceives them as the condition of his own existence. He realizes that he can not be anything (in the sense that we say that someone is witty or nasty or jealous) unless others recognize it as such. In order to get any truth about myself, I must have contact with another person. The other is indispensable to my own existence, as well as to my knowledge about myself. This being so, in discovering my inner being I discover the other person at the same time, like a freedom placed in front of me which thinks and wills only for or against me. Hence, let us at once announce the discovery of a world which we shall call intersubjectivity; this is the world in which man decides what he is and what others are.

Besides, if it is impossible to find in every man some universal essence which would be human nature, yet there does exist a universal human condition. It's not by chance that today's thinkers speak more readily of man's condition than of his nature. By condition they mean, more or less definitely, the *a priori* limits which outline man's fundamental situation in the universe. Historical situations vary; a man may be born a slave in a pagan society or a feudal lord or a proletarian. What does not vary is the necessity for him to exist in the world, to be at work there, to be there in the midst of other people, and to be mortal there. The limits are neither subjective nor objective, or, rather, they have an objective and a subjective side. Objective because they are to be found everywhere and are recognizable everywhere; subjective because they are lived and are nothing if man does not live them, that is, freely determine his existence with reference to them. And though the configurations may differ, at least none of them are completely strange to me, because they all appear as attempts either to pass beyond these limits or recede from them or deny them or adapt to them. Consequently, every configuration, however individual it may be, has a universal value.

Every configuration, even the Chinese, the Indian, or the Negro, can be understood by a Westerner. "Can be understood" means that by virtue of a situation that he can imagine, a European of 1945 can, in like manner, push himself to his limits and reconstitute within himself the configuration of the Chinese, the Indian, or the African. Every configuration has universality in the sense that every configuration can be understood by every man. This does not at all mean that this configuration defines man forever, but that it can be met with again. There is always a way to understand the idiot, the child, the savage, the foreigner, provided one has the necessary information.

In this sense we may say that there is a universality of man; but it is not given, it is perpetually being made. I build the universal in choosing myself; I build it in understanding the configuration of every other man, whatever age he might have lived in. This absoluteness of choice does not do away with the relativeness of each epoch. At heart, what existentialism shows is the connection between the absolute character of free involvement, by virtue of which every man realizes himself in realizing a type of mankind, an involvement always comprehensible in any age whatsoever and by any person whosoever, and the relativeness of the cultural ensemble which may result from such a choice; it must be stressed that the relativity of Cartesianism and the absolute character of Cartesian involvement go together. In this sense, you may, if you like, say that each of us performs an absolute act in breathing, eating, sleeping, or behaving in any way whatever. There is no difference between being free, like a configuration, like an existence which chooses its essence, and being absolute. There is no difference between being an absolute temporarily localized, that is, localized in history, and being universally comprehensible.

This does not entirely settle the objection to subjectivism. In fact, the objection still takes several forms. First, there is the following: we are told, "So you're able to do anything, no matter what!" This is expressed in various ways. First we are accused of anarchy; then they say, "You're unable to pass judgment on others, because there's no reason to prefer one configuration to another"; finally they tell us, "Everything is arbitrary in this choosing of yours. You take something from one pocket and pretend you're putting it into the other."

These three objections aren't very serious. Take the first objection. "You're able to do anything, no matter what" is not to the point. In one sense choice is possible, but what is not possible is not to choose. I can always choose, but I ought to know that if I do not choose, I am still choosing. Though this may seem purely formal, it is highly important for keeping fantasy and caprice within bounds. If it is true that in facing a situation, for example, one in which, as a person capable of having sexual relations, of having children, I am obliged to choose an attitude, and if I in any way assume responsibility for a choice which, in involving myself, also involves all mankind, this has nothing to do with caprice, even if no *a priori* value determines my choice.

If anybody thinks that he recognizes here Gide's theory of the arbitrary act, he fails to see the enormous difference between this doctrine and Gide's. Gide does not know what a situation is. He acts out of pure caprice. For us, on the contrary, man is in an organized situation in which he himself is involved. Through his choice, he involves all mankind, and he can not avoid making a choice: either he will remain chaste, or he will marry without having children, or he will marry and have children; anyhow, whatever he may do, it is impossible for him not to take full responsibility for the way he handles this problem. Doubtless, he chooses without referring to preestablished values, but it is unfair to accuse him of caprice. Instead, let us say that moral choice is to be compared to the making of a work of art. And before going any further, let it be said at once that we are not dealing here with an aesthetic ethics, because our opponents are so dishonest that they even accuse us of that. The example I've chosen is a comparison only.

Having said that, may I ask whether anyone has ever accused an artist who has painted a picture of not having drawn his inspiration from rules set up *a priori?* Has anyone ever asked, "What painting ought he to make?" It is clearly understood that there is no definite painting to be made, that the artist is engaged in the making of his painting, and that the painting to be made is precisely the painting he will have made. It is clearly understood that there are no *a priori* aesthetic values, but that there are values which appear subsequently in the coherence of the painting, in the correspondence between what the artist intended and the result. Nobody can tell what the painting of tomorrow will be like. Painting can be judged only after it has once been made. What connection does that have with ethics? We are in the same creative situation. We never say that a work of art is arbitrary. When we speak of a canvas of Picasso, we never say that it is arbitrary; we understand quite well that he was making himself what he is at the very time he was painting, that the ensemble of his work is embodied in his life.

The same holds on the ethical plane. What art and ethics have in common is that we have creation and invention in both cases. We can not decide *a priori* what there is to be done. I think that I pointed that out quite sufficiently when I mentioned the case of the student who came to see me, and who might have applied to all the ethical systems, Kantian or otherwise, without getting any sort of guidance. He was obliged to devise his law himself. Never let it be said by us that this man—who, taking affection, individual action, and kindheartedness toward a specific person as his ethical first principle, chooses to remain with his mother, or who, preferring to make a sacrifice, chooses to go to England—has made an arbitrary choice. Man makes himself. He isn't ready made at the start. In choosing his ethics, he makes himself, and force of circumstances is such that he can not abstain from choosing one. We define man only in relationship to involvement. It is therefore absurd to charge us with arbitrariness of choice.

In the second place, it is said that we are unable to pass judgment on others. In a way this is true, and in another way, false. It is true in this sense, that, whenever a man sanely and sincerely involves himself and chooses his configuration, it is impossible for him to prefer another configuration, regardless of what his own may be in other respects. It is true in this sense, that we do not believe in progress. Progress is betterment. Man is always the same. The situation confronting him varies. Choice always remains a choice in a situation. The problem has not changed since the time one could choose between those for and those against slavery, for example, at the time of the Civil War, and the present time, when one can side with the Maquis Resistance Party, or with the Communists.

But, nevertheless, one can still pass judgment, for, as I have said, one makes a choice in relationship to others. First, one can judge (and this is perhaps not a judgment of value, but a logical judgment) that certain choices are based on error and others on truth. If we have defined man's situation as a free choice, with no excuses and no recourse, every man who takes refuge behind the excuse of his passions, every man who sets up a determinism, is a dishonest man.

The objection may be raised, "But why mayn't he choose himself dishonestly?" I reply that I am not obliged to pass moral judgment on him, but that I do define his dishonesty as an error. One can not help considering the truth of the matter. Dishonesty is obviously a falsehood because it belies the complete freedom of involvement. On the same grounds, I maintain that there is also dishonesty if I choose to state that certain values exist prior to me; it is self-contradictory for me to want them and at the same state that they are imposed on me. Suppose someone says to me, "What if I want to be dishonest?" I'll answer, "There's no reason for you not to be, but I'm saying that that's what you are, and that the strictly coherent attitude is that of honesty."

Besides, I can bring moral judgment to bear. When I declare that freedom in every concrete circumstance can have no other aim than to want itself, if man has once become aware that in his forlornness he imposes values, he can no longer want but one thing, and that is freedom, as the basis of all values. That doesn't mean that he wants it in the abstract. It means simply that the ultimate meaning of the acts of honest men is the quest for freedom as such. A man who belongs to a communist or revolutionary union wants concrete goals; these goals imply an abstract desire for freedom; but this freedom is wanted in something concrete. We want freedom for freedom's sake and in every particular circumstance. And in wanting freedom we discover that it depends entirely on the freedom of others, and that the freedom of others depends on ours. Of course, freedom as the definition of man does not depend on others, but as soon as there is involvement, I am obliged to want others to have freedom at the same time that I want my own freedom. I can take freedom as my goal only if I take that of others as a goal as well. Consequently, when, in all honesty, I've recognized that man is a being in whom existence precedes essence, that he is a free being who, in various circumstances, can want only his freedom, I have at the same time recognized that I can want only the freedom of others.

Therefore, in the name of this will for freedom, which freedom itself implies, I may pass judgment on those who seek to hide from themselves the complete arbitrariness and the complete freedom of their existence. Those who hide their complete freedom from themselves out of a spirit of seriousness or by means of deterministic excuses, I shall call cowards; those who try to show that their existence was necessary, when it is the very contingency of man's appearance on earth, I shall call stinkers. But cowards or stinkers can be judged only from a strictly unbiased point of view.

Therefore though the content of ethics is variable, a certain form of it is universal. Kant says that freedom desires both itself and the freedom of others. Granted. But he believes that the formal and the universal are enough to constitute an ethics. We, on the other hand, think that principles which are too abstract run aground in trying to decide action. Once again, take the case of the student. In the name of what, in the name of what great moral maxim do you think he could have decided, in perfect peace of mind, to abandon his mother or to stay with her? There is no way of judging. The content is always concrete and thereby unforeseeable; there is always the element of invention. The one thing that counts is knowing whether the inventing that has been done has been done in the name of freedom.

For example, let us look at the following two cases. You will see to what extent they correspond, yet differ. Take *The Mill on the Floss*. We find a certain young girl, Maggie Tulliver, who is an embodiment of the value of passion and who is aware of it. She is in love with a young man, Stephen, who is engaged to an insignificant young girl. This Maggie Tulliver, instead of heedlessly preferring her own happiness, chooses, in the name of human solidarity, to sacrifice herself and give up the man she loves. On the other hand, Sanseverina, in *The Charterhouse of Parma*, believing that passion is man's true value, would say that a great love deserves sacrifices; that it is to be preferred to the banality of the conjugal love that would tie Stephen to the young ninny he had to marry. She would choose to sacrifice the girl and fulfill her happiness; and, as Stendhal shows, she is even ready to sacrifice herself for the sake of passion, if this life demands it. Here we are in the presence of two strictly opposed moralities. I claim that they are much the same thing; in both cases what has been set up as the goal is freedom.

You can imagine two highly similar attitudes: one girl prefers to renounce her love out of resignation; another prefers to disregard the prior attachment of the man she loves out of sexual desire. On the surface these two actions resemble those we've just described. However, they are completely different. Sanseverina's attitude is much nearer that of Maggie Tulliver, one of heedless rapacity.

Thus, you see that the second charge is true and, at the same time, false. One may choose anything if it is on the grounds of free involvement.

The third objection is the following: "You take something from one pocket and put it into the other. That is, fundamentally, values aren't serious, since you choose them." My answer to this is that I'm quite vexed that that's the way it is; but if I've discarded God the Father, there has to be someone to invent values. You've got to take things as they are. Moreover, to say that we invent values means nothing else but this: life has no meaning *a priori*. Before you come alive, life is nothing; it's up to you to give it a meaning, and value is nothing else but the meaning that you choose. In that way, you see, there is a possibility of creating a human community.

I've been reproached for asking whether existentialism is humanistic. It's been said, "But you said in *Nausea* that the humanists were all wrong. You made fun of a certain kind of humanist. Why come back to it now?" Actually, the word humanism has two very different meanings. By humanism one can mean a theory which takes man as an end and as a higher value. Humanism in this sense can be found in Cocteau's tale *Around the World in Eighty Hours* when a character, because he is flying over some mountains in an airplane, declares, "Man is simply amazing." That means that I, who did not build the airplanes, shall personally benefit from these particular inventions, and that I, as man, shall personally consider myself responsible for, and honored by, acts of a few particular men. This would imply that we ascribe a value to man on the basis of the highest deeds of certain men. This humanism is absurd, because only the dog or the horse would be able to make such an over-all judgment about man, which they are careful not to do, at least to my knowledge.

But it can not be granted that a man may make a judgment about man. Existentialism spares him from any such judgment. The existentialist will never consider man as an end because he is always in the making. Nor should we believe that there is a mankind to which we might set up a cult in the manner of Auguste Comte. The cult of mankind ends in the self-enclosed humanism of Comte, and, let it be said, of fascism. This kind of humanism we can do without.

But there is another meaning of humanism. Fundamentally it is this: man is constantly outside of himself; in projecting himself, in losing himself outside of himself, he makes for man's existing; and, on the other hand, it is by pursuing transcendent goals that he is able to exist; man, being this state of passing-beyond, and seizing upon things only as they bear upon this passing-beyond, is at the heart, at the center of this passing-beyond. There is no universe other than a human universe, the universe of human subjectivity. This connection between transcendency, as a constituent element of man—not in the sense that God is transcendent, but in the sense of passing beyond—and subjectivity, in the sense that man is not closed in on himself but is always present in a human universe, is what we call existentialism humanism. Humanism, because we remind man that there is no law-maker other than himself, and that in his forlornness he will decide by himself; because we point out that man will fulfill himself as man, not in turning toward himself, but in seeking outside of himself a goal which is just this liberation, just this particular fulfillment.

From these few reflections it is evident that nothing is more unjust than the objections that have been raised against us. Existentialism is nothing else than an attempt to draw all the consequences of a coherent atheistic position. It isn't trying to plunge man into despair at all. But if one calls every attitude of unbelief despair, like the Christians, then the word is not being used in its original sense. Existentialism isn't so atheistic that it wears itself out showing that God doesn't exist. Rather, it declares that even if God did exist, that would change nothing. There you've got our point of view. Not that we believe that God exists, but we think that the problem of His existence is not the issue. In this sense existentialism is optimistic, a doctrine of action, and it is plain dishonesty for Christians to make no distinction between their own despair and ours and then to call us despairing.

Simone de Beauvoir
1908–1986

Simone Lucie Ernestine Marie Bertrand de Beauvoir was the elder of two daughters born to attorney Georges Bertrand de Beauvoir and his wife, Françoise Brasseur de Beauvoir. The noble-sounding "de" in their name indicated some family prestige, but they were only comfortable, not wealthy. Apart from a five-year period during adulthood, de Beauvoir spent her entire life in the Montparnasse district of Paris. Her mother was a devout Catholic, and as a young girl de Beauvoir regularly attended church and went to confession. She studied in a Catholic school and considered God her personal companion. However, by adolescence she had given up her faith. She later recounted that this loss of belief was both freeing and terrifying: "Alone: for the first time I understood the terrible significance of that word. Alone: without a witness, without anyone to speak to, without refuge."

After World War I, de Beauvoir's father suffered financial setbacks. He was forced to tell his daughters he could not provide them a dowry and concluded, "My dears, you'll never marry; you'll have to work for your livings." De Beauvoir decided to pursue a career as a philosophy teacher. She was drawn to philosophy because

> It went straight to essentials. . . . I had always wanted to know *everything;* philosophy would allow me to satisfy this desire, for it aimed at total reality.

489

She enrolled at the Institut Sainte-Marie in 1925 and studied there for the next four years, simultaneously hearing lectures at the Institut Catholique and the Sorbonne.

In 1929 de Beauvoir met Jean-Paul Sartre and studied with him for the *agrégation* in philosophy (which he had failed the previous year). After both passed the examination with high honors, she agreed to a "two-year lease" relationship with Sartre. During this period she was an assistant at a lycée in Paris. In 1931 de Beauvoir accepted a full-time position at a lycée in Marseille and a year later moved to nearby Rouen. Though Sartre took a similar position at a lycée in Le Havre, on the opposite side of the country, their relationship continued. In fact, their "two-year lease" became a lifelong companionship though they never married and were free to have "contingent" relationships.

By 1936 de Beauvoir was back in her beloved Montparnasse, Paris. For the next eight years she taught at various lycées in Paris until the involvement of a student in her unusual lifestyle led to charges of corrupting a minor and she was suspended. Though reinstated, she resigned in 1944 and supported herself for the rest of her life by her writings. In that year her first novel, *She Came to Stay,* was published to critical acclaim and financial success. She was heralded (with Albert Camus and Sartre) as one of the leaders of the new existentialist movement. The following year with Maurice Merleau-Ponty and Sartre she founded the influential journal *Les Temps modernes* and served as an editor and contributor to the magazine.

In her later years, de Beauvoir became increasingly involved in political issues. With Sartre she visited Cuba, attended the International War Crimes Tribunal on U.S. War Crimes in Vietnam, and joined the student demonstrations at the Sorbonne. On her own she worked vigorously for such feminist issues as legalized abortion and care for unmarried mothers. While leading the involved life of a left-wing political activist, de Beauvoir published a total of five novels, two collections of stories, and a play. She also published five volumes of memoirs, giving a picture of France in the twentieth century and of her relationship to Sartre. But de Beauvoir is best known for her philosophical works, especially the groundbreaking feminist text, *The Second Sex* (1949).

*   *   *

The Second Sex is actually two separate volumes united around the question, "What is woman?" The first section, entitled "Facts and Myths," explores biology, psychology, sociology, history, myth, and literature to explain the answers given to this basic question. The second section, "Woman's Life Today," focuses on women's various roles and explores ways to move beyond these roles.

In the introduction to the work, reprinted here in the H.M. Parshley translation, de Beauvoir presents the basic categories that will guide her exploration of what it means to be woman. According to de Beauvoir, woman is the "second sex" because she is defined by man. Borrowing terminology from Sartre, she claims, "He is the Subject, he is the Absolute—she is the Other." Man sets himself up as the standard, the "One"—the definition of what it is to be human—so that immediately woman becomes the "Other." As the "Other," woman is relegated to existence as *"en-soi"*: a being-in-itself, an object. Woman is not able to exist as *"pour-soi,"* a being-for-itself. She cannot choose her existence because her role is already defined for her as the "Other."

De Beauvoir goes on to ask why women allow this to happen: "Why is it that women do not dispute male sovereignty?" After all, throughout history other groups have been treated as the "Other" and have redefined themselves. Why not women? Later in the book, de Beauvoir speculates that a woman's identity as the "Other" derives in part from her body—especially her reproductive capacity. But in our selection, she points outs that women have always (with rare exceptions) been subordinated to men, "and hence their dependency is not the result of a historical event or a social change—it was not something that *occurred*." Women have accepted their role as the "Other" because otherness "lacks the contingent or incidental nature of historical facts." Women have no past, no history of their own. They are not grouped together *as* women, they have no solidarity of employment since as a rule they work dispersed among men. In short, they do not have the "concrete means for organizing themselves into a unit which can stand face to face with the correlative unit."

The goal of *The Second Sex* is to move beyond analysis to a "concrete means" for organizing women. According to de Beauvoir, there must be two changes in order to accomplish this goal: (1) Women need to act as authentic subjects choosing their own histories and (2) society must be changed to make this possible. The first of these needed changes reflects de Beauvoir's existentialism, the second her Marxism.

While traditionalists condemned the entire work, feminist critics raised questions about some of de Beauvoir's specific analyses. Many contemporary feminists claim that she did not go to the roots of patriarchy and its pervasive infection of even our language. Other feminists question her existentialist or Marxist assumptions (or her apparent hostility to the Femal body). But most feminists salute de Beauvoir for calling attention to feminist issues. As one writer put it, *The Second Sex* is for feminists "the base-line from which other works either explicitly . . . or implicitly . . . take off."

*   *   *

There are several biographies of de Beauvoir, including Axel Madsen, *Hearts and Minds: The Common Journey of Simone de Beauvoir and Jean-Paul Sartre* (New York: Morrow, 1977); Carol Ascher, *Simone de Beauvoir: A Life of Freedom* (Boston, MA: Beacon Press, 1981); Claude Francis, *Simone de Beauvoir: A Life, A Love Story,* translated by Lisa Nesselson (New York: St. Martin's Press, 1987); and the thorough Deirdre Bair, *Simone de Beauvoir: A Biography* (New York: Summit Books, 1990). General studies of her writings include Terry Keefe, *Simone de Beauvoir: A Study of Her Writings* (Totowa, NJ: Barnes & Noble, 1983); Judith Okely, *Simone de Beauvoir: A Re-reading* (London: Virago Press, 1986); Renee Winegarten, *Simone de Beauvoir: A Critical View* (New York: St. Martin's Press, 1988); Catharine Savage Brosman, *Simone de Beauvoir Revisited* (Boston: Twayne Publishers, 1991); and Margaret Crosland, *Simone de Beauvoir: The Woman and Her Work* (London: Heinemann, 1992). For material on her feminist theories specifically, see Jean Leighton, *Simone de Beauvoir on Woman* (Rutherford, NJ: Fairleigh Dickinson University Press, 1975); Mary Evans, *Simone de Beauvoir: A Feminist Mandarin* (London: Tavistock, 1985); Rosemarie Tong; *Feminist Thought: A Comprehensive Introduction* (Boulder, CO; Westview Press, 1989) and Toril Moi, *Feminist Theory & Simone de Beauvoir* (Oxford: Blackwell, 1990). Alice Schwarzer, *After "The Second Sex": Conversations with Simone de Beauvoir* (New York: Pantheon Books, 1984), gives de

Beauvoir's reflections on her classic while Donald L. Hatcher, *Understanding "The Second Sex"* (New York: Peter Lang, 1984), provides a philosophical appraisal of that work.

THE SECOND SEX (in part)

INTRODUCTION

For a long time I have hesitated to write a book on woman. The subject is irritating, especially to women; and it is not new. Enough ink has been spilled in the quarreling over feminism, now practically over, and perhaps we should say no more about it. It is still talked about, however, for the voluminous nonsense uttered during the last century seems to have done little to illuminate the problem. After all, is there a problem? And if so, what is it? Are there women, really? Most assuredly the theory of the eternal feminine still has its adherents who will whisper in your ear: "Even in Russia women still are *women*"; and other erudite persons—sometimes the very same—say with a sigh: "Woman is losing her way, woman is lost." One wonders if women still exist, if they will always exist, whether or not it is desirable that they should, what place they occupy in this world, what their place should be. "What has become of women?" was asked recently in an ephemeral magazine.

But first we must ask: what is a woman? *"Tota mulier in utero,"* says one, "woman is a womb." But in speaking of certain women, connoisseurs declare that they are not women, although they are equipped with a uterus like the rest. All agree in recognizing the fact that females exist in the human species; today as always they make up about one half of humanity. And yet we are told that femininity is in danger; we are exhorted to be women, remain women, become women. It would appear, then, that every female human being is not necessarily a woman; to be so considered she must share in that mysterious and threatened reality known as femininity. Is this attribute something secreted by the ovaries? Or is it a Platonic essence, a product of the philosophic imagination? Is a rustling petticoat enough to bring it down to earth? Although some women try zealously to incarnate this essence, it is hardly patentable. It is frequently described in vague and dazzling terms that seem to have been borrowed from the vocabulary of the seers, and indeed in the times of St. Thomas it was considered an essence as certainly defined as the somniferous virtue of the poppy.

But conceptualism has lost ground. The biological and social sciences no longer admit the existence of unchangeably fixed entities that determine given characteristics, such as those ascribed to woman, the Jew, or the Negro. Science regards any characteristic as a reaction dependent in part upon a *situation*. If today femininity no longer exists, then it never existed. But does the word *woman,* then, have no specific content? This is stoutly affirmed by those who hold to the philosophy of the enlightenment, of rationalism, of nominalism; women, to them, are merely the human beings arbitrarily designated by the word woman. Many American women particularly are prepared to think

From *The Second Sex* by Simone de Beauvoir, translated by H.M. Parshley. Copyright © 1952 by Alfred A. Knopf, Inc. Reprinted by permission of the publisher and Random Century Group.

that there is no longer any place for woman as such; if a backward individual still takes herself for a woman, her friends advise her to be psychoanalyzed and thus get rid of this obsession. In regard to a work, *Modern Woman: The Lost Sex,* which in other respects has its irritating features, Dorothy Parker has written: "I cannot be just to books which treat of woman as woman. . . . My idea is that all of us, men as well as women, should be regarded as human beings." But nominalism is a rather inadequate doctrine, and the antifemininists have had no trouble in showing that women simply *are not* men. Surely woman is, like man, a human being; but such a declaration is abstract. The fact is that every concrete human being is always a singular, separate individual. To decline to accept such notions as the eternal feminine, the black soul, the Jewish character, is not to deny that Jews, Negroes, women exist today—this denial does not represent a liberation for those concerned, but rather a flight from reality. Some years ago a well-known woman writer refused to permit her portrait to appear in a series of photographs especially devoted to women writers; she wished to be counted among the men. But in order to gain this privilege she made use of her husband's influence! Women who assert that they are men lay claim none the less to masculine consideration and respect. I recall also a young Trotskyite standing on a platform at a boisterous meeting and getting ready to use her fists, in spite of her evident fragility. She was denying her feminine weakness; but it was for love of a militant male whose equal she wished to be. The attitude of defiance of many American women proves that they are haunted by a sense of their femininity. In truth, to go for a walk with one's eyes open is enough to demonstrate that humanity is divided into two classes of individuals whose clothes, faces, bodies, smiles, gaits, interests, and occupations are manifestly different. Perhaps these differences are superficial, perhaps they are destined to disappear. What is certain is that right now they do most obviously exist.

If her functioning as a female is not enough to define woman, if we decline also to explain her through "the eternal feminine," and if nevertheless we admit, provisionally, that women do exist, then we must face the question: what is a woman?

To state the question is, to me, to suggest, at once, a preliminary answer. The fact that I ask it is in itself significant. A man would never get the notion of writing a book on the peculiar situation of the human male. But if I wish to define myself, I must first of all say: "I am a woman"; on this truth must be based all further discussion. A man never begins by presenting himself as an individual of a certain sex; it goes without saying that he is a man. The terms *masculine* and *feminine* are used symmetrically only as a matter of form, as on legal papers. In actuality the relation of the two sexes is not quite like that of two electrical poles, for man represents both the positive and the neutral, as is indicated by the common use of man to designate human beings in general; whereas woman represents only the negative, defined by limiting criteria, without reciprocity. In the midst of an abstract discussion it is vexing to hear a man say: "You think thus and so because you are a woman"; but I know that my only defense is to reply: "I think thus and so because it is true," thereby removing my subjective self from the argument. It would be out of the question to reply: "And you think the contrary because you are a man," for it is understood that the fact of being a man is no peculiarity. A man is in the right in being a man; it is the woman who is in the wrong. It amounts to this: just as for the ancients there was an absolute vertical with reference to which the oblique was defined, so there is an absolute human type, the masculine. Woman has ovaries, a uterus; these peculiarities imprison her in her subjectivity, circumscribe her within the limits of her own nature. It is often said that she thinks with her glands. Man superbly ignores the fact that his anatomy also includes glands, such as the testicles, and that they secrete hormones. He thinks of his body as a direct and normal connection with the world, which he believes he apprehends objectively, whereas he regards the body of woman as a hindrance, a prison, weighed down by everything peculiar to it. "The female is a female by virtue of a certain *lack* of qualities," said Aristotle; "we should regard the female nature as afflicted with a natural defectiveness." And St. Thomas for his part pronounced woman to be an "imperfect man," an "incidental" being. This is symbolized in Genesis where Eve is depicted as made from what Bossuet called "a supernumerary bone" of Adam.

Thus humanity is male and man defines woman not in herself but as relative to him; she is not regarded as an autonomous being. Michelet writes: "Woman, the relative being. . . ." And Benda is most positive in his *Rapport d'Uriel:* "The body of man makes sense in itself quite apart from that of woman, whereas the latter seems wanting in significance by itself. . . . Man can think of himself without woman. She cannot think of herself without man." And she is simply what man decrees; thus she is called "the sex," by which is meant that she appears essentially to the male as a sexual being. For him she is sex—absolute sex, no less. She is defined and differentiated with reference to man and not he with reference to her; she is the incidental, the inessential as opposed to the essential. He is the Subject, he is the Absolute—she is the Other.*

The category of the Other is as primordial as consciousness itself. In the most primitive societies, in the most ancient mythologies, one finds the expression of a duality—that of the Self and the Other. This duality was not originally attached to the division of the sexes; it was not dependent upon any empirical facts. It is revealed in such works as that of Granet on Chinese thought and those of Dumezil on the East Indies and Rome. The feminine element was at first no more involved in such pairs as Varuna-Mitra, Uranus-Zeus, Sun-Moon, and Day-Night than it was in the contrasts between Good and Evil, lucky and unlucky auspices, right and left, God and Lucifer. Otherness is a fundamental category of human thought.

Thus it is that no group ever sets itself up as the One without at once setting up the Other over against itself. If three travelers chance to occupy the same compartment, that is enough to make vaguely hostile "others" out of all the rest of the passengers on the train. In small-town eyes all persons not belonging to the village are "strangers" and suspect; to the native of a country all who inhabit other countries are "foreigners"; Jews are "different" for the anti-Semite, Negroes are "inferior" for American racists, aborigines are "natives" for colonists, proletarians are the "lower class" for the privileged.

Lévi-Strauss, at the end of a profound work on the various forms of primitive societies, reaches the following conclusion: "Passage from the state of Nature to the state of Culture is marked by man's ability to view biological relations as a series of contrasts; duality, alternation, opposition, and symmetry, whether under definite or vague

---

*L. Lévinas expresses this idea most explicitly in his essay *Temps et l'Autre.* "Is there not a case in which otherness, alterity [*altérité*], unquestionably marks the nature of a being, as its essence, an instance of otherness not consisting purely and simply in the opposition of two species of the same genus? I think that the feminine represents the contrary in its absolute sense, this contrariness being in no wise affected by any relation between it and its correlative and thus remaining absolutely other. Sex is not a certain specific difference . . . no more is the sexual difference a mere contradiction. . . . Nor does this difference lie in the duality of two complementary terms, for two complementary terms imply a pre-existing whole. . . . Otherness reaches its full flowering in the feminine, a term of the same rank as consciousness but of opposite meaning."

I suppose that Lévinas does not forget that woman, too, is aware of her own consciousness, or ego. But it is striking that he deliberately takes a man's point of view, disregarding the reciprocity of subject and object. When he writes that woman is mystery, he implies that she is mystery for man. Thus his description, which is intended to be objective, is in fact an assertion of masculine privilege.

forms, constitute not so much phenomena to be explained as fundamental and immediately given data of social reality." These phenomena would be incomprehensible if in fact human society were simply a *Mitsein* or fellowship based on solidarity and friendliness. Things become clear, on the contrary, if, following Hegel, we find in consciousness itself a fundamental hostility toward every other consciousness; the subject can be posed only in being opposed—he sets himself up as the essential, as opposed to the other, the inessential, the object.

But the other consciousness, the other ego, sets up a reciprocal claim. The native traveling abroad is shocked to find himself in turn regarded as a "stranger" by the natives of neighboring countries. As a matter of fact, wars, festivals, trading, treaties, and contests among tribes, nations, and classes tend to deprive the concept *Other* of its absolute sense and to make manifest its relativity; willy-nilly, individuals and groups are forced to realize the reciprocity of their relations. How is it, then, that this reciprocity has not been recognized between the sexes, that one of the contrasting terms is set up as the sole essential, denying any relativity in regard to its correlative and defining the latter as pure otherness? Why is it that women do not dispute male sovereignty? No subject will readily volunteer to become the object, the inessential; it is not the Other who, in defining himself as the Other, establishes the One. The Other is posed as such by the One in defining himself as the One. But if the Other is not to regain the status of being the One, he must be submissive enough to accept this alien point of view. Whence comes this submission in the case of woman?

There are, to be sure, other cases in which a certain category has been able to dominate another completely for a time. Very often this privilege depends upon inequality of numbers—the majority imposes its rule upon the minority or persecutes it. But women are not a minority, like the American Negroes or the Jews; there are as many women as men on earth. Again, the two groups concerned have often been originally independent; they may have been formerly unaware of each other's existence, or perhaps they recognized each other's autonomy. But a historical event has resulted in the subjugation of the weaker by the stronger. The scattering of the Jews, the introduction of slavery into America, the conquests of imperialism are examples in point. In these cases the oppressed retained at least the memory of former days; they possessed in common a past, a tradition, sometimes a religion or a culture.

The parallel drawn by Bebel between women and the proletariat is valid in that neither ever formed a minority or a separate collective unit of mankind. And instead of a single historical event it is in both cases a historical development that explains their status as a class and accounts for the membership of *particular individuals* in that class. But proletarians have not always existed, whereas there have always been women. They are women in virtue of their anatomy and physiology. Throughout history they have always been subordinated to men, and hence their dependency is not the result of a historical event or a social change—it was not something that *occurred*. The reason why otherness in this case seems to be an absolute is in part that it lacks the contingent or incidental nature of historical facts. A condition brought about at a certain time can be abolished at some other time, as the Negroes of Haiti and others have proved; but it might seem that a natural condition is beyond the possibility of change. In truth, however, the nature of things is no more immutably given, once for all, than is historical reality. If woman seems to be the inessential which never becomes the essential, it is because she herself fails to bring about this change. Proletarians say "We"; Negroes also. Regarding themselves as subjects, they transform the bourgeois, the whites, into "others." But women do not say "We," except at some congress of feminists or similar formal demonstration; men say "women," and women use the same word in referring to themselves. They do not authentically assume a subjective attitude. The proletarians have accomplished the revolution in Russia, the Negroes in Haiti, the Indo-Chinese are battling for it in Indo-China; but the women's effort has never been anything more than a symbolic agitation. They have gained only what men have been willing to grant; they have taken nothing, they have only received.

The reason for this is that women lack concrete means for organizing themselves into a unit which can stand face to face with the correlative unit. They have no past, no history, no religion of their own; and they have no such solidarity of work and interest as that of the proletariat. They are not even promiscuously herded together in the way that creates community feeling among the American Negroes, the ghetto Jews, the workers of Saint-Denis, or the factory hands of Renault. They live dispersed among the males, attached through residence, housework, economic condition, and social standing to certain men—fathers or husbands—more firmly than they are to other women. If they belong to the bourgeoisie, they feel solidarity with men of that class, not with proletarian women; if they are white, their allegiance is to white men, not to Negro women. The proletariat can propose to massacre the ruling class, and a sufficiently fanatical Jew or Negro might dream of getting sole possession of the atomic bomb and making humanity wholly Jewish or black; but woman cannot even dream of exterminating the males. The bond that unites her to her oppressors is not comparable to any other. The division of the sexes is a biological fact, not an event in human history. Male and female stand opposed within a primordial *Mitsein,* and woman has not broken it. The couple is a fundamental unity with its two halves riveted together, and the cleavage of society along the line of sex is impossible. Here is to be found the basic trait of woman: she is the Other in a totality of which the two components are necessary to one another.

One could suppose that this reciprocity might have facilitated the liberation of woman. When Hercules sat at the feet of Omphale and helped with her spinning, his desire for her held him captive; but why did she fail to gain a lasting power? To revenge herself on Jason, Medea killed their children; and this grim legend would seem to suggest that she might have obtained a formidable influence over him through his love for his offspring. In *Lysistrata* Aristophanes gaily depicts a band of women who joined forces to gain social ends through the sexual needs of their men; but this is only a play. In the legend of the Sabine women, the latter soon abandoned their plan of remaining sterile to punish their ravishers. In truth woman has not been socially emancipated through man's need—sexual desire and the desire for offspring—which makes the male dependent for satisfaction upon the female.

Master and slave, also, are united by a reciprocal need, in this case economic, which does not liberate the slave. In the relation of master to slave the master does not make a point of the need that he has for the other; he has in his grasp the power of satisfying this need through his own action; whereas the slave, in his dependent condition, his hope and fear, is quite conscious of the need he has for his master. Even if the need is at bottom equally urgent for both, it always works in favor of the oppressor and against the oppressed. That is why the liberation of the working class, for example, has been slow.

Now, woman has always been man's dependent, if not his slave; the two sexes have never shared the world in equality. And even today woman is heavily handicapped, though her situation is beginning to change. Almost nowhere is her legal status the same as man's, and frequently it is much to her disadvantage. Even when her rights are legally recognized in the abstract, long-standing custom prevents their full expression in the mores. In the economic sphere men and women can almost be said to make up two castes; other things being equal, the former hold the better jobs, get higher wages, and have more opportunity for success than their new competitors. In industry and politics men have a great many more positions and they monopolize the most important posts. In addition to all this, they enjoy a traditional prestige that the education of children tends in every way to support, for the present enshrines the past—and in the past all history has been made by men. At the present time, when women are beginning to take part in the affairs of the world, it is still a world that belongs to men—they have no doubt of it at all and women have scarcely any. To decline to be the Other, to refuse to be a party to the deal—this would be for women to renounce all the advantages conferred upon them by their alliance with the superior caste. Man-the-sovereign will provide woman-the-liege with material protection and will undertake the moral justification of her existence; thus she can evade at once both economic risk and the metaphysical risk of a liberty in which ends and aims must be contrived without assistance. Indeed, along with the ethical urge of each individual to affirm his subjective existence, there is also the temptation to forgo liberty and become a thing. This is an inauspicious road, for he who takes it—passive, lost, ruined—becomes henceforth the creature of another's will, frustrated in his transcendence and deprived of every value. But it is an easy road; on it one avoids the strain involved in undertaking an authentic existence. When man makes of woman the *Other,* he may, then, expect her to manifest deep-seated tendencies toward complicity. Thus, woman may fail to lay claim to the status of subject because she lacks definite resources, because she feels the necessary bond that ties her to man regardless of reciprocity, and because she is often very well pleased with her role as the *Other*.

But it will be asked at once: how did all this begin? It is easy to see that the duality of the sexes, like any duality, gives rise to conflict. And doubtless the winner will assume the status of absolute. But why should man have won from the start? It seems possible that women could have won the victory; or that the outcome of the conflict might never have been decided. How is it that this world has always belonged to the men and that things have begun to change only recently? Is this change a good thing? Will it bring about an equal sharing of the world between men and women?

These questions are not new, and they have often been answered. But the very fact that woman *is the Other* tends to cast suspicion upon all the justifications that men have ever been able to provide for it. These have all too evidently been dictated by men's interest. A little-known feminist of the seventeenth century, Poulain de la Barre, put it this way: "All that has been written about women by men should be suspect, for the men are at once judge and party to the lawsuit." Everywhere, at all times, the males have displayed their satisfaction in feeling that they are the lords of creation. "Blessed be God. . . that He did not make me a woman," say the Jews in their morning prayers, while their wives pray on a note of resignation: "Blessed be the Lord, who created me according to His will." The first among the blessings for which Plato thanked the gods was that he had been created free, not enslaved; the second, a man, not a woman. But the males could not enjoy this privilege fully unless they believed it to be founded on the absolute and the eternal; they sought to make the fact of their supremacy into a right. "Being men, those who have made and compiled the laws have favored their own sex, and jurists have elevated these laws into principles," to quote Poulain de la Barre once more.

Legislators, priests, philosophers, writers, and scientists have striven to show that the subordinate position of woman is willed in heaven and advantageous on earth. The religions invented by men reflect this wish for domination. In the legends of Eve and Pandora men have taken up arms against women. They have made use of philosophy and theology, as the quotations from Aristotle and St. Thomas have shown. Since ancient times satirists and moralists have delighted in showing up the weaknesses of women. We are familiar with the savage indictments hurled against women throughout French literature. Montherlant, for example, follows the tradition of Jean de Meung, though with less gusto. This hostility may at times be well founded, often it is gratuitous; but in truth it more or less successfully conceals a desire for self-justification. As Montaigne says, "It is easier to accuse one sex than to excuse the other." Sometimes what is going on is clear enough. For instance, the Roman law limiting the rights of woman cited "the imbecility, the instability of the sex" just when the weakening of family ties seemed to threaten the interests of male heirs. And in the effort to keep the married woman under guardianship, appeal was made in the sixteenth century to the authority of St. Augustine, who declared that "woman is a creature neither decisive nor constant," at a time when the single woman was thought capable of managing her property. Montaigne understood clearly how arbitrary and unjust was woman's appointed lot: "Women are not in the wrong when they decline to accept the rules laid down for them, since the men make these rules without consulting them. No wonder intrigue and strife abound." But he did not go so far as to champion their cause.

It was only later, in the eighteenth century, that genuinely democratic men began to view the matter objectively. Diderot, among others, strove to show that woman is, like man, a human being. Later John Stuart Mill came fervently to her defense. But these philosophers displayed unusual impartiality. In the nineteenth century the feminist quarrel became again a quarrel of partisans. One of the consequences of the industrial revolution was the entrance of women into productive labor, and it was just here that the claims of the feminists emerged from the realm of theory and acquired an economic basis, while their opponents became the more aggressive. Although landed property lost power to some extent, the bourgeoisie clung to the old morality that found the guarantee of private property in the solidity of the family. Woman was ordered back into the home the more harshly as her emancipation became a real menace. Even within the working class the men endeavored to restrain woman's liberation, because they began to see the women as dangerous competitors—the more so because they were accustomed to work for lower wages.

In proving woman's inferiority, the antifeminists then began to draw not only upon religion, philosophy, and theology, as before, but also upon science—biology, experimental psychology, etc. At most they were willing to grant "equality in difference" to the *other* sex. That profitable formula is most significant; it is precisely like the "equal but separate" formula of the Jim Crow laws aimed at the North American Negroes. As is well known, this so-called equalitarian segregation has resulted only in the most extreme discrimination. The similarity just noted is in no way due to chance, for whether it is a race, a caste, a class, or a sex that is reduced to a position of inferiority, the methods of justification are the same. "The eternal feminine" corresponds to "the black soul" and to "the Jewish character." True, the Jewish problem is on the whole very different from the other two—to the anti-Semite the Jew is not so much an inferior as he is an enemy for whom there is to be granted no place on earth, for whom annihilation is the fate desired. But there are deep similarities between the situation of woman and that of the Negro. Both are being emancipated today from a like paternalism, and the former master class wishes to "keep them in their place"—that is, the place chosen for them. In both cases the former masters lavish more or less sincere eulogies, either on the virtues of "the good Negro" with his dormant, childish, merry soul—the submissive Negro—or on the merits of the woman who is "truly feminine"—that is, frivolous, infantile, irresponsible—the submissive woman. In both cases the dominant class bases its argument on a state of affairs that it has itself created. As George Bernard Shaw puts it, in substance, "The American white relegates

Migrant Mother, 1936, by Dorothea Lange (1895–1965). This powerful
photograph of a migrant mother in central California reveals both
anxiety and strength. *(The Oakland Museum)*

the black to the rank of shoeshine boy; and he concludes from this that the black is
good for nothing but shining shoes." This vicious circle is met with in all analogous
circumstances; when an individual (or a group of individuals) is kept in a situation of
inferiority, the fact is that he *is* inferior. But the significance of the verb *to be* must be
rightly understood here; it is in bad faith to give it a static value when it really has the
dynamic Hegelian sense of "to have become." Yes, women on the whole *are* today in-

ferior to men; that is, their situation affords them fewer possibilities. The question is: should that state of affairs continue?

Many men hope that it will continue; not all have given up the battle. The conservative bourgeoisie still see in the emancipation of women a menace to their morality and their interests. Some men dread feminine competition. Recently a male student wrote in the *Hebdo-Latin:* "Every woman student who goes into medicine or law robs us of a job." He never questioned his rights in this world. And economic interests are not the only ones concerned. One of the benefits that oppression confers upon the oppressors is that the most humble among them is made to *feel* superior; thus, a "poor white" in the South can console himself with the thought that he is not a "dirty nigger"—and the more prosperous whites cleverly exploit this pride.

Similarly, the most mediocre of males feels himself a demigod as compared with women. It was much easier for M. de Montherlant to think himself a hero when he faced women (and women chosen for his purpose) than when he was obliged to act the man among men—something many women have done better than he, for that matter. And in September 1948, in one of his articles in the *Figaro littéraire,* Claude Mauriac—whose great originality is admired by all—could write regarding woman: "We listen on a tone [*sic!*] of polite indifference . . . to the most brilliant among them, well knowing that her wit reflects more or less luminously ideas that come from *us.*" Evidently the speaker referred to is not reflecting the ideas of Mauriac himself, for no one knows of his having any. It may be that she reflects ideas originating with men, but then, even among men there are those who have been known to appropriate ideas not their own; and one can well ask whether Claude Mauriac might not find more interesting a conversation reflecting Descartes, Marx, or Gide rather than himself. What is really remarkable is that by using the questionable we he identifies himself with St. Paul, Hegel, Lenin, and Nietzsche, and from the lofty eminence of their grandeur looks down disdainfully upon the bevy of women who make bold to converse with him on a footing of equality. In truth, I know of more than one woman who would refuse to suffer with patience Mauriac's "tone of polite indifference."

I have lingered on this example because the masculine attitude is here displayed with disarming ingenuousness. But men profit in many more subtle ways from the otherness, the alterity of woman. Here is miraculous balm for those afflicted with an inferiority complex, and indeed no one is more arrogant toward women, more aggressive or scornful, than the man who is anxious about his virility. Those who are not fear-ridden in the presence of their fellow men are much more disposed to recognize a fellow creature in woman; but even to these the myth of Woman, the Other, is precious for many reasons.* They cannot be blamed for not cheerfully relinquishing all the benefits they derive from the myth, for they realize what they would lose in relinquishing woman as they fancy her to be, while they fail to realize what they have to gain from the woman of tomorrow. Refusal to pose oneself as the Subject, unique and absolute, requires great self-denial. Furthermore, the vast majority of men make no such claim explicitly. They do not *postulate* woman as inferior, for today they are too thoroughly imbued with the ideal of democracy not to recognize all human beings as equals.

---

*A significant article on this theme by Michel Carrouges appeared in No. 292 of the *Cahiers du Sud.* He writes indignantly: "Would that there were no woman-myth at all but only a cohort of cooks, matrons, prostitutes, and bluestockings serving functions of pleasure or usefulness!" That is to say, in his view woman has no existence in and for herself; he thinks only of her *function* in the male world. Her reason for existence lies in man. But then, in fact, her poetic "function" as a myth might be more valued than any other. The real problem is precisely to find out why woman should be defined with relation to man.

In the bosom of the family, woman seems in the eyes of childhood and youth to be clothed in the same social dignity as the adult males. Later on, the young man, desiring and loving, experiences the resistance, the independence of the woman desired and loved; in marriage, he respects woman as wife and mother, and in the concrete events of conjugal life she stands there before him as a free being. He can therefore feel that social subordination as between the sexes no longer exists and that on the whole, in spite of differences, woman is an equal. As, however, he observes some points of inferiority—the most important being unfitness for the professions—he attributes these to natural causes. When he is in a co-operative and benevolent relation with woman, his theme is the principle of abstract equality, and he does not base his attitude upon such inequality as may exist. But when he is in conflict with her, the situation is reversed: his theme will be the existing inequality, and he will even take it as justification for denying abstract equality.*

So it is that many men will affirm as if in good faith that women *are* the equals of man and that they have nothing to clamor for, while *at the same* time they will say that women can never be the equals of man and that their demands are in vain. It is, in point of fact, a difficult matter for man to realize the extreme importance of social discriminations which seem outwardly insignificant but which produce in woman moral and intellectual effects so profound that they appear to spring from her original nature. The most sympathetic of men never fully comprehend woman's concrete situation. And there is no reason to put much trust in the men when they rush to the defense of privileges whose full extent they can hardly measure. We shall not, then, permit ourselves to be intimidated by the number and violence of the attacks launched against women, nor to be entrapped by the self-seeking eulogies bestowed on the "true woman," nor to profit by the enthusiasm for woman's destiny manifested by men who would not for the world have any part of it.

We should consider the arguments of the feminists with no less suspicion, however, for very often their controversial aim deprives them of all real value. If the "woman question" seems trivial, it is because masculine arrogance has made of it a "quarrel"; and when quarreling one no longer reasons well. People have tirelessly sought to prove that woman is superior, inferior, or equal to man. Some say that, having been created after Adam, she is evidently a secondary being; others say on the contrary that Adam was only a rough draft and that God succeeded in producing the human being in perfection when He created Eve. Woman's brain is smaller; yes, but it is relatively larger. Christ was made a man; yes, but perhaps for his greater humility. Each argument at once suggests its opposite, and both are often fallacious. If we are to gain understanding, we must get out of these ruts; we must discard the vague notions of superiority, inferiority, equality which have hitherto corrupted every discussion of the subject and start afresh.

Very well, but just how shall we pose the question? And, to begin with, who are we to propound it at all? Man is at once judge and party to the case; but so is woman. What we need is an angel—neither man nor woman—but where shall we find one? Still, the angel would be poorly qualified to speak, for an angel is ignorant of all the basic facts involved in the problem. With a hermaphrodite we should be no better off, for here the situation is most peculiar; the hermaphrodite is not really the combination of a

---

*For example, a man will say that he considers his wife in no wise degraded because she has no gainful occupation. The profession of housewife is just as lofty, and so on. But when the first quarrel comes, he will exclaim: "Why, you couldn't make your living without me!"

whole man and a whole woman, but consists of parts of each and thus is neither. It looks to me as if there are, after all, certain women who are best qualified to elucidate the situation of woman. Let us not be misled by the sophism that because Epimenides was a Cretan he was necessarily a liar; it is not a mysterious essence that compels men and women to act in good or in bad faith; it is their situation that inclines them more or less toward the search for truth. Many of today's women, fortunate in the restoration of all the privileges pertaining to the estate of the human being, can afford the luxury of impartiality—we even recognize its necessity. We are no longer like our partisan elders; by and large we have won the game. In recent debates on the status of women the United Nations has persistently maintained that the equality of the sexes is now becoming a reality, and already some of us have never had to sense in our femininity an inconvenience or an obstacle. Many problems appear to us to be more pressing than those which concern us in particular, and this detachment even allows us to hope that our attitude will be objective. Still, we know the feminine world more intimately than do the men because we have our roots in it, we grasp more immediately than do men what it means to a human being to be feminine; and we are more concerned with such knowledge. I have said that there are more pressing problems, but this does not prevent us from seeing some importance in asking how the fact of being women will affect our lives. What opportunities precisely have been given us and what withheld? What fate awaits our younger sisters, and what directions should they take? It is significant that books by women on women are in general animated in our day less by a wish to demand our rights than by an effort toward clarity and understanding. As we emerge from an era of excessive controversy, this book is offered as one attempt among others to confirm that statement.

But it is doubtless impossible to approach any human problem with a mind free from bias. The way in which questions are put, the points of view assumed, presuppose a relativity of interest; all characteristics imply values, and every objective description, so called, implies an ethical background. Rather than attempt to conceal principles more or less definitely implied, it is better to state them openly at the beginning. This will make it unnecessary to specify on every page in just what sense one uses such words as *superior, inferior, better, worse, progress, reaction,* and the like. If we survey some of the works on woman, we note that one of the points of view most frequently adopted is that of the public good, the general interest; and one always means by this the benefit of society as one wishes it to be maintained or established. For our part, we hold that the only public good is that which assures the private good of the citizens; we shall pass judgment on institutions according to their effectiveness in giving concrete opportunities to individuals. But we do not confuse the idea of private interest with that of happiness, although that is another common point of view. Are not women of the harem more happy than women voters? Is not the housekeeper happier than the working-woman? It is not too clear just what the word *happy* really means and still less what true values it may mask. There is no possibility of measuring the happiness of others, and it is always easy to describe as happy the situation in which one wishes to place them.

In particular those who are condemned to stagnation are often pronounced happy on the pretext that happiness consists in being at rest. This notion we reject, for our perspective is that of existentialist ethics. Every subject plays his part as such specifically through exploits or projects that serve as a mode of transcendence; he achieves liberty only through a continual reaching out toward other liberties. There is no justification for present existence other than its expansion into an indefinitely open future. Every time transcendence falls back into immanence, stagnation, there is a degradation of existence into the *"en-soi"*—the brutish life of subjection to given conditions—and of liberty into constraint and contingence. This downfall represents a moral fault if the subject consents to it; if it is inflicted upon him, it spells frustration and oppression. In both cases it is an absolute evil. Every individual concerned to justify his existence feels that his existence involves an undefined need to transcend himself, to engage in freely chosen projects.

Now, what peculiarly signalizes the situation of woman is that she—a free and autonomous being like all human creatures—nevertheless finds herself living in a world where men compel her to assume the status of the Other. They propose to stabilize her as object and to doom her to immanence since her transcendence is to be overshadowed and forever transcended by another ego *(conscience)* which is essential and sovereign. The drama of woman lies in this conflict between the fundamental aspirations of every subject (ego)—who always regards the self as the essential—and the compulsions of a situation in which she is the inessential. How can a human being in woman's situation attain fulfillment? What roads are open to her? Which are blocked? How can independence be recovered in a state of dependency? What circumstances limit woman's liberty and how can they be overcome? These are the fundamental questions on which I would fain throw some light. This means that I am interested in the fortunes of the individual as defined not in terms of happiness but in terms of liberty.

Quite evidently this problem would be without significance if we were to believe that woman's destiny is inevitably determined by physiological, psychological, or economic forces. Hence I shall discuss first of all the light in which woman is viewed by biology, psychoanalysis, and historical materialism. Next I shall try to show exactly how the concept of the "truly feminine" has been fashioned—why woman has been defined as the Other—and what have been the consequences from man's point of view. Then from woman's point of view I shall describe the world in which women must live; and thus we shall be able to envisage the difficulties in their way as, endeavoring to make their escape from the sphere hitherto assigned them, they aspire to full membership in the human race.

Willard Van Orman Quine

1908–

Willard Van Orman Quine was the younger of the sons born to Robert Quine and Harriet van Orman Quine of Akron, Ohio. His mother was a schoolteacher and his father a worker in heavy industry. As a child Quine developed a lifelong fascination with travel and maps. On summer vacations he would draw careful maps of nearby lakes and sell copies to local cabin owners. The young Quine also excelled in mathematics and languages. In 1926 he enrolled at Oberlin College, where he majored in mathematics and studied philosophy. His research led him to mathematical philosophy, logic, and the philosophy of Bertrand Russell. In Russell he found a kindred spirit—they shared a logical approach to philosophical problems and a religious skepticism.

Quine went to Harvard University for graduate studies in 1930. He married his college sweetheart, buried himself in studies with such noted philosophers as C.I. Lewis and Alfred North Whitehead, finished his course work, passed preliminary examinations, and received his master's degree—all in a year. The following year he completed a 290-page dissertation on logic and received his Ph.D. degree at age twenty-three. A revision of this dissertation, *A System of Logistic* (1934), became the first of his some fifteen published books.

The year Quine received his doctorate, he was also awarded Harvard's Sheldon Traveling Fellowship. He took the title of the fellowship seriously, and in one year he and his wife visited twenty-seven countries. Quine met several members of the Vienna Circle and studied logic in Warsaw with the great Polish logicians Tarski, Leśniewski, and Lukasiewicz. At the end of the year he was elected into Harvard's Society of Fellows, which gave him, among other emoluments, three years good pay and no duties. Among his five colleagues as junior fellows was the promising young psychologist B.F. Skinner.

Quine taught at Harvard until 1942. During World War II his skill in languages and his gift of logic were put to use translating and analyzing decoded messages from German submarines. In 1946 Quine returned to Harvard and teaching. Except for sabbaticals and visiting professorships (and travelling in over one hundred countries), Quine remained a professor at Harvard until his retirement in 1978. Quine still lives in Boston and uses an office at Harvard—when not travelling.

*   *   *

In his autobiography, Quine explains that he has always despised conceptual constraints and has "been at pains to blur the boundaries between natural science, mathematics, and philosophy." Nowhere is this impatience with divisions more apparent than in Quine's critique of the analytic-synthetic distinction.

Ever since Hume first distinguished between "relations of ideas" and "matters of fact," philosophers have divided all propositions into analytic and synthetic. Yet in his famous paper "Two Dogmas of Empiricism," reprinted here (complete), Quine argues on the basis of various tests of meaning, synonymity, definition, and semantics that such a division has never been clearly made and that there is no compelling reason for believing such a separation *can* be made.

For example, the foundational propositions of logic and mathematics have been held to be true by convention independent of any matters of fact. Thus the proposition (1) "No unmarried man is married" is true regardless of the various interpretations of "man" and "married." But there are also semantic propositions such as (2) "No bachelor is married," which are claimed to be equally analytic. As Quine points out, it is common to believe that this latter (supposed) analytic proposition can be made into a truth of logic by "putting synonyms for synonyms; thus (2) can be turned into (1) by putting 'unmarried man' for its synonym 'bachelor.'" But what is our criterion of synonymity and how is it any more clear than our criterion of "analyticity"? We could say that propositions (1) and (2) are synonymous if the term "bachelor" in (2) is *defined* as "unmarried man." But what is the basis for such a definition? Does analyticity depend on the empirical observations of a lexicographer or the authority of a dictionary? We could say that these propositions are synonymous if proposition (2) is "necessarily true." However, this would be begging the question; to say a proposition is "necessary" is to say it is analytic. Quine concludes that analyticity as a clearly distinguished notion is "an unempirical dogma of empiricists, a metaphysical article of faith."

Having critiqued the analytic-synthetic distinction, Quine next turns his attention to another empirical dogma: the verification theory of meaning and the reductionism that it presupposes. According to this theory of meaning, the meaning of any statement is the "method of empirically confirming or infirming it." But such a theory implies that each meaningful statement can be reduced to an equivalent statement that contains only references to immediate experience. Logical positivists such as Carnap sought to develop such a reductionistic language. But according to Quine, Carnap and the others are relying on the nonexistent analytic-synthetic distinction to separate the "linguistic components" from the "factual components" in any individual statement. Furthermore, *no* statement, taken by itself, could be confirmed or discredited by sensory experience because there could always be a further experience that would overturn the original statement.

Quine concludes:

> The totality of our so-called knowledge or beliefs, from the most casual matters of geography and history to the profoundest laws of atomic physics or even of pure mathematics and logic, is a man-made fabric which impinges on experience only along the edges.

Individual experiences "along the edges" may be dismissed as errors or hallucinations if they disturb more central beliefs. But even our core beliefs of mathematics and logic are subject to possible revision. There is no final truth nor even a clear distinction between the truths of logic and the truths of experience, i.e., between analytic and synthetic.

*   *   *

Alex Orenstein, *Willard Van Orman Quine* (Boston: Twayne Publishers, 1977), provides a good place to begin further study, while Roger F. Gibson, *The Philosophy of W.V. Quine: An Expository Essay* (Tampa: University Presses of Florida, 1982); George D. Romanas, *Quine and Analytic Philosophy* (Cambridge, MA: MIT Press, 1983); Ilham Dilman, *Quine on Ontology, Necessity, and Experience: A Philosophical Critique* (Albany: State University of New York Press, 1984); and Christopher Hookway, *Quine: Language, Experience, and Reality* (Stanford, CA: Stanford University Press, 1988), have written critical investigations. For information on Quine's life, see his autobiography, *The Time of My Life: An Autobiography* (Cambridge, MA: MIT Press, 1985). For collections of essays, see Donald Davidson and Jaakko Hintikka, eds., *Words and Objections: Essays on the Work of W.V. Quine* (Dordrecht, Netherlands: D. Reidel, 1969); Robert W. Shahan and Chris Swoyer, eds., *Essays on the Philosophy of W.V. Quine* (Norman: University of Oklahoma Press, 1979); and especially Lewis Edwin Hahn and Paul Arthur Schilpp, eds., *The Philosophy of W.V. Quine* (La Salle, IL: Open Court, 1986), another volume in the Library of Living Philosophers Series, which includes Quine's responses to critics and a short version of his autobiography.

TWO DOGMAS OF EMPIRICISM

Modern empiricism has been conditioned in large part by two dogmas. One is a belief in some fundamental cleavage between truths which are *analytic,* or grounded in mean-

From Willard Van Orman Quine, *From a Logical Point of View,* Chapter 2, pp. 20–46. Cambridge: Harvard University Press, 1953. Copyright © 1953 by The President and Fellows of Harvard College. Reprinted by permission of Harvard University Press and *The Philosophical Review.*

ings independently of matters of fact, and truths which are *synthetic,* or grounded in fact. The other dogma is *reductionism:* the belief that each meaningful statement is equivalent to some logical construct upon terms which refer to immediate experience. Both dogmas, I shall argue, are ill-founded. One effect of abandoning them is, as we shall see, a blurring of the supposed boundary between speculative metaphysics and natural science. Another effect is a shift toward pragmatism.

1. BACKGROUND FOR ANALYTICITY

Kant's cleavage between analytic and synthetic truths was foreshadowed in Hume's distinction between relations of ideas and matters of fact, and in Leibniz's distinction between truths of reason and truths of fact. Leibniz spoke of the truths of reason as true in all possible worlds. Picturesqueness aside, this is to say that the truths of reason are those which could not possibly be false. In the same vein we hear analytic statements defined as statements whose denials are self-contradictory. But this definition has small explanatory value; for the notion of self-contradictoriness, in the quite broad sense needed for this definition of analyticity, stands in exactly the same need of clarification as does the notion of analyticity itself. The two notions are the two sides of a single dubious coin.

Kant conceived of an analytic statement as one that attributes to its subject no more than is already conceptually contained in the subject. This formulation has two shortcomings: it limits itself to statements of subject-predicate form, and it appeals to a notion of containment which is left at a metaphorical level. But Kant's intent, evident more from the use he makes of the notion of analyticity than from his definition of it, can be restated thus: a statement is analytic when it is true by virtue of meanings and independently of fact. Pursuing this line, let us examine the concept of *meaning* which is presupposed.

Meaning, let us remember, is not to be identified with naming. Frege's example of 'Evening Star' and 'Morning Star,' and Russell's of 'Scott' and 'the author of *Waverley*,' illustrate that terms can name the same thing but differ in meaning. The distinction between meaning and naming is no less important at the level of abstract terms. The terms '9' and 'the number of the planets' name one and the same abstract entity but presumably must be regarded as unlike in meaning; for astronomical observation was needed, and not mere reflection on meanings, to determine the sameness of the entity in question.

The above examples consist of singular terms, concrete and abstract. With general terms, or predicates, the situation is somewhat different but parallel. Whereas a singular term purports to name an entity, abstract or concrete, a general term does not; but a general term is *true of* an entity, or of each of many, or of none. The class of all entities of which a general term is true is called the *extension* of the term. Now paralleling the contrast between the meaning of a singular term and the entity named, we must distinguish equally between the meaning of a general term and its extension. The general terms 'creature with a heart' and 'creature with kidneys,' for example, are perhaps alike in extension but unlike in meaning.

Confusion of meaning with extension, in the case of general terms, is less common than confusion of meaning with naming in the case of singular terms. It is indeed a commonplace in philosophy to oppose intension (or meaning) to extension, or, in a variant vocabulary, connotation to denotation.

The Aristotelian notion of essence was the forerunner, no doubt, of the modern notion of intension or meaning. For Aristotle it was essential in men to be rational, accidental to be two-legged. But there is an important difference between this attitude and the doctrine of meaning. From the latter point of view it may indeed be conceded (if only for the sake of argument) that rationality is involved in the meaning of the word 'man' while two-leggedness is not; but two-leggedness may at the same time be viewed as involved in the meaning of 'biped' while rationality is not. Thus from the point of view of the doctrine of meaning it makes no sense to say of the actual individual, who is at once a man and a biped, that his rationality is essential and his two-leggedness accidental or vice versa. Things had essences for Aristotle, but only linguistic forms have meanings. Meaning is what essence becomes when it is divorced from the object of reference and wedded to the word.

For the theory of meaning a conspicuous question is the nature of its objects: what sort of things are meanings? A felt need for meant entities may derive from an earlier failure to appreciate that meaning and reference are distinct. Once the theory of meaning is sharply separated from the theory of reference, it is a short step to recognizing as the primary business of the theory of meaning simply the synonymy of linguistic forms and the analyticity of statements; meanings themselves, as obscure intermediary entities, may well be abandoned.

The problem of analyticity then confronts us anew. Statements which are analytic by general philosophical acclaim are not, indeed, far to seek. They fall into two classes. Those of the first class, which may be called *logically true,* are typified by:

(1) No unmarried man is married.

The relevant feature of this example is that it not merely is true as it stands, but remains true under any and all reinterpretations of 'man' and 'married.' If we suppose a prior inventory of *logical* particles, comprising 'no,' 'un-,' 'not,' 'if,' 'then,' 'and,' etc., then in general a logical truth is a statement which is true and remains true under all reinterpretations of its components other than the logical particles.

But there is also a second class of analytic statements, typified by:

(2) No bachelor is married.

The characteristic of such a statement is that it can be turned into a logical truth by putting synonyms for synonyms; thus (2) can be turned into (1) by putting 'unmarried man' for its synonym 'bachelor.' We still lack a proper characterization of this second class of analytic statements, and therewith of analyticity generally, inasmuch as we have had in the above description to lean on a notion of "synonymy" which is no less in need of clarification than analyticity itself.

In recent years Carnap has tended to explain analyticity by appeal to what he calls state-descriptions. A state-description is any exhaustive assignment of truth values to the atomic, or noncompound, statements of the language. All other statements of the language are, Carnap assumes, built up of their component clauses by means of the familiar logical devices, in such a way that the truth value of any complex statement is fixed for each state-description by specifiable logical laws. A statement is then explained as analytic when it comes out true under every state description. This account is an adaptation of Leibniz's "true in all possible worlds." But note that this version of analyticity serves its purpose only if the atomic statements of the language are, unlike 'John is a bachelor' and 'John is married,' mutually independent. Otherwise there would be a state-description which assigned truth to 'John is a bachelor' and to 'John is married,' and consequently 'No bachelors are married' would turn out synthetic rather than analytic under the proposed criterion. Thus the criterion of analyticity in terms of state-descriptions serves only for languages devoid of extralogical synonym-pairs, such as 'bachelor' and 'unmarried man'—synonym-pairs of the type which give rise to the "second class" of analytic statements. The criterion in terms of state-descriptions is a reconstruction at best of logical truth, not of analyticity.

I do not mean to suggest that Carnap is under any illusions on this point. His simplified model language with its state-descriptions is aimed primarily not at the general problem of analyticity but at another purpose, the clarification of probability and induction. Our problem, however, is analyticity; and here the major difficulty lies not in the first class of analytic statements, the logical truths, but rather in the second class, which depends on the notion of synonymy.

2. DEFINITION

There are those who find it soothing to say that the analytic statements of the second class reduce to those of the first class, the logical truths, by *definition;* 'bachelor,' for example, is *defined* as 'unmarried man.' But how de we find that 'bachelor' is defined as 'unmarried man'? Who defined it thus, and when? Are we to appeal to the nearest dictionary, and accept the lexicographer's formulation as law? Clearly this would be to put the cart before the horse. The lexicographer is an empirical scientist, whose business is the recording of antecedent facts; and if he glosses 'bachelor' as 'unmarried man' it is because of his belief that there is a relation of synonymy between those forms, implicit in general or preferred usage prior to his own work. The notion of synonymy presupposed here has still to be clarified, presumably in terms relating to linguistic behavior. Certainly the "definition" which is the lexicographer's report of an observed synonymy cannot be taken as the ground of the synonymy.

Definition is not, indeed, an activity exclusively of philologists. Philosophers and scientists frequently have occasion to "define" a recondite term by paraphrasing it into terms of a more familiar vocabulary. But ordinarily such a definition, like the philologist's, is pure lexicography, affirming a relation of synonymy antecedent to the exposition in hand.

Just what it means to affirm synonymy, just what the interconnections may be which are necessary and sufficient in order that two linguistic forms be properly describable as synonymous, is far from clear; but, whatever these interconnections may be, ordinarily they are grounded in usage. Definitions reporting selected instances of synonymy come then as reports upon usage.

There is also, however, a variant type of definitional activity which does not limit itself to the reporting of preexisting synonymies. I have in mind what Carnap calls *explication*—an activity to which philosophers are given, and scientists also in their more philosophical moments. In explication the purpose is not merely to paraphrase the definiendum into an outright synonym, but actually to improve upon the definiendum by refining or supplementing its meaning. But even explication, though not merely reporting a preexisting synonymy between definiendum and definiens, does rest nevertheless on *other* preexisting synonymies. The matter may be viewed as follows. Any word worth explicating has some contexts which, as wholes, are clear and precise enough to be useful; and the purpose of explication is to preserve the usage of these favored contexts while sharpening the usage of other contexts. In order that a given definition be suitable for purposes of explication, therefore, what is required is not that the definiendum in its antecedent usage be synonymous with the definiens, but just that each of these favored contexts of the definiendum, taken as a whole in its antecedent usage, be synonymous with the corresponding context of the definiens.

Two alternative definientia may be equally appropriate for the purposes of a given task of explication and yet not be synonymous with each other; for they may serve interchangeably within the favored contexts but diverge elsewhere. By cleaving to one of these definientia rather than the other, a definition of explicative kind generates, by fiat, a relation of synonymy between definiendum and definiens which did not hold before. But such a definition still owes its explicative function, as seen, to preexisting synonymies.

There does, however, remain still an extreme sort of definition which does not hark back to prior synonymies at all: namely, the explicitly conventional introduction of novel notations for purposes of sheer abbreviation. Here the definiendum becomes synonymous with the definiens simply because it has been created expressly for the purpose of being synonymous with the definiens. Here we have a really transparent case of synonymy created by definition; would that all species of synonymy were as intelligible. For the rest, definition rests on synonymy rather than explaining it.

The word 'definition' has come to have a dangerously reassuring sound, owing no doubt to its frequent occurrence in logical and mathematical writings. We shall do well to digress now into a brief appraisal of the role of definition in formal work.

In logical and mathematical systems either of two mutually antagonistic types of economy may be striven for, and each has its peculiar practical utility. On the one hand we may seek economy of practical expression—ease and brevity in the statement of multifarious relations. This sort of economy calls usually for distinctive concise notations for a wealth of concepts. Second, however, and oppositely, we may seek economy in grammar and vocabulary; we may try to find a minimum of basic concepts such that, once a distinctive notation has been appropriated to each of them, it becomes possible to express any desired further concept by mere combination and iteration of our basic notations. This second sort of economy is impractical in one way, since a poverty in basic idioms tends to a necessary lengthening of discourse. But it is practical in another way: it greatly simplifies theoretical discourse *about* the language, through minimizing the terms and the forms of construction wherein the language consists.

Both sorts of economy, though prima facie incompatible, are valuable in their separate ways. The custom has consequently arisen of combining both sorts of economy by forging in effect two languages, the one a part of the other. The inclusive language, though redundant in grammar and vocabulary, is economical in message lengths, while the part, called primitive notation, is economical in grammar and vocabulary. Whole and part are correlated by rules of translation whereby each idiom not in primitive notation is equated to some complex built up of primitive notation. These rules of translation are the so-called *definitions* which appear in formalized systems. They are best viewed not as adjuncts to one language but as correlations between two languages, the one a part of the other.

But these correlations are not arbitrary. They are supposed to show how the primitive notations can accomplish all purposes, save brevity and convenience, of the redundant language. Hence the definiendum and its definiens may be expected, in each case, to be related in one or another of the three ways lately noted. The definiens may be a faithful paraphrase of the definiendum into the narrower notation, preserving a direct synonymy* as of antecedent usage; or the definiens may, in the spirit of explication, improve upon the antecedent usage of the definiendum; or finally, the definiendum may be a newly created notation, newly endowed with meaning here and now.

In formal and informal work alike, thus, we find that definition—except in the extreme case of the explicitly conventional introduction of new notations—hinges on prior relations of synonymy. Recognizing then that the notion of definition does not hold the key to synonymy and analyticity, let us look further into synonymy and say no more of definition.

3. INTERCHANGEABILITY

A natural suggestion, deserving close examination, is that the synonymy of two linguistic forms consists simply in their interchangeability in all contexts without change of truth value—interchangeability, in Leibniz's phrase, *salva veritate*. Note that synonyms so conceived need not even be free from vagueness, as long as the vaguenesses match.

But it is not quite true that the synonyms 'bachelor' and 'unmarried man' are everywhere interchangeable *salva veritate*. Truths which become false under substitution of 'unmarried man' for 'bachelor' are easily constructed with the help of 'bachelor of arts' or 'bachelor's buttons'; also with the help of quotation, thus:

'Bachelor' has less than ten letters.

Such counterinstances can, however, perhaps be set aside by treating the phrases 'bachelor of arts' and 'bachelor's buttons' and the quotation "bachelor" each as a single indivisible word and then stipulating that the interchangeability *salva veritate* which is to be the touchstone of synonymy is not supposed to apply to fragmentary occurrences inside of a word. This account of synonymy, supposing it acceptable on other counts, has indeed the drawback of appealing to a prior conception of "word" which can be counted on to present difficulties of formulation in its turn. Nevertheless some progress might be claimed in having reduced the problem of synonymy to a problem of wordhood. Let us pursue this line a bit, taking "word" for granted.

The question remains whether interchangeability *salva veritate* (apart from occurrences within words) is a strong enough condition for synonymy, or whether, on the contrary, some heteronymous expressions might be thus interchangeable. Now let us be clear that we are not concerned here with synonymy in the sense of complete identity in psychological associations or poetic quality; indeed no two expressions are synonymous in such a sense. We are concerned only with what may be called *cognitive* synonymy. Just what this is cannot be said without successfully finishing the present study; but we know something about it from the need which arose for it in connection with analyticity in ¶1. The sort of synonymy needed there was merely such that any analytic statement could be turned into a logical truth by putting synonyms for synonyms. Turning the tables and assuming analyticity, indeed, we could explain

---

*According to an important variant sense of 'definition,'the relation preserved may be the weaker relation of mere agreement in reference. . . . But definition in this sense is better ignored in the present connection, being irrelevant to the question of synonymy.

cognitive synonymy of terms as follows (keeping to the familiar example): to say that 'bachelor' and 'unmarried man' are cognitively synonymous is to say no more nor less than that the statement:

(3) All and only bachelors are unmarried men

is analytic.*

What we need is an account of cognitive synonymy not presupposing analyticity—if we are to explain analyticity conversely with help of cognitive synonymy as undertaken in ¶1. And indeed such an independent account of cognitive synonymy is at present up for consideration, namely, interchangeability *salva veritate* everywhere except within words. The question before us, to resume the thread at last, is whether such interchangeability is a sufficient condition for cognitive synonymy. We can quickly assure ourselves that it is, by examples of the following sort. The statement:

(4) Necessarily all and only bachelors are bachelors

is evidently true, even supposing 'necessarily' so narrowly construed as to be truly applicable only to analytic statements. Then, if 'bachelor' and 'unmarried man' are interchangeable *salva veritate,* the result:

(5) Necessarily all and only bachelors are unmarried men

of putting 'unmarried man' for an occurrence of 'bachelor' in (4) must, like (4), be true. But to say that (5) is true is to say that (3) is analytic, and hence that 'bachelor' and 'unmarried man' are cognitively synonymous.

Let us see what there is about the above argument that gives it its air of hocus-pocus. The condition of interchangeability *salva veritate* varies in its force with variations in the richness of the language at hand. The above argument supposes we are working with a language rich enough to contain the adverb 'necessarily,' this adverb being so construed as to yield truth when and only when applied to an analytic statement. But can we condone a language which contains such an adverb? Does the adverb really make sense? To suppose that it does is to suppose that we have already made satisfactory sense of 'analytic.' Then what are we so hard at work on right now?

Our argument is not flatly circular, but something like it. It has the form, figuratively speaking, of a closed curve in space.

Interchangeability *salva veritate* is meaningless until relativized to a language whose extent is specified in relevant respects. Suppose now we consider a language containing just the following materials. There is an indefinitely large stock of one-place predicates (for example, 'F' where 'Fx' means that x is a man) and many-place predicates (for example, 'G' where 'Gxy' means that x loves y), mostly having to do with extralogical subject matter. The rest of the language is logical. The atomic sentences consist each of a predicate followed by one or more variables 'x,' 'y,' etc.; and the complex sentences are built up of the atomic ones by truth functions ('not,' 'and,'

---

*This is cognitive synonymy in a primary, broad sense. Carnap and Lewis have suggested how, once this notion is at hand, a narrower sense of cognitive synonymy which is preferable for some purposes can in turn be derived. But this special ramification of concept-building lies aside from the present purposes and must not be confused with the broad sort of cognitive synonymy here concerned.

'or,' etc.) and quantification. In effect such a language enjoys the benefits also of descriptions and indeed singular terms generally, these being contextually definable in known ways. Even abstract singular terms naming classes, classes of classes, etc., are contextually definable in case the assumed stock of predicates includes the two-place predicate of class membership. Such a language can be adequate to classical mathematics and indeed to scientific discourse generally, except in so far as the latter involves debatable devices such as contrary-to-fact conditionals or modal adverbs like 'necessarily.' Now a language of this type is extensional, in this sense: any two predicates which agree extensionally (that is, are true of the same objects) are interchangeable *salva veritate*.

In an extensional language, therefore, interchangeability *salva veritate* is no assurance of cognitive synonymy of the desired type. That 'bachelor' and 'unmarried man' are interchangeable *salva veritate* in an extensional language assures us of no more than that (3) is true. There is no assurance here that the extensional agreement of 'bachelor' and 'unmarried man' rests on meaning rather than merely on accidental matters of fact, as does the extensional agreement of 'creature with a heart' and 'creature with kidneys.'

For most purposes extensional agreement is the nearest approximation to synonymy we need care about. But the fact remains that extensional agreement falls far short of cognitive synonymy of the type required for explaining analyticity in the manner of ¶1. The type of cognitive synonymy required there is such as to equate the synonymy of 'bachelor' and 'unmarried man' with the analyticity of (3), not merely with the truth of (3).

So we must recognize that interchangeability *salva veritate,* if construed in relation to an extensional language, is not a sufficient condition of cognitive synonymy in the sense needed for deriving analyticity in the manner of ¶1. If a language contains an intensional adverb 'necessarily' in the sense lately noted, or other particles to the same effect, then interchangeability *salva veritate* in such a language does afford a sufficient condition of cognitive synonymy; but such a language is intelligible only in so far as the notion of analyticity is already understood in advance.

The effort to explain cognitive synonymy first, for the sake of deriving analyticity from it afterward as in ¶1, is perhaps the wrong approach. Instead we might try explaining analyticity somehow without appeal to cognitive synonymy. Afterward we could doubtless derive cognitive synonymy from analyticity satisfactorily enough if desired. We have seen that cognitive synonymy of 'bachelor' and 'unmarried man' can be explained as analyticity of (3). The same explanation works for any pair of one-place predicates, of course, and it can be extended in obvious fashion to many-place predicates. Other syntactical categories can also be accommodated in fairly parallel fashion. Singular terms may be said to be cognitively synonymous when the statement of identity formed by putting '=' between them is analytic. Statements may be said simply to be cognitively synonymous when their biconditional (the result of joining them by 'if and only if') is analytic.* If we care to lump all categories into a single formulation, at the expense of assuming again the notion of "word" which was appealed to early in this section, we can describe any two linguistic forms as cognitively synonymous when the two forms are interchangeable (apart from occurrences within "words") *salva* (no longer *veritate* but) *analyticitate*. Certain technical questions arise, indeed, over cases

*The 'if and only if' itself is intended in the true functional sense.

of ambiguity or homonymy; let us not pause for them, however, for we are already digressing. Let us rather turn our backs on the problem of synonymy and address ourselves anew to that of analyticity.

4. SEMANTICAL RULES

Analyticity at first seemed most naturally definable by appeal to a realm of meanings. On refinement, the appeal to meanings gave way to an appeal to synonymy or definition. But definition turned out to be a will-o'-the-wisp, and synonymy turned out to be best understood only by dint of a prior appeal to analyticity itself. So we are back at the problem of analyticity.

I do not know whether the statement 'Everything green is extended' is analytic. Now does my indecision over this example really betray an incomplete understanding, an incomplete grasp of the "meanings," of 'green' and 'extended'? I think not. The trouble is not with 'green' or 'extended,' but with 'analytic.'

It is often hinted that the difficulty in separating analytic statements from synthetic ones in ordinary language is due to the vagueness of ordinary language and that the distinction is clear when we have a precise artificial language with explicit "semantical rules." This, however, as I shall now attempt to show, is a confusion.

The notion of analyticity about which we are worrying is a purported relation between statements and languages: a statement S is said to be *analytic* for a language L, and the problem is to make sense of this relation generally, that is, for variable 'S' and 'L.' The gravity of this problem is not perceptibly less for artificial languages than for natural ones. The problem of making sense of the idiom 'S is analytic for L,' with variable 'S' and 'L,' retains its stubbornness even if we limit the range of the variable 'L' to artificial languages. Let me now try to make this point evident.

For artificial languages and semantical rules we look naturally to the writings of Carnap. His semantical rules take various forms, and to make my point I shall have to distinguish certain of the forms. Let us suppose, to begin with, an artificial language L_0 whose semantical rules have the form explicitly of a specification, by recursion or otherwise, of all the analytic statements of L_0. The rules tell us that such and such statements, and only those, are the analytic statements of L_0. Now here the difficulty is simply that the rules contain the word 'analytic,' which we do not understand! We understand what expressions the rules attribute analyticity to, but we do not understand what the rules attribute to those expressions. In short, before we can understand a rule which begins 'A statement S is analytic for language L_0 if and only if . . .,' we must understand the general relative term 'analytic for'; we must understand 'S is analytic for L' where 'S' and 'L' are variables.

Alternatively we may, indeed, view the so-called rule as a conventional definition of a new simple symbol 'analytic-for-L_0,' which might better be written untendentiously as 'K' so as not to seem to throw light on the interesting word 'analytic.' Obviously any number of classes K, M, N, etc. of statements of L_0 can be specified for various purposes or for no purpose; what does it mean to say that K, as against M, N, etc., is the class of the "analytic" statements of L_0?

By saying what statements are analytic for L_0 we explain 'analytic-for-L_0' but not 'analytic,' not 'analytic for.' We do not begin to explain the idiom 'S is analytic for L' with variable 'S' and 'L,' even if we are content to limit the range of 'L' to the realm of artificial languages.

Actually we do know enough about the intended significance of 'analytic' to know that analytic statements are supposed to be true. Let us then turn to a second form of semantical rule, which says not that such and such statements are analytic but simply that such and such statements are included among the truths. Such a rule is not subject to the criticism of containing the un-understood word 'analytic'; and we may grant for the sake of argument that there is no difficulty over the broader term 'true.' A semantical rule of this second type, a rule of truth, is not supposed to specify all the truths of the language; it merely stipulates, recursively or otherwise, a certain multitude of statements which, along with others unspecified, are to count as true. Such a rule may be conceded to be quite clear. Derivatively, afterward, analyticity can be demarcated thus: a statement is analytic if it is (not merely true but) true according to the semantical rule.

Still there is really no progress. Instead of appealing to an unexplained word 'analytic,' we are now appealing to an unexplained phrase 'semantical rule.' Not every true statement which says that the statements of some class are true can count as a semantical rule—otherwise *all* truths would be "analytic" in the sense of being true according to semantical rules. Semantical rules are distinguishable, apparently, only by the fact of appearing on a page under the heading 'Semantical Rules'; and this heading is itself then meaningless.

We can say indeed that a statement is *analytic-for-L_0* if and only if it is true according to such and such specifically appended "semantical rules," but then we find ourselves back at essentially the same case which was originally discussed: '*S* is analytic-for-L_0 if and only if. . . .' Once we seek to explain '*S* is analytic for *L*' generally for variable '*L*' (even allowing limitation of '*L*' to artificial languages), the explanation 'true according to the semantical rules of *L*' is unavailing; for the relative term 'semantical rule of' is as much in need of clarification, at least, as 'analytic for.'

It may be instructive to compare the notion of semantical rule with that of postulate. Relative to a given set of postulates, it is easy to say what a postulate is: it is a member of the set. Relative to a given set of semantical rules, it is equally easy to say what a semantical rule is. But given simply a notation, mathematical or otherwise, and indeed as thoroughly understood a notation as you please in point of the translations or truth conditions of its statements, who can say which of its true statements rank as postulates? Obviously the question is meaningless—as meaningless as asking which points in Ohio are starting points. Any finite (or effectively specifiable infinite) selection of statements (preferably true ones, perhaps) is as much a set of postulates as any other. The word 'postulate' is significant only relative to an act of inquiry; we apply the word to a set of statements just in so far as we happen, for the year or the moment, to be thinking of those statements in relation to the statements which can be reached from them by some set of transformations to which we have seen fit to direct our attention. Now the notion of semantical rule is as sensible and meaningful as that of postulate, if conceived in a similarly relative spirit—relative, this time, to one or another particular enterprise of schooling unconversant persons in sufficient conditions for truth of statements of some natural or artificial language *L*. But from this point of view no one signalization of a subclass of the truths of *L* is intrinsically more a semantical rule than another; and, if 'analytic' means 'true by semantical rules,' no one truth of *L* is analytic to the exclusion of another.

It might conceivably be protested that an artificial language *L* (unlike a natural one) is a language in the ordinary sense *plus* a set of explicit semantical rules—the whole constituting, let us say, an ordered pair; and that the semantical rules of *L* then are specifiable simply as the second component of the pair *L*. But, by the same token and more simply, we might construe an artificial language *L* outright as an ordered pair whose second component is the class of its analytic statements; and then the analytic statements of *L* become specifiable simply as the statements in the second component of *L*. Or better still, we might just stop tugging at our bootstraps altogether.

Not all the explanations of analyticity known to Carnap and his readers have been covered explicitly in the above considerations, but the extension to other forms is not hard to see. Just one additional factor should be mentioned which sometimes enters: sometimes the semantical rules are in effect rules of translation into ordinary language, in which case the analytic statements of the artificial language are in effect recognized as such from the analyticity of their specified translations in ordinary language. Here certainly there can be no thought of an illumination of the problem of analyticity from the side of the artificial language.

From the point of view of the problem of analyticity the notion of an artificial language with semantical rules is a *feu follet par excellence*. Semantical rules determining the analytic statements of an artificial language are of interest only in so far as we already understand the notion of analyticity; they are of no help in gaining this understanding.

Appeal to hypothetical languages of an artificially simple kind could conceivably be useful in clarifying analyticity, if the mental or behavioral or cultural factors relevant to analyticity—whatever they may be—were somehow sketched into the simplified model. But a model which takes analyticity merely as an irreducible character is unlikely to throw light on the problem of explicating analyticity.

It is obvious that truth in general depends on both language and extralinguistic fact. The statement 'Brutus killed Caesar' would be false if the world had been different in certain ways, but it would also be false if the word 'killed' happened rather to have the sense of 'begat.' Thus one is tempted to suppose in general that the truth of a statement is somehow analyzable into a linguistic component and a factual component. Given this supposition, it next seems reasonable that in some statements the factual component should be null; and these are the analytic statements. But, for all its a priori reasonableness, a boundary between analytic and synthetic statements simply has not been drawn. That there is such a distinction to be drawn at all is an unempirical dogma of empiricists, a metaphysical article of faith.

5. THE VERIFICATION THEORY AND REDUCTIONISM

In the course of these somber reflections we have taken a dim view first of the notion of meaning, then of the notion of cognitive synonymy, and finally of the notion of analyticity. But what, it may be asked, of the verification theory of meaning? This phrase has established itself so firmly as a catchword of empiricism that we should be very unscientific indeed not to look beneath it for a possible key to the problem of meaning and the associated problems.

The verification theory of meaning, which has been conspicuous in the literature from Peirce onward, is that the meaning of a statement is the method of empirically confirming or infirming it. An analytic statement is that limiting case which is confirmed no matter what.

As urged in ¶1, we can as well pass over the question of meanings as entities and move straight to sameness of meaning, or synonymy. Then what the verification theory says is that statements are synonymous if and only if they are alike in point of method of empirical confirmation or infirmation.

This is an account of cognitive synonymy not of linguistic forms generally, but of statements.* However, from the concept of synonymy of statements we could derive the concept of synonymy for other linguistic forms, by considerations somewhat similar to those at the end of ¶3. Assuming the notion of "word," indeed, we could explain any two forms as synonymous when the putting of the one form for an occurrence of the other in any statement (apart from occurrences within "words") yields a synonymous statement. Finally, given the concept of synonymy thus for linguistic forms generally, we could define analyticity in terms of synonymy and logical truth as in ¶1. For that matter, we could define analyticity more simply in terms of just synonymy of statements together with logical truth; it is not necessary to appeal to synonymy of linguistic forms other than statements. For a statement may be described as analytic simply when it is synonymous with a logically true statement.

So, if the verification theory can be accepted as an adequate account of statement synonymy, the notion of analyticity is saved after all. However, let us reflect. Statement synonymy is said to be likeness of method of empirical confirmation or infirmation. Just what are these methods which are to be compared for likeness? What, in other words, is the nature of the relation between a statement and the experiences which contribute to or detract from its confirmation?

The most naive view of the relation is that it is one of direct report. This is *radical reductionism*. Every meaningful statement is held to be translatable into a statement (true or false) about immediate experience. Radical reductionism, in one form or another, well antedates the verification theory of meaning explicitly so called. Thus Locke and Hume held that every idea must either originate directly in sense experience or else be compounded of ideas thus originating; and taking a hint from Tooke we might rephrase this doctrine in semantical jargon by saying that a term, to be significant at all, must be either a name of a sense datum or a compound of such names or an abbreviation of such a compound. So stated, the doctrine remains ambiguous as between sense data as sensory events and sense data as sensory qualities; and it remains vague as to the admissible ways of compounding. Moreover, the doctrine is unnecessarily and intolerably restrictive in the term-by-term critique which it imposes. More reasonably, and without yet exceeding the limits of what I have called radical reductionism, we may take full statements as our significant units—thus demanding that our statements as wholes be translatable into sense-datum language, but not that they be translatable term by term.

This emendation would unquestionably have been welcome to Locke and Hume and Tooke, but historically it had to await an important reorientation in semantics—the reorientation whereby the primary vehicle of meaning came to be seen no longer in the term but in the statement. This reorientation, seen in Bentham and Frege, underlies Russell's concept of incomplete symbols defined in use; also it is implicit in the verification theory of meaning, since the objects of verification are statements.

Radical reductionism, conceived now with statements as units, set itself the task of specifying a sense-datum language and showing how to translate the rest of significant discourse, statement by statement, into it. Carnap embarked on this project in the *Aufbau*.

The language which Carnap adopted as his starting point was not a sense-datum language in the narrowest conceivable sense, for it included also the notations of logic, up through higher set theory. In effect it included the whole language of pure mathe-

---

*The doctrine can indeed be formulated with terms rather than statements as the units. Thus Lewis describes the meaning of a term as "*a criterion in mind,* by reference to which one is able to apply or refuse to apply the expression in question in the case of presented, or imagined, things or situations."

matics. The ontology implicit in it (that is, the range of values of its variables) embraced not only sensory events but classes, classes of classes, and so on. Empiricists there are who would boggle at such prodigality. Carnap's starting point is very parsimonious, however, in its extralogical or sensory part. In a series of constructions in which he exploits the resources of modern logic with much ingenuity, Carnap succeeds in defining a wide array of important additional sensory concepts which, but for his constructions, one would not have dreamed were definable on so slender a basis. He was the first empiricist who, not content with asserting the reducibility of science to terms of immediate experience, took serious steps toward carrying out the reduction.

If Carnap's starting point is satisfactory, still his constructions were, as he himself stressed, only a fragment of the full program. The construction of even the simplest statements about the physical world was left in a sketchy state. Carnap's suggestions on this subject were, despite their sketchiness, very suggestive. He explained spatio-temporal point-instants as quadruples of real numbers and envisaged assignment of sense qualities to point-instants according to certain canons. Roughly summarized, the plan was that qualities should be assigned to point-instants in such a way as to achieve the laziest world compatible with our experience. The principle of least action was to be our guide in constructing a world from experience.

Carnap did not seem to recognize, however, that his treatment of physical objects fell short of reduction not merely through sketchiness, but in principle. Statements of the form 'Quality q is at point-instant $x;y;z;t$' were, according to his canons, to be apportioned truth values in such a way as to maximize and minimize certain over-all features, and with growth of experience the truth values were to be progressively revised in the same spirit. I think this is a good schematization (deliberately oversimplified, to be sure) of what science really does; but it provides no indication, not even the sketchiest, of how a statement of the form 'Quality q is at $x;y;z;t$' could ever be translated into Carnap's initial language of sense data and logic. The connective 'is at' remains an added undefined connective; the canons counsel us in its use but not in its elimination.

Carnap seems to have appreciated this point afterward; for in his later writings he abandoned all notion of the translatability of statements about the physical world into statements about immediate experience. Reductionism in its radical form has long since ceased to figure in Carnap's philosophy.

But the dogma of reductionism has, in a subtler and more tenuous form, continued to influence the thought of empiricists. The notion lingers that to each statement, or each synthetic statement, there is associated a unique range of possible sensory events such that the occurrence of any of them would add to the likelihood of truth of the statement, and that there is associated also another unique range of possible sensory events whose occurrence would detract from that likelihood. This notion is of course implicit in the verification theory of meaning.

The dogma of reductionism survives in the supposition that each statement, taken in isolation from its fellows, can admit of confirmation or infirmation at all. My countersuggestion, issuing essentially from Carnap's doctrine of the physical world in the *Aufbau,* is that our statements about the external world face the tribunal of sense experience not individually but only as a corporate body.

The dogma of reductionism, even in its attenuated form, is intimately connected with the other dogma—that there is a cleavage between the analytic and the synthetic. We have found ourselves led, indeed, from the latter problem to the former through the verification theory of meaning. More directly, the one dogma clearly supports the other in this way: as long as it is taken to be significant in general to speak of the confirmation and infirmation of a statement, it seems significant to speak also of a limiting kind of statement which is vacuously confirmed, *ipso facto,* come what may; and such a statement is analytic.

The two dogmas are, indeed, at root identical. We lately reflected that in general the truth of statements does obviously depend both upon language and upon extralinguistic fact; and we noted that this obvious circumstance carries in its train, not logically but all too naturally, a feeling that the truth of a statement is somehow analyzable into a linguistic component and a factual component. The factual component must, if we are empiricists, boil down to a range of confirmatory experiences. In the extreme case where the linguistic component is all that matters, a true statement is analytic. But I hope we are now impressed with how stubbornly the distinction between analytic and synthetic has resisted any straightforward drawing. I am impressed also, apart from prefabricated examples of black and white balls in an urn, with how baffling the problem has always been of arriving at any explicit theory of the empirical confirmation of a synthetic statement. My present suggestion is that it is nonsense, and the root of much nonsense, to speak of a linguistic component and a factual component in the truth of any individual statement. Taken collectively, science has its double dependence upon language and experience; but this duality is not significantly traceable into the statements of science taken one by one.

The idea of defining a symbol in use was, as remarked, an advance over the impossible term-by-term empiricism of Locke and Hume. The statement, rather than the term, came with Bentham to be recognized as the unit accountable to an empiricist critique. But what I am now urging is that even in taking the statement as unit we have drawn our grid too finely. The unit of empirical significance is the whole of science.

6. EMPIRICISM WITHOUT THE DOGMAS

The totality of our so-called knowledge or beliefs, from the most casual matters of geography and history to the profoundest laws of atomic physics or even of pure mathematics and logic, is a man-made fabric which impinges on experience only along the edges. Or, to change the figure, total science is like a field of force whose boundary conditions are experience. A conflict with experience at the periphery occasions readjustments in the interior of the field. Truth values have to be redistributed over some of our statements. Reevaluation of some statements entails reevaluation of others, because of their logical interconnections—the logical laws being in turn simply certain further statements of the system, certain further elements of the field. Having reevaluated one statement we must reevaluate some others, which may be statements logically connected with the first or may be the statements of logical connections themselves. But the total field is so underdetermined by its boundary conditions, experience, that there is much latitude of choice as to what statements to reevaluate in the light of any single contrary experience. No particular experiences are linked with any particular statements in the interior of the field, except indirectly through considerations of equilibrium affecting the field as a whole.

If this view is right, it is misleading to speak of the empirical content of an individual statement—especially if it is a statement at all remote from the experiential periphery of the field. Furthermore it becomes folly to seek a boundary between synthetic statements, which hold contingently on experience, and analytic statements, which hold come what may. Any statement can be held true come what may, if we make drastic enough adjustments elsewhere in the system. Even a statement very close to the periphery can be held true in the face of recalcitrant experience by pleading hallucination or by amending certain statements of the kind called logical laws. Conversely, by the same token, no statement is immune to revision. Revision even of the logical law of the excluded middle has been proposed as a means of simplifying quantum mechanics; and what difference is there in principle between such a shift and the shift whereby Kepler superseded Ptolemy, or Einstein Newton, or Darwin Aristotle?

For vividness I have been speaking in terms of varying distances from a sensory periphery. Let me try now to clarify this notion without metaphor. Certain statements, though *about* physical objects and not sense experience, seem peculiarly germane to sense experience—and in a selective way: some statements to some experiences, others to others. Such statements, especially germane to particular experiences, I picture as near the periphery. But in this relation of "germaneness" I envisage nothing more than a loose association reflecting the relative likelihood, in practice, of our choosing one statement rather than another for revision in the event of recalcitrant experience. For example, we can imagine recalcitrant experiences to which we would surely be inclined to accommodate our system by reevaluating just the statement that there are brick houses on Elm Street, together with related statements on the same topic. We can imagine other recalcitrant experiences to which we would be inclined to accommodate our system by reevaluating just the statement that there are no centaurs, along with kindred statements. A recalcitrant experience can, I have urged, be accommodated by any of various alternative reevaluations in various alternative quarters of the total system; but, in the cases which we are now imagining, our natural tendency to disturb the total system as little as possible would lead us to focus our revisions upon these specific statements concerning brick houses or centaurs. These statements are felt, therefore, to have a sharper empirical reference than highly theoretical statements of physics or logic or ontology. The latter statements may be thought of as relatively centrally located within the total network, meaning merely that little preferential connection with any particular sense data obtrudes itself.

As an empiricist I continue to think of the conceptual scheme of science as a tool, ultimately, for predicting future experience in the light of past experience. Physical objects are conceptually imported into the situation as convenient intermediaries—not by definition in terms of experience, but simply as irreducible posits comparable, epistemologically, to the gods of Homer. For my part I do, qua lay physicist, believe in physical objects and not in Homer's gods; and I consider it a scientific error to believe otherwise. But in point of epistemological footing the physical objects and the gods differ only in degree and not in kind. Both sorts of entities enter our conception only as cultural posits. The myth of physical objects is epistemologically superior to most in that it has proved more efficacious than other myths as a device for working a manageable structure into the flux of experience.

Positing does not stop with macroscopic physical objects. Objects at the atomic level are posited to make the laws of macroscopic objects, and ultimately the laws of experience, simpler and more manageable; and we need not expect or demand full definition of atomic and subatomic entities in terms of macroscopic ones, any more than definition of macroscopic things in terms of sense data. Science is a continuation of common sense, and it continues the common-sense expedient of swelling ontology to simplify theory.

Physical objects, small and large, are not the only posits. Forces are another example; and indeed we are told nowadays that the boundary between energy and matter is obsolete. Moreover, the abstract entities which are the substance of mathematics—ultimately classes and classes of classes and so on up—are another posit in the same spirit. Epistemologically these are myths on the same footing with physical objects and gods, neither better nor worse except for differences in the degree to which they expedite our dealings with sense experiences.

The over-all algebra of rational and irrational numbers is underdetermined by the algebra of rational numbers, but is smoother and more convenient; and it includes the algebra of rational numbers as a jagged or gerrymandered part. Total science, mathematical and natural and human, is similarly but more extremely underdetermined by experience. The edge of the system must be kept squared with experience; the rest, with all its elaborate myths or fictions, has as its objective the simplicity of laws.

Ontological questions, under this view, are on a par with questions of natural science. Consider the question whether to countenance classes as entities. This, as I have argued elsewhere, is the question whether to quantify with respect to variables which take classes as values. Now Carnap has maintained that this is a question not of matters of fact but of choosing a convenient language form, a convenient conceptual scheme or framework for science. With this I agree, but only on the proviso that the same be conceded regarding scientific hypotheses generally. Carnap has recognized that he is able to preserve a double standard for ontological questions and scientific hypotheses only by assuming an absolute distinction between the analytic and the synthetic; and I need not say again that this is a distinction which I reject.

The issue over there being classes seems more a question of convenient conceptual scheme; the issue over there being centaurs, or brick houses on Elm Street, seems more a question of fact. But I have been urging that this difference is only one of degree, and that it turns upon our vaguely pragmatic inclination to adjust one strand of the fabric of science rather than another in accommodating some particular recalcitrant experience. Conservatism figures in such choices, and so does the quest for simplicity.

Carnap, Lewis, and others take a pragmatic stand on the question of choosing between language forms, scientific frameworks; but their pragmatism leaves off at the imagined boundary between the analytic and the synthetic. In repudiating such a boundary I espouse a more thorough pragmatism. Each man is given a scientific heritage plus a continuing barrage of sensory stimulation; and the considerations which guide him in warping his scientific heritage to fit his continuing sensory promptings are, where rational, pragmatic.